A GUIDE TO
ENGLISH COUNTY HISTORIES

Frontispiece: Christopher Elrington

A GUIDE TO
ENGLISH COUNTY HISTORIES

EDITED BY
C.R.J. CURRIE AND C.P. LEWIS

SUTTON PUBLISHING

First published in the United Kingdom in 1994 by
Alan Sutton Publishing Ltd, an imprint of Sutton Publishing Ltd
Phoenix Mill · Thrupp · Stroud · Gloucestershire · GL5 2BU

Paperback edition first published in 1997

British Library Cataloguing in Publication Data
A catalogue record for this book is available from the British Library

ISBN 0-7509-1505-6

Cover illustration: detail from Braun and Hogenberg's map of London, 1572. (Museum of London)

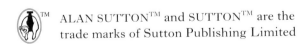
TM   ALAN SUTTON™ and SUTTON™ are the
trade marks of Sutton Publishing Limited

Typesetting and origination by
Sutton Publishing Limited.
Printed in Great Britain by
WBC Limited, Bridgend.

CONTENTS

LIST OF ILLUSTRATIONS

LIST OF CONTRIBUTORS

A. P. Baggs, Architectural Editor, *V.C.H.*

Timothy Baker, Editor, *V.C.H. Middlesex*

Caroline Barron, Reader in the History of London, Royal Holloway, University of London

G. C. Baugh, Editor, *V.C.H. Shropshire*

J. H. Bettey, Reader in Local History, University of Bristol

Beryl Board, formerly Senior Assistant Editor, *V.C.H. Essex*

Diane Bolton, Assistant Editor, *V.C.H. Middlesex*

Janet Cooper, Editor, *V.C.H. Essex*

D. C. Cox, Assistant Editor, *V.C.H. Shropshire*

Patricia Croot, Assistant Editor, *V.C.H. Middlesex*

Alan Crossley, Editor, *V.C.H. Oxfordshire*

Douglas Crowley, Editor, *V.C.H. Wiltshire*

C. R. J. Currie, Deputy Editor, *V.C.H.*

Christopher Day, Assistant Editor, *V.C.H. Oxfordshire*

R. W. Dunning, Editor, *V.C.H. Somerset*

David Dymond, Director of Studies in Local History for the Board of Continuing Education, University of Cambridge

Gordon Forster, Senior Lecturer in Modern History, University of Leeds

Jane Freeman, Assistant Editor, *V.C.H. Wiltshire*

M. W. Greenslade, Editor, *V.C.H. Staffordshire*

Vanessa Harding, Lecturer in London History, Birkbeck College, London; formerly Assistant Editor, *V.C.H. Essex*

Adrian Henstock, Principal Archivist, Nottinghamshire Archives

Nicholas Herbert, Editor, *V.C.H. Gloucestershire*

Michael Hicks, Course Director, B.A. (Honours) History, King Alfred's College, Winchester; formerly Assistant Editor, *V.C.H. Middlesex*

T. P. Hudson, Editor, *V.C.H. Sussex*

D. A. Johnson, formerly Assistant Editor, *V.C.H. Staffordshire*

G. H. R. Kent, Editor, *V.C.H. Yorkshire, East Riding*

Jenny Kermode, Senior Lecturer in Local History, University of Liverpool; formerly Assistant to the General Editor, *V.C.H.*

C. P. Lewis, Assistant to the General Editor, *V.C.H.*

Lionel Munby, formerly Staff Tutor, University of Cambridge Board of Extramural Studies

Margaret O'Sullivan, County Archivist, Derbyshire Record Office

Charles Phythian-Adams, Professor of English Local History, University of Leicester

W. Raymond Powell, formerly Editor, *V.C.H. Essex*

Susan Reynolds, formerly Tutor in Modern History, Lady Margaret Hall, Oxford; previously Editor, *V.C.H. Middlesex*

Ken Rogers, formerly Archivist, Wiltshire Record Office; previously Assistant Editor, *V.C.H. Wiltshire*

W. J. Sheils, Senior Fellow in Economic and Social History, Borthwick Institute, York; formerly Assistant Editor, *V.C.H. Gloucestershire*

Hassell Smith, formerly Director of the Centre for East Anglian Studies, University of East Anglia

Paul Stamper, Shropshire County Council; formerly Assistant Editor, *V.C.H. Shropshire*

Christopher Sturman, Editor, *Lincolnshire History and Archaeology*

Patricia A. Tattersfield was secretary to the General Editor of the *V.C.H.* until her death in 1992

Alan Thacker, Editor, *V.C.H. Cheshire*

Simon Townley, Assistant Editor, *V.C.H. Oxfordshire*

Nigel J. Tringham, Assistant Editor, *V.C.H. Staffordshire*

Roger Virgoe, Senior Lecturer in English History, University of East Anglia

John Walker, Assistant Editor, *V.C.H. Yorkshire, East Riding*

Angus J. L. Winchester, Lecturer in History, University of Lancaster; formerly Assistant Editor, *V.C.H. Shropshire*

A. P. M. Wright, Senior Assistant to the General Editor, *V.C.H.*

Nigel Yates, Consultant Historian to Kent County Council

Joyce Youings, Emeritus Professor, Department of History and Archaeology, University of Exeter

PREFACE

The idea for this book took shape in September 1991. It has always had two aims, one personal and the other academic. The first was to find a framework within which a large number of friends and colleagues of Christopher Elrington could pay tribute to him when he retired from the general editorship of the Victoria County History. The other was to fill a scholarly gap. Although much had been written about the historiography of individual English counties, there was no comprehensive survey offering a qualitative guide to the works of the English county historians and thus also making a contribution to intellectual and cultural history.

From those two aims there emerged the idea of a survey of the historiography of English county history, and a brief for the authors that, in no more than 4,000 words, each chapter should sketch the development of research and writing on the history of a county. They were asked to be interpretative rather than merely bibliographical, and to cover histories—published and unpublished, complete and incomplete—and collections towards projected histories for counties and parts of counties, also taking in bibliographies, outstanding work on individual places and topics, and regional, county, and sub-county historical and kindred societies. No rigid format was prescribed for the chapters, and authors were encouraged to treat what they saw as important and interesting. The chapters that follow thus reflect their authors' interests as well as the variations in chorography among the counties and the extent of earlier work. Most ancient counties have their own chapter, but Monmouthshire is omitted, London is treated separately, Yorkshire is divided between a general chapter and one for each of the ridings, and Cumberland is combined with Westmorland, and Leicestershire with Rutland.

The editors extend their warmest thanks to all who have made this volume possible, not least to a large team of authors who have kept to a tight schedule.

The publication of this book has been assisted by a grant from The Scouloudi Foundation in association with the Institute of Historical Research, and a grant from the late Miss Isobel Thornley's Bequest to the University of London.

LIST OF ABBREVIATIONS

The following abbreviations, sometimes with the addition of -s to indicate plurality, may require elucidation: A.O., Archive[s] Office; Add., Additional; antiq., antiquary *or* antiquarian; Arch., Archaeology *or* Archaeological; Archit., Architecture *or* Architectural; B.L., British Library; B.M., British Museum; Beds., Bedfordshire; Berks., Berkshire; Bodl., Bodleian Library, Oxford; Bucks., Buckinghamshire; Bull., Bulletin; *c.*, *circa*; C.B.A., Council for British Archaeology; Cambs., Cambridgeshire; Cardig., Cardiganshire; Ches., Cheshire; col., column; Com., Commission; Cornw., Cornwall; Cumb., Cumberland; d., died; *D.N.B.*, *Dictionary of National Biography*; Derb., Derbyshire; Dors., Dorset; Dur., Durham; E.P.N.S., English Place-Name Society; E.R., East Riding; ed., edited by *or* editor; edn., edition; esp., especially; f., folio; ff., folios; fl., flourished; *Gent. Mag.*, *The Gentleman's Magazine*; Glos., Gloucestershire; Hants, Hampshire; Harl., Harleian; Herefs., Herefordshire; Herts., Hertfordshire; Hist., History *or* Historical; Hunts., Huntingdonshire; ibid., *ibidem* (in the same place); inf., information; Jnl., Journal; Lancs., Lancashire; Leics., Leicestershire; Lincs., Lincolnshire; Mdx., Middlesex; Mont., Montgomeryshire; MS., manuscript; n.d., no date; N.R., North Riding; no., number; Norf., Norfolk; Northants., Northamptonshire; Northumb., Northumberland; Notts., Nottinghamshire; Oxon., Oxfordshire; para., paragraph; Proc., Proceedings; pt., part; R.O., Record[s] Office; rec., record; Revd., Reverend; Rut., Rutland; s.a., *sub anno* (under the year) *or* *sub annis* (under the years); s.v., *sub verbo* (under the word); s.vv., *sub verbis* (under the words); ser., series; Soc., Society; Som., Somerset; sqq., *sequentes* (following); Staffs., Staffordshire; Suff., Suffolk; Surr., Surrey; Suss., Sussex; trans., translated by; Trans., Transactions; TS., typescript; Univ., University; V.C.H., Victoria County History; V.C.H. recs., Institute of Historical Research, London, Victoria County History records; vol., volume; W.R., West Riding; Warws., Warwickshire; Westmld., Westmorland; Wilts., Wiltshire; Worcs., Worcestershire; Yorks., Yorkshire

CHRISTOPHER ELRINGTON AND THE V.C.H.

Susan Reynolds

Christopher Elrington joined the V.C.H. in May 1954 after completing a London M.A. on John of Salisbury. Before that he had gone through Wellington, national service, and University College, Oxford, together with a variety of holiday jobs. One of them produced an offer of a permanent post as a tea planter. This book is testimony to the unanimous belief among his colleagues that it was a very good thing that Christopher turned the offer down and instead spent his working life with the V.C.H.

Christopher was appointed as the junior of two assistants to the general editor when Peter Tillott left to become editor of York and the East Riding and I moved up into Peter's place and the better desk, facing the door. The office we worked in was a small, cramped, and oddly shaped room partitioned off the Lower Hall on the first floor of the Institute of Historical Research. It was reached through a dark entrance tunnel that is now filled with cupboards of theses. Beyond that were three desks squashed together by a large window from which mildly exciting but never fatal crashes could be seen at the end of Store Street, which was not then one-way. It was a sociable place. Apart from more purely businesslike visits from other county editors and assistants, Peter Tillott remained in particularly close touch and so did Michael Greenslade, who had just started his career on the Staffordshire V.C.H. with a period working with Peter and me in London. In 1956, when I went to work on Middlesex, George Watts came as junior assistant and, a few months later, Barrie Rose was squashed into the third desk as a temporary third assistant. We all worked quite hard but we did quite a lot of talking too. The then Director of the Institute, Goronwy Edwards, once referred to the V.C.H. assistants as the Institute Debating Society: he could hear us from behind the partition when he went through the Lower Hall. Some of our talk was frivolous, as when we composed an examination paper for candidates for V.C.H. jobs. Christopher produced verses on V.C.H. themes from time to time. Some of them are, I believe, somewhere in the files, but one way and another they are not really suitable for quotation here, chiefly because most would now need as much annotation as a school edition of a Shakespeare play.

A good deal of our talk, however, was about history and the V.C.H. Ralph Pugh had been general editor since 1949 and was determined to make the *History* more systematic and up-to-date. Encouraged by him, we thought a lot about what we ought to do and how we did it. One product of all the discussion was the start of the memoranda on different aspects of parish histories. The V.C.H. memoranda have not always been received very enthusiastically by county staff, but they began as a direct result of something like enthusiasm in the cause of improving the standards and scope of the parish histories. Enthusiasm in the assistants' office, however, was never allowed to be thoughtless. Everyone's ideas, even before they came under the general editor's scrutiny, had to be argued every step of the way with the other assistants. Another product of the arguments about method was the assignment of Christopher, soon after his arrival, to take the small Wiltshire parish of Woodford and write it up as a specimen of the new model. It was an unrewarding parish for the purpose because Woodford was so small and poorly recorded but, looking back, it is hard to believe how fiercely Christopher's effort was attacked by one or two senior county editors at the time. One of the milder charges referred to his 'machine-gun style': it is true that Christopher's writing has never wasted words, but most would say that it was neat and felicitous. The episode shows what Ralph was up against and how much he and Christopher have changed the V.C.H. since.

In 1959 Christopher was appointed editor of the newly revived Gloucestershire V.C.H. and moved, with Jean and their young twins, to live first in Newent and then in the splendid ground floor of the 19th-century Tibberton Court. Predictably, his time there was productive: *Gloucestershire*, volume six, came out in 1965 and volume eight in 1968. Of course he did not produce them on his own. Apart from the usual help with architecture, an assistant editor was appointed soon after Christopher started work. All the same, it is no disparagement of Kathleen Thomas or of Nick Herbert, who replaced her in 1965, to see the achievement as primarily Christopher's. One reviewer of *Gloucestershire* volume eight commented, as reviewers will, on the lack of general background to the information provided by the parish histories on subjects that especially interested him, though, to be fair, he admitted that that was inevitable. Another, however, remarked on the conspectus of economic history that could be built up from the parish histories and cited the account of Tewkesbury as one of the substantial studies of urban history that constituted a particularly fruitful recent development in the V.C.H. Meanwhile Christopher completed the work on Bishop Roger Martival's Salisbury register that he had started while he was in London: Ralph Pugh always encouraged his assistants to take on spare-time research. The idea was to advance the assistants' careers and keep their wider historical interest alive, but Ralph was a bachelor. For some parents of young children his benevolent intention might have imposed a greater burden than they could carry, but Christopher's energy seemed adequate for it all—editing a bishop's register and then general-editing the Wiltshire Record Society, as well as doing his V.C.H. work, gardening, ski-ing, playing tennis, squash, and bridge, and doing a good deal of general reading.

In 1968, at Ralph's insistence, Christopher returned to London as deputy editor. It must have been quite a difficult decision. The twins were at school in Newent and Monmouth. Jean was architect to the rural district council, designing much better old people's homes than they were used to, and also doing work that she enjoyed for the Tibberton estate. For the V.C.H., however, the benefits were enormous. Although as deputy Christopher had much less time for writing, which was a serious loss, he did a great deal of the essential drudgery of reading and criticizing and copy-editing typescripts and seeing them through the press. As Ralph got older and more remote Christopher also acted as a buffer between him and the county staff. In spite of Ralph's quirks the two of them made a very strong team. A new county was started in the 1970s and another revived, while on average over two volumes a year came out.

When Ralph Pugh retired in 1977 no outside or inside candidate, even if the most distinguished had been dragooned into applying, could have prevented Christopher from being the best qualified. Ralph once pointed out how valuable Christopher's ability to get on with people was to the V.C.H. It became still more so as the time of expansion gave way to financial stringency. It is not easy to defend the V.C.H. against the economies forced on rate-capped local authorities: an editorial team costs very little, in comparison with local authority departments, but cutting it is generally easy in terms of local politics. Only someone who is capable of arguing with friendly and polite persistence, obvious honesty, no desire to score points for their own sake, and total commitment to the cause could have kept so many counties going as Christopher has. The way that he has done that, has sustained the morale of the V.C.H. staff, and has stimulated them to produce both fast and well, can be better described by the joint editors of this volume than by any outsider. The two following paragraphs are therefore contributed by them.

Christopher's tireless determination has ensured that a great deal more of the *V.C.H.* has appeared since he moved to London. Having assisted as deputy editor at the celebration of 150 volumes in 1970, he was able as general editor to initiate the exhibition held in 1989 to mark the publication of 200 volumes—with several years and more volumes to go before his retirement. He has also made sure that, in several ways, the *V.C.H.* has become more widely available than in the past. One of his first decisions as general editor was to agree, and to persuade the publisher to agree, to allow public library authorities to produce reprints of parts of volumes at a low price. A steady stream of well-produced reprints has resulted, giving further encouragement to local authorities to maintain their support; and all that without abandoning the existing scheme to reprint older volumes in full. When Christopher took over as general editor, academic publishers everywhere were responding to economic difficulties by pushing up prices, cutting printing standards, reducing print runs, and remaindering back stock. The V.C.H. under his guidance took the opposite path of adopting new technology to cut production costs without reducing the physical quality of the books. They now have stronger bindings and more but cheaper illustrations, yet with no loss of elegance in the appearance of the text. Without Christopher's painstaking attention to detail and his patient diplomacy in persuading both local authorities to buy equipment compatible with the Institute's, and local staff to use it, the changes might have brought catastrophe. In the event, the real price of the information to the public has halved.

Christopher is also a brilliant editor, with an enviable knack of making the fewest possible changes for the greatest effect on style, concision, accuracy, and historical intelligibility. Authors whose work Christopher has edited tend to emerge with the feeling that the piece is still entirely in their own words and is what they would have written if they had worked harder at it in the first place. His own prose is so lucid and direct as to be an inspiration to read. On those occasions when a draft parish history seems well and truly stuck in the mire of facts, a look at one of Christopher's Cotswold parish histories in *Gloucestershire*, volume six, can make the contributors feel both that they have known the village since childhood and that they too could write a parish history like that. As a boss, he is always accessible and never makes one feel that one is wasting his time even for the most trivial enquiry or problem. He has seemed as happy to sit down for the two minutes needed to decide the best way of citing some obscure source as to spend hours over the more substantial matters of finance or setting up the 1989 exhibition.

It is difficult to imagine the *V.C.H.* without Christopher Elrington. To imagine it as if he had never existed is to imagine away a very great deal of the value that both professional and amateur historians find in it. Christopher's belief has been that what is wanted from the *V.C.H.* is that it should be scholarly and systematic in coverage and arrangement, but above all that it should be there. Anyone who has needed to find out local information either on other countries or on the bits of England without a *V.C.H.* will agree that the supreme merits of the *V.C.H.* are its presence and its systematic coverage. This book celebrates the chief reason why so much is there now, and why more and more of it is so good. That reason is Christopher Elrington.

BIBLIOGRAPHY OF
C. R. ELRINGTON

Compiled by the late Patricia A. Tattersfield and C. R. J. Currie

1959

'The Fitzwilliam Museum', *V.C.H. Cambs.* iii. 326–7.
'The University Archives', *V.C.H. Cambs.* iii. 327–9.
'The University Seals and Insignia', *V.C.H. Cambs.* iii. 330–1.
'Index', *V.C.H. Wilts.* iv. 461–86.

1962

'Woodford', *V.C.H. Wilts.* vi. 221–7.
'Sir Robert Atkyns and Lower Swell Church', *Trans. Bristol and Glos. Arch. Soc.* lxxxi. 204–7.

1964

'The Survey of Church Livings in Gloucestershire, 1650', *Trans. Bristol and Glos. Arch. Soc.* lxxxiii. 85–98.
'The City of Birmingham: Growth of the City', *V.C.H. Warws.* vii. 4–25 (with P. M. Tillott).
'The City of Birmingham: Communications', *V.C.H. Warws.* vii. 26–42.
'The City of Birmingham: Local Government and Public Services', *V.C.H. Warws.* vii. 318–39, 350–3.
'The City of Birmingham: Churches', *V.C.H. Warws.* vii. 354–96.

1965

Victoria History of the County of Gloucester, vi, ed. C. R. Elrington.
'Topography', *V.C.H. Glos.* vi. 1–258 (with Kathleen Morgan and Helen O'Neil).

1966

'Records of the Cordwainers' Society of Tewkesbury, 1562–1941', *Trans. Bristol and Glos. Arch. Soc.* lxxxv. 164–74.

1968
Victoria History of the County of Gloucester, viii, ed. C. R. Elrington.
'Topography', *V.C.H. Glos.* viii. 1–249, 262–90 (with Kathleen Morgan and
    N. M. Herbert).
'Index', *V.C.H. Glos.* viii. 291–310.

1969
Review of W. E. Tate, *The English Village Community and the Enclosure
    Movements* (1967): *Antiq. Jnl.* xlix. 175–6.

1972
Register of Roger Martival, Bishop of Salisbury, ii (2), ed. C. R. Elrington
    (Canterbury and York Soc. lviii).
Victoria History of the County of Gloucester, x, ed. C. R. Elrington and N. M.
    Herbert.
'Newnham', *V.C.H. Glos.* x. 29–51.
'Frampton on Severn', *V.C.H. Glos.* x. 139–55.
'Fretherne and Saul', *V.C.H. Glos.* x. 155–69.
'Hardwicke', *V.C.H. Glos.* x. 178–88.
'Longney', *V.C.H. Glos.* x. 197–205.
'Moreton Valence', *V.C.H. Glos.* x. 205–15.
'Standish', *V.C.H. Glos.* x. 230–42.
'Wheatenhurst or Whitminster', *V.C.H. Glos.* x. 289–99.

1973
Victoria History of Cambridgeshire and the Isle of Ely, v, ed. C. R. Elrington.
'Great and Little Eversden', *V.C.H. Cambs.* v. 59–68 (with Celia B. Clarke).

1974
Abstracts of Feet of Fines relating to Wiltshire for the reign of Edward III, ed.
    C. R. Elrington (Wilts. Rec. Soc. xxix).
'The Wiltshire Record Society', *British Studies Monitor*, iv (2), 19–23.
Review of P. J. Fowler, *Archaeology and the Landscape* (1972): *Trans. Bristol
    and Glos. Arch. Soc.* xciii. 189–90.

1976
Introduction to James Bennett, *The History of Tewkesbury* (reprint of 1830
    edn.).
Introduction to William Hutton, *An History of Birmingham* (reprint of 1783
    edn.).

1978

Victoria History of Cambridgeshire and the Isle of Ely, vii, ed. J. J. Wilkes and
   C. R. Elrington.

1980

'Fishersgate Half-Hundred', *V.C.H. Suss.* vi (1), 131.
'Kingston by Sea', *V.C.H. Suss.* vi (1), 132–8.
'Old and New Shoreham', *V.C.H. Suss.* vi (1), 138–73.
'Southwick', *V.C.H. Suss.* vi (1), 173–83.

1981

'Ralph Bernard Pugh: an Appreciation', *Wilts. Coroners' Bills, 1752–1796*, ed.
   R. F. Hunnisett (Wilts. Rec. Soc. xxxvi), pp. xiii–xvii.

1983

Review of *Hampshire Studies*, ed. J. Webb, N. Yates, and S. Peacock (1981):
   Southern Hist. v. 281–2.

1984

Review of *Rolls of the Fifteenth of 1225 and the Fortieth of 1232*, ed. F. A. and
   A. P. Cazel (Pipe Roll Soc. new ser. xlv, 1983): *Wilts. Arch. and Natural
   Hist. Magazine*, lxxix. 266.

1985

'Presidential Address: Assessments of Gloucestershire Fiscal Records in
   Local History', *Trans. Bristol and Glos. Arch. Soc.* ciii. 5–15.

1986

'Index', *V.C.H. Suss.* vi (2), 219–39.
Review of *The World of John of Salisbury*, ed. M. Wilks: *Wilts. Arch. and
   Natural Hist. Magazine*, lxxx. 253–4.
Review of *The English Rising of 1381*, ed. R. H. Hilton and T. H. Aston:
   Southern Hist. viii. 160–1.

1987

'Wyndham Half-Hundred', *V.C.H. Suss.* vi (3), 169–70.
'Cowfold', *V.C.H. Suss.* vi (3), 171–89.
'Shermanbury', *V.C.H. Suss.* vi (3), 189–98.

1988

'One Hundred Years of Somerset and Dorset Notes and Queries', *Notes and Queries for Som. and Dors.* xxxii (328), 689–94.

'National Record Societies', *The Blackwell Dictionary of Historians*, ed. J. Cannon, 297–9.

Review of Philip Riden, *Record Sources for Local History* (1987): *Jnl. of the Soc. of Archivists*, ix (3), 159–60.

1989

'Index', *V.C.H. Cambs.* ix. 421–51.

'Lordship and Lineage: the Descent of Manors in the Victoria County History', *Genealogists' Magazine*, xxiii. 41–7.

'Particular Places', *History Today*, xxxix. 61–2.

1990

The Victoria History of the Counties of England: General Introduction: Supplement 1970–90, ed. C. R. Elrington.

'The Victoria County History 1970–1990', *The Victoria History of the Counties of England: General Introduction: Supplement 1970–90*, 1–8.

'State of the V.C.H.', *The Victoria History of the Counties of England: General Introduction: Supplement 1970–90*, 9–14.

Review of *A Professional Hertfordshire Tramp: John Edwin Cussons, Historian of Hertfordshire*, ed. A. Deacon and P. Walne (Herts. Rec. Ser. iii, 1987): *Hist. and Arch. Review*, v. 33–4.

1992

'The Victoria County History', *Local Historian*, xxii (3), 128–37.

Review of Victor Belcher, *The City Parochial Foundation 1891–1991: A Trust for the Poor of London* (1991): *London Topographical Soc. Newsletter*, xxxiv. 7–8.

1993

Review of Kate Tiller, *English Local History: an Introduction* (1992): *Jnl. of Educational Administration and Hist.* xxv (1), 105.

INTRODUCTION:
COUNTY HISTORY

M. W. Greenslade

'**A**fter ignorance of Holy Writ, nothing could be more grave than lack of knowledge of antiquity and histories.' Tudor enthusiasm for antiquarian study and its sources had few bounds. 'Next unto the Holy Scripture chronicles do carry credit', and 'to send them forth abroad among men—for that purpose (I think) God hath in this age given the noble art of printing.'[1] It was against that background that the pursuit of county history emerged.

In the Middle Ages local history was mainly ecclesiastical. Its writers from Bede onwards were concerned with monasteries and bishoprics and with the saints and other leading figures connected with them.[2] In addition London, ever a special case, had its chroniclers from the 13th century. Towards the end of the 15th century topographical curiosity began to spread its wings. In 1478 William Worcester, formerly secretary to Sir John Fastolf, finished winding up his deceased master's affairs, and he spent his remaining years travelling the south of England and recording what he saw. It is possible that he was planning a full-scale study of the antiquities of England, but he died in 1482, leaving only a collection of notes.[3]

The father of English local history was John Leland (*c.* 1503–1552).[4] A clerical scholar who attracted royal favour, he was, as an absentee pluralist, able to pursue his antiquarian interests. In 1534 he set out on a tour of monastic and collegiate libraries with a commission from Henry VIII to bring the work of ancient writers 'out of deadly darkness to lively light'. He compiled a dictionary of British writers, among them over a hundred historians whose work fired him to find out more about the realm. He duly set out on a new tour in 1540. He reported his findings to the king in the form of a New Year's gift in 1546:

---

[1] For the first two quotations, from the Elizabethan John Twyne and from *Hollinshed's Chronicle*, see M. McKisack, *Medieval Hist. in Tudor Age* (1971), 66, 118; for the third, from John Bale in the mid 16th century, see J. Leland, *Itinerary*, ed. L. Toulmin Smith (5 vols. 1907–10), i, p. xii.

[2] See, e.g., T. D. Kendrick, *British Antiquity* (1950), 134; M. W. Greenslade, *Staffs. Historians* (Collections for a Hist. of Staffs. 4th ser. xi; Staffs. Rec. Soc. 1982), chapter i; below, Ches.

[3] A. Gransden, *Hist. Writing in England, c. 1307 to early 16th century* (1982), 327 sqq.; below, Norf.

[4] For Leland see *Itinerary*, ed. Toulmin Smith, i, p. vii sqq.; Kendrick, *British Antiquity*, chapter 4; McKisack, *Medieval Hist.* chapter 1.

I have so travelled in your dominions both by the sea coasts and the middle parts, sparing neither labour nor costs, by the space of these 6 years past, that there is almost neither cape, nor bay, haven, creek, or pier, river or confluence of rivers, brecks, washes, lakes, meres, fenny waters, mountains, valleys, moors, heaths, forests, woods, cities, burgs, castles, principal manor places, monasteries, and colleges, but I have seen them, and noted in so doing a whole world of things very memorable.

He stated that he planned 'a description to make of your realm in writing' within 12 months. It was to be followed by a history of Britain divided 'into so many books as there be shires in England and shires and great dominions in Wales', with six more on the islands of the realm. Finally there was to be a work entitled 'De Nobilitate Britannica'. His topographical work also included two poems, published in his lifetime unlike his more weighty *Itinerary. Genethliacum* (1543) celebrated Prince Edward and the topography of his principality of Wales, his duchy of Cornwall, and his earldom of Chester. *Cygnea Cantio* (1545) is a swan's eye view of the Thames between Oxford and Greenwich.

Leland planned in vain. A fellow antiquary, John Bale, recorded that in 1547 he 'fell besides his wits', and he never recovered. He had, however, introduced the idea of the shire as a unit for studying the history of Britain, and the idea took root. In 1549 Bale, lamenting the destruction of libraries, claimed that the loss could have been made good 'if there had been in every shire of England but one solemn library'.[5] Tudor map-making came to focus on the county. In 1563 the antiquary and map-maker Laurence Nowell, probably a cousin of the dean of Lichfield of the same name, proposed to Sir William Cecil, later Lord Burghley, the mapping of individual 'provinces' as well as the country as a whole. By 1567 he had drawn several county maps in addition to one of the British Isles, evidently with the backing of Cecil. The queen's printer Reyner Wolfe (d. 1573) had plans for maps of England and its regions as part of 'an universall cosmographie'. Between 1574 and 1578 Christopher Saxton published maps of all the counties of England and Wales, again with government backing. Having added a general map, he issued them all as an atlas in 1579.[6]

A 'carde' of Kent already existed in 1570, and it was for Kent that the first county history appeared in 1576, *A Perambulation of Kent* by William Lambarde. A friend and pupil of Laurence Nowell, Lambarde was by the 1560s collecting material for a historical dictionary of the chief places of England and Wales, and in 1571 he described his collection as a store house

---

[5] Leland, *Itinerary*, ed. Toulmin Smith, i, p. xi n.
[6] S. Tyacke and J. Huddy, *Christopher Saxton and Tudor Map-making* (1980). For Nowell see also R. M. Warnicke, *William Lambarde* (1973), 23; McKisack, *Medieval Hist*. 53.

2 John Leland

from which he intended to draw material for histories of all the English counties.[7] He worked up Kent as a *ballon d'essai*—what he described as 'but a bearwhelphe that lacketh licking'.[8] The experience, however, dampened his enthusiasm to proceed further. The preface, by Lambarde's friend and mentor Thomas Wotton of Boughton Malherbe in Kent, expressed the hope

[7] Warnicke, *Lambarde*, chapter 4; Lambarde, *Kent* (1596 edn.), epistle to Thomas Wotton; Tyacke and Huddy, *Saxton*, 29–30.
[8] *Kent* (1596 edn.), epistle to Thomas Wotton.

that Lambarde would go on to do for other counties what he had done for Kent; Lambarde himself had other views:[9]

> And, as touching the description of the rest of the realm, knowing by the dealing in this one that it will be hard for any one man (and much more for myself) to accomplish all, I can but wish in like sort that some one in each shire would make the enterprise for his own country, to the end that by joining our pens and conferring our labours (as it were) *ex symbolo*, we may at the last by the union of many parts and papers compact a whole and perfect body and book of our English antiquities.

Lambarde seems in fact to have gone on toying with the greater project. He finally gave up when William Camden sent him a manuscript of his *Britannia*. That work was in a different class from any previous antiquarian undertaking, and when returning the manuscript in July 1585 Lambarde declared that he might not now 'dwell in the meditation of the same things that you are occupied withal'.[10] Camden (1551–1623), the son of a London painter, had a childhood enthusiasm for antiquities which he continued to indulge at Oxford, encouraged by Philip Sidney, a fellow student.[11] Between leaving Oxford in 1571 and becoming second master at Westminster school in 1575 he travelled around the country making antiquarian collections. From 1575 such excursions continued in the school vacations. He was persuaded to turn his mind to publication—'to restore Britain to Antiquity, and Antiquity to Britain' as he himself put it—by the Flemish map-maker Abraham Ortelius, who visited London in 1577. In 1586 Camden published the first edition of *Britannia, sive Florentissimorum Regnorum Angliae, Scotiae, Hiberniae, et Insularum adjacentium ex intima antiquitate Chorographica Descriptio*. Dedicated to Lord Burghley, it was a small octavo volume in Latin. It was steadily expanded over five more editions, culminating in an illustrated folio in 1607. An English translation by Philemon Holland appeared in 1610. The work has several general sections, but its core is a survey of the British Isles county by county. It was based not only on years of fieldwork but also on wide reading, including documentary research, and on contributions from local correspondents. He drew extensively on Leland, not always with acknowledgement.

Camden became headmaster of Westminster school in 1593, but in 1597 he gave up what a hostile critic called his 'inferior province of boy-beating' to become Clarenceux King of Arms, an appointment secured for him by Sir Fulke Greville. He was a scholar of European standing, and his historical

---

[9] Ibid. (1576 edn.), 387.

[10] Warnicke, *Lambarde*, 26.

[11] For Camden see *D.N.B.*; Kendrick, *British Antiquity*, 143–56; S. Piggott, 'William Camden and the *Britannia*', *Proc. British Academy*, xxviii. 200–17; Camden, *Britannia* (1722 edn.), i, Mr. Camden's preface.

3 William Camden

achievements extended beyond the *Britannia*. That work, however, represents the peak of Tudor and early Stuart antiquarian study and also the foundation of much subsequent writing. Camden himself acknowledged that it was only a beginning:

> A new age, a new race of men will daily produce new discoveries. It is enough for me that I have broken the ice; and I have gained my end if I set others to work, whether to write more or to amend what I have written . . . I frankly own my ignorance, and am sensible that I may oft-times have been mistaken . . . What marksman that shoots a whole day can constantly hit the mark?

It is fitting that the monument above his grave in Westminster Abbey shows him with his hand resting on the *Britannia*.

The 1607 edition of *Britannia* included maps by Saxton and also by the surveyor John Norden (1548–1625).[12] By 1591 Norden had conceived the idea of a 'Speculum Britanniae', a survey covering every county complete with maps. He secured official backing. A Privy Council order of January 1593 described 'the bearer, John Norden, gent.' as 'authorised and appointed by Her Majesty to travel through England and Wales to make more perfect descriptions, charts, and maps'. The first part of the work was published the same year as *An Historicall and Chorographicall Discription of Middlesex*. It included an address to Lord Burghley, who made corrections to a manuscript draft of the work and in 1594 provided Norden with a new testimonial. By 1595 Norden's energy had produced a manuscript dedicated to the queen and entitled 'A Chorographical Discription of the severall Shires and Islands, of Middlesex, Essex, Surrey, Sussex, Hamshire, Weighte, Garnesey, and Jarsay, performed by the traveyle and uiew of John Norden, 1595'.

The enterprise proved over-ambitious. In 1596 he published *Norden's Preparative to his Speculum Britanniae*, describing it as a reconciliation of propositions put forward by various people (critics, wise or otherwise) and complaining that he had been 'forced to struggle with want'. The book was dedicated to Burghley, who in 1597 issued yet another letter of commendation to all justices. He added the request that Norden's 'state and ability being no ways answerable to his good mind, which may cause a hindrance to his good work', the justices should 'use their best favours for some voluntary benevolence or contribution to be given by them well affected to this service, who, as all other Her Majesty's subjects, shall reap the fruit of his labours'. In the event only one other volume, *Hertfordshire* (1598), appeared in Norden's lifetime, although he had completed the survey of Essex in 1594 and went on

---

[12] For Norden see *D.N.B.*; McKisack, *Medieval Hist.* 143–5.

to cover Cornwall, Northamptonshire, and Norfolk *c.* 1610–11. On the other hand several of his county maps were used by John Speed in his *Theatre of the Empire of Great Britain* (1611), a similar scheme to Norden's, though less ambitious.

When Lambarde produced a second edition of his *Perambulation of Kent* in 1596, he admitted that he had learnt a lot about the county from Camden's *Britannia*, but he was not overawed by it. He repeated his conviction expressed in 1576 that it was the local man who was best suited to produce a full-scale county history:

> Nevertheless, being assured that the inwards of each place may best be known by such as reside therein, I cannot but still encourage some one able man in each shire to undertake his own, whereby both many good particularities will come to discovery everywhere, and Master Camden himself may yet have greater choice wherewith to amplify and enlarge the whole.

Kent in fact was the first in the succession of county histories which are described in detail in the chapters that follow.[13] The county was well enough established as a major topic in the study of local history by the mid 17th century for Thomas Fuller to use it as the unit of classification in *The History of the Worthies of England* (1662):

> England may not unfitly be compared to a house, not very great but convenient; and the several shires may properly be resembled to the rooms thereof. Now, as learned Master Camden and painful Master Speed, with others, have described the rooms themselves, so it is our intention, God willing, to describe the furniture of these rooms.

It has to be asked why the county, established as a unit of English local government some six hundred years before, should have emerged as a major object of interest within the Tudor and Stuart renaissance of historical studies generally. The answer cannot be separated from the complex of reasons for that renaissance, but a major element is the new importance of the county in Elizabethan government and of the local gentry who as justices of the peace ran the county. With a practical interest in their pedigrees and title deeds they were readers of local history and often its authors as well. In the preface to Lambarde's *Kent* Thomas Boughton, a former sheriff of the county, commended the book 'to his countrymen, the gentlemen of the county of Kent', and stated:

> I know not (in respect of the place) unto whom I may more fitly thus send it than

---

[13] For a short survey see J. Simmons, 'Writing of English County Hist.', in *English County Historians*, ed. J. Simmons (1978).

unto you, that are either bred and well brought up here, or by the goodness of God and your own good provision are well settled here and here lawfully possess or are near unto sundry of those things that this book specially speaketh of.

William Burton gave local patriotism as his motive for writing *The Description of Leicestershire* (1622): 'rather than my native country should any longer lie obscured with darkness I have adventured (in some sort) to restore her to her wealth and dignity.' Thomas Habington embarked on his study of Worcestershire to refute a remark that there were 'few gentlemen of antiquity' in the county.[14]

Sir William Dugdale provides an example of the gentry network in action. After settling at Blythe Hall in Warwickshire in 1626 he read Burton's *Leicestershire*. Burton lived some eight miles away at Lindley (Leics.); Dugdale was introduced to him by Fisher Dilke of Shustoke, Burton's kinsman and Dugdale's neighbour. Burton then introduced Dugdale to Sir Simon Archer of Tanworth, a man described by Dugdale as 'very much affected to Antiquities', who in turn introduced him to the leading gentry of Warwickshire. They readily gave him access to their muniments, 'being desirous, through Sir Symon Archer's incitation, to preserve the honour of their families by some such public work as Mr. Burton had done by those in Leicestershire'.[15] Dugdale duly acknowledged them in the epistle dedicatory of *The Antiquities of Warwickshire* addressed to 'my honoured friends, the gentry of Warwickshire', and the book was offered to them 'as the most proper persons to whom it can be presented; wherein you will see very much of your worthy ancestors, to whose memory I have erected it, as a monumental pillar.'

The network included the regular meetings of the gentry, which provided further opportunities for antiquarian research. In June 1636 Dugdale asked Sir Simon Archer to remind William Purefoy at the sessions that he had promised to speak to Lord Brooke about his archives. Dugdale also asked Archer to 'speak to Jo. Hunt at the sessions for the seals he promised us of Rich. Beuchamp, E. of War., and what other you can get. Borrow if you can the black book of Warwick.'[16] Similarly in 1638 Archer was asked 'to take the opportunity of your monthly meetings to procure a catalogue of all the constableries in your hundred, with what villages, hamlets, and places of name or note are in each of them, for it will be of good consequence.'[17] It was at a meeting at Devizes in 1660 for choosing two candidates for the county in the forthcoming parliamentary election that John Aubrey and others

[14] Below, Worcs.
[15] *Life, Diary, and Correspondence of Sir William Dugdale*, ed. W. Hamper (1827), 8–9.
[16] Ibid. 155–6.
[17] Ibid. 174.

discussed a plan for a history of Wiltshire along the lines of Dugdale's *Warwickshire*.[18] William Sneyd of Keele (Staffs.) brought 'a little box, a deed and pedigree' to the Epiphany sessions at Stafford in 1679 or 1680, hoping to meet his antiquarian kinsman Walter Chetwynd of Ingestre, who had been asking him about the Sneyd family.[19] In 1684 Chetwynd's chaplain Charles King considered the Stafford assizes an excellent opportunity for promoting Robert Plot's forthcoming *Natural History of Staffordshire* and for distributing the map which had already been published; in a letter to Plot he described the occasion as 'a general meeting of the greatest part of your subscribers, and of the county'.[20] Another of Plot's correspondents informed him in March 1685 that John Beaumont, who was planning a natural history of Somerset, 'was to attend the gentlemen of that county the last week at Taunton assizes, to deliver his proposals and receive their subscriptions'.[21] A negative example of such gentry influence may perhaps be found in Oxfordshire's lack of a large-scale county history, partly explicable by Oxford's minor role as a county town, with the university overawing the gentry.[22]

While county history flourished, general descriptions of Britain continued to appear. In 1673 Richard Blome, a publisher and compiler of somewhat doubtful reputation, issued a *Britannia*, complete with maps, which was branded a 'most entire piece of theft out of Camden and Speed'.[23] John Ogilby (1600–76), a man of varied interests, added surveying to printing after suffering losses during the fire of London in 1666. He secured the titles of king's cosmographer and geographic printer and by the early 1670s was planning a three-volume 'Britannia' consisting of road maps, views of cities, and a topographical description of the kingdom. Only the volume of maps appeared, in 1675, but work had started on the topographical third volume by 1672 when John Aubrey began a survey of Surrey for it.[24] At the same time a plan for continuing the work of Leland and Camden with an emphasis on natural history was launched by Robert Plot (1640–96), an Oxford don who became the first keeper of the Ashmolean Museum in Oxford in 1683.[25] His 'Plinius Anglicus sive Angliae Historia Naturalis ac Artium' was to be a county-based survey of England and Wales, complete with maps. Only volumes on Oxfordshire (1677) and Staffordshire (1686) appeared, but as late as 1694 Plot issued a prospectus for a natural history of London and

[18] Below, Wilts.
[19] Greenslade, *Staffs. Historians*, 17, 166.
[20] R. T. Gunther, *Early Science in Oxford*, xii (1939), 216.
[21] Ibid. 275–8, 285–6.
[22] Below, Oxon.
[23] *D.N.B.*
[24] For Ogilby see *D.N.B.*; below, Surr.
[25] For Plot see Greenslade, *Staffs. Historians*, chapter v.

Middlesex. Both Plot and Ogilby made use of the questionnaire, a tool for research which became the norm for county history and which had been used by George Owen for his *Description of Pembrokeshire* (dated 1603)[26] and by Sir Simon Archer in Warwickshire *c.* 1630. Plot also contributed material on his native Kent and on Middlesex to an enlarged and newly translated edition of Camden which was issued in 1695 by Edmund Gibson, with maps by Robert Morden. Gibson, later bishop of Lincoln and then of London, produced an improved two-volume edition in 1722 but felt it necessary in his preface to defend such pursuits on the part of a bishop—an odd protest, given the increasing involvement of the clergy in local history:

> And though enquiries of this nature may seem less proper for the character and function of a divine, and especially for one of my age and station, yet I hope I shall not be censured for having continued this work under my care and inspection, when it is considered that all ages and stations must be allowed their diversions, and that no diversion can be more innocent or laudable than the history and antiquities of our native country.

One such cleric was Thomas Cox, an Essex pluralist, who produced a new survey entitled *Magna Britannia et Hibernia, antiqua et nova*. It appeared in six volumes published between 1720 and 1731 and was reprinted in 1738. Claiming to be based on Camden with additions, it is a survey of each English county, combining general history with a topographical gazetteer; Morden's maps were again used. Another enlarged edition of Camden with yet another translation was produced by the antiquarian Richard Gough in three volumes in 1789; that edition was reprinted in four volumes in 1806, with revisions to the first volume by Gough. He also turned to the bibliography of local history with his *Anecdotes of British Topography* (1768), a survey of printed and manuscript sources both general and for each county; a second edition in two volumes appeared in 1780 as *British Topography*.

The early 19th century brought an illustrated county series entitled *The Beauties of England and Wales*, published between 1801 and 1816. Originally planned to run to six volumes over three years, it ended as 25 volumes. It was initially the work of E. W. Brayley (1773–1854) and John Britton (1771–1857), who were responsible jointly or individually for nearly half the volumes. Disagreement arose with the publishers and the rest were written by various authors.[27]

Even more ambitious was the *Magna Britannia* of the brothers Daniel and Samuel Lysons.[28] They were members of a family which had bought the manor of Hempsted near Gloucester from the heirs of Sir Robert Atkyns, the

---

[26] *D.N.B.*

[27] For Brayley see *D.N.B.* and below, Surr.; for Britton see *D.N.B.* and below, Wilts.

[28] For the Lysonses see D. and S. Lysons, *Magna Britannia: Berks.* (1978 edn.), introduction by J. Simmons. See also the relevant counties below.

Gloucestershire historian (d. 1711). Daniel (1762–1834), having been appointed curate of Mortlake (Surr.) and later of nearby Putney, published four volumes on the environs of London 1792–6 and a volume on the remaining part of Middlesex in 1800. He inherited Hempsted in 1800, and in 1804 he succeeded his father as rector of Rodmarton (Glos.). Samuel (1763–1819) ceased to practise as a barrister in 1803 when he was appointed keeper of the records in the Tower of London. He contributed etchings to Daniel's *Environs of London*, and his other publications included volumes of plates illustrating Romano-British and Gloucestershire antiquities. He was director of the Society of Antiquaries 1798–1809. The *Magna Britannia*, with the subtitle *A Concise Topographical Account of the Several Counties of Great Britain*, was an attempt to fill the gap between the large-scale county histories and Camden's more general view. As the preface to the first volume (1806) explained, 'it appeared to us that there was still room for a work which should contain an account of each parish, in a compressed form, and arranged in an order convenient for reference'. Lord Brougham described the venture as 'the greatest topographical work ever attempted'. Nine volumes (numbered i–vi, some being in parts) appeared between 1806 and 1822; illustrated with maps and views, they covered Bedfordshire, Berkshire, Buckinghamshire, Cambridgeshire, Cheshire, Cornwall, Cumberland, Derbyshire, and Devonshire. After Samuel's death in 1819 Daniel felt unable to continue the series, recording in volume six that he had completed it after his 'melancholy loss' only because he felt pledged to do so. Even so the scale was expanding as the work progressed, and Daniel admitted that 'our lives would not have sufficed to the completion had they been prolonged even to old age'.

The same problem was experienced by those engaged on a large-scale history of a single county. By the mid 17th century it had been realized that such a project could prove too much for one man, 'being never so inquisitive and laborious', while the problems noted in an early 18th-century scheme for a history of County Durham included the 'incapacity of any writer in respect of the universal learning required'.[29] The problems became greater with the ever growing availability of raw material. William Hamper, the Birmingham antiquary, warned a prospective Staffordshire historian in 1823 to be under no illusions:[30]

> In addition to literary ability, the labour of a County History requires energy, independence, and undivided attention. No man ought to enter upon it who is not perfectly master of his time as well as his subject . . . the time and attention necessary for a County History can only be estimated by those who have engaged

[29] Below, Northumb., Oxon., Wilts.
[30] Greenslade, *Staffs. Historians*, 126, 185–6. See also R. C. Hoare, *Hist. of Modern Wilts.* i (1822), pp. v–vi.

in important literary investigations, where a simple date may occasion a day's labour, and a journey of perhaps 20 miles.

The pursuit all too often proved to be the ruin of health and wealth. The founding father himself, John Leland, went mad, and John Norden soon found himself struggling with poverty. Sampson Erdeswick (d. 1603), Staffordshire's first county historian, was remembered at the College of Arms, according to Anthony Wood, as 'being often-times crazed, especially in his last days', while another Staffordshire historian, Stebbing Shaw (d. 1802), succumbed to the stress of research and financial worries with his *History* only half finished.[31] The Revd. Benjamin Hutchinson circulated proposals for a history of Huntingdonshire in 1792 after 30 years' work but died mad in 1804 with nothing published. Edward Hasted finished the last volume of his history of Kent and the 12 volumes of the second edition during his seven years as a debtor in the King's Bench prison, where he landed in 1795 largely as a result of the expense of his *History*; his library was sold the same year.[32] Charles Gilbert seems to have put his history of Cornwall before his pharmacy business, and he was declared bankrupt in 1825. George Lipscomb, who published a four-volume history of Buckinghamshire between 1831 and 1847, found it too much for him: part of it is said to have been written while he was in the Fleet for debt, and the last volume appeared posthumously. George Baker, the historian of Northamptonshire, abandoned publication in 1841 broken in health and fortune; the next year his collections were sold in a six-day sale. Even the young Dugdale's researches had to be rescued by financial help from Sir Christopher Hatton. The Lysons brothers were notably favoured when in 1802 the Post Office agreed to allow replies by clergymen to Daniel's questionnaire to be sent free of charge.[33] Well might the Herefordshire historian C. J. Robinson in 1877 include among the essential qualities of a county historian vigorous health and a full purse.

In the preface to his *Borough of Stoke-upon-Trent* (1843) John Ward acknowledged that the completion of Stebbing Shaw's scheme for Staffordshire after 40 years was impossible:

All that the literary public can reasonably expect is that every commercial district, large parish, borough, or rural circle should have its particular history . . . If a combination of gentlemen having sufficient leisure and talent could be obtained throughout the county to engage, each in his own sphere, upon one uniform plan, it might then be possible to see a collective county history, worthy of the honour, wealth, and commercial importance of Staffordshire; but this project seems hopeless.

[31] Greenslade, *Staffs. Historians*, 24–5; for the rest of this para. and the next see, unless otherwise stated, the relevant counties below.
[32] *English County Historians*, ed. Simmons, 199 sqq.
[33] Lysons, *Magna Britannia: Berks.* (1978), p. x.

4 Stebbing Shaw

In fact concentration on the history of individual towns and, to a lesser extent, villages had begun in the 17th century, and the process continued apace. Similarly the idea of a collective county history was nothing new. The meeting at Devizes in 1660 produced a scheme for such a history of Wiltshire, even though, in John Aubrey's words, it 'vanished *in fumo tabaci*'. A proposal of 1758 for a history of the East Riding of Yorkshire involved the use of people 'to observe and collect what is remarkable and curious', and John Nichols's history of Leicestershire (1795–1815) was to some extent such a collective work. The founding of county archaeological societies, a feature of the 1840s onwards,[34] often had the stated aim of contributing towards a county history.[35] Northumberland went a stage further: its county history committee was formed in 1890 to complete the project begun by one man in 1814 and brought it to completion in 1940.

The whole movement reached its flowering with the launch in 1899 of the Victoria History of the Counties of England, otherwise known as the V.C.H.[36] Aiming to produce a historical encyclopaedia of England county by county and parish by parish in 160 volumes, it was, in the words of its general editor in 1954, 'an enormous, almost unmanageable, enterprise, such as could only have been conceived in an age of optimistic imperialism'.[37] The idea appears to have originated with G. L. (later Sir Laurence) Gomme, clerk to the London county council, who saw the *History* as a monument to Queen Victoria's Diamond Jubilee. In 1898 he enlisted the support of H. A. Doubleday, a partner in the publishing firm of Archibald Constable & Co., and a prospectus was issued in 1899. With the help of Lord Lorne, soon to succeed as duke of Argyll, the queen was persuaded to allow the enterprise to bear her name, and she became the first subscriber. A royal connexion has been maintained ever since. Argyll was also active in setting up an advisory council consisting of public men and scholars, and in addition local committees were established. In 1900 the County History Syndicate, Ltd., was formed to manage the enterprise.

Gomme soon withdrew owing to pressure of work, and in 1902 William Page, a partner in a firm of record agents, became joint editor with Doubleday. In 1904 he became sole editor. Besides much outside help, he had a full-time staff which included two sub-editors and a team of junior workers, many of them women who had been to university but were still not allowed to graduate. The first volume, for Hampshire, appeared in 1900, and 38 had been published by 1907, when, however, financial problems were being experienced. By 1914

[34] See S. Piggott, *Ruins in a Landscape* (1976), chapter ix.
[35] Below, Som., Staffs., Suss., Worcs.
[36] For the hist. of the V.C.H. see *V.C.H. General Introduction*, ed. R. B. Pugh (1970); *General Introduction: Supplement 1970–90*, ed. C. R. Elrington (1990).
[37] R. B. Pugh, *How to Write a Parish Hist.* (1954), 21.

the total number of volumes stood at 74, with 9 counties completed, but the
First World War brought work to a halt. Attempts to restart it after the war
failed, and in 1920 the enterprise was wound up and a liquidator appointed.
Page, carrying on as editor without a salary, made determined efforts to save
the *History*. Finally in 1923 it was bought from the receiver by W. F. D. Smith,
2nd Viscount Hambleden (of W. H. Smith & Sons), who had become
financially involved in 1906. After his death in 1928 his support was continued
by the 3rd viscount. Meanwhile Page moved in 1923 from Hampstead (Mdx.)
to Middleton near Bognor (Suss.), building a hut in the garden to house 14
tons of material collected for the *History*. Over the next nine years he
produced 16 volumes almost single-handed. The economic crisis of 1931
brought an end to Lord Hambleden's support, and the following year he sold
the *History* to Page. In 1933 Page conveyed it as a gift to London University,
which has continued to manage it through its Institute of Historical Research.

Page died in 1934 and was succeeded as editor in 1935 by Dr. L. F. Salzman,
who had been a sub-editor in the early years of the V.C.H. Financial
constraints and the outbreak of the Second World War reduced output, but
some local financial support was secured, notably from Warwickshire county
council and other Warwickshire local authorities. That pointed the way
forward for expansion after the war. In 1947 a Wiltshire V.C.H. committee was
formed. Funded by the county council, the borough of Swindon, and the city
of Salisbury, and working in partnership with London University, it embarked
on a county for which no volume had so far been produced. It was the first of
10 such county committees formed between 1948 and 1964, each funded out of
the local rates. Two further counties joined in the work in the 1970s, with staff
employed by London University. In 1949 R. B. Pugh, a prime mover in
Wiltshire, was appointed general editor following Salzman's retirement. On
his own retirement in 1977 he was succeeded by C. R. Elrington, deputy editor
since 1968 and local editor in Gloucestershire before that.

The 1899 target of 160 volumes had long been overtaken by events when the
publication of 200 volumes was celebrated in 1989. With 12 counties
completed, 12 in progress, 15 dormant, and 3 unstarted, the 200 volumes were
seen as marking something like the halfway mark, perhaps a somewhat
sanguine estimate. The V.C.H. has been part of the revolution which has
taken place in local history in the later 20th century. New ideas about the
content of local history have meant a widening of the *History*'s scope, and the
simple passage of time constantly produces new topics. The founding fathers
would not have envisaged that nine pages of the article on West Bromwich in
the Staffordshire *V.C.H.* would be devoted to an account of the town's
protestant nonconformity and each of its chapels. Still less could they have
imagined that the section would be followed by one headed Hindus, which
recorded that Ebenezer Congregationalist chapel, closed in 1971, was

5 L. F. Salzman

6 R. B. Pugh

reincarnated in 1973 as Shree Krishna Temple, with the installation of idols in 1974.

The qualities needed by the county historian are unchanged. The need for a full purse also continues, even if it is a public rather than a private purse. There are now wider opportunities, new aids, and fresh insights, but the challenges are correspondingly greater. The 1990s have brought a new problem: with yet another review of local government in progress there is a question mark over the future of the county as a local government unit and so over the future of local records organized on a county basis and the funding of enterprises such as the V.C.H. The heady enthusiasm of Tudor antiquaries amid which county history was born had sobered somewhat by 1714 when a lawyer could praise historical study in more measured terms: 'To know nothing before we were born is to live like children, and to understand nothing but what directly tends to the getting a penny is to live the life of a sordid mechanick.'[38] That perhaps is more in tune with the mood of the centenary decade of the Victoria County History.

[38] Quoted by D. C. Douglas, *English Scholars* (2nd edn. 1951), 14.

ARCHITECTURAL GUIDES AND INVENTORIES

A. P. Baggs

The publication of the final volume of the *Buildings of England* in 1974 was marked by a television programme and celebratory articles in newspapers and magazines. Nikolaus Pevsner had completed in fewer than thirty years and with minimal resources an architectural guide to all the counties of England. It was a feat which caught the public's imagination and the books, which were universally referred to as 'Pevsners', became the travelling companions of thousands of people and, much to their surprise, a source of profit to Penguin, their publishers.

Pevsner used to say that he was inspired to begin the *Buildings of England* partly by the example of the Dehio guides which he had known in his native Germany and partly by the frustrations of waiting for the Royal Commission on Historical Monuments, whose inventories were coming out so slowly that the series had no chance of completion in his lifetime. He was, however, working in a long-established English tradition of commercially published topographical guides. The earliest examples were a product of the picturesque interest of the later 18th century and were the successors of the architectural work of antiquarian writers like William Camden, Thomas Cox,[1] and Browne Willis (*Cathedrals*, 3 vols. 1742). The first multi-volume series which was specifically architectural was Francis Grose's *Antiquities of England and Wales* (6 vols. 1773–87), which is a collection of engravings with commentaries arranged by counties. Less well illustrated but containing much more topographical and architectural information is Britton and Brayley's *The Beauties of England and Wales* (25 vols. 1801–16).[2] Both Britton and Brayley were prolific authors and editors and any deficiency in the number of illustrations in the *Beauties* was largely compensated for by the numerous plates in Britton's *Architectural Antiquities of Great Britain* (4 vols. 1807–14) and his *Cathedral Antiquities* (1814–36). The latter series comprises 15 monographs on individual cathedrals which were published separately but are often found bound up as four or six

---

[1] For Camden's *Britannia* (1586 and later edns.) and Cox's *Magna Britannia et Hibernia* (6 vols. 1720–31) cf. above, Introduction.

[2] Cf. above, Introduction.

volumes. Both series have the advantage of a larger format than that used for the *Beauties*. The contemporary rivals of Britton and Brayley were the brothers Daniel and Samuel Lysons, whose *Environs of London* and *Magna Britannia* emphasized architecture and illustrated it with numerous etchings.[3]

The middle years of the 19th century saw the foundation of many national and local archaeological societies whose journals were to become the principal place for the reporting of new antiquarian research. One of the early projects of the Archaeological Institute was a county-by-county *Ecclesiastical and Architectural Topography of England*. The first two volumes covered the dioceses of Oxford (Bedfordshire, Buckinghamshire, Berkshire, and Oxfordshire) and Ely (Huntingdonshire and Cambridgeshire) and appear to have been largely compiled by ecclesiologists within the older universities. After that only Suffolk was published, in 1855, before the series was discontinued. The volumes are of interest for the thorough coverage of parish churches and as one of the first listings to make use of the architectural terminology which had been originally put forward by Thomas Rickman in *An Attempt to Discriminate the Styles of English Architecture* (1819 and later editions). A potentially more important survey of five and a half thousand English and Welsh churches was compiled by Sir Stephen Glynne between 1825 and 1874. The manuscript is at Hawarden Castle (Flints.) and only the entries for Kent, Gloucestershire, Durham, Wiltshire, Dorset, Yorkshire, Wales, and part of Essex have been published.

Two printed sources which became increasingly detailed during the later 19th century are county directories and general guidebooks. The value of Kelly's *Directories* is not so much in what they say about the early history of houses and churches as in the contemporary record of enlargements, rebuildings, and restorations. Much of that information was supplied by local correspondents and it is not easily available from any other source. The most comprehensive series of guides was Murray's *Handbooks to the English Counties*. Starting in 1851, they completed their coverage in 1899, but because of continuous revision and reprinting the bibliography is complex. For example Oxfordshire, which had occupied 120 pages in a volume shared with Berkshire and Buckinghamshire in 1872, had a volume of 229 pages to itself in 1894. At their best, as in *Lincolnshire* by G. E. Jeans, they were the most reliable architectural guides before the publication of Pevsner. Another completed series of county guides which has good, if brief, descriptions of churches is Methuen's *Little Guides*. Eight volumes are by J. C. Cox and four are by J. E. Morris, and the same authors contributed seven of the 10 volumes of the *County Churches* series which was started by the publisher George Allen in 1910 but did not survive the First World War.

---

[3] For the Lysonses and their work, above, Introduction.

Another near casualty of the war was the *Victoria County History*. As originally conceived in 1899 it was to include architectural descriptions of all the major buildings alongside the topographical histories, and a team of architectural investigators was appointed to work under the direction of a committee made up of some of the best-known architectural historians. By 1914 twenty-three volumes which included architectural topography had been published, most of them in the completed county sets (Bedfordshire, Hampshire, Hertfordshire, Lancashire, and Surrey) and in Worcestershire.[4] The staff, however, had already been reduced both for financial reasons and because the establishment of the Royal Commission on Historical Monuments in 1908 had taken away from the V.C.H. the obligation to produce any sort of inventory as well as opening up the prospect of the description of many smaller buildings. Some of the V.C.H.'s staff were recruited by the Commission, which also adopted the systematic method of describing churches and the standardized scales and date-hatching conventions which the V.C.H. had used on plans. The duplication of some of the text and drawings in both series' accounts of Hertfordshire and Buckinghamshire was the result of an agreed sharing of information. Between 1918 and 1939 the Commission published 15 volumes covering Essex, London, Huntingdonshire, Herefordshire, Westmorland, Middlesex, and the City of Oxford, and its terminal date for the inclusion of buildings, which had originally been 1700, was extended to 1750. Meanwhile the V.C.H. was having severe financial problems which meant that it could no longer employ full-time architectural staff. Nevertheless 13 topographical volumes were issued, completing among other things the sets for Berkshire, Buckinghamshire, Huntingdonshire, Rutland, and the North Riding of Yorkshire. In some the descriptions of buildings had been prepared before 1914, in others they were the work of a variety of contributors or of the editor William Page. Despite the problems of assembling the material the entries continued much as they had done before 1914, including plans of a selection of the churches and houses and with the majority of the photographic plates illustrating architecture.

The billeting of the non-combatant members of the Commission's staff in Cambridge during the war years led to the publication in 1959 of the City of Cambridge inventory. The investigators who had remained there, largely to collect additional material consequent on a decision to move the terminal date to 1850, also completed preliminary fieldwork for the whole of Cambridgeshire. Meanwhile additional provincial offices were established at Bristol (later moved to Salisbury) and York. They were responsible for the

---

[4] The last topographical volume for Worcs. (*V.C.H. Worcs.* iv), though finished before 1914, was not published until 1924

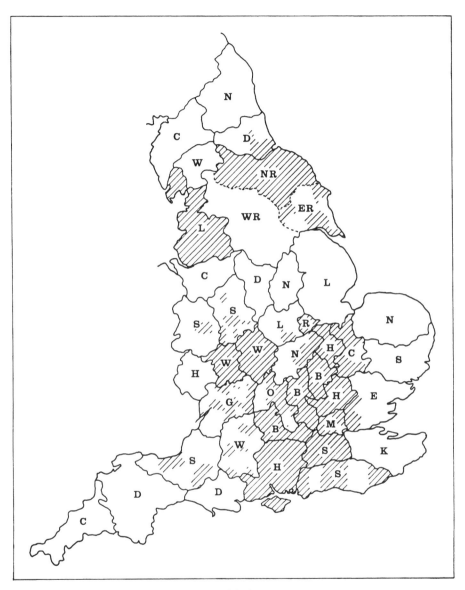

7 V.C.H. topographical coverage to 1993

preparation of inventories of Dorset (5 vols. 1952–75), the City of Salisbury (1980), and York (5 vols. 1962–81), while Cambridge, having revised the material for two areas of the county (1968 and 1972), went on to complete six volumes on Northamptonshire (1975–84) and one on the town of Stamford (1976). An increasing emphasis on non-architectural field monuments, which in the earlier inventories were included with the buildings, led to their separation into dedicated volumes in the Dorset and Northamptonshire series and to the first York volume being devoted to the remains of the Roman city.

New sources of funding after 1949 led to a rapid expansion of the staff of the Victoria County History and the appointment of a full-time architect in 1953. At first the architectural entries were continued in the traditional form but over the last twenty years the emphasis has changed from inventory to historical analysis and the relationship of the buildings to the general history of the places described. Fewer plans have been published although the majority of the plates in most volumes are still chosen for their architectural interest. When the Commission announced that in future it would concentrate on thematic rather than topographical volumes it was suggested that the V.C.H. might return to its more descriptive form of entry. The resources for doing that were not immediately available, and the place of the Commission inventory had to a large extent been taken over by the revised editions of what began as the Ministry of Housing and Local Government lists of buildings of architectural and historic interest. In their original form they were unbound duplicated sheets giving only the briefest description of the buildings. The early lists were frequently inaccurate and unperceptive, and they were not generally available to the public. During the last twenty years many of the lists have been revised. Although they are still not illustrated, more buildings are now included, and the information given about them is detailed and is often backed by historical research and references to other sources of information. The lists have not been published for sale to the public, but they are printed and spirally bound in green card covers which have given rise to the lists' colloquial name of 'Greenbacks', and by law they are available for consultation in local libraries and planning offices.

The Victoria County Histories, Commission Inventories, and Greenbacks have all made the task of the architectural-guidebook compiler easier. The Little Guides continued to be revised in the 1930s, and in 1948 Murray's started a new series of well illustrated *Architectural Guides*, of which only three volumes appeared (Berkshire, Buckinghamshire, and Lancashire). They were soon overtaken by the regular appearance of Pevsners, whose pocket-size format also made them easier travelling companions. Since the completion of the initial coverage of the English counties the Pevsner series has been extended into Wales and Scotland and a major revision of the older volumes has begun. To accommodate the new material, which often includes plans, a larger page size has been adopted, but despite that the books' length and weight is moving them away from the idea of a guidebook and towards classification as reference books. When the revision programme has been completed they will be the most authoritative catalogue of its historic buildings that England has ever had.

BEDFORDSHIRE

Patricia Croot

The county of Bedford, like other midland counties, lacks a strong topographical identity or natural boundaries. Formed in the 10th century when the midland area was divided into shires, its boundaries cut through several existing parishes, and the name Bedfordshire was not mentioned in the Anglo-Saxon Chronicle until 1011.[1] The absence of a distinctive identity may have been the reason for the lack of resident county historians, but paradoxically it may also account for the great output of work on individual parishes, especially since the Second World War.

The historiography of Bedfordshire illustrates the usual pattern of county history: the combination of natural history, topography, and antiquarianism as part of the scientific study of a locality in the 18th and 19th centuries, and the replacement of county history by local parochial history in the 20th. Before the late 18th century the only published accounts of the county of Bedford were by travellers and antiquarians writing about England in general, such as John Leland, William Camden and the successive revisers of his work, and Richard Gough. Though their own contemporary observations are a useful historical source, their historical facts are unreliable, and the vastness of their enterprises meant that they never got to grips with either the topography or the history of Bedfordshire.

From the 18th century a few scholars resident in the county, mainly clergymen, gathered notes on the natural history, topography, and antiquities of the county or of individual towns and villages, but whether from lethargy or the lack of a model or framework in which to present the material amassed, their work was largely unpublished. The only comprehensive treatments of the county were published by non-residents, one of whom expressed surprise in 1812 that the county still awaited its own historian.[2] In 1806 Daniel and Samuel Lysons commented that very little work had been done on the topography of Bedfordshire when they were writing, apart from the material gathered by the Revd. Mr. Cooper.[3]

Oliver St. John Cooper, born in 1741 in Bedfordshire and descended from local gentry families, was a curate at Wymington before becoming vicar of

---

[1] J. Godber, *Hist. of Beds.* (1969), 11.
[2] Thomas Fisher in advertisement to the 1st edn. of his plates, reprinted in T. Fisher, *Collections Historical, Genealogical and Topographical for Beds.* (1838).
[3] D. and S. Lysons, *Magna Britannia: Beds.* (1806), 36.

Podington and Thurleigh, all in Bedfordshire. He amassed many volumes of notes on the churches and the history and genealogy of Bedfordshire, collecting historical documentary evidence mainly from printed works such as Dugdale's *Monasticon*. At his death in 1801 his papers included unpublished histories of Bromham and Turvey, while his work on three parishes was published: notes on the history and natural history of Podington (1783); a narrative account of the parish of Wymington (1785) covering its topography, manorial descent, church architecture and inscriptions, parish charities, and incumbents; and an account of Odell (1787) describing the house on the site of the castle, the manorial descent, church and inscriptions, and notes on some incumbents. Those three accounts all appeared in Nichols's *Bibliotheca Topographica Britannica*, volume four, which also included church notes on Luton by Edward Steele, and an account of the town and abbey of Dunstable taken from *Chronicon sive Annales de Prioratus de Dunstaple*, published by Thomas Hearne in 1733.

Cooper's notes had a history of their own after his death. They were purchased by the Revd. Thomas Orlebar Marsh, and it was he who showed them to the Lysonses.[4] T. O. Marsh (1749–1831) was born and died at Felmersham, and was vicar of Stevington. His major interest was natural history, and he spent many years collecting material for a natural history of Bedfordshire, but it was said after his death that his retiring disposition had prevented his keeping up with new discoveries or publishing his own.[5]

Because topography and antiquities were seen in the 18th century as an extension of natural history, many students of the latter also had an interest in the former, while topographical histories continued to include natural history down to the early volumes of the *Victoria County History*. Marsh was evidently one of those who combined the two interests, but although he assisted the Lysonses and Thomas Fisher of Hoxton with topographical material, he did not manage to make use of Cooper's notes himself. In 1816 he sold Cooper's manuscripts for £157 2s. 6d. to Thomas Fisher, who had spent some time with Marsh in 1811–12 making drawings for a collection of engravings,[6] and a correspondent of Marsh thought that Marsh was wise to dispose of the material, which he might never make use of, to concentrate on buying books for his primary interest, natural history.[7] Fisher's drawings, prints, books, and manuscripts were auctioned in 1837 after his death; the sale catalogues do not specify the Bedfordshire notes though it seems unlikely that he would have disposed of them as he was still working on his plates of Bedfordshire.[8] At

---

[4] B.L. catalogue entry for Add. MSS. 34364–85.
[5] Lysons, *Magna Britannia: Beds.* 36; B.L. Add. MS. 23205, f. 4.
[6] B.L. Add. MS. 23205, ff. 83, 109, 114, 158; below.
[7] B.L. Add. MS. 23205, f. 140.
[8] *Catalogue of Interesting Topographical and Antiquarian Works by T. Fisher; Catalogue of Drawings, Prints, and Library MSS. of T. Fisher* [1837] (copies in B.L.).

some point Cooper's manuscripts were purchased by Sir Gregory Osborne Page Turner, Bt., and then by Sir Thomas Phillipps, Bt., the well known collector and bibliophile; the British Museum bought them, consisting of 22 bound volumes, at a sale of Phillipps's MSS. in 1893. Eleven of the volumes are indexed by parish, other volumes are arranged by source, and there are general volumes, an index volume, and a glossary; a patient searcher would be rewarded with useful items.[9]

Marsh's own manuscript collections, papers, and books were auctioned after his death: a large number of his papers, mainly miscellaneous historical and topographical collections and possibly excluding most of his natural history papers, were deposited in the Bedfordshire Record Office in 1977 by the North Bedfordshire borough council, with papers of the Pearse family who had been clerks of the peace. The papers are not sorted into any particular order and the researcher needs patience to wade through them, but besides Marsh's own notes they include primary sources such as estate and manorial court records.[10]

For Bedfordshire the problem of finding a model for presenting a topographical history was solved by the first work to be published on the county as a whole, in volume one of *Magna Britannia* (1806), by Daniel Lysons and his brother Samuel. Samuel (1763–1819) was an antiquary and keeper of the public records in the Tower from 1803 who made many of the drawings reproduced in their volumes,[11] while Daniel (1762–1834), a clergyman, was an outstanding topographer whose ability to organize a mass of material and establish a pattern in which to present it, together with a scholarly approach in obtaining primary historical evidence and citing the sources for his information, established the pattern for all the major topographical histories that followed, including the *Victoria County History*.[12]

The Lysonses' work was based on unpublished public and ecclesiastical records as well as printed works; they gathered information from landowners and clergy, and visited every parish. The account of Bedfordshire in *Magna Britannia* begins with an account of historical events in the county, then treats various topics such as communications, geology, natural history, and antiquities for the county as a whole, before giving brief topographical accounts of each parish, its manors, church, leading inhabitants, monumental inscriptions, and population from the 1801 census.

The Lysonses' work is still of value today. They never attempted to go beyond their sources to speculate, fabricate, or embellish the ascertainable facts; they often corrected antiquaries such as Leland when documentary sources showed the popular version of events to be untrue. Though

    [9] B.L. catalogue entry for Add. MSS. 34364–85, 'Collections for a Hist. of Beds. made by Oliver St. John Cooper', 22 vols.
    [10] Listed in National Register of Archives, 23412 Pearse, BC 529–36.
    [11] *D.N.B.*
    [12] Daniel's major work was *Environs of London*: below, Mdx.

occasionally they misinterpreted deeds of conveyance, usually because of lack of additional information, the citation of their sources means that it is possible to evaluate their reliability; on the whole their work is remarkably accurate and can be used with confidence.

Magna Britannia provided a model for later histories, and a useful reference point for other publications in the 19th century, particularly of illustrations of antiquities which were enormously popular from the late 18th century. Thomas Fisher, mentioned above, intended to publish a large collection of engravings from the drawings he made of antiquities and buildings in Bedfordshire together with text about them, but was deterred by the government's tax of 11 copies on new publications, against which he campaigned vehemently. The first edition, therefore, though promisingly entitled *Collections Historical, Genealogical and Topographical for Bedfordshire* (1812), was of 95 plates of buildings, brasses, stone carvings, tombs, and earthworks in the county, without text. He was unable to continue his work on the set until he retired in 1834 from his job as Searcher of Records for the East India Company, but he died in 1836 leaving some etchings unfinished and the volume of 114 plates was published with page references to *Magna Britannia* 'for those who wish to use the plates as illustrations to that popular work'.[13]

The Revd. John Docwra Parry, on the other hand, originally undertook to publish plates only, under the title *Select Illustrations, Historical and Topographical of Bedfordshire*, and not a complete history, but when he failed to get enough subscribers for the whole series, he published only one volume, in 1827, which included historical accounts of Bedford, Ampthill, Houghton, Luton, and Chicksands with the plates. He took the work of the Lysonses as a guide, consulted their sources, and transcribed other documents in full with translations from Latin. Parry, who was the son of the incumbent of Woburn, also published the *History and Description of Woburn and its Abbey* when he was 18; a new edition came out in 1823, and another in 1831.[14]

William Marsh Harvey probably used Cooper's manuscripts in producing *The History and Antiquities of the Hundred of Willey in the County of Bedford*, the only other published work of any substance on the county in the 19th century. It was produced for subscribers in parts between 1872 and 1878 and Harvey was obviously greatly influenced by *Magna Britannia* as his work followed very similar lines and included footnotes; it was nevertheless very much longer, using more space to cover a single hundred than the Lysonses had for the whole county. Harvey began with a brief introduction including the basic geography and communications of the hundred, which forms the north-west corner of the county, then gave separate chapters for each parish.

[13] Publisher's introduction to Fisher, *Collections*.
[14] B.L. Add. MS. 21067, f. 126v.; 1831 edn. in Bodl.

8 Samuel Lysons

9 Daniel Lysons

They included the descent of manors with lengthy genealogies of landowners, charities, advowsons, benefices and incumbents, parish church and inscriptions, interesting items from the parish registers, and the population from the censuses.

A hundred years after *Magna Britannia* was published, the only other comprehensive topographical history appeared, and as in the case of *Magna Britannia* Bedfordshire was treated because national coverage was the aim rather than because of a particular interest in the county. The *Victoria History of the County of Bedford* was published in three volumes between 1904 and 1912, with an index in 1914; the whole set was reprinted in 1972. No editor is given for volume one; the other two volumes were edited by William Page. The *Victoria County History* in its earliest incarnation was the last flourish of the 18th-century tradition of the scientific study of the local environment and delighted in the same non-historical subjects as the preceding topographical histories, while giving little space to the local economic and social history that underpins local history in the 20th century. Volume one (1904) therefore includes geology and natural history as well as prehistory, Anglo-Saxon archaeology, Domesday, ecclesiastical history, and religious houses. Volume two (1908) covers Romano-British, political, social, and economic history, industry, agriculture, forestry, schools, and sport, with the topographical accounts of the parishes in the hundreds of Biggleswade, Clifton, and Flitt. Volume three (1912) covers Bedford borough and the parishes in the remaining hundreds of Willey, Stodden, Barford, Wixamtree, Red-bournestoke, and Manshead.

Architecture, antiquities, and natural history continued to be the focus of activity within the county in the 19th century, with the apparently short-lived Bedfordshire Architectural and Archaeological Society, whose annual reports for 1853–67 survive, and some local field clubs. A serious county-wide society was formed only in 1914 when the Bedfordshire Natural History and Archaeological Society came into being, and by then efforts were already being made to preserve and publish local historical records.

In the first half of the 20th century an interest in the local records emerged which laid the foundation for work on local history in the county after the Second World War. Like many of the new county councils after 1889, Bedfordshire county council decided to make some effort regarding the public records they inherited. The county records committee was established in 1898 to take steps to preserve the records then kept in the county muniment room at Shire Hall, and Messrs. Hardy and Page, record agents, were commissioned to restore and arrange the sessions rolls for binding in volumes. Hardy and Page published extracts from some of the documents: sessions rolls 1714–1832 in volume one (1907), sessions minute books 1651–1660 in volume two (1909), and deeds in volume three (1911). The extracts are useful as far as they go but are random, brief, and not very comprehensive.[15]

Activity then seems to have died down until G. H. Fowler took over as chairman of the committee in 1913. He established an organized policy regarding records, with employment of a full-time assistant, introduced a policy of accepting private collections on deposit, proper arrangement of the muniment rooms, the creation of lists and calendars, and a workshop for repair of documents. Bedfordshire is therefore credited with being the first county council in the country to establish a county record office, and it set the example that other counties and repositories elsewhere followed. Fowler's *Care of County Muniments*, published in 1923, was the first printed exposition of the subject; he was also a founder member of the British Records Association.[16]

At the same time the Bedfordshire Historical Record Society came into being and began publishing its excellent series of primary sources for the county in 1913, producing 71 volumes up to 1992, as well as a three-volume survey of ancient buildings by category—windmills, pounds, wells, toll-houses—in the 1930s. The society also published *A Bedfordshire Bibliography* (1962) covering all publications up to 1960, with two supplements in 1967 and 1971, all edited by L. R. Conisbee, and a third supplement for 1971–75 edited by A. R. Threadgill. The bibliography is very wide-ranging and somewhat daunting as it covers contemporary topics, public services, topography, natural history, transport, and so on, as well as historical topics, and includes pamphlets and periodical and newspaper articles. It was compiled by searching libraries and bibliographies, and is particularly useful for local historians in giving the libraries in the county in which the publications can be found.

The county was also fortunate in having all of its parish registers up to 1812 transcribed and published, a useful source of information for the local historian as well as the genealogist. That was due to the efforts of F. G. Emmison when clerk of records in Bedfordshire; from 1927 he began transcribing the registers in his spare time, and duplicated copies of the transcriptions were published from 1931. Publication of the last of the 80 volumes took place in the 1990s, and some Nonconformist registers have also been published by the county record office.

The increasing availability of many parochial and personal records, and the development of economic and social history using material at local level, have together led to the development of local history with its focus on an individual parish, which has in turn encouraged the production of a very

---

[15] *Beds. County Recs., Notes and Extracts* (3 vols. 1907–11).
[16] Ibid. i, introduction; Beds. County Council, *Fifty Years at Beds. County R.O.* [?1963].

different kind of county history. In the 1960s the county council, aware of the fact that the standard history of the county, the *V.C.H.*, had been completed before those new developments and before the availability of the vast mass of local material that found its way to the record office (as they tactfully put it), commissioned their county archivist, Joyce Godber, to produce an authoritative history that would meet the needs of schools and record office users and reflect the modern approaches to local history.[17] Godber's *History of Bedfordshire* was published in 1969 and is one of those rare history books which manages to be both scholarly and entertaining. Though occasionally she was a perhaps a little too speculative and assumed local reactions for which there was no historical evidence, she managed to make an approachable human story out of historical facts to show how national events appeared to, or impinged on, local inhabitants. The *History of Bedfordshire* is divided into eight chronological periods with a pre-Conquest prologue and an epilogue on modern Bedfordshire. Each period is divided into chapters that follow a class hierarchy: upper class and countryside; church; towns; administration and justice; life in general. From 1530 the yeomen, craftsmen, and cottagers get a separate chapter, and roads and transport from 1689. The book is detailed and knowledgeable, covering all the traditional topics of national and local history and based on standard history monographs, the *V.C.H.*, printed national and local primary sources, and the contents of the local record office, with plenty of entertaining detail and quotations, especially from letters illuminating local politics. She also received assistance from scholars of Anglo-Saxon and early medieval history, which are therefore treated in more depth than is usual in local histories.

Godber points out where Bedfordshire evidence runs counter to the general national picture as established in historical writing by the 1960s; though the methodology is not generally innovative, her economic classification of villages in groups according to the number of surviving wills per acre is novel and interesting. Her book provides a wealth of well documented information for social, economic, political, administrative, and family history.

Nevertheless, that type of county history gives little sense of the *county* and there is no sense of what makes Bedfordshire different from any other county: the material presented by Godber is mainly about parishes which all happen to be in Bedfordshire, set against the national background. Her treatment reflects the way that county history generally has become the sum of a number of parish histories. The 19th-century topographical historians of Bedfordshire described the landscape around them with its natural history, roads, and geology which had no particular boundaries, and the ancient buildings and prominent residents for whom the parish in which they were

---

[17] Godber, *Hist. of Beds.* foreword.

located was irrelevant; the county was a manageable unit to work on and one which, moreover, reflected the situation still current then in which political power and administration was organized on a county basis.

With changes in the political and social structure of England, however, and the development of economic and social history, the county has become largely irrelevant to modern local history, and has ceased to form the basis for research, except among historians of the 17th-century 'county communities', where the way county administration brought local gentry together makes the county a logical political and administrative unit to use. Most human activity, though, can be well treated on a parochial basis, and historians seeking a larger unit than the parish tend to look at a region with its economic networks. So although local history in Bedfordshire today flourishes as never before, with hardly a settlement of any size lacking a published account of some kind, the history of the county itself seems to have been a short-lived phenomenon for which there is little rationale today.

BERKSHIRE

Simon Townley

Berkshire, birthplace of Thomas Hearne and for many years home to the historian F. M. Stenton, fared rather worse than some counties in its early historiography. Edward Rowe Mores's lament in 1759 that the county remained 'without an historian'[1] was echoed into the 20th century, and though numerous general histories and county collections were begun, few achieved comprehensiveness and even fewer publication: in 1993 the only reasonably full treatment remained the seriously outdated *Victoria County History*. No comprehensive bibliographical guide then existed, though the *Local Collections Catalogue* produced by Reading Public Library in 1958 (with a supplement in 1967) came closest, listing the library's extensive collection of printed and manuscript material; briefer handlists were produced on local initiative in the late 19th century and early 20th, many in local journals.[2]

As with most counties, the earliest systematic survey was Camden's in *Britannia* (1586), a work rightly characterized by a later Berkshire historian as 'a chorographical description . . . rather than an historical account'.[3] Certainly Camden had no special connexion with Berkshire, and up to and including the pioneering work of the Lysons brothers in the early 19th century the only remotely comprehensive accounts remained those produced as part of national surveys, frequently derived from Camden's work.[4] Traditionally, however, Berkshire's historiography begins rather earlier with the herald and antiquary Elias Ashmole (1617–92), locally applauded as 'first historian of the county . . . and one of the earliest . . . enquirers into the history of people and places', and after whom the county's first historical society was named.[5]

---

[1] J. Nichols, *Bibliotheca Topographica Britannica*, iv (1790), pt. ii, pp. 1–6 (misdated in heading to 1737).

[2] e.g. *Berks., Bucks. and Oxon. Arch. Jnl.* i. 106–7, 138; vii. 90–3; viii. 13–14; *Berks. Notes and Queries*, i (1890), 7–15, 53–7; A. L. Humphreys, *Handbook to County Bibliography* (1917), s.v. Berks. For maps (excluded from the present survey), Reading Public Library, *Local Collections Catalogue of Books and Maps relating to Berks.* (1958, supplement 1967); E. Burden, *Printed Maps of Berks. 1574–1900* (privately printed, 5th edn. 1992): copy in Bodl. G 14/C 17:12 A.

[3] E. Rowe Mores in Nichols, *Bibliotheca Topographica Britannica*, iv (1790), pt. ii, p. 1. For earlier allusions to Berks., J. Leland, *Itinerary*, ed. L. Toulmin Smith (5 vols. 1907–10), *passim*.

[4] In particular T. Cox, *Magna Britannia et Hibernia* (6 vols. 1720–31), i. 162–201; W. Camden, *Britannia*, ed. R. Gough (4 vols. 1806), i. 213–39. For the Lysonses, below.

[5] *Berks., Bucks. and Oxon. Arch. Jnl.* xxviii. 27; below.

Though closely connected with Berkshire through marriage and by his appointment as Windsor herald,[6] Ashmole seems never to have planned a comprehensive history on the lines established by his father-in-law William Dugdale; in connexion with his official duties he did, however, amass extensive notes on monumental inscriptions and genealogy (primarily during his visitations of 1665–6),[7] and more importantly collected voluminous materials for Windsor. Some were incorporated into his *Institutions, Laws and Ceremonies of the Order of the Garter* (1672), still an impressive work of scholarship, but he may have planned further works on the town and borough, and left unpublished collections culled from a wide range of public, corporate, and other records, ranging in date from the Middle Ages to the 17th century.[8] *Antiquities of Berkshire*, posthumously published in 1719, consists chiefly of monumental inscriptions copied during his visitations, and was an unhappy venture from all viewpoints but the printer's: Hearne expressed amazement 'at the abominable Impudence, Ignorance and Carelessness of the Publisher', adding that he could 'hardly ascribe all this to anyone else than to that villain, Curll [the Fleet Street printer]'.[9]

Hearne (1678–1735) himself seems not to have contemplated a thoroughgoing history of his native county, though his manuscripts contain numerous notes and sketches relating to Berkshire places,[10] and he composed a brief general description for an intended work on English topography,[11] besides an even briefer *Letter containing an Account of Some Antiquities between Windsor and Oxford*.[12] Notes left by his predecessor Anthony Wood (1632–95) contain similar jottings, chiefly church notes and genealogies,[13] and not until 20 years after Hearne's death were systematic attempts made at a parochial history of the county. One, apparently the work of James Theobald (fl. 1755) of Waltham Place in White Waltham, would if completed have been an impressive achievement. Opening accounts of White Waltham and of

---

[6] *Berks., Bucks. and Oxon. Arch. Jnl.* xxviii. 27 sqq.; *D.N.B.*

[7] For the date (often given as 1664–6), Harl. Soc. lvii (1907), p. vi.

[8] Bodl. MSS. Ashmole 850–2, 1097–1135 (esp. 1122, 1126), 1137; for visitations, cf. *Four Visitations of Berks.* ed. W. H. Rylands (Harl. Soc. lvi–lvii).

[9] Quoted in *Berks., Bucks. and Oxon. Arch. Jnl.* xxviii. 43; cf., however, the more positive comments of M. F. Bond, *Guide to Books about Windsor Castle and Borough* [Windsor, 1946], p. 4.

[10] e.g. Bodl. MSS. Hearne's Diaries 74, 99; partly printed in *Hearne's Collections* (11 vols., Oxford Hist. Soc. 1885–1921).

[11] Bodl. MS. Rawl. B. 246, pp. 13–22, 477–94.

[12] Written in 1708, printed in vol. v of Hearne's edn. of J. Leland's *Itinerary*, and again in 1725; cf. Bodl. MS. Rawl. D. 1173, f. 22.

[13] Bodl. MSS. Wood D. 4; D. 11; F. 32, f. 121 and v.; partly printed in *Wood's Life and Times*, ed. A. Clark (5 vols., Oxford Hist. Soc. 1891–1900). See also F. Wise, *Letter to Dr. Mead concerning some Antiquities in Berks.* (1738); idem, *Further Observations upon the White Horse* (1742), neither of more than historiographical interest; for miscellaneous early 18th-century notes by Edward Steele, Bodl. MSS. Gough Berks. 24, 26.

nearby parishes, drawing on extensive local knowledge and access to documentary material, contain a wealth of detail on contemporary as well as historical and genealogical matters, all systematically arranged, though descriptions of parishes further afield degenerated into bald (and often incomplete) statements about the church, living, and chief manors, together with transcripts of monumental inscriptions and some well tricked arms.[14]

At virtually the same time an attempt to overcome such limitations was made by the well known antiquary Edward Rowe Mores (1731–78), who although a native of Kent and (in later life) resident in Essex[15] retained a close interest in his ancestral county, producing an account of Great Coxwell (the ancient family seat), and in 1759 circulating a detailed questionnaire to local gentry and clergy with a view to compiling a comprehensive, parish-by-parish history comparable with those for Warwickshire, Hertfordshire, and Nottinghamshire.[16] Quite apart from his methodology, the scope was impressive: besides predictable topics such as manorial descents and country houses, churches, monumental inscriptions, and parochial charities, he sought information on markets and fairs, trade and manufacture, local customs, and archaeology, and attempted to locate privately-held cartularies, rentals, and other documents—the first local attempt to compile an inventory of historical materials. His enthusiasm was not unanimously shared, and he received only a handful of replies of varying fullness, printed posthumously (with additions from Hearne and others) by John Nichols (1745–1826) in his *Bibliotheca Topographica Britannica*. Ten volumes of Mores's own collections for Berkshire (chiefly transcripts from earlier accounts and from original documents, with replies to the questionnaire) were bequeathed by Richard Gough to the Bodleian Library.[17]

Throughout the later 18th century and the 19th a succession of aspiring county historians embarked on the ever-expanding task of collecting and ordering materials. That few achieved publication reflected not only the magnitude of the task but also the financial burdens which publication and research could involve, and it is symptomatic that many (like Theobald and Mores) were landowners or gentry with the necessary time and resources.[18]

---

[14] Reading Local Studies Library, MS. collections attributed to James Whitchurch (c. 1810); Bodl. MS. Top. Berks. c. 53 (unattributed, but clearly a companion volume). Though Whitchurch's name appears (with a note dated 1810) on p. i of the Reading volume, internal evidence shows it to have been written c. 1755–60, probably by Whitchurch's ancestor James Theobald: see esp. pp. v verso, 15. The Bodleian volume was also owned by Whitchurch in 1817. For Theobald, *V.C.H. Berks*. iii. 174, 177; for his researches, Bodl. MS. Gough Berks. 13, f. 82.

[15] *D.N.B.*

[16] Nichols, *Bibliotheca Topographica Britannica*, iv (1790), pts. i–ii.

[17] Ibid.; Bodl. MSS. Gough Berks. 13, 15–23. Though alerted to Theobald's work, Mores seems not to have used it.

[18] For the wealthy farmer and bibliophile Job Lousley (d. 1855), well known in local antiquarian circles though he published little independently, *Berks., Bucks. and Oxon. Arch. Jnl*. xxix. 16; *Berks. Arch. Jnl*. lxiii. 57–65.

Most eminent was Richard Griffin (d. 1858), Lord Braybrooke, the editor of Pepys's diaries, who compiled four volumes of notes (chiefly of transcripts, genealogy, and church matters), but apparently progressed no further.[19] William Nelson Clarke (d. 1855), who corresponded with him,[20] was owner until c. 1833 of Ardington and had more free time than he would have wished, lamenting in later life his lack of 'some profession or business, the want of which I have never ceased to deplore'. Having acquired an interest in antiquities while at Oxford he embarked in the early 1820s on collecting materials for the county, and in 1824 (at the age of 25) published his *Parochial Topography of the Hundred of Wanting*. It was a commercial disaster, but Clarke nevertheless found himself considered 'a regular aspirant to the honor of becoming the county historian', and like Mores circulated printed queries and received 'some few answers'. A few years later personal circumstances forced him to move away, and his extensive collections of transcripts, topographical notes, and pedigrees (with some correspondence) remained unpublished.[21] John Richards (d. by 1871), son of a Reading solicitor and county coroner,[22] also met commercial problems. A prospectus for a projected county history was issued in 1836 and royal patronage was obtained, but by 1839 (when the president of Magdalen College, Oxford, increased his order) there were doubts as to whether there were enough subscribers;[23] in 1871 Richards's unpublished collections were sold by his widow to the British Museum.[24] An earlier attempt c. 1808, when the Revd. Charles Coates (?1746–1813), historian of Reading, was commissioned 'to superintend the compilation of a History . . . upon an extensive plan',[25] was also abandoned. Such problems were highlighted in 1840 by the topographer John Britton (co-author of *Beauties of England and Wales*), who in a letter to the *Berkshire Chronicle* bracketed topography with horse-racing as a pastime suitable only for those (like Robert Surtees or Robert Clutterbuck) with a few hundred pounds to indulge in their 'topographical hobby'.[26]

Other historians had more modest aspirations. Charles Kerry, master of the

---

[19] Berks. R.O., D/EN Z1; the papers, formerly unarranged, were sorted and bound in 1976. For notes on Shrivenham manor and hundred by John, 1st Viscount Barrington (d. 1734), ibid. D/EE 1 E34.

[20] Letter of 2 Apr. 1825 in ibid. D/ECw F15.

[21] W. N. Clarke, *Memorials of his Family* (privately printed, n.d.), 64–79: copy in Berks. R.O., D/ECw F27; *V.C.H. Berks.* iv. 270; for his MS. collections, Bodl. MSS. Top. Berks. b. 2, 4–5; c. 1, 4–8; d. 4–5; e. 2–6; f. 2–3; Berks. R.O., D/ECw F19, F27.

[22] B.L. Add. MSS. 28663, f. 84; 28673, f. 306.

[23] Ibid. Add. MSS. 28660, ff. 142–3; 28670, f. 228; Berks. R.O., D/ESv (M) F92: letter of 16 Dec. 1836.

[24] B.L. Add. MSS. 28660–77, 39989–92.

[25] Ibid. Add. MS. 9409, f. 135 and v.; for Coates, *D.N.B.*

[26] B.L. Add. MS. 28673, f. 312.

Bray and Holyport school and author of the *History and Antiquities of Bray Hundred* (1861), turned later to antiquities in Surrey and Derbyshire;[27] William Hewett of East Ilsley (and later of Reading) confined himself to Compton hundred, while expressing a hope that his labours might one day benefit a county history.[28] Early 19th-century collections by Daniel Benham, a self-taught man with a strong interest in Nonconformist history (and who also published religious polemics) concentrate on Newbury and Reading, though not exclusively,[29] while early 19th-century collections for Berkshire and Oxfordshire by Henry Hinton (1749–1816) and James Hunt (1795–1857) consist mostly of church notes.[30] Different in kind are two volumes compiled from medieval records in his care by John Caley (d. 1834), assistant sub-commissioner of records, not from antiquarian zeal but in support of contemporary legal disputes;[31] in contrast with his antiquarian fellows, Caley (true to character) was presumably well remunerated.

The usefulness of such collections to modern researchers inevitably derives less from their historical content than from contemporary information and, sometimes, inclusion of obscure source material. Theobald and Hewett both gave details of contemporary agriculture, most described churches (and other buildings) before the onslaught of Victorian restoration, and the local correspondence contained in several collections is especially valuable. By contrast much of the purely historical material has since become easily available, though like their modern counterparts the early historians exploited whatever contacts they could. Ashmole transcribed a vast range of documents from New Windsor's corporate records, Kerry (two centuries later) made much of his privileged access to privately-owned manorial court rolls (chiefly for genealogical purposes), and Clarke made limited use of the archives of Worcester College, Oxford, for South Denchworth and Lyford, though for other parishes he had to rely almost entirely on the more accessible public records.[32] Richards's collections include some original documents and two volumes of 18th- and 19th-century correspondence,[33] and several contain

[27] C. Kerry, *Hist. and Antiquities of Bray Hundred* (1861); *Hist. of Waverley Abbey* (1872); *Smalley in County of Derby* (1905–7).

[28] W. Hewett, *Hist. and Antiquities of Compton Hundred* (1844), p. vii. The preface implies an earlier edn. of 1842.

[29] Reading Local Studies Library, MS. collections of D. Benham, listed in *Local Collections Catalogue* (1958–67); see D. Benham, *Reflections on Genealogy of Christ* (1836), preface; idem, *Notes on Origin and Episcopate of the Bohemian Brethren* (1867).

[30] *Oxoniensia*, xxxvii (1972), 215–20.

[31] Reading Local Studies Library, bound as 'Feudal Hist. of Berks.' (2 vols.). The collection, arranged chronologically by Caley, was rearranged by county before being sold.

[32] Clarke, *Parochial Topography of Wanting*, pp. iii–iv.

[33] B.L. Add. MSS. 28670–1.

invaluable printed ephemera and newspaper cuttings. That of the antiquary A. J. Dunkin (1812–79) contains little else.[34]

From the 19th century collections increasingly featured topographical drawings. Benham's and (earlier) Theobald's compilations included sketches, church plans, or architectural details in their own hands, and Richards devoted a large scrapbook to (mostly printed) engravings and drawings.[35] The widespread topographical work of (among others) Samuel Grimm (1734–94), the Bucklers, and Edward Blore (1787–1879), grandfather of a future president of the Berkshire Archaeological Society,[36] includes Berkshire materials, and unpublished drawings prepared by Samuel Lysons for the Berkshire portion of *Magna Britannia* survive in manuscript.[37]

More interesting historiographically is what such historians believed themselves to be achieving. Most lamented the pitiful tally of publications to date, and clearly considered it beyond contention that Berkshire deserved and needed a general history on the lines of those existing for other counties. Clarke, rightly divining that his book on Wantage hundred would be little read, quoted in defence Bishop Kennett's hyperbolic assertion that 'historical antiquities . . . will make [the student] understand the state of former ages . . . and, indeed, the nature of mankind'—though in later life he viewed the book as juvenilia fit only for 'the trunkmakers'.[38] Hewett hoped only to 'supply in some measure that great lack of topographical literature relating to Berkshire', and defined the topographer's task as to describe the present state of his region and narrate its past, omitting nothing 'seeming worthy of preservation'.[39] Most—understandably, given their backgrounds and the need for wealthy subscribers—concentrated on the traditional areas of genealogy, manors, country houses, church history, and the more obvious archaeological remains, though Clarke sought information on economic life,[40] and Richards's collections include demographic, social, and economic information culled partly from parliamentary papers,[41] an indicator both of widening horizons and of increasing source materials. For all, however, the chief impetus was a keen amateur interest in their surroundings and the pleasure of discovery. Sir Thomas Phillipps, writing to Clarke in 1821, regretted that they could not

[34] Reading Local Studies Library, MS. collections of A. J. Dunkin (for whom see *D.N.B.*).
[35] B.L. Add. MS. 28676A.
[36] *Berks., Bucks. and Oxon. Arch. Jnl.* xxxii. 65.
[37] B.L. Add. MSS. 9460 (Lysons), 15537–48 (Grimm), 36356–7 (Buckler), 42000–47 (Blore). For other collections of drawings, Bodl. MSS. Top. Berks. a. 1; c. 49–51; ibid. MS. Top. gen. d. 16, ff. 115–80.
[38] Clarke, *Parochial Topography of Wanting*, pp. iv–v; idem, *Memorials of his Family*, 76.
[39] Hewett, *Hist. of Compton Hundred*, p. v.
[40] *Queries proposed by Mr. Clarke, to the Nobility, Gentlemen, and Clergy of Berks.* [c. 1826]: copy in Bodl. Caps. 6.24.
[41] e.g. B.L. Add. MS. 28660, ff. 65 sqq.

devote more time to 'our favourite pursuit',[42] while Hewett cited as the chief motivation his 'fond regard for that place, with its vicinity, which gave me birth',[43] a view with which Mores (who also began with his ancestral home) might have concurred. Occasionally topographical notes were taken not as part of a systematic plan, but in hurried moments during trips made for other reasons, as with Benham's excursion to Reading in 1843 or his brief trip to Tadley (Hants) 'for . . . my health' in 1822.[44]

   Similar compilations continued into the late 19th century, though they were then rather anachronistic and may not have been seriously intended for publication.[45] By 1840 the unlikelihood of an individual singlehandedly producing a modern county history was publicly acknowledged, prompting calls for a county historical society to spread the burden,[46] and in the same year the Berkshire Ashmolean Society was formed to publish historical materials 'in private collections and libraries'. The society, with a membership of 300 (confined to men), 'bristled with F.S.A.s', among them John Richards and the young J. O. Halliwell, and published three volumes before disappearing presumably through lack of support.[47] It was followed in 1871 by the Berkshire Archaeological Society (B.A.S.),[48] founded (as the Reading Architectural Association) by a group of young architects associated with Charles Smith (the first president). Besides organizing lectures and excursions the society published from 1878 its own *Transactions*, succeeded in 1889 by the *Quarterly Journal* and in 1895 by the *Berkshire, Buckinghamshire and Oxfordshire Archaeological Journal*, brainchild of the Oxford bookseller James Parker, who recognized that three societies could meet the rising costs of publication more effectively than one. Though 'not a very lucrative venture, as many people forgot to pay their subscriptions', the journal survived the later withdrawal of the two other counties, continuing after 1930 as the *Berkshire Archaeological Journal*. From the beginning the society aimed at the 'examination of historic sites and ancient buildings, the encouragement of historical and architectural study, the preservation and restoration of

[42] Berks. R.O., D/ECw F15; for some of Phillipps's Berks. material, Bodl. MSS. Phillipps-Robinson b. 33; c. 261.

[43] Hewett, *Hist. of Compton Hundred*, p. vii.

[44] Reading Local Studies Library, Benham MSS. vol. i, pt. ii (1822), pp. 540 sqq.; ibid. 'Excursion to Reading, 1843'.

[45] In particular N. J. Hone's collections for Beynhurst hundred [*c.* 1886] and various collections by E. E. Thoyts, all in Reading Local Studies Library; cf. *Berks., Bucks. and Oxon. Arch. Jnl.* xxviii. 80. For church notes collected by W. H. Rylands (1847–1922), Blanche C. Wroughton, and J. M. Falkner: Bodl. MSS. Rylands e. 34–52; MSS. Top. Berks. a. 2–4; b. 8; c. 26; d. 14–16; e. 7–8, 16–17; MSS. Top. eccles. e. 14–17.

[46] B.L. Add. MS. 28673, f. 312.

[47] Ibid.; *Berks., Bucks. and Oxon. Arch. Jnl.* xxvii. 76–7.

[48] For the following, *Berks., Bucks. and Oxon. Arch. Jnl.* xxvii. 77–86; xxix. 44; *Berks. Arch. Jnl.* lxvi. 1–5.

historic monuments', and at disseminating information on 'topography, genealogy, heraldry, numismatics, prehistoric remains, and . . . archaeology', and by 1921 had 'earned the character of an active Society'; a local history recording scheme (concerned with oral history) was established in 1924. Less successful was an intention to publish original documents: as late as 1960 Stenton highlighted the lack of printed records as the chief weakness of local studies in the county.[49] A Berkshire Record Society was launched in 1993.

More localized societies arose during the same period, to such an extent that by 1921 they were viewed by some as a positive handicap to co-ordinated research.[50] The *Transactions* of the Newbury District Field Club (established in 1870 to 'promote knowledge of the natural history and antiquities' of west Berkshire and north Hampshire) continued in 1991, when they included recollections, popular history, and amateur research in contrast to the more academic *Berkshire Archaeological Journal*.[51] More short-lived were the Maidenhead Naturalists' Field Club (later Maidenhead and Taplow Field Club), the Thames Valley Antiquarian Society,[52] and the quarterly *Berkshire Notes and Queries* (published from 1890 to 1891). The backbone of such ventures were upper middle-class landowners, professionals, and clergy, who typically split their time between historical pursuits and public works; among them were C. E. Keyser (d. 1929), president of the B.A.S. and author of a standard work on church murals, Walter Money (d. 1926), historian of Newbury, John Hautenville Cope (later involved with the Victoria County History) and his wife Emma (née Thoyts), and P. H. Ditchfield (d. 1930), rector of Barkham, author of popular histories (and later co-editor of the V.C.H.), and for 35 years editor of the *Berkshire Archaeological Journal*.[53] A later B.A.S. president was Sir Frank Stenton (1880–1967),[54] formerly professor of modern history at Reading University, whose presidency marked a shift towards greater professionalization and whose other contributions to Berkshire historiography included his *Place-Names of Berkshire* (1910) and *Early History of Abingdon Abbey* (1913). A further development of the later 19th century was the opening in 1883 of Reading Public Library, which quickly acquired impressive local collections through the gifts of donors such as Money, A. E. O. Slocock of Newbury, and A. L. Humphreys,[55] author

[49] *Berks. Arch. Jnl.* lxiii. 4.

[50] *Berks., Bucks. and Oxon. Arch. Jnl.* xxvii. 85.

[51] *Trans. Newbury District Field Club*, i (1870–1); xiv (1) (1991).

[52] Reading Public Library, *Local Collections Catalogue*, s.v. Maidenhead; cf. *Berks., Bucks. and Oxon. Arch. Jnl.* xvii, title page.

[53] *Berks., Bucks. and Oxon. Arch. Jnl.* xxvii. 77 sqq.; xxx. 158–9; xxxii. 65–70; xxxiv. 50–3; and *passim.*

[54] Obituary in *Berks. Arch. Jnl.* lxiii. 1–4.

[55] *Berks., Bucks. and Oxon. Arch. Jnl.* xxix. 16–20; xxxi. 200; Reading Public Library, *Local Collections Catalogue*, introduction.

(*inter alia*) of curious compilations for East Hendred (1923) and Bucklebury (1932); a county record office, for which the B.A.S. had long campaigned, was finally opened in 1948.[56]

Despite such initiatives, the only comprehensive histories of Berkshire to be produced arose from external stimuli.[57] The first, in the early 19th century, was the Berkshire portion of the Lysonses' *Magna Britannia et Hibernia* (1806), about which much has been written;[58] suffice it to say that although Berkshire was one of the first counties tackled and the account is extremely compressed, the work was nevertheless a landmark in its comprehensiveness, methodology, and in the range of topics covered, which aimed to go beyond the traditionally antiquarian, prompting one contemporary local criticism that there were no arms, epitaphs, or pedigrees.[59] The unfinished series marked the limit of what was possible on individual initiative, and perhaps the most revolutionary aspect of the second great project to cover Berkshire, the Victoria County History, was its insistence that the work must be 'not the labour of one or two men, but of many . . . a system of co-operation between experts and local students'.[60] Work began by 1902 and was completed by 1914, though publication of the last two (topographical) volumes was delayed until 1924;[61] editorship was shared by William Page (general editor of the series) and Ditchfield (with help from Cope), and nearly 60 contributors received acknowledgment.

Local pride in the venture was unmistakable: A. L. Humphreys called it 'one of the greatest historical enterprises of modern times', and drew attention to its innovative exploitation of public records and comprehensive footnoting. His chief comments on the content, however, were to commend the manorial descents and accompanying pedigrees,[62] and certainly it is easy to find fault with the volumes from a modern perspective. Topography, settlement, and landscape were hardly discussed; economic and social history were treated in the general volumes but ignored at parish level; nonconformity was scarcely alluded to; and individual parish histories still rested primarily on descents of manors and advowsons, on architectural descriptions of churches and the grander houses, and on genealogy and heraldry. While the shortcomings are undoubtedly frustrating, it should

---

[56] *Berks. Arch. Jnl.* lxvi. 2.

[57] Excepting the popular and anecdotal accounts of C. C. King, *Hist. of Berks.* (1887), and P. H. Ditchfield, *Bygone Berks.* (1896).

[58] D. and S. Lysons, *Magna Britannia: Berks.* ed. J. Simmons (1978), pp. i–xxvii.

[59] Clarke, *Parochial Topography of Wanting*, p. ii.

[60] *V.C.H. Berks.* i, p. viii.

[61] Ibid. vols. iii–iv, title pages; *Berks., Bucks. and Oxon. Arch. Jnl.* viii. 1; ix. 1–3, 8–22, 36–7.

[62] *Berks., Bucks. and Oxon. Arch. Jnl.* xxvii. 52–5; xxxi. 205–7.

nevertheless be remembered that nothing on such a scale had previously been attempted, and that the only models available were existing county histories. Acknowledgments to Sir Paul Vinogradoff and J. H. Round (who contributed an extensive introduction to Berkshire Domesday) indicate the academic level sought if not always attained, while the introductory accounts of prehistoric and later archaeological remains (with gazetteers of finds) were the first surveys of their kind in Berkshire, within a relatively new discipline. The general volumes and accounts of towns (especially borough government) remain useful, and for all its faults it may at least be said of the *Victoria County History* (as it has been said of the Lysonses' work)[63] that for a century it provided the foundation of knowledge of the county as a whole.

If Berkshire had to wait until the 20th century for a comprehensive history, its chief towns fared little better until the 19th. Ashmole's collections for Windsor were mentioned above, and predictably Windsor dominated the county's historiography, usually with reference to the castle rather than the borough; significant works treating the latter included R. R. Tighe and J. E. Davis's *Annals of Windsor* (1858), and James Hakewill's *History of Windsor and its Neighbourhood* (1813).[64] A prototype popular history was Joseph Pote's *History and Antiquities of Windsor Castle* (1749), unashamedly aimed at those who found Ashmole 'too minute and circumstantial to be read with pleasure', and subsequently reworked as a successful guide.[65] Valuable accounts of Reading, Wallingford, and Newbury, based at least partly on archival research, appeared during the 19th century,[66] though Abingdon (for which unpublished collections were made by John Stevenson in the 18th)[67] remained neglected until 1910.[68] Among rural parishes, Wargrave was the subject in 1690 of a short unpublished account by a former vicar (whose motive was, however, preservation of the church's rights rather than historical interest),[69] and until the *Victoria County History* most parishes remained without a written history.

Berkshire's 20th-century historiography is too diverse for treatment here,

---

[63] Lysons, *Magna Britannia: Berks.* ed. Simmons, p. xxvii.

[64] Bond, *Guide to Books about Windsor.*

[65] J. Pote, *Hist. and Antiquities of Windsor* (1749), p. ii; *Les Delices de Windesore* (1755); for Pote, *D.N.B.*

[66] C. Coates, *Hist. and Antiquities of Reading* (1802); J. Man, *Hist. and Antiquities of Borough of Reading* (1816); J. K. Hedges, *Hist. of Wallingford* (1881); W. Money, *Hist. of Ancient Town and Borough of Newbury* (1887); for some of Coates's papers, Berks. R.O., D/P 96/28/1.

[67] Bodl. MSS. Gough Berks. 4–10.

[68] J. Townsend, *Hist. of Abingdon* (1910), essentially a chronological compendium; cf. J. G. Davis, *Short Hist. of Abingdon* (1894); W. H. Richardson, *Short Bibliography of Abingdon* (1902).

[69] Berks. R.O., D/P 145/3/1 (including additions by later vicars); it formed the basis of Theobald's account.

though a few themes may be identified. That no new county history has been produced (one or two popular and school histories excepted)[70] is unsurprising, given not only increased specialization and the explosion of source materials but also the current preference for regional rather than local, county, or parish history, which in an area as diverse as Berkshire militates against treatment of the county unit. Local government reorganization in 1974 accentuated the fact by merging the Vale of White Horse with Oxfordshire, and even the disposition of regional historical societies reflects the county's divisions, the Newbury society catering primarily for the south-west, the B.A.S. for the south-east, and the Oxfordshire Architectural and Historical Society traditionally claiming the Vale of White Horse.[71] Thus most recent studies treating Berkshire have been monographs dealing with particular historical problems, exploiting the county (or a part of it) almost incidentally and often because of availability of sources.[72] The literature on individual places is immense, ranging from institutional studies of individual towns,[73] to archaeological reports scattered through numerous journals, to historical case studies of particular villages.[74] Vernacular architecture has excited recent interest, owing primarily to the large number of surviving timber-framed buildings of medieval origin in the north.[75]

Yet the notion of the ancient county as a legitimate area of study persists. The Berkshire Local History Association, formed in 1976, explicitly claims the whole of the former county, and from 1983 has published its own journal, *Berkshire Old and New*.[76] The Berkshire Family History Society (formed 1975)[77] is also county-based, and record offices have retained intact their archives relating to pre-1974 counties, which for archival (and arguably for historical) purposes continue to have meaning. Last but not least, the

---

[70] Notably E. A. Greening Lamborn's innovative *School Hist. of Berks.* (1908).

[71] *Oxoniensia*, i (1936), p. 2.

[72] e.g. R. Faith, 'Berkshire', *Peasant Land Market in England*, ed. P. D. A. Harvey (1984), 107–77; P. J. Jefferies, 'Consideration of some Aspects of Landholding in Medieval Berks.' (Reading Univ. Ph.D. thesis, 1972–3); C. G. Durston, 'Berks. and its County Gentry, 1625–49' (Reading Univ. Ph.D. thesis, 1977); M. I. Connolly, 'The Godly in Berks. from Reign of Elizabeth to *c.* 1642' (Reading Univ. M.Phil. thesis, 1977); R. J. Williams, 'Crime and the Rural Community in 18th-Century Berks.' (Reading Univ. Ph.D. thesis, 1986). See also J. E. Brooks, 'Deserted Medieval Villages of North Berks.' (Reading Univ. Ph.D. thesis, 1983); K. G. Burton, *Early Newspaper Press in Berks. 1723–1855* (privately printed, 1954); E. A. Payne, *Baptists of Berks.* (1951).

[73] e.g. N. M. Herbert, 'Borough of Wallingford, 1155–1400' (Reading Univ. Ph.D. thesis, 1971).

[74] e.g. M. A. Havinden, *Estate Villages: Study of Berks. Villages of Ardington and Lockinge* (1966).

[75] e.g. *Oxoniensia*, xxvi/xxvii. 207–14; xxxii. 13–33; xxxiii. 71–88; xxxvii. 177–86; lvii. 81–244; *Berks. Arch. Jnl.* l. 30–48; lvi. 34–45; lvii. 86–98; lviii. 1–19; lxii. 45–70.

[76] *Berks. Old and New*, nos. 1–9 (1983–92).

[77] B.F.H.S. publicity leaflet.

historiographical tradition represented by Berkshire's would-be historians remains embedded in their collections, which, incomplete and unfashionable though they are, continue to be mined for information. They deserve preservation, not only as a resource but for the valuable insights which they provide into a vanished historical outlook.

BUCKINGHAMSHIRE

Diane Bolton

Buckinghamshire,[1] a 10th-century creation named after the stronghold or town in the north of the county,[2] was treated by most of the national topographers and historians from Leland and Camden. White Kennett, bishop of Peterborough 1718–28, referred to the county in his *Parochial Antiquities*, first published in 1695, although its focus was on Oxfordshire. A greatly enlarged edition in 1818 treated Chilton, near the Oxfordshire border. The first Buckinghamshire historian was Browne Willis (1682–1760),[3] a local squire who spent his time and money restoring churches, publishing surveys of cathedrals, and collecting antiquities. In 1712 he sent out a list of questions to incumbents to further his announced intention of writing a history of the county. He produced a list of all the knights of the shire (*Notitia Parliamentaria*) in 1715 and published a history of the hundred and deanery of Buckingham in 1755. It contained much undigested information from original records and was poorly received. His collection of material, catalogued by the Revd. William Cole, the Cambridge antiquarian, whom Willis had presented to Bletchley, was bequeathed to the Bodleian Library and became the starting point for subsequent histories. Cole's own collections[4] have been little used although his Bletchley diary for 1765–7 was edited by F. G. Stokes and published in 1931.

There is little evidence of historical interest in the county during the second part of the 18th century. Francis Grose's Buckinghamshire section of the first volume of *Antiquities of England and Wales* [*c.* 1787], for example, was very sketchy although he did list 15 market towns and calculate that the county contained 615 villages. In 1797 Thomas Langley published his *History of the Hundred of Desborough and Deanery of Wycombe*, in which he quoted extensively but without much understanding from records which he had found in the Tower, the British Museum, and Lincoln cathedral library.

---

[1] The assistance is gratefully acknowledged of Eileen Scarff (editor of Bucks. Rec. Soc.), Julian Hunt (Local Studies Librarian, Aylesbury), and Hugh Hanley (County Archivist).

[2] A. H. J. Baines, 'The Danish Wars and Establishment of Borough and County of Buckingham', *Recs. of Bucks.* xxvi (1984), 11–27.

[3] Based on A. C. Ducarel, *Some Account of Browne Willis* [1760], printed at end of Willis's *Hist. and Antiquities of Buckingham* (1755); J. G. Jenkins, *The Dragon of Whaddon* (1953).

[4] B.L. Add. MSS. 5839–40.

Several books were published in the early 19th century, though mostly as part of national series. Volume one of the *Beauties of England and Wales*, published in 1801, was later described as 'the earliest book with anything resembling a history of the county'.[5] George A. Cooke produced a pocket-sized *Topographical and Statistical Description of the County of Buckingham* in the Modern British Traveller series *c.* 1802. Daniel and Samuel Lysons, whose Buckinghamshire in their *Magna Britannia* series was published in 1806,[6] included information supplied by local clergymen and others and visited some parishes, but the work lacked the solid base of Daniel's Middlesex volumes. The Revd. Edward Cooke (d. 1824), rector of Haversham, gathered material for a county history, never published, and the duke of Buckingham sent out a questionnaire with a view to sponsoring a county history. Parochial returns made in 1826–7 form part of the Stowe collection.[7]

George Lipscomb (d. 1846),[8] as Edward Cooke's executor, gained access to his collection. Lipscomb, a medical doctor resident at Whitchurch, was already author of several books both on medical subjects and on British topography. He later claimed that he had begun collecting material on Buckinghamshire *c.* 1800, apparently as part of a plan for a history of Ashendon hundred, and his *Journey into South Wales* (1802) contained 78 pages on the topography and antiquities of the county. For his main work on Buckinghamshire he allegedly searched all the main national repositories and libraries, as well as those of the universities, and the archives of local families. Nevertheless Lipscomb's was an effort in the cumulative tradition: his own research had 'thus greatly increased the stores previously collected' by Kennett, Willis, Cole, Langley, and others, and the 'still more valuable materials' of Edward Cooke. Lipscomb's four-volume *History and Antiquities of the County of Buckingham* was published in parts from 1831 to 1847 (the last part thus appearing posthumously). It was dedicated to William IV and the 'nobility, gentry, and clergy of the county', but his success in obtaining subscriptions from those classes was very limited and his health and wealth, like those of so many county historians, were adversely affected by the work. Part of it was allegedly written while he was imprisoned in the Fleet for debt. It remained, however, the most complete history of the county until the advent of the *Victoria County History*.

Lipscomb's book was thoroughly traditional in form. It consisted of parish histories, with only a brief 32-page introduction discussing place names,

---

[5] [H. Gough], *Bibliotheca Buckinghamiensis* (1890).

[6] Issued with a new title page in 1813.

[7] J. G. Jenkins, *Hand-List of Stowe Collection in Huntington Library, California* (Bucks. Rec. Soc. 1956). For Stowe collection, below.

[8] This and next para. based on G. H. Wyatt, 'Lipscomb and his Hist. of Bucks.' *Recs. of Bucks.* xix (1971–4), 272–97; Lipscomb, *Hist. and Antiquities of County of Buckingham* (4 vols. 1831–47).

boundaries, rivers, geology, and Roman roads, and ending with lists of sheriffs, names of families recorded in visitations, and parish statistics reprinted from census reports. The parish statistics were thus detached from the histories of the parishes to which they refer. The topography was overwhelmingly dominated by descents of manors and advowsons, pedigrees, and lists of inscriptions on church monuments, lists which vastly outweighed the often terse architectural descriptions of the churches themselves. A few documents, notably letters relating to the siege of Boarstall Tower in 1844, some Buckingham corporation records, and the extent of Eton College's estates from the *Valor Ecclesiasticus* of 1535, were printed or reprinted *in extenso*. The illustrations were similarly dominated by views of churches and country houses and drawings of church monuments, very few plates being devoted to other types of building, to townscapes, or to excavated antiquities. Besides maps of hundreds Lipscomb included a few redrawings of early estate maps, though he was not the first English county historian to have done so.

The year 1847 was the turning point in the study of the county's history, for in addition to Lipscomb's work it also saw the foundation of the Buckingham-shire Archaeological Society.[9] There was no connexion between the two. Where Lipscomb's emphasis was on the local aristocracy, the society, which dismissed his work as 'incomplete and inaccurate', was heavily biased towards the Church. Most members were clergymen, the bishop was president,[10] the driving force from 1858 to 1890 was the secretary, Charles Lowndes, rector of Hartwell, of which he published a history in 1862, and the primary interest of the society was ecclesiastical. Even the recording of archaeological finds owed much to consciousness of the destruction wrought by church restoration. The society read papers, made outings which usually culminated in excellent food and wine, collected records and other material, and from 1854 published *Records of Buckinghamshire*. A county museum opened in Aylesbury in 1907 to house the society's collections. From 1937 a separate series, called *Buckinghamshire Record Society*, was published, initially by J. G. Jenkins, editor of several early volumes, on a private press in his garden. In 1947[11] the branch became entirely separate with the volumes devoted to single subjects, for example cartularies, charters, eyre and subsidy rolls, and episcopal visitations. *Records of Buckinghamshire* lost its ecclesiastical emphasis and carried several articles within one volume, archaeological reports and useful notes on accessions to the museum and record office, and research of a high quality on a variety of local historical topics. Between them the two series

   [9] E. Viney, 'Hist. of Soc. pt. 1, 1847–97', *Recs. of Bucks.* xxx (1988), 170–6.
   [10] William Stubbs, as bishop of Oxford, was president from 1890 although he was an honorary official only, never attending meetings.
   [11] The 7th vol., published in 1947, has 1943 on the title page, delayed no doubt by the war.

form the backbone of subsequent historical writing on the county. A natural history section was formed in 1947.

Some important source material had found its way into print before the establishment of the record society. Family papers, among the most important sources for the history of the county, were among the first. Those for the Verneys were published by the Camden Society in 1845 and 1853, by Frances Parthenope Verney in 1892,[12] and by Margaret Maria, Lady Verney, in 1930. Another collection, the *Purefoy Letters 1735–53*, was edited by G. Eland in 1931.[13] He also edited the *Shardeloes Papers* in 1947. The most important family papers, however, the Stowe collection, in the Huntington Library of California, remains unpublished although J. G. Jenkins produced a *Handlist* of the collection for the Buckinghamshire Record Society in 1956. Other records published early included the sessions records (by a Records Joint Committee of the County Council), charters of the borough of Chipping Wycombe in 1817, *Calendar of Pipe Rolls for Bucks. and Beds. 1189–99*, edited by G. H. Fowler and M. W. Hughes for the Bedfordshire Record Society in 1923, Burnham church deeds in 1913, and a series of church registers published between 1902 and 1916 by the Buckinghamshire Parish Register Society. They included the first church register of Chesham edited in 1904 by J. W. Garrett-Pegge.[14] F. G. Parsons produced *Old Records of Monks Risborough* in 1936–8.

A history and topography of the county by James Joseph Sheahan (who was not a member of the Archaeological Society), published in 1862, was castigated by Henry Gough (who was) as 'abounding with errors', although it provided useful information about the contemporary parish and did not confine itself to the manor and church. Gough himself issued a prospectus for a history of the 'three hundreds of Newport etc.' in 1863. Although the work was never published his notes remain, deposited in the Bodleian Library. Gough did, however, produce *Bibliotheca Buckinghamiensis* (1890), which was originally issued with the *Records of Buckinghamshire*. As well as books, court cases and local sermons were listed and there was a section on local newspapers, starting with the *Buckinghamshire Herald*, published in 1792. Robert Gibbs, another member of the Archaeological Society, whose main interest was his native town, Aylesbury, produced a four-volume *Buckinghamshire* (1878–82), a selection of miscellaneous events arranged like a chronicle from 1400 onwards and including, in its last volume, material from contemporary newspapers. His *Buckinghamshire Miscellany* (1891) was a similar mixture of quotations from published sources. He also produced *Worthies of Bucks.* (1888).

---

[12] A 4-vol. edn. appeared in 1899, vols. iii and iv being by Margaret Maria, Lady Verney.
[13] Eland's edn. is better than that by L. G. Mitchell (1973).
[14] Its sequel, 1637–1730, was published by the Chess Valley Arch. and Hist. Soc. in 1984.

The *Victoria County History of Buckinghamshire* (1905–28) completed the history of the county in five volumes including the index volume. Particularly detailed on manors and churches, it was typical of its time in its neglect of economic and social history at the parochial level. There have been several general histories of the county since, almost entirely based on secondary sources. John Camp's *Portrait of Buckinghamshire* (1972), readable and anecdotal, is a good example of the genre. Even more anecdotal and impressionistic is *The Buckinghamshire Village Book* by the Buckinghamshire Federation of Women's Institutes, published in 1987. Michael Reed's *A History of Buckinghamshire* (1992) has been called a 'model of readable scholarship'.

Buckinghamshire possessed neither city nor large town until the development of Slough[15] (which was removed from the county in 1974) in the 1920s, followed by that of Milton Keynes, the new town and now the county's largest conurbation, from the 1970s. Milton Keynes has attracted several books. Frank Markham wrote a two-volume *History of Milton Keynes and District* (1973–5), which covered the area up to 1950, before the building of the new town. The county abounded with small towns, many of which attracted individual histories from the mid 19th century onwards. Such were the histories of Newport Pagnell by Joseph Staines (1842) and by Joseph Simpson (1868); of High or Chipping Wycombe by Henry Kingston (1848), by John Parker[16] (1878 and 1881), and by L. J. Ashford and L. J. Mayes, both published in 1880;[17] of Buckingham by H. Roundell (1857 and 1864); of Aylesbury by Robert Gibbs (1885); and of Winslow by Arthur Clear (1890). Several of those towns attracted new histories in the later 20th century.[18] Few town histories appeared between 1900 and 1945, but since the Second World War, and particularly in the 1980s, new histories have covered several towns previously unchronicled.[19] In 1974 Clive Birch, a member of both the Buckinghamshire Archaeological and Record Societies, founded Barracuda Books, based at first at Chesham and later at Buckingham. The firm specialized in community histories, many written by Birch himself. Generously illustrated, they treated the history of towns in the 19th and early 20th centuries.[20] Also associated with the company was Clive Birch's *Mixed Pack* (1983), the history of the Vale of Aylesbury hunt.

---

[15] *Story of Slough* by Judith Hunter appeared in 1983 in the Town Hist. ser.

[16] Parker's sons were respectively editor of *Recs. of Bucks.* and Oxford bookseller.

[17] Ashford, who dealt with the town up to 1880, used borough records, but Mayes, on the town after 1880, listed no sources.

[18] e.g. Buckingham by M. T. Vernon and D. C. Bonner (1969) and D. J. Elliott (1975), and Winslow by A. Wigley (1981).

[19] e.g. Wing [c. 1985] and Wavenden [c. 1986] by R. and R. Marks, and Wendover by M. Summerell (1989).

[20] Chesham (1975, 1977, and 1979), Aylesbury (1975), Amersham (1976 and 1991), Chesham Bois (1976), Beaconsfield (1976), Bletchley (as *Town of Trains 1838–1980* by A. E. Grigg), Olney (1981), Burnham (1984), Buckingham (1988), and Winslow (1989).

Eton attracted histories from 1713 but the best history of the college, by H. C. Maxwell Lyte, was first published in 1875. Country houses and gardens were an object of picturesque descriptions in the 18th century, of histories from the 19th. The gardens of Stowe, seat of Viscount Cobham and then of the dukes of Buckingham, were described in 1744 and the house in 1777 by B. Seeley.[21] Other houses with published histories are Hartwell by William Henry Smyth (privately printed, 1851–64) and Hughenden by Henry W. Taunt (1882). The 19th century also saw an attempt at the history of a group of villages in Gordon Willoughby James Gyll's *History of the Parishes of Wraysbury, Ankerwych Priory, Horton and Colnbrook* (1862), but village histories did not become a common subject until the 20th century. A. C. Chibnall's noteworthy study of *Sherington* (1965) was followed by others in the 1970s and 1980s. Other places attracted attention because of their association with the famous. Stoke Poges, where Thomas Gray (d. 1771) supposedly wrote his *Elegy in a Country Churchyard*, had a history by John Penn in 1813 and another, anonymous one in 1844. Olney, associated with Thomas Cowper, Chalfont St. Giles, with John Milton, Marlow, with Percy Shelley, and West Wycombe and Medmenham, with Sir Francis Dashwood and the Hellfire Club, were written about only as backdrops to their protagonists.

The first attempt at systematic architectural history, partly an indirect result of the work of the *Victoria County History*, was the Royal Commission on Historical Monuments's two volumes on the county published in 1912–13. Apart from guides in national series[22] the only later survey of note, *Nonconformist Chapels and Meeting Houses in Buckinghamshire* (1986), was also published by the Commission. The *Place-Names of Buckinghamshire* by A. Mawer and F. M. Stenton (1925) was the first in the county series of the English Place-Name Society.

Other special aspects of local history began to be treated in a more scholarly way after the Second World War, perhaps partly because of the increased availability of local records. A county archivist was appointed in 1938, the year after the Record Society published its first volume, and a purpose-built county record office opened in Aylesbury in 1966, about the same time as the local history library developed as a specialist part of the Aylesbury reference library. One of the major contributions of the latter is a comprehensive bibliography which aims to include all printed books on the county held in the county library in Aylesbury, in High Wycombe library, in the collections of the county museum, record office, and Buckinghamshire

---

[21] Cf. also *Drawings of Stowe by John Claude Nattes* (Bucks. County Museum, 1983); *Descriptions of Lord Cobham's Gardens at Stowe (1700–1750)*, ed. G. B. Clarke (Bucks. Rec. Soc. xxvi, 1990).

[22] J. Betjeman and J. Piper, *Murray's Bucks. Archit. Guide* (1948); N. Pevsner, *Buildings of England: Bucks.* (1960).

Archaeological Library, and including some books in the British Library and the Bodleian. It was compiled by C. Rippon, a former county librarian, to include all books up to 1969. It was continued to 1984 when the practice was abandoned. Divided alphabetically under subjects and places, its big disadvantage is that it is only available on microfiche in Aylesbury. In addition to the catalogues available in the record office itself and the reports in the *Records of Buckinghamshire*, the record office has published useful handlists like *Education Records* (1961) and a *Catalogue of Maps 1440–1850*. Elizabeth M. Elvey compiled a *Handlist of Buckinghamshire Estate Maps* for the Record Society in 1963 and other books on county maps were produced by Gordon Wyatt in 1978 and Valerie Scott and Eve McLaughlin in 1984.

Articles in *Records of Buckinghamshire* had dealt with individual excavations and other archaeological subjects but it was not until 1955 that J. F. Head's *Early Man in South Buckinghamshire* drew conclusions from them. He also provided a gazetteer and a summary of the relevant societies and museums. More recent work covering similar ground has tended to focus on the region or the locality rather than the county.[23]

The county was the focus of Richard W. Davis's *Political Change and Continuity 1760–1885: A Buckinghamshire Study* in 1972. Alison Cole's *The Aylesbury Duck* [1981] appeared under the auspices of the county museum. From the 1970s the landscape and its relation to history has formed the subject of several books,[24] though only Michael Reed's *The Buckinghamshire Landscape* (1979), a good starting point for more detailed research, treated the county as a unit. Other subjects treated in recent years include traditional industries,[25] railways,[26] crime prevention,[27] the county's volunteer forces,[28] health,[29] and the county's gentry families, some by members of the families themselves,[30] others by unrelated writers, of which G. and E. Elvey, *The Wiggs*

---

[23] e.g. K. Rutherford Davis, *Britons and Saxons: the Chiltern Region 400–700* (1982); K. Branigan, *The Catuvellanni* (1985); *Roman Milton Keynes: Excavations and Fieldwork 1971–82*, ed. D. Mynard (Bucks. Arch. Soc. 1987); P. T. Marney, *Roman and Belgic Pottery from Excavations in Milton Keynes 1972–82* (ibid. 1989).

[24] e.g. D. and J. Hay, *Hilltop Villages of Chilterns* (1971); L. W. Hepple and A. M. Doggett, *The Chilterns* (1992).

[25] L. J. Mayes, *Hist. of Chairmaking in High Wycombe* (1960). Books on other traditional crafts like lace-making and straw-platting are not exclusive to the county.

[26] R. Davies and M. D. Grant, *Forgotten Railways: Chilterns and Cotswolds* (1975).

[27] E. Viney, *The Aylesbury Association for the Protection of Persons and Property, 1785–1985* (1985).

[28] I. F. W. Beckett, *Call to Arms* (1985).

[29] V. E. Lloyd Hart, *Health in the Vale of Aylesbury, 13th–20th Centuries* (1979) and *John Wilkes and the Foundling Hospital at Aylesbury, 1759–68* (1979).

[30] e.g. Sir Francis Dashwood, *Dashwoods of West Wycombe* (1987); Sir Harry Verney, *Verneys of Claydon* (1968), an abridged version of *Memoirs of Verney Family during the Civil War* by Lady Frances P. Verney; Mrs. James de Rothschild, *Rothschilds at Waddesdon Manor* (1979).

of Mentmore (1984), was reviewed as a model of family history. More unusual is the autobiography of an early 19th-century labourer, Joseph Mayett, edited by Ann Kussmaul for the Record Society (1986).

The county contains a family history society and numerous local history societies. The Wolverton and District Archaeological Society collects old photographs, many of which were published in *Victorian and Edwardian Buckinghamshire* by Margaret and Ivan Sparkes (1976) in the Batsford series. Others, like Beaconsfield and District Historical Society, which compiled a *History of Beaconsfield*, ed. A. W. Taylor (1976, revised edn. 1983), published. A Workers' Educational Association class studied Slough in 1971–4 and published *A Town in the Making, Slough 1851*. There are other W.E.A. local history groups and Oxford University runs extra-mural classes on Buckinghamshire history. The University of Buckingham has shown little interest but several theses have been completed for the Open University, itself based mostly in Milton Keynes, and for other universities.

CAMBRIDGESHIRE

A. P. M. Wright

Despite the presence at its heart of a large colony of learned men, and despite the persistent interest during four centuries of diligent and increasingly scholarly antiquaries, Cambridgeshire did not begin until almost the mid 20th century to acquire a systematic and full-scale treatment of its past such as many others had received in the 18th or 19th. The delay meant, however, that when its history began to be written, in the national series named from Queen Victoria, it paid rather more attention to the affairs of those below the ranks of the gentry and clergy than would have been attempted earlier. Meanwhile the work of previous students had at least provided a good foundation for handling the more traditional topics of local history.[1]

John Layer, squire of Shepreth, south-west of Cambridge, who worked into the 1630s to compile an account of his native shire, was among the pioneers of the subject.[2] Before his death early in 1641 he had completed a manuscript history covering, relatively briefly, the borough and university of Cambridge (about whose most legendary origins he showed a marginal scepticism) and most of the county south of the Isle of Ely. At some stage he had drafted an ambitious scheme covering numerous aspects of the county as a whole and of individual places within it. What he actually achieved (in which he was also, perhaps unhappily, somewhat of an innovator) was related to the predilections of his social class: a fairly continuous account for each parish of the descent since Domesday Book of the estates owned by his contemporary county gentry. In the course of preparing those descents Layer busily transcribed old deeds from his own estate papers and those of neighbouring gentlemen. He probably did not undertake much personal investigation into the records of the Crown. For information from them he relied partly on extracts from Chancery and Exchequer rolls made available by the Yorkshire antiquary Roger Dodsworth (1585–1654), partly on a compilation by unknown hands, which survives at Trinity College, of records concerned with feudal tenures

---

[1] No attempt has been made here to discuss the historiography of Cambridge Univ., its colleges, or its members.

[2] W. M. Palmer, *John Layer, 1586–1640, of Shepreth* (Cambridge Antiq. Soc. octavo ser. liv, 1935).

within the county. Layer's contribution was to arrange the facts systematically by parishes and within each parish by manors, completing the most recent portion of each descent from his personal knowledge of his neighbours' affairs. He also treated rather briefly the status and ownership of the advowson of each parish church. When he journeyed around Cambridgeshire to inspect the churches his main concern was to note inscriptions and the heraldry on monuments and glass, much of which was destroyed soon after. He seldom noted any purely architectural features. His long recitals of the names of successive manorial lords were only occasionally interspersed with notices of the more immediate past, for instance of the deer and rabbits in a knight's park feeding over the site of a depopulated village, or of a tradition about pilgrimages to a hill-top chapel of the Virgin.

Layer's history, unperfected at his death, survives in several versions, one in virtually continuous narrative. His earlier failure to get printed one of the two handbooks that he had written for justices and constables might have discouraged him from attempting publication even if he had lived longer. For almost a century his manuscripts and notes were obscurely preserved at his family's Shepreth manor house, narrowly escaping destruction after his male line became extinct in 1717. One section sold as waste paper was recovered from being used to wrap drugs at an apothecary's. In the mid 18th century copies of Layer began to be made and studied by a circle of clerical antiquaries, some of whom also transcribed extracts from episcopal registers and similar records. Another who examined the registers was the Norfolk county historian Francis Blomefield (1705–52). His notes combined lists of parish clergy with records of surviving brasses and inscriptions, the latter based on fresh visits between 1724 and 1734 to about 35 of the county's 150 rural churches, besides the churches and colleges in Cambridge. They were eventually put into print in 1750.[3]

Almost simultaneously the first printed work to call itself a history of the county was produced by a Cambridge writing master, Edmund Carter.[4] Despite its name it is essentially a gazetteer, parish by parish, of the contemporary state of the county, following an account of the borough and university. It was largely a mere compilation, though containing some useful information about Carter's own day, such as the management of Stourbridge fair, besides reports of recent curious or disastrous events. In treating the churches he included from manuscript sources accounts of the expulsion of royalist clergy and the destruction of 'popish' church decorations during the Puritan domination of the 1640s. In handling the landholdings of the gentry, however, he troubled to trace them back beyond the 17th century for only a

[3] F. Blomefield, *Collectanea Cantabrigiensia* (1750).
[4] E. Carter, *Hist. of County of Cambridge* (1753).

few places apparently chosen at random. The book was padded out with summary lives of local worthies, borrowed from Fuller, and even a modernized version of Chaucer's Reeve's Tale, apropos of Trumpington and its mill.

Far more useful to later historians of the county, even though he published nothing himself about it, was the life's work of the indefatigable William Cole (1714–82).[5] He was brought up in the 1720s at Babraham, where he remembered the ornate mansion built by an Elizabethan financier, and the chalk-cut giant figure which probably gave the neighbouring Gogmagog Hills their name. Given independence by a small estate built up by his father, Cole could devote his early manhood, living in college at Cambridge, to the steady collection of material on the past of his native county. He transcribed in bulk bishops' registers and those of wills and church courts, often borrowing rare volumes to work on in his rooms, and copied lists of incumbents originally produced by fellow antiquaries, sometimes with caustic comments on their carelessness or inaccuracy. Because of personal disputes he particularly depreciated the work of Robert Masters, whom he later served briefly as curate at Waterbeach. (Masters's brief history of that parish, printed in 1795, was the first for any individual Cambridgeshire village.) Cole also calendared deeds (some now lost) from college archives, and also those of his friend Henry Bromley, Lord Montfort, at whose home, Horseheath Hall, he was a frequent and convivial visitor. During the 1740s, too, he explored all but five of the parish churches in the county, recording and illustrating not only their fabric, but also screens, other woodwork, and every single monument, inscription, piece of medieval glass, and hatchment then extant, all too many of which fell victim to 19th-century restorations. Sometimes Cole retrieved missing parts of brasses from church chests. He did not neglect the houses of the gentry, many also since demolished or rebuilt, carefully noting their structures and contents, especially when bearing heraldry. Having returned to live in Cambridgeshire in 1767 after 14 years holding a Buckinghamshire rectory, he continued into a gout-ridden late middle age to bring his earlier parochial topographies up to date with notices of recent changes and extracts from the newly established local press.

Although Cole may have contemplated writing a history of the county as a distant project, he made few efforts to put his almost embarrassingly large collections into publishable form. He did compile an account, not always accurate in its earliest stages, of the ancestry of one line of baronets, the Cottons, and devoted much effort to gathering, and alphabetically ordering, materials for an *Athenae* for Cambridge to match Anthony Wood's for

5 W. M. Palmer, *William Cole of Milton* (1935).

Oxford. His true preference, however, was for the sheer accumulation of knowledge in his chosen field. In a similar fashion he amassed numerous fragments of stained glass to fill the study windows of the lightly Gothickized house at Milton, north of Cambridge, where he spent his last years between 1769 and his death in 1782. He served posterity by leaving over 80 volumes of his notes to the British Museum.[6] About a third are principally concerned with the county rather than the university. The slightly malicious pleasure with which he scattered through them a *chronique scandaleuse* of the foibles, failings, and not infrequent lunacies of the contemporary gentry and clergy led him to forbid public access for 20 years from his death.

The first scholarly study of any part of the county to be printed was the *History of Ely Cathedral*, prepared between 1756 and 1764 and eventually published in 1771 by Cole's friend James Bentham (1708–94),[7] for many years a minor canon there. The handsome folio, whose large plates were accompanied by a pioneering discrimination of the different periods of medieval architectural style, was based on thorough research. In stately periods Bentham paraphrased the history of the cathedral and its community from the chronicles then available in print, also making extensive use of the 12th-century *Liber Eliensis*, which was not printed in full for another 200 years. Bentham also consulted the episcopal cartularies and registers for particular points. He related the founding and refounding of the monastery to a discussion of the whole Anglo-Saxon Church, although inevitably he took as authentic some stories and charters rejected by more recent criticism. The main history, however, consisted of biographies of bishops, priors, and deans, concerned primarily with their public careers. He noted only in passing their administration of the diocese and the liberty of the Isle, although he did procure an essay on the origin and maintenance of that franchise, whose later parts were based on reliable documentation.

In the volume devoted to Cambridgeshire in their incomplete *Magna Britannia*, for which they were collecting materials in 1806–7, the brother antiquaries Daniel and Samuel Lysons provided the first, and before the late 20th century the only, systematic history to cover the whole county.[8] Their histories of individual parishes, which comprise over two thirds of the volume, followed the by then customary emphasis on the manor and the church. For the earlier portions of their summary manorial descents (which through shortage of space often dealt with the succession of families rather than mentioning each individual lord) they were largely guided by Layer, and

[6] B.L. Add. MSS. 5802–87.
[7] J. Bentham, *Hist. and Antiquities of Conventual and Cathedral Church of Ely* (1771; 2nd edn., including memoir of author, 1812).
[8] D. and S. Lysons, *Magna Britannia: Cambs.* (1808); *D.N.B.*

those of his own sources then available. As a result for many villages they left
dead ground between the mid 17th century and the late 18th, except where a
landowner or his lawyer volunteered information from title deeds or manorial
court books in response to the Lysonses' standard questionnaire.[9] Many of
the facts supplied by their correspondents on charity schools and almshouses
were not published. Although the brothers travelled through the countryside
to study churches for the detailed account of medieval architecture which they
compiled, they largely neglected secular buildings save for brief notices of
some gentlemen's seats. The summaries of parish history in county
directories and similar publications of the later 19th and early 20th century
were largely derived from the Lysonses' work.

    In the mid 19th century the town clerk of Cambridge C. H. Cooper
(1808–66) produced for the borough and university a wide-ranging and
painstakingly compiled *Annals of Cambridge*, the fifth of five thick volumes
being supplemented by his son.[10] It arranged the main documentary sources
purely in chronological order without any attempt at interpretation. That lack
was partly supplied, for Cambridge's earlier history, by the fortunate decision
of F. W. Maitland to use the town where he lived to exemplify the growth of
an English borough against its agrarian setting.[11] The only other 19th-century
history covering the whole county, that by J. W. E. Conybeare, vicar of
Barrington, was an avowedly popular book, including very little original
research.[12] It was concerned largely with the involvement of the county in
national events and trends, and devoted much space to the university.
Conybeare briefly discussed Cambridgeshire's prehistory as then understood,
but gave little attention to the period after 1660. His scanty notices of life at
village level were to some degree supplemented by other volumes taking his
readers through various villages with accounts of picturesque buildings and
incidents.[13]

    Cambridgeshire long lacked a society specifically devoted to its local
history. The Cambridge Antiquarian Society founded in 1840 was initially
sponsored by university graduates, including distinguished natural scientists,
from among whom its membership and management long continued to be
mainly drawn.[14] Originally intended to provide a forum for relatively private
discussion, it nevertheless shortly began to publish occasional essays by its
members, being among the earliest local antiquarian societies to do so, besides

[9] Their correspondence for Cambs. is preserved as B.L. Add. MSS. 9412–13.
[10] C. H. and J. W. Cooper, *Annals of Cambridge* (1846–53 and 1908). For the father, *D.N.B.*
[11] F. W. Maitland, *Township and Borough* (1898).
[12] J. W. E. Conybeare, *Hist. of Cambs.* (1897).
[13] e.g. idem, *Highways and Byways in Cambridge and Ely* (1910).
[14] M. W. Thompson, *Cambridge Antiq. Soc. 1840–1990* (1990).

summary records of the subjects examined at its meetings. At first its attention was as likely to be directed to antiquities from outside the county as to those found locally, although it soon began to obtain coins, prehistoric weapons, pottery, and similar objects, discovered in the surrounding area. In 1885 those collections were given to the University Archaeological Museum newly established with the society's assistance. Of about 55 volumes published under the society's auspices between 1851 and 1942 (other than its *Proceedings*), almost a third were linked in some way with the university, and barely a third treated parts of Cambridgeshire outside the borough boundaries. From the 1870s, however, a few parish clergy and members of their families did contribute histories of their own and neighbouring parishes, sometimes partly based on considerable research in parochial, diocesan, and even national archives. Some incumbents also sent to the society's *Proceedings* detailed accounts of discoveries made while their churches were being restored.

After the society had been revived by an energetic secretary, having almost expired in the early 1870s for lack of members, it began to recruit more widely within the county. From the 1890s interest in local archaeology and topography was stimulated by regular excursions to view churches, manor houses, ruins, and earthworks. Even though the public lectures which helped the growth in its membership in Edwardian times might, as later, be as often concerned with ancient Egypt as with prehistoric Cambridgeshire, from the 1890s it was sponsoring excavations at nearby dykes, barrows, and villas by such notable archaeologists as Cyril Fox, whose *Archaeology of the Cambridge Region*, first published in 1923,[15] remains the most comprehensive survey of the area, and the sometimes eccentric T. C. Lethbridge.[16]

The society was, however, relatively slow to concern itself with the medieval or later history of the county, and in 1900 another was started to cover those periods for both Cambridgeshire and Huntingdonshire. Its somewhat autocratic founder, C. H. Evelyn-White,[17] had from 1885 until it collapsed in 1910 edited the *East Anglian*, covering Cambridgeshire, Essex, Norfolk, and Suffolk. In it he published numerous brief notes of his own, as well as several extensive series, compiled by others, of calendars and lists of records concerning Cambridgeshire in the Public Record Office. Meanwhile Canon J. H. Crosby printed in the *Ely Diocesan Remembrancer* a complete calendar of the bishops' registers from the mid 14th century to the late 16th.[18]

[15] C. Fox, *Arch. of Cambridge Region* (1923).
[16] Lethbridge's speculations relating earthworks to ancient mythology are contained in, e.g., *Gogmagog: the Buried Gods* (1957).
[17] Below, Hunts.
[18] Published monthly in *Ely Diocesan Remembrancer* between 1889 and 1914.

The most industrious and productive antiquary to study Cambridgeshire in that period was W. M. Palmer, who worked through many classes of older documents at the Public Record Office, besides much local material.[19] After his death in 1939 his extensive series of notebooks were deposited at Cambridge University Library. Palmer concerned himself particularly with the southern edges of the county, near both his birthplace at Meldreth, and Linton, from which he carried on a country medical practice between 1900 and 1925. His many publications included curious incidents as brief notes in the *East Anglian*, longer articles on individual manors, families, and churches, and short collections of documents on particular subjects. Before 1920 his articles largely appeared in the *Transactions of the Cambridgeshire and Huntingdonshire Archaeological Society*. Thereafter he also wrote frequently in the *Proceedings* of the Antiquarian Society, which from the early 1920s gave more space to the county's social and economic history. Between the 1930s and the 1960s scholars such as Helen Cam and J. S. Roskell also contributed discussion of its medieval administrative élite and parliamentary representatives. In 1952 the Antiquarians incorporated the declining Archaeological Society. From the late 1960s, however, the pages of *Proceedings* began again to be dominated by archaeology, both prehistoric and medieval. Another journal, issued from 1951 by the newly founded Cambridgeshire Local History Council,[20] provided an outlet for shorter articles, especially on the rural parts of the county.

In 1899 the Cambridge Antiquarian Society had projected the compilation of a history of the county to include detailed accounts of individual parishes, for each of which there were to be sections on its manors, church, charities, natural history, and general antiquities. References were soon being assembled from the national medieval records then in print, and authors were found for almost 30 parishes. The society shortly became aware, however, that its intended publication would compete with the Victoria County History, just then being organized. Although at first the society proceeded with its plans, by 1902 it was satisfied, on seeing an early volume, that the V.C.H. would accomplish what it had wanted for the county, and abandoned its project, handing over what material had been collected.[21] Initially work on Cambridgeshire for the V.C.H. was mainly concerned with the county as a whole.[22] Conybeare was recruited in 1908 to prepare its ecclesiastical history,

---

[19] For Palmer, *Proc. Cambridge Antiq. Soc.* xxxix. 1–4; *Trans. Cambs. and Hunts. Arch. Soc.* vi. 99–101.

[20] *Bull. Cambs. Local Hist. Council* [later *Soc.*] (1952 onwards).

[21] *Proc. Cambridge Antiq. Soc.* x. 68, 156–9, 269–70.

[22] V.C.H. recs., A 2 and other correspondence files, analysed in an unpublished paper by C. R. J. Currie.

and several articles were commissioned on its natural history and geology. The financial crisis that overtook the whole V.C.H. in 1908, however, meant that Cambridgeshire was effectively left dormant, with not a single volume published, until the V.C.H. was taken over in the 1930s by the University of London. An appeal for funds met with generous contributions from several Cambridge colleges. For the two volumes then written (publication of one being delayed by the Second World War) attempts were made, unsuccessfully, to entice country gentlemen to write on Cambridgeshire sports. The political, economic, and ecclesiastical aspects of the county were mostly entrusted to established academics including H. C. Darby, with his deep knowledge of the Fens, J. Otway-Ruthven, who handled Domesday Book, and Kathleen Wood-Legh. E. M. Hampson, who had already published a thorough study of the local administration of the old poor law,[23] contributed the account of local government and a section on schools.

Increasing public interest in local history from the 1960s encouraged many people to attempt detailed histories of their native or adopted villages. One by Rowland Parker for Foxton, south-west of Cambridge, in which diligent study of unprinted records was informed by a sometimes over-active imagination, achieved wide celebrity in the 1970s.[24] The more restrained and scholarly work of J. R. Ravensdale skilfully related the economic development of some fen-edge parishes to the resources available from their environment.[25] Several academic historians have also handled aspects of Cambridgeshire's medieval and early modern history. Edward Miller's book on Ely's lands was among the first to trace the feudal and agrarian development of a single large estate in the High Middle Ages within its regional context,[26] while Margaret Aston's account of the early career of one late medieval bishop also contains a lively narrative of the conflicts between the local agents of the bishop and archdeacon of Ely.[27] In 1974 Margaret Spufford revealed how changes in the early modern social life of three villages could be related to their differing situations on the county's chalk downlands, upland clays, and fen edge, and explored the early development of dissent in its social context.[28]

Meanwhile work resumed in the early 1950s on the volumes of the *V.C.H.* intended to cover local topography. The county was among the first in the series to benefit from the enlargement of the range of subjects treated beyond

---

[23] E. M. Hampson, *Treatment of Poverty in Cambs. 1597–1834* (1934).
[24] R. Parker, *The Common Stream* (1975).
[25] J. R. Ravensdale, *Liable to Floods: Village Landscape on the Edge of the Fens, A.D. 450–1850* (1974).
[26] E. Miller, *Abbey and Bishopric of Ely* (1951).
[27] M. Aston, *Thomas Arundel: a Study of Church Life in Reign of Richard II* (1967).
[28] M. Spufford, *Contrasting Communities: English Villagers in 16th and 17th Centuries* (1974).

such traditional topics as manors and churches to include economic and social life, the history of landscape and settlement, dissenting chapels, and village schools. The second volume to be published under the new dispensation, in 1959, covered Cambridge and contained the first analytical history of the city and an account of the university. The Isle of Ely had had a volume to itself in 1953, and from the late 1960s the rural hundreds of the county were slowly but steadily covered. The first volume, published in 1973, also at last treated Cambridgeshire sporting life. The account of horse-racing contrived to deal with Newmarket without including the name of a single horse or the result of a single race. In common with the rest of the *V.C.H.*, the parish histories for Cambridgeshire have over the years become longer and more elaborate with the addition of new sources and new topics. When the Victoria History first approached the county, three volumes were expected to suffice to cover it, but in the event the concluding volume of the set projected for publication in the mid 1990s will be the tenth.

CHESHIRE

A. T. Thacker

Cheshire's early history rendered it distinctive among English counties, if not perhaps as distinctive as some of its more ardent sons have claimed. Though the great fief established by the Conqueror for Hugh of Avranches was not (as Cheshire antiquaries long believed) a quasi-regal palatinate, royal officials were nevertheless entirely excluded from the county under the Norman earls, and by the early 13th century its ruler could style himself *princeps*.[1] Such special status found expression in the early historiography of the county, most strikingly in the late 12th-century tract 'De Laude Cestriae' by Lucian, a monk of Chester abbey.[2] A remarkably early example of local patriotism, the work extols the author's native city and treats the *Cestrienses*, men of Cheshire, as a distinctive and superior *gens* separate from the English and the Welsh.[3] It stands at the beginning of a powerful historiographic tradition. In the late 12th century Lucian's fellow monks recorded material about their patron, the Mercian princess Werburg, in a book known as the 'third passionary';[4] under Abbot Simon Whitchurch (1265–91) annals were compiled;[5] and in the earlier 14th century Ranulph Higden, head of the monastic scriptorium, wrote his 'Polychronicon', which, though not a work of local history, embodied much local material.[6] The tradition attained a final flowering in the early 16th century with the verses of the monk Henry Bradshaw. Nominally a Life of St. Werburg, his work included a history of early medieval Chester, its

[1] *V.C.H. Ches.* ii. 1–6; A. T. Thacker, 'Earls and their Earldom'; C. P. Lewis, 'Formation of Honor'; D. Crouch, 'Administration of Norman Earldom', all in *Earldom of Chester and its Charters*, ed. A. T. Thacker (Chester Arch. Soc. lxxi, 1991), 7–22, 37–95. I am grateful to the staffs of the Cheshire and Chester City Record Offices for their assistance, and especially to the county archivist, Ian Dunn, who generously made available an unpublished paper and helped in many other ways.

[2] *Liber Luciani de Laude Cestriae*, ed. M. V. Taylor (Rec. Soc. Lancs. and Ches. lxiv, 1912).

[3] Ibid. 61, 65; Crouch, 'Administration', 71.

[4] H. Bradshaw, *Life of St. Werburge*, ed. C. Horstmann (Early English Text Soc. [original ser.] lxxxviii, 1887), esp. 188.

[5] *Annales Cestrienses*, ed. R. C. Christie (Rec. Soc. Lancs. and Ches. xiv, 1886).

[6] *Polychronicon*, ed. C. Babington and J. R. Lumby (9 vols., Rolls Ser. 1865–86), ii. 78–80; A. Gransden, *Hist. Writing in England, c. 1307 to early 16th Century* (1982), 43–57; J. Taylor, *Universal Chronicle of Ranulph Higden* (1966).

minster and Benedictine abbey, culled largely from earlier texts in the monastic library.[7]

If not in the first rank of historical scholarship, such works nevertheless represented an enduring interest in the local past fostered by a persistent awareness of its distinctiveness. They laid the groundwork for Cheshire's enthusiastic response to the general growth in local history in the later 16th century. While neither Leland's nor Camden's account of the county was particularly distinguished,[8] by the 1560s there was already a locally-based antiquary: Laurence Bostock of Bostock in Davenham,[9] who made a number of journeys round the county to record details of monuments and inscriptions,[10] and composed a curious set of verses on the Norman earls of Chester and a history of the barons of Halton. Though he published nothing, a notebook and other transcripts from his collections circulated among later historians of Cheshire.[11]

Almost contemporaneously, the herald William Smith of Warmingham (c. 1550–1618) compiled what may be regarded as the first history of Cheshire, which with obvious partiality he entitled the 'Vale Royal of England'.[12] It contained sketchy accounts of Cheshire's pre-Conquest rulers, followed by a description of the shire, its topographical 'particularities', and miscellaneous information about the Norman earls and the later gentry.[13] Hardly comprehensive and well below the standard of the best work of the time, it was nevertheless a pioneering survey, and its stress on the Norman earls and the palatinate helped to establish a pattern generally followed until the early 19th century.

By the early 17th century a considerable corpus of material was accumulating in manuscript. In the 1590s Sampson Erdeswick, whose family originated in Erdeswick in Minshull Vernon but later moved to Staffordshire, embarked upon an ambitious 'View' of the two counties with which he was connected.[14] Before his death in 1603 he had finished Staffordshire but, except for a brief account of Beeston and its castle, had proceeded no further than the collection of materials for Cheshire.[15] His work circulated in manuscript

[7] Bradshaw, *Life of Werburge*.

[8] J. Leland, *Itinerary*, ed. L. Toulmin Smith (5 vols. 1907–10), iv. 2–5; W. Camden, *Britannia*, ed. R. Gough (4 vols. 1806), iii. 39–46.

[9] G. Ormerod, *Hist. of Ches.* ed. T. Helsby (3 vols. 1882), i, pp. xxxix, 258. All later references are to that edn.

[10] B.L. Harl. MS. 139.

[11] Ibid.; Harl. MS. 506, ff. 56–61; Harl. MS. 2113, f. 117v.; Add. MS. 6032, p. 92; Ches. R.O., DLT/B1, ff. 116–21.

[12] *D.N.B.*; Ormerod, *Hist. of Ches.* i. 119; A. Wagner, *Heralds of England* (1967), 226; A. Wood, *Athenae Oxonienses*, ed. P. Bliss (4 vols. 1813–20), ii, cols. 223–4.

[13] *Vale Royal of England*, ed. D. King (1656), [i]; E. Berry, 'Vale Royal of England, i', *Ches. Round*, i (9) (1968), 308–10.

[14] M. W. Greenslade, *Staffs. Historians* (Staffs. Rec. Soc. 4th ser. xi, 1982), 22–36.

[15] B.L. Harl. MS. 506 ('Erdeswick's Book of Ches.').

before its publication in 1717,[16] and some of his notes on Cheshire were transcribed by later historians.[17] Other early Cheshire antiquaries included Ralph Starkey of Darley (d. 1628),[18] John Woodnoth of Shavington (fl. *c.* 1600),[19] and John Booth of Twemlow (1584–1659).[20] Like their predecessors they were from the local gentry, and their interests were primarily genealogical. Their work was much copied,[21] and the local demand thus stimulated was sufficient also to support a few professionals, above all the Chaloner and Holme families, herald painters at Chester, whose labours produced the largest collection of Cheshire manuscripts ever assembled. Particularly active in the earlier 17th century were Thomas Chaloner, appointed a deputy herald by the College of Arms in 1598,[22] Randle Holme I (*c.* 1571–1655), who married Chaloner's widow and in 1601 succeeded to his office,[23] and Randle's son Randle II (1601–59).[24]

In the late 16th century the growing pride of Chester's civic élite found expression in the compilation of lists of mayors and sheriffs augmented by annalistic entries, a genre given definitive shape in 1594 by the mayor, William Aldersey.[25] About the same time Robert Rogers (d. 1595), archdeacon of Chester, embarked upon a history of the city,[26] eventually completed between 1609 and 1637 in several recensions by his son David.[27] The Rogers's 'Breviary' exhibits a desire to promote and embellish a partly mythological civic past, an objective its authors shared with their contemporary William Webb (fl. *c.* 1580–1620), a clerk in the mayor's court, whose work dwelt lovingly on the antiquity of his city's institutions.[28] Webb, who later extended

[16] Greenslade, *Staffs. Historians*, 35–6.

[17] e.g. Leycester's Liber H: Ches. R.O., DLT/B7; possibly also B.L. Harl. MS. 2113.

[18] Ormerod, *Hist. of Ches.* i, p. xlii; ii. 103–4; [T. F. Gower], *Sketch of Materials for New Hist. of Ches.* (1771), 34. Starkey's signature occurs on the flyleaf of B.L. Harl. MS. 139.

[19] Ormerod, *Hist. of Ches.* i, p. xlii; iii. 507. For a transcript from his work, possibly by Francis Bassano, see B.L. Add. MS. 6032.

[20] Ormerod, *Hist. of Ches.* i, pp. xxxviii–xxxix; iii. 137.

[21] Esp. Booth's pedigrees: Ches. R.O., DLT/B3, f. 27v.; B5, f. 61; [Gower], *Sketch*, 44.

[22] For his collections see B.L. Harl. MSS. 1971–5, 1979, 2088–9, 2164–5, 2167, 2169, and pts. of 2120 and 2163.

[23] Wagner, *Heralds of England*, 239–40.

[24] J. P. Earwaker, 'Four Randle Holmes of Chester', *Jnl. Chester Arch. Soc.* new ser. iv (1892), 113–37.

[25] Chester City R.O., AB 1, ff. 11–24; CR 469/542; L. M. Clopper, *Recs. of Early English Drama: Chester* (1979), pp. xxii–xxiv, xxvi–xliv; *Vale Royal*, [i]. 62–89; [ii]. 161–221; P. Clark, 'Visions of Urban Community', *Pursuit of Urban Hist.* ed. D. Fraser and A. Sutcliffe (1983), 110–11.

[26] Clopper, *Recs. of Early English Drama*, p. xxxii; Ormerod, *Hist. of Ches.* i, p. xlii.

[27] There are five different versions, representing stages in David's completion of his father's work: Chester City R.O., CX 3; Ches. R.O., DCC 19; B.L. Harl. MSS. 1944, 1948; Liverpool Univ. MS. 238. See Clopper, *Recs. of Early English Drama*, pp. xxii–xxxvi, 232–54.

[28] Berry, 'Vale Royal, ii', *Ches. Round*, i (10) (1969), 338–9; *Vale Royal*, [ii]. 4–49, 154–221, esp. 161–2.

his history to cover the whole county, claimed to have derived inspiration from London's historian, John Stow, and from the Cheshire-born cartographer John Speed (?1552–1629), who had already provided shire and city with excellent maps.[29] Like Smith, Webb made no pretension to scholarship. His work was essentially little more than a description of the contemporary city and county, complemented by short accounts of the earls and bishops and lists of local officials. Undoubtedly, however, it was the fullest and best organized history thus far produced.[30]

Smith's and Webb's compilations, long available only in manuscripts owned by the local gentry,[31] were eventually published in 1656 by the engraver Daniel King (d. ?1664),[32] who added a history of the Isle of Man[33] and a fresh 'Chronicon Cestriense', commissioned from the puritan divine Samuel Lee (1625–91).[34] Lee's work, though competent, was brief; it comprised little more than a chronology of county administration together with yet another account of the bishops and earls.[35] King did not attempt to integrate his texts and the resultant repetitious and disorganized compilation, which he entitled *Vale Royal of England*, found little favour then or later.[36] The quest for a worthy history of Cheshire had, however, entered a new phase well before 1656. The disturbances of the 1640s and the political changes which followed engendered a fresh approach to antiquarian studies; gentlemen detached from the conflict or isolated by unfashionable sympathies devoted their enforced leisure to the study of a local past whose legacy seemed under threat. A striking instance is the anonymous compiler of an uncompleted history of the county, who in a preface, composed in 1649, remarked that he took up his long neglected studies in the second year of the Civil War in Cheshire because the time was unpropitious for any other activity.[37] Foremost among the new generation was William Vernon (*c.* 1585–1667), who was linked by birth and marriage to several Cheshire gentry families, and whose father-in-law, Philip Oldfield,

---

[29] *Vale Royal*, [ii]. 1; *D.N.B.*; J. Speed, *Theatre of Empire of Great Britain* (facsimile of 1676 edn., 1991), p. v; J. B. Harley, 'From Saxton to Speed', *Ches. Round*, i (6) (1966), 174–84.

[30] Berry, 'Vale Royal, ii', 339–41.

[31] Ormerod, *Hist. of Ches.* i. 119; *Vale Royal*, King's 'address to reader'. For early MSS. of Smith see Bodl. MS. Rawl. B. 282; Ches. R.O., DAR/I/52.

[32] Berry, 'Vale Royal, i', 307–8.

[33] Wood, *Athenae Oxonienses*, iii, cols. 502–3. The author had also made collections relating to Staffs., Salop., and Ches.

[34] For Lee's connexions with Ches. see his preface to the 'Chronicon'. On Lee himself see *D.N.B.*; Ormerod, *Hist. of Ches.* i. 119.

[35] Berry, 'Vale Royal, ii', 342–3.

[36] Wood, *Athenae Oxonienses*, iii, col. 503; *Epistolary Relics of Ches. Antiqs.* ed. G. Ormerod (Chetham Soc. [1st ser.] iv, 1851), 5–7; [Gower], *Sketch* (1771 edn.), 5; D. and S. Lysons, *Magna Britannia: Ches.* (1810), 465.

[37] Ches. R.O., DBC 4868. I am grateful to Ian Dunn and Jonathan Pepler for drawing my attention to this recently discovered material.

also had antiquarian interests.[38] By 1647 Vernon was in correspondence with Dugdale, who had a high opinion of his abilities and clearly hoped that he would produce a definitive history of Cheshire along the lines of the projected work on Warwickshire. Dugdale put Vernon in touch with other eminent antiquaries, eased his access to public and diocesan records, and most importantly obtained for him an excellent transcription of the Domesday text for Cheshire.[39]

How much Vernon accomplished is doubtful. Though he produced some 16 or 17 notebooks,[40] they contain little original composition[41] and as early as 1648 he seems to have begun doubting his ability to complete the project.[42] By 1652 he was probably concentrating upon helping his friend Peter Leycester (1613–78), with whom he had already collaborated in 1649 in the purchase of the Domesday transcript.[43] A cultivated country gentleman with wide scholarly interests[44] and a long-standing enthusiasm for original records,[45] Leycester began to work seriously on his local hundred of Bucklow from 1646 when as a royalist he found himself excluded from other responsibilities.[46] Like Vernon he made contact with leading antiquaries, for example Dodsworth, Dugdale, d'Ewes, and 'my cousin Booth of Twemlow', and transcribed his collections into a series of notebooks.[47] Leycester, however, was far more methodical, accurate, and diligent than his friend.[48] His standing as a leading member of the Cheshire gentry ensured the co-operation of his peers, and he ransacked all the main local family collections for material relating to his chosen hundred.

Apart from a brief interruption c. 1655, when he was imprisoned and forced to compound for his estates, Leycester was busy until 1660. Though the

---

[38] Ormerod, *Hist. of Ches.* i, pp. xxxi–xxxii, 197.

[39] Ibid. i, p. xxxv; B.L. Harl. MS. 1967, ff. 67, 73–4, 76, 80–2, 85–7; *Life, Diary, and Correspondence of Sir William Dugdale*, ed. W. Hamper (1827), 205–17, 237–8, 251–3, 258–64, 266–8; *Epistolary Relics*, ed. Ormerod, 6; Ches. R.O., DSS 3991, box 22 (no. 11).

[40] B.L. Harl. MS. 1967, ff. 93–140; Harl. MSS. 2007–8, 2074. They may be identified with some 18 notebooks containing material relating to Lancs. and Ches. in the family papers of Vernon's wife's first husband, Peter Shakerley: Ches. R.O., DSS 3991, box 22.

[41] Apart from an account of the Norman earls in Ches. R.O., DSS 3991, box 22 (no. 2), which differs from that published in P. Leycester, *Hist. Antiquities* (1673), but must be by Leycester since the author expressly referred to Sir Randle Mainwaring as his maternal grandfather.

[42] B.L. Harl. MS. 1967, ff. 80–1; *Life of Dugdale*, ed. Hamper, 215–17.

[43] Leycester, *Hist. Antiquities*, 393.

[44] Ches. R.O., DLT/B87; Ormerod, *Hist. of Ches.* i, pp. xxxii–xxxiii, 623–5.

[45] See, e.g., his treatise on Saxo-Norman words (c. 1640): Ches. R.O., DLT/B97.

[46] Ibid. DLT/B3 (Liber C); Ormerod, *Hist. of Ches.* i. 623–5; *Amicia Tracts*, i, ed. W. Beamont (Chetham Soc. [1st ser.] lxxviii, 1869), p. xii.

[47] Ches. R.O., DLT/B1–15.

[48] Ormerod, *Hist. of Ches.* i, p. xvii.

Restoration brought public office and with it delay,[49] he had resumed his studies by the mid 1660s[50] and thereafter laboured uninterruptedly until in 1673 he was able to publish *Historical Antiquities*. The core of the work was the second book, devoted to Cheshire. Its quality is immediately apparent in the opening accounts of the pre-Conquest rulers and Norman earls, which though apparently following the pattern established by Smith and Webb represented a real advance, based as they were upon the most systematic assessment of the sources thus far attempted.[51] Leycester's principal effort was, however, reserved for the section on Bucklow hundred, in which, township by township, he recorded descent of land, gentry pedigrees, churches and advowsons, local customs and events. There again the thoroughness and accuracy with which he had searched the local collections, his inclusion of original material, and his care in recording his sources place his work on a different plane from that of his predecessors.

Perhaps the most original element in Leycester's compilation was its concluding section, the text of the Cheshire Domesday. The first portion of the Survey to be published *in extenso*, it was based upon Leycester's own copy of the transcript which he and Vernon had obtained from Domesday's custodian, Scipio Squire.[52] Clearly the existence of the transcript had generated considerable local interest, for by 1660 at least two further copies had been made.[53] Leycester's pioneering decision to publish in full represented an enlightened attempt to spare the local gentry the 'great charge' involved in making such transcriptions.[54]

Despite Leycester's labours the task of compiling a county history was becoming ever more daunting as unpublished material unremittingly accumulated. A major factor was the zeal of Randle Holme III (1627–1700) and his son Randle IV (c. 1659–1707), who continued to augment their family collections, amassing in all some 270 manuscripts which ultimately passed to the British Museum.[55] For Cheshire historians the assemblage has been, perhaps, a mixed blessing. Though undoubtedly industrious, the four Randle Holmes were neither scholarly nor intellectual. Their manuscripts are valuable in preserving some original documents and transcripts of others now lost, but consist largely of copies (often inaccurate) of extant material best

[49] *Amicia Tracts*, i, pp. xiii–xv.

[50] List of parish churches and chapels later published in *Hist. Antiquities*, 192–9.

[51] For published material available to Leycester see his library catalogue: Ches. R.O., DLT/B87.

[52] Ibid. DLT/B9; *Hist. Antiquities*, 393–436.

[53] Ches. R.O., DAR I/46; DBC 4868; DSS 3991, box 22 (no. 11).

[54] *Hist. Antiquities*, 'To reader'.

[55] B.L. Harl. MSS. 1920–2177, 5955, 7568–9; they were purchased by Robert Harley at the instance of Bishop Gastrell: [Gower], *Sketch* (1771 edn.), 40; letter in Ches. R.O., DCC 22; Earwaker, 'Randle Holmes', 163.

consulted in the original. The necessary but laborious task of sifting through their vast collections undoubtedly inhibited the writing of a county history.

In the early 18th century attempts were made to produce digests. In particular, in 1701 Edward Williamson (fl. to 1719),[56] a Chester physician, compiled his 'Villare Cestriense', in which he arranged by township material culled from the Holmes and other collections. Later scholars found his work invaluable,[57] and several copies were made.[58] Another systematizer was Francis Gastrell (1662–1725), bishop of Chester, who trawled the diocesan records and the Holmes collection to produce the first detailed survey of the diocese of Chester. The 'Notitia Cestriensis' consists primarily of a gazetteer, arranged by archdeaconry, rural deanery, and parish, replete with details of patrons and advowsons, livings, church buildings, chapels, schools, charities, and parochial customs. The manuscript was preserved in the registry at Chester where it was consulted by all succeeding county historians until its publication in the mid 19th century.[59]

Though the digests further stimulated antiquarian activity,[60] publication remained rare, and in 1778 the lack of a comprehensive history of the county had become so acute that John Poole, a local printer, could reissue King's *Vale Royal* on the specious ground that it formed 'a complete description of the county'.[61] By then a more ambitious project had been set in motion. In 1771 Thomas Foote Gower (?1726–1780),[62] Cheshire-born though resident in Chelmsford (Essex), produced his *Sketch* of the unpublished collections and unveiled a scheme for a grand new history, intended to be 'infinitely superior' to all comparable works.[63] Gower reissued the *Sketch* in 1772 together with an 'Address' which disclosed plans for a copiously illustrated work in three volumes. The scheme, in his view 'entirely different from that of any other provincial history', required 4,000 guineas to be raised by subscription.[64] Gower corresponded with other antiquaries interested in Cheshire, including Thomas Pennant[65] and Richard Gough, who was sufficiently impressed by

[56] B.L. Add. MS. 36663, ff. 85–6.

[57] Ormerod, *Hist. of Ches.* ii. 751–2.

[58] B.L. Add. MS. 6031; Ches. R.O., DCC 20; Lysons, *Magna Britannia: Ches.* 467–8.

[59] *Notitia Cestriensis or Hist. Notices of Diocese of Chester*, ed. F. R. Raines (Chetham Soc. [1st ser.] viii, xix, xxi–xxii, 1845–50).

[60] e.g. William Cooper (1701–67) of Chester: Chester City R.O., P/Cowper [1956], i, ff. 138–287; ii, ff. 1–41; iiA; Ches. R.O., DCC 1–7, 14, 19, 24, 26, 47.

[61] J. Poole, *Hist. of Ches.* (2 vols. 1778).

[62] *D.N.B.*

[63] Ormerod, *Hist. of Ches.* i, p. xl; J. Hemingway, *Hist. of City of Chester* (2 vols. 1831), i. 240; [Gower], *Sketch* (1771 edn.), esp. 68–9.

[64] Gower, *Sketch* (2nd edn. 1772), esp. pp. iv–v.

[65] *Tour in Wales* (1778), i; *Journey from Chester to London* (1782), 1–44; *D.N.B.*; Ches. R.O., D 4784.

the *Sketch* to invoke the support of the Society of Antiquaries, of which he was director.[66] Work, however, proceeded slowly and when Gower died in 1780 he left only a single volume of text, dealing with the early history of the county.[67] His real achievement was to record and thereby help to preserve Cheshire's numerous manuscript collections.[68]

Publication along the lines laid down by Gower was planned successively by Dr. John Wilkinson and William Latham, a London antiquary of Cheshire descent who in 1800 issued a third edition of Gower's *Sketch*.[69] Their failure to go further was doubtless due to the paucity of Gower's remains, which, as Ormerod observed with characteristic if uncharitable irony, comprised only some four or five notebooks together with 'numerous volumes of blank paper on which the intended history was to have been written'.[70] It was presumably to remedy that deficiency that a remarkable questionnaire was prepared and printed at some unknown point in the long gestation of the project. Intended for despatch to the nobility, gentry, and clergy of the county, it comprised a comprehensive sequence of 74 questions; whether it was distributed or answered cannot now be determined.[71]

While Gower's scheme thus languished another, less ambitious, survey was successfully concluded. In 1810 the topographer Samuel Lysons (1763–1819) and his brother Daniel (1762–1834) completed Cheshire for their *Magna Britannia*.[72] The largest of the five accounts to date, as the authors acknowledged, it had been 'extended to a much greater length than . . . expected', mainly because of the 'great mass of unpublished materials'.[73] Their work was thoroughly professional. Divided into two parts, an historical introduction and a topographical survey based on the ancient parishes, it was well-grounded in the sources and ranged unusually widely, with excellent sections on population, commodities, manufactures, communications, and antiquities.

The Lysonses' publication did not deter a new protagonist from taking up Gower's more elaborate project. George Ormerod (1785–1873),[74] who first examined Gower's papers in 1809, had definitely decided upon his history by 1813. A Mancunian, his interest in Cheshire doubtless owed something to his marriage in 1808 to the daughter of a Cheshire-born physician in touch with a

---

[66] *D.N.B.*; Ches. R.O., D 4784; Camden, *Britannia*, ed. Gough, iii. 47–63.
[67] B.L. Add. MS. 11338.
[68] Ormerod, *Hist. of Ches.* i, p. xxxiii.
[69] Ibid. i, pp. xxxiii–xxxiv; Gower, *Sketch* (3rd edn. 1800), p. vi.
[70] B.L. Add. MSS. 11334–7; Ormerod, *Hist. of Ches.* i, p. xxxiv.
[71] B.L. Add. MS. 11334, ff. 18–19v.
[72] *D.N.B.*
[73] Lysons, *Magna Britannia: Ches.* advertisement.
[74] *D.N.B.*; J. Hess, *George Ormerod, Historian of Ches.* (1989).

former owner of Gower's papers.[75] Ormerod, who never regarded himself as a Cheshire man, and who in 1817 left the county for good,[76] undoubtedly laboured hard and long at his *History*; just how hard is revealed by his frequent complaints on the subject in his letters and by his unbroken determination never to undertake such a demanding project again.[77] He examined a wide range of sources, including almost everything mentioned by Gower in his *Sketch*, as well as a far wider selection of the public and ecclesiastical records than had hitherto been attempted.[78] From 1813 to 1817 he worked regularly in London each autumn and winter, returning to Cheshire for the summer months to make expeditions around the county and to work on the palatinate records at the castle, where he was greatly assisted by the archivist Faithful Thomas.[79] His working methods and order of priorities are illustrated by his letters to his fellow antiquary William Hamper, to whom he submitted proofs of the *History* before publication.[80] Genealogy and descent of land were clearly of overriding interest and eclipsed textual matters: 'Though I should cheerfully gallop twenty miles to obtain a deficient date for a pedigree, my eyes and head are instantaneously abroad when I sit down to collate the i's and y's of old writing.'[81]

Two important networks of contacts helped Ormerod greatly in his labours. His fellowship of the Society of Antiquaries of London put him in touch with leading local historians, and indeed 11 fellows are named in his acknowledgements and a further 43 among the subscribers.[82] Even more important were his contacts with the Cheshire gentry, who granted access to their papers and whose 'kindness', as he wrote to Hamper, 'nearly carried me through'.[83] Like Gower, Ormerod sought to fund the project through subscriptions. A prospectus was issued in 1814 and by 1816, on the basis of 304 subscribers, the decision had been taken to produce 350 standard and 65 large paper copies.[84] Issued in nine parts between 1816 and 1819, the complete work formed three

---

[75] William Latham, to whom Ormerod's father-in-law was not closely related, if at all: Hess, *Ormerod*, 32.

[76] Ibid. 32, 42; Ormerod, *Hist. of Ches.* i, p. xxi; Birmingham Central Library Archives Department [hereafter B.C.L.A.D.], no. 125538 (30 June 1816; 19 Dec. 1818).

[77] B.C.L.A.D., no. 125538 (7 Aug. 1815; 29 May 1817; 9 Dec. 1818; 4 Sept. 1819).

[78] Ormerod, *Hist. of Ches.* i, pp. xxxv–xlii, 360–2.

[79] Ibid. i, pp. xxi, 360–1; Hess, *Ormerod*, 36; D. J. Clayton, 'An Early Ches. Archivist, Faithful Thomas (c. 1772–1844)', *Archives*, xvii (1986), 5–6.

[80] *D.N.B.*; correspondence for 1814–24: B.C.L.A.D., no. 125538.

[81] B.C.L.A.D., no. 125538 (30 June 1816). Cf. ibid. (13 Dec. 1815; 3 Sept. 1816; 29 May 1817); Ormerod, *Hist. of Ches.* i, pp. xliii, 421–5.

[82] Ormerod, *Hist. of Ches.* i, p. xliii; Ches. R.O., D 4299/1.

[83] Ormerod, *Hist. of Ches.* i, p. xliii; B.C.L.A.D., no. 125538 (9 Dec. 1818). Cf. Hess, *Ormerod*, 39. Hugh Cholmondeley, dean of Chester (1806–15), was especially helpful: Ormerod, *Hist. of Ches.* i, pp. xlii–xliii; B.C.L.A.D., no. 125538 (13 Dec. 1815).

[84] Ches. R.O., D 4299/1.

volumes handsomely illustrated with engravings, many from originals by
Peter de Wint.[85] The work sold well and in general was favourably received.
The only substantial criticism emanated from Joseph Hunter, a fellow
Antiquary, who in 1822 complained of 'a want of cohesion', arguing that
insufficient attention had been paid to the way in which manors related to
one another or to the parishes and no attempt made to show how one parish
might be carved out of another.[86] There was some justice in his criticism.
Ormerod's strengths lay in traditional topics: the established church and its
buildings, and above all the gentry—their pedigrees, houses, and the descent
of their lands. His heart was not in topographical description and all too
often his analysis of the physical appearance of a settlement was confined to
the parish church and the local manor house. Moreover his coverage was
uneven and became less thorough as he progressed.[87] Yet despite such
weaknesses the *History* embodies a prodigious amount of generally accurate
information arranged systematically by hundred, ancient parish, and
township. It undoubtedly ranks among the great antiquarian undertakings of
the period.

The appearance of Ormerod's *History* was a milestone in Cheshire's
historiography. No further comprehensive history was attempted in the 19th
century, with the single exception of that by James Hanshall, published
almost contemporaneously in 22 parts.[88] Hanshall, who was editor of the
Chester Chronicle, addressed a highly local audience and did not seek to
emulate Ormerod's 'splendid and costly volumes',[89] but even so his work was
deeply resented. Outraged by what he regarded as Hanshall's 'barefaced
piracy', in 1818 Ormerod condemned the unfortunate editor as 'a conceited
illiterate prig'.[90] Thereafter the main thrust of Cheshire's historiography was
towards the study of sub-county units. Among the numerous works
produced[91] perhaps the most original, and certainly still one of the most
useful, was the first full-scale history of Chester, by Joseph Hemingway,
Hanshall's successor as editor of the *Chronicle* (1824–30), who, refreshingly,
gave attention to the city's relatively recent past.[92] Other works of similar

[85] Ormerod's own copy, bound in 10 folio vols. with numerous original drawings and
watercolours by de Windt, is in Bodl.
[86] *Ches. Sheaf*, 3rd ser. xx (1923), nos. 4893, 4921.
[87] Hess, *Ormerod*, 52.
[88] J. Hanshall, *Hist. of Ches.* (1817–23).
[89] H. Hughes, *Chronicle of Chester, 1775–1975* (1975), 36–7, 40, 43, 78. The original parts with
subscription lists survive at Ches. R.O.
[90] B.C.L.A.D., no. 125538 (30 June 1818).
[91] For full bibliographies see J. H. Cook, *Bibliotheca Cestriensis* (1904); A. C. Walsh, A. R.
Allen, and B. E. Harris, *Hist. of County Palatine of Chester: Short Bibliography and Guide to
Sources* (1983).
[92] J. Hemingway, *Hist. of Chester* (2 vols. 1831); Hughes, *Chronicle of Chester*, 36, 42–5.

scope, if less individuality, were produced throughout the century.[93] An especially substantial contribution was made by J. P. Earwaker (1847–95), whose numerous studies culminated in an ambitious account of the hundred of Macclesfield, which Ormerod had treated relatively cursorily. Despite its author's claims to 'modernity', his work offered no real advance upon Ormerod.[94]

More significant was Thomas Helsby's revision of Ormerod issued in 18 parts between 1876 and 1882.[95] A second edition had been mooted as early as 1836, but Ormerod consistently opposed the idea, and the project could only be undertaken after his death.[96] Helsby, like Ormerod himself, was not a Cheshire man. A Mancunian lawyer, he seems to have been inspired primarily by respect for his predecessor,[97] whose unemended *ipsissima verba* he augmented or corrected in numerous supplementary footnotes or insertions scrupulously marked by square brackets. The resultant compilation doubled the size of the original. Though inelegant and unwieldy, it was full of fresh information culled from both public and private records and manifestly did not merit Earwaker's tart dismissal as new 'only in name'.[98]

Perhaps the most important development in Cheshire's historiography after 1819 was the emergence of an unusually numerous and active group of learned societies. The earliest was the Chetham Society, founded in 1843 at Chetham's Library by a group of Manchester *literati* to publish literary and historical texts pertaining to Lancashire and Cheshire.[99] Its pioneering linkage of the two north-western palatinates was followed at Liverpool in 1848 by the Historic Society of Lancashire and Cheshire, whose *Transactions* were focused upon local historical writing rather than the editing of texts.[1] Manchester remained the more active centre of local studies with the foundation of the Record Society of Lancashire and Cheshire (an offshoot of the Chetham Society) in 1878, and of the Lancashire and Cheshire Antiquarian Society in 1883.[2] Only with the removal of the Record Society from Manchester to Liverpool in 1918 was the present equilibrium

---

[93] H. Heginbotham, *Hist. of Stockport* (2 vols. 1882); J. Hall, *Hist. of Nantwich* (1883); W. W. Mortimer, *Hist. of Hundred of Wirral* (1847); P. Sulley, *Hundred of Wirral* (1889).

[94] *D.N.B.*; B. E. Harris, 'A 19th-Century Ches. Historian: John Parsons Earwaker', *Jnl. Chester Arch. Soc.* lxi (1978), 51–9; J. P. Earwaker, *East Ches. Past and Present* (2 vols. 1877–80).

[95] G. Ormerod, *Hist. of Ches.* ed. T. Helsby (3 vols. 1882).

[96] Ches. R.O., D 4299/1.

[97] Ormerod, *Hist. of Ches.* i, p. xv.

[98] *East Ches.* ii, p. xxiv.

[99] A. Crosby, *Chetham Soc. 1843–1993* (Chetham Soc., 3rd ser. xxxvii, 1993).

[1] B. B. B. Benas, 'Centenary Hist.' *Trans. Historic Soc. Lancs. and Ches.* c (supplement) (1950), 11; J. T. Danson, 'Uses of Learned Soc.: in particular Historic Soc.' ibid. [1st ser.] xi (1859), 233–42.

[2] B. E. Harris, *Centenary Hist. and Guide to Publications* (Rec. Soc. Lancs. and Ches. cxviii, 1978); 'Rules' and 'Report of Council', *Trans. Lancs. and Ches. Antiq. Soc.* i (1884), 5–9.

established with each local metropolis hosting two societies, one publishing original sources, the other historical articles.

Within Cheshire itself the most notable development was the foundation in 1849 of the Architectural, Archaeological, and Historic Society of Chester and North Wales, based at Chester and dominated by an influential group of local ecclesiastics, architects, and architectural historians.[3] Later a number of less weightily academic periodicals appeared, often initially as columns in local newspapers.[4] Especially significant was the *Cheshire Sheaf*, published from 1878 in weekly instalments in the *Chester Courant* and established by its first editor, Thomas Hughes (1826–90), as a major outlet for short notes and documents.[5]

By the end of the century it was apparent that the outpouring of publication stimulated by the societies required expression in a fresh survey. The intended vehicle was the Victoria County History, which by 1904 had begun on a set of four volumes. Over the next five years many general chapters were written, among them natural history, geology, forestry, and agriculture; particularly notable were Professor James Tait's edition of Domesday and lengthy contributions on ecclesiastical history, religious houses, and social and economic history by the Chester historian Canon Rupert Morris (1844–1918).[6] In 1907 John Brownbill (*c.* 1860–1931),[7] then assistant editor of the Lancashire V.C.H., was commissioned to write the topography, but in 1909 because of the V.C.H.'s financial difficulties the offer was withdrawn and publication of the Cheshire volumes deferred. Tait's typescript was returned to him and subsequently published, but Morris's chapters were retained by the V.C.H. and unfortunately lost.[8]

As the V.C.H. was abandoned, the history of the palatinate was placed upon a new footing by scholars such as Tait (1863–1944),[9] Brownbill,[10] Ronald Stewart-Brown (1872–1940),[11] and William Fergusson Irvine (1869–1962).[12]

---

[3] Personal comment by P. de Figureido.

[4] e.g. *Notes and Queries*, published in *Stockport Advertiser* (1882–1906); *Wirral Notes and Queries* (1893–4).

[5] Obituary, *Ches. Sheaf*, [1st ser.] iii (1891, for 1883), pp. i–vii. For his papers see Chester City R.O., CR 60.

[6] R. H. Morris, *Chester in Plantagenet and Tudor Reigns* [1894]; obituary, *Jnl. Chester Arch. Soc.* xxii (1918), 208–12. For his papers see Chester City R.O., CR 59.

[7] Obituary, *Hoylake and West Kirby Advertiser*, 29 May 1931, p. 5.

[8] V.C.H. recs., A 38–9, 52, 57, 67; B 6.

[9] *D.N.B. 1941–50*; *Domesday Survey of Ches.* (Chetham Soc. 2nd ser. lxxv, 1915); *Chartulary of Abbey of St. Werburgh, Chester* (Chetham Soc. 2nd ser. lxxix, lxxxiii, 1920–3).

[10] e.g. as editor of *Ledger Book of Vale Royal Abbey* (Rec. Soc. Lancs. and Ches. lxviii, 1914).

[11] e.g. *Ches. Chamberlains' Accounts, 1301–60* (Rec. Soc. Lancs. and Ches. lix, 1910); *Ches. in Pipe Rolls, 1158–1301* (ibid. xcii, 1938). See also obituary, *Trans. Hist. Soc. Lancs. and Ches.* xci (1940), 209–14.

[12] G. Barraclough, *Early Ches. Charters* (1957), pp. vii–ix. See also obituary, *Trans. Hist. Soc. Lancs. and Ches.* cxiii (1962), 215–19.

Their work, largely published by the local societies with which all were closely connected, concentrated on the medieval period,[13] and the more recent history of the county was opened up only after the appearance in 1950 of W. H. Chaloner's pioneering study of Crewe.[14] Yet despite the wealth of recent publication on individual aspects of the county (beyond the scope of the present study), the need for a new and comprehensive history of Cheshire continued to be felt. Cheshire Rural Community Council planned a series of 'historical handbooks' in the 1930s, but the war interrupted progress and only one appeared.[15] In 1958, however, the council, which already issued a journal,[16] revived the project,[17] and between 1964 and 1985 it published 11 volumes, under the editorship of J. J. Bagley.[18]

Interest in the medieval palatinate revived, after pioneering work by Professor Geoffrey Barraclough,[19] and since the 1970s there has been an impressive flow of publication.[20] Recent doctoral research has ranged widely—from the Vikings to the 18th century[21]—but perhaps the most

---

[13] Cf. also J. H. E. Bennett (1873–1956): obituary, *Jnl. Chester Arch. Soc.* xliii (1956), 52–3. For his papers see Ches. R.O., DBE.

[14] W. H. Chaloner, *Social and Economic Development of Crewe, 1780–1923* (1950). For Chaloner see *Trans. Lancs. and Ches. Antiq. Soc.* lxxxv (1988), 5–105. Other works include C. S. Davies, *Hist. of Macclesfield* (1961); J. M. Lee, *Social Leaders and Public Persons* (1963); *Hist. of Congleton*, ed. W. B. Stephens (1970); J. S. Morrill, *Ches. 1630–60* (1978).

[15] W. J. Varley and J. W. Jackson, *Prehistoric Ches.* (1940).

[16] *Ches. Historian* (1951–60); continued as *Ches. Round* (1961–9); *Ches. Local Hist. Committee Newsletter* (1971–7); *Ches. Hist.* (from 1978).

[17] With *Hist. Atlas of Ches.* ed. D. Sylvester and G. Nulty.

[18] W. J. Varley, *Ches. before Romans* (1964); F. H. Thomson, *Roman Ches.* (1965); J. D. Bu'lock, *Pre-Conquest Ches.* (1972); B. M. C. Husain, *Ches. under Norman Earls* (1973); H. J. Hewitt, *Ches. under Three Edwards* (1967); J. T. Driver, *Ches. in Later Middle Ages* (1971); J. Beck, *Tudor Ches.* (1969); R. N. Dore, *Civil Wars in Ches.* (1966); J. H. Hodson, *Ches. 1660–1780: Restoration to Industrial Revolution* (1978); G. H. Scard, *Squire and Tenant: Life in Rural Ches. 1760–1900* (1981); R. E. Tigwell, *Ches. in 20th Century* (1985). A 12th volume on towns in Cheshire 1760–1900 was planned but never written. For Bagley: *Trans. Hist. Soc. Lancs. and Ches.* cxxxii (1983), pp. xi–xiv; ibid. cxxxviii (1989), 233–4.

[19] G. Barraclough, 'Earldom and County Palatine of Chester', *Trans. Hist. Soc. Lancs. and Ches.* ciii (1952), 23–57; *Early Ches. Charters* (1957); *Charters of Earls of Chester* (Rec. Soc. Lancs. and Ches. cxxvi, 1988). See also R. H. C. Davis, 'Geoffrey Barraclough and the Lure of Charters', and D. Quinn, 'Bibliography of Published Work of Geoffrey Barraclough', both in *Earldom of Chester and its Charters*, 23–34, 199–222.

[20] e.g. *Medieval Ches.* ed. J. I. Kermode and C. B. Phillips, being *Trans. Hist. Soc. Lancs. and Ches.* cxxviii (1979); P. H. W. Booth, *Financial Administration of Lordship and County of Chester, 1272–1377* (Chetham Soc. 3rd ser. xviii, 1981); P. Morgan, *War and Society in Medieval Ches.* (Chetham Soc. 3rd ser. xxxiv, 1987); D. J. Clayton, *Administration of County Palatine of Chester, 1442–85* (Chetham Soc. 3rd ser. xxxv, 1990).

[21] e.g. S. I. Mitchell, 'Urban Markets and Retail Distribution, 1730–1815, with particular reference to Macclesfield, Stockport and Chester' (Oxford Univ. D.Phil. thesis, 1975); D. Griffiths, 'Anglo-Saxon England and Irish Sea Region, A.D. 800–1100' (Durham Univ. Ph.D. thesis, 1992); T. J. Thornton, 'Political Society in Ches. 1480–1560' (Oxford Univ. D.Phil. thesis, 1993).

significant development has been the re-establishment of the Cheshire V.C.H. In 1972, when Cheshire was one of the few counties for which no V.C.H. volume had been published, the county council, in partnership with the Leverhulme Trust and in response to initiatives from Professor Alec Myers (1921–80), agreed to fund the project.[22] Since 1972 three general volumes have been published,[23] and a topographical volume is in preparation.[24]

[22] V.C.H. General Introduction Supplement, 5.
[23] Devoted to physique, prehist., arch., and Domesday: V.C.H. Ches. i (1987); political and parliamentary hist.: ii (1979); religious hist. and education: iii (1980).
[24] V.C.H. Ches. v: City of Chester.

CORNWALL

John Walker

The history and topography of Cornwall have long been a subject of study. The earliest works dealing with the county were those of early travellers, map-makers, and writers who published general works on Britain as a whole. By the early 17th century, however, detailed studies of the county were being produced and during the 19th century accounts of individual parishes and towns were also completed, a trend which has continued into the 20th century.

John Leland was the first writer to take an interest in the history and topography of Cornwall. His pioneering *Itinerary*, the result of his journeys through England and Wales in 1535–43, includes a detailed description of the county in two overlapping sections.[1] Leland's travels took him from Launceston to Bodmin, via the north Cornish coast; from Bodmin to Land's End; and along the south coast, through Truro and Falmouth, to Plymouth. His account of Cornwall was similar in style to those of the other counties he visited, and included many descriptions of churches and ecclesiastical buildings, together with other detailed references to castles and bridges. He did, however, pass comments of a more general and occasionally critical nature, describing Boscastle as 'a very filthy town' and Padstow as 'uncleanly kept'. He also mentioned genealogical details relating to important families including the Godolphins of Kerthen.

Although Leland's work remained unpublished until the 18th century, it had a great influence on a number of later topographical writers including William Camden. Camden's description of Cornwall in the English edition of *Britannia* (1610)[2] was relatively brief, but it too was influential on later writing, including Daniel Defoe's *Tour through the Whole Island of Great Britain* (1724). Defoe's account includes a number of fascinating tales, but his imagination often obscures factual reporting and the work cannot be completely trusted.[3] A more valuable account of Cornish life was written by Celia Fiennes about thirty years earlier. She produced a first-hand

---

[1] J. Leland, *De rebus Britannicis Collectanea*, ed. T. Hearne (1715); J. Leland, *Itinerary*, ed. L. Toulmin Smith (5 vols. 1907–10), i–iii; cf. above, Introduction.

[2] W. Camden, *Britannia*, trans. P. Holland (1610); cf. above, Introduction.

[3] D. Defoe, *Tour through Whole Island of Great Britain*, ed. P. Rogers (1971).

description of the county with a number of highly detailed sections, including one describing tin mining and blowing at St. Austell.[4]

Those early accounts were complemented by the production of a number of maps and plans of the county. The first county map of Cornwall was that designed by Christopher Saxton in 1576.[5] A great influence on later maps, it was copied and used in the early editions of Camden's *Britannia*. John Norden probably visited Cornwall in the 1580s and again between 1597 and 1601, when he carried out the survey work for his maps. His observations on the county were published in *Speculi Britanniae Pars: A Topographical and Historical Description of Cornwall*, written *c.* 1604, which included a new county map of Cornwall together with more detailed maps of the nine hundreds.[6] Although Norden's work remained unpublished until 1728 it was much sought after by his contemporaries and the maps were used by William Kip and Robert Morden respectively in the 1607 (Latin) and 1695 (English) editions of Camden's *Britannia*. John Speed also made use of Norden's work for his map of Cornwall in *Theatre of the Empire of Great Britain* (1611).[7] Indeed it was not until the very end of the 17th century that Norden's work was finally superseded. That achievement was the work of Joel Gascoyne, a leading land surveyor who moved from London to Cornwall in 1693 at the instigation of John Grenville, earl of Bath. He was employed in a series of detailed surveys of manors, and was probably responsible for the production of the Stowe and Lanhydrock Atlases. The detailed work involved in the production of those documents enabled Gascoyne to carry out a ground survey of Cornwall which in turn led to the production of his map of Cornwall in 1699.[8] The map was of great significance because it was the first county map to include parish boundaries and to be produced on the relatively large scale of one inch to the mile.

In addition to those developments in map-making the 17th century also saw the beginnings of detailed topographical studies centred exclusively on Cornwall. The first writer who studied Cornwall in that way was Richard Carew, a member of one of the county's leading families, who became an active member of the Society of Antiquaries from 1589. In the same year he

[4] C. Fiennes, *Journeys*, ed. C. Morris (1947). For a compilation of the work of early travellers see *Early Tours in Devon and Cornw.* ed. R. Pearse Chope (1967 edn. with an introduction by A. Gibson). See also T. Cox, *Magna Britannia et Hibernia* (1720–31); R. Blome, *Britannia* (1673).

[5] In C. Saxton, *Atlas of England and Wales* (1579).

[6] J. Norden, *Speculi Britanniae Pars: a Topographical and Hist. Description of Cornw.* (1728); *John Norden's Manuscript Maps of Cornw. and its Nine Hundreds*, with an introduction by W. Ravenhill (1972).

[7] J. Speed, *Theatre of Empire of Great Britain* (1611).

[8] J. Gascoyne, *Map of Cornw.* (1700); 'Map of Cornw. by Joel Gascoyne', *Devon and Cornw. Rec. Soc.* new ser. xxxiv (1991), introduction by W. L. D. Ravenhill and O. J. Padel.

began work on the compilation of a history of the county, which was finally published in 1602 as *The Survey of Cornwall*.[9] The first part of the book dealt with a general description of the county including its climate, geology, industry, education, and recreation. The second part comprised an introductory section on Cornish history followed by a more detailed description of the hundreds on a parish-by-parish basis. The importance of the book was recognized by Carew's contemporaries and one modern commentator has described it as 'a very delightful book . . . perhaps the most attractive of Elizabethan topographical and historical descriptions of counties'.[10] The author himself was rather more critical, and he soon planned a second edition, which he was unable to complete before his death. In 1811 Francis Basset, Lord de Dunstanville, published another edition incorporating comments made on the text by Thomas Tonkin.

Thomas Tonkin became interested in the topography and genealogy of the county *c.* 1700 and in 1737 he put forward proposals for a county history to be published in three volumes. Presumably as a result of financial problems, however, the work was never published, and the manuscript passed after his death from his niece first to Francis Basset and eventually to the British Museum. A second work by Tonkin, which comprised an alphabetical account of all the Cornish parishes as far as the letter O, passed to another topographer, William Borlase. Tonkin's studies were embodied in a number of later county histories, including that of Gilbert Davies, and he has been described as 'one of the most enlightened antiquaries of his day'.[11] A slightly more successful attempt to produce a parochial history of the county was that begun by William Hals, who devoted about fifty years in the late 17th and early 18th century to the collection of relevant materials but who died before it could be completed. It appears that he suffered from a lack of encouragement and patronage, which was presumably connected with his unfortunate tendency to include abusive anecdotes about principal inhabitants of the county. Although the first part of his work remains in manuscript, the second part was published in 1750 as *The Compleat History of Cornwall*, by Andrew Brice, a Truro printer, and comprises an account of 72 parishes from Advent to the first six lines of Helston.[12]

Another influential writer of the 18th century was William Borlase, an Oxford scholar who became vicar of Ludgvan, near Penzance, in 1722. He was originally interested in the natural history of the county, and in 1758

[9] R. Carew, *Survey of Cornw.* (1602); *D.N.B.*
[10] A. L. Rowse, *Tudor Cornw.* (2nd edn. 1969), 19.
[11] B.L. Add. MS. 29763; *D.N.B.*; below.
[12] B.L. Add. MS. 29762; W. Hals, *Compleat Hist. of Cornw. (pt.)* (1750).

published *The Natural History of Cornwall*.[13] By that date, however, his attentions had been diverted towards archaeology and topography and in 1754 he published *Observations on the Antiquities of the County of Cornwall*, 'the first chronological account of the antiquities of the county', which was followed by a second edition in 1769.[14] Both editions contained the author's own illustrations and comprised four parts including a chronological history of the county, details on religious and military history, and a detailed study of the origins and development of the Druids. Borlase's work has been described as 'the foundation of archaeological research in the county'. Nevertheless it has been criticized as inaccurate, and his interest in, and concentration on, the Druids included some rather fanciful speculations. Borlase's other topographical work included *Observations on the Ancient and Present State of the Islands of Scilly* in 1756, based on observations made on a visit to the islands in 1752, and in his later years he turned his attention to a parochial history of the county which was never completed.[15]

In the 19th century there was an increase in the number of books published on topographical matters. The Revd. Richard Polwhele had originally been interested in the history of Devon, but following his move to Cornwall at the end of the 18th century, he began work on a history of that county which was published in three volumes in 1803, and improved and enlarged in seven volumes in 1816. The work provided a general survey of the county rather than the detailed parochial history associated with the studies of some earlier writers.[16] Charles Sandoe Gilbert began his working life as an itinerant vendor of medicines but his interest was aroused in antiquities, genealogy, and topography after learning that he might have a claim to the inheritance of Compton castle in Devon. That interest eventually led to the publication in 1817 and 1820 of the *Historical Survey of the County of Cornwall* in two volumes. Gilbert and his associates had collected the material for the study while travelling round the county selling medicines. It appears that his obsession with Cornish history led to the decline of his vending business and in 1825 he was declared bankrupt.[17]

Many of the 19th-century topographical publications on Cornwall made use of the works of earlier writers. Daniel and Samuel Lysons's *Magna Britannia* included a general description and detailed parochial history of Cornwall in the third volume (1814).[18] In 1838 Davies Gilbert, or Giddy, published *The*

[13] W. Borlase, *Natural Hist. of Cornw.* (1758, new edn. 1970), introduction by F. A. Turk with a biographical note by P. A. S. Pool; *D.N.B.*

[14] W. Borlase, *Observations on Antiquities Hist. and Monumental of Cornw.* (1754, 2nd edn. 1769).

[15] W. Borlase, *Observations on Ancient and Present State of Islands of Scilly* (1769).

[16] R. Polwhele, *Hist. of Cornw.* (1803, new edn. enlarged in 7 vols. 1816).

[17] C. S. Gilbert, *Hist. Survey of Cornw.* (2 vols. 1817–20); *D.N.B.*

[18] D. and S. Lysons, *Magna Britannia: Cornw.* (1814). See also F. Hitchens and S. Drew, *Hist. of Cornw.* (2 vols. 1824).

Parochial History of Cornwall in four volumes. It was a study based on the manuscript histories of Hals and Tonkin. Owing to the ill health of the author much of the work was carried out by others on his behalf, and their less than meticulous efforts ruined the reputation of the whole enterprise.[19] A similar idea was developed by Joshua Polsue, who published his *Parochial History of Cornwall* (known, after one of the publishers, as *Lake's Parochial History*) in four volumes between 1867 and 1872. That study, an alphabetical description of the Cornish parishes, contained prefaces to each section outlining the work of Hals and Tonkin.[20]

The 19th century also saw the development of more localized studies of towns, parishes, and other divisions of the county. One of the most important was John Maclean's *The Parochial and Family History of the Deanery of Trigg Minor*, published in three volumes between 1872 and 1879.[21] Other local studies of the period include Thomas Bond's *Topographical and Historical Sketches of the Boroughs of East and West Looe in the County of Cornwall* (1823); John Allen's *History of the Borough of Liskeard* (1856); and Richard and Otho Peters's *A History of Launceston and Dunheved, in the County of Cornwall* (1885). Those developments have continued into the 20th century, with a proliferation, as in other counties, of histories of most of the Cornish villages, towns, and parishes. The Royal Institution of Cornwall, founded in 1818, the Devon and Cornwall Record Society, founded in 1904, and the West Cornwall Field Club, founded in 1933, which became the Cornwall Archaeological Society in 1962,[22] are just some of the organizations to have published valuable materials relating to the history of Cornwall.

The proposal made by Thomas Tonkin in 1737 for the publication of a county history was met before the 20th century by several writers. No large-scale work, however, has been published, despite the efforts of the *Victoria History of the Counties of England*, founded in 1899.[23] In contrast to some counties, which have received extensive coverage, only one complete volume and two parts of a second volume have been published for Cornwall.[24] In 1906 volume one of the county set included sections on the natural history, zoology, and industries of the county, and in 1924 volume two, part three, dealt with Romano-British Cornwall, and part five provided a transcription and analysis

---

[19] D. Gilbert, *Parochial Hist. of Cornw.* (4 vols. 1838); *D.N.B.*

[20] J. Polsue, *Complete Parochial Hist. of Cornw.* (4 vols. 1867–72).

[21] J. Maclean, *Parochial and Family Hist. of Deanery of Trigg Minor* (3 vols. 1872–9).

[22] *Report of Royal Institution of Cornw.* i–xlv (1818–63); *Jnl. of Royal Institution of Cornw.* i–xxv (1864–1942), new ser. (1951 onwards); *Devon and Cornw. Rec. Soc.* i–lx (1905–54), new ser. (1955 onwards), extra ser. i–ii (1973–9); *Proc. West Cornw. Field Club: Arch.* (1936 onwards); *Cornish Arch.* (1962 onwards).

[23] *V.C.H. General Introduction.*

[24] *V.C.H. Cornw.* i (1906); ii (3 and 5) (1924).

of the Domesday Survey of the county. The experiment of selling the *History* in parts was, however, a financial failure, and plans to complete the publication of the county's general and more detailed topographical volumes remain unfulfilled. A considerable financial outlay would be required to restart and complete that ambitious but important project.

CUMBERLAND AND WESTMORLAND

Angus J. L. Winchester

Despite an antiquarian tradition reaching back to the early 17th century, many facets of the history of the 'sister counties' of Cumberland and Westmorland remain comparatively under-researched. The explanation lies partly in the absence of some of the local institutions through which local historical study has been fostered in other parts of England since the mid 19th century. The two counties possess no record society of their own, nor, until 1992, have they had a resident university, and it is striking that Westmorland remains the only county (apart from Northumberland, which boasts its own county history) untouched by the Victoria County History. However, the strong regional identity of the northern twins has given a distinctive flavour to their historiography.

Cumberland and Westmorland have been bound together in the national consciousness by their proximity to Scotland, their comparative poverty and remoteness from southern England, their distinctive institutions (such as their division into wards instead of hundreds, and the much discussed tenure known as 'Border tenantright'), and their ethnic identity, the most tangible expression of which is the survival of a strong dialect, rich in Scandinavian words. The heartland of the two counties lay in that fertile belt of red-earthed lowland which stretches from the Irish Sea coast of west Cumberland, across the broad and open Carlisle plain, and up the rich Eden valley. There, north of the Lake District, lay the county towns of Carlisle and Appleby and the bulk of the gentlemen's seats of both counties. It also coincided approximately with the diocese of Carlisle, the southern boundary of which ran from the coast at Workington, through the heart of the Lake District, to the Shap fells on the southern edge of the upper Eden valley. Cumberland south of the Derwent and the southern half of Westmorland were, until 1856, far-flung northern territories of the dioceses of, successively, York and Chester. Westmorland was a county which faced two ways: the 'bottom' (that is, the barony of Westmorland with its seat at Appleby) in the upper Eden valley gave the county its name; the 'barony' (that is, the medieval barony of Kendal) to the south of Shap fells became the county's economic heartland by the later Middle Ages. The division between northern- and southern-facing territories, imposed by geography and reinforced by ecclesiastical organization, is a theme which recurs in the historiography.

The 'discovery' of the Lake District in the second half of the 18th century broke down the region's isolation but, it could be argued, increased its distinctive regional identity, not only as a sought-after landscape but also as a society whose inhabitants were viewed as curiosities in their own right. 'Their ideas are simple, and their notions confined to the narrow rules of nature; yet honesty, integrity, and heart-felt happiness are no strangers to this sequestered land', wrote John Housman in 1794.[1] That image of an ideal society was developed and disseminated by Wordsworth, who described the Lake District communities as a 'pure Commonwealth', 'a perfect Republic of Shepherds and Agriculturalists'.[2] As tourism developed, Cumberland and Westmorland gradually came to be synonymous with the Lake District to the extent that the traveller entering the modern county of Cumbria is greeted by road signs proclaiming 'Cumbria: The Lake District', despite the fact that only 31 per cent of the historic counties of Cumberland and Westmorland falls within what is now the national park. As will be seen, the development of 'the Lake Counties' as a convenient unit of study has had a subtle but profound effect on the historiography of the two counties, by inverting former perceptions and concentrating on those parts which had earlier been perceived as an inhospitable, mountainous backdrop, peripheral to the centres of population and wealth in each county.

The first separate history of the two counties to appear in print was Nicolson and Burn's *History and Antiquities of the Counties of Westmorland and Cumberland* (1777), which will be discussed further below. It relied heavily on unpublished material collected by a series of local antiquaries during the 17th century. The earliest attempt to outline the history of Cumberland was John Denton's 'Accompt of the most considerable estates and families in the county of Cumberland from the conquest unto the beginning of the reign of K. James', compiled *c.* 1610.[3] Denton (d. 1617) was a lawyer and gentleman of Cardew, near Dalston. In 1595 he was appointed as a Crown agent in Cumberland to discover concealed lands, a task which both gave him access to the records in the Tower of London and made him unpopular with his gentry neighbours. He also gained entry to the Carlisle

---

[1] W. Hutchinson, *Hist. of Cumb.* (1794), ii. 135. The author wishes to record his thanks to Bruce Jones for reading and commenting on an earlier draft of this chapter.

[2] *Wordsworth's Guide to the Lakes: the Fifth Edn. 1835*, ed. E. de Selincourt (1906), 67–8.

[3] An edn. by R. S. Ferguson was printed as Cumb. and Westmld. Antiq. and Arch. Soc. [hereafter C.W.A.A.S.] Tract ser. ii (1887). For a modern discussion of Denton's MS. see D. J. W. Mawson, 'Another Important Copy of John Denton's Manuscript', *Trans. C.W.A.A.S.* lxxviii. 97–103.

diocesan records through his kinsman Henry Robinson, bishop of Carlisle 1598–1616. In 1612 hostile witnesses claimed that Denton had

> had the secrett fingering of all the evidences of the church of Carlile. He hath insinueated himself into as many of the gentlemen's evidences in his countrie as wold give him any creditt. He hath whole loads of old evidences gotten heere and there.[4]

Denton's account was thus based on a solid foundation of documentary research. It was essentially a tenurial history, taking as its framework the county's division into baronies, and tracing the descent of the principal manors in each barony. The copies of Denton's work which had been made by the mid 18th century formed the basis on which much of the later work on the county's history was built, as repetition of Denton's inaccuracies demonstrates. Seven manuscripts were known when the 'Accompt' was published in 1887. The printed edition made use of two of them and included in footnotes additional manorial descents added to their copies of Denton's original c. 1687 by William Gilpin (d. 1724) of Scaleby Castle and c. 1749 by William Milbourne (1717–69) of Armathwaite, both in their time recorders of Carlisle.

The later decades of the 17th century witnessed a flowering of work on the history of both counties which resulted in three further manuscript historical descriptions of Cumberland, one of Westmorland, and the collection of a voluminous body of material towards a history of the latter county. The earliest were the descriptions of Cumberland, Westmorland, and the Furness district of Lancashire (that is of the whole of the Lake Counties) written in 1671 by the Westmorland squire Sir Daniel Fleming (1633–1701) of Rydal.[5] Fleming was a leading member of county society in both Cumberland and Westmorland and a keen antiquary. He drew on Camden and on John Denton's manuscript, from which he reproduced extracts almost verbatim, but he also included contemporary observations and material drawn from his own muniments relating to his family's estates in all three counties. Indeed, in the early 1680s he wrote a careful and scholarly memoir of the Fleming family and their estates, based on the original records in his possession.[6] His descriptions of Westmorland and Cumberland were arranged by ward, brief accounts of the market towns in each prefacing treatment of 'other places of note', which are mostly gentlemen's seats. His brief and factual sketch is of particular interest for its

[4] J. Wilson, 'The First Historian of Cumb.' *Scottish Hist. Review*, viii. 5–21.

[5] Fleming's descriptions of Cumb. and Westmld. were printed from imperfect copies as C.W.A.A.S. Tract ser. iii, ed. R. S. Ferguson (1889) and i, ed. G. F. Duckett (1882) respectively. The original MS. (now Cumbria R.O. (Carlisle), D/Sen/7/1) was printed in *Fleming-Senhouse Papers*, ed. E. Hughes (Cumb. Rec. Ser. 1961), 1–27, 34–64.

[6] Printed as *Memoirs of Sir Daniel Fleming*, ed. R. E. Porter and W. G. Collingwood (C.W.A.A.S. Tract ser. xi, 1928).

contemporary descriptions of market towns and its references to industrial developments.

Edmund Sandford, a member of a gentry family from Askham, Westmorland, compiled a 'cursory relation' of the antiquities and county families of Cumberland *c.* 1675.[7] His account is a delightful, anecdotal tour of the gentry seats, conducted by a circuitous route through the county. Sandford's genealogical knowledge was often vague and sometimes inaccurate but his account was lively and laced with personal reminiscence. He was no dry scholar: his interests often strayed from antiquities to horse-racing, hunting, and fishing, and the 'cursory relation' provides a vivid insight into the life of the Cumberland gentry during the 17th century.

Thomas Machell (1647–98), rector of Kirkby Thore and a member of a family whose seat was at Crackenthorpe, near Appleby, began to collect materials for a history of Cumberland and Westmorland while at Oxford in the 1670s. By his own account, he was encouraged to undertake the task by Sir William Dugdale and Anthony Wood, and his intention was 'to leave such collections behind me, though I never print, as may afford matter for after Aiges to compile a large volume of the 2 sister-countyes'. By the end of his life his collections, though substantial, fell far short of what was necessary for a full history. Perhaps not surprisingly, his papers show a pronounced bias towards Westmorland barony in general, and towards the Machell family in particular. His material was drawn from a wide range of sources: copies of documents, answers to questions sent to local clergy and gentry, and his own observations from what would now be described as fieldwork. In particular, his journeys on horseback across southern Westmorland between 1691 and 1693 provide a lively description of the barony of Kendal and have been printed.[8] Machell's own inclinations, no doubt encouraged by his friendship with Dugdale, were towards genealogy and heraldry, and his collections form an important quarry for the history of gentry families in the 'bottom' of Westmorland. His material on Cumberland was much less extensive than that on his native county, but his papers included copies of John Denton's and Edmund Sandford's manuscript histories, as well as an account of 'the present state of the parish and manor of Melmerby' supplied by the rector, Richard Singleton, in 1677. Machell had sought information under several headings, including the boundaries, extent, and configuration of the parish; soils; the church, rectory, parsonage house, and glebe; the descent of the manor; and wells and streams.[9]

---

[7] Printed as *Cursory Relation of all Antiquities and Familyes in Cumb. c. 1675 by Edmund Sandford*, ed. R. S. Ferguson (C.W.A.A.S. Tract ser. iv, 1890). The only known MS. is that in Cumbria R.O. (Carlisle), Machell MSS., vol. vi.

[8] *Antiq. on Horseback*, ed. J. M. Ewbank (C.W.A.A.S. Extra ser. xix, 1963).

[9] Cumbria R.O. (Carlisle), Machell MSS., vol. vi, pp. 705–22.

After Machell's death his collected papers passed to William Nicolson, bishop of Carlisle, who had them bound into six large volumes which were placed in the library of the dean and chapter of Carlisle. Nicolson was realistic about their value: 'upon perusal of 'em, I found the collection so imperfect, Raw and indigested, that 'twas impossible to bring them (of 'emselves) to any such Account as the good man hoped for'.[10] Nevertheless being bound and preserved in the Dean and Chapter library ensured that Machell's papers were readily available to later county historians.

In contrast the manuscript history of Cumberland compiled by his contemporary Thomas Denton (1638–95) was destined to obscurity for at least a century. Denton, probably a distant kinsman of John Denton of Cardew, was a lawyer, recorder of Carlisle, and lord of Warnell, a small manor in Sebergham parish. His account, compiled at the request of Sir John Lowther of Lowther, was entitled 'A Perambulation of Cumberland ['and Westmorland' interlined] containing the Description, Hystory, and Customes of those Counties, written in the yeares 1687 & 88'. It is essentially an account of Cumberland, arranged on a plan similar to that of John Denton earlier in the century, the parishes being arranged by barony and, by Thomas Denton's own admission, following the antiquarian framework established by Camden. He clearly knew Cumberland well and appears to have visited most parts of the county collecting data for his account. From the perspective of the modern local historian, Thomas Denton's greatest contribution was to include a wealth of contemporary detail, including estimates of population and figures on the values of estates, manors, fisheries, and mines. His own unease about including such potentially sensitive information stresses that his history was a private report for an individual patron:

> Now as I have (in the Description of this County) been in many things too remiss for want of true information, so have I, in other things, been more particular than did befitt me; in putting a yearly estimate upon most Gentlemen's estates, and discovering their Customes & Tenures, which I am sure might give greate occasion of offence, if some had the purusall hereof, but, as I was desired to mention such particular instances, and what I have here incerted is onely designed for your own private satisfaction, I hope this errour may the sooner receive your favourable construction.[11]

To his account of Cumberland Denton added material on Hadrian's Wall, a very sketchy attempt at a history of Westmorland (largely confined to

---

[10] Ibid. vol. i, Nicolson's preface, dated 10 Aug. 1711.
[11] Cumbria R.O. (Carlisle), D/Lons/L, 'Denton MSS.' box, Thomas Denton's preface addressed to Sir John Lowther.

accounts of the lords of the barony of Westmorland and of Border tenantright), and brief accounts of the Isle of Man, Dublin, and Ulster. That they were afterthoughts was made clear in Denton's disarming preface addressed to Lowther: 'finding soe much wast paper in this book as would contain a cursory discription of your county [i.e. Westmorland], I attempted it.' Like the descriptions compiled by Fleming and Sandford, Thomas Denton's account of Cumberland is important to the modern historian, not so much for its antiquarian information as for its contemporary description of the county. It has never been published; the one original manuscript, of which later historians appear to have been unaware until 1808, remains in the Lonsdale muniments in Cumbria Record Office.[12]

The decades either side of 1700 saw attempts to compile histories of the diocese of Carlisle, rather than either of the counties, by two churchmen, William Nicolson and Hugh Todd, who are remembered as much for their personal animosity to each other as for their antiquarian labours. William Nicolson (1655–1727), author of *The English Historical Library* (3 vols. 1696–9), was archdeacon of Carlisle from 1682 and bishop from 1702 to 1718. His collected materials for a history of the diocese are found in four volumes in the Dean and Chapter archives. They consist largely of extracts from the diocesan records but also include a manuscript glossary of the dialect of Cumberland and Westmorland, prepared by Nicolson when a student at Oxford in 1677.[13] Nicolson's contemporary and fellow antiquary Hugh Todd (*c*. 1657–1728) was vicar of Penrith from 1699. He compiled two manuscript accounts of the diocese, a single-volume 'History of the Diocese of Carlisle' in 1685–7, and a more substantial 'History of the Bishopric of Carlisle' in two volumes *c*. 1720.[14]

The two counties shared in the great wave of county history publishing in the later 18th century. From that period date the two histories which provide the first full treatment of the counties, parish by parish, namely *The History and Antiquities of the Counties of Westmorland and Cumberland* by Joseph Nicolson and Richard Burn (1777) and William Hutchinson's *History of the County of Cumberland* (1794–7). The former was the product of collaboration between two men from very different backgrounds.[15] Joseph Nicolson (1706–77) was a member of the close-knit ecclesiastical élite which clustered around the diocesan seat at Carlisle. A nephew of Bishop William Nicolson

[12] Ibid.

[13] Cumbria R.O. (Carlisle), Dean and Chapter archives, Nicolson's MSS. The dialect glossary is in vol. i, pp. 355–507.

[14] Oxford, St. Edmund Hall MSS. 7/1–3. See D. J. W. Mawson, 'Dr. Hugh Todd's Account of Diocese of Carlisle', *Trans. C.W.A.A.S.* lxxxviii. 207–24.

[15] For Nicolson and Burn and a fuller account of their work, see B. C. Jones's introduction to their *Hist.* in the 1976 reprint.

and son of the diocesan registrar and chapter clerk, Joseph Nicolson inherited a small estate from his mother, at Hawksdale, near Dalston, close to the bishop's palace at Rose Castle. He was thus ideally placed, both by residence and by connexion, to have access to the diocesan records and those of the dean and chapter, which included the papers of Machell and William Nicolson.

Richard Burn (1710–84) was the dominant member of the partnership, taking overall editorial responsibility for the history and having the financial ability to publish it. He was a self-made man, the son of a yeoman from Winton, Westmorland. After university, he was appointed schoolmaster at Kirkby Stephen and in 1736 was ordained priest and appointed to the vicarage of Orton, which he held until his death. He became a magistrate in 1747, and as a newcomer to the bench, without legal training, he kept notes which formed the basis of his *Justice of the Peace and Parish Officer* (first published 1755). It passed through many editions and became a standard reference work. His careful legal mind, combined with a deep local knowledge of Westmorland, provided firm foundations for the history.

Nicolson and Burn's work was, by their own admission, a compilation which drew heavily on the accounts of John Denton and Daniel Fleming and on the materials collected by Machell, Bishop Nicolson, and others: 'these are now collected, digested, and offered to the public view', they wrote in their introduction. The account of Westmorland (compiled by Burn) was considerably fuller than that of Cumberland (compiled by Nicolson). Burn's general introduction to Westmorland was particularly wide-ranging, containing information on housing, clothing, tenures, and communications, and even a description of a children's game called Scotch and English, which he described as 'a very active and violent recreation'. Those parts of both counties which lay outside Carlisle diocese were treated much less thoroughly than places within the diocese. Of the two parts of Westmorland, the account of the 'bottom' (in Westmorland barony and Carlisle diocese) was more detailed than that of Kendal barony, and the account of Allerdale above Derwent ward (that part of Cumberland forming Copeland deanery in Chester diocese) was particularly thin. The whole work was prefaced by a long essay on the ancient and modern state of the Border, which drew heavily on Bishop Nicolson's *Border Laws* (1705), itself based on a manuscript history of the Borders compiled in the early 17th century by Richard Bell, a former clerk of the Western March.[16]

Within twenty years the deficiencies of Joseph Nicolson's account of Cumberland were at least partly rectified by the publication of William Hutchinson's *History of the County of Cumberland* (2 vols. 1794–7). William

---

[16] Cumbria R.O. (Carlisle), Dean and Chapter MSS., Richard Bell's Hist. of the Borders.

Hutchinson (1732–1814), a lawyer practising at Barnard Castle, Co. Durham, had already completed a history of Durham. He was no stranger to Cumberland, having visited the Lake District in 1773 and published an account of his visit (*An Excursion to the Lakes*, 1776), which was one of the early Lake District guides, appearing just as the area was being 'discovered' by fashionable society. The idea of publishing a *History of Cumberland* probably originated when Hutchinson approached Francis Jollie, a Carlisle printer, for help in printing the final volume of his history of Durham. Jollie seems to have agreed on condition that Hutchinson turned his attention to Cumberland. The resulting work, bearing Hutchinson's name as author and Jollie's as 'proprietor and editor', was the product of several hands. How much was written by Hutchinson himself is not clear. Jollie probably contributed material, and the text contained extensive quotations from John Denton's manuscript and drew heavily on Camden and other published sources. A substantial introductory section on the natural history of the county was the work of the Carlisle physician John Heysham (1753–1834) (on animals), the Revd. William Richardson (on botany), and John Losh of Woodside (on geology). Two other contributors played a major part in shaping the body of the work. The Revd. Jonathan Boucher (1738–1804), a native of Bromfield, wrote the accounts of Bromfield, Caldbeck, and Sebergham parishes, as well as contributing the brief biographies signed 'Biographia Cumbria'. John Housman of Cumwhitton, described by Hutchinson as 'a skilfull person who lately traversed the county', provided for each parish a wealth of contemporary detail, including information on soils, agriculture, land tenure, population, and education, which were signed 'Housman's Notes'.[17] They give the *History* a distinctive quality which is reflected in its dedication to Sir John Sinclair, president of the Board of Agriculture. The spirit of agricultural improvement pervades its pages, Housman's contributions providing a contemporary survey akin to the Statistical Account of Scotland which was being compiled at the same time.

Hutchinson's *Cumberland* also devoted space to descriptions of the beauties of the Lake District. Given Hutchinson's own interest in the Lakes and the burgeoning fashionability of the area in the 1780s and 1790s, it is not surprising that his was the first history in which the weight of attention began to shift from the Cumberland lowlands, where the native gentry resided, to the Lake District, which was rapidly becoming a playground for fashionable society. The editors justified the inclusion of so much non-historical material by claiming that 'we should hold ourselves highly blameable, were we to pass negligently over those subjects of fashionable curiosity, the Lakes.' The result

---

[17] Housman later wrote his own *Topographical Description of Cumb., Westmld., Lancs. and pt. of West Riding of Yorks.* (1800).

is that the accounts of Ullswater, Keswick, Derwentwater, Borrowdale, and Buttermere are well padded with long descriptions of the landscape in the picturesque idiom, extracted from the works of Thomas West, William Gilpin, and others.[18]

When it appeared, Hutchinson's *Cumberland* received critical reviews. Its publication had been heralded by a series of caustic attacks on Hutchinson and Jollie in the *Gentleman's Magazine* from Richard Gough, the antiquary.[19] While it is true that much material had been recycled from earlier authors and that Hutchinson's literary style could be cumbersome and pompous, his *Cumberland* remains a useful source for modern historians, particularly in view of the social and economic data in Housman's notes.

Nicolson and Burn and Hutchinson became the standard histories of the two counties. Their words, often borrowed from the 17th-century antiquarians whose works they quarried, were recycled throughout the 19th century. The two histories of Westmorland from the early 19th century were both largely derivative. Indeed John Hodgson's *Topographical and Historical Description of the County of Westmoreland* [*c.* 1815] was simply a rebinding of the relevant section of Britton and Brayley's *Beauties of England and Wales* as a separate volume. The second, Sayer's *History of Westmorland* (2 vols. 1847–8), admitted on its title page that it contained 'the substance of all the remarkable events recorded by Burn and Nicolson', but also claimed to present material from 'ancient MSS. never before published', though there is little evidence that it did so. In Cumberland, John Wilkins advertised his intention to produce a four-volume history of the county under the title 'Cumbria Antiqua', but it does not appear to have been published, nor has a manuscript version been found.[20]

New sources of evidence, however, were also drawn into the corpus of published history during the century. First of all, Thomas Denton's manuscript description of Cumberland, written in 1687–8, was rediscovered among the muniments at Lowther Castle and was lent to Daniel and Samuel Lysons when they were compiling the Cumberland volume of their *Magna Britannia*, probably in 1808 when they visited the county.[21] As a result, material recorded by Thomas Denton was also included in the next major attempt to write a detailed history of Cumberland, that made, unsuccessfully, by Samuel Jefferson (1809–46). Jefferson was a Carlisle bookseller whose chief interests lay in church history. Seeing the scant attention which had been paid to the county's churches by earlier authors, Jefferson returned to the

---

[18] The principal quotations are from T. West, *Guide to the Lakes* (1778); W. Gilpin, *Observations relative to Picturesque Beauty made in 1772, in several pts. of England, particularly the Mountains and Lakes of Cumb. and Westmld.* (2 vols. 1786).

[19] C. R. Hudleston's introduction to Hutchinson's *Cumb.* in the 1974 reprint.

[20] *Carlisle Jnl.* 30 Mar. 1822. The author is grateful to D. R. Perriam for this reference.

[21] D. and S. Lysons, *Magna Britannia: Cumb.* (1814), 1–3.

original sources (including the collections of Machell and Bishop Nicolson) and to field observation. His intention was to publish a history of Cumberland in seven volumes, one each for the city of Carlisle and the county's six wards (the five ancient wards plus the new division, Derwent ward, created in 1840). Only three of the projected volumes were published: *The History and Antiquities of Carlisle* (1838), *The History and Antiquities of Leath Ward* (1840), and *The History and Antiquities of Allerdale Ward above Derwent* (1842).

Jefferson's histories concentrated on the descent of the manor and the history of the parish church. For the former he drew heavily on the accounts by Hutchinson, John Denton, and Sandford, but he also incorporated later information gleaned from more recent sources, including the Lysonses' *Magna Britannia* and Parson and White's *Directory of Cumberland and Westmorland* (1829). It was in his architectural and historical accounts of Cumberland's parish churches that Jefferson made a significant contribution to the historiography of the county. He attempted to trace advowsons and the value of livings, to compile lists of clergy, to record monumental inscriptions, to list parochial charities, and to describe the past and present fabric of the church. His descriptions were full and detailed, particularly in the volume on Leath ward. For Allerdale above Derwent, outside Carlisle diocese and thus less readily documented, his briefer descriptions are enlivened by scathing attacks on improvements which concealed or destroyed a church's antiquity. He thought the windows at Gosforth 'all modern and barbarous in design' and attributed the removal of the south porch at St. Bridget Beckermet to 'the idea that it was no longer necessary to have an appendage to the church which modern utilitarians consider as convenient only for scraping shoes in'.[22]

In 1860 William Whellan, a compiler and publisher of directories, published a new *History and Topography of the Counties of Cumberland and Westmorland* in an attempt, as he put it, 'to supply to the people of [the two counties] a complete and modern history'. Whellan's single volume treated the parishes in each county alphabetically by ward and was prefaced by a substantial introduction composed of essays on the 'general history' of the counties by Thomas Wright (1810–77), the antiquary; geology, with particular reference to the Lake District, by J. G. Cumming (1812–68), professor of geology at Queen's College, Birmingham; and a 'survey of the Lake District' by Harriet Martineau (1802–76), that shrewd observer of Lake District society and friend of Wordsworth. Whellan's parish histories were brief and drew heavily on earlier writers, the manorial descents often being close paraphrases of Nicolson and Burn, themselves borrowed from John Denton. But it would be unfair to dismiss Whellan's history as simply a regurgitation of the words of others. He used recent and contemporary data, gleaned from directories and official sources, and he also appears to have had

---

[22] S. Jefferson, *Hist. and Antiquities of Allerdale Ward above Derwent* (1842), 301, 308.

access to manuscripts not used by earlier historians, including the detailed and extensive 'Percy survey' of 1578 in the muniments at Cockermouth castle, which describes estates in western Cumberland.[23]

Modern historical scholarship reached Cumberland and Westmorland in the later 19th century when, under the stimulus of a group of educated and leisured men infused with the regional pride of Victorian society, a determined attempt was made to cultivate the study of the two counties and to move beyond heavy reliance on the less than perfect work of the 17th-century antiquarians. The turning point came in 1866 with the foundation of the Cumberland and Westmorland Antiquarian and Archaeological Society, largely by churchmen and gentlemen. Through its *Transactions* were reported the findings of research on a wide range of fronts, while its record, tract, and extra series provided vehicles for the publication of original manuscripts. The society stimulated not only archaeological investigation, notably concerning the legacy of the Roman period in Cumberland, but also investigation into documentary sources. By the end of the century its *Transactions* had published papers exploring the potential of parish registers, vestry books, and manor court records, as well as numerous articles on the history of landed families and their houses and seminal excursions into the industrial history of west Cumberland.[24]

Perhaps the leading figure in the new society was Richard Saul Ferguson (1837–1900), the founding editor of its *Transactions*, its president from 1886, and active in the establishment of Tullie House museum, Carlisle, in 1893. Ferguson was a Carlisle man and the archetypical gentleman antiquary of the Victorian period, combining his scholarly interests with wide-ranging public service. He was a lawyer by profession, and was active in local affairs as chairman of the Cumberland quarter sessions, mayor of Carlisle, and chancellor of the diocese. As well as contributing numerous papers to *Transactions*, he also edited for publication much primary source material which appeared as volumes in the society's tract and extra series. They included the manuscript histories by John Denton, Fleming, and Sandford, the account of Bishop Nicolson's visitation of the diocese in 1703, Todd's history of Carlisle, corporation records of Carlisle and Kendal, and a volume of early wills proved at Carlisle.[25]

[23] Cumbria R.O. (Carlisle), D/Lec/301.

[24] The last were I. Fletcher, 'Arch. of West Cumb. Coal Trade', *Trans. C.W.A.A.S.* [old ser.] iii. 266–313; H. A. Fletcher, 'Arch. of West Cumb. Iron Trade', *Trans. C.W.A.A.S.* [old ser.] v. 5–21.

[25] *Miscellany Accounts of Diocese of Carlisle by William Nicolson*, ed. R. S. Ferguson (C.W.A.A.S. Extra ser. i, 1877); *John Denton's Accompt of Cumb.* (C.W.A.A.S. Tract ser. ii, 1887); *Some Municipal Recs. of City of Carlisle*, ed. R. S. Ferguson and W. Nanson (C.W.A.A.S. Extra ser. iv, 1887); *Description of County of Cumb. by Sir Daniel Fleming of Rydall, A.D. 1671* (C.W.A.A.S. Tract ser. iii, 1889); *A Cursory Relation by Edmund Sandford* (C.W.A.A.S. Tract ser. iv, 1890); *Hugh Todd's Account of City and Diocese of Carlisle* (C.W.A.A.S. Tract ser. v, 1891); *The Boke off Recorde of the Burgh of Kirkbie Kendall* (C.W.A.A.S. Extra ser. vii, 1892); *Testamenta Karleolensia* (C.W.A.A.S. Extra ser. ix, 1893).

Chancellor Ferguson contributed the volumes on *Cumberland* (1890) and *Westmorland* (1894) to Elliot Stock's 'Popular County Histories' series. Noting that local history had become so specialized that the student of the subject required 'a whole bookcase' of books 'devoted exclusively to one subject', he saw his task as being to 'attempt to discharge the functions of the "General Introduction" to an old-fashioned county history.'[26] Ferguson therefore took a broad brush to his canvas, though the accent of both volumes fell on the archaeological evidence for the prehistoric and Roman periods, on feudal and ecclesiastical aspects of medieval history, and on local political history ('national history writ small'). The last substantive chapter in both volumes was entitled 'The '15 and the '45' and the only attempt to cover the history of the two counties since 1750 was in a final 'Miscellaneous' chapter. The Cumberland volume leant heavily towards the history of Carlisle and the Border, with extensive treatment of Hadrian's Wall, the medieval city, and the Scottish wars. The sister county was less familiar to Ferguson, and his treatment of Westmorland is altogether thinner and is padded out by long extracts from primary sources and detailed descriptions of archaeological sites. Ferguson acknowledged that many of the essential materials for the history of the two counties remained unprinted and inaccessible.

In the last years of his life R. S. Ferguson turned to a project which was intended to take the history of Cumberland a major step forward. This was the projected four-volume *Victoria History of Cumberland*, of which he was appointed editor and to which he intended to contribute. He died before any of the volumes appeared in print and his place as editor was taken by Canon James Wilson (1856–1923), the vicar of Dalston, who was a medievalist and a careful and productive scholar. Under Wilson's editorship two volumes of the Cumberland *V.C.H.* were published. Volume one (1901) contained, as well as the obligatory introductory section on natural history, three major essays: on early man (by Ferguson), pre-Norman remains (by W. G. Collingwood), and an introduction to the texts of the Cumberland material in Domesday Book, the early Pipe Rolls, and *Testa de Nevill* (by Wilson himself). The last remains to this day an important discussion of the feudal history of the county in the 11th and 12th centuries. Volume two (1905) included articles on ecclesiastical history, religious houses, and political history, all contributed by Wilson, and sections on industries, sport, and forestry typical of the Edwardian *V.C.H.*

Other noteworthy products of the Victorian period included two sets of biographical essays recounting the lives of notable natives and a body of literature on the region's distinctive ethnic and cultural identity. George

---

[26] R. S. Ferguson, *Hist. of Cumb.* (1890), p. vii.

Atkinson's *The Worthies of Westmorland: or Notable Persons born in that County since the Reformation* (2 vols. 1849–50) was heavily weighted towards churchmen, though it did include some legal, literary, and military figures as well. More substantial was Henry Lonsdale's *The Worthies of Cumberland* (6 vols. 1867–75), which concentrated on men of science and the arts, including agricultural improvers, astronomers, geologists, physicians, and poets. Henry Lonsdale (1816–76) had been physician to the Cumberland Infirmary. His 28 lives, some brief, others full-length biographies, provide a useful, if selective, dictionary of county biography for Cumberland.

Work on Cumbria's cultural identity developed through the study of its place names, dialect, and customs. The earliest significant studies were Robert Ferguson's *The Northmen in Cumberland and Westmorland* (1856) and J. Sullivan's *Cumberland and Westmorland, Ancient and Modern: the People, Dialect, Superstitions and Customs* (1857). The study of those aspects of history was fostered by a second county society, the Cumberland (from 1884, Cumberland and Westmorland) Association for the Advancement of Literature and Science. In contrast to the Antiquarian and Archaeological Society, the Association's founders were men of science from the industrial towns of west Cumberland. They interpreted their brief widely, to include 'local customs, peculiarities and history', and the 17 volumes of the Association's *Transactions*, published 1876–92, included several papers on language and place names.

The revolution in the conception of local history which has taken place during the 20th century has been accompanied by three interrelated developments which have changed significantly the perspective from which the history of Cumberland and Westmorland has been viewed. First has been the revolution in the study of local history itself. No longer is it the purely documentary and architectural study of the twin pillars of English rural society, the parish church and the manor house. The growth of social and economic history in general and of the concept of community in particular has encouraged local historians to take a much broader approach to the study of local and regional communities. In Cumbria, as will be seen, that has been expressed in the rapid growth in the study of archaeology, place names, vernacular buildings, dialect, and folk life, topics which received considerably more attention than documentary history until comparatively recently. A second development has been the move towards viewing 'the Lake Counties' or 'Cumbria' (Cumberland, Westmorland, and Lancashire north of the Sands) as a convenient unit of study, and the growth of a body of literature treating the history of the region as a whole. Behind that lay the 'discovery' of the Lake District and the realization that the ancient county boundaries divided a region which possessed much in common. The growth of a Lake Counties school of regional history may be thought of as the logical

development of the consciousness of the Lake District as an entity seen in the
earlier histories of Hutchinson and Whellan. A third and equally important
shift of emphasis lies in the geographical direction from which the study of
the two counties has been conducted. Until 1900, as has been seen, most of
the historians writing about the counties lived north of the great physical
divide created by the Lake District mountains. They looked to Carlisle as
their centre and viewed both counties from a northern perspective. The
growth of history as a profession and the failure of Carlisle to attract a
university have resulted in most of the 20th-century writing on the histories
of Cumberland and Westmorland being carried out from outside their
boundaries, mainly by scholars who have viewed Cumbria from a Lancashire
perspective. The result has been to produce a shift in focus, away from the
Border and the Cumberland lowlands, which preoccupied much of the earlier
literature, and south to the Lake District and the lowlands skirting
Morecambe Bay. It is striking, for example, that the only 20th-century
attempt to collect and publish materials towards a county history was focused
on the Kendal area. It was the project to publish *Records Relating to the
Barony of Kendale* (3 vols. 1923–6) undertaken by the great historian of
Lancashire, William Farrer (1861–1924).[27]

   The study of dialect and place names, which, as has been noted, began in
the mid 19th century, combined with work on pre-Norman sculpture, drew
attention to the links between Scandinavia and Cumbria and opened a field
of study which continues to be tilled[28] and which has led to the Viking
legacy in Cumbria holding a central place in the popular conception of the
region's history. The Scandinavian connexion was a central interest of W. G.
Collingwood (1854–1932), whose *Lake District History* (1925) pioneered the
broader treatment of the region's economic, settlement, and landscape
history. Collingwood, professor of fine art at University College, Reading,
and formerly secretary to John Ruskin, was a man of wide interests. He
contributed profusely to the *Transactions* of the Cumberland and Westmorland Antiquarian and Archaeological Society (which he edited for 32
years), his contributions spanning both archaeological and documentary
subjects. As well as his seminal work on pre-Norman sculpture, which
culminated in his *Northumbrian Crosses of the Pre-Norman Age* (1927), he

---

[27] The trilogy was completed and edited by J. F. Curwen, who also compiled a companion
volume, *Later Recs. relating to North Westmld. or Barony of Appleby* (1932).
   [28] See A. Sparke, *Bibliography of Dialect Literature of Cumb., Westmld. and Lancs. North-of-the-
Sands* (C.W.A.A.S. Tract ser. ix, 1907). The seminal study of the place-name evidence was W. J.
Sedgefield, *Place-Names of Cumb. and Westmld.* (1915). The study of sculpture was established by
W. S. Calverley, *Early Sculptured Crosses, Shrines and Monuments in Present Diocese of Carlisle*,
ed. W. G. Collingwood (1899). For a review of recent work see *Scandinavians in Cumbria*, ed. J. R.
Baldwin and I. D. Whyte (1985).

contributed to the study of industrial history in Cumberland with his volume on the 16th-century Mines Royal in the Keswick area, published as *Elizabethan Keswick* (1912). His *Lake District History* was conceived as an 'interim report' to make available to a wide audience the new light that had been shed on the history of the region since the 19th century. Collingwood's history was firmly rooted in the landscape, and the book contained discussions of archaeological and place-name evidence, industrial history, the social history of Lakeland yeoman society, and the influence of the quest for mountain scenery and the growth of tourism. Collingwood had constructed a template which continues to shape popular histories of the region.[29]

A second strand in the study of the Lake Counties has been the study of the region's social history. The seminal work in that area was *Prelates and People of the Lake Counties: a History of the Diocese of Carlisle, 1133–1933* (1948) by C. M. Lowther Bouch (1890–1959). Canon Bouch, the last of the gentleman amateurs and the first of the modern historians of Cumberland and Westmorland, came to Cumberland as a vicar in Carlisle in 1932 and was rector of Clifton and Brougham near Penrith from 1946. He was a gifted historian and he saw *Prelates and People* as an attempt to fulfill A. L. Rowse's call for 'a synthesis of local and national history'.[30] He believed that church history could not be understood if it were divorced from political and social history and his book was an important landmark in the historiography of Cumberland and Westmorland, providing for the first time a comprehensive, modern history of the counties from the 12th century to the 20th.

Bouch wrote before the arrival of the county record offices. Those in Cumbria were finally established in 1962 by a joint committee of the county councils of Cumberland and Westmorland and the city council of Carlisle, though Cumberland had a county archivist (mostly on a part-time basis) from 1942. The increased accessibility of county and church records and the deposit of many of the major family and estate collections in what are now the offices of Cumbria Archive Service at Carlisle and Kendal have enabled work on the history of the Lake Counties to develop rapidly. Studies of the region's social and economic history have been provided for the early modern period by Bouch and Jones[31] and by Appleby,[32] for the 19th and early 20th century by

[29] e.g. W. Rollinson, *Hist. of Man in Lake District* (1967); R. Millward and A. Robinson, *Lake District* (1970); *Lake District, Landscape Heritage*, ed. W. Rollinson (1989).

[30] A. L. Rowse, *Tudor Cornw.* (1941), 10, quoted by C. M. L. Bouch, *Prelates and People of Lake Counties: Hist. of Diocese of Carlisle, 1133–1933* (1948), p. vi.

[31] C. M. L. Bouch and G. P. Jones, *Short Economic and Social Hist. of Lake Counties, 1500–1830* (1961).

[32] A. B. Appleby, *Famine in Tudor and Stuart England* (1978). Despite its title it is an historical demography and economic hist. of Cumbria.

Marshall and Walton,[33] and for the medieval period by Winchester.[34] Both counties have been surveyed by the English Place-Name Society,[35] and other specialist studies include surveys of traditional life and vernacular architecture[36] and studies of the industrial development of west Cumberland during the 17th and 18th centuries.[37] A popular history of the two counties was provided by William Rollinson's volume in the Darwen County History series.[38] The only bibliographic guide to the literature on the two counties is the *Bibliography of Cumberland and Westmorland* issued by the Joint Archives Committee for Cumberland, Westmorland, and Carlisle in 1968 and edited by H. W. Hodgson. Its usefulness is severely limited, however, by the editor's decision to omit all publications concerning individuals, as he considered them to constitute biography, not history.

Many of the scholars who have contributed to the Lake Counties school of regional history since 1950 have viewed the region from the south: G. P. Jones, J. D. Marshall, William Rollinson, and John K. Walton have all tended to focus on the southern half of the modern county of Cumbria, concentrating on communities in Furness and southern Westmorland. The result is that our understanding of the history of the Lake District has developed at the expense of that of the Lake Counties as a whole. The popular literature on the Lake District has endowed it with an historic personality which has been disseminated in print and through the media of television and adult education classes to the population at large. In contrast, the historic heartland of Cumberland and Westmorland in the Carlisle plain and the Eden valley, which received so much attention from the 17th- and 18th-century antiquaries, has been comparatively neglected. The villages and market towns of the northern half of Cumbria continue to offer a rich and undercultivated field for future local historians.

---

[33] J. D. Marshall and J. K. Walton, *Lake Counties from 1830 to mid-20th Century* (1981).

[34] A. J. L. Winchester, *Landscape and Society in Medieval Cumbria* (1987).

[35] A. M. Armstrong and others, *Place-Names of Cumb.* (3 vols., E.P.N.S. xx–xxii, 1950–2); A. H. Smith, *Place-Names of Westmld.* (2 vols., E.P.N.S. xlii–xliii, 1967).

[36] W. Rollinson, *Life and Tradition in Lake District* (1974); R. W. Brunskill, *Vernacular Archit. of Lake Counties* (1974); S. Denyer, *Traditional Buildings and Life in Lake District* (1991).

[37] E. Hughes, *North Country Life in 18th Century, Volume II: Cumb. and Westmld. 1700–1830* (1965); J. V. Beckett, *Coal and Tobacco: Lowthers and Economic Development of West Cumb. 1660–1760* (1981).

[38] W. Rollinson, *Hist. of Cumb. and Westmld.* (1978).

DERBYSHIRE

Margaret O'Sullivan

One of the characteristics of Derbyshire historiography is the abundance of printed descriptions of parts of the county but the absence of a large-scale, conventional topographical study of the whole. Unlike its neighbours, Derbyshire has had no Dugdale, Thoroton, or Nichols,[1] and local historians have rarely failed to comment on the lack. For example, the county history planned by Thomas Blore (1764–1818) met with 'a lack of proper encouragement'. Local support, especially financial, for such ventures was the more uncertain when descriptive guides to Derbyshire were readily available. The fact that the county has had its share of ambitious projects, imperfectly realized, should not detract from the value of contributions towards its history of enduring quality and originality by a number of antiquaries and historians from the 17th century. Intellectual life in Derbyshire was not cut off from developments elsewhere. When Erasmus Darwin (1731–1802) established the Derby Philosophical Society in the early 1780s as an offshoot of the Lunar Society of Birmingham, he actively promoted contacts between the two associations. Over the next 75 years his society built up a library and organized lectures, chiefly on topics of contemporary scientific interest, which enabled its members to share in new ideas. Darwin's friend Joseph Wright of Derby (1734–97) likewise made experimental and industrial activity the subjects of some of his best known paintings.[2]

The spirit of enquiry in antiquarian form was demonstrated by a later Derbyshire worthy, Sir George Sitwell (1860–1943) of Renishaw. His son Osbert was surprised to see his father setting off uncharacteristically late one night in a very old carriage. '"Just driving down to Eckington Church to observe the effect of moonlight on the spire", explained Sir George with a flutter of his hand, as if conferring a favour on the edifice; "I want it for my chapter, *Eckington Church in the Thirteenth Century*, in *Tales of My Native*

---

[1] W. Dugdale, *Antiquities of Warws.* (1656); R. Thoroton, *Antiquities of Notts.* (1677); J. Nichols, *Hist. and Antiquities of County of Leicester* (1795).

[2] Derby Philosophical Soc. *Rules and Catalogue* (1835); R. Schofield, *The Lunar Soc. of Birmingham* (1963), 236–7; B. Nicholson, *Joseph Wright of Derby* (2 vols. 1968).

Village".[3] Sir George's idiosyncrasies were as unique to him as the special boxes he had made for his working notes, 'fashioned of a material the colour of an aubergine, and in texture like a skin with gooseflesh',[4] but he did see at least some of his work in print, unlike many of his predecessors.

One notable example was the appearance after more than 270 years of William Woolley's *History of Derbyshire*.[5] Woolley's editors identified both his sources and the succession of local researchers and record collectors familiar with his account in one or other version. From about 1715 his unpublished manuscript was a prime source for the county's history, known amongst a restricted but well informed circle who recognized the value of his work and the problems he had experienced.

Woolley (?*c.* 1655–1719) had access to a manuscript volume on Derbyshire's history compiled in the early 1660s by his step-uncle Samuel Sanders (1641–88), the product of detailed research into public records in London.[6] A contemporary but apparently unrelated enterprise by Philip Kinder (b. 1597) appears to be known only in the form of a manuscript synopsis, his 'Prolusion', now in the Bodleian Library, published by the Revd. W. G. Dimock Fletcher in *The Reliquary*.[7] William Woolley was a subscriber to Charles Leigh's *Natural History of Lancashire, Cheshire, and the Peak in Derbyshire*, privately printed in 1700,[8] but his enthusiasm for historical research was tempered by his awareness of local difficulties. He doubted whether he could complete genealogies from a base in Derbyshire 'considering the many families whose chiefs are minors and many who belong to this county properly live in others or in London, and so could not easily be met withall'.[9] Nevertheless between 1710 and 1715 he put together chapters on the southern part of the county, the hundreds of Morleston and Litchurch, Appletree, and Repton and Gresley, together with Wirksworth wapentake. His work was later annotated by an anonymous writer, possibly Sir Thomas Abney (1691–1750) of Willesley Hall (now demolished), who echoed Woolley's frustration in his remarks on 'the great difficulties I have found in getting new light from the natives, the . . . peevish answers of some gentlemen and

---

[3] O. Sitwell, introduction to G. Sitwell, *On the Making of Gardens* (1949), p. xiii.

[4] Ibid. p. xviii; G. Sitwell, *Tales of My Native Village* (1933).

[5] *William Woolley's Hist. of Derb.* ed. C. Glover and P. Riden (Derb. Rec. Soc. vi, 1981) [hereafter *Woolley's Hist.*]. The writer is indebted to Dr. Philip Riden for permission to quote from his introduction to that volume.

[6] Ibid. introduction, pp. xxvi–xxxii.

[7] Bodl. MS. Ashmole 788; E. B. Thomas, 'Philip Kinder: author of "Hist. of Derbyshire"', *Derb. Miscellany*, iv (2) (1967), 99–109; *Woolley's Hist.* introduction, p. xi; W. G. Dimock Fletcher, *The Reliquary*, xx (1881–2); xxiii (1882–3); J. C. Cox, *Notes on Churches of Derb.* i (1875), p. xvii.

[8] C. Leigh, *Natural Hist. of Lancs., Ches., and the Peak in Derb.* (1700); *Woolley's Hist.* introduction, p. xix.

[9] *Woolley's Hist.* introduction, pp. xxv, 4.

the ignorant answers of some others [which] has made me despair of finishing the whole'.[10]

Owners of copies of Woolley's *History* included the antiquary and early field archaeologist Samuel Pegge (1704–96), the majority of whose Derbyshire collections are now in the College of Arms and the Bodleian Library, and Adam Wolley (d. 1827), whose papers were mostly bequeathed to the British Museum. Before that, in 1818, another Derbyshire antiquary, Godfrey Meynell, had transcribed William Woolley's text from the version owned by Adam Wolley.[11] This list is by no means exhaustive. Of county historians whose work was published, amongst the most influential users of William Woolley's manuscript were the Lysonses, Daniel and Samuel, whose Derbyshire volume in their *Magna Britannia* series appeared in 1817.[12] Another copy of Woolley was acquired by a well known compiler of local directories and guides, Stephen Glover, who eventually saw in print only two volumes of his proposed *History of the County of Derby*, in 1829 and 1833.[13] Glover's first volume included wood engravings by the young Thomas Orlando Sheldon Jewitt (1799–1869), born at Chesterfield. The Jewitt family were well represented in Derbyshire historiography, both popular and scholarly, in the 19th century. Orlando's father Arthur (1772–1852) was a prolific writer of local histories and guidebooks, including the *History of Buxton* (1811) and the *Matlock Companion* (1832).[14] Orlando Jewitt produced wood engravings for some of his father's publications, for Robert Simpson's *A Collection of Fragments Illustrative of the History and Antiquities of Derby*, as well as, later, for a different but distinguished tradition of local writing on natural history, through his much admired illustrations to *A True Treatise on the Art of Fly-Fishing as Practised on the Dove* by William Shipley.[15] Orlando's youngest brother, Llewellynn Frederick William Jewitt (1816–86), was also a wood engraver, but his major contribution was to Derbyshire antiquarian writing. In 1860 he was the originator, and from then until his death the editor, of *The Reliquary*, the medium for many articles of his own. That innovative quarterly journal antedated the foundation of a county archaeological society, elsewhere often the main focus of later Victorian local historical research and publishing. Jewitt's *Reliquary* had been established for 18 years when the Derbyshire Archaeological and Natural History Society began in 1878. '*The Reliquary* filled a genuine gap in available outlets for the

---

[10] Ibid. p. xlvii.
[11] Ibid. pp. xlviii, lvii.
[12] D. and S. Lysons, *Magna Britannia: Derb.* (1817).
[13] *Woolley's Hist.* introduction, pp. xlix–li; S. Glover, *Hist. of County of Derby* (2 vols. 1829–33).
[14] H. Carter, *Orlando Jewitt* (1962), 8; A. Jewitt, *Hist. of Buxton* (1811) and *Matlock Companion* (1832).
[15] R. Simpson, *Collection of Fragments Illustrative of Hist. and Antiquities of Derby* (1826); W. Shipley, *True Treatise on Art of Fly-Fishing as Practised on the Dove*, ed. E. Fitzgibbon (1838).

kind of work it published'[16] and, although pieces in it did not have to relate to Derbyshire, there was a natural tendency on Jewitt's part to favour such a provenance. The existence of *The Reliquary* enabled much original material on local historical topics to reach a wider audience for the first time. Ironically, those articles included in 1870 Jewitt's proposals for his own history of Derbyshire, apparently never executed. He referred to previous projects, including those of his father, of Thomas Blore, and of Samuel Mitchell of Sheffield (Yorks.) who had died in 1869, 14 years after the appearance of his prospectus for a similar history, though to be confined to the two northern hundreds of High Peak and Scarsdale.[17]

That last scheme would have been a development from the many descriptions of scenery and natural features, particularly in the north and west of the county, popular since the 17th century. Numerous authors have expatiated on the 'Wonders of the Peak'. Thomas Hobbes's Latin poem *De Mirabilibus Pecci* (1636) was published in an English translation in 1678 and the title, though not the contents, were repeated in another verse work by Charles Cotton in 1681. Six of Cotton's seven wonders were the outlandish phenomena of 'A Country so deform'd, the Traveller/Would swear those parts Nature's Pudenda were', where a hill was a 'wart', for instance; the seventh was the 'pallace' and improved landscape at Chatsworth which was 'far above' any 'painter's baffl'd Art'.[18] Admiration for nature succeeded dislike of the 'houling Wilderness' in later rhapsodic pieces such as *The River Dove: A Lyric Pastoral* by Samuel Bentley (1768).[19] Similar romantic effusions continued to be composed well into the 19th century to overlap with the production both locally and nationally of guides for travellers whether by road, rail, or on foot. After Charles Leigh in 1700, major writers on Derbyshire's topography included James Pilkington (1789), John Aikin (1795), John Hutchinson (1809–10), the Revd. D. P. Davies (1811), the Lysons brothers (1817), and John Britton and Edward Brayley, whose Derbyshire section in their *Beauties of England and Wales* was first published in 1802.[20]

---

[16] *The Reliquary: a Depository of Precious Relics Illustrative of the Habits, Customs and Pursuits of our Forefathers* (1860–1909); *Index to the Reliquary, First Ser.* ed. P. Riden (Derb. Rec. Soc. Occasional Paper ii, 1979), introduction, p. vi.

[17] *Index to the Reliquary, First Ser.* ed. Riden, pp. viii, x; *The Reliquary*, x (1869–70), pp. 255–6; William Henry Goss, *Life and Death of Llewellynn Jewitt* (1889).

[18] T. Hobbes, *De Mirabilibus Pecci, being the Wonders of the Peak in Derb.* (1678); C. Cotton, *The Wonders of the Peak* (1681).

[19] S. Bentley, *The River Dove: a Lyric Pastoral* (1768).

[20] J. Pilkington, *View of Present State of Derb.* (2 vols. 1789); J. Aikin, *Description of Country from 30 to 40 Miles round Manchester* (1795); J. Hutchinson, *Curiosities of Derb. including Description of Celebrated Baths of Buxton and Matlock* (1810); D. P. Davies, *New Hist. and Descriptive View of Derb.* (2 vols. 1811); D. and S. Lysons, *Magna Britannia: Derb.* (1817); J. Britton and E. W. Brayley, *Beauties of England and Wales*, iii (1802).

Interest did not decline with familiarity. As an example, two years after John Ruskin's observations on Matlock Bath and the Peak,[21] there appeared in 1886 James Croston's edition of *Chantrey's Peak Scenery* with engravings taken from drawings by the Derbyshire-born Sir Francis L. Chantrey, R.A. (1781–1842).[22] Beauty was complemented by salubriousness: the health-giving properties of spa waters in Derbyshire had been promoted as early as 1572 by John Jones and 1697 by Sir John Floyer.[23] Later surveys of the county frequently emphasize both aspects.[24]

Seventeenth-century accounts of curiosities and the grandeurs of the landscape developed into more thorough and scholarly studies of Derbyshire's industry, geology, and mineral resources. A work which had wide currency despite, or perhaps because of, its format was the versified account of lead-mining customs in Wirksworth by the Ashbourne attorney Edward Manlove, first published in 1653.[25] Twenty-eight years later they were described in prose by Thomas Houghton in his *Rara Avis in Terris*,[26] followed much later by writers including William Hardy, James Mander, and Thomas Tapping.[27] Topographers such as Pilkington described the county's lead and textile undertakings, as well as its agriculture, but it was John Farey's work (1811) which first made the connexion between farming and manufacturing innovation and which examined in detail what physical characteristics made Derbyshire different from neighbouring counties.[28] Contemporaneously the geologist White Watson published his *Delineation of the Strata of Derbyshire*.[29]

Derbyshire is well supplied with those antiquities likely to appeal to early researchers with archaeological interests, the most distinguished of whom in the 18th century was Samuel Pegge. His *Roman Roads Discovered and Investigated through the Country of the Coritani or the County of Derby* (2nd

---

[21] *Mr. John Ruskin on Matlock Bath and the Peak of Derb.* (1884).

[22] *Chantrey's Peak Scenery or Views in Derb.* (1886); cf. E. Rhodes, *Peak Scenery* (1818); W. Adam, *Gem of the Peak* (1838).

[23] J. Jones, *The Benefit of the Auncient Bathes of Buckstones* (1572); J. Floyer, *Enquiry into Right Use and Abuses of Hot, Cold, and Temperate Baths in England* (1697).

[24] T. Short, *Natural, Experimental, and Medicinal Hist. of Mineral Waters of Derb.* (1734); A. Greeves, *Account of Medicinal Water of Ilkeston* (1833); W. H. Robertson, *The Peak of Derb. and Buxton Mineral Waters* (1854); J. V. Stephens, *Wells and Springs of Derb.* (1929).

[25] E. Manlove, *Liberties and Customs of Leadmines within Wapentake of Wirksworth in County of Derby* (1653, reprinted in facsimile 1977).

[26] T. Houghton, *Rara Avis in Terris* (1681).

[27] W. Hardy, *Miners' Guide* (1762); J. Mander, *Derb. Miner's Glossary* (1824); T. Tapping, *Treatise on High Peak Mineral Customs and Mineral Courts Act* (1851); idem, *Treatise on Derb. Mining Customs and Mineral Courts Acts of 1852* (1854).

[28] J. Farey, *General View of Agriculture and Minerals of Derb.* (3 vols. 1811–17); cf. J. Mawe, *Mineralogy of Derb.* (1802).

[29] W. Watson, *Delineation of Strata of Derb.* (1811); idem, *A Section of the Strata forming Surface in Vicinity of Matlock Bath* (1813).

edn. 1784) marked a considerable advance in knowledge of the subject.[30] Another
pioneer was Thomas Bateman (1821–61), whose early death occurred just after
publication of his major work on barrow digging, an activity which continued to
attract later 19th-century writers. William Boyd Dawkins (1837–1929) included
Derbyshire examples in his *Cave Hunting* (1874), although it was published
before he began excavations at Creswell Crags in 1875, and the county also
featured in numerous articles by his disciple Dr. J. Wilfrid Jackson (1880–1978).[31]

Despite many descriptions of its great houses, architectural history in
Derbyshire, secular or ecclesiastical, has been less well served. A noteworthy
exception is the detailed study of South Wingfield manor and its manor
house, published separately in 1793 by Thomas Blore, all of substance that
emerged of his intended county history, the notes for which survive in
Cambridge University Library.[32] William Woolley's descriptions of
churches have been characterized as showing 'a studied lack of interest'[33]
and a comprehensive printed work did not appear until the Revd. John
Charles Cox's *Notes on the Churches of Derbyshire*, published between 1875
and 1879,[34] which drew on unpublished collections by Francis Bassano.[35]
Cox (1843–1919) succeeded Llewellynn Jewitt as editor of *The Reliquary*
from 1886 to 1909, but by that time it had a rival in the Derbyshire
Archaeological Society's *Journal*, first published in 1879. Both periodicals
shared energetic contributors, such as the antiquary the Revd. Charles
Kerry, and village or township studies began to appear more frequently, to
complement the few printed histories of single parishes, such as Melbourne
and Repton.[36] The growth of interest in local history research bore rather
strange fruit in the 10-volume *Feudal History of the County of Derby (chiefly
during the 11th, 12th and 13th centuries)*, published by and for John Pym
Yeatman between 1892 and 1912, which included Sir George Sitwell's work
on Scarsdale hundred. Yeatman (1830–c. 1908) was a combative and litigious
figure. Twice declared bankrupt, a fierce critic of the Victoria County
History and of the Public Record Office, he described his vicissitudes as an

---

[30] S. Pegge, *The Roman Roads, Ikenild Street and Bath Way through the Country of the Coritani
or County of Derby* (2nd edn. 1784).

[31] T. Bateman, *Vestiges of Antiquities of Derb.* (1847); *Ten Years' Diggings in Celtic and Saxon
Grave Hills in Counties of Derby, Stafford and York from 1848 to 1858* (1861, reprinted 1978); Ll.
Jewitt, *Grave Mounds and their Contents* (1870); R. Pennington, *Notes on Barrows and Bone-Caves
of Derb.* (1877); W. B. Dawkins, *Cave Hunting* (1874); *Cave Hunters*, ed. M. J. Bishop (1982).

[32] T. Blore, *Hist. of Manor and Manor House of South Winfield in Derb.* (1793); Cambridge
Univ. Library, Add. MSS. 3874–3920.

[33] *Woolley's Hist.* introduction, p. xxxvii.

[34] Cox, *Notes on Churches of Derb.* (3 vols. 1875–9).

[35] Ibid. i, introduction, p. xvi.

[36] *Jnl. Derb. Arch. and Natural Hist. Soc.* (1879 to date); J. Briggs, *Hist. of Melbourne* (1852); R.
Bigsby, *Hist. of Repton* (1854).

historian in his prefaces and in a lengthy petition in Chancery in 1907.[37] Houses and genealogy were the chosen fields of a more populist contemporary, Joseph Tilley, whose *Old Halls, Manors and Families of Derbyshire* appeared between 1892 and 1902.[38]

John Charles Cox was also the author of *Three Centuries of Derbyshire Annals as illustrated by the Records of Quarter Sessions*, in which he included 'explanatory disquisitions . . . to try to make these . . . fairly acceptable and interesting to the ordinary reader'.[39] Indefatigable, nine years later he issued a supplement, *The Calendar of the Records of the County of Derby*, a project emulated for Derby borough by Isaac Jeayes in 1904.[40] Cox then became a supporter of a new venture, the *Victoria County History of Derbyshire*. Only two volumes were published (1905–7) before financial problems overtook the scheme, no doubt to the gratification of Yeatman, who had condemned it as 'folly' and 'a wild project, doomed sooner or later to utter failure'. Derbyshire had 'three or four editors palmed upon her who had all thrown up the task with disgust'. The first volumes, 'consisting, no doubt, of very valuable essays on botany, concology [*sic*], mineralogy, with all the other ologies, [were not] a county history'. Moreover, what historical merit could there be in the work of contributors who were all, unlike Yeatman, 'worshippers of rank and wealth'?[41] In fact the two published volumes included, besides the natural-history articles attacked by Yeatman, standard chapters on prehistoric, Roman, and Anglo-Saxon antiquities, social and economic history, and industries, which, though since superseded by more modern work, were pioneering studies in their time; as well as a translation of the Domesday text for Derbyshire and short histories of religious houses which remain useful works of reference.

The early abandonment of the *Victoria County History* for Derbyshire did not hinder the publication of a variety of articles and texts relating to the county's history. The Derbyshire Archaeological Society's *Journal* has been supplemented from 1956 by *Derbyshire Miscellany* and from 1959 by the specialist *Bulletin* of the Peak District Mines Historical Society. Since its inception in 1977, Derbyshire Record Society has sustained an active publications programme of the highest quality. That is particularly important since the demise of the record series published by the Archaeological Society. In addition, reprints of more popular 19th-century works have been undertaken by both local and national publishers.

[37] J. P. Yeatman, *Feudal Hist. of County of Derby* (10 vols. 1886–1912); *Recs. of Borough of Chesterfield*, ed. idem (1884). The writer is indebted to Dr. P. Riden for reference to the petition.

[38] J. Tilley, *Old Halls, Manors and Families of Derb.* (4 vols. 1892–1902).

[39] J. C. Cox, *Three Centuries of Derb. Annals* (2 vols. 1890), esp. i, preface, p. x.

[40] J. C. Cox, *Calendar of Recs. of County of Derby* (1899); I. H. Jeayes, *Calendar of Ancient Recs., Borough of Derby* (1904); idem, *Derb. Charters* (1906).

[41] *V.C.H. Derb.* (2 vols. 1905–7); Yeatman, *Feudal Hist.* prefaces to vols. viii and ix.

Easier access to new technology has enabled many societies and groups to produce pamphlets and books, chiefly on particular localities or subjects, while universities such as Nottingham have revived regional local history journals.[42] In conclusion, the wealth of unpublished original sources available to the historian in the county archives has been summarized in the Derbyshire Record Office *Guide*.[43]

---

[42] From 1992 summary details of recent publications are given in Derb. Rec. Soc.'s *Booklist*.

[43] Derb. R.O. *Guide* (1992). J. M. Bestall (1921–73), general editor of Derb. Rec. Ser. from 1966, attributed lack of progress on Derb.'s hist. to the inaccessibility of original recs.

DEVON

Joyce Youings

Anyone embarking on a study of the county histories of Devon could do worse than seek out a copy of the Revd. Thomas Moore's *History of Devonshire*, published in unbound parts between 1829 and 1836. Moore had read all the published work of his predecessors, the medieval chroniclers, John Leland, the Elizabethans, Camden and Sir William Pole, Tristram Risdon, John Prince, Richard Polwhele, and the Lysons brothers, and most remarkably had obtained access to the unpublished histories of John Hooker and Thomas Westcote. His ample footnotes provide a useful bibliography.[1]

Moore's medieval sources dealt very largely with national events and he was hard pressed to winkle out of them any of Devon's early history. With John Leland he was on firmer ground, for in the course of traversing the two coasts of the county in or about 1540 the roving reporter learned, by observation and from those with whom he conversed, a good deal about its antiquities. Leland had an especially quick eye for its terrain and in particular, no doubt with an appreciation of his royal master's interests, for its maritime potential. In Exeter, for instance, he not only described the cathedral but noted the city fathers' plans to deepen the river and 'bring the haven' for seagoing vessels to the city gates.[2]

It was indeed a characteristic of all Devon's early histories that the past and the present, and indeed sometimes even future prospects, were only roughly distinguished. There existed a real sense of obligation to pass on to posterity how the contemporary world ran its affairs, not without an occasional invidious comparison of past and present times. That was true particularly of the earliest of Devon's own local historians, John Hooker alias Vowell (1525–1601) of Exeter. Although born a gentleman he was essentially a city dweller, like his immediate merchant forebears. Educated at Oxford in the civil law, nurturing Protestantism well in advance of most of his fellow

---

[1] T. Moore, *Hist. of Devonshire from earliest Period to Present* (3 vols. 1829–36); *The Devon Union List: a Collection of Written Material relating to Devon*, ed. A. Brockett (1977) is useful for locating copies of the histories, but James Davidson's *Bibliotheca Devoniensis* (1852) provides fuller details of the early books relating to the county.

[2] J. Leland, *Itinerary*, ed. L. Toulmin Smith (5 vols. 1907–10), i. 244.

citizens, he 'managed' Elizabethan Exeter as the city's chamberlain, and occasionally one of its M.P.s. Among a multitude of chores he rescued the city records, leaving them in an amplitude and order for which alone later generations of historians must be grateful. Unfortunately he had no access to the county records.

As early as 1578 Hooker's *Lives of the Bishops of Exeter* demonstrated his considerable talents as an historian, not least, although he complained of obstacles having been put in his way, in his use of original sources.[3] Thereafter his involvement in public affairs, far from curtailing his local endeavours, inspired him to even greater labours. His later literary 'remains', few of them published either during his lifetime or later, are to a large extent works of reference for his professional successors and have been extensively quarried. They include manuscript 'Annals' of the city, for which he drew on not only Exeter's own medieval archives but also his own vivid memory of men and events, enlarged perhaps by the recollections of his elders.[4] They are especially valuable for the period of the Henrician Reformation and the siege of Exeter in 1549. The city of Exeter, as the county's administrative, judicial, and ecclesiastical centre, as well as its social, industrial, and commercial focus, the hub of its communications, and indeed its military and strategic stronghold, reflected in its own history much of that of the county at large. Towards the end of his life Hooker turned his attention to Devon as a whole. His 'Synopsis Corographical' or, as entitled in another version, his 'Description', is a curious compilation.[5] Largely a work of reference, in parts almost a notebook, it is prefaced by an analysis of Devon's contemporary economy which, though brief, contains some quite extraordinary insights. Its categorization of local society, however, owes much to the *Description of England* (1577) of William Harrison,[6] the Essex parson with whom Hooker collaborated on the revision of Holinshed's *Chronicles*. Brief descriptions of the county's institutions of government, ecclesiastical as well as secular, are followed, *inter alia*, by lists of the county's parishes arranged by hundreds with their taxation assessments and leading families; by the names of its towns (some with interesting pen portraits), parks, and castles; and by biographies of those he identified as the county's literary worthies. He included a detailed account of his own career, in which he attributed his

    [3] J. Youings, 'John Hooker and Tudor Bishops of Exeter', *Exeter Cathedral: a Celebration*, ed. M. Swanton (1991), 202–7.

    [4] Devon R.O., Exeter City Recs., Book 51. The best of the many printed texts of his account of the siege is in *Description of Excester*, ed. W. J. Harte, J. W. Schopp, and H. Tapley-Soper (Devon and Cornw. Rec. Soc. 1919–47), 55–96.

    [5] Devon R.O., H 783 and, slightly shorter, B.L. Harl. MS. 5827.

    [6] *Description of England by William Harrison*, ed. G. Edelen (1968).

failure to live up to early academic promise to his having entered into the state of holy matrimony. The 'Synopsis' without doubt laid the foundations for the near-contemporary work of Thomas Westcote and Tristram Risdon. Each acknowledged the help he had received from Hooker, but the extent of their shameless plagiarism will be revealed only when the older man's text is published, as he clearly intended it should be. His 'Synopsis' is very neatly complemented by Christopher Saxton's exquisitely satisfying map of the county published in his *Atlas* of 1579, alongside which should be displayed the equally magnificent bird's-eye view of Elizabethan Exeter drawn by an unknown hand in 1587 and engraved by Remigius Hogenberg, under the watchful eye of Hooker, its undoubted promoter.[7]

Probably the only early historian of Devon who owed nothing to Hooker was his much younger contemporary Sir William Pole (1561–1635) of Shute in east Devon. A member of the county establishment, he no doubt gathered his material, largely genealogical, from fellow magistrates and their records. Much that he had assembled was lost during the Civil War, but what remained, including lists of holders of baronies and Crown offices, a county survey of landowners by hundred and parish, an armory, and the names of resident gentry, past and present, survived to be published in 1791.[8]

Such histories, even while in manuscript, were not lost to view: indeed all were copied and quarried by later authors. Tristram Risdon referred gratefully to Pole, 'from whose lamp I have received Light in these my Labours', and it is even more likely that the rather older Thomas Westcote (?1567–*c.* 1640) was similarly privileged. Born at West Raddon in Shobrooke, north-west of Exeter, as a young man Westcote saw the world as a soldier and courtier, being with Drake on the Portuguese expedition in 1589, before settling down on his inheritance *c.* 1600. According to his own statement he turned to a study of his native county at the suggestion of his kinsman William Bourchier, earl of Bath. Whatever his exact relationship with the aged Hooker, of whom he wrote somewhat disparagingly, he certainly followed where Hooker 'only chalked the way'. His treatise begins with a description of the county, rather longer but very like that in the 'Synopsis'. The style of his peregrination of the county, in which for the most part he follows the course of Devon's many rivers, has, unlike that of the civil lawyer Hooker, a lyrical, almost Shakespearean quality, such as when he wrote of one of the river Exe's tributaries:

---

[7] W. L. D. Ravenhill and M. Rowe, 'Decorated Screen Map of Exeter based on John Hooker's Map of 1587', *Tudor and Stuart Devon: Common Estate and Governance*, ed. T. Gray, M. Rowe, and A. Erskine (1992), 1–12. See also 'John Hooker: Life and Writings', in V. F. Snow, *Parliament in Elizabethan England* (1977), 3–28.

[8] W. Pole, *Collections towards a Description of Devon* (1791).

> Creedy here seems to vaunt of the fruitful soil he passeth through which never
> proves ungrateful to the labourer for his pains nor deceiveth the husbandman's
> hope of expected or wished increase, thinking it the richer for being bathed by his
> stream, and so it is found indeed to be.

What better description of the rich water meadows that still make it such
valuable farming country!

Where Hooker had adopted a more literary style, Westcote followed, not
shrinking from lifting passages from the 'Synopsis' verbatim. Here and there
he added new historical detail, such as on the Combe Martin silver mines, and
although uncertain of his dates he knew about the short-lived Council of the
West of 1539–40 and suggested, with some shrewdness, that Devon (unlike
Cornwall) had no stomach for home rule. One of his aims was to establish,
with extensive recourse to classical authors, the superiority of Devon over less
fortunate counties. The sentiment was by no means foreign to Hooker, who
had declared that Devon could get along without the help of the rest of
England better than it without her, an opinion often expressed but never put
to the test in respect of the county's militia. Westcote also included pedigrees
of no fewer than 300 of the county's gentry. Besides using Pole he hinted at
other sources when he wrote of 'meeting casually or purposely with some of
the heirs of such families . . . and by way of discourse or some entreaty . . . I
have moved them to give me sight of their pedigree'. He went on to tell of one
who, to the amusement of other gentlemen present, declared that he did not
know his father, who died when he was young, and 'indeed he spake no more
than the world knew to be true'. In defence of his use of epitaphs he declared
that none are 'so silly or simple but that somewhat may be learned out of
them, or some while spent in laughter at them'.

The old soldier did not aspire to publication and it was not until over 200
years had passed that one of the many copies of his work in circulation was
printed.[9] The editors, one of whom was the eminent Victorian scholar Dr.
George Oliver, took the liberty of correcting what they considered to be
errors, brought many of his pedigrees up to date, and less forgivably
modernized his spelling, but by and large they treated his text with respect.

Not so fortunate was Westcote's near-contemporary Tristram Risdon
(c. 1580–c. 1640). Born at Winscott near Torrington in west Devon, he went to
Oxford and later, like Westcote, enjoyed the leisure of a moderately wealthy
country gentleman. His 'Chorographical Description or Survey of the county
of Devon . . . for the Love of his Country and Countrymen in that Province',
like Westcote's *View*, circulated (and still exists) in several manuscripts. In
spite of the efforts of John Prince to call a halt, it was shamefully hacked
about by a rogue London publisher, Edmund Curll, in the early 18th century;

---

[9] T. Westcote, *View of Devonshire in MDCXXX*, ed. G. Oliver and P. Jones (1845).

the missing parts were made available but in a revised form by Thomas Chapple in 1785; and finally it was reprinted *in toto* in Plymouth in 1811. The anonymous editors even then could not resist amending and extending what they claimed to be 'the most correct' text available, claiming in part justification that the transcripts of deeds were in many cases 'quite unintelligible'. Whether the fault lay with Risdon himself will only emerge at such time as all the texts, manuscript and printed, have been collated.[10] The short general description of the county has many echoes of Hooker but the 300 pages of topographical peregrination from the Dorset border round to north Devon make very tedious reading, Risdon's style being decidedly inferior to Westcote's.

The first of Devon's clerical antiquaries was John Prince (1643–1723), vicar of Berry Pomeroy in south Devon from 1681. His main contribution to the county's history took the form of a collection of biographies of notable Devonians, a substantial number of which (192) were first published in his lifetime (1701) and reprinted in 1810.[11] Others remain in manuscript.[12] Again the early 19th-century editors, no doubt with their principal market in mind, could not resist extending the genealogical details where possible. Apart from some rearrangement the author's text was unchanged. Although Prince no doubt made maximum use of his predecessors' work, his own has much material of independent value.

The first large-scale map of Devon was made by Benjamin Donn of Bideford in north Devon, a schoolmaster and self-taught practitioner (1765). It appeared over half a century later than Joel Gascoyne's comparable map of Cornwall, but still, for its time, was an outstanding feat. With its meticulous depiction at one inch to the mile of topographical features, settlements large and small, important country houses, and especially the county's road system, it is an invaluable tool for the historian.[13]

As the late Georgian county prepared itself to withstand a possible invasion by Napoleon the magistracy was provided with ample recreation by the appearance of a new and altogether much more elaborate history by the Revd. Richard Polwhele (1760–1838), vicar of Kenton in Devon and later of parishes in his native Cornwall, whose own history he had already published. His method, however, in practice if not in principle, was a considerable advance

---

[10] T. Risdon, *Chorographical Description or Survey of Devon*, ed. E. Curll (1714); *Continuation of Survey of Devonshire*, ed. E. Curll (1714–33); and *Chorographical Description* (1811). For more details see J. M. Hawker, 'Sketch of Risdon', *Trans. Devonshire Association*, vii (1875), 79–83.

[11] J. Prince, *Danmonii Orientales Illustres or Worthies of Devon* (1701, 2nd edn. 1810).

[12] West Devon R.O. (Plymouth), 373/1/1–2. For the provenance of the manuscript see J. Stevens, 'Prince's Worthies of Devon, Part II', *Devon and Cornw. Notes and Queries*, xxxi (1968), 67–70.

[13] *Benjamin Donn's Map of Devon, 1765*, introduction by W. L. D. Ravenhill (Devon and Cornw. Rec. Soc. 1965).

on that of his predecessors, being that of the historian-entrepreneur, taking advantage of the more widespread circulation of the printed word. He inserted a note in the *Gentleman's Magazine* for 1791 entitled 'Queries for a History of Devon'. His massive text, published in three volumes between 1793 and 1797, followed by a revised edition in 1809, embodied both the responses of his correspondents and what he himself could gather from his reading. His opening narrative, the first real chronology to be attempted by any historian of the county, though in places very dubious, purported to cover the most important events in Devon's history but was in fact very largely confined to those which brought the county on to the national stage. Concerning the ordinary people of the county it is far inferior to Hooker, of whose work Polwhele seems to have been ignorant. There follows what is basically an encyclopaedia of parish histories, arranged by deanery, as befitted an Anglican parson; that was a break with his predecessors, all of whom had used the hundred as their division. Coverage of the parishes and where appropriate of their separate hamlets was uneven, but more comprehensive than anything hitherto published. At best the text, not forgetting the substantial footnotes, is full of invaluable details concerning the descent of landed property, the local economy, and, here and there, crude population data. Thomas Moore thought some of his 'notions' contained 'more of poetry in them than truth', but the sources of his information are often well worth following up by modern scholars.[14]

Were it not for Polwhele, who had just about cornered the market, there would have been a warmer local reception for the equally, if not more, magnificent achievement of the brothers Daniel and Samuel Lysons, especially as both were virtually strangers to the west country. Devon was the ninth and last county they tackled, Daniel publishing the work in two volumes in 1822, after Samuel's death.[15] Readers will vary in their preferences, but most find the Lysonses' work more immediately useful than Polwhele's as a work of reference, and certainly easier to handle in the physical sense. It followed the traditional pattern, beginning with a general history, in the writing of which, being strangers, they dwelt less on the county's historic glories and the achievements of her traditional heroes, and (an innovation) included natural history. The second Devon volume consisted of short parish histories in alphabetical order. With the 1801 census returns now to hand they were able to include far more population data.

So we come again to Thomas Moore, better able to appreciate both how much was available to him (including Westcote's then unpublished history) and what a useful task he performed for a more popular audience than can

---

[14] R. Polwhele, *Hist. of Devonshire* (3 vols. 1793–1806).
[15] D. and S. Lysons, *Magna Britannia: Devon* (1822).

have been commanded by any of his predecessors. He is thought to have been a London clergyman but Moore was a common local name and he showed great familiarity with the county and its people. His 234 biographies, some including more than one member of a family, occupied 908 pages of text and were no doubt avidly read by his subscribers. Owing to difficulties with his publisher, however, his parish histories never saw the light of day, and none has survived. The 94 plates of contemporary prints which occupy volume three of the bound version add very considerably to the undoubted charm of his undervalued work.[16] Moore lived in the great age of topographical drawings, the wealth of which for Devon is amply demonstrated in Somers Cocks's exhaustive catalogue.[17]

With the Lysonses and Thomas Moore the age of the county history writ large came to an end in Devon for well over a century, although a place must be found for George Oliver's magisterial *Monasticon Diocesis Exoniensis*, well able to stand comparison with William Dugdale's national achievement, especially for its complement of edited texts.[18] There was no comparable Victorian publication on the county's secular history. As far as works of reference were concerned there was little progress until the publication by J. L. Vivian in 1895 of the findings of the heralds' visitations of 1531, 1564, and 1620, extensively augmented by parish registers, probate and other public records, a work not without errors but still enormously valuable for identifying the early modern gentry and their relations.[19]

The most important legacy of the reign of Queen Victoria to Devon's historical studies was the founding in 1862, largely by the scientist William Pengelly, of the Devonshire Association for the Advancement of Science, Literature, and Art (*now* the Arts). Admittedly in no way a 'popular' organization, its membership contained, then and for a century or more to come, most of those (ladies and gentlemen) with the means, the inclination, the leisure, and the capacity for extending the frontiers of knowledge, especially of local history.[20] They not only created their own publishing outlet and the essential financial patronage to sustain it, in the Association's *Transactions*, but by regular meetings and field trips built up a local network of specialized knowledge. Not that their gatherings were always all sweetness and light: feathers often flew, the ladies being well to the fore, especially after

[16] Above, n. 1.

[17] J. Somers Cocks, *Devon Topographical Prints, 1660–1870* (1977).

[18] First edn. 1846, reprinted with supplement 1854 and with index 1889. See also T. N. Brushfield, 'Bibliography of Rev. George Oliver, D.D., of Exeter', *Trans. Devonshire Assoc.* xvii (1885), 266–76.

[19] J. L. Vivian, *Visitations of Devon* (1895).

[20] H. H. Walker, 'Story of Devonshire Association', *Trans. Devonshire Assoc.* xciv (1962), 42–110.

the First World War. In the early 1920s the Association established one of its many committees, with the object of assembling a slip index of all printed references, primary and secondary, to the history of Devon. Thus began the project which came to be associated primarily with the name of R. Burnet-Morris, the millionth slip of which he added in 1940 just after the outbreak of the Second World War. Miraculously, the Burnet-Morris Index survived the war intact, together with the local history collections and most of the original records of the county and of the city of Exeter. Now housed in Devon Library Services' Westcountry Studies Library in Exeter, it is known and envied world-wide, and has recently been microfilmed.

By 1900 the time was ripe for advancing from local antiquarianism, with all its virtues of enthusiasm and local knowledge, into the more rarefied and rigorous historical studies then typified by the Rolls Series, the Calendars of State Papers, and the *Dictionary of National Biography*. Pride of place in the county must go to the inauguration of the *Victoria History of the County of Devon*. The local initiative in 1899 came from a country gentleman, Sir Roper Lethbridge, who, together with the Lord Lieutenant, Lord Clinton (whom Lethbridge sought out at the Hotel Metropole in Cannes), assembled an impressive local committee, few if any of whose members were capable of contributing to the project except in the form of cash, which never materialized in any quantity. The Devonshire Association, at least in the person of its honorary secretary J. Brooking Rowe, and in spite of the promptings of his friend Lethbridge, by then the Association's president, held aloof for fear that the *History* was being planned 'on too popular lines'! Two other local scholars were at loggerheads over their reading of the text of Domesday. After intervention by J. H. Round, the Revd. O. J. Reichel's version won the day.[21] It was virtually the only historical content of volume one, published in 1906, which was otherwise confined to natural history. Other chapters were written or at least commissioned but none was printed except Michael Oppenheim's 'Maritime History of Devon', which languished in proof on the shelves of the central V.C.H. office until it was eventually published by the University of Exeter as a separate book in 1968.

Left to itself, the local antiquarian fellowship did not flag in its enthusiasm and industry. Genealogy, a rather more limited pursuit than what is now called family history, was always an absorbing preoccupation, and when, in 1904, the Devon and Cornwall Record Society was founded, some 90 per cent of its publications, issued inconveniently but presumably under the limitations of cash flow in unbound parts, consisted of parish registers. Not

---

[21] R. Dunning, 'V.C.H. in Devon: a Story of Hopes so far Unfulfilled', *Devon Historian*, xl (April 1990), 9–13. For one who practised what he preached see P. O. Hutchinson, 'Scheme for Hist. of Devonshire', *Trans. Devonshire Assoc.* ix (1877), 292–5.

until the early 1950s, with the inauguration of its New Series, each annual volume complete in itself, was the content of the society's publications enlarged to cover a wide spectrum of historical sources. To date there have been 36 volumes in the New Series and two 'Extra Volumes'. The editors are now largely university teachers and archivists.

Apart from parish histories and monographs on particular topics, books on Devon's history as a whole, even covering limited periods, seemed between the two world wars to be beyond the capacity of local scholars, even with the growth of historical studies at the University College of the South West. Again with an emphasis on genealogy, the annual *Transactions of the Devonshire Association* offered its subscribers a wealth of historical papers, and from 1900 *Devon and Cornwall Notes and Queries* provided a vehicle for the publication of short articles. Among the growing body of well informed or at least enthusiastic public, in 1965 there was felt to be a need to complement the somewhat genteel parochial history section of the Devonshire Association with the foundation of what eventually became the more workaday Devon History Society. The society organizes conferences throughout the county and publishes the *Devon Historian*. Twenty years later there was pressure for a regional organization and in 1985 the University of Exeter picked up the then somewhat bare threads of its pre-war History of Exeter and the South West Research Group and set up the Centre for South-Western Historical Studies, which organizes regional conferences and publishes a *Register of Current Research* and a twice-yearly *Newsletter*. The Devon Archaeological Society is a separate organization with its own *Proceedings*.

None of what is now a vast industry of research and publication could have been achieved without libraries and record offices and the services of their professional staff. Readers living within reach of Exeter are especially well provided with the Westcountry Studies Library, the Devon and Exeter Institution Library and Reading Rooms, Exeter Cathedral Library, and Exeter University Library. The Westcountry Studies Library maintains parish history files and a collection of typed calendars of Devon wills, invaluable in view of the wartime loss of the locally registered copies.

With such resources the post-war output of substantial books dealing with the county as a whole has been remarkably small. That may be partly because one book in particular, in both the quantity and quality of its contents, has outdistanced all competitors. Indeed no other county in England has a post-war history to compare with *Devon*, by W. G. Hoskins, first published in 1954 and many times reprinted, most recently in 1992 to commemorate the death early in that year of its distinguished author.[22] A huge book, as its subject

---

[22] C. Phythian-Adams, 'Hoskins's England: a Local Historian of Genius and the Realisation of his Theme', *Local Historian*, xxii (1992), 120–53.

demands, it is the first real history of the county and its people to have been published, but it combines the best of the old and the new history. Based firmly on previous published work, of which the author had an unrivalled knowledge, it is enlarged and illuminated with his own research and historical insight. Its 16 chapters deal with each of the main topics of Devon's history in turn, their strength being in social and economic rather than political history, much of which still remains to be explored. Its value is enormously increased by the addition of a gazetteer drawing attention to each parish's topographical and other features, especially historic buildings. The recent reprint, with a fairly complete supplementary bibliography, makes unnecessary any attempt here to list the best of the many scholarly monographs and postgraduate dissertations which, in addition to the works of Hoskins and his occasional collaborator H. P. R. Finberg, have placed the county of Devon in the second half of the 20th century in the forefront of English local history.

DORSET

J. H. Bettey

Students of Dorset history are fortunate in having an excellent bibliography of printed works relating to the history of the county.[1] It is entitled *A Handbook of Local History: Dorset* and was compiled by Robert Douch in 1952 and revised by him in 1960. It lists printed material on all aspects of local history and provides an invaluable tool for researchers. An earlier though less ambitious bibliography was produced in 1885 by C. H. Mayo and typically for its period was entitled *Bibliotheca Dorsetiensis*.[2]

The earliest systematic attempt to describe the history and topography of Dorset and the descent of its most prominent families was made during the 1620s by Thomas Gerard of Trent (Som. until 1895), near Sherborne. His work was not published until 1732 and it was not until the 20th century that its true authorship was recognized. Gerard (1592–1634) was a member of a wealthy Dorset family with numerous connexions in both Somerset and Dorset. His marriage to Anne, daughter of Robert Coker of Mappowder, brought him into contact with even more of the leading gentry of the county, and he used those connexions to prepare his *General Description of the County of Dorset*. Gerard's work provides valuable information about topography, agriculture, markets, and ports in the county, although his main concern was with the gentry families, their lineage, estates, and houses. He was inordinately proud of his own family and decorated the transept arch of his parish church at Trent with 40 armorial shields representing the marriage connexions of the Gerard and Coker families. The authorship and date of his work is evident from numerous references in the text, but when he died in 1634 the manuscript passed into the hands of his Coker relatives, and when it was eventually printed and published in 1732 by John Wilcox, a London bookseller, it was alleged to be the work of the Revd. John Coker (d. 1635), who had been rector of Mappowder. A facsimile of the book was produced in

[1] R. Douch, *Handbook of Local Hist.: Dors.* (1962). Dors. County Library also keeps a valuable catalogue of books on Dors. in the reference library at Dorchester. I am grateful for the comments and suggestions on an earlier draft of this chapter by Jude James, Hugh Jaques, Laurence Keen, Robert Machin, and Roger Peers.

[2] C. H. Mayo, *Bibliotheca Dorsetiensis* (1885).

1980 with an informative introduction by Rodney Legg, establishing beyond doubt the true authorship and date of the work.[3]

Since the 16th century numerous travellers have produced accounts of their journeys through Dorset, providing useful material about the landscape, agriculture, roads, and society of the county. Among the most informative are those of John Leland; the diary of the remarkable Cornish traveller Peter Mundy, who visited Dorset in 1636; the journals of Celia Fiennes; and the Dorset sections of Defoe's *Tour through England and Wales*. Arthur Young included useful information even on Dorset in his *Farmer's Tour through the East of England* (1771).[4] Defoe's account is particularly full and provides details of matters such as the trade in oysters from Poole; the stone quarries of Purbeck and Portland; duck decoys; fishing; the swannery at Abbotsbury; farming, especially the vast sheep flocks; manufactures, including textiles, rope, lace, silk, and sailcloth; trade from the Dorset ports; and the genteel society of the Dorset towns. Defoe was obviously impressed by Dorchester and wrote that

> Dorchester is indeed a pleasant agreeable town to live in . . . a man that coveted a retreat in this world might as agreeably spend his time and as well in Dorchester, as in any town I know in England.[5]

Apart from the chapter in Camden's *Britannia*, which was written *c.* 1586, and a useful section on the history and topography of the county in Thomas Fuller's *The Worthies of England*, first published in 1662, which was written from first-hand knowledge since Fuller was vicar of Broadwindsor 1634–41,[6] the first attempt to provide a full-scale history of the county was Thomas Cox's *Compleat History of Dorsetshire* (1730), part of the author's six-volume *Magna Britannia* (1720–31).

Incomparably the fullest and most detailed work on the history of Dorset and the essential starting point for any historical research in the county is the massive *History and Antiquities of the County of Dorset* by John Hutchins (1698–1773). Hutchins was born in Dorset, where both his father and grandfather had been parsons, and after education at Dorchester grammar school and Oxford, he spent the rest of his life as a parish clergyman in the county, eventually becoming rector of Wareham in 1744. The great *History* was his life's work, started while he was a curate at Milton Abbas; the first edition, in two volumes, was published in 1774, a year after his death. A second and considerably enlarged edition was published in four volumes by

[3] *Thomas Gerard's General Description of Dors.* ed. R. Legg (1980).

[4] Peter Mundy's travels in Europe and Asia 1608–67, including his visit to Dors., are described in Hakluyt Soc. 2nd ser. xlv (1919), 4–12.

[5] D. Defoe, *Tour through England and Wales* (Everyman edn. 1927), i. 210–11.

[6] T. Fuller, *Hist. of Worthies of England*, ed. J. Freeman (1952).

R. Gough and J. B. Nichols during the years 1796–1815, while the third and fullest edition, which is now the standard text, was edited by W. Shipp and J. W. Hodson in four large volumes between 1861 and 1870.[7] The third edition in particular is a magnificent source of information on Dorset history, and includes 124 plates illustrating mansions, churches, monuments, prehistoric remains, armorial bearings, tokens, seals, and town plans. Hutchins was encouraged and occasionally financed by some of the county gentry, so that genealogy, descent of land, ecclesiastical patronage, and manorial history all figure large in his pages. His work was firmly based on original sources, many of which he quoted extensively. In spite of the difficulties of travel and of his duties as a conscientious parish clergyman, Hutchins travelled throughout Dorset and made visits to Oxford and London as well as to the diocesan registry at Salisbury to consult documents. His *History* has become such an indispensable tool for local historians that it is salutary to be reminded how narrowly it twice escaped destruction. The unfinished manuscript and Hutchins's notes were only saved from a disastrous fire at the rectory in Wareham through the heroism of his wife, while another fire at the printer's in 1808 destroyed all except one copy of the third volume.

After the publication of Hutchins's comprehensive *History* there were no further attempts at county history in Dorset for more than a century, although topographical works and descriptions of the county continued to be produced, many aimed at the growing number of tourists who followed the royal example of enjoying holidays and sea bathing along the Dorset coast. Among the most useful, both for its text and for its illustrations, was *The Topographical and Historical Description of Dorset* by J. Britton and E. W. Brayley, first published in 1804 as part of their series *The Beauties of England and Wales*.

The number and prominence of the prehistoric and Roman monuments in the county meant that many local gentlemen and antiquaries from the later 19th century onwards were led to the study of archaeology. Charles Warne published *The Celtic Tumuli of Dorset* in 1866, followed in 1872 by *Ancient Dorset*. In 1880 General Pitt-Rivers moved to Cranborne Chase and began the archaeological investigations which created new standards of excavation technique, laying the foundations for modern archaeology, and resulting in the seminal four-volume *Excavations in Cranborne Chase* (1887–98). H. J. Moule, who became curator of the Dorset County Museum, published an account of geology and prehistory entitled *Old Dorset* in 1893; and that was followed by Alfred Pope's *The Old Stone Crosses of Dorset* in 1906 and by

---

[7] This account is based on the introduction written by Robert Douch for the reprint of the 3rd edn. (1973). That introduction is reprinted in *English County Historians*, ed. J. Simmons (1978), 113–58.

Memorials of Old Dorset, edited by T. Perkins and H. Pentin, in 1907. The growth of interest in the archaeology, history, and natural history of the county was marked by the foundation in 1875 of the Dorset Natural History and Antiquarian Field Club, later called the Dorset Natural History and Archaeological Society. From 1877 the society began to publish annual *Proceedings*, which contain scholarly contributions on all aspects of Dorset archaeology and history, as well as on geology and natural history. The society is based at the Dorset County Museum in Dorchester, whose new building was opened in 1884. Its library includes a fine collection of printed works on Dorset as well as numerous manuscript volumes of notes, extracts from public records, wills, inventories, legal proceedings, and many other subjects relating to the history of the county.

Another remarkable source of information and an invaluable quarry for research on all aspects of the history of Dorset is the volumes of the *Somerset and Dorset Notes and Queries*, which began publication in 1888 and have continued ever since. The history of that publication and its contribution to historical scholarship was described by Christopher Elrington in an article in the centenary issue in 1988.[8] The first Dorset editor was Charles Herbert Mayo, vicar of Longburton, who served from 1888 to 1921. During that time he also edited various important records relating to the county, including the *Municipal Records of Shaftesbury* (1889), the *Minute Book of the Dorset Standing Committee, 1646–50* (1902), and the *Municipal Records of Dorchester* (1908).[9] Among the contributors to *Somerset and Dorset Notes and Queries* was the Dorset poet and philologist William Barnes, whose work made a significant contribution to local history in Dorset, as well as fostering the study of folklore, dialect, and archaeology. Barnes regarded his *Poems of Rural Life in the Dorset Dialect* (1844) and *Glossary of Dorset Dialect* (1886) as a contribution to the history of the county. Likewise, the novels, articles, and poems of Thomas Hardy, firmly based in his native Dorset, helped to inspire research into the society, customs, farming, and economic conditions which he so memorably described. The study of folklore was continued by J. S. Udal in *Dorsetshire Folklore* (1922), for which William Barnes wrote an introduction. A facsimile edition of Udal's work with a foreword by Roger Peers was published in 1989. The illustrations which William Barnes provided for numerous historical and other works on Dorset are described and reproduced in Laurence Keen and Charlotte Lindgren, *William Barnes, the Dorset Engravings* (1986; 2nd edn. 1989).

Early in the 20th century work was begun on Dorset by the Victoria

---

[8] C. R. Elrington, 'One Hundred Years of Som. and Dors. Notes and Queries', *Som. and Dors. Notes and Queries*, xxxii (1988), 689–94.

[9] C. H. Mayo was the foremost among several scholarly clergymen in Dors. during the 19th century; it was largely due to their antiq. interests that many of the municipal and parish recs. have survived.

County History and in 1908 the first volume (volume two) was published. It dealt with the ecclesiastical history of the county, and also included general accounts of its political, social, and economic history. Much of that pioneering work has inevitably been superseded by more detailed research, especially on the economy and society of the county. The second volume of the *V.C.H.* (volume three) appeared in 1968. It was an edition of and introduction to the Dorset Domesday Survey and Geld Rolls by Ann Williams. Sadly, work on further volumes of the *V.C.H.* did not continue in Dorset, although another ambitious project has been completed during the second half of the 20th century. That is the eight-volume survey of all existing buildings and earthworks dating from before 1850, completed by the Royal Commission on the Historical Monuments of England. The first volume covering west Dorset was published in 1952 (2nd edn. 1974), and the task was completed with the publication of the final volume on east Dorset in 1975. The magnificently detailed and beautifully illustrated surveys mean that Dorset is 'better recorded architecturally than any other English county'.[10]

The later 20th century has seen an increasing flow of books, articles, and theses on every aspect of the archaeology, history, landscape, economy, society, and buildings of Dorset, and only a few of the most significant of them can be mentioned here. Naturally, much attention has continued to be focused on the great prehistoric monuments and Roman remains of the county. Good general surveys include L. V. Grinsell, *The Archaeology of Wessex* (1958) and N. H. Field and J. Bugler, *Guide to the Field Monuments of Dorset* (1973). Detailed investigations of particular sites or monuments include Mortimer Wheeler's influential report of his excavations at *Maiden Castle, Dorset* (1943). There have been a few attempts to write short accounts of the county's history, among them J. H. Bettey, *Dorset* (1974) and C. N. Cullingford, *A History of Dorset* (1980).

The development of the Dorset landscape has been described by Christopher Taylor in *The Making of the English Landscape: Dorset* (1970), part of an uncompleted national series. The Dorset volume adopted an innovative approach and is particularly important for its elucidation of the early landscapes of the county. The landscape history of one estate has been interpreted in *The Historic Landscape of the Weld Estate*, ed. Laurence Keen and Ann Karreck (1987), in which the text is accompanied by a series of maps illustrating the landscape of the estate at different periods. Medieval life in the county has been described by Joseph Fowler in his masterly survey *Mediaeval Sherborne* (1951), and by K. L. Wood-Legh in her remarkably full account of the life of the chantry priests serving John Munden's chantry at Bridport during the period 1453–60, entitled *A Small Household of the Fifteenth*

---

[10] J. Newman and N. Pevsner, *Buildings of England: Dors.* (1972), 57.

Century (1953). Little has been written on the early 16th century or on the Reformation in Dorset, although Dorset life during the later 16th century has been explored in Rachel Lloyd's book *Dorset Elizabethans* (1967).

Throughout its history Dorset has been dominated by great landowners and large estates, and the county is notable for the number and excellence of its manor houses and elegant residences. They have been described and illustrated most fully by A. Oswald, *Country Houses of Dorset* (1959). Because of its wealth and strategic importance Dorset suffered greatly from the passing and repassing of rival armies during the Civil War, the course of which has been described in detail by A. R. Bayley, *The Great Civil War in Dorset, 1642–1660* (1910); although so densely packed with information that it is not always easy to read or understand, it remains the standard work on the period. An insight into the economic, social, and religious history of the county during the 17th century is provided by two books by David Underdown: *Revel, Riot and Rebellion: Popular Culture in England, 1603–1660* (1985) and *Fire from Heaven: Life in an English Town in the Seventeenth Century* (1992). Much of the evidence for the first is derived from Dorset and the West Country, while the second deals with the history of Dorchester during the 17th century, particularly the influence of the puritan rector John White (1575–1648). An earlier study of John White and his part in sending parties of puritan colonists to the New World was made by Frances Rose-Troup in *John White, the Patriarch of Dorchester* (1930). More recently the part played by Dorset exiles in the colonial ventures has been described by Frank Thistlethwaite in *Dorset Pilgrims* (1989). The involvement of many Dorset men, particularly from the villages and farms of west Dorset, in the ill-fated rebellion of the duke of Monmouth in 1685, and the terrible retribution which awaited them at the hands of Judge Jeffreys at the Dorchester assizes has been chronicled and analysed by numerous writers.[11] A detailed examination of farming, trades, rural crafts, forestry, landowners, labourers, and the treatment of the poor in several villages across Dorset has been made by Barbara Kerr in *Bound to the Soil* (1968), and the harsh treatment accorded to the unfortunate labourers of Tolpuddle following their disastrous attempt to secure better conditions has attracted many writers.

There are a few notable early maps of Dorset which provide a great deal of historical and archaeological information. The earliest printed map of Dorset is Christopher Saxton's map of 1575, and it was followed by William Kip's map which was published in 1607 but had originally been produced for Camden's *Britannia* in 1586. More detailed and informative is John Speed's

---

[11] Among recent studies of the Monmouth rebellion and its effects in Dors. are: P. Earle, *Monmouth's Rebels* (1977); W. M. Wigfield, *Monmouth Rebellion* (1980); R. Dunning, *Monmouth Rebellion* (1984); *Monmouth Rebels, 1685*, ed. W. M. Wigfield (Som. Rec. Soc. lxxix, 1985).

map of 1610 which shows the hundred boundaries and includes the first plan
of Dorchester. Even more informative is Isaac Taylor's map of Dorset dated
1765 which shows many settlements, archaeological features, roads, and
boundaries, as well as including excellent drawings of Maiden Castle,
Maumbury Rings, the castles of Corfe, Sherborne, and Lulworth, the
observatory tower at Horton, and numerous other features. Another fine
county map is Greenwood's (1825–6), which was part of a national survey. It
includes the boundaries of hundreds, liberties, and parishes, as well as
turnpike roads, toll bars, woods, parks, commons, and the sites of mills both
wind and water.

The enormous growth in the popularity of local history during the past few
decades has led to the formation of many local history societies in the county,
and to the production of numerous histories of individual towns and villages,
so that few places are now without a history of some sort, although space does
not permit a survey here. Active research by dedicated individuals continues
on many aspects of local history in the county, notwithstanding the warnings
of some 19th-century Dorset historians against the perils of such local studies
and the poor rewards to be expected by their authors. George Ellis, who
produced a detailed *History of Weymouth* in 1829, wrote:

> the most ungrateful task which any writer can undertake, is that of a work of
> entirely local character, for with whatever discretion he may proceed, he must
> offend that mighty phalanx who think they cannot be too lightly censured or too
> highly praised; and the Author is placed between the perilous alternative of either
> drawing down hatred on himself or of sacrificing his duty.[12]

Likewise in 1839 John Sydenham, the joint proprietor of the *Dorset County
Chronicle*, published a history of his native town, which since 1568 had also
possessed the dignity of county status, *The History of the Town and County of
Poole*. It is a remarkably full account of all aspects of the history of Poole,
beginning with the archaeological evidence for the earliest human habitation
and concluding with the contemporary state of the town. Sydenham was
under no illusions as to the difficulties of his subject:

> Topography is, at the best, an uncompromising and unthankful branch of literature.
> Neither in the pecuniary return which is customarily its lot, nor in the reputation
> awarded to its student, does it offer any inducement to undertake that labour and
> expend that time which it rightly requires.[13]

---

[12] G. Ellis, *Hist. of Weymouth* (1829).
[13] J. Sydenham, *Hist. of Town and County of Poole* (1839).

COUNTY DURHAM

Nigel J. Tringham

Pride of place among the historians of County Durham belongs to Robert Surtees, whose *History and Antiquities of the County Palatine of Durham* was published in folio in four parts between 1816 and 1840.[1] Nevertheless, Surtees was not the first historian to publish, still less the first to collect material, on the county.

In the introduction to the first volume of his *History*, Surtees discussed the work of earlier collectors of historical material in County Durham.[2] The earliest was Christopher Watson, a native of Durham and a cleric, who in 1573–4, when in his late 20s and living in Norfolk, completed four 'Bookes of Durham History' in manuscript. Only two of them, in fact, related to the history of the county, and even then the information was restricted to brief accounts of its bishops.[3] A contemporary, William Claxton of Winyard (d. 1600), was more extensive in his interests. He collected much information generally on the county and was able to supply details to William Camden, who incorporated his researches in the Durham sections of his book. Other notable collectors were James Mickleton (1637–93), a barrister; John Smith, D.D. (1659–1715), a canon of Durham who apparently supplied the material for the Durham section of Thomas Cox's *Magna Britannia et Hibernia* (1720–31); and Dr. Christopher Hunter (1675–1757).[4] Many of Hunter's manuscripts survive in the library of the dean and chapter of Durham, and include a proposal circulated in 1743 for printing a 'Parochial History of the Diocese of Durham'. Nothing came of that venture.

Of greater significance were the researches of George Allan (1736–1800) of the Grange, Darlington.[5] A lawyer by profession, Allan built up an extensive

---

[1] The years of publication were 1816, 1820, 1823, and (posthumously) 1840. The work was republished in 1972. I am most grateful to Dr. David Watkinson, deputy librarian of Durham Univ. Library, for helpful comments on this article in draft and for supplying information.

[2] Earlier survey of Durham historians in [R. Gough], *British Topography* (2 vols. 1780), 329–44. Also of interest is C. E. Whiting, 'Historians of Diocese of Durham', *Durham Univ. Jnl.* xxvii. 239–63.

[3] The MSS. are now B.L. Cott. MS. Vit. C. ix. For Watson (d. 1581) see *D.N.B.*

[4] For Smith see R. Surtees, *Hist. and Antiquities of Co. Dur.* iv. 100, and for Hunter ibid. ii. 287–8.

[5] For Allan see Surtees, *Hist.* iii. 370–2; *D.N.B.*

10 George Allan and William Hutchinson

collection of manuscripts and transcripts of documents, a number of which he printed on his own press, set up in 1768. In 1774 he circulated a request for information in connexion with a history of the county, at a time when general interest in such a work would have been stimulated by Andrew Armstrong's large-scale map of the county, produced in four parts in 1768.[6] In his circular Allan praised recent initiatives to compile county histories in Yorkshire and Cheshire, and gave advice on how such new-style histories should be researched. Hitherto, he claimed, most county histories had comprised 'futile etymologies, verbose disquisitions, crowds of Canterbury stories and legends, incorrect pedigrees, lying epitaphs, lists of landowners, and such farrago'. 'Injudicious and sedentary compilers' had found it much easier to arrange material which had come into their hands, rather than 'to ramble about and examine every remnant of antiquity'. Emphasis was laid on the need to check sources, and to correspond with local informants. Allan acknowledged that such works required time, but he counselled patience: 'this study [of local history] suffers by nothing so much as by productions hurried into light, without proper correctness or maturity'. Understandably he was reluctant to undertake the task himself, but his library was put to good use by his friend William Hutchinson (1732–1814), the first writer to publish a history of the county.[7] A lawyer who practised at Barnard Castle, Hutchinson was already the author of *Views of the English Lakes and Northumberland* when, in 1785, he published in quarto the first volume of his *History and Antiquities of the County Palatine of Durham*; two further volumes appeared in 1787 and 1794. Although the work includes North Durham, it is not entirely complete for the county itself, as parts of Chester ward were never written.

Hutchinson's main interests, apart from the county's Roman antiquities, centred on the twin pillars of village life, the church and the gentry. Footnotes were used extensively to record the text of charters and other documents upon which pedigrees were constructed, somewhat shakily at times: when attempting the descent of the manor of Mordon (in Sedgefield parish), Hutchinson admitted that the details he gave were contradictory, but he consoled himself with the thought that the reader would make 'his own conclusions touching the variances'. A man of polite society, his comments on the contemporary scene are of interest: houses around the recently built town square of South Shields 'border on elegance, though most of them have shops', and Stockton was the 'handsomest town in the north of England' despite the presence in the main street of a shambles whose survival was regretted. At times his criticism was

---

[6] For a catalogue of county maps see R. M. Turner, *Maps of Durham, 1576–1872* (Durham Univ. Library Publications, no. 1 (1954), with supplement of 1960).

[7] For Hutchinson see *D.N.B.* and T. Stewart's introduction to his 1987 edn. of Hutchinson's *Spirit of Masonry*.

less restrained, as when dismissing as fanciful a legend which had attached itself to the place name Worm Hill (in Washington parish). He was also easily persuaded: he felt that a folk custom of dressing 'a figure of Ceres', which took place at harvest time in Easington parish, 'evidently derived from the Romans'. Hutchinson was not insensitive to the importance of industrial and commercial activity in the county, but it was a world which intimidated him: when questioning the ironworkers of Winlaton (in Ryton parish) about their trade, he neatly attributed his inability to get information about the scale of manufacture there to 'an eye of jealousy on enquiry'.

As the 'first adventurer' in publishing a history of County Durham, Hutchinson sought to excuse himself from adverse criticism by drawing his readers' attention at the outset to 'the toil of arranging such a chaos of materials' as lay before him.[8] Other commitments, as well as a disconcerting quarrel with his printer which delayed the publication of the third volume of his work, denied Hutchinson the time needed to reflect on how best to use the information at his disposal, and even the kindly Surtees was unable to characterize the finished product as more than 'a constant and useful index'.[9]

The publication of Hutchinson's third volume in 1794 coincided with Joseph Granger's *General View of the Agriculture of the County of Durham*, a pocket-size book commissioned by the Board of Agriculture.[10] A more detailed and authoritative survey under the same title was produced in 1810 by John Bailey, a land agent at Chillingham (Northumb.), again at the request of the Board of Agriculture.[11] Meanwhile, Edward Brayley had written generally on the county for volume five of *The Beauties of England and Wales*, published in 1803.

The popular market at which that series was aimed was also met in County Durham by a number of town histories, of which the first was *An Account of Durham &c Intended for the Information and Amusement of Strangers who Visit this Part of the Kingdom*, published in 1804 by a Durham bookseller and printer, Lewis Pennington. The author is unknown, but he evidently drew much material from Hutchinson's *History*. A revised version appeared in 1813 under the title *A View of the City of Durham and its Environs*. The county town also benefited from the attention of Robert Henry Allan, the great-nephew of the antiquary George Allan. His *Historical and Descriptive View of the City of Durham and its Environs* was published in 1824.[12] Elsewhere in the

[8] Preface to vol. i.
[9] Surtees, *Hist.* i. 8.
[10] Granger was a land surveyor from Heugh, in Esh.
[11] *D.N.B.*
[12] Biographical note in *Archaeologia Aeliana* [hereafter *Arch. Ael.*], 3rd ser. x. 172–3. I am esp. grateful to Dr. Watkinson for information confirming Allan's authorship.

county, Sir Cuthbert Sharp published his *History of Hartlepool* in 1816. The son of a Hartlepool shipowner, Sharp (knighted in 1814) was mayor of the town in 1816; he died in 1849.[13] An avid collector of manuscripts, most of his archive survives in the library of the dean and chapter at Durham. His *History* treated both the town's past and its present condition; the writer's natural concern for the prosperity of his home town is shown especially when he wrote about its fisheries. The book includes a town plan drawn by Sharp himself. In 1819 another coastal town was celebrated when George Garbutt published his own *Historical and Descriptive View of the Parishes of Monkwearmouth and Bishopwearmouth, and the Port and Borough of Sunderland*.[14] William Longstaffe's *The History and Antiquities of the Parish of Darlington*, published in parts between 1848 and 1854, was a much more substantial town history.[15] Longstaffe (1826–98), a solicitor, was a prodigious writer on antiquarian matters, notably in articles for *Archaeologia Aeliana*, of which he was sometime editor.[16] Far from being 'of the light, sketchy, amusing character' he had first envisaged, his history of Darlington became in his own words 'a magazine of evidences', crowded with detail, including pedigrees of leading families.

Those localized works were eclipsed by the history of the county written by Robert Surtees. It is an outstanding achievement: a work of scholarship enhanced by the author's enjoyment of the subject and his sympathetic interest in people. Surtees was born in Durham city in 1779, the only surviving child of Robert Surtees of Mainsforth, a landowner with cultured interests.[17] The future historian attended Christ Church, Oxford, before becoming a student at the Middle Temple. On his father's death in 1802 he abandoned a legal career and, establishing himself at Mainsforth, devoted much of his time to the history of County Durham. The interest had shown itself in his school days: as early as 1790, it seems, he envisaged writing a county history, and to that end he began to collect material from a wide range of sources, notably from private archives to which his position in society allowed him easy access. A plan which he sketched out in 1804 reveals that he meant his history to appeal mainly to antiquaries, whilst hoping that lawyers would also find it useful as a reference book. The driving force behind the enterprise was probably his simple conviction that 'All persons love to see their County illustrated'.[18]

---

[13] Biographical note in *Arch. Ael.* 3rd ser. x. 138–9; and see *D.N.B.*

[14] Garbutt (1792–1859) was a printer and stationer and towards the end of his life was librarian of Sunderland Subscription Library: *Proc. Soc. Antiq. Newcastle-upon-Tyne*, 4th ser. ii. 83–4.

[15] Reprinted, with an introduction by Robert Wood, in 1973.

[16] *Arch. Ael.* 3rd ser. x. 229–31. For the journal see below, Northumb.

[17] A memoir of Surtees by his friend George Taylor was bound up with Surtees, *Hist.* iv. It was reprinted, with additional material added by another friend, the Revd. James Raine, in Surtees Soc. xxiv (1852). Eric Birley contributed an appreciation of Surtees in the 1972 reprint of the *Hist.*

[18] The plan is reproduced in the introduction to the 1972 reprint (vol. i, p. xv).

By good fortune it is possible to observe the historian at work in the words of a friend, Sir Cuthbert Sharp, who frequently stayed at Mainsforth:[19]

The manner in which Mr. Surtees wrote his History was very peculiar. He never sat down 'doggedly' to write; but would wander about on a spacious gravel-walk in front of his house; and having well considered his subject, he would come to his library, and hastily write down the result of his musings. But his ideas crowded on his mind so rapidly, and his fancy was so exuberant, that his pen could not keep pace with his creative imagination; and the consequence was, that his words were but half written, or simply hieroglyphic indications; and nobody but himself could read what he had written; and that not always. Yet he would afterwards amplify, and make his words more legible. For sending his 'copy' to the press the different paragraphs and sentences were generally pinned or wafered together, and numbered. The compositor had many difficulties to encounter in decyphering his writing; and frequently mistook his meaning altogether; yet he never found fault; but, on the contrary, he was amused with the mistakes of the press: and he could recall, at pleasure, his former thoughts;—for, the ideas having been once fixed in his mind, the correction of the press was a matter of little difficulty. He never had any 'copy' ready until it was absolutely wanted: he said, he never held a 'stock in hand', but he could always provide for the current day's work.

Remarkably, the finished work shows hardly any signs of such an *ad hoc* approach to composition.

In a review, the poet Robert Southey described the first volume of the *History* as 'a farrago in folio'. Although duly acknowledging its methodical structure, he was as much taken with the author's humour as with his erudition and perseverance, delighting in the unexpected passages of playfulness which caused the reader to smile.[20] Surtees, indeed, retained a boyish enthusiasm for history as an entertaining and amusing pursuit, and he was not above enlivening his footnotes with verses of his own composition.[21] None the less the work is a considerable achievement, not least in its impressive use of local records. After discussing the county's early history and giving biographies of the bishops of the diocese in the first part of volume one, Surtees covered the topography of the county in a systematic way, parish by parish. The four volumes, however, are not a complete survey, as much of the western part of the county was still unwritten at Surtees's death in 1834. Although the price of the volumes was to some extent lessened by subscribers paying for plates which illustrated monuments, country houses, churches, and worthies,[22] the costs of printing were borne by Surtees. He ran into debts on

[19] Cited in Taylor's memoir (*Hist.* iv. 13).
[20] Ibid. 64–5.
[21] Birley's appreciation in the 1972 reprint of the *Hist.* i, pp. viii, xiii.
[22] *Hist.* i, introduction, 10–11; iv [memoir], 74–5.

his estate as a result, and after his death his library and collection of coins had to be sold, much to the distress of his family and friends.

Surtees's main interest lay in the fortunes of the county's aristocracy and gentry. Parish histories are principally accounts of the leading families, displayed in annotated pedigrees and illustrated by copious extracts from the relevant archive. The writer evidently found the topic satisfying. The need to record the demise of a gentry family was distressing, as is seen in comments intruded into the middle of a section otherwise devoted to documents relating to the Trollop family of Thornley (in Kelloe parish), and the unreasonable operation of the common law in the descent of the Surtees family of Dinsdale was a matter for censure. It was pleasanter to record the lives of those who adorned their families, and parish histories commonly include lengthy biographies of such worthies. Although impressed by the physical setting of country houses, Surtees seems less interested in the changing face of the landscape. Indeed, his descriptions of towns are sometimes jejune, and for reflection on townscapes, the modern reader still needs to consult the earlier work of Hutchinson. When relating the text of a medieval charter to the landscape, however, Surtees showed much greater enthusiasm, and on several occasions he skilfully interpreted place names after personally inspecting sites.

Although a countryman, and inordinately fond of dogs, Surtees announced that it was not his intention 'to trespass on the province of the Agriculturist'.[23] His lack of interest in the subject was evident in the 1804 plan for the history, where he allowed for the inclusion of agricultural facts 'if certain and they come my way', and grudgingly contemplated a print to illustrate the Blackwell and Ketton oxen. The illustration never appeared. Fascinated by the past, Surtees was little moved by the contemporary scene. For details of the recent history of the county's industrial areas he was much indebted to the research of others, often rehearsing their notes with little attempt at incorporating them into the narrative. When treating the ironworks at Winlaton (in Ryton parish), he mentioned the extraordinary charities established for the workers at the end of the 17th century and then noted that they all ceased in 1816. The reader longs to know why, but is not told.

In his researches Surtees was driven about the county in a gig by his groom, who soon found the employment tiresome: 'it was weary work; for master always stopped the gig: we never could get past an auld beelding'.[24] Surtees himself often felt the strain of the undertaking: when on a research visit to York he promised his wife in a letter not to overtire himself and 'to rest like a decent Christian on Sunday'.[25] He was not without assistance,

[23] Ibid. i (2), 148 note t.
[24] Ibid. iv [memoir], 13.
[25] Ibid. 76.

however. In 1812 he met the Revd. James Raine (1791–1858), then a tutor at Durham grammar school and later librarian to the dean and chapter of Durham, and the two men collaborated extensively.[26] Soon after the publication of the first volume of the *History*, Raine undertook, at Surtees's request and to ease his burden, the task of writing the history of North Durham, a detached part of the county north of the Tyne comprising Holy Island and the nearby mainland, Norham, and Bedlington, most of which was added to the county of Northumberland in 1844. Raine's *History and Antiquities of North Durham*, completed in 1852, was published in folio to complement Surtees's *History*. After Surtees's death, it was Raine who edited his notes and saw the fourth volume of the *History* through the press in 1840.

Surtees and Raine were also involved in a scheme for the publication of a journal for editions of historical records relating to the northern counties. The idea, mooted in 1818, apparently came from the Revd. John Hodgson, co-secretary of the recently formed Society of Antiquaries of Newcastle upon Tyne. Nothing came of the plan.[27] In 1834, however, Raine became secretary of the Surtees Society, established as a memorial to the historian; its purpose was and is to publish manuscripts relating to the history of the north of England and the southern part of Scotland, 'a region which constituted the Ancient Kingdom of Northumberland'.[28]

Only two other general histories of the county were completed in the 19th century. In 1834 *An Historical, Topographical, and Descriptive View of the County Palatine of Durham* was published in two volumes under the joint authorship of Eneas Mackenzie and Metcalfe Ross. Wholly self-taught, Mackenzie had already published histories of Northumberland (in which North Durham was treated) and of Newcastle, before starting work on Durham.[29] At his death in 1832 most of the first volume had been set in type, and the task of completing the work was undertaken by Ross, a fellow Newcastle printer. Ross had Mackenzie's notes to work from, but he undertook research himself, claiming that the descriptions of churches and other public buildings were generally made after personal examination. The works of Hutchinson and Surtees were naturally used extensively, but Mackenzie and Ross covered the ground in a more popular and discursive manner, with less emphasis on matters of interest to the antiquary and genealogist. In particular, the inclusion in the first volume of a lengthy 'Geographical and Statistical Description' of the county reflected Mackenzie's interest in providing information needed for self-improvement;

[26] Ibid. i. 10; iv. 64. For Raine see *D.N.B.* and *Raine Miscellany* (Surtees Soc. cc).

[27] Below, Northumb.

[28] Only records before the Restoration were to be published. A hist. of the soc. by A. H. Thompson was published in 1939: *The Surtees Soc. 1834–1934* (Surtees Soc. cl).

[29] For Mackenzie's background, below, Northumb.

he was a keen promoter of the Newcastle Mechanics' Institution and was active in working men's politics. His enthusiasm for the cause of the working classes is reflected in the use he made of parliamentary reports to compile accounts of the county's charities in the belief that 'these inheritances of the poor have been too frequently lost or misappropriated' and that 'it is highly desirable to render their nature and extent generally known, and to record them to posterity'.[30]

The other general history of the county was William Fordyce's *The History and Antiquities of the County Palatine of Durham*, published in two volumes in 1857 and dedicated to Robert Henry Allan. Like Mackenzie, Fordyce (d. 1865) pursued a number of occupations, but was chiefly a printer and bookseller in Newcastle upon Tyne.[31] His history of County Durham followed a pattern similar to that of Mackenzie and Ross but is somewhat less detailed.

An attempt to complete Surtees's history of the county was undertaken in the 20th century by a relative, Brig.-Gen. Sir Conyers Surtees (d. 1932). Between 1919 and 1930 he published in a series of pamphlets 21 parish histories, relating mainly to places in the west of County Durham. In that covering Witton le Wear (1924) Sir Conyers noted that it was his ambition 'to eventually combine this and similar booklets in folio form', but the project was never completed.

Although not a history of the county, mention should be made of a valuable architectural study written in 1892 by J. R. Boyle and entitled *The County of Durham: its Castles, Churches, and Manor-Houses*. It is still of great use, in conjunction with Pevsner's Durham volume of *The Buildings of England*, published in 1953 and revised by Elizabeth Williamson in 1983.

Beside the Surtees Society, which continues to publish the texts of documents, the county's main local history organization is the Architectural and Archaeological Society of Durham and Northumberland, established in 1862.[32] A volume of transactions was first brought out in 1870. Since the late 1960s the publication has concentrated on archaeological reports, and in 1984 the title was altered to the *Durham Archaeological Journal*. Articles on the history of the county now appear in the *Bulletin* of the Durham County Local History Society, established in 1964. Elsewhere in the county the Sunderland Antiquarian Society was founded in 1899 and has published transactions since 1902.

---

[30] Preface to vol. i.

[31] Biographical details are given by Frank Atkinson in his introduction to the 1973 reprint by Frank Graham of Newcastle upon Tyne of Fordyce's *Hist. of Coal, Coke, [and] Coal Fields* (1860).

[32] Preface to vol. i of the soc.'s transactions. There is a centenary hist. of the soc. in vol. xi (editorial to pts. 3 and 4).

A county archivist was not appointed until 1961, and the present record office in County Hall was opened in 1963.[33] Historians of the county also benefit from collections in Durham University Library, including the Archives and Special Collections at no. 5 The College, and the library of the dean and chapter of Durham.

At the time of writing (1993) it seems possible that the task of writing the county's history may be resumed by the Victoria County History. Three volumes were published in 1905, 1907, and 1928, the first two covering general topics and the third the city of Durham and the south-eastern portion of the pre-1974 county (Stockton ward). When publication was suspended the histories of Chester ward and most of Darlington ward were in galley proof and manuscripts of the histories of the rest of Darlington ward and of Easington ward were ready for the press. Local interest in completing the enterprise surfaced in the early 1990s, when subscribers were invited to contribute to a trust fund intended to assist in the costs of revising what remains to be published. If work is indeed restarted it will go far towards illuminating what Sir Nikolaus Pevsner called 'one of the least known parts of England'.

---

[33] *Northern Hist.* i. 110–11.

ESSEX

W. Raymond Powell

Essex references can be found in Roman and Anglo-Saxon histories, and while some of them—particularly in Bede—are of great local significance, they are incidental to wider themes.[1] This applies to most historical writing before the 16th century, though after the Conquest the local element becomes more prominent: a chronicle of Walden abbey, for instance, gives fascinating glimpses of 12th-century life and thought through the careers of Geoffrey de Mandeville and Prior William, first head of the house.[2]

William Camden's *Britannia* (1586 in Latin; first English edn. 1610) tends to be depreciated in Essex, perhaps because he identified Camulodunum with Maldon, and thought that Colchester castle was built by Edward the Elder. But he correctly identified Othona and Ythancæstir with Bradwell-juxta-Mare, and combined fieldwork with documentary research; while his occasional descriptions of the contemporary scene—as at Saffron Walden[3]—are of permanent value. For each county, *Britannia* provided a brief guide: in the 1610 edition the Essex section amounts to 18 pages. A revised edition was published in 1695 by Edmund Gibson, later bishop of London and patron of Philip Morant; he was assisted for Essex by John Ouseley (below).

John Norden's *Speculi Britanniae Pars: an Historical and Chorographical Description of Essex* was compiled in 1594 as part of a projected series of county histories under Lord Burghley's patronage.[4] Several versions have survived in manuscript;[5] the following comments refer to the version printed in 1840.[6] Norden's map shows hundreds, towns, parishes, hamlets, greater houses, parks, and other features. It is the first Essex map to delineate roads, though they need to be viewed with caution. Norden's brief text describes the county, its

---

[1] For Essex references in some early narrative sources see W. R. Powell, 'Beyond the "Morant Canon"', *Essex Arch. and Hist.* xxiv (1993).

[2] C. H. Empson and H. Collar, 'The Foundation of Waltham Abbey', *Essex Rev.* xlv. 73, 147, 224; xlvi. 12, 88, 164, 227; xlvii. 36, 94, 150, 216; J. H. Round, *Geoffrey de Mandeville* (1892), 38 n.; W. R. Powell, 'Norman Essex and its Historian', *Essex Jnl.* xviii (1983), 30.

[3] *Britannia* (1610 edn. trans. P. Holland), 452–3.

[4] *D.N.B.* s.v. Norden, John (1548–?1625).

[5] F. G. Emmison and R. A. Skelton, 'The Description of Essex by John Norden', *Geographical Jnl.* cxxiii (1957), 37.

[6] Ed. H. Ellis (Camden Soc. [old ser.] ix). Another version of the map was published in 1957: Essex R.O., Publication 29.

topography, agriculture, and industries; and lists places, houses, and prominent residents. Barstable, Rochford, and Dengie hundreds yield 'great store of ottes . . . whence Her Majestie hath greate store of provision'; Canvey Island provides pasture for ewes 'which men milke and thereof make cheese (such as it is) and of the curdes of the whey they make butter once a year, which serveth the clothier'.[7] Cloth is produced at Colchester, Coggeshall ('the best whites in England'), Bocking, Dedham, and Halstead. But, says Norden, 'I cannot commend the healthfulness [of Essex] and especially nere the sea coastes, which gave me a most cruel quarterne fever.' A manuscript of his 'Essex', said to have been 'in Sir John Turner's library', was often used by later writers.[8]

Research for a full-scale history of Essex was launched by Thomas Jekyll (1570–1652) of Bocking, a King's Bench lawyer.[9] His notes from the public records and other sources passed to his grandson Nicholas Jekyll, who put them at the disposal of John Ouseley (1645–1709), rector of Panfield, near Bocking.[10] Ouseley's projected history of Essex never appeared but, besides helping Gibson to revise *Britannia*, he collaborated generously with another scholar, Richard Newcourt.

Newcourt (d. 1716) was registrar of London diocese 1669–96. His *Repertorium Ecclesiasticum* (2 vols. 1708–10) is an 'Ecclesiastical Parochial History' of the diocese, and its second volume covers Essex. For each parish there is an account of the advowson and of the property of the benefice, followed by a list of incumbents, with biographical notes and patrons' names. This information comes mainly from the London diocesan archives, with occasional use of other church records. Newcourt also used printed sources, especially Dugdale's *Monasticon* and *Baronage*. Among private manuscript sources often quoted is Norden's 'Description of Essex'. Newcourt's biographical notes draw heavily on Anthony Wood's *Athenae Oxonienses*. In detailing grants and appointments he often cites patent rolls and other public records; most of this material came from his friend William Grimes, a Chancery official, and from John Ouseley. To Ouseley, Newcourt was also indebted for encouragement and for advising him to list the incumbents under each parish: 'This I looked upon as a laborious task, but was resolved to undergo it.' Over 100 of Newcourt's Essex parishes contain information from Ouseley, sometimes accompanied by further tributes to him.

[7] Cf. *V.C.H. Essex*, i. 571–2.

[8] [R. Gough], *British Topography* (2 vols. 1780), i. 343.

[9] For Jekyll and his successors see E. A. Fitch and C. F. D. Sperling, 'Historians of Essex', *Essex Rev.* vols. ii, iii, v, viii, and ix: cf. *V.C.H. Essex Bibliography* (1959), 7–8; C. M. Cobbold, 'Writing of Essex County History, *c.* 1600–1768', *Essex Jnl.* viii. 2; P. Morant, *Hist. of Essex* (1978 reprint), intro. by G. Martin; *D.N.B.* s.v. Thomas Jekyll, William Holman, Nicholas Tindal, Nathaniel Salmon, and Philip Morant; [Gough], *British Topography*, i. 343 sqq. is also useful, but sometimes inaccurate.

[10] M. Christy, 'The Revd. John Ouseley', *Essex Rev.* xxi. 132.

Newcourt's *Repertorium* has obvious limitations, as he himself admitted.[11] Since his lists of incumbents are based mainly on the bishops' registers, there are few entries earlier than 1306 or between 1642 and 1660. There are many unexplained gaps in the lists; for places exempt from episcopal jurisdiction, like Hornchurch, Writtle, and Roxwell, there are no lists; and while church dedications are sometimes given, there are few architectural details. Newcourt cannot have done much fieldwork, nor did he use many Essex sources of information, apart from Ouseley's collection. Throughout the book there are errors of transcription or printing. But *Repertorium* contains an immense amount of information, and it is still very useful. To volume two there are several published supplements, notably Percy H. Reaney's *Early Essex Clergy* (1947);[12] and two unpublished, by George Hennessey and John L. Fisher.[13] Harold Smith's *Ecclesiastical History of Essex under the Long Parliament and Commonwealth* [*c.* 1931] supplies the names of additional clergy, many of them from the returns to the Parochial Inquisition of 1650.[14] Smith omitted from the book his lists of parochial clergy for the period, but they survive in typescript.[15]

About 1710 William Holman, minister of Halstead Independent chapel, put in hand a history of Hinckford hundred, under the patronage of John Morley, a local butcher and landowner, who introduced him to neighbouring gentry and to Humfrey Wanley, librarian to Robert Harley, earl of Oxford.[16] Anthony Holbrook, John Ouseley's son-in-law, took an interest in Holman's work, and sold him some of Ouseley's papers. Nicholas Jekyll lent Holman some of Thomas Jekyll's Essex papers. Samuel Dale (?1659–1739) of Braintree, apothecary and antiquary, helped Holman with documentary research, fieldwork, and editorial advice. Holman was soon planning a history of the whole county. He supplied Essex information to Thomas Cox for his *Magna Britannia* (1720–31), and to Thomas Wotton for his *English Baronage* (1727); and corresponded with many other scholars.[17] Having travelled the county recording antiquities, he drafted detailed notes on each of the 400 parishes;[18] but he died in 1730 leaving them unpublished.[19]

Nicholas Tindal, vicar of Great Waltham, undertook to edit and publish Holman's drafts. In 1732 he published two parts of *A History of Essex*, relating to six places in Hinckford hundred, but then abandoned the task. About 1739

[11] Vol. i, intro.
[12] *V.C.H. Essex Bibliography*, 17; *V.C.H. Essex Bibliography Supplement* (1987), 10.
[13] In Chelmsford Cathedral Library (copies in Essex R.O., T/A 547 and T/A 237).
[14] H. Smith, *Ecclesiastical Hist. of Essex*, 233–321.
[15] Chelmsford Cathedral Library, 'Sequence of the Parochial Clergy in Essex, 1640–64'.
[16] For Wanley see D. C. Douglas, *English Scholars* (2nd edn. 1951), 98–118.
[17] For Dale, Cox, and Wotton see *D.N.B.*
[18] Now Essex R.O., T/P 195.
[19] Holman's history of *Halstead* (ed. T. G. Gibbons) was published in 1902; 2nd edn. 1909.

Holman's drafts were acquired by Nathaniel Salmon, a nonjuring cleric who had already published histories of Surrey and Hertfordshire, and had supplied Holman with Essex material.[20] Between 1740 and 1742 Salmon published 19 parts of *The History and Antiquities of Essex*, covering about 250 parishes; but he died in 1742. Like Tindal, he had followed Holman's drafts closely, concentrating on manorial descents, church advowsons, and monumental and fenestral antiquities.

Salmon's Essex papers, including Holman's parish drafts, eventually passed to John Booth, a lawyer who was undersheriff of Essex. During the 1740s Booth visited many parishes, made additional notes, and collated the Domesday extracts made by the previous scholars with the original. About 1750 he handed over all his material to Philip Morant, rector of St. Mary's, Colchester. Morant also obtained access to the cream of Thomas Jekyll's Essex collection, including abstracts of inquisitions *post mortem* (1242–1639), and of letters patent (1483–1618).[21]

Morant (1700–70) had been Nicholas Tindal's curate and literary assistant at Great Waltham; and in 1748 he had published a history of Colchester (below). He now undertook to complete Salmon's book, but 'observing what a poor use he had made of the excellent materials in his possession', he proceeded to compile an entirely new and complete *History and Antiquities of Essex* (2 vols. serialized, 1762–8). The first volume includes a revised version of Morant's *Colchester*. Morant's parish histories are similar in scope to those of Tindal and Salmon except that he omitted the epitaphs recorded by Holman. He was criticized for that by Richard Gough, but defended himself stoutly: to have included epitaphs would have 'swelled the book immeasurably'.[22] Gough also charged Morant with failing to describe the face of the county and the ancient monuments. 'Recluse and sedentary antiquarians', he wrote, 'find it much easier to arrange materials put into their hands than to ramble about the country, and to examine every remain of antiquity.'[23] Is this a fair criticism? Much of the local information and fieldwork incorporated in the *History* appears to have come from Holman's out-of-date drafts. There is no evidence that Morant himself did much fieldwork, but he certainly added material supplied by local correspondents like Lord Dacre[24] and George Scott.[25] If he had tried to do more the work would have been prolonged, and he might never have finished it.[26]

[20] For Salmon and Holman see Essex R.O., D/Y 1, Nicholas Jekyll to Holman 27 July 1730.
[21] J. Nichols, *Literary Anecdotes of 18th Century* (9 vols. 1812–15), ii. 706.
[22] W. R. Powell, 'Antiquaries in Conflict: Philip Morant versus Richard Gough', *Essex Arch. and Hist.* xx (1989), 143–6.
[23] Ibid.
[24] N. Briggs, 'Lord Dacre and Morant', *Essex Jnl.* ii (1967), 6–12.
[25] A. Searle, 'George Scott of Woolston Hall', *Essex Jnl.* i. 191.
[26] Cf. Morant's remark in the preface to volume one of his *Essex*: 'But finding, beyond what I could expect, a continuance of life and strength'.

The *History* describes churches briefly but systematically, and notes the location of each manor house—a feature most helpful to the compiler of the recent map of Domesday Essex.[27] Secular buildings, apart from the greatest, are rarely described. Morant says little, except in the towns, about local government, poor relief, religious, social, or economic life. Yet, as Professor Martin says, 'most aspects of life are to be found in the *History* if one looks for them'.[28] Morant's indexes are inadequate, but his book is admirably arranged and cross-referenced, with sources cited. In one respect, perhaps, he can be said to have failed even by his own standards: his early manorial descents, based largely on the inquisitions *post mortem* and the patent rolls, have many gaps, particularly between 1086 and *c.* 1250. The Feet of Fines, invaluable for that period, are hardly ever used, except in occasional references taken second-hand from Thomas Madox.

Morant's *History*, reprinted in 1816 and 1978, has not yet been entirely superseded. Between 1769 and 1772 a concise version was issued anonymously under the title *A New and Complete History of Essex by a Gentleman* (6 vols.).[29] The publisher was Peter Muilman of Castle Hedingham, a rich merchant of Dutch birth who had been 'a most generous encourager' of Morant's *History*.[30] The book included some new material: many illustrations and details of sepulchral monuments, and a little information on other matters, particularly those concerning Muilman himself.[31] Thomas Wright's *History and Topography of Essex* (2 vols. serialized, 1831–6) is a rehash of Morant, partly updated, with a substantial introduction and good engravings. Wright, who was a Cambridge undergraduate when the book was commissioned, is said to have visited Essex only once or twice in his life.[32]

Daniel Lysons's *Environs of London* (1796, revised 1811) includes 11 Essex parishes.[33] These, while owing much to Morant, provide a wider range of information, notably on epitaphs, baptisms and burials, and agriculture. The same parishes, with 10 more adjoining, figure in Elizabeth Ogborne's unfinished *History of Essex* (parts 1–3, 1817).[34] Mrs. Ogborne's book was illustrated by her husband John, who had been born in Chelmsford; it includes useful church notes and biographical details.

[27] W. R. Powell, *Essex in Domesday Book*, Gazetteer, p. 8.

[28] P. Morant, *Hist. of Essex* (1978 reprint), intro. p. xiii.

[29] E. A. Fitch, 'Historians of Essex: a Gentleman', *Essex Rev.* v. 106; viii. 20.

[30] Morant, *Essex*, ii. 301 n. Six members of the Muilman family subscribed to Morant's book: ibid. i, list p. vi.

[31] *Hist. of Essex by a Gentleman*, i. 92 (Chelmsford: this reference was kindly supplied by Miss H. E. P. Grieve); ii. 108 (Castle Hedingham); ii. 182–3 (Little Yeldham); iii. 381–4 (Greenstead).

[32] E. A. Fitch, 'Historians of Essex: Thomas Wright', *Essex Rev.* ix. 65.

[33] In vol. iv. For Lysons (1762–1834) see *D.N.B.*

[34] E. A. Fitch, 'Historians of Essex: Elizabeth Ogborne', *Essex Rev.* viii. 129.

Philip Benton's unfinished *History of Rochford Hundred* (3 vols. serialized, 1867–86), covers 15 places and part of a sixteenth, leaving eight places in the hundred untreated.[35] Benton, a local farmer, described the descent of manors; churches and charities; worthies and burials; buildings, bridges, and earthworks; and agriculture and industries. The style is discursive but lively and there is much original material. Benton had talked to people whose memories went back to the 18th century and who told him, for instance, how *c.* 1750 a poor man and wife, accused of witchcraft, were subjected to the water ordeal. *Rochford Hundred* was reprinted in 1991 (2 vols.) with a new companion volume containing a memoir of Benton, a bibliographical note, and indexes.

William Palin's *Stifford and its Neighbourhood* (1871) and *More about Stifford and its Neighbourhood* (1872) contain sections on 20 parishes in south Essex. He was rector of Stifford 1834–82, a prolific writer, and a magistrate;[36] interested in topography and social life as well as antiquities; and he printed many extracts from parish records.

Few monographs on Essex places appeared before the 19th century. Thomas Fuller's *History of Waltham Abbey* (1655) is a brief account of the abbey with little further information on the town or parish; it does, however, use the churchwardens' accounts in narrating the post-Dissolution history of the abbey church. Fuller, then incumbent of Waltham, is better known for his *Worthies of England*.

The earliest parish history is *The History and Antiquities of Harwich and Dovercourt* by Silas Taylor and Samuel Dale. Taylor (1624–78), who had previously worked on the history of Herefordshire, was keeper of naval stores at Harwich. His *History*, compiled *c.* 1676, was extended, edited, and published by Dale in 1730. It is a sumptuous volume with much original material, fine engravings, a memoir of Taylor, and a bibliography. Dale—previously Holman's assistant—punctiliously distinguished his own work from that of Taylor. The book is too long and contains many irrelevancies; but there is much of value on topography, industries, maritime history, local government, and public services, as well as the churches and the manor. There are also lighter touches. Henry Smith, benefactor to the parish, was rich but mean. 'He had the nickname of "Dog" Smith, because he dined at his friends' houses and then desired a bit for his dog, which was to refect himself.'[37]

The History of Waltham Abbey (1735) by John Farmer, 'Gent.', is much

---

[35] The book includes South Benfleet (Barstable hundred) and Canvey Island (partly in Barstable hundred), which were transferred to Rochford poor-law union in 1847.
[36] *D.N.B.*
[37] S. Taylor and S. Dale, *Hist. of Harwich and Dovercourt*, 91.

slighter. Dedicated obsequiously to the lord of the manor, it has pretensions
to scholarship, with charters quoted at length, but the arrangement is poor.
There are many illustrations, including one of the gunpowder mills, and a
copy of the 1641 perambulation of Waltham forest.

Philip Morant's *History and Antiquities of Colchester* (1748) is an
encyclopaedic work displaying great erudition and industry.[38] As the
history of an ancient community it is less successful, partly because the
general narrative (book one) is inflated with much that is common to the
history of England; but Morant lived in the borough and made good use of
its records, and this is a fine book. The revised edition of 1768 was
reprinted in 1970.

Thomas K. Cromwell, author of *The History of Colchester* (2 vols. 1825) was
a young writer who later became a Unitarian minister.[39] Besides antiquities,
he mentions recent events: a new library (1803), a malt distillery (1812), and a
Philosophical society (1820). There is also information on neighbouring
places: Mersea Island, Wivenhoe, and St. Osyth. Aimed at a more popular
readership than that of Morant, the book is well written.

From the mid 19th century historians, in Essex as elsewhere, began to
collaborate more formally. The British Archaeological Association and the
Royal Archaeological Institute, both founded in the 1840s, were based in
London but held provincial congresses like that of the R.A.I. at Colchester in
1876.[40] Next came county societies, facilitated by the railways.

The Essex Archaeological Society, formed at Colchester in 1852, brought
together gentry, clergy, and professional men. The historian William Stubbs,
then vicar of Navestock, was a founder member. From its earliest days the
society has published *Transactions*, now called *Essex Archaeology and History*.
J. Horace Round (1854–1928), historian and genealogist (president 1916–21),
contributed more than 170 items to this journal over 50 years.[41] Among other
early contributors were Henry W. King of Leigh (honorary secretary
1866–93), whose collections are in the Essex Record Office;[42] Henry Laver,
family doctor, and George Rickword, borough librarian, both of Colchester;
Frederic Chancellor, architect, of Chelmsford; W. Chapman Waller, barrister,
of Loughton; and Robert C. Fowler of Witham.[43] Fowler, an assistant keeper
in the Public Record Office, edited the *Transactions* 1918–29. He also
transcribed the *Essex Feet of Fines*, which the society began to serialize in

---

[38] It was satirized by J. Clubbe in *Hist. and Antiquities of Ancient Villa of Wheatfield* (1768).
[39] *D.N.B.*
[40] *Essex Arch. and Hist.* xxiii (1992), 80.
[41] Ibid. xii (1980), 31–2; J. H. Round, *Family Origins* (ed. W. Page, 1930), pp. lxi–lxv.
[42] Essex R.O., T/P 73.
[43] *Essex Arch. Trans.* new ser. xv. 82 (Laver); xxi. 343 (Rickword); xv. 85 (Chancellor); xiv. 356
(Waller); xix. 328 (Fowler).

1899. Since 1945 several other occasional papers have been published. G. Montagu Benton, vicar of Fingringhoe, was the society's editor from 1929 to 1959, as well as secretary 1923–53 and president 1950–5.

The Essex Field Club, founded in 1880 and based in south-west Essex, has always been primarily concerned with natural history but its journal, *Essex Naturalist*, includes some archaeology and history.

The *Essex Review* (1892–1957) was an independent quarterly covering history, literature, and current affairs, founded by Edmund Durrant of Chelmsford and later published for many years by Benham of Colchester. The first editor was Edward A. Fitch of Maldon, farmer, naturalist, and antiquary.[44] Miss Charlotte Fell Smith held the post from 1898 to 1933.[45] The *Review* was attractively produced and contains much good work.

The first two volumes of the *Victoria History of the County of Essex* (1903; 1907) contain all the 'general' articles originally planned except 'Roman Essex'. J. H. Round, who helped to edit both volumes, compiled the 'Domesday' section for volume one. Most of volume two was the work of local scholars, including R. C. Fowler ('Religious Houses'), Miller Christy ('Industries'), and Charlotte Fell Smith ('Schools'). No more was published at that period.

Between 1850 and 1914 there was an increasing flow of monographs on individual places. Some of the authors were Anglican clergy, like John P. Shawcross, whose history of *Dagenham* (1904) was illustrated by A. Bennett Bamford. George F. Beaumont, historian of *Coggeshall* (1890), was a solicitor.[46] Edward P. Dickin (*Brightlingsea*, 1913, revised 1939) was a family doctor.[47] George Terry (*Memories of Old Romford*, 1880) was a Wesleyan minister.[48] As reprinted in 1979, with chapter headings and illustrations, his book became more useful. William Winters (*Waltham Abbey*, 1888) was a Strict Baptist minister, journalist, and bookseller.[49] Thomas L. Wilson (*Upminster*, 1856, revised 1880) was a builder and undertaker.[50] W. C. Waller's substantial history of *Loughton* was published in the parish magazine (1889–1900); a few bound sets were later made up.

The expansion of London in the late 19th century stimulated interest in the places that were being so rapidly transformed. *East and West Ham* (1888) by Katharine Fry (1801–86) was revised and published by Gustav Pagenstecher, a local land agent, who received much information on East Ham from Walter

---

[44] Ibid. xiii. 69; *Essex Rev.* xxi. 191. For the early history of *Essex Rev.* see xvii. 36.
[45] Ibid. xlvi. 133.
[46] *Essex Arch. Trans.* new ser. xix. 137.
[47] Ibid. xxiv. 168.
[48] For Terry see J. Hall, *Hall's Circuits and Ministers* (1897), 256.
[49] *Essex Rev.* ii. 204.
[50] His MSS. are now in Essex R.O., T/P 67. Cf. *V.C.H. Essex*, vii. 148.

Crouch.[51] Miss Fry, who lived in East Ham, was the daughter and biographer of Elizabeth Fry.[52] Her book is an antiquarian study with little on recent events. John Kennedy's *Leyton* (1894) is more up-to-date: he was a young local vicar.[53] *West Ham: a Study in Social and Industrial Problems* (1907), by (Sir) Edward Howarth and Mona Wilson, is focused on present conditions, but also surveys the recent history of the borough. Howarth, then head of the Trinity College (Oxford) settlement at Stratford, was later a civil servant; Miss Wilson eventually became a literary biographer.[54]

Between 1850 and 1914 several important books were published on particular aspects of the county's history. *Annals of Evangelical Nonconformity in Essex* (1863) is a pioneer work by Thomas W. Davids, a Colchester Congregational minister.[55] It has no personal name index; but one compiled in typescript by W. T. Whitley is in the Essex Record Office. William R. Fisher, author of *The Forest of Essex* (1887), was a barrister who had represented the City of London in the recent Epping Forest litigation. The index is poor but this is still the best book on the subject.[56] Frederic Chancellor's *Ancient Sepulchral Monuments of Essex* (1890) is a huge tome containing measured drawings by his assistants along with genealogical information. *Church Bells of Essex*, by Cecil Deedes, a former Essex rector, and Henry B. Walters of the British Museum, was the fruit of many years work by several scholars. It is beautifully produced, with special typefaces depicting inscriptions on the bells, and many photographs.[57]

By 1914 Essex had over one million residents. About half of them lived in the metropolitan south-west, for whom, in those days, the Essex Archaeological Society was too exclusive and remote. More attractive would be societies with open and inexpensive membership, meeting in the local public libraries and concentrating on the history of the immediate district.[58] Such was the Walthamstow Antiquarian Society, formed in 1915, initially to serialize a history of the town already compiled by George F. Bosworth, a local schoolmaster.[59] Strongly supported by the town council and its librarian George Roebuck, the W.A.S. had by 1940 published some 40 monographs. Several of these were the work of Percy H. Reaney, another Walthamstow

[51] *Essex Rev.* xxvii. 139.
[52] *Katharine Fry's Book*, ed. J. Vansittart (1966); *V.C.H. Essex Bibliography*, 86 and author index.
[53] *V.C.H. Essex*, vi. 226.
[54] For Howarth (d. 1953) and Wilson (d. 1954) see *Who Was Who*. For the Trinity Coll. settlement see *V.C.H. Essex*, vi. 141-2.
[55] *D.N.B.*; Davids's MSS. are in Dr. Williams's Library, London.
[56] It is well summarized in *V.C.H. Essex*, ii. 614 sqq.
[57] For Deedes (d. 1920) and Walters (d. 1944) see *Who Was Who*.
[58] For Essex public libraries: *V.C.H. Essex Bibliography*, 324 sqq.
[59] W. G. S. Tonkin, *Diamond Jubilee: Walthamstow Antiq. Soc. 1915-75* (1975).

schoolmaster.[60] A second series, owing much to W. Gregory S. Tonkin, had produced 25 more by 1982. Similar societies were formed in several other Essex towns before 1945, and others later. Many have published journals or occasional papers.[61] In 1964 the societies formed a federal body, the Essex Archaeological and Historical Congress, which since 1966 has published the *Essex Journal* on the lines of the old *Essex Review*.

Essex is one of the few counties for which the Royal Commission on Historical Monuments published a detailed *Inventory* (4 vols. 1916–23).[62] Details of church plate were included in the *Inventory*, but they were superseded by *The Church Plate of Essex* (1926), compiled by William J. Pressey, G. Montagu Benton, and Francis W. Galpin, three vicars who were all members of the Essex Archaeological Society.[63]

The Essex Record Office, opened by the county council in 1938, had by 1992 issued 119 publications, including guides to the records; progress reports; reproductions of maps (including the fine county map of 1777 by John Chapman and Peter André); exhibition booklets; teaching portfolios; source books; studies of particular places, topics, and persons; and sound recordings. During the same period many postgraduate theses were based on the Essex records, and several later became books.[64]

The Essex V.C.H. was revived in 1951, under a committee financed by the local authorities, in association with the University of London. The honorary secretary of the committee was John G. O'Leary, borough librarian of Dagenham, who was himself a local historian and, for many years, a driving force in promoting Essex history. By 1987 eight more volumes had been published. Volume three ('Roman Essex', 1963) was compiled by M. Reginald Hull, curator of Colchester museum, with contributions by John G. S. Brinson, president of the E.A.S.; Sir Ian Richmond wrote the introductory survey. Volumes four to eight (1956–83) cover the topography of south-west Essex, including the London boroughs east of the river Lea. Volume four (Ongar hundred) was the first V.C.H. volume to include local government as a standard feature; it also contains an appendix analysing medieval and 17th-century tax assessments. Volume five contains an article by William Ashworth on 'Metropolitan Essex since 1850'. The *Essex Bibliography* (1959) and its

---

[60] Reaney's *Place-Names of Essex* (E.P.N.S. xii, 1935), an admirable companion to local studies, is beyond the scope of this survey.

[61] For 'profiles' of Essex local history societies see *Essex Jnl.* xxiii (1988), 70, and later vols.

[62] Above, Architectural Guides and Inventories.

[63] *Essex Arch. Trans.* new ser. xxiii. 369 (Pressey); ibid. new ser. xxv. 379 (Benton); ibid. new ser. xxiv. 172 (Galpin). A review article by J. H. Round on *Church Plate of Essex* belongs to the Essex Society for Archaeology and History, which intends to publish it soon.

[64] In 1992 Essex R.O. library held about 130 theses based on the county records, including 82 submitted for doctors' or masters' degrees.

Supplement (1987)—which are unique within the V.C.H.—comprise sections on the county; persons and families; individual places and regions. They list books, pamphlets, and sale catalogues in the libraries of the county, the London boroughs, the Essex Record Office, the E.A.S., and Chelmsford cathedral; also articles identified by searching the *Dictionary of National Biography*, some 2,000 volumes in 50 periodicals, and 8,500 volumes of parliamentary papers. A set of articles on the history of Essex libraries is appended to the *Bibliography*.

The extensive literature on Essex history published in recent years can be seen from the *Bibliography Supplement*. There has been growing interest in vernacular architecture, industrial archaeology, working-class history, women's history, and family history. Publishing bodies have included, besides those already mentioned, various departments of the county, district, and borough councils; Essex University; the Workers' Educational Association; churches, chapels, schools, and hospitals; industrial and commercial firms; and societies and clubs. A few resourceful historians have published their own books. Important excavations at Mucking, Colchester, and elsewhere have been documented. Outstanding among general books has been *Essex Windmills* (5 vols. 1981–8) by Kenneth G. Farries, a schoolmaster who had begun his research as a boy, when living beside the mill at Upminster. Like many other scholars over the centuries covered by this chapter, he was most generous in sharing his knowledge.[65]

ACKNOWLEDGEMENT

This chapter was put onto computer disk by Mrs. Pamela Studd, a kindness generously offered and very much appreciated.

[65] For K. G. Farries (1916–86) see *Essex Windmills*, v. 15–16.

GLOUCESTERSHIRE AND BRISTOL

Nicholas Herbert

Gloucestershire, with boundaries that took in upper Thames valley meadowland, river cliffs on the Wye, the south end of the Malvern hills, and some of the outer hamlets of Bristol, was not a county with a readily definable personality. Nor was it one whose natives in exile were easily recognizable. Some of those living in London formed a Gloucestershire Society and even sang an unofficial county anthem called 'George Ridler's Oven', but there were probably no 'professional' Gloucestershiremen. Loyalty was as much to individual regions, such as the Forest of Dean and the Vale of Berkeley. There was, however, pride in the county and in its diversity of landscape and economic activity, one indication of which is the number of historical works in which it was celebrated. In the 18th century three full-scale antiquarian histories appeared—massive, expensively-bound folios of a familiar type but proving to be much more than mere ornaments for the shelves of country-house libraries: all three have been republished recently.[1]

Among the county's antiquaries an early and unusual figure was John Smith (1567–1641), for many years steward to the Berkeleys of Berkeley Castle. His principal work was a remarkable history of the Berkeleys, including detail of estate management as well as the more expected biographical matter and providing full references to the family's muniments.[2]

In the late 17th century the first attempt was made at a county history. The author was the unlikely figure of Abel Wantner, son of a Gloucester innkeeper and probably himself in that trade at Minchinhampton.[3] In his later years he was parish clerk at a Gloucester city church. He began work on his county

---

[1] Much of the biographical and bibliographical detail that follows is taken from two standard reference works: I. Gray, *Antiq. of Glos. and Bristol* (1981) and *Bibliographer's Manual of Glos. Literature*, ed. F. A. Hyett and W. Bazeley (3 vols. 1895–7). The best general account of the county's historians is E. A. L. Moir, 'Historians of Glos.: Retrospect and Prospect', in *Glos. Studies*, ed. H. P. R. Finberg (1957). I am grateful to Brian Frith and Dr. Joe Bettey for comments and suggestions.

[2] Published as *Berkeley Manuscripts: Lives of Berkeleys with Description of Hundred of Berkeley*, ed. J. Maclean (3 vols. 1883–5); for an early appreciation of Smith's achievement, S. Seyer, *Memoirs of Bristol and Neighbourhood*, i (1821), pp. vii–viii.

[3] B. Frith, 'Abel Wantner: an Unpublished Glos. Historian', *Trans. Bristol and Glos. Arch. Soc.* xcix. 170–2. Wantner's MS. is Bodl. MSS. Top. Glouc. c. 2–3.

history *c*. 1673, and in 1686 issued specimen pages with a prospectus inviting
subscriptions. An updated fair copy is dated 1714 and probably represents a
last effort to leave something completed. He died later that year. For
Gloucester and some other towns Wantner's manuscript provided much
useful information of a kind ignored by historians of greater pretension. By
that and by the inclusion of some dubious anecdotal material, he laid himself
open to the scorn of those for whom antiquarianism was a pursuit for the
clergy or for those of the gentry unfitted by temperament for politics, field
sports, or estate management. The antiquary Bishop William Nicolson stated
that Wantner was 'busy meddling in things beyond his sphere'.[4] Nicolson
would have found the next aspirant from a more reassuring mould. Richard
Parsons, a clergyman from a clergy family, was chancellor of Gloucester
diocese from 1677 until his death in 1711.[5] His manuscript, entitled 'A
Parochial Visitation of the Diocese of Gloucester' and arranged by rural
deaneries, owes its form to the episcopal visitation and was a direct
development from his professional duties. However, a printed questionnaire
prepared by Parsons shows that he intended to include much secular detail,
mainly contemporary rather than historical. What he left is still largely in
note form, his manuscript becoming like Wantner's a quarry for others.

The first of the 'big three' Gloucestershire antiquaries, Sir Robert Atkyns
(1647–1711), was from an established Gloucestershire landowning family.[6] He
trained as a lawyer and was M.P. for Cirencester and the county, but, as a
Tory, withdrew from public office after the Revolution of 1688 and devoted
his time to historical research. Atkyns's *Ancient and Present State of
Glostershire* (1712) is much what might be expected of his background. His
parish histories very largely comprised manorial descents, and, as for many
years no one else tackled the records of national government with his
application, it was long before his descents were bettered; they were borrowed
wholesale by his successors. Church history and other detail was based mainly
on Parsons's manuscript. For the Tory author one purpose of local history
was as cement for those pillars of ordered society, the Church and the landed
interest: his preface is an attempt to demonstrate its practical and instructive
value, suggesting unconvincingly that details of the population of outlying
hamlets and the value of church livings might encourage church building, and
that manorial descents might inspire present-day landowners to emulate the
best in their predecessors. Among the features that have made the book a

---

[4] Quoted in T. Fosbrooke, *Hist. of Gloucester* (1819), 124; and cf. Fosbrooke's comment, ibid.
157.
[5] B. S. Smith, introduction to R. Atkyns, *Ancient and Present State of Glos.* (reprint 1974), pp.
viii–ix. Parsons's MS. is Bodl. MS. Rawl. B. 323.
[6] Smith, introduction to Atkyns, *Glos.*

collectors' item is the series of over 60 engravings by Johannes Kip, who by happy coincidence was then preparing his *Britannia Illustrata*. They form a gallery of the mansions and manor houses of a prosperous county, and were not matched later in quality. The failure of Atkyns's successor Samuel Rudder to get many landowners to pay for views of their houses meant the loss of an equivalent visual record for the later years of the 18th century.

Samuel Rudder (1726–1801), whose *New History of Gloucestershire* was published in 1779, had a very different background.[7] His father was a Uley shopkeeper and sometime pig-killer, and Samuel himself earned his living at Cirencester as a printer with sidelines as auctioneer and dealer in patent medicines. A thorough, painstaking man, he took 12 years over the preparation and printing of his book. Originally intending a revision of Atkyns, his own wider range of interest and the unwelcome competition from a new edition of Atkyns (1768) led to something much more. By means of a printed questionnaire and by extensive travelling, which took him to every parish in the county, he collected a substantial helping of contemporary information. His details of markets, trade, agricultural improvements, and some brief topographical descriptions give him more lasting value than Atkyns, who, wedded to his beloved documents, mistrusted 'message-information' and had no taste for fieldwork. The *New History* gave particularly detailed treatment to Gloucester city, because for that part Rudder was able to use a manuscript compiled by the Revd. Richard Furney (d. 1753), who had been a schoolmaster at Gloucester in the 1720s.[8] Although more open than Atkyns to the idea that local history had an intrinsic interest, Rudder too sometimes adopted a didactic tone, including, for example, strictures on absentee landowners who deserted their estates for the London season. In other ways Rudder is the Gloucestershire historian to whom his modern successors find it easiest to relate, for he left some detail of the experience of compiling his county history. Lunches with hospitable landowners, the occasional snub, the submission of a draft to a landowner who failed to return it, the constant enquiries about the length of time his book was taking all have a familiar ring to today's county historians. Leading a horse through the deep, mud-filled lanes of north-west Gloucestershire or a night in a flea-ridden inn near Cheltenham are, happily, outside their experience.

In Gloucestershire, historians trod hard on the heels of their predecessors. Samuel Rudder in his preface mentioned that a 'gentleman [employed] in the heralds office' was collecting monumental inscriptions for publication. That

---

[7] N. M. Herbert, introduction to S. Rudder, *New Hist. of Glos.* (reprint 1977).
[8] Copies of Furney's MS. hist. are Bodl. MSS. Top. Glouc. c. 4–5 and Glos. R.O., D 327.

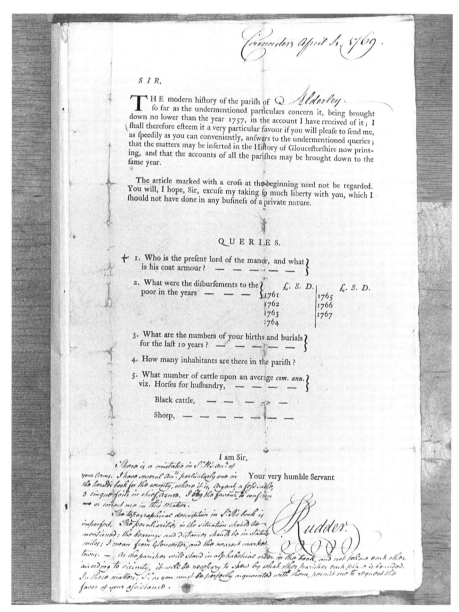

Cirencester April 4, 1769.

SIR,

THE modern history of the parish of *Alderley* so far as the undermentioned particulars concern it, being brought down no lower than the year 1757, in the account I have received of it; I shall therefore esteem it a very particular favour if you will please to send me, as speedily as you can conveniently, answers to the undermentioned queries; that the matters may be inserted in the History of Gloucestershire now printing, and that the accounts of all the parishes may be brought down to the same year.

The article marked with a cross at the beginning need not be regarded. You will, I hope, Sir, excuse my taking so much liberty with you, which I should not have done in any business of a private nature.

QUERIES.

+ 1. Who is the present lord of the manor, and what is his coat armour? — — — —

2. What were the disbursements to the poor in the years — — — —

	£. S. D.		£. S. D.
1761		1765	
1762		1766	
1763		1767	
1764			

3. What are the numbers of your births and burials for the last 10 years? — — — —

4. How many inhabitants are there in the parish?

5. What number of cattle upon an average *com. ann.* viz. Horses for husbandry, — — — —

Black cattle, — — — —

Sheep, — — — —

I am Sir,

Your very humble Servant

Rudder.

There is a mistake in Sir R's acct of your Arms. I have several acct. particularly one in the herald's book for the county, where it is, Argent a fess sable, 3 cinque foils in chief Azure. I beg the favour to confirm me or correct me in this matter.

The topographical description in Sir R's book is imperfect. The peculiarities in the situation should be mentioned; the bearings and distances should be in statute miles; I mean from Gloucester, and the nearest market town. — As the parishes will stand in alphabetical order in the book, and not follow each other according to vicinity, it will be necessary to shew by what other parishes each place is bounded. In these matters, Sir, as you must be perfectly acquainted with them, permit me to request the favor of your assistance.

11 Samuel Rudder's questionnaire for the *New History of Gloucestershire*

was Ralph Bigland (1711–84), who had begun planning an updated edition of Atkyns even before Rudder but was led by the announcement of Rudder's plans and by his own special interest to a different production; his *Historical, Monumental, and Genealogical Collections relative to the County of Gloucester* were published in part in 1791 but not fully until 1889.[9] Born into a minor gentry family from the north of England, Bigland was apprenticed to a London cheesemonger, and it was evidently that business which took him to Gloucestershire's Vale where he married the daughter of a Frocester cheesemonger. It has been suggested that his interest in genealogy was prompted by a demonstration of its practical value when his family successfully established their claim to an inheritance. It was certainly already evident in the 1740s when he collected monumental inscriptions in the Low Countries, where he was selling cheese to the armies engaged in the War of the Austrian Succession. Making his hobby a profession, he became a junior herald in 1757, rising to the rank of Garter King at Arms in 1780. Bigland had a mission to promote accurate genealogy. A booklet published in 1764[10] was a plea for the fuller and more methodical keeping of parish registers and included far-sighted proposals—for the establishment of a national marriage register and for each parish church to keep a record of its monumental inscriptions—that, if carried out, would have made him the patron saint of modern genealogists. His own main contribution was to record hundreds of inscriptions from Gloucestershire churches and churchyards, many since lost. The long saga of the publication of Bigland's work involved several other notable antiquaries, including John and J. B. Nichols, the London publishers specializing in local history, the Gloucestershire-born Revd. James Dallaway, and Sir Thomas Phillipps, whose celebrated collection of manuscripts was once located within the county, at his house in Cheltenham.[11]

Two more county histories appeared in the first decade of the 19th century, but in a less expensive and more convenient format; one of the authors, the Revd. Thomas Fosbrooke, remarked that 'subscribers wisely objected to the clumsy lumbering inconvenience of folios'.[12] Fosbrooke (1770–1842)[13] was very much the professional antiquary and not a good advertisement for the type. Typical of his usual tone is a pompous letter giving evidence to a government

---

[9] I. Gray, 'Ralph Bigland and his Family', *Trans. Bristol and Glos. Arch. Soc.* lxxv. 116–33; T. Prince, 'Ralph Bigland and his Kin' (TS. in Glos. R.O. library). The *Collections* were reprinted (ed. B. Frith) by the B.G.A.S. Rec. Ser. in three vols. 1989–92, with the final vol. planned for 1995.

[10] R. Bigland, *Observations on Marriages, Baptisms, and Burials, as preserved in Parochial Registers* (1764).

[11] Hyett and Bazeley, *Manual of Glos. Literature*, i. 31–44.

[12] Preface to his county history.

[13] P. Ripley, introduction to T. Fosbrooke, *Original Hist. of City of Gloucester* (reprint 1976).

commission on the Forest of Dean in 1832, in which he felt it necessary to
mention the irrelevant facts that he was 'author of the [sic] History of
Gloucestershire' and 'member of the great learned societies'.[14] He was often
querulous about criticism of his work and about his failure to secure ecclesiastical
advancement, which he seemed to think should result naturally from antiquarian
endeavour. His county history, published in 1807, is as unappealing as its title
promises: *Abstracts of Records and Manuscripts respecting the County of Gloucester;
formed into a History, correcting the very erroneous accounts, and supplying numerous
deficiencies in Sir Rob. Atkins, and subsequent writers.* After some introductory
general matter his parish sections concentrate almost wholly on manorial
descents, presented in a dense form with little attempt at readability. A
determination to display the breadth of his scholarship led him to encumber his
text with unnecessary reference and example, and the unattractive typography
provided by his printer is a further disincentive to the reader.

The Revd. Thomas Rudge (1753–1825), a schoolmaster, pluralist incumbent,
and eventually archdeacon of Gloucester, was a more worldly man and a less
pretentious historian. His *History of the County of Gloucester, compressed and
brought down to the year 1803* (1803) did exactly what it set out to do, presenting
a résumé of Atkyns with updating. Concerned simply 'to amuse and to
inform', Rudge gave a workmanlike account, keeping his own views and
personality well in the background. Compared to many of his contemporaries,
he carried dispassionateness to extremes, claiming to have included 'nothing
that will hurt the feelings of the living, insult the memory of the dead, or pass
censure on any public establishment'.[15] A feature that sets both books firmly in
their period is the inclusion of sections on the 'picturesque' in Gloucestershire
with the heavy-handed discussion of the visual merits of particular landscape
features favoured by William Gilpin and his followers; Fosbrooke later himself
contributed a 'Wye Tour' to that genre of literature.[16] A more practical
approach to the countryside is found in Thomas Rudge's other main work, his
survey of Gloucestershire agriculture for the Board of Agriculture.[17] In the
same period Gloucestershire produced two more eminent figures in the field
of antiquarianism, but the brothers Daniel and Samuel Lysons, from a family
of landowners and clergy based at Hempsted, near Gloucester, did not reach
their native county in their unfinished *Magna Britannia* (1806–22).[18]

---

[14] *3rd Report of Dean Forest Commissioners*, pp. 22–3, House of Commons sessional paper 515
(1835), xxxvi.

[15] Rudge's preface to his county history.

[16] T. D. Fosbrooke, *The Wye Tour, or Gilpin on the Wye* (1818).

[17] T. Rudge, *General View of Agriculture of County of Gloucester* (1807).

[18] Samuel's other works included *Account of Roman Antiquities discovered at Woodchester* (1797);
and *Collection of Glos. Antiquities* (1803).

Historians often find it difficult to give due credit to their predecessors, on whose work they always build but whose mistakes, to one covering the same ground, are very apparent. The chain of Gloucestershire historians has links of competitive sourness as well as grateful dependence. Sir Robert Atkyns, though including a tribute to Richard Parsons, failed to acknowledge the extent of his debt. Samuel Rudder, whose attitude to Atkyns was affected by a public controversy with the publisher of the rival second edition of the *Ancient and Present State*, was stung by critics of his own book into inserting a new preface, itemizing some of Atkyns's many mistakes. Among those critics was Thomas Rudge, who was perhaps already contemplating a similar venture.[19] Thomas Fosbrooke, in his advance publicity and in his very title, also directed his fire at Atkyns's descents. Almost seeming to relish what he called 'the slander incident to such publications', he hit out at contemporaries even before his book's publication,[20] and in his preface he launched an extraordinary pre-emptive strike at the antiquary Richard Gough.[21] Rudge, with whom he was in direct competition, was dismissed by Fosbrooke as a 'scissors and paste' historian.[22]

For modern readers a fair appreciation of the work of the old county historians is difficult unless we keep in mind both the scholarly interests of their own times and their problems in locating and collecting material. Living at a time when local history knows few limits in terms of subject matter or access to source material, our main prejudice is against the lack of interest in economic, social, and topographical history. It is hard now to recapture a time for which the narration of the main lines of political, tenurial, and ecclesiastical history came fresh and new. Discovering details about a vanished monastery or finding that a local manor was once owned by some baronial warlord was as exciting for the early antiquaries and their readers as uncovering the rich patterns of trade, topography, and townscape is for historians today. Gloucestershire is lucky that, though to modern eyes limited in scope, each of its main historians brought from their background something of particular benefit: for Atkyns, the landowner with legal training, it was an interest in and ability to use the sources for manorial descents; for Rudder, the tradesman, a curiosity about commerce and agriculture; for Bigland, the herald, an insatiable appetite for collecting monumental inscriptions.

Of the individual towns of the county Gloucester inevitably attracted fullest treatment, but with Furney's work never appearing in its original form,

[19] Herbert, introduction to Rudder, *Glos.*
[20] *Gloucester Jnl.* 29 Mar., 2 Aug. 1802; 24 July 1809.
[21] Preface and vol. i. 5 n. of his county history.
[22] Gray, *Antiquaries of Glos.* 23.

the first publications exclusively concerned with the city were by Rudge
(1811) and Fosbrooke (1819).[23] The abilities and scope of interest of neither
were adequate to the task. For Cirencester, Samuel Rudder published the
relevant section from his county history as a separate volume and later
expanded it to a useful town history.[24] Tewkesbury's first history was written
and published by a printer and bookseller of the town, William Dyde, in
1790,[25] and a successor in the same trades, James Bennett, prompted by
numerous enquiries at his bookshop, produced a more detailed history in
1830.[26] Bennett also produced an annual supplement until 1849, under the title
of the *Tewkesbury Register*. For Cheltenham, as a result of the particular
circumstances of its sudden rise to fame in the late Georgian period, the
earliest published works were in the form of guides, designed to promote its
attractions; at least 15 appeared in the period 1781–1850.[27] By their nature they
contain mainly contemporary description, so that the best of them give as
good value to the modern historian as the antiquarian histories of other towns.
The histories of the various smaller towns of the county that appeared in
Victorian times are generally undistinguished, with the exception of P. H.
Fisher on Stroud (1871).[28] Fisher, a Stroud solicitor, wrote when aged over 80,
using his own memories to particular effect in chapters in which he
perambulated the streets. A history of the Forest of Dean produced in 1858 by
the Revd. Henry Nicholls made an effective first attempt at the complex story
of one the most idiosyncratic regions of any county.[29]

The earliest scheme to establish a county archaeological society for
Gloucestershire, in the mid 1840s, was unsuccessful, but in 1876 historical and
archaeological studies in the region found a new focus with the foundation of
the Bristol and Gloucestershire Archaeological Society.[30] The society's most
lasting achievement will probably be the annual *Transactions*, in the pages of
which the wealth of local source material for the county first became evident.
In the early and mid 20th century some of the editors were slow to banish the

[23] T. Rudge, *Hist. and Antiquities of Gloucester from Earliest Period to Present Time* (1811); T. D.
Fosbrooke, *Original Hist. of City of Gloucester almost wholly compiled from New Materials.*
Fosbrooke's history, which was produced by the Nicholses, included Bigland's inscriptions for
the city's churches.
[24] S. Rudder, *Hist. and Antiquities of Cirencester* (1780); *Hist. of Ancient Town of Cirencester*
(1800).
[25] W. Dyde, *Hist. and Antiquities of Tewkesbury* (1790).
[26] J. Bennett, *Hist. of Tewkesbury* (1830); C. R. Elrington, introduction to reprint (1976).
[27] Hyett and Bazeley, *Manual of Glos. Literature*, ii. 88–98.
[28] P. H. Fisher, *Notes and Recollections of Stroud, Glos.* (1871); N. M. Herbert, introduction to
reprint (1975).
[29] H. G. Nicholls, *Forest of Dean: Historical and Descriptive Account* (1858); the book was
reprinted, together with Nicholls's *Iron Making in Forest of Dean* (1866), in 1966.
[30] E. Ralph, 'The Soc. 1876–1976', *Essays in Bristol and Glos. Hist.* (B.G.A.S. 1976).

discursive class of articles with titles like 'Some Notes on the History of . . .' in favour of those with a less parochial and more analytical approach, but later a range of high quality historical articles provided a suitable counterpoint to the less readable but equally necessary 'pots and bones' archaeological reports. In the days when individual personalities still loomed large in antiquarian studies the society attracted formidable adherents. Sir John Maclean (d. 1895) edited the *Transactions* for 16 years and was himself a contributor on a heroic scale. The Revd. William Bazeley (d. 1925) and Sir Francis Hyett (d. 1941), collaborators in the 1890s on the standard work on Gloucestershire bibliography,[31] were particularly active representatives of the clergy and gentry who took the lead in the society's earlier years. With Roland Austin (d. 1954), for some years secretary, treasurer, and editor of the B.G.A.S., the age of the leisured amateur began to give way to that of the professional, employed in libraries, museums, archives, and educational establishments. As the Gloucester city librarian, Austin amassed and catalogued one of most comprehensive local history collections of any civic library[32] before moving in 1936 to become archivist of the new county record office.[33]

The early years of the Victoria County History produced only a single volume of general articles for Gloucestershire (1907), and it was not until 1960 that the project was revived in the county. Gloucestershire's county council was one of the few which agreed to shoulder the whole burden of the research costs of a county V.C.H.,[34] and the resulting close connexion with the county record office proved of great benefit. Christopher Elrington served as the first county editor until 1968 and set the pattern which by 1988 had produced topographical volumes covering Gloucester, eight of the principal market towns, and over 100 rural parishes. As the more specialized and analytical approach of the academic historian gained ground, a volume of essays edited by H. P. R. Finberg in 1957 was influential in setting the agenda for new departures.[35] Although the county had no university within its borders, Bristol from one direction and Birmingham from another began to give it due attention. During the late 20th century local history in the county developed as in the country as a whole, with the widening of amateur involvement and an acceleration in publication, aided by a specialist local publisher and, from 1987, by a B.G.A.S. record series.

---

[31] Hyett and Bazeley, *Manual of Glos. Literature* (1895–7); two supplementary vols. were later produced by Hyett and Roland Austin (1915–16).

[32] R. Austin, *Catalogue of Glos. Collection in Gloucester Public Library* (1928).

[33] I. E. Gray, 'Glos. Recs.: a Retrospect', *Trans. Bristol and Glos. Arch. Soc.* lxxxvii. 9.

[34] *V.C.H. Glos.* vi (1965), p. xv; *V.C.H. General Introduction*, 19.

[35] Finberg, *Glos. Studies* (1957).

The wide and multi-faceted study of the history of an English county will continue to develop in ways we cannot envisage. In the antiquarian age, when Samuel Rudder found in some parishes 'nothing worth the traveller's attention' and when Thomas Fosbrooke had to refute the claim that the available records for the history of the county had been 'exhausted' by his predecessors,[36] the new approaches of the 20th century were impossible to foresee. Our own successors, while acknowledging our achievements in opening up new topics, bringing to light new sources, and making fresh use of old ones, may conclude that in terms of interpretation we hardly scratched the surface.

BRISTOL

Bristol was severed from Gloucestershire and gained county status in 1373 but continued to cast its shadow over much of the county, maintaining a dominant role in its economic life. The story of the great trading centre has left a wealth of archives and a rich antiquarian literature,[37] beginning with the survey of his native town compiled by William Worcester c. 1480. Worcester's street-by-street description of Bristol is one part of his *Itineraries* that amply justifies his title as the first English antiquary.[38] A contemporary of Worcester, Bristol's town clerk Robert Ricart, was asked by the mayor in 1478 to compile a memoranda book of the town's liberties and customs, and he included in his 'Mayor's Calendar' annual lists of officers and notes of local and national events.[39] Such collections of annals were later a feature of Bristol's historiography: in the 1820s some 40 or 50 manuscript annals, mostly compiled in the 17th and 18th centuries, were thought to be in the possession of old city families.[40]

The history of the city did not attract sustained attention until fairly late in the antiquarian age. The surgeon William Barrett (c. 1727–1789) and the

[36] Rudder, *New Hist. of Glos.* 221, 383, 636; *Gloucester Jnl.* 29 Mar. 1802, advertisement by Fosbrooke.

[37] For detail on Bristol's historians, see Gray, *Antiquaries of Glos.* and Hyett and Bazeley, *Manual of Glos. Literature*; and for a brief general account, H. A. Cronne in *Bristol Charters, 1378–1499* (Bristol Rec. Soc. xi), 1–10.

[38] Published in J. Dallaway, *Antiquities of Bristow in the Middle Centuries; including the Topography by William Wyrcestre* (1834). For Worcester, cf. W. Worcester, *Itineraries*, ed. J. H. Harvey (1969), introduction.

[39] Published as *The Maire of Bristowe is Kalendar by Robert Ricart*, ed. L. Toulmin Smith (Camden Soc. new ser. v, 1872).

[40] S. Seyer, *Memoirs of Bristol and Neighbourhood*, i (1821), pp. x–xi. That by William Adams (d. c. 1650), which Seyer described as the best he had seen, was published as *Adams's Chronicle of Bristol*, ed. F. F. Fox (1910).

clergyman and Bristol schoolmaster Samuel Seyer (1757–1831) then produced substantial works, very different in character but in many ways complementary. The two authors, inspired by pride in 'the second city in the kingdom' and 'the metropolis of the West of England',[41] enjoyed a friendship and mutual respect that is refreshing when compared to some of their Gloucestershire contemporaries. Barrett's *History and Antiquities of the City of Bristol* (1789) unfortunately became associated chiefly in the minds of contemporaries and successors with the purportedly late-medieval 'Rowley' manuscripts, produced and supplied to Barrett by the precocious and disturbed Bristol teenager Thomas Chatterton. It is easy to ridicule Barrett for his credulity but, given the ingenuity of the young poet and the limits of contemporary scholarship, he can be forgiven. The inclusion of the Chatterton fabrications has led sometimes to an unfair dismissal of the whole volume,[42] which includes rich contemporary description of the city's trade and topography. Barrett's work was, however, easily outshone by that of Samuel Seyer. Seyer's first antiquarian publication, an edition of the city's charters, was hampered by the city corporation's reluctance to give him access to the originals,[43] but in his major work, *Memoirs Historical and Topographical of Bristol and its Neighbourhood* (1821–3), he encountered no such problem and made good use of the corporation archives and other original sources. Seyer's preface to the *Memoirs*, a full and careful evaluation of his sources, inspires immediate confidence in what follows, and the humble spirit of scholarship, careful testing of evidence, readable style, and, in the account of the early archaeology, intelligent use of fieldwork made it one of finest town histories of the period. Although Seyer gave due weight to local topography and administrative history, he was sufficiently a man of his time to feel happier when he could set Bristol's story within the march of great national events and his narrative picks up momentum when dealing with periods such as the Civil War.

Seyer sensibly rejected the annalistic format, which became something of a fixation for Bristol historians. Barrett had used it in a final section, and it was adopted by John Evans (d. 1828), a Bristol printer and journalist, whose unoriginal and uninspired *Chronological Outline of the History of Bristol* (1824) was not a financial success. Some years before Seyer (in 1816) another John Evans (d. 1831), a Bristol schoolmaster and Presbyterian minister, and a London-based author John Corry,[44] one of those 'miscellaneous' writers able to turn his hand to any genre, had produced another unremarkable city

---

[41] Dedications (to Bristol corporation) by Barrett and Seyer in their histories.
[42] e.g. the entry for Barrett in *D.N.B.*
[43] *Charters and Letters Patent granted to Town and City of Bristol*, ed. S. Seyer (1812), preface.
[44] For Evans, *Trans. Bristol and Glos. Arch. Soc.* lxi. 198–200; and for Corry, *D.N.B.*

history, though attractively illustrated.[45] Among later histories, that by two Bristol librarians James Nicholls and John Taylor[46] has a particularly useful section on ecclesiastical history and many excellent text illustrations, but the most significant works of the late Victorian period were the series of volumes by the journalist John Latimer (d. 1904).[47] Latimer collected a vast amount of information, much of it from local newspapers, but the result was flawed by his adoption of the annal format and his failure to include any references to his sources. During the 20th century Bristol's history was especially fostered by the establishment of the Bristol Archives Office in 1924[48] and the Bristol Record Society in 1929.[49]

[45] *Hist. of Bristol, Civil and Ecclesiastical* (2 vols.).

[46] *Bristol Past and Present* (3 vols. 1881–2). For the authors, *D.N.B.*

[47] *Annals of Bristol in 19th Century* (1887); *Annals of Bristol in 18th Century* (1893); *Annals of Bristol in 17th Century* (1900); *16th Century Bristol* (1906). For an appreciation of Latimer's work, P. McGrath, introduction to *Annals of Bristol* (reprint 1970), vol. i.

[48] *Guide to Bristol A.O.* (1971), p. xi.

[49] *Bristol Charters, 1155–1373* (Bristol Rec. Soc. i), 224.

HAMPSHIRE AND THE ISLE OF WIGHT

Michael Hicks

'Hampshire has received, perhaps, less attention at the hands of topographers, historians, and antiquaries than any other county in England', remarked the Hampshire *V.C.H.* in 1900. 'Why a district so intimately connected with the history of the country should have been so neglected it is difficult to understand.'[1]

Here the *V.C.H.* echoed such earlier antiquaries as Sir Richard Worsley (1781), the Revd. Richard Warner (1793), and T. W. Shore (1892), who remarked on the paradox that a county of such interest and abundant source material should lack a county history.[2] Not until the late 18th century did Winchester, Southampton, and Selborne attract historians[3] and were sustained attempts made to remedy the absence of a county history.

Ironically everyone overlooked the survey of Hampshire and the Isle of Wight of John Norden in 1595, which briefly described the topography and listed hundreds, towns, mansions and their occupiers, the nobility, and the leading gentry.[4] Already there existed a 'General Survey of the Isle of Wight, with all the fortresses and castles near adjoining' by Sir Francis Knollys (d. 1596), last recorded in the possession of the earl of Anglesey in the late 17th century.[5] Another history of the Isle of Wight was proposed by Dr. Richard James (d. 1638), who prepared a Latin preface and collected early material. Much larger collections made by Sir John Oglander (d. 1655) of Nunwell have

---

[1] *V.C.H. Hants*, i, p. xix.

[2] R. Worsley, *Hist. of Isle of Wight*, ed. R. M. Robbins (1975); R. Warner, *Topographical Remarks on South-western Pts. of Hants* (1793), i, pp. ii–iii; T. W. Shore, *Hist. of Hants* (1892), pp. vi–vii.

[3] G. White, *Natural Hist. and Antiquities of Selborne* (1789); J. Milner, *Hist. Civil and Ecclesiastical, and Survey of Antiquities of Winchester* (2 vols. 1798–1801); J. Speed, *Hist. and Antiquity of Southampton 1770*, ed. E. R. Aubrey (Southampton Rec. Soc. v, 1909).

[4] 'Chorographicall Description of the Seuerall Shires and Islands of Middlesex, Essex, Surrey, Sussex, Hampshire, Wight, Jersey and Guernsey': B.L. Add. MS. 31853, pp. 37–48; cf. F. Kitchen, 'John Norden's "*Speculum Britanniae: Pars; the Isle of Wight*" and some Elizabethan Manuscript Maps of the Island', *Proc. Hants Field Club* [hereafter *P.H.F.C.*], xlvii (1992).

[5] A. Wood, *Athenae Oxonienses*, ed. P. Bliss (4 vols. 1813–20), i. 654; T. Philipps, *Bibliotheca Angleseiana* (1686); W. Nicolson, *English, Scottish and Irish Hist. Library* (1736), i. 14.

been published in part.[6] From 1702 or earlier William Pavey of Clements Inn visited over forty Hampshire churches and recorded their inscriptions; in 1717–19 he was writing up his data and had drafted a title page for his collections.[7] Nothing remains of the county history proposed by Alexander Thistlethwayte, M.P., in 1754.[8]

The History of the Isle of Wight (1781) of Sir Richard Worsley of Appuldurcombe House was the culmination of three generations of endeavour by a particularly well educated and widely travelled family. Sir James Worsley (d. 1757) researched on the Oglander papers and wrote something publishable before his death; his son Sir Thomas (d. 1768) prepared the first chapter by 1765; and Sir Richard completed the 'publication as the discharge of a family duty'. Work was intensified in 1777, the year of Sir Richard's election as F.S.A., and help was sought systematically from local and national sources, leading antiquaries, and local parsons. If Sir Richard orchestrated and financed the project, the Newport solicitor Richard Clarke made substantial unacknowledged contributions, as R. M. Robbins showed in his valuable modern edition. Clarke's supplementary notes down to 1807 are in Carisbrooke Castle Museum. Bar carping comments from Horace Walpole and criticism of the illustrations, Worsley's *History* was deservedly well received. It was well researched, organized, and written, and handsomely produced. Of 440 pages, it falls into three main parts. Seven general chapters of 190 pages describe the island itself (extent, soil, population) and treat its military history, government, the three boroughs of Newport, Newtown, and Yarmouth, religious houses, and churches. Chapter eight treats the island in alphabetical order of places, typically covering the advowson and church, the lordships and country houses, curiosities, and subsidiary places, sometimes at considerable length. There is little architectural detail. Entries are genuinely historical, though early evidence is sparse, and there is an appendix of 160 pages of documents from 1086 to the 17th century. The *History* is informative about the 18th-century Isle of Wight. It was supplemented but not superseded by the histories of the island by J. Albin (1795) and George Hillier (1856), only two parts of whose high quality production were published; by Warner (1795), Sir Henry Engelfield (1816), and Percy Stone (1891), whose strengths were respectively in natural history, geology, and architecture; and by successive county histories.[9]

---

[6] 'Antiquitates Insulae Vectae': Bodl. MS. James 9; *D.N.B.*; *Oglander Memoirs*, ed. W. H. Long (1888); C. F. Aspinwall-Oglander, *Nunwell Symphony* (1945); *Royalist's Notebook: Commonplace Book of Sir John Oglander of Nunwell*, ed. F. Bamford (1936).

[7] B.L. Stowe MS. 845, esp. f. 31; Add. MS. 14296; *Catalogue of Stowe MSS. in B.M.* i. 591.

[8] *Letters from Thomas Herring, Archbishop of Canterbury, to William Duncombe, 1728–57* (1777), 168.

[9] Worsley, *Hist. of Isle of Wight, passim*; for the other hists., below.

Sir Thomas Gatehouse's deliberately brief 'History of Hampshire' or 'Survey of the County of Southampton' now survives as a manuscript volume at the University of Southampton. A fair copy written and corrected in a single hand, presumably Gatehouse's, it was still in the family in 1832, when on loan to Sir Thomas Phillipps, Bt. (d. 1872), and consulted by Sir Frederic Madden (d. 1873). It was sold in 1886 by the Hartley Library to Henry Knatchbull-Hugessen, 1st Lord Brabourne (d. 1893), passed to the Revd. Sir William Cope, Bt., of Bramshill, and was left by him to the Hartley Institution (later Southampton University) in 1892. A second copy belonged to Montagu Samuel, Lord Swaythling (d. 1919), a member of the V.C.H. county committee, and was used by the Hampshire V.C.H.[10]

The author, Sir Thomas Gatehouse of Nether Wallop, was a former sheriff of Hampshire (1762), who had fallen on hard times.[11] A native of Hampshire, Gatehouse prided himself on his knowledge of his county, its history, and its legends. He saw himself as a member of the county élite, dedicating his book to the lord lieutenant James Brydges, duke of Chandos (d. 1789), and identified 'the Nobility and Gentry of the county' as his intended readership. He was introduced into literary circles by his father-in-law William Huggins (d. 1761), the translator and friend of Smollett, whose *History of England* Gatehouse frequently cited. As Huggins's library, inherited by Gatehouse, was put up for sale by his creditors in 1776,[12] Gatehouse presumably did his research somewhat earlier.

It is not altogether clear what were the 'accounts of this kind . . . too frequently drawn from Tradition only' from which Gatehouse dissociated himself. He claimed that his 'Survey' was 'founded partly on observation, partly on the best private information', and compiled from a variety of the 'best and most authentic materials'. The only unpublished sources acknowledged were Eton College charters (for Ellingham), manuscripts of the bishop of Winchester (on Winchester), and a roll of Henry VI, but he cites, not always accurately, the printed authorities available in his own day, monumental inscriptions, and correspondence of the Society of Antiquaries on Christchurch and Portchester. More seriously, Gatehouse was wholly uncritical of local traditions, accepting absurdities about Winchester on the authority of Thomas Rudborne's *Chronicle*. Actually what Gatehouse called the 'abstracted detail of antiquities' does not bulk large either in the 'Survey'

---

[10] Southampton Univ. MS. 5/15 (formerly Ao 202); C. M. Woolgar and K. Robinson, *Guide to Archives and Manuscript Collections of Hartley Library* (1992); B.L. Add. MS. 33279, ff. 37, 42; *V.C.H. Hants*, i, p. xiii. The next three paras. are based on Southampton Univ. MS. 5/15.

[11] M. A. Hicks, 'Lessor v. Lessee: Nether Wallop Rectory 1701–1870', *P.H.F.C.* xlvi (1990), 145–57.

[12] *D.N.B.*; *Hants Chronicle*, 23 Sept. 1776.

itself or his plan. His objective was to describe the city of Winchester, boroughs, market towns, hundreds, and estates, with their distances from London and one another, and to state the foundation and dissolution of any religious house or public structure. That often produced extremely brief descriptions of important places and institutions.

The 'Survey' runs to 303 pages, of which 130 are devoted to the topography of Hampshire and a further 50 to Wight and the Channel Isles. Gatehouse divided the county into sections, broadly defined by river basins, and discussed places in geographical order. He did not include all parishes, churches, or estates. Though the value and patronage of most livings and the occupants of most gentlemen's seats are stated, entries vary greatly. There is little about buildings. Occasionally he is more expansive: on Alresford, especially Alresford pond, he writes at length about birds; about Winchester, especially the lost hospital of St. Mary Magdalen; and about Nether Wallop, his home, for which he adds nothing to what can be seen today. The topographical survey completed, Gatehouse lists the members of Hampshire corporations, Hampshire's M.P.s, militia officers (1771), the poor rate by divisions, turnpikes, main roads, churches of Winchester, and details of the royal review of 1778. The 'Survey' contains little of value about the past but is informative about Hampshire in the 1770s.

In 1791 the Revd. Richard Warner (1763–1857) issued his 'Proposals for compiling and publishing a general history of the county of Southampton'. He too was conscious that such works were often criticized as 'dull accumulations of dry materials', interesting, at most, to local residents, but argued that they could be useful and informative evidence of the character of the past and of human progress.

Subscriptions were invited to a fund held by six trustees, including George Rose, M.P. (d. 1818), of Lyndhurst and Warner's patrons Sir Harry Burrard, Bt., of Walhampton, and William Gilpin, vicar of Boldre, for three volumes. Volume one would contain civil, military, and ecclesiastical history, the history of every religious house and of the Isle of Wight, Winchester, Southampton, and the New Forest. Volume two and much of volume three would consist of a topographical history of parishes arranged alphabetically and containing the descents of manors and estates, notices of their owners and local notables, prehistoric and historic antiquities, and the natural history of each place. There was also to be a large appendix of documents or *Chartularium Hantoniense*, and copious indexes. The whole project was to be completed within ten years. It was to be based on manuscripts already collected or purchased, including Speed's 128-folio history of Southampton, to be collected by Warner himself or supplied by others, and illustrated with drawings already acquired from the estate of Capt. Francis Grose (d. 1791) and others yet to be commissioned. Evidently the 150 subscriptions sought by

1 March 1792 were not received,[13] but a further attempt was made in 1793 and advertised in Warner's *Clausentum*, this time for 300 subscriptions to a revised publishing schedule, with better security for publication, and under the patronage of George III's brother William, duke of Gloucester (d. 1805).[14] The subscription closed in May, apparently with 492 subscribers, but on 28 August 1793 Warner abandoned the project. He stated then that he was unequal to the task and much later recollected that the project was unduly ambitious both financially and academically for him alone to undertake. It would, he later estimated, 'have required at least half a dozen lettered men of various accomplishments, and ten whole years'. A contributory factor may have been the hostile review given to his *Topographical Remarks* by the *Gentleman's Magazine*.

Although still aged only 27 in 1791, Warner was already an experienced and confident author and had published extensively on Hampshire's past. Brought up at Lymington, educated at Christchurch and Oxford, he was curate successively at Boldre, Fawley, and from 1794 in Bath, where he became the leading literary figure. He wrote in quick succession his *Companion in a Tour round Lymington* (1789); *Hampshire Extracted from Domesday Book with Translation, Preface, Glossary* (1789), inspired by H. P. Wyndham's *Wiltshire* (1788); *Attempt to Ascertain the Situation of Ancient Clausentum* (1792); *Topographical Remarks on the South-Western Parts of Hampshire* in two volumes (an expanded version of the *Tour of Lymington*) in 1793; the Isle of Wight section of Abraham and William Driver's *General View of Hampshire Agriculture* (1794); and a *History of the Isle of Wight* in 1795, besides other works. He knew his locality, consulted and transcribed documents, and even excavated some barrows himself. On the other hand, he relied overwhelmingly on existing publications, wrote freely about what he knew very little, and borrowed from or even plagiarized other authors. He was successfully prosecuted for pirating one print and his *Isle of Wight*, he later admitted, was suggested by Sir Richard Worsley's *History* and indebted to it for most of its materials. He was criticized for inaccuracy, inappropriate citations, and failure to employ technical architectural terms. Some such faults were due to the speed with which he wrote, with an eye both to fame and profit. He lost on his *Tour of Lymington*, but made a handsome profit from *Clausentum*. His *Topographical Remarks* aimed not only to inform about

---

[13] R. Warner, *Literary Recollections* (1830), ii. 315–20; B.L. Add. MS. 33279, f. 42; Hants R.O. [hereafter H.R.O.], 14M86/1, p. 29.

[14] 'Proposals for Compiling and Publishing a Hist. of Hants': B.L. Add. MS. 42780A, ff. 119v.–120 (MS. of George Rose, signed by Warner); H.R.O. 16M79/127, pp. 2–3; and often appended to Warner's *Clausentum*. The next three paras. are based on *D.N.B.*; *Gent. Mag.* lxiii (2), 724, 742–4; Warner, *Topographical Remarks* (1793), i, pp. i–iii, 223–7, 266–7, 280–91; idem, *Literary Recollections*, i. 86, 190, 196, 248, 284 n., 285–6; ii. 320; H.R.O. 16M79/127; B.L. Add. MS. 33279, f. 42.

localities, but also 'to render it amusing to readers unconnected with the tract I have gone over' as well as to residents. Such motives explain his discussion of sanctuary under Beaulieu and the Templars under South Baddesley. This resulted in an extremely long-winded and self-consciously elegant prose, adorned with literary allusions and heavily footnoted. His model, he later admitted, was Dr. Johnson. The review in the *Gentleman's Magazine* found Warner's style affected and amplified by incorrect spellings, manufactured words, unnecessary Latinisms, and trite verses.

That Warner was ill-suited by objectives and competence to write a satisfactory county history is borne out by his notes, passed via Rose to William Bingley, who rebound them as one volume in 1809. Only 62 places are treated, many by notes only a few lines long, and only half a dozen short articles on places such as Ashe, Avington, and Crondall and families such as Brocas had been written. Longer than Gatehouse's 'Survey' and more elegantly written but addressed to the same audience, the notes consist of cursory accounts of the main estates, livings, and monuments, derived from printed sources and the Bodleian and British Museum libraries; there are no architectural descriptions and the bishops' registers were not used. Bar Speed's *Southampton*, Madden considered them 'very trifling' when shown them by Sir Thomas Phillipps, to whom Bingley sold them. Since 1979 they have been at Hampshire Record Office.[15]

Both when issuing his proposals and abandoning his 'History', Warner earnestly hoped that 'this desirable work may be speedily undertaken by someone more equal to the task than myself'. His wish was fulfilled in 1795 by *Collections for a History of Hampshire* by D.Y., five volumes in six, which is commonly known as Warner's *History of Hampshire* because of the prominence with which his name appears on the title-page. Warner denied any part in it and later denounced it as 'one of the most barefaced *piracies* ever committed on the literary property of an unfortunate author'. He did not sue, he claimed, only because of the lavish praise of himself included in the introduction, yet presumably it was he who had sold Grose's engravings to D.Y.[16] D.Y.'s own identity is not recorded: he claimed to have served James Harris, earl of Malmesbury (d. 1822), at Brookwood near Alresford and showed a muddled interest in law reform in his dedication to Francis Seymour-Conway, marquess of Hertford (d. 1820). Volume one, in two parts, is topographical; the next three are reprints, volume two of Warner's *Hampshire Domesday*, volume three of the Drivers' *General View of Agriculture*, and volume four of Philip Falle's *History of Jersey* (1734); volume five, on Guernsey and Sark, which runs to 14 lines, was plagiarized.

---

[15] Warner, *Literary Recollections*, i. 268–71; *Gent. Mag.* lxvii (2), 44.
[16] D.Y. *Collections*, i–vi, *passim*; *Gent. Mag.* lxvii (1), 44–7.

Only the topographical survey was new text and most of it was derivative. Much of the preliminary material is derived from Camden's *Britannia*, Thomas Cox's *Magna Britannia*, and the Drivers' *General View*. The alphabetical entries relate not to parishes or estates of Hampshire and the Isle of Wight but to places on which the author had information. Entries range from a sentence or a paragraph to the 63 pages on Christchurch taken from Warner's *Topographical Remarks*. That book and Worsley's *History* are reproduced almost in their entirety at different points and other entries are taken from *The Topographer* of Stebbing Shaw (d. 1802), Camden's *Britannia*, White's *Selborne*, and the *Progresses of Elizabeth I*. Apart from what is acknowledged, much else comes from the same sources, and the rest may also be plagiarized, since for many places no information is provided. So slavish are the borrowings that even footnotes are repeated, often giving the text an undeservedly learned appearance. The style varies with the source, new errors are introduced, and accounts from different authors are muddled or repeated. It cannot even be trusted for its own day, since accounts of the current situation are taken verbatim from sources published much earlier. Nor did the *Collections* popularize rarer works, since only 225 copies were published of the small paper edition and 25 of the larger.[17]

Having acquired Warner's collections, George Rose commissioned a history of Hampshire and the Isle of Wight from the Revd. William Bingley (1774–1823) on his appointment as curate of Christchurch in 1802. Bingley produced annual reports on progress in 1808–13. Already a botanist and author of distinction, he proved a good researcher and historian. He worked methodically through published books and the manuscripts of earlier compilers. He arranged notes by hundreds and parishes and composed articles on every parish until he needed only to consult the bishops' registers and current property owners for completion. Apart from manorial descents and advowsons, he treated population, land tax and poor rate, schools, charities, friendly societies, and other modern institutions concisely, precisely, and with appropriate technical terms. This was a worthy county history, but only the article on Bosmere hundred—212 pages long—was published, posthumously. Whilst Bingley blamed non-publication on financial difficulties and on Rose, his 6,000 pages of notes accumulated in 1802–17 vastly exceeded the three short volumes that Rose had wanted published in three years. Sir Thomas Phillipps bought Bingley's collections, which now consist of 141 items, mainly volumes, at Hampshire Record Office, two at the Bodleian Library, and the Christchurch volume in private hands.[18]

---

[17] *D.N.B.*
[18] H.R.O. 16M79/1–141, esp. 122; Bodl. MSS. Phillipps-Robinson e. 152; e. 154; W. Bingley, *Topographical Account of Hundred of Bosmere* (1817).

There were at least three other major 19th-century projects. By 6 January
1823 Nathaniel Lipscombe Kentish of Winchester had persuaded the duke of
Wellington and others to subscribe to a large-scale map of Hampshire and
supporting topographical survey, which he called 'Kentish's History'.
Material was collected and surveys undertaken but nothing was published
before Kentish's emigration to Australia.[19] Sir Frederic Madden (1801–73)
briefly planned a history in the early 1830s. Keeper of manuscripts at the
British Museum and the foremost palaeographer of his day, Madden was
'indefatigable in amassing manuscript material, much of which remains
unused'. Starting as a boy in Portsmouth, Madden assembled masses of notes
and transcripts, correspondence, and illustrations mainly on that area and
now split between the British and Bodleian libraries and Portsmouth Record
Office. He had consulted Gatehouse's 'Survey' and the collections of Warner
and Bingley and methodically listed materials for what promised to be the
most systematic, scholarly, and wide-ranging of county histories. Apart from
articles, nothing came of the project, presumably because his employment and
his other major publications constantly took priority.[20] So too did those of
Francis Joseph Baigent (d. 1918), whose more specific projects evidently came
first. Thirty-one volumes of notes in the British Library presented by
Cardinal Gasquet (d. 1929) include 14 arranged by parishes towards a
parochial history of Hampshire. The notes relate almost entirely to
ecclesiastical history, and mingle material from bishops' registers and modern
newspaper cuttings. Apparently little was written before the project was
superseded by the *V.C.H.*[21]

What was actually published in the 19th century was much less
impressive. Thomas Mudie's *Hampshire* of 1839 was a gentle perambulation
in three volumes. More substantial was the three-volume *General History of
Hampshire*, begun by B. Woodward, who treated Winchester at length, and
continued, corrected, and co-ordinated by T. C. Wilks. Published in 1861–9,
it consists principally of a topographical survey; the Isle of Wight was
treated by C. Lockhart. More of an incomplete perambulation than a
history, it is more valuable for the time when written than the past and
never 'could it have aspired to the position of a county history in any case',
as the *V.C.H.* somewhat unkindly put it. Nobody was more critical than
Wilks himself, hard though he had worked, who nevertheless deserves
credit for his criticism of long-established and groundless local legends.

---

[19] B.L. Add. MS. 33279, f. 33v.; *Hants Chronicle*, 6 Jan. 1823; *Hants Telegraph*, 13 Jan., 7 Apr.
1823; H.R.O. 3M60/9.
[20] *D.N.B.*; J. Webb, *Sir Frederick Madden and Portsmouth* (Portsmouth Paper xlvii, 1987); B.L.
Add. MSS. 33279–86; *Archaeologia*, xxiii (1831), 374–80.
[21] B.L. Add. MSS. 39959–94, esp. 39985, p. 184.

The weaknesses he ascribed particularly 'to the very scanty and meagre fruits of the literature which has the history of Hampshire for its subject'.[22] Less ambitious and more scholarly was the *History of Hampshire* (1892) of T. W. Shore of the Hartley Institution, who feared that 'owing to the increase of historical knowledge, the time for attempting to write the history of such a county as Hampshire, in one comprehensive work, may have passed away'.[23] Fortunately he was wrong, for the *Victoria History of the County of Hampshire and the Isle of Wight* was published in five volumes in 1900–12.

Few counties have owed as much to the *V.C.H.* as Hampshire. Where formerly there was nothing, every place was now provided with accounts of manors and churches that provided an essential framework for future local histories. The articles on the different boroughs and on the religious houses (by J. C. Cox) have also proved valuable, the other general articles less so. The *V.C.H.*, unlike earlier county histories, was strong on the public records; it was weak on records held locally and on local topography. Thus Benstead St. Clair was placed near Alton rather than Droxford.[24] In some respects it has been outdated by more modern surveys, such as Barbara Carpenter-Turner's *History of Hampshire*, first published in 1963, and the more academic *Portsmouth Region* (1989), and its treatment of Domesday Book has been superseded several times, most notably in Frank Barlow's *Winchester in the Early Middle Ages* (Winchester Studies i, 1976), but the manorial descents and advowsons remain invaluable.

One reason for the *V.C.H.*'s failings was its direction from London and apparent neglect of such local figures as Baigent and Shore, who were not members of the county committee. In 1885, somewhat belatedly by the standards of neighbouring counties, Hampshire acquired its own county society, the Hampshire Field Club, with Shore as the secretary, and in 1888 its own record society. The record society was anticipated by other editions printed by Warrens of Winchester[25] and by such works as Baigent and Millard's *History of Basingstoke* (1889). The *V.C.H.* built on such work and should have stimulated history locally, but it did not do so. Indeed there was a relative decline.

Several factors can be cited here. One was the nature of the county society.

[22] B. Woodward, T. C. Wilks, and C. Lockhart, *General Hist. of Hants*, esp. i, pp. vii, ix; *V.C.H. Hants*, i, p. xix.

[23] Shore, *Hist. of Hants* (1892), pp. vi–vii.

[24] *V.C.H. Hants*, ii. 485; C. L. Sinclair Williams, 'Manor of Bensted St Clair', *P.H.F.C.* xlii. 109–23. See also Hants Field Club [hereafter H.F.C.] *Newsletter*, new ser. xiii (1990).

[25] e.g. *Charter of Edward III Confirming and Enlarging Privileges of St. Giles Fair, Winchester, 1349*, ed. G. W. Kitchin (1886); *Consuetudinary of Refectory of House of St. Swithin in Winchester*, ed. G. W. Kitchin (1886).

Unlike its Dorset and Wiltshire counterparts, the Hampshire Field Club did
not include a county museum; it was founded late; and it was a field club rather
than an archaeological society, interested initially in excursions rather than
research and publication and lacking a library and a centre. When its character
changed, it became primarily concerned with archaeology in the modern
sense, adding 'and Archaeological Society' to its name in 1921, and contributed
substantially to an exceptionally distinguished record of archaeological
advance that still continues. J. P. Williams-Freeman, Heywood Sumner,
O. G. S. Crawford, Christopher Hawkes, Martin Biddle, and Barry Cunliffe
were all members of the Field Club. In 1985 Professor Cunliffe stated that more
Iron Age sites had been excavated in Hampshire than in the whole of the rest of
the country.[26] In recent years Cunliffe and M. Millett's excavations of Anglo-
Saxon villages at Chalton and Cowdery's Down, the campaigns of Biddle and
his successors on Winchester, and the city archaeological unit at Southampton
have made major contributions to Hampshire's medieval past. Apart from
articles in the Field Club's *Proceedings* and the national journals, archaeological
monographs are published nationally and under the aegis of the Field Club,
Biddle's *Winchester Studies*, and the city of Southampton.[27] Local history still
takes second place to archaeology within the Field Club.

Another factor was that interest was decentralized. The county record society
last published in 1897, perhaps because Latin ecclesiastical records had limited
appeal. Initiated by Dean G. W. Kitchin and dominated by the clergy, it
published 12 volumes in all, only two not primarily ecclesiastical.
Understandably, perhaps, Southampton established its own record society, now
the Southampton Record Series, which since 1905 has published over 50 volumes,
mainly on post-medieval records, but including relevant cartularies and the
unique brokage books.[28] Similarly the other Hampshire conurbation,
Portsmouth, set up its own record series (7 vols. 1971–90) and has now published
59 Portsmouth Papers. Postgraduate research at Southampton and Portsmouth
universities has focused on those cities rather than the rest of the county. The
joint directors of the Portsmouth local history diploma, Barry Stapleton and

---

[26] E. Taylor, 'One Hundred Years of Hants Field Club' and R. Whinney, 'One Hundred Years
of Hants Arch.' *P.H.F.C.* xli. 5–35; 'Reports on Centenary Year', ibid. xlii. 169–70; H.F.C.
Newsletter, new ser. x (1988), 7; R. T. Schadla-Hall and S. H. Shennan, *Arch. of Hants* (H.F.C.
monograph i, 1980).

[27] e.g. D. Keene, *Survey of Medieval Winchester* (2 vols., Winchester Studies ii, 1985); B.
Cunliffe and C. Poole, *Danebury: Iron Age Fort* (5 vols., C.B.A. Reports lii, lxxiii, 1984–91); B.
Cunliffe and J. Munby, *Excavations at Porchester Castle* (4 vols., Soc. of Antiq. Reports
xxxii–xxxiv, xliii, 1973–85); P. Holdsworth, *Excavations at Melbourne Street, Southampton* (C.B.A.
Report xxxiii, 1980); V. Evison, *Anglo-Saxon Cemetery at Alton* (H.F.C. monograph iv, 1988).

[28] E. L. C. Mullins, *Texts and Calendars* (2 vols., Royal Hist. Soc. Guides and Handbooks vii
and xii, 1958–83).

James Thomas, edited a thoroughly up-to-date history of the *Portsmouth Region* (1989). That Hampshire has contained such self-sufficient cities has detracted from local history elsewhere, which has been channelled into a host of very local societies, over 100 by 1990, their publications being predominantly on modern history, and into amateur parish histories published by Phillimore's.[29] Not surprisingly, some of the major editions of the early and mid 20th century were the work of the Canterbury and York and Royal Historical societies.[30]

The 1980s, in contrast, were a period of development. In 1979 the Field Club was reorganized with a local history section and with its *Proceedings* initiated regular publication of quality local history. Important factors here were the emergence of a large history department at King Alfred's College, Winchester, the growth of Hampshire Record Office, and the low-cost computer typesetting pioneered by Alan Sutton Publishing (then of Gloucester). Under the aegis in turn of Miss M. Cash and Miss R. Dunhill and encouraged by the leader of Hampshire county council Mr. F. A. J. Emery-Wallis, Hampshire Record Office established the Hampshire Record Series, which since 1976 has published 12 volumes of records in English and of somewhat wider range than the Hampshire Record Society; the Hampshire Field Club local history section (1979); the Hampshire Archives Trust (1986); and Hampshire Papers (1991). So successful was the trust's archivist in seeking out new records that a much larger purpose-built record office was opened in 1993.

The change should not be exaggerated. The amount that has been achieved remains relatively small. Hampshire still lacks an English Place-Name Society volume, editions of its sessions records and the collections of earlier county historians, and those accounts of county society in the 15th, 16th, and 17th centuries and the later Middle Ages that exist for so many other counties.[31] Very few research students or academics are undertaking original work on Hampshire and in particular little has been made of the exceptional riches of the bishop of Winchester's pipe rolls, though the county council has agreed to finance the three-year appointment of an editor. Much depends on the financial backing of the county council, which cannot be guaranteed. But certainly more is now being written and published on the history of Hampshire than ever before.

---

[29] e.g. C. Knowles, *Hist. of Sparsholt and Lainston* (1981); F. G. Standfield, *Hist. of East Meon* (1984).

[30] e.g. *Registrum Johannis de Pontissara*, ed. C. Deedes (2 vols., Canterbury & York Soc. xix, xx, 1915–24); *The Account-book of Beaulieu Abbey*, ed. S. F. Hockey (Camden 4th ser. xvi, 1975); also *Pipe Rolls of Bishopric of Winchester, 1208–9*, ed. H. Hall (1903).

[31] But see A. M. Coleby, *Central Government and Localities: Hants 1649–89* (1987).

HEREFORDSHIRE

Janet Cooper

Several attempts have been made since the mid 17th century to compile a history of Herefordshire, but although over 40 manuscript volumes of notes were accumulated, nothing was published until John Duncumb, under the patronage of the duke of Norfolk, published the first volume of his *Collections* for a history of the county in 1804. Between then and 1913 a further seven volumes of *Collections* were published, but the series remains incomplete. Contemplating the daunting amount of manuscript material and the lack of a published history, C. J. Robinson commented to the meeting of the Archaeological Institute at Hereford in 1877, 'To be a good historian of a county, a man should possess a variety of qualifications. Vigorous health, studious habits, untiring patience, and a facile pen should be his; but above all things he should have a full purse and a vein of stubborn but unobtrusive scepticism.'[1] It has been Herefordshire's misfortune that its would-be historians have lacked some of those qualifications, notably the vigorous health and the full purse.

Silas Taylor or Domville, who came from Harley near Much Wenlock in Shropshire, began work on a history of Herefordshire in the later 1650s, while he was a sequestrator of royalist lands in the county.[2] He planned to publish his work, and drafted an elaborate title-page and an introduction covering the political history of the county from Caratacus to 1135.[3] His sources included chronicles, bishops' registers, and other manuscripts from Hereford cathedral library, charters, Domesday Book, and other material from the public records. He illustrated his notes with some drawings of arms and of seals, but there are no other drawings. He added his own pungent observations on some places, such as Amberley,

> A small church . . . the ruins of which complain of bad neighbourhood subject to all the incommodities and disasters of despicableness, the churchyard being eaten up by the patrons, the steeple turned to a pigeon house, those birds not frightened by the noise of the bells because stolen away by a tinker.

At Goodrich he recorded the local belief that the floors of the castle were

---

[1] *Arch. Jnl.* xxxiv. 423.
[2] S. Taylor and S. Dale, *Hist. and Antiquities of Harwich* (1730), pp. viii–xi.
[3] B.L. Harl. MS. 6766, ff. 189–212v.

made of Irish earth 'so that if ever they brought a toad in and laid it on the floor it would die.'[4] Taylor's collections and drafts, in five or six volumes, came into the hands of Sir Edward Harley,[5] and are now part of the Harleian collection in the British Library.

Taylor left Herefordshire at the Restoration, and his work seems to have been unknown to the next collector of materials for the history of the county. Thomas Blount of Orleton (d. 1679) was a recusant lawyer and the author of several legal and antiquarian works, including a law dictionary or *Nomolexicon* (1670), *Animadversions upon Sir Richard Baker's Chronicle* (1671), and *Fragmenta Antiquitatis. Ancient Tenures of Land* (1679). He corresponded with other antiquaries, among them William Dugdale and Anthony Wood. In the 1670s he compiled two volumes of notes for a history of Herefordshire, arranged alphabetically by parishes, drawing on Domesday Book and other central government records as well as local charters and chronicles. His secondary sources included Leland's 'Itinerary' and Camden's *Britannia*. In addition, by 1678 he had visited 60 churches in the county. He recorded some traditions and legends, such as the story of St. Catherine Audley of Ledbury, and he described churches and their monuments, and other major buildings, but on the whole his work contains less personal comment than Taylor's.[6] The volumes remained in the Blount family, but the first one, covering the parishes whose names began with the letters A–K, was lost about the middle of the 18th century, apparently lent to Sir Robert Cornwall and not returned. The remaining volume was sold to Hereford City Library in 1956.[7]

In the early 18th century another Herefordshire antiquarian, William Brome of Withington, planned a book on the county, probably one concerned more with its archaeology than its history. Brome was a collector of antiquities who corresponded with Thomas Hearne, a fellow nonjuror, and he was one of those consulted by Browne Willis for help with his detailed account of Hereford cathedral.[8] In 1714 Hearne, writing to Brome to return some Roman coins found at Ariconium, said he supposed that other antiquities had been found there, 'of all of which we do not doubt but that you will give an exact account in your discourse on the county.' In 1724 Hearne noted, 'Mr. Brome told me today his book on the antiquities of Herefordshire is a folio, and I am

[4] Ibid. Harl. MS. 6726, ff. 90v., 118v.

[5] Ibid. Harl. MSS. 4046, 6726, 6766, 6856, 6868; Harl. MS. 4174 may also be Taylor's.

[6] Hereford Library, surviving vol. of Blount MSS.; Herefs. R.O., B56/12; T. Bongaerts, *Correspondence of Thomas Blount* (1978), *passim*; *Wood's Life and Times*, ii (Oxford Hist. Soc. xxi), 286; iv (Oxford Hist. Soc. xxx), 229; *D.N.B.*

[7] Bongaerts, *Correspondence of Thomas Blount*, 62–3.

[8] B. Willis, *Survey of Cathedrals of York, Durham, Carlisle, Chester, Man, Lichfield, Hereford, Worcester, Gloucester, and Bristol* (1727), p. vi.

apt to think 'tis large.'[9] In addition to his own collection of antiquities, Brome probably had access to Blount's notes on Herefordshire. His own work was known to Roger Gale and William Stukeley as well as to Hearne,[10] and his notes seem to have passed to another Herefordshire antiquary, Richard Walwyn (d. 1750).

Richard, the son of James Walwyn of Longworth, was working on the history of Herefordshire *c.* 1746 when he made notes from Blount's volumes. In 1749 he circulated 'Queries Relating to the County of Hereford', which he prefaced with the statement that he intended to 'attempt rescuing the small remains of former ages from the obscurity they are now buried in, that they may not be wholly lost to posterity.' The questionnaire was comprehensive, asking for information about the location and extent of each parish, its markets and fairs, trades, customs and tenures, 'fields of battle or burial places', place names, 'natural rarities', and medicinal springs, as well as about the manors, the church, religious houses, antiquities, and earthworks.[11] The book would have been a comprehensive one, but the project probably lapsed on Richard Walwyn's death in 1750, although his father James (d. 1766) added to the material he had collected on the county history; their manuscripts passed eventually to the Phillipps family, connexions by marriage of the Walwyns.[12]

Blount's volumes were also used by James Hill of Hereford, a barrister in the Middle Temple,[13] who amassed seven manuscript volumes of notes on Herefordshire between *c.* 1715 and 1722. He drafted a prospectus for a history in two volumes, one on the city and the other on the rest of the county. The scope of the second volume was ambitious. It was to contain a transcript of the Herefordshire Domesday and to deal with 'the ancient state of [the county's] inhabitants, of the several hundreds, their ancient names, extent, lords, privileges, and courts, of the foundation and endowment of parochial churches, of their monuments, inscriptions, chantries, and rights of incumbents, of monasteries, preceptories, and chapels' as well as with manors, honors, castles, and tenures, and with the families who had owned them. Finally it was to 'treat of the rise and privileges of boroughs, of their M.P.s and tenures, of Roman towns, urns, coins, pavements, as likewise of British, Saxon, and other pieces of Antiquity'.[14] It is perhaps not surprising that by

---

[9] *Hearne's Collections*, iv (Oxford Hist. Soc. xxxiv), 296, 304–7, 312, 317, 332; v (Oxford Hist. Soc. xlii), 79, 170, 176; viii (Oxford Hist. Soc. l), 211.

[10] Bongaerts, *Correspondence of Thomas Blount*, 207; *Memoirs of William Stukeley*, i (Surtees Soc. lxxiii), 204–5.

[11] Herefs. R.O., B56/12.

[12] Bongaerts, *Correspondence of Thomas Blount*, 67; C. J. Robinson, *Historic Mansions and Manors of Herefs.* (1872), 189 n.; Burke, *Landed Gentry* (1848 edn.), s.v. Phillipps of Longworth.

[13] *Alumni Oxonienses, 1500–1714*, ed. J. Foster (4 vols. 1891), ii. 710.

[14] Hereford Library, Hill MS. 5, f. 7.

1720 Hill had decided to publish only a history of the city, although one dealing mainly with the cathedral had been published, anonymously, by Richard Rawlinson in 1717,[15] and soon afterwards he seems to have abandoned the project altogether. In 1722 Hearne recorded that 'a worthy clergyman of Herefordshire' had told him that Mr. Hill had laid aside his Antiquities of Herefordshire, 'and that he hath little skill in these matters'.[16] The last judgement was probably too harsh. Hill was clearly well regarded as an antiquarian, and his manuscripts contain useful descriptions of churches and the monuments in them, some illustrated with good drawings.[17] Hill died late in 1727 or early in 1728, and his father at his request sent his collections to Roger Gale, who reported to Stukeley that although Hill had 'performed a good deal more than most people believed', he had left still 'a mere embryo of what he had promised'.[18]

Gale appears to have returned Hill's collections to his family. In 1752 they were bought from Hill's brother by Isaac Taylor of Ross-on-Wye, a surveyor who published a county map, on a scale of about 1 inch to the mile, in 1754. Taylor was clearly interested in antiquities, and his map shows churches, old 'seats' and newly built 'seats', castles, churches, chapels, foundations of ruined chapels, and 'camps' as well as hundreds, towns and villages, roads, rivers, and parks.[19] By 1753, however, he had given or lent Hill's volumes to John Roberts of Ross, a physician and antiquary, who added a further 10 manuscript volumes, including an index.[20] Roberts was presumably already working on Herefordshire history in 1749, when he was the recipient of one of Richard Walwyn's questionnaires, and he was still working on it in 1768, but he was forced by ill health to abandon thoughts of publication.[21] On his death in 1776 his manuscripts were left to, or reverted to, Taylor, who sold them at auction to Thomas Clarke of Hereford, the diocesan registrar. On Clarke's death c. 1780 they passed to James Clarke and then to John Allen, who repaired some of them in 1818.[22] By 1833 they belonged to Thomas Bird of Hereford (d. 1836) who collected a further 13 volumes of material on the

[15] [R. Rawlinson], *Hist. and Antiquities of City and Cathedral of Hereford* (1717).

[16] Hereford Library, Hill MS. 1, f. 1; *Memoirs of William Stukeley*, i. 205 n.; *Hearne's Collections*, viii. 7.

[17] e.g. Hereford Library, Hill MS. 1, ff. 285, 317, 333; MS. 3, ff. 9, 339, 359.

[18] *Memoirs of Stukeley*, i. 204–5.

[19] [R. Gough], *British Topography* (2 vols. 1780), i. 418; I. Taylor, *New Map of County of Hereford* (1754, reissued 1786).

[20] Hereford Library, Hill MSS.; Bodl. MS. Phillipps-Robinson e. 167, ff. iv.–2; *Alumni Oxonienses, 1715–1886*, ed. J. Foster (4 vols. 1888), iii. 1207.

[21] Herefs. R.O., B56/12; Hereford Library, Hill MS. 3, f. 82; ibid. Duncumb MS. Wormelow Hundred (2), letter from Walter Hill to Duncumb.

[22] Hereford Library, Hill MS. 5, pp. 1, 369, and last page in vol.; *D.N.B.* s.v. James Hill; [Gough], *British Topography*, i. 418.

county. Unlike the earlier collections Bird's notes are not arranged by place
and are in no sense a draft history. He used mainly printed sources, and
indexed parts of the *Annual Register* and the *Gentleman's Magazine*. His
collections, but not those of Hill and Roberts, passed to his brother and heir
Charles John Bird, who added several volumes to them.[23] The Bird collection
was given to Hereford Public Library by W. H. Vale in 1878.[24] Hill's and
Roberts's collections belonged in 1840 to Robert Biddulph Phillipps of
Longworth in Lugwardine, who had been working on the history of the
county as early as 1833.[25] One or two of Roberts's manuscripts were kept by
his widow and passed on her death to Roberts's great-nephew Walter Hill. In
1804 he made them available to Duncumb.[26]

Several attempts were made in the late 18th century to write a county
history. Richard Blyke (d. 1775), a member of the editorial committee for the
rolls of parliament, filled 22 volumes with notes on Herefordshire, taken
largely from the public records and arranged by subject. They were bought in
1780 by Lord Howard, later duke of Norfolk.[27] John Lodge of Leominster in
1793 published *Introductory Sketches towards a Topographical History of the
County of Hereford*, in fact the introductory chapters to a proposed county
history. The first chapter covered the physical appearance of the county, its
agriculture, customs, and climate, the second the pre-Roman and Roman
history, including a long account of the capture of Caratacus, and the third the
centuries from the departure of the Romans to the Civil War of the 1640s.
Lodge hoped, if given access to the 'libraries of the nobility and gentry of the
county', to publish a full history, devoting one volume to each hundred. He
appended to the published volume a long questionnaire, asking for
information on place names, the extent and population of parishes, customs,
manufactures, Nonconformist chapels, and natural history, as well as the
standard subjects, manors, antiquities, churches, and religious houses.[28] He
presumably abandoned the project on learning of the work being done by
John Duncumb. From *c.* 1790 John Price, also of Leominster, collected
material for the history of the county, but was for some reason unable to
complete the work. He did publish histories of Leominster in 1795 and of
Hereford in 1796. Both are substantial works, dealing with the history and
topography of the two towns, and including descriptions of public buildings,

---

[23] Bodl. MS. Phillipps-Robinson e. 167, f. 1v.; Hereford Library, Bird MSS.; Burke, *Landed
Gentry* (1937 edn.), s.v. Bird.

[24] Hereford Library, note in 1st vol. of T. Bird's collection.

[25] Ibid. Hill MS. 1, bookplate, f. 312v.; MS. 2, f. 297; Bodl. MS. Phillipps-Robinson e. 167, ff.
1v.–2, 5; ibid. d. 54; e. 168, *passim*.

[26] Hereford Library, Duncumb MS. Wormelow Hundred (2), letter from Hill to Duncumb.

[27] [Gough], *British Topography*, i. 410.

[28] J. Lodge, *Introductory Sketches towards Topographical Hist. of County of Hereford* (1793).

Nonconformist chapels, hospitals, and almshouses. The history of Hereford contains a map of the town and a ground plan of the cathedral. Price drew on Blount's manuscript and on local material including, for Leominster, the archives of Viscount Malden at Hampton Court; for Hereford he had the use of material collected by John Lodge.[29] A later historian of Leominster also drew on Blount's manuscript as well as on the borough muniments. George Fyler Townsend, vicar of Leominster, wrote his detailed account of *The Town and Borough of Leominster* about 1863; E. A. Freeman contributed a chapter on the parish church and priory.

John Duncumb, a Sussex man presented by the duke of Norfolk to the livings of Abbey Dore and Mansell Lacy, was employed by the duke, who held extensive lands in the county, to compile a history of Herefordshire. The duke had bought 'several' manuscript collections for the history of the county, including those of Richard Blyke and perhaps some of Roberts's volumes.[30] Duncumb also had access to Blount's and Walwyn's work, and used other manuscripts in the British Museum, the Bodleian Library, and the Augmentation Office in the Tower of London. Like Walwyn and Lodge he sent out lists of queries, asking about the boundaries of each parish, the owners of its manors, and about its rivers, mills, and turnpikes. He also asked about the soil and crops, and tried to get details of the amount of timber, meadow, pasture, arable, coppice, and waste in each parish. Finally he asked about the land tax and poor rates, and about the number of houses rated to or exempt from the window tax.[31] Had he been able to get the information his *Collections* would be a useful source of information about the early 19th century, but the questionnaires do not seem to have been answered. Duncumb's first volume, covering the city of Hereford, was published in 1804, and part of the second, covering Broxash hundred and Ewyas Lacy hundred, in 1812. Funding presumably ceased on the duke's death in 1815, but the remaining part of volume two, covering part of Greytree hundred, was issued by Thomas Thorpe, bookseller, in 1837. George Strong published in 1848 his *Heraldry of Herefordshire*, 'adapted to form a Supplement to Duncumb's County History'. The book is arranged by families, but contains brief notes of their seats, and a continuation of Duncumb's list of high sheriffs of Herefordshire from 1800 to 1847.

Robert Biddulph Phillipps, a wealthy landowner who was working on the history of the county by 1833, intended to complete Duncumb's work. To that

---

[29] J. Price, *Hist. and Topographical Account of Leominster and Vicinity* (1795); *Hist. Account of City of Hereford, with some Remarks on River Wye from Brobery to Wilton* (1796).

[30] J. Hutchinson, *Herefs. Biographies*, Appendix, p. 8; J. Duncumb, *Collections for Hist. of Herefs.* p. i; *D.N.B.* s.v. Blyke; Hereford Library, Duncumb MS. Wormelow Hundred (2), letter from Hill to Duncumb.

[31] Hereford Library, Duncumb MS. Broxash Hundred.

end he accumulated further notes, making use of title deeds and other material in the hands of his neighbours and other country gentlemen. He even appears to have gained access to the cathedral manuscripts, later said to be 'so jealously guarded that we are without any definite idea of their character'; he also acquired Hill's, Roberts's, and Walwyn's collections. Like so many of his predecessors, Phillipps died, in 1864, without having published anything. He bequeathed his papers to Belmont priory (later abbey) near Hereford, but several volumes of his notes became part of the collection of Sir Thomas Phillipps.[32]

Duncumb's work was continued, largely from his own manuscripts, by William Henry Cooke, a lawyer and deputy lieutenant of Herefordshire. Cooke published volume three, Greytree hundred, in 1882, and volume four, Grimsworth hundred, in two parts in 1886 and 1892; other work prevented him from doing more. About 1896 a committee, composed of Sir G. H. Cornewall, Bt., Sir Herbert Croft, Bt., the Revd. W. Poole, Michael Biddulph, M.P., and Paul Foley, was formed to continue the history, and two more volumes, on Huntington hundred and Radlow hundred, were published in 1897 and 1902, edited by Morgan G. Watkins, vicar of Kentchurch, mainly from Duncumb's manuscripts. By 1903 Watkins had proved 'quite incapable of the task' of completing the publication of Duncumb's work, and the committee had to find a new editor.[33] The search seems to have been difficult, but J. H. Matthews published Wormelow hundred, in two parts, in 1912 and 1913. The manuscript collections for Radlow, Stretford, Webtree, Wigmore, and Wolphy hundreds have been acquired by Hereford Library.

Publication of the later volumes of Duncumb's *History* was not easy. Funds were raised by subscription in 1900, and in the same year the committee overseeing the publication of the work approached Arthur Doubleday, editor of the *Victoria History of the Counties of England,* proposing that the V.C.H. should take over both the name of Duncumb's *History* and the *c.* £300 collected for it. Such an idea was, however, unacceptable to Doubleday. Part of the money was presumably used for Watkins's second volume and Matthews's two volumes. The residue, £120, was given by the trustees to the Woolhope Club in 1921, to be used if possible to continue Duncumb's *History* or else to publish in the Club's *Transactions* material which would advance the knowledge of the antiquities of the county. The club concluded that the continuation of the county history was impossible and established the Duncumb Fund to assist the publication of research.[34]

[32] *Arch. Jnl.* xxxiv. 429; Bodl. MSS. Phillipps-Robinson b. 47; c. 217; d. 54; e. 167–9, esp. e. 169, ff. 64v.–66v.; A. N. L. Munby, *Dispersal of Phillipps Library* (Phillipps Studies v, 1960), 110–11, 115.
[33] V.C.H. recs., A 8, Herefs.
[34] *Trans. Woolhope Naturalists' Field Club* (1921), pp. lxi–lxii, lxvi, lxxxvi.

The volumes produced by Duncumb and his successors were collections of material rather than finished histories. Duncumb himself started his account of each parish with a brief statement of its location, usually simply naming the neighbouring parishes. That was followed by an account of the church, with detailed descriptions and transcriptions of all monuments in it. Thereafter the parish collections are just that, a collection of excerpts from charters and other documents which do not necessarily tell a full, or even an accurate, story. The later Herefordshire historian, C. J. Robinson, commented, 'Mr. Duncumb's account of Brockhampton is singularly incorrect, and he has confused the descent of the place with that of Brockmanton in the parish of Pudleston'.[35] The fact that he did not even attempt to write a connected history made Duncumb particularly prone to confusion of that sort. Cooke and Watkins followed Duncumb's drafts closely, perpetuating his style and errors. J. H. Round's view of Cooke's continuation of Duncumb was characteristically caustic; he wrote of the account of Much Marcle, 'It would be difficult to compress more errors into thirteen lines (pp. 2–3) than has here been done in the early history of the Ballon family. It is worse than worthless.'[36] Matthews, perhaps because Duncumb had done less work on Wormelow hundred, or because he was a more competent historian, did search a wider range of sources for some parishes than his predecessors, but his work is patchy and remains a collection of notes and transcripts.

The nearest thing Herefordshire has to a county history is not Duncumb, but two volumes by Charles J. Robinson, *A History of the Castles of Herefordshire and their Lords* (1869) and *Historic Mansions and Manors of Herefordshire* (1872). The latter volume in particular does attempt to give a coherent account of every parish in the county, at least of its manors. Robinson himself disclaimed any pretence of writing a county history, saying in his preface, 'The following pages may be compared to a tesselated pavement wherein are *tesserae* both small and great of all shapes and shades. Some are mere fragments, others tolerably perfect'. His main interest seems to have been genealogy,[37] but he included architectural descriptions of churches and manor houses and noted recent rebuildings or restorations. He made use of charters, title deeds, court rolls, and parish registers, as well as the collections of Taylor, Blount, Hill, and Phillipps. Both volumes are well illustrated, mainly with contemporary drawings, although in the account of Sellack there is a drawing of the 'quaint old hall' demolished in 1826.

The Victoria County History published only one volume on Herefordshire, volume one. It contained articles on natural history, early man, Romano-

[35] Robinson, *Mansions and Manors of Herefs*. s.v. Bromyard.
[36] J. H. Round, *Studies in Peerage and Family Hist*. (1901), 206.
[37] B.L. Add. MS. 35280, *passim*.

12 The Woolhope Naturalists' Field Club at Goodrich, 1917

British remains, ancient earthworks (including Offa's Dyke), Domesday Book, political history, and agriculture. J. H. Round, with characteristic lack of modesty, described his own introduction to Domesday as being, 'apart from its learning . . . readable and interesting'.[38] An article on sport was written for volume two, and work had started on articles on ecclesiastical history and religious houses for the same volume when in 1909 the Herefordshire *History* had to be discontinued because of 'financial difficulties'.[39] The series has not been resumed.

The Woolhope Naturalists' Field Club was founded in 1851 for the 'practical study in all its branches of the Natural History of Herefordshire and the districts immediately adjacent'. As early as 1855 the club members visited a 'cromlech', perhaps as much to study its geology as its archaeology, and in 1869 an article on the 'Ancient Forest of Deerfold' contained an

[38] V.C.H. recs., A 47, 29 Jan. 1908.
[39] Ibid. A 8, Herefs., 12 Oct., 24 Nov. 1908; 22 June 1909.

account of Lollardy in the area and descriptions and drawings of old buildings. The club merged with the Herefordshire Philosophical, Literary, Antiquarian, and Natural History Society in 1862, but its stated aims were confined to natural history until 1893, when the study of archaeology was formally added to them.[40] The club, which continued in 1993, has published an increasing number of historical and archaeological articles in its *Transactions*.

[40] *Trans. Woolhope Naturalists' Field Club*, 'Rules' 1852, 1893; (1855), 151; (1862), 283.

HERTFORDSHIRE

Lionel Munby

Until the 20th century Hertfordshire was predominantly a rural county, though one within easy striking distance of London for those richer Londoners intent on retiring to the countryside. It was also blessed with a great many small market towns which often provided a focus for local loyalties stronger than that of the county itself, particularly as the county has always had a split personality between the western, Chiltern, half, looking to St. Albans, and the eastern portion, which had Hertford at its centre. Those features may help to explain the two outstanding facts about the local historiography of the county before 1945: an extremely vigorous tradition of small-town histories, but one which co-existed with an exceptionally large number of full-scale county histories. Since 1945, alongside the flowering of amateur local history that has affected all parts of England, there has been the added spice of the enormous changes in the balance of rural and urban within Hertfordshire which is essentially a result of the growth and overspill of the metropolis.[1]

Five completed county histories even before the *Victoria County History* is an unusually large number. The earliest, John Norden's *Description of Hartfordshire* (1598; later edns. 1723 and 1903), was 'rather the survey of a geographer, than the description of an historian', in the words of one of his successors.[2] Norden travelled in order 'to make more perfect descriptions, charts, and maps', and both described and extolled the soil, parks, woods, rivers, thoroughfares, and the healthful air. In his alphabetical table of towns, parishes, and hamlets the place names are eccentric, but there is also a sense of history, as in his observation that 'Hartford . . . hath beene most rob'd of her glory, by Wayres advancement, since the turning of the highway through it'.[3]

Sir Henry Chauncy's *Historical Antiquities* (1700; 2nd edn. 1826) was the first full county history. Originating at Ardeley, Chauncy was a lawyer and recorder of Hertford, besides being from a local family. He was 'conversant socially with

---

[1] L. M. Munby, *Herts. Landscape* (1977), esp. 25–41, 234–54.
[2] R. Clutterbuck, *Hist. and Antiquities of County of Hertford* (1815–27), i, p. i.
[3] J. Norden, *Speculi Britaniae pass: A Description of Hartfordshire* (1903 edn.), pp. ii, 2, 9, 18.

many of the families about whom he wrote',[4] and indeed aimed 'to serve such gentlemen as have lost their grants or charters' through contemporary upheavals. His social attitudes may be gauged from his comment that

> Mechanics ambitious of rule and government educate their sons in [the Inns of Court]; the gentry . . . prefer them in their business . . . qualifying their servants . . . to purchase their estates . . . whilst they . . . cause a scarcity of husbandmen, artificers, and servants.

At the same time, he had some views which seem more modern: properly educated, women would reveal their 'extraordinary qualifications'. Best of all, however, is his facility in describing his contemporaries. Ralph Freeman, for example,

> in the time of rebellion did quit all public imployments, affected a retired life, and pleased himself with the conversation of his children. He made his house neat, his gardens pleasant, his groves delicious, his children cheerful, his servants easie.[5]

The next Hertfordshire historian was the less well known Nathaniel Salmon, whose *History of Hertfordshire* (1728) describes the county's 'ancient monuments particularly the Roman, the chief possessors of the lands, and the most memorable occurrencies', as his title-page puts it. Salmon was curate at Westmill, a nonjuror in 1702, and then practised medicine at Bishop's Stortford. It has to be said that his treatment of place names and topography was distorted by his idiosyncratic views of Roman influence, but he also had many merits. In the first place he had access to unpublished additions and continuations left by Chauncy. On to that he grafted 'considerable material from his own research', and he was an acute observer of economic, especially agrarian, conditions.[6] Above all he wrote vividly, as in the phrase which he used of Kings Langley: 'The situation is well chosen, has a prospect down to the road . . . upon which the church and most of the houses stand . . . Here the rubbish of royalty exists'.[7]

Robert Clutterbuck published *The History and Antiquities of the County of Hertfordshire* between 1815 and 1827, in three giant folio volumes beautifully printed and illustrated with maps and drawings. According to Cussans he committed suicide by cutting his throat. A brewer of Watford with an ample fortune, he was 'on that account only, eminently qualified to write a county history'; 'he obtained access to many important muniment chambers [but]

---

[4] W. Branch Johnson, *Local Hist. in Herts.: a Brief Retrospect* (1964), 5, to which I owe much of the information in this chapter.

[5] H. Chauncy, *Hist. Antiquities* (1826 edn.), i, pp. xiii, xvii, 248–9; ii. 435.

[6] S. Doree, 'Nathaniel Salmon: Herts.'s Neglected Historian', *Herts. in Hist.* ed. D. Jones-Baker (1991), 207–9, 213, rehabilitates Salmon while making clear his faults.

[7] N. Salmon, *Hist. of Herts.* (1728), 113.

personally visited but few parishes [trusting] almost entirely to paid assistants'. As a result, it was only around Watford that his records of church inscriptions and monuments were accurate. Few people consult him with pleasure. While Cussans admitted that 'to Clutterbuck I owe very much', he added, 'I do not love him as I do Chauncy'. Clutterbuck followed the established pattern of county histories: in Branch Johnson's words, his achievement was that 'the story of Hertfordshire manors, churches and landed gentry is brought a century nearer our own time; [but] the short and simple annals of the poor will be looked for in vain'.[8]

The last of the Hertfordshire county historians was John Edwin Cussans. Although he never lived in the county, his *History of Hertfordshire* (1870–81; reprinted 1972) is the best of the pre-*V.C.H.* histories, mainly as the result of his conscientious labour. 'I have visited every parish and church in the county', he claimed.[9] Cussans carried Clutterbuck's book with him, a considerable muscular exercise in itself. Cussans's career was unusual for a county historian. Until 1863 he worked in the U.S.A. and Russia as a photographer and newspaper correspondent. From then until 1881 he lived by writing, though he was never well off and indeed lost £3,000 on *Hertfordshire*. While following the traditional pattern, Cussans added a great deal to it from his own likeable personality: 'more than any of his predecessors (and far more than the V.C.H.) Cussans liked people for their own sake, irrespective of social status—especially when he could take a humorous view of them'. His sympathetic wit can be seen, for example, in the moral that he drew from the absence of brass plates from many of the county's gravestones. Chauncy had simply complained that it made tracing manorial descents difficult. Cussans instead turned it into a jibe at the Protectorate's ban on Sunday games: 'it is but natural that the people forbidden to play at bowls on the green, should have sought amusement by the innocent relaxation of despoiling tombs of their brasses and church windows of their stained glass'.[10] Cussans's trenchant comments in a grangerized edition of his own book (now in the county record office) were at the time unprintable, but they have since been published in *A Professional Hertfordshire Tramp* (1987), Cussans's own description of himself.

The *V.C.H.* for Hertfordshire, completed in four volumes in 1914, thus represented the culmination of several hundred years of antiquarian and historical scholarship in the county. Its parish histories are much more reliable than anything earlier, though even they, by following the traditional

---

[8] J. E. Cussans, *A Professional Herts. Tramp*, ed. A. Deacon and P. Walne (1987), 39, 103; Branch Johnson, *Local Hist. in Herts.* 9.

[9] Cussans, *Professional Tramp*, 103.

[10] Chauncy, *Hist. Antiquities* (1826), i, p. xviii; J. E. Cussans, *Hist. of Herts.* (1972 edn.), i, Introduction, p. x; Braughing hundred, p. 15.

path of tracing the ownership of the manor, omit what was often the most important factor influencing the lives of other residents, namely who actually occupied the manor house. In other respects they broke new ground. The Hertfordshire volumes were edited by William Page, the general editor of the *V.C.H.* Page was a pioneer topographer, whose paper on the origins and forms of Hertfordshire towns and villages anticipated W. G. Hoskins and other modern historians.[11] Page had strong Hertfordshire connexions, since his sister was the wife of the Hertfordshire antiquary and record agent W. J. Hardy, and he himself lived at St. Albans between 1896 and 1902, when he moved to London on being appointed editor of the *V.C.H.*[12] His strength of feeling for the county is evident in what he wrote for *V.C.H. Hertfordshire*: many of the general descriptions and manorial descents, some parish histories, the pre-Conquest sections of the ecclesiastical and St. Albans histories, and an essay on Celtic and Romano-British Hertfordshire. As general editor, he was also largely responsible for the outline history and topographical description which opens each parish history and in which important residences and their contemporary owners are named, information which has now become historically important.

Genealogy bulks large in all the county histories up to and including the *V.C.H.*, where Hertfordshire was one of only two counties to have an accompanying volume of pedigrees, Duncan Warrand's *Hertfordshire Families* (1907). Similar volumes had originally been projected for all counties. Warrand's volume gives full pedigrees of 12 families 'whose long association with their county has made them a part of its history [and who possess] a freehold domain of such importance that the phrase "a seat and landed estate" may be reasonably used concerning it'.[13] Warrand's introduction to the volume mentioned more briefly another 57 families.

The vast expenditure of effort on full-scale county histories did not preclude much that was worth while in the way of town histories. The earliest (1631) was John Shrimpton's *Antiquities of St. Albans* (ed. Carson I. A. Ritchie, 1966). Shrimpton, son of an ale brewer in the town, concentrated on the abbey and the three parish churches, and notably on their monumental and other inscriptions, but he also alluded incidentally to local people and events. Much of what he wrote is in verse. Of the other towns, Hitchin has been much the best served, though the first effort, Isaac James's manuscript history written between 1785 and 1826, is more compilation than history proper.[14] More interesting and durable was the work of his contemporary

---

[11] W. Page, 'Origins and Forms of Herts. Towns and Villages', *Archaeologia*, lxix (1917); ibid. 2nd ser. xix (1920), 47–60.
[12] *V.C.H.* Rut. ii, pp. ix–xi.
[13] *V.C.H. Herts. Families*, p. xviii.
[14] R. L. Hine, *Hist. of Hitchin*, i (1927), 314–16.

13 William Page

William Dunnage, successively bank clerk and postmaster in Hitchin, who began a manuscript history in 1776 and completed it in 1815. His work has been much used by later historians and may be printed in the near future.[15]

The first modern town history in Hertfordshire (modern in its critical use of sources) was Lewis Turnor's *Hertford* (1830). In his preface Turnor justifiably claimed that 'he has never taken any statement upon trust, however imposing might be the name with which it is associated; neither has he set down any fact without having the best evidence of its authenticity'.[16] He combined antiquarian thoroughness with much institutional, political, and social history. In contrast to Hitchin, Hertford has no later all-embracing town history, though there have been specialized studies of the castle, Christ's Hospital, and the Quakers.[17]

For Berkhamsted, pride in local improvements suffuses J. W. Cobb's *History and Antiquities of Berkhamsted* (1855 and 1883), originally written as two lectures to the Mechanics' Institute, each of 50 printed pages. Cobb's local pride is evident in his peroration: 'Our canal, our railway, our gas, and last, though not least, our Mechanics' Institute, are all proofs of advancement in civilization . . . they are tokens of essential prosperity'. Alfred Kingston's *Royston* (1906), which makes full use of quoted local sources, reveals just how intellectually lively a small country town could be 200 years ago; he also wrote with affection of the uniqueness of Royston heath, 'a never failing attraction to all residing in the town'.[18] J. A. Tregelles's *Hoddesdon* (1908) was based on manuscripts and notes by the late Alexander McKenzie, moving remorselessly to a 'chronicle' 159 pages long; its author admitted that it 'may be very like dry bones'.[19]

Hitchin continued to attract historians of the first calibre in the late 19th century and the 20th. Frederic Seebohm, from a local family, wrote his classic *English Village Community* (1883) on the basis of investigating its open fields. Seebohm was a pioneer in the study of field systems and the book closes with far-sighted ideas about continuity from Roman times into the medieval period. The outstanding Hertfordshire town historian of the 20th century, however, was Reginald L. Hine, who published a two-volume *History of Hitchin* (1927–9) and *Hitchin Worthies* (1932). Hine was an original, his writing anything but dreary or dry-as-dust. By profession he was a solicitor in an ancient Hitchin firm; by inclination he soaked himself in their accumulated

[15] W. Dunnage, 'Hist. of Hitchin' (MS. in Hitchin Museum).
[16] L. Turnor, *Hist. of Ancient Town and Borough of Hertford* (1830), pp. vi–vii.
[17] H. C. Andrews, *Chronicles of Hertford Castle* (1947); W. Lempriere, *Hist. of Girls' School of Christ's Hospital* (1924); F. M. Page, *Christ's Hospital, Hertford* (1953); V. A. Rowe, *The First Hertford Quakers* (1970).
[18] A. Kingston, *Hist. of Royston* (1906), 196.
[19] J. A. Tregelles, *Hist. of Hoddesdon* (1908), p. viii.

records. His autobiography, *Confessions of an Uncommon Attorney* (1946–63), is very revealing about him. St. Albans and its Roman predecessor Verulamium have been much studied in the 20th century.[20] The best general history was that in volume two of the *V.C.H.*, until Elsie Toms published her scholarly and readable *The Story of St. Albans* in 1962. Other towns with histories published since 1945 have been Ware, Stevenage, Hitchin (again), and Hemel Hempstead.[21]

Meanwhile, from the late 19th century onwards, there was a huge increase in the publication of local history. The existence of two sub-county publishing societies dates back to the county's split personality already mentioned. Because east–west communications were bad, the county until 1874 had two separate quarter sessions, and from 1889 the new county council also met, alternately, in both Hertford and St. Albans. It was 50 years before it settled in Hertford. No wonder two archaeological societies were created: the St. Albans and Hertfordshire Architectural and Archaeological Society in 1845 (its *Transactions* began in 1884) and the East Herts. Archaeological Society and its *Transactions* in 1898. The two *Transactions* merged into *Hertfordshire Archaeology* only in 1968. In the late 19th century an explosion of local history writing began among groups of people who gathered round each society: Page, Hardy, Gibbs, Seebohm, and the Evans brothers at St. Albans; the Andrewses, Glasscock, Tregelles, and Gerish in the East Herts. Society. The first interest of most of them was the Church. J. L. Glasscock's *Records of St. Michael's Parish Church, Bishop's Stortford* (1882) was a transcript of churchwardens' accounts for 1431–1847 with full notes. The monumental *Nonconformity in Herts.* (1884) by William Urwick, a St. Albans Congregational pastor, started with the Lollards but emphasized the 17th century. In 1895 the first of four volumes of W. J. Hardy's *Middlesex and Hertfordshire Notes and Queries* and the first of three volumes of William Brigg of Harpenden's *Herts. Genealogist and Antiquary* appeared. Hardy spanned everything from parish history to vanishing landmarks; Brigg transcribed ecclesiastical and genealogical documents in maddeningly chaotic instalments (on the grounds that his 'work was almost entirely done in spare time').[22]

Interest in the development of local government explains both Glasscock's

[20] L. F. Rushbrook, *Hist. of Abbey of St. Albans* (1917); A. E. Levett, 'Studies in Manorial Organization of St. Albans Abbey', *Studies in Manorial Hist.* ed. H. M. Cam, M. Coate, and L. S. Sutherland (1938), 69–286; P. Corder, 'Verulamium, 1930–40', *Antiquity*, xv (1941), 113–24; S. S. Frere, 'Verulamium, Three Roman Cities', *Antiquity*, xxxviii (1964), 103–12; E. Roberts, *Hill of the Martyr* (1993).

[21] E. Hunt, *Hist. of Ware* (1946–9); R. Trow-Smith, *Hist. of Stevenage* (1958); A. Foster, *Market Town: Hitchin in 19th Century* (1987); *Hist. of Hemel Hempstead*, ed. S. Yaxley (1973).

[22] W. Brigg, *Herts. Genealogist and Antiq.* i (1895), prefatory note.

inclusion of secular records and A. E. Gibbs's *Corporation Records of St. Albans* (1890), which summarizes 'every event of local or antiquarian interest' mentioned in the manuscripts.[23] The county council entrusted W. J. Hardy with the editing of two volumes of quarter sessions rolls, published in 1905 with a third volume in 1910. There were also notable developments before 1914 in architectural history, in both cases as part of series conceived on a national scale. Herbert Tomkins's *Little Guide* (1903) was one of the best in its series, catholic in its coverage, and the Royal Commission on the Historical Monuments of England's *Inventory* (1910) for Hertfordshire was the very first one published. Both volumes, though quite different in concept, have comprehensive and enlightening introductions.

Between the wars there was something of a lull in publishing, though further volumes of quarter sessions records appeared (1923–39) and there was the important work on St. Albans and Hitchin already mentioned. The most interesting and influential work on a single parish was *Hexton: A Parish Survey* (1936), compiled by children in the village elementary school under the guidance of their headmaster Ralph Whiteman. It included both history and contemporary description and became a model copied elsewhere.

After the Second World War new county and local societies and adult education classes reflected and in turn fostered renewed interest in local history. The Local History Council (1949/50), now the Hertfordshire Association for Local History, published *Hertfordshire Past and Present* between 1960 and 1976, which was succeeded in 1976 by *Hertfordshire Past* with the collaboration of the Archaeological Council, itself founded in 1966. The Family and Population History Society, established in 1977, publishes *Hertfordshire People*. The Local History Council also publishes occasional papers, the first being M. F. Thwaite's *Hertfordshire Newspapers, 1772–1955* (1956). The series became Hertfordshire Publications in 1978, since when it has been produced jointly with the county library service. Books and substantial booklets by authors from all kinds of background have appeared under the two imprints, ranging from Rutherford Davis's *Deserted Medieval Villages* (1973; 2nd edn. 1982) to Allen Eyles and Keith Skone's *Cinemas* (1985).

Adult education classes have also been active in publishing both local histories and transcripts of wills. *Hatfield and its People* (1959–64) and *Wheathampstead and Harpenden* (1973–91) were both the result of co-operative authorship, resulting in series of booklets which amount to comprehensive book-length histories. *Life and Death in Kings Langley, 1498–1659* (1981) is a scholarly edition of local wills. The Hertfordshire Record

---

[23] A. E. Gibbs, *Corporation Recs. of St. Albans* (1890), preface.

Society, publishing annually from 1985, concentrated on the Tudor and Stuart periods, with Anthony Palmer's *Tudor Churchwardens' Accounts* (1985), my *Early Stuart Household Accounts* (1986), which contains transcripts of a 1635 account of the earl of Salisbury's clerk of the kitchen and the 1637–9 house book of Gorhambury, and Stephen Doree's *Parish Register and Tithing Book of Thomas Hassall of Amwell* (1989), whose illuminating introduction casts light on the tribulations of a 17th-century parson. So many individual monographs and theses have appeared in recent years that it would be invidious to pick out what seem at the moment to be the more outstanding or interesting examples, except perhaps for B. J. Davey's *Ashwell 1830–1914: the Decline of a Village Community* (1980), which traces the disappearance of what the author calls the 'old community', attributing much to the effects of rising and falling population, and explaining Ashwell's particularities, especially the importance of craftsmen. *Ashwell* crystallizes many of the ideas of the 'Leicester school' of English local history. Mention must also be made of the extensive work of W. Branch Johnson.[24]

The county council, formed in 1889, has had an influential role in the development of local history in Hertfordshire, because from the first it showed a strong interest in its own history. As early as 1895 it appointed a committee to 'report upon the question of the county records'.[25] Sir John Evans, better known in connexion with Knossos, had been chairman of quarter sessions, then chaired the Hertfordshire Records Committee, and in 1901 became chairman of the county council. The Records Committee 'resolved that a properly built strong room should be provided, fire, burglar, and damp proof'; it was completed in 1909, with heating and air conditioning. The room, approved in 1927 for the storage of manorial records, continued in use until 1952. In August 1939 up-to-date strong rooms and offices in the new county hall were ready and a permanent records clerk was appointed.[26]

The records were sorted and listed from 1895 by Page and Hardy, brothers-in-law and partners in a firm of record agents; Hardy became record agent to the county, serving until 1919. His son Col. William Le Hardy succeeded him and in 1946 became county archivist. Under them the county council published 10 volumes of quarter sessions records, seven edited by Le Hardy, whose *Guide to the Hertfordshire Record Office: Part I* (1961) has not been continued, though there are useful short guides to parts of the collections. Le Hardy's prefaces are in effect a running history of quarter sessions

---

[24] *Carrington Diary, 1797–1810* (1956); *Companion into Herts.* (1957); *Little Guide: Herts.* (1957); *Herts. Inns* (1962–3); *Herts.* (1970); *Industrial Arch. of Herts.* (1970); and (as editor) '*Memorandums for . . .': Diary of John Carrington* (1973).

[25] G. Sheldrick, *Hart Reguardant: Herts. County Council, 1889–1989* (1989), 24.

[26] *Guide to Herts. R.O.: Part 1*, ed. W. Le Hardy (1961), pp. x–xi.

government, full of information about social, economic, and religious history. The county council has also given financial support to the Local History Council, the Hertfordshire Record Society, and Hertfordshire Publications. With justifiable pride it published under the last imprint *The Hart Reguardant* (1989), Gillian Sheldrick's centenary history, which tells of growing administrative responsibilities, a corresponding apparatus, and the changing nature of councillors and officials. It is a pleasure to find a book which makes modern local government history interesting.

A distinctive feature of Hertfordshire's history in the 20th century has been the planning of garden cities and new towns, topics covered in C. B. Purdom, *Letchworth Achievement* (1963), R. E. Pahl, *Urbs in Rure* (1964), and my own *Hertfordshire Landscape* (1977). A recurrent refrain among commentators on the changing scene has been that of protest against the latest arrivals by those established only a little longer. *Notes and Queries* in 1897 wrote that 'new railways soon bring with them the means for destroying rusticity' and urged 'let the residents who need a rustic home within easy reach of London [refuse] to sell their land for building'.[27] The final word of disillusionment with the charms of Hertfordshire should perhaps be left to the vicar of St. Ippolyts: in 1857 he thought that 'this is undeniably a gentlemenly county', but years later, knowing his village better, he condemned it as 'a nest of typhoid and scarlet fever, involving difficult sewage questions'.[28]

[27] *Mdx. and Herts. Notes and Queries*, iii. 4, 167.
[28] D. Rance, *St. Ippolyts* (1987), 95, 97.

HUNTINGDONSHIRE

C. P. Lewis

It is difficult to find a precise reason why Huntingdonshire was so badly served by antiquarian scholarship before 1900, though later successes are more easily explained.[1] The county was small, low in population, almost wholly agricultural, and with no large or even middling town. Even in the 20th century those factors affected its treatment, since country-wide series, whether popular or scholarly, tended to add Huntingdonshire to some other county (normally Bedfordshire) rather than lavish a separate volume on it.[2] Because there were fewer parish clergy and gentry than in larger counties, the market for county histories and the pool of potential authors were both small. The only one completed on the traditional model was the *Victoria County History* (1926–38), a success based firmly on the co-operation of local funding, central organization, and the expertise and sources available in London and locally.

Huntingdonshire historiography is scattered (though not liberally) with proposed histories that failed to get subscribers, and manuscript collections that were begun and abandoned or were completed and then lost. The most tantalizing might-have-been came at the beginning, in the county history contemplated in the late 16th century by one of the greatest scholars of the age, Robert Cotton (1571–1631). Cotton had the perfect background for a pioneering county historian: born to a long-established local landed family, educated at Westminster school under no less an antiquary than William Camden (at that precise moment preparing *Britannia*), and sufficiently leisured in his early maturity to indulge antiquarian tastes. Cotton began collecting material in his youth for a county history, and later started a second and more detailed Huntingdonshire notebook, but pursued neither. By his early 20s he was concentrating instead on his library and on contacts with scholars throughout western Europe. In comparison with the breadth of his

---

[1] The help of Dr. Philip Saunders, archivist at Cambs. R.O., Huntingdon [hereafter Hunts. R.O.], in providing much additional information is gratefully acknowledged.

[2] e.g. P. Bigmore, *Beds. and Hunts. Landscape* (1979); E. A. R. Ennion, *Cambs., Hunts., and Isle of Ely* (1951); H. W. Macklin, *Beds. and Hunts.* (1917; 2nd edn. revised by P. G. Langdon, 1929); A. Mawer and F. M. Stenton, *Place-Names of Beds. and Hunts.* (E.P.N.S. iii, 1926); A. Mee, *The King's England: Beds. and Hunts.* (1939; 2nd edn. revised by J. Godber and P. Dickinson, 1973); N. Pevsner, *Buildings of England: Beds. and County of Huntingdon and Peterborough* (1968).

later career, his early passion for topography looks like a youthful enthusiasm that was soon forgotten.[3] Two of his notebooks survive. One, written in 1588 when he was 18, has extracts from Ramsey abbey's Anglo-Saxon charters, Domesday Book, and the *Nomina Villarum* of 1316, and from a wider range for his home parish of Conington.[4] The other extended the fuller set of sources to more places, making use of at least five monastic cartularies and several classes of public records scattered in London. The order of the parishes is rather haphazard, but an alphabetical index was added in 1630 by Robert Bernard,[5] later recorder of Huntingdon and a prominent figure in the county.[6] Several of Cotton's sources were either already in his library or ended up there, including a transcript of Domesday Book for Huntingdonshire,[7] and the cartulary of Northampton abbey, which probably belonged to a fellow antiquary, Francis Tate (1560–1616), when Cotton used it.[8] Another manuscript which he may have known is a compilation of sources for Cambridgeshire and Huntingdonshire, including the *Nomina Villarum*, close, patent, and hundred rolls, and inquisitions *post mortem*, though it has no proven connexion with him.[9] Cotton did not lose all interest in his native county on reaching manhood, since he can plausibly be identified as the 'right worthy and learned Friend' who supplied John Speed with the description of Huntingdonshire printed in *The Theatre of the Empire of Great Britain* (1611). The piece is prolix and erudite, with copious marginal references to the sources appearing in Cotton's later notebook, and dwells at some length on Conington and the Cottons.[10] Disguised as Speed, Cotton passed into the mainstream of England-wide topographical compilations.[11] Judging from Speed, a larger work of county history from Cotton's pen would have been scholarly and full of insights but almost unreadable. As it was, Cotton was simply a false start.

Cotton's successor in Huntingdonshire was Richard Astry (?1632–1714), son of a small landowner, educated at Cambridge University, and an alderman of Huntingdon.[12] Astry kept a notebook of county topography, arranged

---

[3] *D.N.B.*; K. Sharpe, *Sir Robert Cotton, 1586–1631: Hist. and Politics in Early Modern England* (1979), esp. 11–13, 19, 24, 41–2, 50, 198, 219; [R. Gough], *British Topography* (2 vols. 1780), i. 435.

[4] Cambs. R.O. 588/Z 1; photocopy of relevant parts in Hunts. R.O., Acc. 4179.

[5] Hunts. R.O., M20B/10.

[6] G. E. C[okayne], *Complete Baronetage* (6 vols. 1900–9), iii. 249–50; *V.C.H. Hunts.* ii. 17, 131, 179, 184, 306.

[7] B.L. Cott. MS. Tib. E. viii, ff. 265–279v.

[8] Ibid. Cott. MS. Tib. E. v; G. R. C. Davis, *Medieval Cartularies of Great Britain* (1958), no. 698; *D.N.B.* s.v. Tate.

[9] B.L. Add. MS. 33358; inf. from Dr. Nigel Ramsay, B.L.

[10] J. Speed, *Theatre of Empire of Great Britain* (facsimile of 1676 edn., 1991), 57–8; Sharpe, *Cotton*, 38.

[11] e.g. T. Cox, *Magna Britannia et Hibernia* (6 vols. 1720–31, reissued 1738), ii. 1043–70 at 1044.

[12] *D.N.B.*; R. E. C. Waters, *Genealogical Memoirs of Families of Chester and Astry* (1881), 69–70.

alphabetically from Abbotsley to Yelling, which he added to at intervals over some 40 years.[13] Among secondary works he made use of Leland, Camden, and Speed; his original sources included Domesday Book, charters, and the heraldic visitation of 1613; and he appears to have visited the county's churches fairly systematically. Astry is most useful for his own period: one-line descriptions that bring places alive (like the 'delectable additions' at Hinchingbrooke), glimpses of the Church (an 'exceeding good preacher' at Eynesbury),[14] and priceless notes on changes in the ownership of manors and local manorial customs. Although he supplied information to the antiquary Edmund Gibson, later bishop of Lincoln,[15] Astry's main scholarly interest was not local history at all: he was fascinated by personal names.[16] The man who first gleefully recorded the surnames of the Huntingdonshire grand jury of 1619 (King, Prince, Duke, Marquess, Earl, Baron, Lord, Knight, Squire, Gentleman, Yeoman, Pope, Cardinal, Abbot, Monk, Friar, Priest, Prior, Archdeacon, Bishop, Dean, and Deacon)[17] would surely have revelled in the most famous (but fictitious) list of names from the county, Beachcomber's *Huntingdonshire Cabmen*, especially the final volume (Ruxton–Zoroaster).[18] Oddly, and despite its internal dating evidence, Astry's notebook was long believed to be Cotton's.[19] It was mined by later county antiquaries and the V.C.H. but its main effect is to cause regret that such an acute observer did not write more.

The middle years of the 18th century saw a quickening of antiquarian activity, even in Huntingdonshire. Part of the stimulus there may have come from the establishment in 1730 of the Gentlemen's Society of Peterborough (Northants.) in imitation of the older society at Spalding (Lincs.). Its early members included two of the most active Huntingdonshire antiquaries of that era, John Clement and the Revd. Robert Smyth.[20] Clement (1711–42), whose father was lessee of part of Woodston rectory land,[21] was probably the more ambitious of the two. He gathered information on lords of manors from inquisitions *post mortem* and heraldic visitations, on incumbents and patrons from the diocesan registry at Lincoln, and by visiting the county's churches. By 1739 he had a clear plan:

---

[13] B.L. Lansd. MS. 921.

[14] Ibid. ff. 7, 31v.

[15] [Gough], *British Topography*, i. 435; for Gibson as antiquary: *D.N.B.*

[16] *D.N.B.*

[17] B.L. Lansd. MS. 921, f. 90; the story behind the summoning of the jury is well told in W. H. B. Saunders, *Legends and Traditions of Hunts.* (1888), 202–3.

[18] No copy of that important work in B.L.; see instead *Beachcomber: the Works of J. B. Morton*, ed. R. Ingrams (1974), 152, 213, 254; *Best of Beachcomber*, ed. M. Frayn (1963), 207–9.

[19] *D.N.B.* s.v. Astry.

[20] 'Gentlemen's Soc. of Peterborough', *Fenland Notes and Queries*, iv. 384–91; v. 12–16, 53–6.

[21] Ibid. iv. 386; G. C. Gorham, *Hist. and Antiquities of Eynesbury and St. Neot's (Hunts.) and St. Neot's (Cornw.)* (2 vols. 1820–4), i. 163–4; inf. from Dr. Saunders, citing Woodston parish recs. in Hunts. R.O.

I purpose in the first place treating of the County in general, next of the
Hundreds & the Towns in each of them in alphabetical order, giving an account
Genealogical & historical from the Norman Conquest to the present time of the
Lords of them, with Pedigrees of other remarkable families. Also an account of
the several Churches & Chapels, their founders, (as many as I can recover)
dimensions, monuments, funeral inscriptions, arms, number of bells, &
inscriptions thereon, benefactions to Churches & Poor, remarkable Transactions,
& in an appendix the most material charters &c. & for the ornamental part of the
work I intend Draughts of the Gentlemen's Seats & of every Church & Chapel in
the county & of the most remarkable monuments therein, & of any other
Antiquity which occurs worth preserving.[22]

Clement's history would have been of a conventional enough kind, but he
died too young to complete it.

Clement's papers probably passed to the Revd. Robert Smyth (*c.*
1700–1761),[23] who was rector of Woodston from 1730.[24] Smyth worked on
other counties besides Huntingdonshire, though his main interest was not
antiquities or parochial history but the history of sheriffs.[25] He never
published, apparently because he was 'too confined in circumstances, either to
afford the leisure, or to run the hazard, of committing the result of his
researches to the press', and many of his papers were destroyed after his death
by his illiterate brother, though others survived and in the early 19th century
were in the hands of the topographical printer John Nichols (1745–1826). For
Huntingdonshire they included collections of monumental inscriptions which
built on and corrected those made by Clement.[26]

Other mid 18th-century collections which included a little Huntingdonshire material acquired in the course of other interests were those of the
Cambridgeshire antiquaries Brock Rand (1697–1753)[27] and William Cole
(1714–82),[28] and that of the Bromley house-painter Edward Steele,[29] whose
slim Huntingdonshire notebook contains perfunctory lists of 18th-century
parish clergy, notes of arms and inscriptions in churches, and records of fires,

---

[22] Bodl. MS. Willis 39, ff. 231–3 (Clement to Browne Willis, 4 Dec. 1739; 6 Sept. 1740).

[23] Gorham, *Hist. Eynesbury and St. Neot's*, i. 163–4.

[24] *Trans. Cambs. and Hunts. Arch. Soc.* iii. 276; *Alumni Cantabrigienses to 1751*, ed. J. and J. A.
Venn (4 vols. 1922–7), iv. 108.

[25] e.g. J. and J. B. Nichols, *Illustrations of Literary Hist. of 18th Century* (8 vols. 1817–58), iv.
355–7; T. Harwood, *Survey of Staffs.* (1844 edn.), pp. lxxxiv–lxxxv; B.L. Stowe MS. 753, ff. 33–4.

[26] J. Nichols, *Literary Anecdotes of 18th Century* (9 vols. 1812–15), v. 47–50.

[27] B.L. Add. MS. 5847, ff. 55v.–58v., 63, 65v. (Cole's extracts from Rand's MS.); *Alumni
Cantabrigienses to 1751*, iii. 418.

[28] e.g. B.L. Add. MSS. 5837–8; *D.N.B.*

[29] For whom: B.L. Add. MS. 6223, esp. ff. 30v., 37–40v.; *Catalogue of Books, Tracts, MSS., and
Coins of Edward Steele, Painter* (1758) and *Catalogue of Natural and Artificial Rarities and Other
Curiosities of Edward Steele, Painter* (1759): copies in B.L. printed books, C.119.h.3 (39–40); and
Summary Catalogue of Western MSS. in Bodl. vii (1953), s.v. Steele.

floods, and drownings in the county.[30] From a little later there is a scrappy notebook of Huntingdonshire material by Sir Joseph Ayloffe (1709–81) and Richard Gough (1735–1809), mainly consisting of notes on churches.[31] All in all, though, one of the most prolific periods for county history proved a virtual blank in Huntingdonshire.

Just as Robert Smyth died, in 1761, another clergyman and would-be historian of Huntingdonshire was appointed to a parish in the county. Benjamin Hutchinson was rector of Kimbolton 1761–94 and of Holywell cum Needingworth 1788–1804 (besides holding other ecclesiastical preferments).[32] A later reference suggests that he set to work on the county in the 1770s. In 1787 and 1794 he circulated a prospectus for 'The Natural History and Antiquities of Huntingdonshire'; the volume was to have a map and plates, and include a translation of Domesday Book. Nothing came of it, Hutchinson went mad, and died unpublished in 1804.[33] His collections passed first to Thomas Martyn, the absentee professor of botany at Cambridge.[34] By 1814, when it was claimed that they were 'all ready for the press after a labour of 30 years', they had been bought by John Symmons (1781–1842) of Paddington, who also acquired Smyth's heraldic collections from Nichols. In 1814 Symmons was letting it be known that his Huntingdonshire manuscripts were available for use by others:

> if any one were inclined to give a full and complete publication of that hitherto inedited county, the materials are all ready to his hand, wanting nothing but a little arrangement to render it in all respects a perfect work of the kind.[35]

That was optimistic. No one took up the offer and by 1824 Smyth's and Hutchinson's manuscripts had been bought by the wealthy collector Sir Richard Colt Hoare, Bt. (1758–1838), and were in his library at Stourhead (Wilts.).[36] The scope of Hutchinson's collections remains somewhat obscure. In the 1820s they were cited as an authority for the existence of Roman remains in the parishes of Holywell, Eynesbury, and St. Neots, and for an estimate that St. Neots market place covered 71,000 square feet,[37] which

[30] Bodl. MS. Gough Hunts. 2.

[31] Ibid. MS. Gough Hunts. 4; *D.N.B.* for both.

[32] *Trans. Cambs. and Hunts. Arch. Soc.* iii. 123, 138; J. Le Neve, *Fasti Ecclesiae Anglicanae*, ed. T. D. Hardy (3 vols. 1854), ii. 233.

[33] Bodl. MS. Gough Gen. Top. 364, ff. 131, 134: reproduced in J. P. Feather, *Book Prospectuses before 1801 in Gough Collection, Bodl.* (1980), fiche 02, frames B03, B04; *Gent. Mag.* lxxiv (1), 282.

[34] E. W. Brayley, *Beauties of England and Wales*, vii (1808), unpaginated list of books at end; *V.C.H. Cambs.* iii. 234.

[35] *Gent. Mag.* lxxiv (2), 445–6; *D.N.B.* s.v. Symmons, Charles (1749–1826).

[36] Gorham, *Hist. Eynesbury and St. Neot's*, ii, p. clxxxi; [J. B. Nichols], *Catalogue of Hoare Library at Stourhead* (1840), 205; *D.N.B.*

[37] Gorham, *Hist. Eynesbury and St. Neot's*, i. 5, 12, 15, 138.

To be Publiſhed, in Folio, by Subſcription,

WITH A MAP OF THE COUNTY AND OTHER PLATES,

T H E

Natural Hiſtory and Antiquities

O F

Huntingdonſhire ;

W I T H

An EXTRACT and TRANSLATION

O F

DOOMSDAY-BOOK,

RELATIVE THERETO, BY

B. Hutchinſon,   A. M.

PREBENDARY of LINCOLN, RECTOR of RUSHDEN, in *Northamptonſhire ;*
and of HOLYWELL with NEEDINGWORTH, in *Huntingdonſhire ;* and
CHAPLAIN to his GRACE the DUKE of BEDFORD.

To defray the Expence of the Undertaking, which will be conſiderable,
the firſt *Subſcription* to be ONE GUINEA, and a GUINEA more, on
the Delivery of the BOOK, in *Boards.*

RECEIVED   Day of   1794

of   *One Guinea,* being

the firſt *Subſcription* to this Work.

Mr H is so totally decayed as the under confinement. June 1803 Mar 1804

14 Benjamin Hutchinson's prospectus for a history of Huntingdonshire

makes them sound eclectic at least, but their description by Nichols in 1808 suggests that they mainly covered natural history, and in the catalogue of the Stourhead library they were listed simply as 'Twenty small 8vo. Memorandum Books relative to the History of Huntingdonshire (Natural History, &c.)'.[38] They have not been traced since they were sold in 1888.[39] It is very doubtful whether they would have made a real county history even if they had been published as Hutchinson and others hoped: one of his intended chapters was apparently a detailed vindication of the healthfulness of the Fen air.[40]

The paucity of accessible information about the topography of the county was shown up in Edward Brayley's Huntingdonshire section of *The Beauties of England and Wales*, published in volume seven in 1808. The 250 pages given over to the county at first sight look impressive; but 100 pages nominally about Huntingdon were actually on the Cromwell family, and mainly devoted to a general history of Oliver Cromwell's career in the Civil Wars. Brayley himself as much as admitted that there was nothing new in his account of the county apart from his own observations based on just three short visits.[41]

By the early 19th century the focus of interest in English local history was shifting away from the counties towards more manageable projects such as individual towns. Huntingdonshire was no exception and the years 1820–31 saw the publication of works on Huntingdon, Godmanchester, and St. Neots. The historian of the county town, Robert Carruthers (1799–1878), was master of its National school in the mid 1820s.[42] His *History of Huntingdon* (1824) covered institutions, churches, historical events, eminent natives, M.P.s, mayors, and a description of the town. The author's intention was to be encyclopaedic and impartial: 'to bring to the task all the information he could collect from authentic sources'.[43] Carruthers was no native wedded to a life-long study, but an ambitious autodidact Scotsman who returned north in 1828. He later distinguished himself as a newspaper editor and literary and antiquarian author.[44] At least one of his friends thought the Huntingdon book well done but the subject unworthy of his talents.[45] Huntingdon was shortly followed into print by Godmanchester, perhaps spurred on by the traditional

[38] [Nichols], *Catalogue of Hoare Library*, 205.
[39] *V.C.H. Hunts.* i, p. xvi.
[40] [S. J.] Pratt, *Gleanings in England* (2nd edn., 2 vols. 1801), ii. 569–75.
[41] Brayley, *Beauties of England and Wales*, Hunts. [4].
[42] *D.N.B.*; B.L. Eg. MS. 2246, ff. 282–283v. (Carruthers to John Clare, 8 Feb. 1824).
[43] [R. Carruthers], *Hist. of Huntingdon* (1824), esp. pp. v, xiii.
[44] *D.N.B.*
[45] National Library of Scotland, Acc. 10097, vol. i, no. 1 (Allan Cunningham to Carruthers, 23 Dec. 1824): photocopy in Hunts. R.O., Acc. 4101.

rivalry between the two towns.[46] *The History of Godmanchester* (1831) by Robert Fox (?1798–1843) was the work of a surgeon and bailiff of the town.[47] Fox admired Carruthers, whom he called 'well-informed and ingenious', and may have modelled his own book on the earlier work, since it covered roughly the same ground and similarly claimed to be based on 'laborious investigation into every circumstance immediately or remotely connected with the Town'.[48] In fact Fox had far more sources available locally for Godmanchester than Carruthers had for Huntingdon.

The third of the town histories, G. C. Gorham's *History and Antiquities of Eynesbury and St. Neot's* (2 vols. 1820–4), was more idiosyncratic but a more scholarly work. Gorham (1787–1857), a native of St. Neots, was then a fellow of a Cambridge college, held a curacy in Surrey, and had already been embroiled in a doctrinal dispute with the bishop of Ely, a prelude to his more famous tangle with the bishop of Exeter in the late 1840s.[49] His history covered not just St. Neots in Huntingdonshire (and its mother parish of Eynesbury) but St. Neot in Cornwall, and not just the places but St. Neot the saint. In fact the focus of the book was as much on the saint and his two churches as on Huntingdonshire topography. The latter part was nevertheless a thorough account, based on extensive and critical use of sources, including (unlike Carruthers's and Fox's works) those to be found in London. Gorham also collected two volumes of material for a 'Monasticon Huntingdoniense', which he never published.[50]

Three town histories, even three substantial and interesting ones, were no substitute for a county history. The mid 19th century was a particularly barren period for Huntingdonshire history. Cambridgeshire antiquaries like Rand and Cole had never taken much interest in it, and that pattern was confirmed by the Cambridge Antiquarian Society, established in 1840. Its *Proceedings* scarcely ever looked beyond Cambridgeshire and the 98 other volumes that appeared between 1840 and 1951 variously in the octavo, quarto, occasional, and extra series included only one on Huntingdonshire.[51] More attention was paid in the pages of *Fenland Notes and Queries*, which ran in quarterly parts from 1889 to 1909. Its founder, W. H. B. Saunders of Peterborough, had in 1888 published *Legends and Traditions of Huntingdonshire*, with limited ambitions that showed how far local historians had abandoned the traditional concept of county history:

[46] e.g. [Carruthers], *Hist. of Huntingdon*, between pp. 35–6, s.a. 1625.
[47] *D.N.B.*
[48] R. Fox, *Hist. of Godmanchester* (1831), esp. pp. vii, 18.
[49] *D.N.B.*
[50] [Nichols], *Catalogue of Hoare Library*, 205.
[51] G. J. Turner, *Calendar of Feet of Fines for Hunts.* (1913); M. W. Thompson, *Cambridge Antiq. Soc. 1840–1990* (1990).

the present volume will, in a small and concise form, supply a general review of
the history of the County, in a manner suitable to popular tastes . . . It is not
intended to be a manorial history; it does not profess to give a record of the
County families; it does not touch the all absorbing subject of the Parish
Churches in the County.[52]

The most substantial book on the county to appear in the 19th century was
James Hatfield's 783-page *History, Gazetteer and Directory of the County of
Huntingdon* (1854). An unusually detailed work of its type, it built on existing
published material but is especially useful in the gazetteer sections for the
towns, where it preserved much first- and second-hand knowledge of recent
history. Conversely, the most interesting book not published must be the
history of the county projected by Cuthbert Bede, a curate at Glatton while
he was writing *The Adventures of Mr. Verdant Green* (published in parts
1853–6), and later rector of Denton 1859–71.[53] His notes were used by the
editor of Murray's *Handbook* for Huntingdonshire,[54] but a history from his
own hand would surely have been more entertaining.

Huntingdonshire in 1900 was arguably the least studied and least published
English county. There was no full-scale history of the traditional kind. To the
piecemeal histories of Huntingdon, Godmanchester, and St. Neots had been
added only a book on Ramsey (whose authors, though Wise and Noble,
produced more a compendium of information from original sources than a
full history), substantial histories of Elton and Great Gransden, and short
accounts of St. Ives and a handful of villages, reprinted from articles in the
Hunts. County Guardian.[55] As has been seen, the antiquarian manuscript
collections which survived were few and slight. There was no county
archaeological society. The turn of the century, however, saw great
improvements: Herbert Norris, originally from St. Ives, was amassing a vast
collection of books, pamphlets, and notes on the county in Cirencester
(Glos.);[56] the first scholarly book to make full use of the remarkable medieval
archive of Ramsey abbey appeared in 1899;[57] the Victoria County History was
established the same year; and a local archaeological society was formed in
1900. In all four cases the impulse came from outside Huntingdonshire.

---

[52] Saunders, *Legends and Traditions of Hunts.* pp. [xiii–xiv].
[53] *D.N.B. Supplement*, s.v. Bradley, Edward (1827–89).
[54] *Handbook for Herts., Beds., and Hunts.* (1895), preface.
[55] J. Wise and W. M. Noble, *Ramsey Abbey: its Rise and Fall* [1881]; R. F. Whistler, *Hist. of
Elton* (1892); [A. J. Edmonds], *Hist. of Great Gransden* (1892); H. E. Norris, *Hist. of St. Ives*
(1889); idem, *Wyton and its Church* (1888); S. G. Jarman, *Village of Wood Hurst* (1888); idem,
Village of Old Hurst (1893).
[56] e.g. *Catalogue of Hunts. Books collected by Herbert E. Norris* (Cirencester, privately printed,
1895); A. L. Humphreys, *Handbook to County Bibliography* (1917), 90–3.
[57] N. Neilson, *Economic Conditions on Manors of Ramsey Abbey* (1899).

The local society was not even exclusive to the county, as its name shows. The Cambridgeshire and Huntingdonshire Archaeological Society (C.H.A.S.) was founded virtually single-handedly by the Revd. C. H. Evelyn-White (1850–1938), rector of Rampton (Cambs.) and already editor of the antiquarian monthly the *East Anglian* (which did not cover Huntingdonshire). Evelyn-White, an effective organizer and a good scholar but at times a difficult man, objected that the Cambridge Antiquarian Society 'concerned itself too much with general archaeology to the neglect, as it seemed to some, of matters affecting the County', and was 'so closely bound up with the University that the members generally had no practical share in its management'.[58] Evelyn-White's interest in a society run by its members was make-believe: he intended the C.H.A.S. to be a publishing society with himself as secretary-editor and treasurer. The *Transactions* started appearing in 1901 and two thirds of the first volume, for 1900–3, was Evelyn-White's own work. That could not go on, and between 1904 and 1906 the society rebelled. He ceased to be treasurer in 1904 and the rules were revised so that the editor was not also the secretary and so that the council (not the editor) 'shall decide what papers are to be published in the annual volume of the Society's Transactions, and determine all questions relative to plans and illustrations for the same'. Evelyn-White resigned both as editor and member of the society in 1906.[59]

Freed from Evelyn-White's oppressive personality, the C.H.A.S. rapidly became more of a Huntingdonshire society. Only 12 of the original 57 members had been from the county but by 1908 they formed half the membership and later outnumbered Cambridgeshire members three to one.[60] The articles published in the *Transactions* reflected the change. The editors after Evelyn-White were Huntingdonshire clergymen and from 1906 more than half the space was always devoted to Huntingdonshire material. Growing publishing costs and the failure to raise membership above *c.* 70 led the C.H.A.S. to be incorporated into the Cambridge Antiquarian Society in 1952, after which that society's *Proceedings* carried much more Huntingdonshire material.[61] The foundation of the Huntingdonshire Local History Society in 1957 showed the demand for a more popular body specifically devoted to the county; it published a *Bulletin* 1958–62 and a slim journal, *Records of Hunts.*, from 1965, and continued to thrive after Huntingdonshire ceased to be an administrative county in the latter year.[62]

---

[58] *Trans. Cambs. and Hunts. Arch. Soc.* i. 86–9, 99; vi. 55–61; vii. 48–9.
[59] Ibid. i, p. [i]; ii, between pp. 104–5; vi. 57; vii. 47–9.
[60] Membership lists: ibid. i, pp. ii–iv, 435–6; ii. 270–1; iii. 412–13; iv, pp. [xi–xii]; v, pp. [x–xi], 399–400; vi, at end; vii. 78–9.
[61] Ibid. vii. 101; Thompson, *Cambridge Antiq. Soc.* 75.
[62] *Recs. of Hunts.* i (10) (1980), 12–16.

The Victoria County History, established in 1899, published nothing on Huntingdonshire before the 1920s. Although some general articles had been written before 1909, when lack of money temporarily halted the whole series, the county was not one of the ten selected for completion when work resumed in 1910.[63] The county was restarted in 1924 after the general editor, William Page, elicited an offer to underwrite the costs of research and publication.[64] The man with the money was Granville Proby (1883–1947), then in his early 40s, member of a gentry family which had owned Elton Hall since the 1660s, and newly interested in the history of his county.[65] Proby also gave money to the Royal Commission on Historical Monuments, enabling it to undertake the fieldwork for its Huntingdonshire volume. Backed by Proby, the Commission and the V.C.H. began work on the county at almost the same time and co-operated closely. Page was himself a Commissioner.[66]

V.C.H. Huntingdonshire was a collaborative enterprise, more so even than the new model *V.C.H.* of the years after 1950.[67] Page persuaded Proby to be his assistant editor for the county, and the two worked together at every stage of research, writing, and publication. Page signed up specialist contributors for the general chapters; hired researchers, authors, and reference-checkers for the parish histories; and maintained close editorial control over everything that was published, rewriting substantial parts himself. Proby advised, smoothed things over with difficult contributors, and did a little research and writing, but his most important contribution other than financial was as the conduit by which Page tapped the wealth of knowledge available in the county. Proby put Page in touch with the most active members of the C.H.A.S., notably the Cirencester jeweller Herbert Norris (1859–1931) and the Huntingdon architect Sidney Inskip Ladds (1867–1950). The parish histories were based not only on the established systematic methods of the V.C.H. but also on Norris's notes and library and Ladds's 'almost encyclopaedic knowledge of the county', especially its buildings. The papers of both men later went to the Norris Library and Museum in St. Ives, opened in 1933.[68] Although the V.C.H. volumes published between the wars lack the detail on economic and social history of those written since the 1950s, the

[63] *V.C.H. General Introduction*, 1–27, for hist. of V.C.H.; V.C.H. recs., A 57, William Page to James Tait, 27 Apr. 1910; A 67; B 6, MS. chart of sections planned and completed.

[64] *Elton Manorial Recs. 1279–1351*, ed. S. C. Ratcliff (1946), pp. xi–xii; V.C.H. recs., B 6, TS. 'Method as to Guarantees', appendix 1.

[65] *Trans. Cambs. and Hunts. Arch. Soc.* vi. 262–3; *The Times*, 14 Mar. 1947, p. 6, col. d; *Who's Who* (1947); *V.C.H. Hunts.* iii. 160.

[66] Royal Com. on Hist. Monuments (England), *Inventory of Hist. Monuments of Hunts.* (1926), pp. xxv, xxviii–xxix.

[67] Paragraph based on V.C.H. recs., A 9.

[68] *Trans. Cambs. and Hunts. Arch. Soc.* vii. 45; *Recs. of Hunts.* i (10) (1980), 16–19; inf. on Norris from Mr. Bob Burn-Murdoch, Norris Museum, St. Ives.

team assembled and led by Page and Proby produced a fine county history. Much of it was on the traditional lines planned in 1899, but some new ground was broken, notably by the article on the reclamation of the Middle Level of the Fens.

The county record office came late to Huntingdonshire, in contrast with other south-east midland counties.[69] The county council was poor and many of the earlier county records had not survived—two partial explanations why there was no archivist continuously in post until 1947, no record office until 1952, and no full-time archivist (though the assistant's post was full-time) until the succession of amateur part-timers, either still in or retired from other professions, ended in 1968. By then the collections had grown through the deposit of estate papers from Kimbolton, Ramsey Abbey, and Hinchingbrooke, the archdeaconry records, and borough records from Huntingdon and Godmanchester. The county thus obtained a record office meeting modern standards only after it had lost its administrative independence; it was under the management of the Northamptonshire Record Office 1968–74 and of Cambridgeshire after 1974.[70]

The fourth new shoot of interest in the county remained rooted elsewhere and bore fruit of a rather different sort. Modern academic interest in the rich medieval documentation for Ramsey abbey's manors was initiated by a Russian, Paul Vinogradoff (1854–1925),[71] and an American, Nellie Neilson (1873–1947),[72] and has been sustained since the 1950s by a whole team of Canadians.[73] Theirs is not county history, but its detail serves to underline the fact that even the *V.C.H.*, the only county history of Huntingdonshire ever published, has left plenty for others to do.

[69] Above, Beds., Bucks., Herts.; below, Northants.
[70] Information from Dr. Saunders, Hunts. R.O.
[71] P. Vinogradoff, *Villainage in England* (1892; Russian edn. 1887); *D.N.B. 1922–30*.
[72] *Jnl. of British Studies*, xviii (2) (Spring 1979), 142–5.
[73] e.g. J. A. Raftis, *Estates of Ramsey Abbey* (1957); *Tenure and Mobility* (1964); *Warboys* (1974); *Small Town in Late Medieval England: Godmanchester* (1982); *Early Tudor Godmanchester* (1990); E. B. DeWindt, *Land and People in Holywell-cum-Needingworth* (1972); E. Britton, *Community of the Vill* [Broughton] (1977).

KENT

Nigel Yates

The history of Kent has always presented a special temptation to local historians, and not to local historians alone: the temptation to see the county as a small kingdom unto itself, sharply demarcated in important respects from the rest of the country, even long after it had lost its political independence in the eighth century. Much of the time that temptation has to be resisted, and local events placed firmly in a national perspective.[1]

Kentish historiography is not only weakened by misrepresentation but in many respects is simply non-existent. A county which has contributed more than its fair share to national history is one of the poorest in terms of published historical research.

At the time of writing, the authoritative history of Kent is still that produced by Edward Hasted two centuries ago. The first edition in four folio volumes was published between 1778 and 1799. A second, substantially revised and corrected, edition, designed for a more popular market in 12 octavo volumes, was published between 1797 and 1801.[2] Hasted, of course, was not the first to work on the history of Kent. Indeed his *magnum opus* can be seen as the climax of two centuries of scholarship, beginning with William Lambarde (1536–1601), whereas in the two centuries since Hasted wrote, the published county histories have, in the main, relied on his work and developed it little further. Lambarde published his *Perambulation of Kent* in 1576, the result of a combination of a legal career with strong antiquarian interests. Its chief value lies in its very detailed descriptions of Kentish customs and its economic survey of the county. Lambarde was followed by Richard Kilburne (1605–78), another lawyer, whose *Survey of Kent* was published in 1659. Unlike Lambarde's, Kilburne's work is more in the nature of a directory, providing a useful list of contemporary facts about the county's geographical and political divisions. A much more substantial work is Thomas Philipot's *Villare Cantianum*, also published in 1659. Despite its haphazard arrangement, Philipot was clearly aiming at the sort of county

---

[1] R. Eales, 'Introduction to Kent Domesday', *Kent Domesday* (Alecto Hist. Edns. 1992), 1.
[2] The second edn. was reprinted in 1972 with an authoritative introductory essay by Alan Everitt.

15 William Lambarde

history that Hasted eventually published. By the standards of the time it was a scholarly antiquarian study which was ambitious enough to attempt an appendix on the supposed etymology of Kentish place names. Rather less successful was the first volume of a proposed county history published by John Harris (1667–1719) in the year of his death. Although Harris attempted to write a much more wide-ranging study of Kent's history than had been attempted before, he clearly lacked the scholarship necessary to undertake it, and the published volume is now valuable chiefly for the superb engravings of country houses with which it is illustrated. The last of Hasted's precursors in the writing of Kentish history was Charles Seymour, whose *New Topographical, Historical and Commercial Survey* appeared in 1776. Its usefulness was so overshadowed by Hasted's work that it is now largely, and perhaps unfairly, forgotten.[3]

Kentish historiography is dominated by Hasted's *History and Topographical Survey of the County of Kent*. Its value as a work of scholarship has been much debated.[4] Edward Hasted (1732–1812) was, like Lambarde and Kilburne before him, a lawyer, though his approach was closest to Philipot's in his attitude to historiographical method. He says remarkably little about the general history of the county. He is concerned to present for the bulk of his work, as the *Victoria County History* itself aimed to do a century later, a detailed study of each parish in the county. Like the *Victoria County History*, the work is arranged by political divisions: in Kent that meant dealing with parishes not only on the basis of hundred divisions but within their respective lathes as well. The parish studies are arranged in a standard manner, beginning with the descents of the various manors, and moving on to a history of the advowson and fabric of the parish church, a survey of the parochial charities, and a list of incumbents and patrons. The municipalities receive more extensive treatment though, with the exception of Canterbury, very much less than they deserve. The overall accuracy of the work is high and the sources reasonably acknowledged, but there is no doubting that as a history of Kent and its individual communities it is limited and often very irritating in what it omits. Nevertheless there is much of value. As well as relying on records available to him, either in the original or more probably in transcript form, at Lambeth Palace and Canterbury cathedral libraries, at the Canterbury Prerogative Office, and above all in the collections built up by the Dering family at Surrenden, he had visited every parish in Kent to ensure that he was able to give a personal description of them. The maps provided at the beginning of each hundred entry are particularly useful.

    [3] On the pre-Hasted historians see F. Hull, 'Kentish Historiography', *Archaeologia Cantiana*, lxx (1956), 221–30.

    [4] See Alan Everitt's introduction to the 1972 reprint of the 2nd edn.; J. Boyle, *In Quest of Hasted* (1984); and J. Thirsk, 'Hasted as Historian', *Archaeologia Cantiana*, cxi (1993), 1–15.

Hasted's successors as county historians failed to build on what he had achieved. W. H. Ireland's *History of Kent*, published between 1828 and 1830, in its best parts does no more than repeat verbatim passages from Hasted. In recent years a few one-volume surveys of the county's history have been attempted, of which by far the best is that by Frank Jessup.[5] There has, however, been a strong tradition of municipal as opposed to county history, which goes back to the 17th century. One thinks of the work by William Somner on Canterbury,[6] John Bavington Jones on Dover,[7] Edward Jacob on Faversham,[8] Robert Pocock and Robert Cruden on Gravesend,[9] William Newton and J. M. Russell on Maidstone,[10] Frederick Smith on Rochester,[11] and William Boys on Sandwich.[12] In roughly the same category was John Lewis's *History and Antiquities of the Isle of Thanet*, published in 1723. Attention should also be drawn to John Dunkin's important *History and Antiquities of Dartford*, published in 1844, and Charles Woodruff's scholarly *History of the Town and Port of Fordwich*, which, though the size of a small village, had its own corporation until it was dissolved in 1885. Woodruff's book was published 10 years after that crucial event. In 1871 there appeared Robert Furley's *History of the Weald of Kent*, which was more wide-ranging than its title would suggest, and which can almost be counted as a county history. Furley's work suffered from the faults of much late 19th-century historiography: a belief that the distant past was more interesting than the recent past. Thus his study of Kent up to the 17th century supplied a great deal omitted by Hasted, though it suffered from an arrangement designed to make local history fit into periods that are only really relevant to national history. By the time he reached the 18th century he had little to communicate to the modern reader.

The Kent Archaeological Society has made an important contribution to the study of Kent's history in its journal, *Archaeologia Cantiana*, first published in 1858. It has to be acknowledged that in more recent years the historical content of *Archaeologia Cantiana* has been somewhat weaker than its archaeological content. Kent has also suffered from not being able to establish a separate record society. The record publications produced by the Kent Archaeological Society have been sporadic and only rarely of

---

[5] F. W. Jessup, *Hist. of Kent* (1958, revised edn. 1984).
[6] W. Somner, *Antiquities of Canterbury* (1640).
[7] J. B. Jones, *Annals of Dover* (1916) and *Recs. of Dover* (1920).
[8] E. Jacob, *Hist. of Town and Port of Faversham* (1774).
[9] R. Pocock, *Hist. of Incorporated Towns and Parishes of Gravesend and Milton* (1797); R. P. Cruden, *Hist. of Town of Gravesend* (1843).
[10] W. Newton, *Hist. and Antiquities of Maidstone* (1741); J. M. Russell, *Hist. of Maidstone* (1881).
[11] F. F. Smith, *Hist. of Rochester* (1928).
[12] W. Boys, *Collections for Hist. of Sandwich and Richborough* (1792).

exceptional quality. Nevertheless after more than a century without any serious competition the Kent Archaeological Society, whatever its defects, remains the only voluntary body dedicated to promoting and publishing historical studies in Kent. The former County Local History Committee, more recently known as the Kent History Federation, is no more than a quarterly meeting of the county's small local history societies, and its *Journal of Kent Local History* is little more than an extended newsletter. A more serious journal, *Cantium*, folded through lack of support after only a few issues in the 1970s. The more recent *Bygone Kent*, as its name implies, is angled very clearly towards the more popular end of the local history market.

The defects in the historiography of Kent would have been made good, to some extent at least, had it been possible to complete more than the three general volumes for Kent in the *Victoria County History*. They were published between 1908 and 1932. They are now very dated and even at the time their publication was not universally well received. Indeed it was dissatisfaction with the published results which led to the project's being abandoned for lack of a local endowment after the production of the third volume. Attempts to relaunch work on the *History*, by continuing with the topographical volumes, in both the 1950s and the 1980s, failed through lack of local support. In 1989 the county council, faced with the realization both that existing histories were unsatisfactory and that it was not financially feasible to relaunch the *Victoria County History*, agreed to commission a more limited history of Kent under the general editorship of the present writer. The door was not firmly slammed in the face of the *Victoria County History*. The editorial board was permitted to include in what was to be known as the Kent History Project both the directly commissioned volumes, two specialist monographs already in preparation, and future topographical volumes of the *Victoria County History* if the finance for them can be raised. No such volume has been agreed to date though at least one may emerge in due course. The first of the other volumes in the project should appear in 1994.

In other respects Kent has made more of a mark on the national historical scene. Its work in the saving of the raw material of history and the creation of well appointed archive repositories has been considerable. It began with the archive collections accumulated by Maidstone Museum and the Kent Archaeological Society, both of which were established in 1858. In 1933 W. L. Platts, the autocratic clerk of Kent county council between 1929 and 1953, appointed an archivist to sort and catalogue the large collection of official records that the county council had inherited from its predecessor authorities. In 1938 a purpose-built archive repository was opened, one of the earliest in Britain built by a local authority. Platts had very firm views about archive services and was reluctant to take on responsibility for collections that did not belong to the county council except under special legal arrangements designed to protect the county council from financial embarassment if collections were subsequently withdrawn. With Platts's departure the archives service was able to expand in the 1950s and soon became what has been accurately termed 'a place of pilgrimage for archivists from all over the world'.[13] A guide to its holdings, which by then included the former accumulations of the Kent Archaeological Society and after 1975 those of Maidstone Museum as well, was published in 1958, with supplements appearing at regular intervals thereafter. Between 1976 and 1989 further expansions took place in the archives service so that by the latter year the archives of the Rochester Bridge Trust and Tunbridge Wells borough council were the only significant collections in the county not to be the responsibility of the enlarged archives service. Branch repositories were opened in libraries at Folkestone, Ramsgate, and Sevenoaks; agreements were made with local councils at Hythe and in the Medway towns; most importantly, a partnership developed between the county council, the city council, and the cathedral chapter for the future management of important archive collections in Canterbury cathedral library. Although the post of county archivist was abolished in 1990 as part of a major reorganization of services by Kent county council, the former archives service forms the main component part in the integrated archives, museums, and local studies functions provided by the Heritage Services Group of the new Arts and Libraries Department. The establishment of archive repositories in Kent did not just succeed in rescuing and making accessible the materials for the writing of Kent's history. From the 1950s the staff of the county archives service made an important contribution to Kentish historiography. It included publications by the service itself, such as the 10 volumes of the *Kentish Sources* series published between 1959 and 1987, as well as monographs and articles in learned journals by archivists.[14]

The establishment of the University of Kent at Canterbury in 1965 should have given a major impetus to Kentish historiography. It is generally admitted that this has not really been the case,[15] though there are welcome signs of change. Unlike some universities, Kent did not see local or regional history as a particularly important aspect of its role in the provision of facilities for adult or continuing education. The research interests of many members of the board of studies in history lay not just beyond the boundaries

[13] E. Melling, *Hist. of Kent County Council* (1975), 56.

[14] For work by Felix Hull and Elizabeth Melling, see *Studies in Modern Kentish Hist.* ed. A. P. Detsicas and W. N. Yates (1983), 3–9; other important work by present or former archives staff includes C. W. Chalklin, *17th Century Kent* (1965), and articles on Kentish topics by Anne Oakley and Nigel Yates.

[15] F. Hull, 'Kentish Historical Writing 1956–83: an Assessment', *Archaeologia Cantiana*, c (1984), 1–14.

of Kent, but beyond the boundaries of the British Isles altogether. By contrast the board of studies in economic and social history always had some interest in promoting Kentish history, encouraging dissertations on relevant topics among both undergraduate and postgraduate students, and eventually playing a major part in the development of the university's part-time diploma in local history. The launching of the Kent History Project by the county council in 1989 was only made possible by the active involvement of most members of the economic and social history board, and it is pleasing to record that individual members of the history board are also involved. The role of the university in the promotion of Kentish historiography, once severely limited, seems destined to grow substantially in the future.

In the absence until recently of major historiographic initiatives in Kent, the number of publications on aspects of Kentish history has been limited and only a few of those have been significant contributions to Kentish historiography. Many aspects of Kent's history have no recent academic literature at all; that is particularly true of the medieval period, but also in large measure of the 18th and 19th centuries; by far the best work on Kentish history has been concentrated in the 16th and 17th centuries. Particular attention needs to be drawn to the work of Christopher Chalklin, Peter Clark,[16] Alan Everitt,[17] David Ormrod, and Michael Zell. Useful work on the medieval period has been done by Irene Churchill, Robin du Boulay, Elizabeth Murray, William Urry, and Brian Woodcock.[18] John Whyman and Michael Winstanley[19] have enriched our knowledge of the later modern period with their work on different aspects of social history.[20] An indispensable guide to Kentish historiography is the *Kent Bibliography* and its supplement published by the London and Home Counties branch of the Library Association in 1977 and 1981 respectively.

Although it is true that Kentish historiography is still dominated, and to some extent even undermined, by Hasted's great work, the picture is beginning to change. Recent work has opened up an improved understanding of some aspects of Kent's history. There is growing dissatisfaction with the lack of work in other areas and a desire to remedy those deficiencies. It may

---

[16] P. Clark, *English Provincial Soc. from Reformation to Revolution* (1977).

[17] See esp. A. M. Everitt, *Community of Kent in the Great Rebellion* (1966); *Patterns of Rural Dissent* (1972); and *Continuity and Colonisation: Evolution of Kentish Settlement* (1986).

[18] I. J. Churchill, *Canterbury Administration* (1933); F. R. H. du Boulay, *Lordship of Canterbury* (1966); K. M. E. Murray, *Constitutional Hist. of Cinque Ports* (1935); W. Urry, *Canterbury under Angevin Kings* (1967); B. L. Woodcock, *Medieval Ecclesiastical Courts in Diocese of Canterbury* (1952).

[19] M. J. Winstanley, *Life in Kent at the Turn of the Century* (1978).

[20] The contributions of Chalklin, Ormrod, Whyman, and Zell to modern Kentish hist. are to be found not in one major work but in various contributions to learned journals, volumes of essays, and specialist monographs.

be that movements in the University of Kent, and the launching of the Kent History Project, will transform the quality and quantity of work on the history of Kent dramatically over the next decade or two. But old myths die hard. The warning in the opening quotation of this paper should still be heeded. It is of course true that Kent's proximity to the rest of Europe has made it, more than other parts of Britain, receptive to imports from the Continent whether in terms of ideas, refugees, or trade. Nevertheless that does not mean that the county's history can be considered as a thing apart, unconnected to the national background. Yet popular images which distort the county's history are still actively promoted, whether it be the 'Garden of England' label (never more than a gross over-simplification) or the assertion in a recent publicity handout that Kent was the oldest place name in Britain, whatever that is supposed to imply. The history of Kent does not need popularization by the image-makers and the writers of advertising copy. It needs long, hard, and sustained research leading to publications that will place the history of Kent firmly in the context of British history as a whole.[21]

---

[21] The author is grateful to Debbie Saunders, Local Studies Librarian at the Centre for Kentish Studies (the union of the former Kent Archives Office and the former County Local Studies Library) for reading and commenting upon this paper, though she bears no responsibility for the opinions expressed.

LANCASHIRE

Jenny Kermode

Lancashire is a large county with a varied topography and several distinct economic areas, based on the extraction of iron ore in the north and coal in the south, animal husbandry and domestic industry along the Pennine uplands, arable farming, fishing, coastal and overseas trade, chemicals, processing industries, and textile manufacturing. Local government boundary changes have created problems of continuity, something that John Harland was aware of in 1868 when he wrote that 'the old boundaries and landmarks of parishes, and to some extent, even of counties, have been greatly disturbed . . . in many cases utterly overthrown'. He cautioned the future historian to adopt a structure different from that of the traditional township and parish.[1] Earlier historians avoided such dilemmas by treating the county as an unchanging unit.

Collectors and historians have proliferated in Lancashire,[2] eager to celebrate the singular and superior qualities of their county. It was an impressive tradition which began with two 17th-century antiquarians wishing to 'retrieve the Glory of their Palatine out of the Monumental Ashes' of the Civil War:[3] Christopher Towneley (1604–74) of Carr Hall near Burnley, and Dr. Richard Kuerden (1623–?1690) of Cuerden near Preston.[4] Towneley's family was at the centre of a flourishing scientific movement in the north,[5] although he was himself a lawyer. Kuerden was a staunch royalist, educated at Oxford and Cambridge. It was said that he neglected his duties as a physician to collaborate with Towneley in gathering and transcribing materials for a projected history of Lancashire which was frustrated by Towneley's death in 1674. Kuerden inherited all Towneley's manuscripts and, encouraged by Sir

---

[1] E. Baines, *Hist. of County Palatine and Duchy of Lancaster*, i (1868), preface.

[2] The earliest, Roger Dodsworth (1585–1654), transcribed records relating to Lancs. in the Tower of London as part of his antiq. activities. He planned a hist. of Yorks. but not of Lancs. His collection is in the Bodleian Library, those relating to Lancs. being Bodl. MSS. Dodsw. 39, 54, 61–2, 70, 87, 131, 142, 149, 153. Christopher Towneley copied Dodsworth's transcriptions of Lancs. inquisitions *post mortem*: *D.N.B.* s.v. Dodsworth.

[3] B.L. Harl. MS. 2042 (8).

[4] *D.N.B.* s.vv. Jackson or Kuerden; Towneley.

[5] C. Webster, 'Richard Towneley (1629–1707), the Towneley Group and 17th-Century Science', *Trans. Historic Soc. Lancs. and Ches.* cxviii (1966), 51–76.

William Dugdale, whom he served as a marshal during an heraldic visitation of Lancashire, he issued proposals in 1688 for a work entitled 'Brigantia Lancastriensis Restaurata; or History of the Honourable Dukedom or County Palatine of Lancaster' in five volumes. It was not accomplished and all Kuerden left was 11 volumes of almost illegible transcripts. John Harland later prepared an index to part of the collection.[6]

Kuerden and Towneley concentrated on transcribing family muniments, wills, pedigrees, and deeds, and included copies derived from other collections such as those of Roger Dodsworth and William Vernon. Towneley attempted to organize his material with indexes and letter pagination for cross-referencing but it remains muddled. The bulk of his transcripts are in the British Library, Manchester Central Library Archives Department, and Chetham's Library, which also has his correspondence. Leeds City Archives Department and the Bodleian Library have others. The original manuscripts in Towneley's collection are scattered among the same repositories and Burnley Central and Cambridge University libraries.[7] The Kuerden and Towneley manuscripts include copies of many items now lost and were heavily consulted by later Lancashire historians, most notably William Farrer in preparing the *Victoria County History*.

Most county histories published in the 18th and earlier 19th century reflected the gentry culture of their authors and subscribers. In the Lancashire histories pretentious and irrelevant classical references were cited to place the county at the centre of Roman Britain and provide a context for meticulous drawings of Neolithic and Roman artefacts excavated locally. Sherds, sculptures, and other objects from the Roman fort at Ribchester excited classically educated scholars, and an interest in archaeological remains has survived as a feature of the county's learned societies and historians. One of the first of them was Charles Leigh (1662–?1701), a physician educated at Oxford and Cambridge and a contributor to the Royal Society.[8] His *Natural History of Lancashire, Cheshire, and the Peak in Derbyshire: with an Account of the British, Phoenician, Armenian, Greek and Roman Antiquities in those Parts* (1700) contains a significant description of Lancashire's antiquities.

It became common to draw a trail connecting Ptolemy and other classical writers through Camden and Clarendon to the time of the author, augmented by events and legends specific to Lancashire such as the creation of the palatinate, the descent of the duchy, and the Civil War. Lengthy political

[6] Manchester Central Library, Farrer Collection, vol. 123. Kuerden's transcripts are now B.L. Harl. MS. 7386; College of Arms, Kuerden MSS.; and Chetham's Library, Manchester, MUN.C.6.1–2.

[7] Hist. MSS. Com. *Guide to Location of Collections* (1982), 61.

[8] *D.N.B.*

narratives persisted as part of most Lancashire histories until the beginning of the 20th century and served as introductions to the topographical accounts which were the authors' main goal.

Around 1800 three histories were published: Thomas West, *Antiquities of Furness* (1774), John Aikin, *A Description of the Country from 30 to 40 Miles round Manchester* (1795), and the Revd. Thomas D. Whitaker, *A History of the Original Parish of Whalley and the Honor of Clitheroe* (1801). They were early exponents of an interesting feature of Lancashire's histories, the study of a region smaller than the county. West was born in Scotland in 1720. He became a Jesuit and after studying at Lille went to Furness in 1769. He was buried at Sizergh (Westmld.) in 1779. The focus of *Antiquities of Furness* was the abbey and important local families, but he also described the region's topography, economy, and social conditions.[9] He related the Furness economy to its communications and trade network, noted prices and wage rates, and appended population figures abstracted from parish registers. He drew on manuscripts in the British Museum and in the collections of local families such as the Flemings at Rydal, printing full transcripts of some. His description of Whiteridge near Ulverston as 'the Peru of Furness' suggests a lively mind. *Antiquities* includes a good map surveyed by William Brasier in 1745 at one inch to the mile.

The Revd. Thomas D. Whitaker (1759–1821) produced two editions of his *History of Whalley*.[10] In the preface to the 1818 edition he admitted to a common fault, 'as a young and zealous antiquary, prone, from local attachment, to ascribe to some objects a degree of importance to which they were not entitled'. He rectified many factual mistakes for that edition but his strong personal opinions remained. Whitaker was born in Norfolk, the son of a curate. His father returned with his young family to his ancestral home in Cliviger. Thomas graduated from St. John's College, Oxford, in 1781, was ordained in 1785, and settled at Holme in Cliviger. He conceived the passionate ambition to become vicar of the exceptionally large parish of Whalley, 105,249 acres, and did so in 1809. Estate improvement was one of his cherished causes and the Society of Arts gave him an award for planting larches.[11]

His history is a classic of its time, prefaced by a chronological account of the parishes of Whalley and Cartmel and the honor of Clitheroe. Each

---

[9] New edn. 1805, reprinted 1977. He also wrote a *Guide to the Lakes* (1778) and *Antiquities Discovered in Lancaster* (1776). See also *D.N.B.*

[10] First edn. 1801; 2nd 1806; 1818 edn. included the parish of Cartmel; 4th edn. 1872–6 revised and enlarged by J. G. Nichols and P. A. Lyons. He also wrote *Hist. and Antiquities of Deanery of Craven* (2 vols. 1805) and *Hist. of Richmondshire in North Riding of Yorks.* (2 vols. 1823).

[11] *D.N.B.*

township was surveyed, with a focus on county society, pedigrees, descents of estates, and engravings and descriptions of gentry houses and their occupants. Some of his comments on the latter are entertainingly acerbic. Although he used original duchy of Lancaster sources he relied heavily on existing manuscript and transcript collections such as those of James Torre, Dodsworth, and especially Towneley. Whitaker somewhat patronizingly described Towneley as the 'indefatigable transcriber', but then gratefully lifted many of his family histories and a transcript of the Cockersand cartulary. *Whalley* is infused with moralizing comments on the decline of husbandry, the decayed state of the peasantry, and their excessive consumption of alcohol: opinions common to agricultural improvers of the time. The fourth and enlarged edition of 1872 included Slaidburn and incorporated much new material.

Dr. John Aikin's *Description* is refreshingly free of the gentry and adopted a remarkably modern approach. Aikin was a doctor of medicine, a graduate of Aberdeen, Edinburgh, and Leiden universities, and taught chemistry, anatomy, and physiology at Warrington Academy from 1772 until 1783. His father, John senior, was a key figure there. Aikin junior reflected the educational philosophy of the Academy, which had broken through the classics barrier and offered a modern education to Nonconformists. Aikin's other published work included a handbook on chemistry and geographical descriptions of England. His fellow scholars educated at Warrington, including T. Percival and T. R. Malthus, had an interest in the past which was not class-based and a concern to gather facts and figures for objective analysis.[12]

Quite whose idea *A Description* was remains contentious. In the preface the publisher, John Stockdale, claimed it was his, whereas Aikin's daughter Lucy insisted it was her father's: Stockdale was to collect the materials and Aikin was to do the collation and writing, but 'in fact, from his exertions and the communications of his personal friends, the most valuable part of the work proceeded'. Her judgement, that 'the absence of vulgar prejudices and partialities, strongly distinguish it . . . among the works of English topography', is well borne out by *A Description*.[13] In it, links with Rome were

---

[12] *D.N.B.*; R. Frankenberg, 'John Aikin (1747–1822), Doctor and Philosopher', *Manchester Literary and Philosophical Soc.* cvi (1963–4), 74–93. I am grateful to Michael Powell for this reference. See also H. McClachlan, *Warrington Academy, its Hist. and Influence* (Chetham Soc. new ser. cvii, 1943), 31, 69, 75–7, 104–5; *Warrington Academy, Part II: Hist. Account of Students*, ed. W. Turner and G. A. Carter (1957), 90–2.

[13] According to Lucy, Aikin made the acquaintance of Thomas Pennant during a brief residence in Chester, and published proposals for a hist. of Lancs. sometime before 1783. They failed through lack of support. Aikin was closely associated with another Warrington Academy lecturer, the Revd. Dr. William Enfield, author of an equally pioneering urban hist. of Liverpool: L. Aikin, *John Aikin* (2 vols. 1823).

replaced by an account of the region's morphology. The inclusion of north Wales as well as the counties adjacent to Manchester reveals a striking commercial and economic perspective and his subscribers included brokers, industrialists, and merchants. He dwelt more on open fields, canals, and rivers than on county society. Although 30 to 40 miles round was taken to include almost the whole of Lancashire except Lonsdale hundred, there was an emphasis on the south and on towns. Urban institutions, living conditions, trade, and industry moved centre stage, gentlemen and their seats to the edge.

It is not surprising, given the precocity of urbanization in Lancashire, that a number of individual town histories had been completed by 1800 and more followed.[14] Space precludes discussion of them here, but town studies provided material incorporated into later county histories. Matthew Gregson, for instance, drew heavily on Enfield's *Liverpool*.

Early 19th-century compilers began to move closer to the goals and methods of modern historical research. There was an increasing interest in presenting original documents. In tune with the statistical faith of the age, comprehensive tables of population, county rate assessments, the distribution of mills, and quantities and destinations of traded commodities began to appear alongside manorial descents and family pedigrees, though discussion of such statistics was limited. Most county histories still relied on gentry subscribers.

Matthew Gregson's *Portfolio of Fragments relative to the History and Antiquity of the County Palatine and Duchy of Lancaster* (1817) is an example of county history in transition. Gregson (1749–1824),[15] the son of a Liverpool shipbuilder, was an upholsterer active in local art and craft circles. He was awarded a gold medal by the Society of Arts but refused the offer of a knighthood from the prince regent. His historical endeavours were motivated by pride in his county, but also by an intention to give employment to local artists. *Fragments* is lavishly illustrated with 800 engravings, mostly by local artists.[16] His other purpose was to create a sound base of documentary evidence for later historians and the book includes tables of local statistics and extracts from sources such as Domesday Book, charter rolls, inquisitions *post mortem* and *ad quod damnum*, the *Nomina Villarum, Testa de Nevill*, county

[14] B. T. Barton, *Hist. of Borough of Bury and Neighbourhood* (1874); W. Beamont, *Annals of Lords of Warrington and Bewsey, 1587 to 1833* (1873); W. Enfield, *Essay towards Hist. of Liverpool* (1774); H. Fishwick, *Hist. of Parish of Rochdale* (1889); idem, *Hist. of Parish of Preston* (1900); D. Sinclair, *Hist. of Wigan* (2 vols. 1882); R. Simpson, *Hist. and Antiquities of Town of Lancaster* (1852); J. Whitaker, *Hist. of Manchester in Four Books* (1771).

[15] 2nd edn. 1824, 3rd edn. by J. Harland 1869; *D.N.B.*

[16] H. A. Taylor, 'Matthew Gregson and the Pursuit of Taste', *Trans. Hist. Soc. Lancs. and Ches.* cx (1959), 157–76. See also the Gregson collection in Liverpool City R.O. and Liverpool Univ. Library.

16 Initial from Matthew Gregson's *Portfolio of Fragments*

records, and medieval duchy records. The extracts were scarcely discussed and, as the author admitted, he had 'not attempted to give his materials the order of argument which the rules of historical composition require . . . having in view the value of each individual document rather than the composition of a connected chain of events'. His parish histories were taken up with heraldry and pedigrees, the latter 'because all agree that genealogy is so importantly connected with historical knowledge that it is impossible to arrive at any proficiency in the one without being minutely versed in the other.'

John Corry's two-volume *History of Lancashire* (1825) was a poor imitation of Gregson. His slide into disrepute was hastened by the advent of Edward Baines (1774–1848).[17] Baines was born in Walton-le-Dale, educated in Preston, and rose from printer's apprentice to become the proprietor of the *Leeds Mercury* in 1801 and Liberal M.P. for Leeds 1834–41. He published historical gazetteers for Yorkshire in 1824 and Lancashire in 1824–5,[18] enlarging his

[17] *D.N.B.*
[18] *Hist., Directory, and Gazetteer of County Palatine of Lancs.*

Lancashire study into four volumes published in 1836. How much of it was
Baines's own work remains a mystery. He certainly took full advantage of the
manuscript collections of Kuerden, Towneley, and Dodsworth, and of the
engravings of Thomas Binns of Liverpool. Employing transcribers and
researchers was a tradition among gentlemen scholars, and Baines
acknowledged the biographical research of William R. Whatton, a Mr.
Hampson (as his 'humble but confidential amanuensis'), and Edwin
Butterworth, who 'visited all the parishes and townships of the county,
without a single exception, for the purpose of collecting local information'.
The last two were credited with ensuring the accuracy of the publication,[19] a
claim which Baines might have regretted had he lived to see the revised
edition of his work, published in two volumes by John Harland in 1868.

Baines's ambitious history was a more informed and comprehensive study
than his predecessors'. The standard general historical narrative was
augmented with greater detail on the development of the county's
administration, the Dissolution, witchcraft, parliamentary representation, and
a useful summary of the debate over the origins of the palatinate. Gentry
pedigrees persisted in the topographical chapters but were complemented by
local annals and laconic physical descriptions. Thus Sefton parish was 'a
range of dreary sand-hills . . . along the shore, lined with marshes and covered
with rabbit warrens', Hoole 'flat and the scenery uninteresting'. Economic
and institutional developments were included and major towns separately
described. The history of cotton manufacture had its own section, though it
concentrated on the wonders of technology, making only slight reference to
the conditions of workers.

Baines's history dominated 19th-century Lancashire historiography and
remains an important text, even though subsequent editions of 1868 and
1888–93 substantially revised the original. The first and most fundamental
revisions were undertaken by John Harland, who was born in Hull in 1806
and became a respected reporter with the *Manchester Guardian*, retiring in
1860. He published several antiquarian works, edited 13 volumes in 12 years
for the Chetham Society, and undertook the revision of Baines into two
volumes. Harland died in 1868, the year volume one of Baines was published,
and Brooke Herford completed the revisions for volume two, published in
1870.[20] The revisions combined the entire rewriting of some sections, such as
the history of Manchester, with factual corrections and the insertion of new
material to bring the work up to date: charities, institutions, and local
government finances were especially favoured but railways were mentioned
only in passing. Harland omitted entirely 'the very inaccurate family

---

[19] Baines, *Hist. Lancs.* i, pp. x–xi; *D.N.B.* s.v. Butterworth; cf. his papers in Oldham public library.
[20] *D.N.B.* s.v. Harland; *D.N.B. 1901–11*, s.v. Herford.

pedigrees' of the first edition, on the grounds that corrections would be too time-consuming, and preferred English translations or précis of documents to Baines's Latin versions.

It is clear from Harland's references how much better placed he was, benefiting from the scholarly interest in historical matters which surged through mid 19th-century Lancashire and Cheshire. Chetham's Library had begun to acquire local collections and learned papers as a matter of policy in the late 18th century and was the natural home for the Chetham Society, founded in 1843 to publish 'historical and literary remains' of Lancashire and Cheshire.[21] The Record Society of Lancashire and Cheshire emerged as an offshoot for the same purpose in 1878.[22] The forum for learned papers had grown from the Manchester Philosophical and Literary Society of 1781 and its Liverpool counterpart of 1812 to include the annual transactions of the Historic Society of Lancashire and Cheshire and the Antiquarian Society of Lancashire and Cheshire, founded in 1848 and 1883 respectively. The officers and membership of all the societies were interlinked and, although never large, were admirably enthusiastic in making editions of important documents available and in generating productive discussion about the region's history.[23] They also continued to collect manuscripts and transcripts: one of the founders of the Chetham Society, Francis Raines, being one of the more energetic. He was born in Whitby in 1805, and served as an apprentice surgeon before being ordained in 1828. As vicar of Milnrow near Rochdale he could develop his antiquarian interests, and produced 44 volumes of transcripts ranging from the 13th to the 18th century, many of which were published by the Chetham Society. The society published other collectors' transcripts, for example those of the Revd. John Piccope.[24]

Access to documents through the local and national publishing societies and the Record Commission made the county historian's task both easier and more complicated. It was now possible to move beyond simple pedigrees and

---

[21] M. Powell, 'Chetham's Library, Manchester', *Local Historian*, xx (1990), 31–6; J. Tait, 'Chetham Soc.: a Retrospect', *Chetham Miscellanies, New Ser. VII* (Chetham Soc. 2nd ser. c, 1939), 1–23.

[22] B. E. Harris, 'Centenary Hist. of Rec. Soc. of Lancs. and Ches.' in *Index to Wills and Administrations formerly preserved in Probate Registry, Chester, 1831–1833*, ed. R. and F. Dickinson (Rec. Soc. Lancs. and Ches. cxviii, 1978), pp. vii–li.

[23] e.g. J. E. Bailey, born Edgbaston in 1840, educated in Warrington and Owen's College, Manchester, employed as a counting-house clerk until 1886, and died in 1888. He became honorary secretary of the Chetham Soc. and in 1881 began a monthly antiquarian magazine, *Palatine Notebook*, which survived for nine issues and four years: *D.N.B.*; Chetham's Library, Bailey MSS. Other enthusiasts included William Beamont, James Crossley, J. H. E. Bennett, J. P. Earwaker, Lt.-Col. Henry Fishwick, W. Fergusson Irvine, John Paul Rylands, and R. Stewart-Brown.

[24] Chetham's Library, Raines collection, MUN.C.6.34–80; Piccope collection, MUN.C.6.12–33.

narrative both in depth and detail. The focus, however, was resolutely on the more distant past and even the most up-to-date historians felt compelled or preferred to linger over pre-industrial Lancashire. Their ambivalence towards the more romantic and the recent past could be difficult to resolve, but Edward Baines's son Thomas conceived a two-volume history of Lancashire and Cheshire which managed to accommodate both. Introducing his *Lancashire and Cheshire Past and Present* in 1867, he acknowledged the importance of the Chetham Society's publications for his chapters on the earlier centuries. Nevertheless he invited William Fairbarn[25] to write the section on 'The Rise and Progress of Manufactures and Commerce, and Civil and Mechanical Engineering in these Districts', which was a paean of praise to industrializing Lancashire and municipal public services. His section was paginated in roman numerals, separate from the arabic pagination of the main text. It was distinct in other ways, being illustrated with town prospects, engineering drawings of docks, and sections through the Longdendale reservoir scheme, whereas Baines's chapters were more conventionally illustrated with views of famous sights such as Beeston castle, Chester, and Lancaster, and portraits of persons of importance.

One 19th-century oddity which saw Lancashire in terms of the new manufacturers was the Revd. G. N. Wright's *History*.[26] He followed Edward Baines in describing the processes of textile production, but most of his two-volume work was a pot-pourri of biographical sketches of 'remarkable men who have been the architects of their own fortunes [and of] legends and traditions connected with the crumbling abodes of departed power'.

It would be particularly pleasing to be able to welcome the advent of the *Victoria County History* as a turning point for Lancashire history, and in some respects it was. Its senior editor, William Farrer, had strong medieval interests, which are echoed in the *V.C.H.* volumes. He was born in Little Marsden near Burnley in 1861, educated at Rugby, and entered the family business. He abandoned that in 1896 to devote his life to local history. In the same year he bought J. P. Earwaker's Lancashire history collection, having already acquired a dozen volumes of Towneley's transcripts.[27] His co-editor John Brownbill emerged from a very different career. He was born *c.* 1860 into a family of Liverpool watchmakers. John was a brilliant mathematician, educated at Oates Academy, Everton, and Cambridge. His conversion to Roman Catholicism ended earlier plans to enter the ministry and instead he

---

[25] Probably Sir William Fairbairn (1789–1874): *D.N.B.*

[26] *Lancs.: Hist., Legends and Manufactures* (2 vols. n.d. but probably before *c.* 1845); *D.N.B.*

[27] He edited several important medieval manuscripts for the Chetham Soc. and Rec. Soc. between 1898 and 1915: *D.N.B.* See also the collection of his papers in Manchester Central Library Archives Department.

was briefly a schoolmaster before joining the *Liverpool Courier* as a copy-editor. His articles for the *Cheshire Sheaf* attracted the attention of Farrer, who persuaded him to become sub-editor of *V.C.H. Lancashire*. After the completion of the *V.C.H.*, Brownbill continued his historical interests, contributing to the *Complete Peerage*, editing the *Transactions of the Historic Society of Lancashire and Cheshire* from 1911 to 1928 and several volumes for the Record and Chetham Societies, and publishing a number of local studies.[28]

The eight volumes of *V.C.H. Lancashire* were published between 1906 and 1914. Eminent historians such as James Tait, F. M. Powicke, and A. F. Leach wrote on their specialisms, Farrer on Domesday Lancashire, and he and Brownbill were responsible for the topographical chapters. They laboured under the same sorts of disadvantages as their recent predecessors and did not yet have the advantages of a well ordered local archives service. It is apparent that Farrer expended much time and effort trying to gain access to family muniments. Transcripts completed by local scholars such as W. Fergusson Irvine, J. P. Earwaker, James Tait, and W. H. Price of Chester were used, and a London agent was employed.[29] Inevitably the topographical chapters relied heavily on earlier transcripts and even the 'crabbed hand' of Kuerden's collections was deciphered to advantage. The resulting volumes continue to be the standard reference work for many aspects of Lancashire history. The most original contributions at the time were the general sections, especially those on industries, sport, and education.

In the inter-war period two pioneering regional histories were published by the Chetham Society, focused on areas of the county defined by their economic coherence: G. H. Tupling, *Economic History of the Forest of Rossendale* (1927) and F. Walker, *Historical Geography of Southwest Lancashire before the Industrial Revolution* (1939). Tupling's study remains essential reading for economic historians of any county. The author was born in Hull in 1883 and taught at Haslingden grammar school for 37 years. His curiosity about the impact of the industrial revolution on the town led him into an extensive study of the Rossendale district. On his retirement in 1943 he became the first holder of the Farrer Fellowship at Manchester University.[30]

---

[28] He moved to Ilford to be closer to the B.M. and P.R.O. and, perhaps as a consequence, his obituary in *Trans. Hist. Soc. Lancs. and Ches.* lxxii (1930), 245, is remarkably brief. I am grateful to Jim O'Neil and esp. to Mrs. Gillian Ingram who unearthed a fuller memoir in the *Hoylake and West Kirby Advertiser*, 29 May 1931.

[29] Farrer papers L1/58, *passim*, and for named historians, L1/58/1/339–41, 381–5, 451–8; L1/58/3/236–73.

[30] Obituary in *Haslingden Observer*, 22 Dec. 1962, kindly supplied by Haslingden District Library. Obituary and list of his main writings, *Trans. Antiq. Soc. Lancs. and Ches.* lxxii (1962), 177–9.

His book was a turning point in local studies and moved Lancashire history away from the merely descriptive to a more sophisticated and dynamic level. Tupling wanted to know why and how a domestic woollen industry was superseded by the factory cotton industry and sought an explanation in the morphology of the region. His research used landscape forms and original documents, explaining the changing pattern of settlement and economic systems from the 13th to the 19th century. The directness of his curiosity shows in his hand-copied plans of field shapes, which have an engagingly personal quality.[31]

Walker, a postgraduate student at Liverpool University, was equally curious about the interplay between the land and those human agencies which altered the landscape. His theme was the extent to which the differences in the physical geography between south-west and south-east Lancashire were permanent and had influenced their histories.

Few of the more recent historians have attempted the total history of Lancashire. Good popular studies such as those of Joe Bagley and P. J. Gooderson[32] have selected a number of topics and events to convey the flavour of the county's past quickly. Other studies have examined more substantial themes in greater depth. The county's economic giant was finally given a worthy history in *The Cotton Trade and Industrial Lancashire 1600–1780*, by Alfred P. Wadsworth and Julia De Lacy Mann in 1968. Eric Midwinter's *Social Administration in Lancashire 1830–1860* (1969) is still the best introduction to the development of the police, poor-law, and public health agencies county-wide. A very different approach has been adopted by the most important recent history. John Walton's *Lancashire: a Social History, 1558–1939* (1987), which accommodates all levels of society. Thomas Baines had observed the 'heroic patience with which the sufferings of the cotton district were borne [in the 1860s], and . . . the noble generosity with which they were relieved' but he was one of the few to glance down at the workers. Walton's history is a synthesis of published and unpublished work, woven into a wide-ranging history of the county: a worthy successor to Edward Baines as the new Lancashire textbook.

The Record Society began to meet in Liverpool in 1918, where the Historic Society was already based.[33] Those two societies have developed a gentle

---

[31] *Trans. Antiq. Soc. Lancs. and Ches.* xlix–li, lviii, lix (1935–7, 1945, 1947, 1948).

[32] J. J. Bagley was Lancs. hist. for many years after the Second World War, teaching and writing extensively on many aspects of the county. See the introduction to *17th-Century Lancs.* being *Trans. Hist. Soc. Lancs. and Ches.* cxxxii (1983), pp. xi–xiii, for a list of his writings, and *Trans. Hist. Soc. Lancs. and Ches.* cxxxviii (1989), 233–4 for his obituary. P. J. Gooderson, *Hist. of Lancs.* (1980).

[33] G. C. F. Forster, 'Record Publishing in North-West in Retrospect and Prospect', *Northern Hist.* xiv (1978), 243–51.

rivalry with the Antiquarian and Chetham Societies, based in Manchester. All four have maintained a programme of publications, with those in the south-west perhaps achieving greater regularity. In recent years the Chetham Society has moved away from publishing documents in favour of monographs.

An avalanche of small books and pamphlets is published each year on every conceivable aspect, and local history societies from all parts of the county meet together in the Lancashire Federation of Local History Societies, publishing a regular newsletter. Encouraged by the Standing Conference for Local History, a Joint Committee on the Lancashire Bibliography was set up in 1950 to compile a comprehensive bibliography of printed material relating to Lancashire. The first editor was G. H. Tupling and volume one, *Lancashire Directories 1684–1957*, was published in 1968. The bibliography is currently under the auspices of Terry Wyke at Manchester Metropolitan University. A directory of north-west local studies resources was published in 1993.[34] Interest in Lancashire's history is stronger than ever in the 1990s.

[34] Inf. from Miss Diana Winterbotham, Lancs. Local Studies Librarian. I am indebted to her, Michael Powell of Chetham's Library, and Michael Winstanley of Lancaster Univ. for invaluable help in the preparation of this chapter.

LEICESTERSHIRE AND RUTLAND

Charles Phythian-Adams

While penning his valediction to what he mistakenly hoped in 1641 would soon be a second enlarged edition of his *Description of Leicestershire*, William Burton seems to have been sufficiently afflicted by that very melancholia which so fascinated his brother Robert, to have felt the need to defend his own work in advance against 'supersilious criticks' and 'carpers'. As he then emphasized,

> I may truly affirm, that there is no one sailing upon a vast and unknown sea, can still stop shipwreck; nor wandering in a wild desert, where no path is extant, can justly hit his intended way; none passing in the dark can always find his end; so in that vast, wild and dark study, what hope is there always to find the certain truth, and never to be misled by error?[1]

How often must the general editor of so huge an enterprise as the *Victoria History* feel the same, as endless copy from far-flung parts of the realm passes before his eyes? Fortunately for us the beneficiaries of Christopher Elrington's calm, efficient, and discriminating scholarly skills, where error there is he can be depended upon in kindly wise to scotch it, and what he writes himself he pens with masterly precision and lucidity.

That, sadly, has not been always so in the curious and sometimes wild development of the writing of county histories and certainly not in the more particular experiences of Leicestershire and Rutland. For that situation, however, the very object of study itself is perhaps partly to blame. In the historiographical tradition of the genre, indeed, there may be said to have rapidly evolved a fundamental tension that only now shows some small sign of being resolved: the tension between on the one hand the introductory survey of the shire as a whole or, in its absence, the overall impression created by the accumulated massing of the detail, and on the other the microscopic matter of the parochial gazetteer. For, separately and therefore paradoxically, as is still the case with the *Victoria History*, county history is usually also both parochial and, indeed, hundredal history at the very same time. In the case of

---

[1] J. Nichols, *Hist. and Antiquities of County of Leicester* (4 vols. in 8 pts. 1795–1811, reprinted 1971), iii (1) p. xxii; D. Williams, 'William Burton's Revised Edition of "Description of Leicestershire"', *Trans. Leics. Arch. and Hist. Soc.* [hereafter *T.L.A.S.*], l (1974–5), 30–40.

the *V.C.H.* at least we may be thankful that that division remains. Christopher Elrington rightly has ever been the staunchest defender of the topographical volumes as the bedrock of the whole project, and should the *V.C.H.* not complete the toilsome task of laying those foundations, certainly no one else ever will. But if that work may be left in the safe hands of the contributors to the great *descriptio*, the technical matter of how *in principle* the characterization of a county as a whole and a gazetteer of its parts might be logically reconciled elsewhere remains to be explored. Since the counties of Leicester and Rutland have often been the objects of historical experiment, their ever-changing treatment by successive generations of historians may constitute a particularly appropriate measure both of the evolving stance of the traditional county history in those respects and of the implications of those matters for historians today.

Leaving aside the passing interest of John Rous, the continuous historiography of both counties strictly begins not with William Burton, squire of Lindley near Hinckley, but with William Wyrley, from 1604 Rouge Croix Pursuivant of Arms, who, from the year after the Armada, was already exploring and noting the heraldry in the churches of both Leicestershire and Rutland (as well as those of other counties) and who later was to accompany Burton himself on similar visits in the 1600s.[2] Begun in 1597, *The Description of Leicestershire* itself, when eventually it appeared in 1622, was advertised in its subtitle as *containing Matters of Antiquitye, Historye, Armorye, and Genealogy*, having previously been no less accurately entitled 'Collectio armorum, insignium gentilitiorum, tumulorum, et eorum inscriptionum, monumentorum' etc.[3] As such, it was later to be the chosen model for James Wright's *The History and Antiquities of the County of Rutland: Collected from Records, Ancient Manuscripts, Monuments on the Place, and other Authorities*, which was published in 1684, although researched over many years before. With Burton, whose work was licensed by the Earl Marshal, Wright too affirmed 'the Antiquity of a Church Window, for the proof of a match and issue had', but since so much armorial glass had been smashed during the Civil War period, Wright's work also highlighted 'The violation of funeral Rites' and criticized 'the disornament of Churches' as blinding 'the truth of History'. Both writers have thus to be seen against the background not only of the heraldic visitation but also of the long-term development, through the Reformation period into contemporary times, of the elaborate monumental tomb with its heraldic adornments, the heraldic funeral itself, and hence the mental world represented by John Weever's *Ancient Funerall Monvments within the*

---

[2] Nichols, *Leics.* iii (1), p. xv and n. 1; ibid. iii (2), 992.
[3] Ibid. iii (1), p. xv.

Vnited Monarchie of Great Britain (1631), which work Wright specifically cites.[4]

Burton's introduction was scrappy, and it is Wright who is usually credited with producing the first brief overall introductory survey of an English county, but the cumulative effect of the work of both writers was identical.[5] In theirs, the earliest stage of local historical writing, the Midland emphasis was not on contemporary regional description or chorography as in the south-west, but on the county history as a retrospective ceremonial substitute for the perpetual chantry. This then was essentially a newly invented cult of the gentle dead within its own traditionally bounded arena of local influence; a collective recitation of distinguished forefathers; a hymn to the descent of provincial property and office; and through that—but only lastly—a legitimization of the current realities of *county* leadership on the one hand and, through the gazetteer, of *manorial* lordship on the other. The two spatial levels were thus for the first and possibly only time logically connected, and without reference to any intervening grouping by hundred.

A century later, a second phase of historiographical development marked a widening of emphasis to a point where the image of 'the county' visibly shifted. True there were many continuities between the old and the new modes. Wright, for example, had illustrated a number of Rutland's greater mansions and churches in ways that were to be more strongly developed by both John Nichols and John Throsby, while the gazetteer format too continued to thrive in amplified form: Nichols indeed cannibalized Burton's work in its entirety. Yet to those evolving approaches were added others.

The Baconian distinction between civil and natural history was but tardily explored in the region and never accomplished systematically.[6] The fragments of an attempt made by Francis Peck (1692–1743)—the historian of Stamford and the author of an unfinished *History and Antiquities of Rutland*—to compile 'the Natural History and Antiquities of Leicestershire' were described as 'slender' by John Nichols, who nevertheless absorbed what little there was into his own gigantic *History and Antiquities*. There he also summarizes Peck's somewhat idiosyncratic plan to digest his scientific materials into 'Stones, Salt, Long Life, Herbs, Earthquakes, Crevaces and Apparitions'.[7] For 'A catalogue of some of the more RARE PLANTS found in the Neighbourhood of LEICESTER, LOUGHBOROUGH and in

    [4] J. Wright, *Hist. and Antiquities of County of Rutland*, 'Preface to Reader', unpaginated (1973 reprint); C. Gittings, *Death, Burial and the Individual in Early Modern England* (1984), chapter 8.
    [5] J. Simmons, 'Writing of English County Hist.' in *English County Historians*, ed. J. Simmons (1978), 10.
    [6] S. A. E. Mendyk, *'Speculum Britanniae': Regional Study, Antiquarianism and Science in Britain to 1700* (1989), 116–35.
    [7] Nichols, *Leics.* ii (1), 203; i (1), pp. clxxxvii–cxc.

CHARLEY FOREST', however, Nichols had to rely on the celebrated botanist Dr. Richard Pulteney (1730–1801), while for 'THE NATURAL HISTORY OF THE VALE OF BELVOIR', he found himself dependent on no less a person than the poet, the Revd. George Crabbe, rector of Muston; and for problems of stratification and 'fossiology' in the same vicinity, on the work of the Revd. William Mounsey.[8]

As Professor Jack Simmons has rightly emphasized, one of the more important of Nichols's own innovations was his extraordinary expansion of the supporting visual materials,[9] into what might almost be described as a visual gazetteer of the parishes in its own right. His illustrations, which directly reflect the curiosity he could show about anything, thus range from earthworks and architecture via monumental brasses, carved stones, cast-off fonts, prehistoric axe-heads, seals, coins, fossils, through to portraits of people. Frequently buildings are shown in their settings—the ultimate example being the two 'prospects' exhibiting the provincial palace of the dukes of Rutland: Belvoir Castle brooding like an English Versailles over its formal gardens and landscaped parkland with the subjugated landscape of the Vale beyond.[10] At the very moment that Versailles itself symbolically fell, indeed, that last was the approach that had been taken more specifically still by John Throsby in his *Select Views in Leicestershire from Original Drawings containing Seats of the Nobility and Gentry, Town Views and Ruins*, of 1789. A year later—and so betraying his visual priorities—he was to add *The Supplementary Volume to the Leicestershire Views containing a series of Excursions in the year 1790 to the Villages and Places of Note in the County*.

The 'Leicestershire' evoked by Throsby and more especially Nichols (the publication of whose eight enormous tomes spanned the years 1795–1815), therefore, directly reflected the contemporaneous apotheosis of the country house in two ways. If the landscape of the county itself could be treated almost as a cultivated landed estate—even a formal country park or a garden—replete with visual surprises or curiosities to be absorbed, 'The Ruins . . . and the Churches' were now to be regarded, in Throsby's fashion-conscious words, as 'sources for contemplation'.[11] John Nichols's Leicestershire, however, was effectively also a country-house museum: a showcase in which were exhibited either those curious local objects—whether archaeological or natural—that appealed to the acquisitive collecting urges of the late 18th-century gentleman, or documents, laudatory poems, memoirs of the famous or eccentric, and even inventories of other men's pictures.

[8] Ibid. i (1), pp. cciii–ccvii.
[9] J. Simmons, 'Introduction' to Nichols, *Leics.* i (1) (1971), pp. [x–xi].
[10] Nichols, *Leics.* ii (1), plates vii and viii opposite p. 25.
[11] Throsby, *Select Views*, p. iii.

Meanwhile, still available for consultation—as it were, in the adjoining library—there remained a more exhaustive catalogue than ever before of local manorial descents, to which numerous other unconnected details of parish interest were now randomly added. Where the historical county had been dimly perceived by the 17th century midst the melancholy gloom of parochial chancels, a later version of it was observed by the 18th century through the study window-panes of the country mansion. The view was thus a proprietary one with the county boundary now assumed to form a logical distant horizon for no other reason than that it, the hundreds which determined it, and the ruling families within it, had anciently been there.

Nichols represents a major transitional figure in the crafting of county history in ways that are worthy of note. First, his is the last of that tradition locally of county history as a process of *cumulative* correction and writing, one in which therefore previous perceptions are simply carried over from the old to the new. He acknowledged over 100 helpers in his preface, while for his detailed gazetteer alone, he consulted nearly two dozen corrected versions of the first edition of Burton which had been lovingly annotated by local landowners (and frequently brought to his attention by them) and triumphantly included relevant parts of Burton's own lost corrections and additions when the revised manuscript came to light. Numerous too were Nichols's other 'co-adjutors' whose own work was sometimes absorbed with open acknowledgement *in toto* into his: more or less the entire text of *The History and Antiquities of Claybrook in the County of Leicester*, which had been published as recently as 1791, for example, was included by Nichols with the willing assent of its author, the Revd. A. Macaulay.[12] Distance from such national records as were accessible, the existence of private family muniments and personal collections of documents, transcripts, and antiquarian writings, made essential such collaboration through constant correspondence, visiting, and lending amongst enthusiasts from Burton to Nichols. The outcome of inevitably uneven help of that kind, however, was a lack of system in the approach.

There is another and not wholly unconnected way in which Nichols's work may be seen as marking a stage in the historiography of the region. Like those of other authors, his generalized prefatory observations about the county as a whole are meagre. Instead, he adopts two other means of introduction to his detailed text. His first solution is to print documents of as near county-wide coverage as possible: not only Farley's text of Domesday—which he himself had previously published—but also a whole range of sources both ecclesiastical and lay from the *Matriculus* of Bishop Hugh of Wells through

---

[12] C. J. Billson, 'Predecessors and Coadjutors of John Nichols, Historian of Leics.' in *Leicester Memoirs* (1924), 123–42; for Burton, above, n. 1.

subsidy rolls and muster lists down to some of the governmental sources that were now becoming publicly available on, significantly, a county-by-county basis, like the parliamentary returns on charities and, in the last volume to be published, the overall figures from both the 1801 and 1811 censuses.[13] With that new and fashionable statistical aid, those interested in a particular place—as opposed to a manor—could choose, if they wished, to see its standing exhibited comparatively with other places across the county at specific dates. Highly significant, here, was the incorporation of printed information from national outlets, a process that increasingly did much to undermine the interdependence of the former antiquarian tradition. It also helped to encourage a more systematic approach.

That historiographical shift was reflected in two contrasted ways in our area. The traditional concentration on the pedigrees of noble and gentle families and the careers of important individuals was taken to new heights of documentary precision and detail in Thomas Blore's *The History and Antiquities of the County of Rutland* (1811), although only the second part of the first volume on *The East Hundred* was actually published, so that we lack his introductory material and therefore a statement of his historical intentions.[14] Blore's main interest, however, was the impact of his local dignitaries on the national scene. The new model was more sternly signalled, secondly, by the headmaster of the free grammar school at Ashby-de-la-Zouch in 1831, the Revd. J. Curtis, in his preface to *A Topographical History of the County of Leicester, The Ancient Part Compiled from Parliamentary And Other Documents And the Modern From Actual Survey*:

> Topography, in the estimation of writers on that subject, comprises a history of whatever was, or is; . . . and hence arises the confusion, the irregularity, and the want of order in almost all works on the subject, with scarcely any exception. It might be affirmed . . . that in the great mass of them, it would be in vain to seek for precisely the same species of information, running uniformly and invariably through all their parts and subdivisions.[15]

His personally preferred solution, therefore, was a condensed, mechanistic account:

> The same description of information will be found in every Parish and Hamlet, and in the same situation; so that there can be no difficulty in seeking what is required in its proper place: and however brief in many cases the notices may be considered, still they are uniform and invariable.

---

[13] Nichols, *Leics.* i (2) (1815), 10 pp. added before the index.
[14] See also 'Bibliography of Rut.' *Rut. Magazine*, i (1904), 54–61.
[15] Curtis, *Topographical Hist.* p. iii.

Curtis listed each place (including Leicester) in alphabetical order regardless of hundred. The history of every place was then reconstituted from a systematic regional index compiled, in chronological order, from each of the 11 medieval national sources now conveniently published by the Record Commissioners (the *Valor Ecclesiasticus* in particular being quoted where appropriate *in extenso*), to which were added information from the 1821 census, figures for poor-rate expenditure in 1824, and the values of glebe land, each article ending, almost dismissively, with a page reference to Nichols. Curtis's book was designed to be the first in a national series and to be economically priced, a revealing further step forward in widening the audience for county history.[16] It was no accident, therefore, that in 1846 Curtis's work would provide the historical core of the Leicestershire sections of William White's *History, Gazetteer, and Directory of Leicestershire and the small County of Rutland*, where the emphasis, of course, was commercial, and in which the two counties were treated together in print for the first time.

If the direction of county history was thus now changing, Nichols himself had played a further important part in that process. His own work was prefaced not only by some cursory general remarks, and by transcribed county documents, but also, and deliberately, with an account of the town from which the shire took its name. In that he was again very lucky to have had material from Throsby, from Samuel Carte, and more particularly from the unpublished papers of William Staveley (which had almost reached print under the editorship of Dr. Richard Farmer).[17] As a result, Nichols effectively used the largely political history of Leicester as itself a surrogate historical introduction—well salted, as was customary, with events and people of national significance—to the county at large. He thus skilfully evaded the central historiographical issue concerned here.

That towns at last should be given increasing local prominence, however, was not simply because they were growing in population and industrial employment as never before, but also because rather belatedly, by comparison with many other centres like Stamford, Leicester and its smaller neighbours were only then beginning to attract sufficiently influential numbers of the 'polite', who now began to project their own residential area as a collective image of the country house, with its more refined architecture, its elegant facilities for recreation and learning, musical performances, formal gardens, and so on. Nor, equally, was it coincidental that urban antiquities themselves also began to attract increasing attention. Nichols—but as a Londoner marrying into the area—had cut his own teeth in 1782 on the history of

---

[16] Ibid. p. iv.
[17] J. Throsby, *Hist. and Antiquities of Ancient Town of Leicester* (1791); Billson, *Leicester Memoirs*, 128–32, 137–8.

Hinckley, which he later incorporated in its entirety into his larger work. If, from Market Harborough, he was able to assimilate the work of another antiquary, Rowland Rouse, that town was to produce its own published history in 1808.[18] Leicester itself was covered chronologically by John Throsby, parish clerk to the civic church, in his *The History and Antiquities of the Ancient Town of Leicester* (1791). The outstanding local urban historian of the 19th century, however, was James Thompson, whose *History of Leicester, from the Time of the Romans to the End of the Seventeenth Century* appeared in 1849, and a second volume, *History of Leicester in the Eighteenth Century*, 22 years later. Here at least was a work based on extensive documentary research that had been properly digested to create a coherent narrative of the town's development.

If the county town was thus soon to replace the country house as the sophisticated prism through which the rustic history of the region might now be refracted, Leicester itself was poised simultaneously between what was new and challenging in the present on the one hand and a newly stimulated apprehension of the past on the other. The former was best expressed intellectually in the largely scientific preoccupations of the local Literary and Philosophical Society founded in 1835, which, however, did include an historical section. It was pressure from that society, combined with the donation of its collections, that led to the establishment of the town's museum in 1849 with its marked bent towards the natural history of the county. Equally innovatory was the founding in 1838 of the Church Building Society of the County and Town of Leicester to provide new churches for the growing population.[19]

By contrast, the historically minded were concentrating on what was being lost. The last days of the timber-framed medieval town were recorded by a local watercolourist, John Flower (d. 1861), who himself nevertheless lived in one of the smarter new quarters of the town.[20] In 1855, under the influence of a number of the leading donors to the Church Building Society, there was founded the Leicestershire Architectural and Archaeological Society in direct imitation of the nationally influential Ecclesiological Society (formerly the Cambridge Camden Society 1839–45). The objects of the new society echoed almost precisely the declared aims of its model. Its concern for the authentic preservation of medieval arrangements as then interpreted was soon amplified by other activities: the reading of papers, 'the exhibition of relics of

---

[18] *Bibliotheca Topographica*, vii (1782); Billson, *Leicester Memoirs*, 139–40; W. Harrod, *Hist. of Market Harborough and Vicinity* (1808).

[19] G.K. Brandwood, *Anglican Churches of Leicester* (Leics. Museums Publication v, 1984), 26.

[20] R. Gill, *Book of Leicester* (1985), 27; J. Simmons, *Leicester Past and Present*, i, *Ancient Borough* (1974), 182.

antiquarian interest'—a continuing reflection of Nichols's concern for museum objects—and regular excursions, most frequently to Gothic churches. If Leicester itself was to become the centre of such activities, it was appropriate to a county society that its annual general meetings should now usually be held in one of the local market towns. Leicestershire, finally, joined the existing union of architectural and archaeological societies of Bedfordshire, Lincolnshire, St. Albans, and the archdeaconry of Northampton and contributed its section annually to their *Reports and Papers*, continuing to do so even after establishing its own series of *Transactions* for papers given before the society since 1855.[21]

The concern for the relics of medievalism was also reflected in a very different way. A rare local historical genre emanating from the 18th-century interest in 'popular' or 'vulgar' antiquities had found expression in the writings of one of Nichols's correspondents, Thomas Sharp (whose *Dissertation on the Pageants or Dramatic Mysteries Anciently performed at Coventry, by the Trading Companies* had appeared in 1825), as well as more recently in Muskett's *Notices and Illustrations of the Costume, Processions, Pageantry etc., formerly Displayed by the Corporation of Norwich* of 1850. At Leicester in 1865 the borough accountant and leading freemason William Kelly produced an unusual local survey that widened those preoccupations even further, and was entitled *Notices Illustrative of the Drama and Other Popular Amusements, Chiefly in the Sixteenth and Seventeenth Centuries, Incidentally Illustrating Shakespeare and his Contemporaries; Extracted from the Chamberlains' Accounts and other Manuscripts of the Borough of Leicester*. It was followed in 1866 by a scholarly work, more liturgical in its interests, by the honorary secretary of the new society, Thomas North—*A Chronicle of the Church of S. Martin in Leicester during the Reign of Henry VIII, Edward VI, Mary and Elizabeth with Some Account of its Minor Altars and Ancient Guilds*.

Those less socially exalted concerns for students of local pasts were thus quite unlike those of their country-house predecessors, albeit the viewpoint was still an educated one. On a wider front and interestingly, however, it was still the county, not the parish, which was regarded as the appropriate spatial expression of regional popular culture. It was symptomatic that in 1881, for example, a local glossary could be entitled *Leicestershire Words, Phrases and Proverbs* by A. B. and S. Evans. With contemporary folklore survivals now fashionably being seen as clues to an understanding not merely of medieval but even of prehistoric practices, and with the *Transactions* of the society

---

[21] Brandwood, *Anglican Churches of Leicester*, 26; *Trans. Leics. Archit. and Arch. Soc.* i (1854–9), 13–20; Anon. *Leics. Arch. Soc. 1855–1955* (1955), 3–10; J. Simmons, 'Papers relating to Leics. Published in *Reports and Papers of Associated Archit. Socs.* 1877–1931', *T.L.A.S.* xxviii (1952), 84–8.

becoming disorganized and scrappy, moreover, it was perhaps not surprising that in 1889 a new quarterly magazine was founded, the *Leicestershire and Rutland Notes and Queries and Antiquarian Gleaner*, edited, published, and sold by Leicester booksellers John and Thomas Spencer. The avowed aim was

> to place on permanent record the Antiquities, Archaeology, Folk-lore, Quaint Manorial Customs, Popular Superstitions, Old Wives' Fables, Provincial Dialects, Old Records of our County (Leicester), and the adjoining County (Rutland, with which it was once connected) and see them regulated and localized, before they pass down the stream of time into the ocean of oblivion.

On the death of one of the editors that promising enterprise came to a sudden end in 1895, the very year in which C. J. Billson published his *Leicestershire and Rutland: County Folk-lore*. In 1902, however, a meeting was held at Oakham to establish an Archaeological and Natural History Society for the County of Rutland, two members of the Leicestershire Architectural Society being invited to 'explain the steps to be taken for carrying out an Archaeological Survey in conjunction with the Leicestershire committee'.[22] Also launched was a new periodical, *The Rutland Magazine and County Historical Record: An Illustrated Quarterly Journal Devoted to the History, Antiquities, Biography, Dialect, Folk-lore, Legend, Genealogy, Topography, Natural History Etc. of the County of Rutland*, edited by G. Phillips. Appearing first in 1903–4, with some papers of sufficient scholarship to be quoted by William Page in the *V.C.H.*, that journal too foundered within a few years. If in the meantime both Leicestershire and Rutland had vastly expanded the storehouse of local knowledge to an unparalleled degree of unconnected detail, that new accumulation would resist any attempt to impose some overall pattern on it. Simultaneously, with the subordination of place to theme, the old established tradition of the manorially based gazetteer was quietly dying except where plagiarized, largely in the commercial directories with their restricted emphasis on helping trade.

The intellectually heady decades that had seen the beginnings of such unprecedented thematic interests, whether cultural or social, now drew to a sudden close with the advent of the new 'scientific study of genealogy'. That austerely disciplined approach to both the analysis of Domesday Book and the reconstruction of manorial descents, which is to be associated above all with Horace Round, first found expression in the region in the early volumes of the *Victoria History*, edited for both Leicestershire (volume one, 1907) and Rutland (volume one, 1908; volume two, 1935) by William Page. The

---

[22] *T.L.A.S.* ix (1899–1904), 147–8.

Domesday sections of each were written under Round's own supervision by
his protégé, F. M. Stenton, who was then making the Danelaw his speciality.
The essential base, the early outline history of any county, was for the first
time thereby laid down in a manner that would remain broadly acceptable for
the next half century and more. In the case of Rutland, the completion of the
topographical volume, which contained Page's obituary, both marked the
recrudescence locally of the parochial gazetteer (each entry being introduced
by one of Page's own pioneering introductions on settlement morphology),
and the stifling of any remaining ambitions on the parts of others to analyse
the county further for years to come.

In Leicestershire, however, where the topographical volumes had to be
postponed, an unlikely alliance forged between Alexander Hamilton
Thompson, reader in medieval history and later professor at the University of
Leeds 1919–39, and George Farnham, scion of an ancient Leicestershire
gentry family, nevertheless led to the radical reconstruction of the contents of
the *Transactions* and a flow of articles tracing with icy precision the descents
of a sequence of local manors, the advowsons of the churches, and their
architectural histories.[23] Farnham, whose bump for local topography was said
to have stemmed from youthful days in the hunting saddle, had the means
and the leisure to make constant visits to the Public Record Office, where he
took meticulous transcripts of documents—especially plea rolls—at first only
as they related to his own family, but later more extensively. In 1912 he had
published his massive *Quorndon Records*—the history of the Farnhams of
Quorn—before collaborating in a series of articles with Hamilton Thompson
and, eventually, concentrating on his own six volumes of *Leicestershire
Medieval Village Notes* (1929–33), with their ordered extracts from a
staggering range of sources. Hamilton Thompson had declared at the time of
the publication of the first four volumes, 'A county history is inevitably a
family history'.[24] If that be so, then the achievement of Farnham's surely
unique gazetteer was to have laid the accurate manorial foundations for every
subsequent history of Leicestershire.

That concern for the highest academic standards in exploiting the source
materials also lay behind the major editions of largely town-centred sources—
both lengthy and brief—that marked the earlier 20th century, including Mary
Bateson's *Records of the Borough of Leicester*, Henry Hartopp's *Register of the
Freemen of Leicester* for 1196–1770 in 1927, and for 1770–1930 in 1933, and

---

[23] *Leics. Arch. Soc.* 15, 20–7; Anon. 'Professor A. Hamilton Thompson', *T.L.A.S.* xxix (1953),
13–14; A. Hamilton Thompson, 'Leics. Arch. Soc. in Present Century', *T.L.A.S.* xxi (1939–41),
122–48.
[24] A. Hamilton Thompson, 'Mr Farnham's Contribution to Hist. of Leics.' *T.L.A.S.* xvi
(1929–31), 12.

Hamilton Thompson's own edition of *A Calendar of Charters and Other Documents belonging to the Hospital of William Wyggeston at Leicester* in 1933. Those and other materials were now rapidly accumulating, but of a history of the county other than a helpful Oxford County History in 1915, written by C. E. Kelsey for 12–16 year olds, there was no sign. For all that had happened in the interval, and despite the advertised intentions of Thomas Potter to publish one in 1849,[25] a whole century later than Curtis's wooden presentation there was still no general reinterpretation of Leicestershire's past. The nearest that anyone came was a valuable collection of otherwise unconnected essays edited by Alice Dryden, entitled *Memorials of Old Leicestershire* (1911), in which she herself sought to provide a brief introductory survey concentrating largely on notable people and events.

The scene was now unconsciously set for little short of a quiet revolution in attitude towards the writing of county history. With the appointment of W. G. Hoskins to the University College of Leicester in 1931, his admission to the Archaeological Society in 1934–5, and the withdrawal of Hamilton Thompson, the manor as the foremost object of analysis was rapidly displaced by the village and its fields, the lord by the peasant, gentry families by the names and lineages of humbler folk, county power-structures by settlement patterns and population fluctuations over the centuries, municipalities by occupational structures and a new curiosity about urban origins and comparative developments. Above all, of course, Hoskins sought to integrate topographical evidence with the documentary, at the same time as he extended pre-existing local interests on the Middle Ages back to the days of settlement, and forward into the pre-industrial period. In a succession of remarkable articles and larger studies spanning the years 1935–51, Hoskins laid the foundations not only of the modern local historical study of Leicestershire, and to a lesser extent Rutland, but also of that of England generally. Leicestershire, indeed, was used by him to test many of his ideas, and it was with his studies of that county that he developed his essentially double-edged approach. In the first instance, and through a series of thematic studies both topographical and socio-economic, Hoskins built up a sparklingly fresh picture of peasant life and material culture—what, borrowing from George Bourne, he came to call 'the peasant civilization' as opposed to 'the country house civilization'.[26] It now seems clear that that portrayal was beginning to coalesce in his mind during the closing years of the Second World War, though it was to be sophisticated both through his

[25] R. A. Rutland, 'Leics. Arch. to 1849: Development of Chronological Interpretation', *T.L.A.S.* lxv (1991), 39.

[26] C. Phythian-Adams, 'Hoskins's England: a Local Historian of Genius and the Realisation of his Theme', *T.L.A.S.* lxvi (1992), 143–59.

own edited volume of 1948, *Studies in Leicestershire Agrarian History*, with amongst others notable contributions from L. A. Parker and M. W. Beresford, and also by the talented team of young writers—R. H. Hilton, R. A. McKinley, J. H. Plumb, and Joan Thirsk—whom he recruited to contribute to a volume of the revived *V.C.H.* on political and agrarian matters (1954). Of them, R. H. Hilton had already published his major study on *The Economic Development of some Leicestershire Estates in the 14th and 15th Centuries* (1947). With the third *V.C.H.* volume (1955) and its crucial sections on industries, communications, and, most notably, 'Population' by C. T. Smith; and a fourth volume on Leicester (1958), the first of its kind on a city alone, only the topographical volumes on each hundred with their component market towns now remained to be written. Of those, Gartree hundred (including Market Harborough) by Janet Martin, Richard McKinley, and J. M. Lee was soon to appear in 1964. Once again survey and gazetteer (which now at last covered economic matters separately in each entry) had been brought back into some sort of conjunction.

Although he never wrote a history of Leicestershire, how Hoskins saw that subject synoptically in terms of economic and social history is clear from his notebooks, his extra-mural teaching programme, and from the pages of his classic work, *The Midland Peasant*, as it came to be called when eventually it was published in 1957 over a decade after its conception. His view is summed up in the description of a course which he taught in 1947:

> The old country civilization and its characteristics. The self-sufficient Leicestershire village, its economic integration and social structure. The squires and their homes, farming and domestic life. Husbandmen, cottagers and labourers and the open-field system, their homes and domestic economy. The village craftsmen and their supreme importance to the village. Village architecture in Leicestershire. The break-up of the old country civilization: enclosure, decay of domestic industry, coming of railways. Decay of the market-town. Leicestershire today.[27]

The second new approach to county history that Hoskins pioneered was closely connected to the first and has proved subsequently to be hugely influential in moulding later 20th-century expectations of what is county history. In *Leicestershire: An Illustrated Essay on the History of the Landscape* (1957), a tiny book (which, however, derived from extensive fieldwork and its crystallization not only in formal articles but also in local handbooks), he sought to express in thematic terms the physical evolution of the local countryside and its towns. It was an approach which brought with it a

---

[27] Leicester Univ. Department of English Local Hist. Archive, Hoskins's papers, hardback notebook H.

number of unintended implications. First, as with his other work locally, Leicestershire was simply taken as a given entity (obviously different in kind from his home county of Devon) and therefore as something that might be characterized in its own right whatever the relationship, or lack of it, between an historic unit of local government and politics on the one hand, and the socio-economic development of the same area and its landscape on the other. Second, the county boundary therefore remained a frame (a state of affairs greatly aided by the growing accessibility in the county of its own records) *within which* local studies could be confined. Third, within that frame those local studies now took on an increasingly spatial content. The map of the county would be used thenceforward increasingly as itself a finite visual 'gazetteer' of places distributed comprehensively according to selected themes, and therefore deployed for such highly specific purposes in relation only to each other and to locally restricted physical features like rivers, roads, or the underlying geology. A new analytical tool had thus come usefully to hand and might thenceforward be employed on such topics as the distribution of evidence for early settlement from prehistoric to Anglo-Saxon, the Domesday county, the incidence of medieval rural markets, the location of deserted village sites, the extent of enclosure at various dates, the mapping of the 1801 crop returns, the spread of industries, the development of modern communication systems, and above all the changing distributions of the county's population over the centuries. That mode has come to dominate the major overall surveys of the county which have been attempted since Hoskins's day: the relevant historical sections of the British Association volume on *Leicester and its Region* (1972), edited by the geographer Professor Norman Pye, and, in 1985, *A History of Leicestershire and Rutland*, by another geographer, an erstwhile colleague of Hoskins and early contributor to his *Making of the English Landscape* series—Roy Millward. To those may also be added the second of two excellent archaeological surveys of the county together with Rutland by Peter Liddle, *Leicestershire Archaeology: the Present State of Knowledge*, ii, *Anglo-Saxon and Medieval Periods* (1982). That cartographic version of historic Leicestershire and more recently Rutland, albeit with different emphases, thus tends to be an efficient, regionally compressed construct of the historical geographer: a spatially organized academic summary paced within a sequence of time-frames.

A byproduct of that approach in the case of Leicestershire has been the continuing emphasis given to the centrality of Leicester by virtue both of its seemingly unambiguous position on minimal base-maps and, of course, of its general predominance in the county in various roles and periods. The publication in 1958 of Leicester as a separate urban volume for the first time in the *Victoria History* underlined its centrality, as did also the two most

important other works on the city: implicitly in A. Temple Patterson's
Radical Leicester (1954) and explicitly in Jack Simmons's masterly two-
volume synopsis, *Leicester Past and Present* (1974).

By the later 1980s, therefore, it looked at first sight as though a satisfactory
modern view of Leicestershire's past had at last emerged, although only one
topographical volume of the *V.C.H.* had been published and therefore of the
local market towns of the county only Harborough had received modern
scholarly attention in print. With the filling of such *vacua*, it might seem, the
story would eventually be complete. Leicestershire would be treated
thenceforward as a tidy administrative and socio-economic entity: a region
focusing in on its own county town, with an overall history which united a
succession of predominantly economic themes experienced to varying degrees
by its constituent rural and urban settlements as opposed to manors. Since 1974,
moreover, in much of the literature Rutland has tended to be merged into the
historic easterly margin of Leicestershire (the ancient boundary between the two
being simply ignored on some distribution maps). There could be no more vivid
indication of the degree to which the silent adoption of the area as a 'region' has
thus displaced the primacy of the 'county' as the object of historical study.

So summary a view of course masks the notice that has long been taken by
historians of the more subtle interior variations of terrain within the area,
and thereby the tacit subdivision of that 'region' into entities other than
hundreds. The most notable of those, Charnwood forest, or more accurately
the waste of Charnwood, has drawn the attention of all local writers and has
attracted *inter alia* two notably wide-ranging studies: Thomas Potter's *The
History and Antiquities of Charnwood Forest* (1842), and more recently
Charnwood Forest: A Changing Landscape, edited by John Crocker for the
Loughborough Naturalists Club in 1981. Both those studies take account of
the natural terrain in a way that G. F. Farnham, *Charnwood Forest and its
Historians and the Charnwood Manors* (1930), with its otherwise valuably
corrective emphasis on the tenurial history, does not. The broader approach
also characterizes the useful study of *Leicester Forest* by Levi Fox and Percy
Russell in 1948. The cumulative effect of such concentration on the pastoral
western side of the county, taken in conjunction with the work of W. G.
Hoskins on the easterly distribution of deserted villages and the mapping of
his material on the 1801 crop returns by H. C. K. Henderson, led to the
recognition of a crucial division between the eastern landscapes of the lower
Lias and those of the Keuper Marl to the west, a division which appears to
have underlain the long-term shift of population from the east to the west of
the county, first revealed by C. T. Smith.[28] If the royal forest of

---

[28] H. C. K. Henderson, '1801 Crop Returns: Geographical Distributions', *T.L.A.S.* xxvii (1951),
100–2; Hoskins, *Leics.* fig. 3 on p. 28; C. T. Smith, 'Population', *V.C.H. Leics.* iii. 128–55.

Leicestershire and Rutland in that eastern zone has only received attention in the *V.C.H.*, the most crucial breakthrough in our understanding of the agricultural sub-regions of the area has come from recent analyses of the wold countrysides that more or less ring the county round from the Nottinghamshire-Leicestershire wolds to the north, via east and south Leicestershire, and north again along the Leicestershire-Warwickshire border towards the 'wolds' around Ashby-de-la-Zouch. Together, therefore, the wold areas physically separate the core of Leicestershire from its county neighbours to the east, south, and west.[29]

Those usually underpopulated watershed landscapes may be treated as a type of *pays* in its own right or, as for long periods, countrysides linked to the more populous valleys or vales on both sides of them. In either case, historians increasingly focus on the changing character of the *societies* that have inhabited them as opposed to their agricultural biases. Such a development potentially shifts the perspective of the modern county historian yet again, towards a consideration of how far the county unit expresses a recognizable local society and culture. At present it is too early to tell with certainty, but work on both Lutterworth and Melton Mowbray for the early modern period indicates that each acted as a centre for an identifiable area.[30] Melton's hinterland extended to inner Leicestershire, but Lutterworth's stretched over the county boundary into contiguous parts of Warwickshire. Similarly, unpublished work on the Welland valley seeks to indicate the separateness of the society on both sides of it and therefore of the county boundary both from inner Leicestershire to the north, *and* from Northampton and the Nene valley to the south.[31] In other words, the Welland line links southern Leicestershire more with southern Rutland and Stamford than with northern Leicestershire. To the north-west of the county, meticulously detailed work on the origins of the county boundary is showing how necessary it is to take account of the adjacent parts of Derbyshire.[32] Separate studies of the western margins of the county, however, tend to show that the ancient boundary, which for a stretch coincides with the watershed between the Trent drainage basin to the north and that of the Severn-Avon to

[29] J. C. Cox, 'Forestry', *V.C.H. Rut.* i. 251–7; R. A. McKinley, 'Forests of Leics.' *V.C.H. Leics.* ii. 265–6; A. Everitt, 'The Wolds Once More', *Jnl. Hist. Geography*, v (1) (1979), 69–70; H. S. A. Fox, 'People of Wolds in English Settlement Hist.' *Rural Settlements of Medieval England*, ed. M. Aston, D. Austin, and C. Dyer (1989), 77–101.

[30] D. Fleming, 'Local Market System: Melton Mowbray and the Wreake Valley, 1549–1720' (Leicester Univ. Ph.D. thesis, 1981); J. D. Goodacre, *Transformation of a Peasant Economy* (forthcoming 1994).

[31] C. Phythian-Adams, 'The Market Harboroughs of England' (J. C. Davies Memorial Lecture, 1992, unpublished).

[32] M. J. Tranter, 'A View from Across the Border', *Anglo-Saxons in Leics.* ed. J. Bourne (forthcoming).

the south-west, was a significant cultural and societal barrier.[33] Nevertheless, to understand that, it is still necessary to look beyond Leicestershire itself into Warwickshire. Finally, empty for much of its extent, east Leicestershire turns its back on northern Rutland, the river valleys of which face eastward. No wonder that, despite an increasingly shared historiography, Leicestershire and Rutland have ever remained obstinately different even to the extent that today each boasts its own separate and excellent 'popular' county journal.[34]

If, however, Leicestershire might be regarded in that way as having a delimited inner societal integrity, we shall in future be needing to distinguish the core area (within which Leicester itself is indeed the central place) from several outer areas that may overlap—to greater or lesser degrees—into neighbouring shires, and which are consequently more loosely connected with the county town. Within that more flexible spatial framework, a new kind of county history might thus become possible: one which accepts not only that county-areas help to give identity to both societies and cultures within them, but also that, paradoxically, the county boundary itself—as an immediate cut-off point for analysis—no longer invariably delineates a study area acceptably.[35] And if general 'county' surveys are to continue to be matched by gazetteers in future, rather different *sub*-divisions of the county (to which now should be added relevant adjacent areas) from the old hundredal unit (usually relevant only to early local government)[36] would similarly have to be envisaged. Whatever the case, given often radical redistributions of local populations from time to time, it seems doubtful in future whether, outside the ever-essential pages of the *Victoria History*, it will any longer be possible meaningfully to retain component places within the same gazetteer-grouping for every century to be surveyed. A more flexible approach by period, inevitably involving some chronological and spatial overlap as places are moved from one grouping to another, might be worth seriously considering if historians are finally to slip the conceptual shackles into which generations of illustrious predecessors have unwittingly locked them. Deliberately relating the county as a formal institution to a society inhabiting *approximately* the same area, moreover, might now make better sense than pretending that a local government area, whatever the social needs

[33] C. Phythian-Adams, *Continuity, Fields and Fission: Making of a Midland Parish* (Leicester Univ. Department of English Local Hist. Occasional Papers, 3rd ser. iv, 1978), 27, 33; *Re-thinking English Local Hist.* (ibid. 4th ser. i, 1987), 37–42

[34] *Leics. Historian* (1967 onwards); *Rut. Rec.* (1980 onwards).

[35] *Societies, Cultures and Kinship 1580–1850*, ed. C. Phythian-Adams (1993).

[36] C. Phythian-Adams, 'Rut. Reconsidered', *Mercian Studies*, ed. A. M. Dornier (1977), 63–84; idem, *Norman Conquest of Leics. and Rut.: Regional Introduction to Domesday Book* (Leics. Museums Publication lxxiii, 1986), 9–11.

reflected in its origins, is automatically a continuously appropriate, finite entity within which to study all other aspects of the past. Perhaps we historians have made our study so 'wild and dark' that we have sometimes even obscured it for ourselves.

LINCOLNSHIRE

Christopher Sturman

Lincolnshire, with a rich tradition of historical scholarship, has nevertheless proved relatively barren ground for county historians: the size of the county and the high costs of publication have undoubtedly militated against the completion of a full survey. Many have collected material but published results are few and incomplete; much energy, however, has been channelled into the history of its wapentakes and hundreds and its distinctive regions, notably the fenland and the Isle of Axholme. Only in recent years has anything approaching a rigorous county history been undertaken.

Historical research on Lincolnshire began in the 17th century, stimulated to some extent by earlier heralds' visitations.[1] That is certainly evident in the heraldic and genealogical work of the Lincoln blacksmith James Yorke, whose *Union of Honour* was printed in 1640. It is evident, too, in the detailed church notes collected by Gervase Holles (1607–75) in the 1630s and early 1640s,[2] and in his history of the Holles family written in 1658, but, as Holles explained in that work, his interests went much further:

> Amongst those other innocent entertainments with which I have pleased my selfe in my life, it hath not beene a litle time or paynes that I have spent in investigating the antiquities and families of my owne country. Nor have I done it without some intention of publique benefit, designing with my selfe . . . to have digested a relation both historicall and genealogicall concerning the county of Lincolne . . . And to that purpose I had gathered together very many materialls out of history, recordes, charters, and church monuments; and more I had enriched my selfe with every day had not this damned and dire Rebellion . . . rob'd me of my whole leisure, and of a great part of my collections.

Holles managed to transport the 'remaynder of the wrack' to the Netherlands but was unable to complete his history: 'for he that will erect such a structure must have all his materialls ready before he can build anything'.[3]

---

[1] See also D. Owen, 'Development of Hist. Studies in Lincs.' *Some Historians of Lincs.* ed. C. Sturman (1992), 7–12.

[2] *Lincs. Church Notes made by Gervase Holles, A.D. 1634 to A.D. 1642*, ed. R. E. G. Cole (Lincoln Rec. Soc. i, 1911).

[3] *Memorials of Holles Family 1493–1656 by Gervase Holles*, ed. A. C. Wood (Camden 3rd ser. lv, 1937), 8.

At the same time that Holles was gathering material in the north of the county, in the south Robert Sanderson (1587–1663), rector of Boothby Pagnell until 1643, and from 1660 bishop of Lincoln, was working with equal industry.[4] The history of Sanderson's collection, especially the index to his notes arranged by wapentake,[5] illuminates much later antiquarian activity in the county. His heraldic collections were known to Abraham de la Pryme in the 1690s[6] and his notes on the monuments of Lincoln cathedral, made in 1641, were first published by Francis Peck in 1735.[7] Sanderson's index was augmented by Thomas Sympson between 1741 and 1743;[8] by the 1790s it had been acquired by Sir Joseph Banks,[9] who made it available to Edmund Turnor of Grantham;[10] it was later bought by William John Monson, 6th Lord Monson, from a London bookseller.[11]

De la Pryme (1671–1704), curate of Broughton, made extensive collections for north-west Lindsey and published the results of some of his field surveys in the *Philosophical Transactions of the Royal Society*. He was the product of the newly invigorated antiquarian movement of the time. The role played by Lincolnshire men in it is further seen in the foundation of the Spalding Gentlemen's Society in 1712 by Maurice Johnson (1688–1755) and in the archaeological investigations of his friend William Stukeley (1687–1765). Stukeley published some of his findings in *Itinerarium Curiosum* (1724).[12] The Gentlemen's Society started as a literary meeting and its early minute books reflect the catholic nature of its members' interests. The communications of such antiquarians as Francis Peck (1692–1743), Thomas Sympson (1702–50), and Samuel Pegge (1704–96) are thus found alongside medical matters, botany, and natural history.[13] With Maurice Johnson's death there was a waning in the society's interests; the decline was perhaps more general: in terms of historical work, the mid 18th century was a relatively unproductive period for Lincolnshire.

---

[4] See in particular G. G. Walker, 'Dr. Robert Sanderson', *Associated Archit. Socs.' Reports and Papers* [hereafter *A.A.S.R.P.*], xxxi (1) (1911), 25–7.

[5] Lincs. A.O., Monson 7/43; Bodl. MS. Gough Lincs. 4, including additionally Beltisloe wapentake.

[6] *Diary of Abraham de la Pryme*, ed. C. Jackson (Surtees Soc. liv, 1870), 83.

[7] *Desiderata Curiosa* (2 vols. 1732–5), ii, Liber VIII, pp. 1–31.

[8] E. M[ansell] S[ympson], 'Thomas Sympson', *Lincs. Notes and Queries*, ix (1906), 75, 77, 81.

[9] Lincs. A.O., Monson 7/11/81.

[10] E. Turnor, *Collections for Hist. of Town and Soke of Grantham* (1806), p. v.

[11] Bound into vol. ii is a statement, dated 14 June 1839, by the bookseller John Russell Smith: 'This Manuscript was rescued from the hands of a butcher in Soho, who was using it as waste paper & was purchased by me of the person who discovered it': Lincs. A.O., Monson 7/43.

[12] *Minute Books of Spalding Gentlemen's Soc. 1712–1755*, ed. D. M. Owen and S. W. Woodward (Lincoln Rec. Soc. lxxiii, 1981); [J. Nichols], 'Some Account of Gentlemen's Soc. at Spalding', *Bibliotheca Topographica Britannica*, xx (1784). Stukeley's drawings are listed in Appendix D of the first edn. of S. Piggott, *William Stukeley: an 18th-Century Antiq.* (1950).

[13] Bodl. MSS. Gough Lincs. 1, 5–10, 12.

Towards the end of the century, renewed stimulus came through Sir Joseph Banks (1743–1821), president of the Royal Society, who from 1779 made annual visits in September and October to Revesby Abbey, his Lincolnshire estate. Banks had extensive notes made on Lincolnshire materials, and collected manuscripts and engravings. Between 1789 and 1805 he employed the artist John Claude Nattes to produce a series of views, principally of gentlemen's seats and churches.[14] Lincolnshire-born artists were also active, notably William Fowler of Winterton (1761–1832),[15] who produced remarkable hand-coloured engravings of stained-glass windows and mosaic pavements, and Thomas Espin of Louth (1767–1822).[16] From 1797 the Louth-born engraver Bartholomew Howlett (1767–1827) began to issue a series of views of churches, gentlemen's seats, and antiquities in the county, including several of Nattes's and Espin's works.

The first known proposal for a full county survey was made by John Cragg of Threekingham in the *Lincoln, Rutland and Stamford Mercury* of 7 March 1800:

A VILLARE LINCOLNIENSE; or an Alphabetical List of all the Towns, Villages, Hamlets and Manors in the county of Lincoln, describing the Wapentake they are situated in and the Place they are near, with the present Owners of the said Manors, as far as the same could be ascertained; and to show the comparative Size of the Parishes, the number of taxable Houses are figured opposite thereto; with the Date annexed when many of their Inclosures took place. Also the name of High sheriffs and Members of Parliament for the County, City and several Boroughs, from the earliest Accounts of Time.

To which will be added, the Places contained in Domesday Book, with their present Names assigned to each, and the Reference to the Pages wherein the Survey thereof may be found: This Part, it is hoped, will be an acceptable Acquisition to the Antiquary and to such Gentlemen who have Property in any Village referred to in that venerable Record.

Cragg's *Villare* was never published.[17] The first decades of the 19th century, however, saw a flowering of publishing activity, including the first county surveys, many embellished by engravings and vignettes. Howlett's *Selection of Views in the County of Lincolnshire*, with brief historical descriptions by F. Vincent, appeared in 1805;[18] volume nine of E. W. Brayley and J. Britton's

[14] As early as 1786 Banks was considering a county hist.: *Banks Letters*, ed. W. R. Dawson (1958), 434. Banks used his copy of Holles's church notes as a filing-system for Lincs. material: Lincoln Central Library, Banks MSS. 4–9. The library also houses the Nattes drawings; the Lincs. engravings are in the library of the Spalding Gentlemen's Soc.

[15] *Correspondence of William Fowler of Winterton*, ed. J. T. Fowler (1907).

[16] [R. S. Bayley], *Notitiae Ludae* (1834), 270.

[17] Formerly Lincs. A.O., Cragg 1/2 (present location unknown); ibid. Cragg 1/1 is a later version (*c.* 1824–31) of the topographical directory.

[18] Howlett later (*c.* 1820) proposed to issue in parts 'Ecclesiastical Antiquities of County of Lincoln' with text by John Caley: Lincs. A.O., Monson 7/40/4.

Beauties of England and Wales (1807) included Lincolnshire.[19] Both had undoubted appeal to the county gentry whose patronage Cragg had failed to solicit and who were not too concerned about historical accuracy. The beginnings of a proper county history were made by the Boston printer William Marrat (1772–1852) with his *History of Lincolnshire, Topographical, Historical and Descriptive* (1814–16). The work was issued in parts but was never finished (volumes one to three, covering much of Holland and Kesteven, are complete, but volumes four and five are fragmentary): Marrat alleged that publication was curtailed because Sir Joseph Banks had refused him access to his collections.[20] George Weir's *Historical and Descriptive Account of Lincolnshire* (1828) progressed no further than the first volume (Lincoln and Lindsey). Thomas Allen (1803–33), whose publications included histories of London, Surrey, and Sussex, began to issue in parts from 1830 *The History of the County of Lincoln* but it was suspended at his death. Publication was taken over by John Saunders of Lincoln, but only two volumes (1833–4) were completed. Saunders later issued *Lincolnshire in 1836*, a return to the somewhat anodyne formula of Howlett's compilation.[21] One other planned work deserves mention: *c.* 1819 the genealogist T. C. Banks (1765–1854) issued a prospectus to print, preparatory to a county history, a one-volume folio edition of Domesday Book, the Book of Fees, and other medieval records,[22] but like Cragg's more modest proposal it came to nothing.

At the same time Lincolnshire printers and London publishers issued a number of histories dealing with smaller regions. The beginnings were not entirely propitious: Edmund Turnor's *Collections for the History of the Town and Soke of Grantham* appeared in 1806 but only one number of John Moore's *Collections for a Topographical, Historical, and Descriptive Account of the Hundred of Aveland* (1806) was issued and only one of the two projected volumes of W. Peck's *Topographical Account of the Isle of Axholme* (1815) was printed. However, Pishey Thompson's *Collections for a Topographical and Historical Account of Boston and the Soke of Skirbeck* (1820),[23] George Weir's *Historical and Descriptive Sketches of the Town and Soke of Horncastle* (1820), Richard Yerburgh's *Sketches Illustrative of the Topography and History of Old and New Sleaford and of Several Places in the Surrounding Neighbourhood*

---

[19] Reissued as *Topographical and Hist. Description of County of Lincoln* [*c.* 1817].

[20] *D.N.B.* s.v. Marrat.

[21] It was conceived as the first part of a much more ambitious project, 'England in 19th Century': Lincoln Central Library, Banks MSS. 20/20/7–9.

[22] Lincs. A.O., Monson 7/40/12 (3 copies). Banks and the chess virtuoso J. H. Sarratt (d. 1819) were listed as the compilers. In another copy of his prospectus, Banks deleted Sarratt's name and described himself as 'Antiquary and Professor of Genealogy &c &c &c'.

[23] Revised as *Hist. and Antiquities of Boston and Villages of Skirbeck, Fishtoft, Freiston, Butterwick, Benington, Leverton, Leake, and Wrangle* (1856). See also I. Bailey, *Pishey Thompson: Man of Two Worlds* (1991).

(1825), and W. B. Stonehouse's *History and Topography of the Isle of Axholme* (1829) show that local antiquarian activity was in a lively state. At least one author recognized that a Lincolnshire county history could be achieved only through pooling the efforts of several historians working on their own areas of the county: in the prospectus (*c.* 1821) for his *Topographical and Historical Account of Wainfleet and the Wapentake of Candleshoe*, Joshua Cheffins stated:

> The publication of detached portions of Local History, by persons resident in the immediate vicinity of the places described, will furnish the best possible materials, for a GENERAL HISTORY of this important division of the kingdom; the compilation of which is certainly a work beyond the accomplishment of any one individual.[24]

Such sentiments did not deter workers in the mid 19th century from gathering material. The artist, architect, and antiquary E. J. Willson of Lincoln (1787–1854) certainly planned to write a history of the county. He acquired William Marrat's collections and made his own notes by parish and wapentake, but was increasingly preoccupied with the city of Lincoln. His library and manuscript collections were dispersed by auction in 1888.[25] Another Lincolnian, John Ross (1801–70), made equally extensive historical notes and drawings,[26] and the printer Adam Stark (1784–1867) also gathered material for a county history.[27] The outstanding collector of Lincolnshire material in the first half of the 19th century, however, was William John Monson, 6th Lord Monson (1796–1862): his zeal in making notes on churches and manuscripts was matched by his enthusiasm for purchasing original documents. He was encouraged by his brother-in-law A. S. Larken, who later became Richmond Herald. At one stage they evidently planned a county history, to judge from Larken's enthusiastic comment when Monson purchased Bishop Sanderson's index: 'What a man in 10,000 this Bishop was! He really ought to be canonized by all Lincolnshire Antiquaries. We must get the finest Portrait we can of him to put in our History.'[28]

---

[24] Lincs. A.O., Monson 7/40/10. Cheffins's work was seen through the press in 1829 by Edmund Oldfield.

[25] Sotheby, Wilkinson and Hodge, sale catalogue, 30 May 1888, pp. 16–32. Some of Willson's collections are in the library of the Soc. of Antiq., e.g. 786/3 (Local Notes by Parishes and Wapentakes, II), 786/11–12 (Marrat).

[26] Lincoln Central Library, Ross MSS.; his antiq. correspondence (1823–70) is at Lincs. A.O., Hill 40.

[27] Lincs. A.O., Brace 14/6–10. For Stark see J. S. English, 'Adam Stark, Charles Moor, and other Historians of Gainsborough', *Some Historians of Lincs.* 83.

[28] Lincs. A.O., Monson 7/30/110, 29 Jan. 1839; also *Lincs. Church Notes made by William John Monson*, ed. J. Monson (Lincoln Rec. Soc. xxxi, 1936). Monson's original church notebooks and his miscellaneous notes relating to the county (including the 'Collectanea Lincolniensia') are respectively Lincs. A.O., Monson 27/1 and 27/3. Monson gathered his antiq. correspondence,

A Lincolnshire Topographical Society, under Monson's patronage, existed briefly from 1841 to c. 1843.[29] The first lasting county antiquarian society, the Lincolnshire Society for the Encouragement of Ecclesiastical Antiquities, was formed at Louth in 1844. Possibly as a result of the influential meeting of the Archaeological Institute at Lincoln in 1848, it eventually moved to Lincoln in 1856, having changed its name in 1849 to the Lincolnshire Architectural Society and in 1853 to the Lincoln Diocesan Architectural Society.[30] At first it issued brief annual reports, but in 1850 joined with other societies to issue the *Reports and Papers* of the Associated Architectural Societies (a practice which continued until 1936). Interest in distinct areas of the county was maintained in the annual excursions, reported in full, often alongside papers relevant to the locality. A further change of name to the Lincolnshire and Nottinghamshire Architectural and Archaeological Society was made in 1885 following the removal of the archdeaconry of Nottingham from the diocese; in 1902 Nottinghamshire was dropped from its title.

During the 1870s there was a stirring of interest once more in a full county history. When the society's librarian John Ross died in 1870, an obituarist, describing him as 'one of the most industrious and skilful antiquaries of Lincolnshire', lamented:

> Had he been spared he would probably have completed his collection of materials and moulded them into a history of this county which is so greatly needed: but unfortunately those materials alone now remain, and a master head and hand are still more than ever necessary to mould these and other sources of information into a work worthy of being called a History of Lincolnshire.[31]

In 1872 Edward Trollope dedicated his *Sleaford, and the Wapentakes of Flaxwell and Aswardhurn* to the bishop of Lincoln, Christopher Wordsworth:

> I beg leave most respectfully to dedicate this little volume to you, as one which may supply some future materials towards a future History . . .
>   I have often been urged to undertake the task of compiling such a History; but have ever felt that the labour required would be too great for me, engaged as I constantly am in more urgent and ceaseless professional duties, as well as from the fact that the cost of its production would be very great, if illustrated and

---

principally that with Larken, in the 6-vol. 'Scrinia Lincolniensis' (Lincs. A.O., Monson 7/29–36). For a description of the important Monson collection at Lincs. A.O. see Lincs. Archives Committee, *Archivists' Report* (1951–2), 5–36.

[29] *Selection of Papers relative to County of Lincoln read before Lincs. Topographical Soc. 1841, 1842* (1843).

[30] Francis Hill, 'Early Days of Soc.' *Lincs. Hist. and Arch.* i (1966), 57–63. The proceedings of the 1848 meeting were published as *Memoirs Illustrative of Hist. and Antiquities of County and City of Lincoln* (1850).

[31] *A.A.S.R.P.* x (i) (1869), p. ix.

printed in a form worthy of the County of Lincoln, and of comparison with the
already published Histories of other Counties.[32]

Bishop Wordsworth became the most enthusiastic champion of a county
history. At his triennial visitation of 1873, concerned that 'the clergy in our
county have usually much time at their disposal', he urged on them the
collecting and writing of historical material:

> Bishop Saunderson, in his 'Articles of Enquiry' issued before his Visitation of the
> Diocese of Lincoln in 1662, requested the clergy to furnish him with any
> interesting particulars which they could discover in their parish churches, such as
> coats of heraldry and ancient inscriptions, illustrative of the history of the county.
> We have no good county history of Lincolnshire. Might not the parochial clergy
> employ some of their spare time in collecting the historical records of their
> respective parishes?[33]

Wordsworth returned to the theme in an address to the Lincoln Diocesan
Architectural Society in 1876,[34] and in 1878 at the conference of archdeacons
and rural deans; their resolution was passed to the Diocesan Society, which
established a committee to examine the proposal. Trollope, the chairman of
the committee, reported back cautiously:

> The first measure essential for the completeness and accuracy of such a work is
> the thorough examination of all such documentary authorities, as the Records of
> the Realm, Calendars of Wills, Episcopal Registers, Heraldic Visitations, and
> other similar sources . . . It would then be necessary that all the extracts derived
> from these materials should be sorted and arranged, according to the Hundreds,
> Parishes, Manors, &c., to which they belong . . .
>   Such extracts can only be supplied by experts, accustomed to the deciphering
> of ancient records . . . but the agency of these experts would necessarily involve a
> considerable expenditure of money, far larger than a Committee of voluntary
> workers could possibly undertake. It is therefore absolutely essential that a
> sufficient *publication-fund* should be provided before any steps can be taken
> towards the production of this important and most desirable work.[35]

By the end of 1879 an exceptionally thorough 'scheme for promoting
uniformity in the arrangement of the materials' and a copy of J. C. Cox's *How
to Write the History of a Parish* (1879) had been issued to all the clergy in the

---

[32] See also T. Leach, 'Edward Trollope and Lincoln Diocesan Archit. Soc.' *Some Historians of
Lincs.* 13–26.
[33] 'The Studies of the Clergy', *Twelve Addresses Delivered at Visitation of Cathedral and Diocese
of Lincoln in the Year MDCCCLXXIII* (1873), 247. For Sanderson's 1662 Articles of Visitation
see *Works of Robert Sanderson*, ed. W. Jacobson (6 vols. 1854–8), iv. 464.
[34] *A.A.S.R.P.* xiii (2) (1876), p. lxi.
[35] Ibid. xiv (2) (1878), pp. lxxvi–vii; Lincs. A.O., A.S. 1A/2, pp. 247–50.

diocese.[36] Although Wordsworth's proposal came to nothing, the foundations for such a work were beginning to be laid, notably from 1874 through the work of J. F. Wickenden (d. 1883) on the cathedral muniments.[37] A. R. Maddison (1843–1912) expressed his feelings forcibly in relation to his work on the bishops' transcripts:

> You may pass resolutions by the score, to the effect that it is desirable that this great important County should have its history worthily written; you may talk and talk by the hour as to how it is to be done, and draw up schemes and prospectuses by the dozen. All this is weaving ropes of sand. The foundations of a County History are laid in work such as I have described.—Cleaning, arranging, docketting, labelling.[38]

Maddison is chiefly remembered for his important four-volume *Lincolnshire Pedigrees* (Harleian Society, 1902–6) and his editions of Lincolnshire wills, but over the years he produced numerous articles, notably on Lincolnshire families, for the *Reports and Papers* and for *Lincolnshire Notes and Queries*. The latter was established in 1888 and had a considerable influence on historical work in the county for nearly 50 years. Other significant contributions along the lines adumbrated by Maddison were made by A. R. Gibbons, Edmund Venables, R. E. G. Cole, and W. O. Massingberd, whilst T. W. Longley, in relative isolation in a remote marshland parsonage, worked on a pioneering (though unpublished) study of the Lincolnshire Domesday and early feudal surveys for the county.[39]

The period also witnessed the final flowering of the area histories, notably for the Fens. W. H. Wheeler, *History of the Fens of South Lincolnshire* (1860; substantially revised 1896), S. H. Miller and S. B. J. Skertchly, *The Fenland Past and Present* (1878), and J. S. Padley, *Fens and Floods of Mid Lincolnshire* (1882) all reflected a growth of interest in a distinctive region for which the quarterly *Fenland Notes and Queries* was issued between 1889 and 1909. Elsewhere, James Conway Walter charted the history of some 70 parishes in

---

[36] *A.A.S.R.P.* xv (1) (1879), p. viii; Lincs. A.O., R.D. 3/1, pp. 112–15. The preface to Cox's book shows that it had been prepared specifically for the project: 'Some of the Clergy of the Diocese of Lincoln are responsible for the issue of this booklet. A much-needed County History of Lincolnshire is now being projected upon the basis of separate parochial histories.' When Wordsworth later reprinted 'The Studies of the Clergy' (above, n. 33) he added a note apropos the county hist., 'This suggestion is now being acted on, 1879': *Miscellanies Literary and Religious* (3 vols. 1879), iii. 332.

[37] D. M. Williamson, *Lincoln Muniments* (1956), 13–16.

[38] 'Transcripts in the Bishop of Lincoln's Registry', *A.A.S.R.P.* xvi (2) (1882), 163–4. See also N. Bennett, 'A. R. Maddison and Development of Local Hist. in Lincs.' *Some Historians of Lincs.* 27–31.

[39] D. Owen, 'William Oswald Massingberd' and C. Sturman, 'Thomas Longley', *Some Historians of Lincs.* 39–44.

the Horncastle area in three volumes: *Records of Woodhall Spa and Neighbourhood* (1899), *Records, Historical and Antiquarian, of Parishes Round Horncastle* (1904), and *A History of Horncastle* (1908); Charles Moor ('Oxoniensis') brought together in *Historical Notes Concerning the Deanery of Corringham* (1907) his histories of parishes in the Gainsborough area first published in the *Gainsborough News*.[40] The only substantial county bibliography, A. R. Corns's *Bibliotheca Lincolniensis*, was printed in 1904.

The establishment of the Victoria County History in 1899 once again revived the possibility of a county history. Canon G. T. Harvey, secretary to the Diocesan Architectural Society 1867–86, reflected on the past and the present in a letter to H. A. Doubleday:

> Some 20 years ago an attempt was made to collect material for a County History of Lincolnshire, but the matter failed for lack of interest taken in such things by the laity. Possibly now that greater interest is being taken in old things, & that the proposed History is backed up by the prestige of a central authority, the movement as regards this county may be more successful.[41]

He later commented (prophetically as regards the fate of Lincolnshire):

> I should be glad to know something about the financial basis on which the history is being begun—though copies of the History will be sold in the County, I should not be very hopeful of success, if the movement as regards Lincolnshire depend upon a large County contribution.
> The first question which people ask me, when I mention the matter is 'where is the money to come from?'[42]

In the early years Doubleday made contact with scholars and specialists in the county with respect to the general volumes in the series. Amongst them was W. O. Massingberd, who expressed his reservations in trenchant manner:

> There is the question of the History of Lincolnshire as a whole. What satisfies you ought to satisfy me. But are you satisfied that there is a reasonable hope that the Lincolnshire part of VCHs will be done well? I rather doubt whether the VCH authorities realise the difficulties. We have a large county, a huge mass of records, very little done, & very few workers. We have no layman of means who takes any active part in the work. We cannot maintain a Record Society, & a volume of records does not obtain sufficient subscribers to cover the expense of printing. I cannot therefore at present see how the history is to be written.[43]

---

[40] For Charles Moor see J. S. English, 'Adam Stark, Charles Moor, and other Historians of Gainsborough', *Some Historians of Lincs.* 85.

[41] V.C.H. recs., A 12, Lincs., 22 Apr. 1899.

[42] Ibid. 25 May 1899.

[43] Ibid. A 44, 12 Aug. 1901. The following paragraphs which provide an outline of the Lincs. V.C.H. are derived substantially from that file of Massingberd's correspondence with H. A. Doubleday and his successor William Page.

Massingberd's fears were no doubt allayed by Doubleday, for over the years he became the driving force behind the Lincolnshire V.C.H. A county committee and an executive committee were formed in April 1904. In 1905 Massingberd was appointed editor for Lincolnshire and plans were made for two general and three topographical volumes. Massingberd's correspondence with the general editor, William Page, shows that he was extremely thorough in editing volume two (1906). With progress on volume one continuing, early in 1907 Massingberd began work on the topographical volumes, starting with the material sent from London for Yarborough wapentake. He found the suggested word limit per parish 'most unsatisfactory':

> The topographical work is to be 'approved' by me as representing the County Committee, and I shall certainly decline to approve of such parochial histories as might appear in White's or any other Gazette. I have been warned that this was to be little more than a 'glorified guide book', and have always said that if that was to be the case I should have nothing more to do with the work.[44]

An additional topographical volume was soon agreed by Page. From 1908 Massingberd began to obtain the help of other local scholars in writing up the parish histories, but progress was halted by external events. Page first advised Massingberd of the financial difficulties which affected the whole scheme at the end of the year. Massingberd was not optimistic of local help: 'Lincolnshire is unfortunately now a very poor County, and the Landowners have no thousands to play with . . . I fear the very few who have any money have comparatively little interest in the work'.[45] Massingberd continued to soldier on with the parish histories for volume three until his death in September 1910, though, as had become apparent in May, there was little chance of Lincolnshire's being completed.[46] There was an attempt to revive the scheme in 1912, but Page soon asked for the return of material from the writers in Lincolnshire; the drafts and notes remain in the V.C.H. archives.

Massingberd's correspondence over the V.C.H. shows that he was acutely aware of the limitations of a history written largely from national records. Though he and his contemporaries had worked hard to calendar and edit Lincolnshire materials, a new professionalism came through the work and vision of one man, Canon C. W. Foster (1866–1935). In 1910, the year of

[44] Ibid. 16 Aug. 1907.
[45] Ibid. 15 Apr. 1909.
[46] On 5 May 1910 Page advised Massingberd that the cost of completing the remaining five vols. would be £9,181 whilst estimated sales amounted only to £5,500; an additional (undated) memorandum indicates the sales of vol. ii to have been only £308 9s. 6d.

Massingberd's death, Foster founded the Lincoln Record Society. Appropriately, its first published volume was an edition of Gervase Holles's church notes. Foster's achievement should, however, not be measured solely in terms of scrupulous editing. He began to create interest in the records and history of the county among professional historians, notably Frank and Doris Stenton.[47] Furthermore, Foster hoped that the Old Gaol in Lincoln castle would become the repository for diocesan and county archives: a diocesan record office was established in 1935 and the Lincolnshire Archives Office in 1948 (though it was not until 1961 that the search rooms in the castle were opened).[48] The wealth of material deposited at Lincoln was soon highlighted by Joan Thirsk's *English Peasant Farming: The Agrarian History of Lincolnshire from Tudor to Recent Times* (1957).

To understand more recent developments it is necessary to chart the varying fortunes of periodical publications and the county societies. *Lincolnshire Notes and Queries* ceased publication in 1938, but already the increased interest in local studies was catered for by the Lindsey Local History Society (founded 1930) and its quarterly *Lincolnshire Magazine* (1932–9); renamed the Lincolnshire Local History Society, it published the *Lincolnshire Historian* from 1947 to 1965. In 1965 it merged with the Lincolnshire Architectural and Archaeological Society to form the Lincolnshire Local History Society (with a journal *Lincolnshire History and Archaeology*). In 1974, following a further merger with the Lincoln Archaeological Research Committee, it became the Society for Lincolnshire History and Archaeology. In 1966 the new society established a History of Lincolnshire Committee, with the aim of publishing 'a series of volumes which would be at the same time both scholarly and of general interest, written by specialists already engaged on particular periods and subjects'. Twelve volumes were proposed, covering prehistoric times to the 20th century. Inevitably there have been some changes to the scheme, but in 1993 the History of Lincolnshire was nearing completion,[49] and a new series of Studies in the History of Lincolnshire was being planned.

---

[47] K. Major, 'Canon Charles Wilmer Foster', *Archives*, xviii (1987), 42–9; K. Major, 'Canon C. W. Foster and Sir Frank and Lady Stenton', *Some Historians of Lincs.* 55–60.

[48] F. Hill, 'From Canon Foster to the Lincs. A.O.' *Lincs. Hist. and Arch.* xiii (1978), 71–3. Following local government reorganization an archives office for South Humberside was established in Grimsby in 1976.

[49] Vols. so far published are: J. May, *Prehistoric Lincs.* (1976); J. B. Whitwell, *Roman Lincs.* (1970, revised edn. 1992); G. Platts, *Land and People in Medieval Lincs.* (1985); D. M. Owen, *Church and Soc. in Medieval Lincs.* (1971); G. A. J. Hodgett, *Tudor Lincs.* (1975); C. Holmes, *17th-Century Lincs.* (1980); T. W. Beastall, *Agricultural Revolution in Lincs.* (1978); R. J. Olney, *Rural Soc. and County Government in 19th Century Lincs.* (1979); N. R. Wright, *Lincs. Towns and Industry 1700–1914* (1982); *20th Century Lincs.* ed. D. R. Mills (1989).

The great 17th-century county historian Robert Thoroton described Gervase Holles as a 'great Lover of Antiquities' and Robert Sanderson as 'the most diligent collector of Genealogies I ever knew in these parts'.[50] Many labourers in the vineyard of antiquarian and historical scholarship have followed their example, but a full county history remains to be written. Given the scale of such an enterprise and the current parlous nature of finance to support any such scheme, the completion of such a work remains but a faint hope.

[50] *Antiquities of Notts.* (1677), 443, 475.

LONDON

Caroline Barron and Vanessa Harding

L ondon is not strictly a county, nor has it ever been. London was the largest and most populous of the *burh*s which grew up in southern England in the wake of the Viking invasions of the 9th century. Authority in the city appears to have been divided between the bishop and a portreeve appointed by the king.[1] London was not self-governing but it enjoyed a measure of independence from the developing feudal network. About 1130 Henry I granted the citizens the right to elect their own sheriff and justiciar, and thus implicitly raised London to the status of a shire.[2] It was also in the 12th century that the first historian of London emerged, William FitzStephen, a Londoner and a member of the household of Thomas Becket. After Becket's murder in 1170 FitzStephen, like many others, felt compelled to write his life; but, as he honestly acknowledged, he seized the opportunity also to describe the situation and constitution of London.

FitzStephen's account is topographical rather than historical:[3] he described London as one might describe a person, delineating some distinguishing characteristics and giving a little genealogy. In spite of his clerical status, FitzStephen's account is studded with allusions to classical authors, and the prevailing spirit is secular: it was the cookshops, the horses, and the antics of schoolboys that really aroused his enthusiasm. True to his classical models, FitzStephen provided a description of the situation of London, but he was primarily concerned with the inhabitants of the city rather than its buildings. Although his was the first account of a British town, yet it fell within a long tradition of Latin accounts of cities stretching back to the 8th century.[4] Most recently, Benedict, a canon of St. Peter's, had written his *Mirabilia Urbis*

---

[1] Writ of King William I, printed most recently in S. Reynolds, W. de Boer, and G. MacNiocaill, *Elenchus Fontium Historiae Urbanae* (Leiden, 1988), 34.

[2] Ibid. 62–4.

[3] Printed in, e.g., ibid. 76–83; *Materials for Hist. of Thomas Becket, Archbishop of Canterbury* (3 vols., Rolls Ser. 1887), iii. 2–13; translated by H. E. Butler in F. M. Stenton, *Norman London: an Essay* (1934, reprinted 1990).

[4] J. K. Hyde, 'Medieval Descriptions of Cities', *Bull. John Rylands Library*, xlviii (1965–6), 308–40; A. Gransden, 'Realistic Observation in 12th-century England', *Speculum*, xlvii (1972), 29–51. We are very grateful to John Scattergood for letting Dr. Barron see a typescript of his paper 'Misrepresenting the city: Genre, Intertextuality and William FitzStephen's *Description of London (c. 1173)*', read at Queen Mary Westfield College in autumn 1992.

Rome in 1143, and FitzStephen's lead was followed by the monk Lucian for Chester,[5] but their example was not rapidly copied by others. Moreover, FitzStephen's account of London was not widely popular, nor widely known, judging by the surviving manuscripts: only two from the 13th century, one from the 14th, and one from the 15th.[6]

Although there were no further historians of London in the medieval period, a number of London chroniclers incorporated into their annalistic accounts brief references to events in London or to changes in the way the city was governed. In truth they were chronicles of England in which passing reference was made to London, but they were distinguished from other chronicles by their organization of material by mayoral, rather than regnal, years and, from the late 14th century, by their almost exclusive use of English.[7] In the course of the 15th century their authors emerge with names, personalities, and opinions, but they cannot really be considered to have written histories of London.

It was John Stow, writing in the 1590s, who took up the mantle which FitzStephen had laid down three hundred years earlier. Stow, who lived through the dissolution of the monasteries in the 1530s and witnessed the dramatic rise in London's population from *c.* 50,000 to 200,000 in the course of his lifetime, may have been impelled to write his monumental *Survey of London* by the pace of obliterating change all about him. Significantly, he printed FitzStephen's account as an appendix, and he saw his *Survey* as an expansion, or updating, of the earlier description. Like his predecessor, Stow incorporated oral tradition, his own observations, and a certain amount of 'speculative archaeology', but he largely abandoned FitzStephen's classical allusions and tropes, and relied to a far greater extent on documentary and chronicle sources. In the first 13 chapters Stow consciously followed the format of the earlier work and wrote on general topics such as 'Sports and Pastimes' and the 'Honour of Citizens', but from chapter 14 he broke out of the medieval carapace and provided a detailed description of the city, ward by ward. He included the wards outside the walls, the suburbs, and Westminster. The work was an immediate success and has been in print more or less continuously ever since.[8]

Stow also consciously intended the *Survey* to be a 'county' history of

---

[5] Above, Ches.

[6] J. Stow, *Survey of London*, ed. C. L. Kingsford (2 vols. 1908), ii. 387.

[7] C. L. Kingsford, *Chronicles of London* (1905); idem, *English Hist. Literature in 15th Century* (1913). The most recent study of the chronicles is M.-R. McLaren, 'London Chronicles of 15th Century: the Manuscripts, their Authors and their Aims' (Melbourne Univ. Ph.D. thesis, 1991).

[8] Edns. since 1598 listed in Stow, *Survey*, ed. Kingsford, i, p. lxxxv. Kingsford's definitive edn. (1908) was reprinted in 1971. H. B. Wheatley produced an edn. for the Everyman Library (1912) which was reprinted in 1956 and again in 1978 with a new introduction by Valerie Pearl.

London such as other Elizabethan antiquaries and historians were providing
for other English counties.[9] In his preface, he acknowledged the inspiration of
William Lambarde's *Perambulation of Kent* (1576) and John Norden's
Middlesex (1593) and 'Essex' (written in 1594).[10] In emulation of those works,
and to encourage others to take up their pens and write the histories of their
native shires to 'make the whole body of the English chorography amongst
ourselves', Stow 'attempted the discovery of London, my native soil and
country'.[11]

In fact the monumental success of Stow's *Survey* tended to discourage
further histories of London. Instead his work was expanded and updated,
by Anthony Munday in 1618, by Humphrey Dyson in 1633, and, most
famously, by the Revd. John Strype in 1720. Richard Blome, the
cartographer, had considered producing a new version of Stow's *Survey* as
early as 1694 and had produced a newly-engraved series of ward maps.
Strype took over the project in 1702 but the new edition did not appear until
1720, by which time Blome's maps were nearly 30 years out of date. Just as
Stow had been provoked by the changes of the 16th century, so Blome and
Strype were influenced by the dramatic destruction of the fire of 1666 and
the rapid rebuilding which removed what the fire had not already destroyed.
In his preface Strype stated that he intended to remove the errors that had
crept into Stow's text, to add information about 'ancient times', and to
bring the work up to date.[12] It has, perhaps, been customary for more recent
historians of London to see Strype's main use in his detailed account of the
changes in the fabric of London since 1603, and indeed he has much to
recount on that score, but there is much more information about medieval
and 16th-century London than is usually thought. In his preface Strype
described the remarkable range of new material that he had consulted,
including the records in the Tower, the library of Robert Cotton, and a
considerable amount of parish material.[13] Strype has much to tell the
historian of medieval London as well as the enthusiast for the 17th-century
city.

There were few impressive historians of London in the 18th century. An
exception to that possibly cavalier dismissal is William Maitland. His
biographer in the *Dictionary of National Biography* snobbishly dismissed him

---

[9] F. S. Fussner, *The Historical Revolution: English Historical Writing and Thought, 1580–1640*
(1962), esp. chapter 8; M. McKisack, *Medieval Hist. in Tudor Age* (1971), esp. chapter 6.

[10] Stow, *Survey*, ed. Kingsford, i, p. xcvii. Stow is known to have owned a copy of Norden's
Herts. (1598): ibid. i, p. lxxxvii.

[11] Ibid. i, p. xcvii.

[12] J. T. Morrison, 'Strype's Stow: the 1720 Edn. of *A Survey of London*', *London Jnl.* iii (1977),
40–54.

[13] J. Strype, *Survey of Cities of London and Westminster* (2 vols. 1720), i, p. xxix.

as a hair merchant who acquired some wealth and then produced 'several ponderous compilations, which were well received at the time, but are now of small repute'.[14] The book may have had a ponderous title—*The History of London from its Foundation by the Romans to the Present Time, with Several Accounts of Westminster, Middlesex and Southwark and other parts within the Bill of Mortality* (1739)—but it contains much of interest, particularly in the author's attempt to describe the present condition of London, its population, government, commerce, schools, and hospitals. The book is lavishly provided with engravings but also, more unusually, with copious tables of statistics. In defining the area to be covered as that lying 'within the bill of mortality', Maitland aimed to include large tracts of Middlesex and Surrey which formed part of the 'greater London'.[15]

Most later historians of London in the 18th and early 19th century tended simply to mix together an amalgam of Stow, Strype, and Maitland in varying proportions and with different illustrative material. John Noorthouck, who brought out his *New History of London* in 1773, admitted that his main purpose was to produce a volume of 'more convenient size and purchased at an easier price'. With engaging candour he continued:

> It will neither be supposed, nor is it pretended, that no use has been made of Stow and Maitland in the ensuing work: as Maitland followed Stow and Strype, so an acknowledgement is here made that his work has been consulted as a general guide throughout. When different persons travel the same journey, it will be almost impossible for those who follow last to avoid tracing the footsteps of those who went before; especially in places where the road happens to be confined and narrow.[16]

The resulting volume may, perhaps, have been cheaper than Maitland's but it is scarcely more convenient in size, although comprising one volume rather than two.

One of the distinctive features of Strype's edition of Stow had been the quantity and quality of the illustrations: not only Blome's ward maps, but also engraved plates of churches, public buildings, and hospitals, and the only known drawings of several of the city gates which were swept away in the mid 18th century.[17] Stow's *Survey* had had no illustrations, although it has been argued that he used a copy of the mid 16th-century copper-plate map to help

[14] *D.N.B.*

[15] On the vexed question of the area covered by the bills of mortality, see V. Harding, 'The Population of London, 1550–1700: a Review of the Published Evidence', *London Jnl.* xv (1990), 111–28.

[16] J. Noorthouck, *New Hist. of London including Westminster and Southwark to which is added a General Survey of the Whole* (1773), p. v.

[17] Strype, *Survey*, i, facing p. 14.

him in his perambulations.[18] From the end of the 16th century, however,
London was increasingly sketched, drawn, engraved, mapped, and, finally,
properly surveyed by John Ogilby and William Morgan in 1676.[19] Numerous
maps followed in the course of the 18th century, including John Rocque's
attractive and well-known maps from the 1740s.[20] Following the establishment
of the Ordnance Office for England in 1783, Richard Horwood in the 1790s
produced his *Plan of the Cities of London and Westminster, the Borough of
Southwark and Parts Adjoining*, which accurately delineated every house site
in London.[21] The title of his maps indicates the scale of the problem which
was facing both cartographers and historians of London: the phenomenal
growth of the city was making it increasingly difficult to comprehend the
built-up area of London in its entirety, or indeed to govern it effectively.

If the century following the publication of Maitland's volume produced no
great historians of London, yet those were years when cartographers and
artists made an incomparable contribution to the history of the city. Whereas
Strype and Maitland and John Entick, who produced a new edition of
Maitland in 1775,[22] were anxious to illustrate their volumes with pictures of
the fine new churches, public buildings, and hospitals in the classical style
which were being built across the face of London, by the end of the century
other writers and artists were increasingly sensitive to the fragmented and
battered remains of the medieval city. Among the earliest of the
'archaeological artists' of London were John Carter, J. T. Smith, and Jacob
Schnebbelie (the last being followed by his son Robert). They rushed to the
bedsides of dying buildings and made their death-masks. Leadenhall Market,
Guildhall Chapel, Crosby Place, Old London Bridge, and numerous coaching
inns and timber-framed houses were recorded by them.[23] Many of

---

[18] M. Holmes, 'A Source-book for Stow', *Studies in London Hist. presented to Philip E. Jones*,
ed. A. J. Hollaender and W. Kellaway (1969), 275–85; S. P. Marks, *The Map of mid 16th-century
London* (London Topographical Soc. c, 1964).

[19] I. Darlington and J. Howgego, *Printed Maps of London, c. 1553–1850* (1964); P. Glanville, *London
in Maps* (1972); *The London Surveys of Ralph Treswell*, ed. J. Schofield (London Topographical Soc.
cxxxv, 1987); A. Griffiths and G. Kesnerova, *Wenceslaus Hollar: Prints and Drawings* (1983). Most of
the important maps of London have now been published by the London Topographical Soc., e.g.
A to Z of Restoration London based on Ogilby and Morgan, 1676, ed. R. Hyde (1992).

[20] *A to Z of Georgian London based on Rocque's Plan of 1747*, ed. R. Hyde (London
Topographical Soc. cxxvi, 1982).

[21] *A to Z of Regency London based on Horwood's Map of 1813*, ed. P. Laxton (London
Topographical Soc. cxxxi, 1985).

[22] J. Entick, *William Maitland's Hist. of London from its Foundation to the Present Time,
Continued to 1772* (2 vols. 1775).

[23] H. L. Mallalieu, *Dictionary of British Watercolour Artists to 1920* (1976); examples reproduced
in, e.g., J. Schofield, *The Building of London from the Conquest to the Great Fire* (1984); C. M.
Barron, *The Medieval Guildhall of London* (1974). The most recent study of Carter is J. M. Crook,
'John Carter and the Mind of the Gothic Revival' (paper delivered at Soc. of Antiq. Feb. 1990; to
be published as Soc. of Antiq. Occasional Paper).

their watercolours were engraved, and the London buildings which George Shepherd and his sons delineated not only appeared in contemporary accounts of London but have been reproduced in calendars and stamped upon the surfaces of innumerable tablemats.[24]

In 1842 the Library Committee of the Corporation of the City of London took a decision which had far-reaching consequences for the history of the city. It was decided to spend £400 on repairing, arranging, and indexing the City's records, and William Turner Alchin was employed as archivist. The committee's main concern seems to have been the publication of the City's records, and the man who did much of the work was Henry Thomas Riley, a graduate of Clare College, Cambridge.[25] In the 1850s and 1860s Riley edited the City's custumals, the *Liber Albus* and the *Liber Custumarum*, and produced his miscellaneous and enticing selection of translated material culled from a wide range of City records under the title *Memorials of London and London Life* (1868).[26] Eight years later the incomparable Reginald R. Sharpe was appointed to the permanent position of Records Clerk or Deputy Keeper at the Corporation, and for nearly 40 years he worked indefatigably, if not always amiably, to care for, index, calendar, and publish the records.[27] Sharpe produced calendars of the wills enrolled in the Husting Court, the coroner's rolls, letters under the mayor's seal, and the 11 volumes of the City's medieval letter books. Almost single-handedly he revolutionized the study of London's history. It was possible now to go back beyond Stow and to write the constitutional and political history of London from the documents. Not surprisingly, Sharpe himself was among the first to make use of the wealth of new material in his *London and the Kingdom* (1894–5).[28] Although his preoccupation with kings, battles, and 'great events' may now be unfashionable, his work has not been superseded, for his house was built upon the rock of documentary evidence. Moreover the lead set by the Corporation of London was followed elsewhere as the City companies began to publish their records, and ecclesiastical

---

[24] Shepherd (c. 1782–c. 1830) drew for Wilkinson's *Londina Illustrata* (1808); his son George illustrated C. Clarke's *Architectura Ecclesiastica Londini* (1820); and his second son, Thomas Hosner, illustrated J. Elmes, *Metropolitan Improvements* (1827) and idem, *London and its Environs in 19th Century* (1829).

[25] *D.N.B.* s.v. Riley.

[26] *Munimenta Gildhallae Londoniensis: Liber Albus, Liber Custumarum et Liber Horn* (3 vols., Rolls Ser. 1859–62); *Memorials of London and London Life, 1276–1419* (1868); *Liber Albus: the White Book of the City of London* (1861); *Chronicles of Mayors and Sheriffs of London, and the French Chronicle of London* (1863).

[27] B. Masters, 'Local Archivist 1876–1914: Dr. Reginald R. Sharpe', *Jnl. Soc. Archivists*, v (1976), 275–82.

[28] Cf. W. J. Loftie, *Hist. of London* (2 vols. 1883), which was more concerned than Sharpe with social history.

institutions sifted and published the dusty contents of muniment rooms and parish chests.[29]

It was not only the history of London which was being revolutionized. In 1889 the government of the 'great wen', except the City, was brought under the control of the London county council. The latter took up its responsibilities for health, housing, and transport with great seriousness; nor did it neglect history. A committee was established to survey the memorials of greater London and compile lists of those buildings which should be preserved because of their historic interest. In 1900 the first volume of the *Survey of London* was published, a study of the parish of Bromley by Bow. Forty-two further volumes had appeared by 1986.[30]

The time also seemed right for a more comprehensive study of the history of London: printed source material was abundant, archive repositories were largely accessible, and local societies reflected and encouraged enthusiasm for London history. The London and Middlesex Archaeological Society had been founded in 1855 and the London Topographical Society in 1880. Both published the fruits of archaeological and archival research.[31] Moreover the history of London had recently attracted a scholar of outstanding ability: Charles Lethbridge Kingsford. In 1905 he published his *Chronicles of London*, which restored to serious historical scholarship the vernacular chronicles compiled for 15th-century London citizens, and in 1908 he brought out his new edition of Stow's *Survey*, still the definitive edition and a dazzling work of scholarship.[32]

When the *Victoria County History* was founded in 1899, there was no intention of treating London separately from Middlesex. Relatively soon, however, there was a change of mind, arising perhaps from the editor William Page's own interest in London's history, and volume one of *The Victoria History of London* appeared in 1909. It was a 'general' volume, and included sections on Romano-British London, Anglo-Saxon Remains, and Ecclesiastical History. No further volumes were published, partly as a result of the crisis in the *History*'s finances which temporarily stopped work on all counties in 1909, but also perhaps owing to the difficulty of accommodating a useful account of London's complex development in the emerging format for *V.C.H.* volumes. Page remained keen on the idea, however, endeavouring

---

[29] e.g. *Accounts of Churchwardens of St. Michael Cornhill, 1456–1608*, ed. W. H. Overall (1869); *Facsimile of First Vol. of MS. Archives of Worshipful Company of Grocers, 1345–1463*, ed. J. A. Kingdon (2 vols. 1886).

[30] *Survey of London: Parish of Bromley le Bow*, ed. C. R. Ashbee (1900). See F. Sheppard, 'Sources and Methods used for the *Survey of London*', *Study of Urban Hist*. ed. H. J. Dyos (1968), 131–45; anon. 'Francis Sheppard and the *Survey of London*', *London Jnl*. xii (1986), 3–7.

[31] *Trans. London and Mdx. Arch. Soc.* (from 1868); *London Topographical Soc. Rec.* (from 1901).

[32] *D.N.B.* s.v. Kingsford. Henry Harben had been preparing a new edn. of Stow's *Survey* but was forestalled by Kingsford; he used his materials in his *Dictionary of London* (1918).

unsuccessfully to obtain guarantees for the remaining proposed London volumes in 1925, and evidently still hoped to complete work on at least some of them up to his death in 1934. Thereafter, however, the plan for continuing *V.C.H. London* was dropped.[33]

Since that time, there has been no attempt at a large-scale general history of London, though there have been several publication series, either on aspects of London, such as its architectural history, or with a less ambitious remit than the *V.C.H.* might have claimed. One of the problems is that the sprawling size of the metropolis and its confused governmental history make it difficult to find a consistently satisfactory definition of London for the purposes of historical enquiry extending over a long period. A narrow definition is inadequate for studies extending into the modern period; too broad a definition is inappropriate for Roman and medieval studies. The definition settled on for the planned *V.C.H.* volumes (the City, plus Westminster and Southwark) was satisfactory for the Roman and Anglo-Saxon chapters, but rather less so for that on ecclesiastical history. It could not be consistently observed for the religious history of London in the 18th and 19th centuries, and certainly led to anomaly in the treatment of the religious houses of the London area.

Another major problem with devising a successful independent series on the history of London is the absence of an obvious patron for a history of the whole metropolis. The University of London was apparently ready to co-operate on the London volumes of the *V.C.H.* in 1925, but the relationship that later developed was with the *V.C.H.* as a whole. No municipal body has been prepared to take on responsibility for a large-scale historical series, though all have supported museums and other educational enterprises. In the 1960s Secker and Warburg planned an eight-volume series telling 'the first full history of the world's greatest city', and commissioned an independent academic author to write each volume; so far, however, only three volumes have appeared, and while each is of high quality and individuality the original idea of a complete series has not been achieved.[34]

That is in marked contrast to Paris, where the extent of municipal jurisdiction has been periodically redefined to include the whole metropolis (at least up to the 20th century), and the Ville de Paris has taken an active interest in promoting its own historiography. The result has been an impressive series, the *Nouvelle Histoire de Paris*,[35] combining chronological

---

[33] *V.C.H. General Introduction*, 3, 12, 14.

[34] C. N. L. Brooke and G. Keir, *London 800–1215: the Shaping of a City* (1975); G. Rudé, *Hanoverian London, 1714–1808* (1971); F. Sheppard, *London 1808–1870: the Infernal Wen* (1971).

[35] Published by Hachette for the Association pour la Publication d'une Histoire de Paris, Bibliothèque Historique de la Ville de Paris.

volumes and thematic studies (urbanism, civic ritual and celebration), which together provide a very substantial account of the development of the city and its role in the political, social, and cultural life of France.

If there has been no successful 'county history' of London in the 20th century, there has certainly been no dearth of historical writing and publication, in the form of monographs, more popular works, journals and periodicals, and editions of historical documents. The historiography of London has tended to fragment: the better and more serious works are usually rather narrowly focused on a theme, period, or topic, while in general the more ambitious the scope, the more superficial the treatment. That is not invariably the case, since there are both general books which are good and detailed studies (especially works of local or institutional piety) which are not, but there seem to be two distinct markets for books on London, the popular and the academic, though books of maps and pictures can bridge that gap.[36]

Page's preface to the V.C.H. London volume gives some indication of contemporary approaches to research. Interest in municipal history, especially the evolution of institutional forms, was strong: Page's own book on early medieval London, which was clearly related to his V.C.H. work, focused on that, and J. H. Round and Laurence Gomme, both closely associated with the inception and early years of the V.C.H., had already published books on aspects of the subject. George Unwin's study of the City guilds and livery companies examined constitutional as well as economic issues.[37] Page also noted the growth of archaeology and the improved accessibility of manuscript sources for the history of London, and excavation and documentary research have indeed made an enormous contribution to London's historiography since 1900. The period also saw the formal recognition of the importance of London's history as an academic subject with the foundation of a readership in the history and records of London at University College in 1922.[38]

In the period since the Second World War, our view of Roman London, and our whole thinking about Anglo-Saxon London, have been changed by

[36] e.g. F. Barker and P. Jackson, *London: 2000 Years of a City and its People* (1974) is a useful sourcebook for visual material; Celina Fox's generously-illustrated *Londoners* (1987) has a good text as well.

[37] W. Page, *London, its Origins and Early Development* (1923), dedicated to Viscount Hambleden and published by the V.C.H.'s publisher, Constable and Co.; J. H. Round, *The Commune of London, and other studies* (1899); G. L. Gomme, *The Governance of London: Studies on the Place Occupied by London in English Institutions* (1907); G. Unwin, *Gilds and Companies of London* (1908).

[38] The post was held successively by Miss Eliza Jeffries Davis, Professor T. F. Reddaway, and Professor Valerie Pearl. It has been frozen since 1981.

new excavation and by reinterpretation of earlier archaeological discoveries.[39] The war itself offered new opportunities for archaeological investigation, but the establishment of professional archaeological units for the City of London and for Greater London, and the great boom in rescue archaeology resulting from the pressure for commercial property development in the 1970s and early 1980s produced a wealth of discovery and publication.[40] Architectural history has also been well served, by the *Survey of London* (taken over by the Greater London Council on its creation in 1965), and by the Royal Commission on Historical Monuments, which took over the *Survey* when the Greater London Council was abolished in the mid 1980s and whose own five-volume set, published between the wars, described buildings subsequently lost to demolition and bomb damage, as a comparison with Pevsner's *London* (1957) makes clear.[41]

London, especially the City, is extremely rich in medieval and early modern records, many more of which are now accessible for study than Page can ever have imagined. He was familiar with the Public Record Office and with the medieval muniments of the Corporation of London, but new classes have been exploited since his time (perhaps most notably the records of the Court of Chancery and of the Corporation's Court of Husting), while deposits in the manuscript section of Guildhall Library have greatly expanded the range of possible enquiry. Nearly all the City parishes and the majority of the livery companies have lodged their own records there, it holds the London diocesan archive, including probate records, the immense medieval archive of St. Paul's cathedral was transferred there in the early 1980s, and the archives of some city firms are now facilitating the study of business history.[42]

The publication of historical records has continued, but in the second half of the 20th century the main focus has shifted from the archive holders to independent bodies, notably the London Record Society, founded by William

[39] W. F. Grimes, *Excavation of Roman and Medieval London* (1968); R. B. Merrifield, *Roman City of London* (1965), revised as *London, City of the Romans* (1983); P. Marsden, *Roman London* (1980); A. Vince, *Saxon London: an Arch. Investigation* (1990).

[40] M. Biddle and D. Hudson with C. Heighway, *The Future of London's Past, a Survey of the Arch. Implications of Planning and Development in the Nation's Capital* (1973); Museum of London, Department of Urban Arch. *Annual Reviews* (to 1989); B. Hobley, *Roman and Saxon London: a Reappraisal* (1986); articles in *London Archaeologist, Popular Arch., Trans. London and Mdx. Arch. Soc.*, and special volumes published by London and Mdx. Arch. Soc. and the Museum of London.

[41] Royal Com. on Hist. Monuments (England), *Inventory of Hist. Monuments in London* (5 vols. 1924–30); N. Pevsner, *Buildings of England: London 1, Cities of London and Westminster* (1957; 3rd edn. 1973); see also H. Hobhouse, *Lost London: a Century of Demolition and Decay* (1971); B. Cherry and N. Pevsner, *London 2: South* (1983); B. Cherry, *London 3: North West* (1991).

[42] Compare P. E. Jones and R. Smith, *Guide to Recs. at Guildhall* (1951) with E. M. Scudder, *Guide to London Local Hist. Resources: Corporation of London* (1991), and J. Bullock-Anderson, *Guide to Archives and Manuscripts at Guildhall Library* (2nd edn. 1990). See also D. Keene and V. Harding, *Survey of Documentary Sources for Property Holding in London before Great Fire* (London Rec. Soc. xxii, 1985).

Kellaway in 1966.[43] One of the most valuable single publications has surely been the complete edition of Samuel Pepys's *Diary*.[44] Libraries and record offices have tended to concentrate on the publication of guides and lists, though the Corporation of London has also supported record publication. The London Topographical Society has played an important role in publishing facsimiles of historic maps and plans.[45]

The increased wealth of available documentation has influenced all serious work on London. There have been many important monographs on aspects or periods of London's history. An early and still valuable study of London as a whole was M. D. George's *London Life in the 18th Century* (1925); later works include Sylvia Thrupp's *The Merchant Class of Medieval London* (1948), Donald Olsen's *The Growth of Victorian London* (1976), and Peter Earle's *The Making of the English Middle Class: Business, Society, and Family Life in London, 1660–1730* (1989). Religious life has been well covered,[46] and attention has also been paid to the mechanisms of social stability, class relations, crime, and order.[47] The debate about the role of the Greater London Council, and its abolition in the 1980s, focused attention again on London's government and politics.[48] Recent historical interest in the community of the locality, even within a communal urban entity, is reflected in books on medieval Westminster and early modern Southwark, and in some more modern studies published by History Workshop.[49]

Archival research on London had an outlet in the periodical *Guildhall Miscellany*, subsequently *Guildhall Studies in London History*, from 1952 to

[43] J. M. Sims, *London and Mdx. Published Recs.: a Handlist* (London Rec. Soc. Occasional Publication i, 1970), and the lists of serial publications in E. L. C. Mullins, *Texts and Calendars* (2 vols., Royal Hist. Soc. Guides and Handbooks vii and xii, 1958–83).

[44] *Diary of Samuel Pepys*, ed. R. C. Latham and W. Matthews (11 vols. 1970–83).

[45] Above. See also *British Atlas of Historic Towns*, iii, *London from Prehistoric Times to c. 1520*, ed. M. D. Lobel (1990), a map reconstructed from historical sources.

[46] S. Brigden, *London and the Reformation* (1989); P. Seaver, *The Puritan Lectureships, the Politics of Religious Dissent, 1560–1640* (1970); Tai Liu, *Puritan London, a Study of Religion and Society in the City Parishes* (1986).

[47] S. Rappaport, *Worlds within Worlds: Structures of Life in 16th-century London* (1989); I. Archer, *Politics of Stability: Social Relations in Elizabethan London* (1991); T. Harris, *London Crowds in Reign of Charles II* (1987); R. B. Shoemaker, *Prosecution and Punishment: Petty Crime and the Law in London and Mdx. c. 1660–1725* (1991); G. S. Jones, *Outcast London: a Study in the Relationship between Classes in Victorian Society* (1971).

[48] D. Owen, *Government of Victorian London 1855–1889* (1982); K. Young and P. Garside, *Metropolitan London: Politics and Urban Change 1871–1981* (1982); J. Davis, *Reforming London: the London Government Problem 1855–1900* (1988); *People and Politics: the LCC 1889–1965*, ed. A. Saint (1989).

[49] G. Rosser, *Medieval Westminster, 1200–1540* (1989); J. Boulton, *Neighbourhood and Community: a London Suburb in the 17th Century* (1987); J. White, *The Worst Street in North London: Campbell Bank, Islington, between the Wars* (1986); *Metropolis London: Histories and Representations since 1800*, ed. D. Feldman and G. S. Jones (1989).

1981, and still has in the *London Journal* ('a review of metropolitan society past and present'), a bi-annual journal established in 1975.

The past twenty years have seen a considerable growth in academic interest in London. The historiography of the capital has generally been characterized by the individual academic researcher, and that will undoubtedly continue to be an important sector, but more recently several collaborative research projects have got under way, some under the direction of the Centre for Metropolitan History at the Institute of Historical Research, University of London, others in history and geography departments of individual colleges of the university. Though dependent on outside funding for individual projects, and not always certain of core support, enterprises of that kind offer new opportunities to tackle major outstanding problems in the study of London's history in ways that would be difficult or impossible for the lone researcher.[50] They may not follow the V.C.H.'s prescribed methods or approaches, but they share its willingness to embark on ambitious historical projects.

---

[50] Annual reports of the Social and Economic Study of Medieval London to the Board of the Institute of Historical Research, 1980–8, and of the Centre for Metropolitan History, from 1989. The Centre's activities include the preparation of a bibliography of printed works on London history to 1939, edited by Heather Creaton with Tony Trowles, to be published in 1994.

MIDDLESEX

Timothy Baker

'An acre in Middlesex is better than a principality in Utopia'. Macaulay, like many before him, was merely acknowledging the advantage of being next door to London. Most of Middlesex's traditional attractions owed something to the capital, from villages on radiating roads to scenes of national events and seats of the rich or the famous. The county was modest in size, as in scenery. It had no obvious northern boundary and, before and after building swept across it, had little to distinguish it from the inner parts of other counties bordering the metropolis.

Historians, from the first, have seen a county physically and officially under threat. Westminster, while remaining in the old hundred of Ossulstone, was evolving its own government before it secured an Act, as a city and a liberty, in 1585. Soon Middlesex parishes were being brought within the area of London's bills of mortality, in a process which led to the mid 19th-century encroachments of metropolitan boards and foreshadowed the end. Middlesex lost more than other shires to the new London county council (L.C.C.) in 1889, although the rump was considered sufficiently non-urban to be left as an administrative county. It survived, bigger only than London itself, Rutland, the Isle of Wight, and the soke of Peterborough, until swallowed by the Greater London Council (G.L.C.) in 1965.

Consequently there are accounts of London which touch on Middlesex, of London's environs which include Middlesex, of an ancient Middlesex which embraces Westminster and sometimes even London, and of a truncated Middlesex alone. The environs themselves have overleaped Middlesex, which was wrapped around three sides of London, to take in parts of Essex and Hertfordshire. The area considered below is the historic (pre-1889) county but ignores Westminster in so far as it is treated in harness with London by writers who look no further afield.

If a blurred identity has dampened county patriotism, Middlesex has enjoyed disproportionate notice as an appendage of the capital. In the 18th century it appears hesitantly on its own, and, to more effect, as part of London's environs. In the 19th century it figures with them in much derivative writing. Its final 75 years have inspired many exclusive, often nostalgic, works. Today it may still be the subject of an illustrated county book, although the name is more likely to receive an incidental mention in general accounts of Greater London, the Thames, or the home counties.

A 'Middlesex Bibliography', compiled in 1956 and with a supplement to 1965, covers only the post-1889 county. Archives, purely pictorial records, and newspapers are excluded. Books, articles, and typescripts or manuscripts are listed for 'Outer' Middlesex and for each of its 27 boroughs or urban districts, together with collections in London libraries and rare items in national institutions.[1] Concise bibliographical notes for the same county, with many judgements that are echoed below, are in Michael Robbins's *Middlesex* (1953).[2] Absorption into Greater London has encouraged treatment of a wider area, as in J. M. Sims's *London and Middlesex Published Records* (1970), a handlist for the London Record Society. The *Bibliography of Greater London*, to be published by the Library Association in 1994 for the Centre for Metropolitan History, takes in the whole of Middlesex, covering its history to 1939 as reflected in publications up to 1990.[3] Inevitably its 260-odd entries with Middlesex in the title do not include all those descriptions in works vaguely claiming to be about the metropolis or its surroundings; individual places, however, are entered separately.

Middlesex first appears in general topographies: in John Leland's 'Itinerary' of *c.* 1534–43,[4] in William Camden's *Britannia* of 1586 (translated from the Latin by Philemon Holland, 1610), briefly in the 16th song of Michael Drayton's *Poly-Olbion* (1622), in the first book of John Speed's *Theatre of the Empire of Great Britain* of 1627, and, preceding London and Westminster, in volume three of Thomas Cox's *Magna Britannia*, a recension of Camden, in 1724.

Nominally, the county boasts an early topography of its own in John Norden's *Speculum Britanniae, The First Part, An Historical and Choro-graphical Description of Middlesex* of 1593.[5] Norden supplied a list of places, supported by a map and starting with Acton, where London and Westminster were kept in alphabetical order. The device is clumsy, however, since the two cities between them took up almost half of the gazetteer. A thread of inconsistency can be traced back to Norden, for whom the small but fertile shire was graced above all rivals by the capital, 'which as an adamant draweth unto it all the other parts of the land'. His successors increasingly were torn between city and country, between the splendour of Londoners' seats and the charm of rural survivals. Ventures into Middlesex by civic chroniclers began with John Stow's *Survey of London* of 1598 and 1603.[6] Sandwiched between

---

[1] *London and Mdx. Arch. Soc. Trans.* [hereafter *L.A.M.A.S. Trans.*], xxii (1), 18, 20. Duplicated copies were distributed among the county's libraries and several metropolitan centres.

[2] Below.

[3] Inf. from Heather Creaton, Centre for Metropolitan Hist., Institute of Hist. Research.

[4] J. Leland, *Itinerary*, ed. L. Toulmin Smith (5 vols. 1907–10), i and ii.

[5] Facsimile edn. (1971).

[6] J. Stow, *Survey of London*, ed. C. L. Kingsford (1908).

Southwark, duchy of Lancaster liberties, and Westminster were such 'suburbs without the walls' as Hoxton, Shoreditch, Finsbury, and Clerkenwell. The second volume of an enlarged edition by John Strype of 1720 had additional details on the suburbs and an appendix of 'circuit walks' as far as Hackney, where Strype himself preached, with many monumental inscriptions.

For Thomas Fuller, a resident of Cranford, the county was 'but the suburbs of London, replenished with the retiring houses of the gentry and citizens thereof'. His *History of the Worthies of England*, published posthumously in 1662,[7] hinted at an educated class that was largely self-made, lacking the inborn loyalties of a provincial readership. Such a public may explain why John Bowack, a writing master, ended his *Antiquities of Middlesex* (1705–6) after two volumes on Chelsea and five neighbouring parishes. The prolific Richard Rawlinson, while feeling that Bowack deserved no better, himself failed to find a publisher for a projected history of Middlesex based on Norden.[8] Also curtailed were a *Description* of the county printed for R. Snagg in 1775, which did not proceed beyond London and Middlesex as promised, and Luke Pope's *History* of 1795, which stopped while still on London.

Visitors' curiosity proved more rewarding than did natives' pride. Particular places drew pleasure- or health-seekers from London, including Pepys and Evelyn, besides more committed travellers such as Celia Fiennes, who died at Hackney, in the 1690s and Daniel Defoe, who lived at Stoke Newington, in the 1720s. The extended title of Snagg's *Description* shows that it was aimed at tourists. Sights were noted alphabetically in *London and Its Environs Described*, six volumes printed for R. and J. Dodsley in 1761 and purporting to cover the country 20 miles around. A successor was *The Ambulator, or the Stranger's* [later *a Pocket*] *Companion in a Tour Round London*, whose 12 editions from 1774 to 1820 contained material 'collected by a gentleman for his amusement' extending to 25 miles.

Historical and more ambitious than anything earlier was the Revd. Daniel Lysons's *Environs of London within Twelve Miles of that Capital*, whose second and third volumes of 1795 dealt with Middlesex parishes as far out as Harrow and Enfield. They were followed by *An Historical Account of those Parishes in the County of Middlesex which are not Described in the Environs of London* of 1800 and by a reissued *Environs* with a supplement of 1811. Whereas other home counties have their own majestic histories, Middlesex's classic account is that of a national topographer, the holder of a family living in Gloucestershire.

---

[7] T. Fuller, *Hist. of Worthies of England*, ed. P. A. Nuttall (1840).
[8] *L.A.M.A.S. Trans.* xix. 44–51.

Lysons, with his footnotes, is not often to be faulted. His comparative sketchiness on economic history was partly counterbalanced by the issue of reports to the Board of Agriculture by Thomas Baird in 1793, Peter Foot in 1794, and, most notably, John Middleton in his *View of the Agriculture of Middlesex* in 1798. Despite its title, George Alexander Cooke's *Topographical and Statistical Description of the County of Middlesex* [1805] is more of a guidebook, where London and Westminster take up over half of the text.

Many of Lysons's contemporaries were concerned with the picturesque and of value more for scraps of up-to-date information or for fine engravings than for historical comments. There was no agreement as to what should appear under London or Westminster rather than Middlesex. B. Lambert's *History and Survey of London and Its Environs*, volume four (1806), separated suburban parishes from those farther out, as did David Hughson's *London, The British Metropolis and Its Neighbourhood*, volumes four (1811) and six (1813). Both were dismissed as tedious by James Thorne, who did not deign to notice the Revd. Henry Hunter's *History of London and its Environs*, where Middlesex was treated briefly in volume two (1811), the painter John Hassell's *Picturesque Rides and Walks Thirty Miles Round the British Metropolis* (2 vols. 1817–18), which takes places almost at random, or Edward Brayley and John Britton's *Beauties of England and Wales*, where Middlesex was described by J. N. Brewer in that part of volume ten variously published as fourth or fifth (1816).

Slightly later topographies showed the same preoccupation with sights. Titles can mislead: James Elmes's *Topographical Dictionary of London and Its Environs* (1831) barely strayed into Middlesex. William Edward Trotter's *Select Illustrated Topography of Thirty Miles Round London* (1839) was written round a collection of views, John Fisher Murray's *Environs of London: Western Division* (1842) was quick to exploit the opportunity for excursions offered by the Great Western railway, and William Keane's *Beauties of Middlesex* (1850) was concerned with 190 landscaped gardens. William Pinnock's *History and Topography of Middlesex* (1824, published in the six unnumbered volumes of Pinnock's County Histories 1825) consisted mainly of elementary questions and answers and left much of Middlesex to an account of London in the same successful series. Separate treatment was given in Samuel Tymms's *Middlesex, London, and Westminster* (1843, the last of seven volumes of his England-wide *Family Topographer*), where a directory preceded a gazetteer which said nothing new. Peter Cunningham's *Handbook for London Past and Present* (2 vols. 1849) noticed parts of 'Inner' Middlesex.

Parish histories began as early as that of William Bedwell, the vicar who in 1631 wrote *A Brief Description of the Town of Tottenham High Cross* (printed in W. J. Roe, *Ancient Tottenham* [1950]). They multiplied with the works of William Robinson, a solicitor of private means, born in St. Luke's, Old

Street, and later resident at Tottenham. *The History and Antiquities of Tottenham High Cross*, published as two volumes in 1818 and substantially revised in 1840, preceded similarly titled histories of *Edmonton* (1819), *Stoke Newington* (1820 and 1842), *Enfield* (2 vols. 1823), and *Hackney* (2 vols. 1842–3). His works, despite much general padding, are particularly valuable for Tottenham and Hackney and made him probably the most prolific of all writers on the parishes north and north-east of London.[9] Elsewhere he was matched only by Thomas Faulkner, a printer-antiquary of Chelsea, whose *Historical and Topographical Description of Chelsea* (1810) was followed by one of *Fulham*, including Hammersmith (1813), and by the *History and Antiquities of Kensington* (1820), of *Hammersmith* (1839), and of *Brentford, Ealing, and Chiswick* (1845).

It remained hard to interest a wide enough public. Faulkner could print for profit, with help from private patrons, but Robinson lost money, at least on Hackney, which was not alone in its indifference. Islington already had its own *History* by John Nelson (1811); when Thomas Edlyne Tomlins brought out the first part of *Yseldon: A Perambulation of Islington* in 1844, it found so little favour that no more appeared until 1858. Yet Robinson may have been the inspiration of younger local historians, among them William John Pinks, the ragged-school teacher who died in 1860 after spending six of his 31 years preparing a *History of Clerkenwell* (edited with additions by E. J. Wood, 1865).

Ranking second only to Lysons's *Environs* for the county as a whole, although without footnotes, is James Thorne's *Handbook to the Environs of London* (2 vols. 1876). Observing a 'curious abundance' of borrowed or perfunctory works, and rightly fearing Lysons's to be too bulky for republication, Thorne's gazetteer extended to 20 miles round London, with historical notices which themselves have saved later writers much labour. A slightly smaller area is treated in greater detail in Edward Walford's *Greater London*, whose first volume (1882) included most of 'Outer' Middlesex. The omitted parishes were covered by Walford in volume four, for Westminster and the innermost area, and volume six of his and Walter Thornbury's *Old and New London* (6 vols. 1873–8). Thorne (d. 1881) is also to be remembered as an artist employed by Charles Knight, and Walford (d. 1897), a Balliol contemporary of Matthew Arnold, as an editor of the *Gentleman's Magazine* and of Knight's *London*.[10] John Timbs's *Curiosities of London* (1876) had entries for inner parishes, H. J. Foley's *Our Lanes and Meadowpaths* (1887)

   [9] A. Abrahams, *Life and Works of William Robinson* (1925). A seven-volume manuscript collection for Stepney cannot be traced.
   [10] F. Boase, *Modern English Biography* (6 vols. 1892–1921). Walford, a parson's son, was twice converted to Rome and twice returned to Anglicanism: *The Times*, 7 Sept. 1881, p. 10F; 22 Nov. 1897, p. 6B; 23 Nov. 1897, p. 6C.

tried to open north Londoners' eyes to the country on their doorstep, and Henry B. Wheatley's *London Past and Present* (3 vols. 1891) expanded Cunningham's *Handbook*.

An antidote to antiquarianism, Charles Booth's *Life and Labour of the People in London*[11] dealt with social and related problems, which were pinpointed in his 'Descriptive Map of London Poverty' in 1889.[12] It concerned only 'Inner' Middlesex, as did the *New Survey of London Life and Labour* by H. Llewellyn Smith and others (9 vols. 1930–5). R. Mudie-Smith's *Religious Life of London* (1904), added to parts of Booth. *North of the Thames* (1911), an addition to Walter Besant's 10-volume *Survey of London* (1906–8), was lighter and more historical.

After 17 counties had established archaeological societies since 1840, the London and Middlesex Archaeological Society (L.A.M.A.S.) followed in 1855 and published its first *Transactions* in 1860.[13] Although archaeology and history have had to compete for space, the *Transactions* have ensured some coverage for an ancient county that has not managed to sustain an historical society of its own. Today they also publicize local groups. The London Topographical Society, founded in 1880, has featured inner parts of Middlesex in its later *London Topographical Record* and in maps such as Milne's or Booth's.

Administrative changes focused attention on the county's historical records. A special committee appointed by the magistrates in 1882 reported that the sessions records, derived from four commissions, surpassed those of any other shire in interest and probably in extent; the earliest, of 1549, were antedated only by those of Norfolk and the East Riding.[14] Their transfer from the sessions house at Clerkenwell (from 1889 taken over by London) to Middlesex's guildhall (ironically in Westminster) led in 1899 to an action in Queen's Bench between the dukes of Westminster and Bedford as custodes rotulorum. Judgement was given for the duke of Bedford on the grounds that London was not an ancient county, although costs were refused to protect the taxpayer from 'this lamentable litigation'.[15] Selections from the 4,916 bundles, containing half a million documents, had already been published for a short-lived Middlesex Record Society, founded in 1884.[16]

Serious contributions to Middlesex history were now being made almost as a family affair. Among the record society's vice-presidents was Sir William

[11] 17 vols., revised edn. 1902–3.

[12] *Charles Booth's Descriptive Map of London Poverty, 1889* (London Topographical Soc. 1984).

[13] *L.A.M.A.S. Trans.* xviii (1), 1.

[14] W. J. and W. Le Hardy, *Mdx. County Recs. Reports, 1902–28* (1928).

[15] Greater London Record Office [hereafter G.L.R.O.], *Guide to Mdx. Sessions Recs. 1549–1889* (1965), 3; *The Times*, 19 Dec. 1899, p. 15B; 23 Dec. 1899, p. 12E.

[16] *The Times*, 29 Nov. 1889, p. 3D.

Hardy (d. 1887), successor to his brother Sir Thomas as deputy keeper of the public records, and father of William John Hardy (d. 1919),[17] who did more than anyone to publicize the county's historic identity. From 1885 until 1902 W. J. Hardy was in partnership as a record agent with his brother-in-law William Page (d. 1934); both were inspectors under the Historical Manuscripts Commission and later responsible for organizing the collection of material for the *Victoria History of the Counties of England*.[18] A further debt was to be owed by Middlesex to W. J. Hardy's son Col. William Henry Clement Hardy (from *c.* 1922 Le Hardy), who was to be appointed part-time archivist in 1945 and for a time was to act for Middlesex and Hertfordshire together.[19]

The division of 1889 is necessarily ignored in most publications of earlier documents. Four volumes of *Middlesex County Records* for 1550–1688[20] were followed by a fifth for 1689–1709.[21] Duplicated calendars of later records were described by the Hardys in their *Reports*. A full calendar for 1612–18 formed four volumes of *Middlesex Sessions Records*.[22] A *Calendar to the Feet of Fines for London and Middlesex* (2 vols. 1892–3), from Richard I to 1569, represented the partnership of Hardy and Page. 'Outer' Middlesex alone was the subject of *Middlesex Parish Registers* (8 vols. 1909–30) in the ambitious series begun by W. P. W. Phillimore (d. 1913) and continued by his company.

Popular periodicals needed more readers than could be won in Middlesex. A *London and Middlesex Notebook*, edited by Phillimore (1892), extended to only one issue; *Middlesex and Hertfordshire Notes and Queries*, edited by W. J. Hardy, reached four volumes (1895–8) and was superseded for a wider area, including London, by *The Home Counties Magazine* (1898–1912), with Hardy as editor of the first six volumes.

Practical guidebooks, illustrated sketches, and anecdotal ramblings have abounded from the 1890s. A few mark the dutiful inclusion of 'Outer' Middlesex in country-wide series, among them John B. Firth's *Middlesex* (1906) in Methuen's Little Guides;[23] others, such as R. H. Ernest Hill's *Picturesque Middlesex* (1904), A. R. Hope Moncrieff's *Middlesex* (1907), and Walter Jerrold's *Highways and Byways in Middlesex* (1909), chiefly illustrated the past, in Jerrold's case with generous helpings of poetry. All shed some light on the contemporary scene. History advanced with *Memorials of Old Middlesex*, edited by J. Tavenor-Perry (1909), one of a counties series begun

[17] Boase, *Modern English Biography*, i, col. 1334; *Who Was Who, 1916–28*.
[18] *V.C.H. General Introduction*, 4; *The Times*, 5 Feb. 1934, p. 17B; *Who Was Who, 1929–40*.
[19] *G.L.R.O. and Library Report* (1974), 7–8; inf. from G.L.R.O.
[20] Ed. J. C. Jeaffreson (1886–92).
[21] Ed. W. J. Hardy (1905).
[22] Ed. W. Le Hardy (1935–41).
[23] Revised by R. L. P. Jowitt (1930).

in 1901; the longest article, by J. Charles Cox on churches of the ancient county, recorded changes since the appearance of John Hanson Sperling's ecclesiological *Church Walks in Middlesex* (1849; 1853) and the three small volumes of Frederick Cansick's incomplete *Collection of Curious Epitaphs* (1868–75). Arthur Mee's romantic *Middlesex: Little Home County* (1940) in the King's England series was one more general summary preceding a gazetteer. Martin Briggs's *Middlesex Old and New* (1934), 'the best general survey of the modern county',[24] concentrated on scenes increasingly under threat. The author, an architect, lamented the suburban county's unhelpful booksellers and its apathetic public.

Middlesex county council from 1898 could use money from the rates on the care and publication of records. A muniment room was included in the new Middlesex Guildhall, opened in 1913, where conservation was praised by the Historical Manuscripts Commission. The most notable archives apart from those of the sessions were those of the Middlesex Registry of Deeds, containing all land transactions from 1709 to 1837; later deeds remained with the L.C.C.[25] Both the Middlesex Record Office (M.R.O.), rehoused in 1954 in Dartmouth Street, and the L.C.C.'s records at County Hall passed in 1965 to the G.L.C. London's head archivist then took charge of a Greater London Record Office (G.L.R.O.) and Middlesex's county archivist became deputy head, with special responsibility for Middlesex records. The arrangement persisted until the Dartmouth Street records were moved in 1979 to County Hall and in 1982 to the new G.L.R.O. in 'Inner' Middlesex's Clerkenwell. Since 1986 the record office and adjoining history library have been administered by the Corporation of the City of London.[26]

The most scholarly national series have failed to agree on a uniform area. The Middlesex volumes of the *V.C.H.*, planned to exclude an undefined 'Westminster', began in 1911 with volume two, where general articles preceded accounts of seven south-western parishes which were dwarfed by a history of Hampton Court. The Royal Commission on Historical Monuments's *Middlesex* (1937) treated only 'Outer' Middlesex and went no later than 1714. Nothing of similar quality supplemented it except such detailed parish accounts or monographs of the L.C.C.'s (continued as the G.L.C.'s) *Survey of London* as concerned some of the older parts of Middlesex. The English Place-Name Society's 18th volume, *The Place-Names of Middlesex* (1942), included Westminster but was far too thin for its subject.

---

[24] Robbins, *Mdx.* 401.

[25] Ibid. 397–8; *Mdx. County Recs. Reports*, 105.

[26] C. Radcliffe, *Mdx.* [1954], 79; *G.L.C. Library and R.O. Report* (1965, 1966); *G.L.R.O. and Library Report* (1967 and later edns.); inf. from G.L.R.O.

Continued threats to the amputated county brought an Indian summer of historical writing. The 'Middlesex Bibliography', noted above, is a legacy of the Middlesex Local History Council, which was formed in 1951 and produced useful short articles in its *Bulletin*. The past, together with municipal achievements, is celebrated by the clerk of the peace Sir Clifford Radcliffe in *Middlesex*, initially for the council's jubilee in 1939 and reissued in 1954. Authoritative thematic histories were Norman G. Brett-James's *Middlesex* (1951), one of Robert Hale's County Books, and Michael Robbins's *Middlesex* (1953), which included a gazetteer and is a reminder of the loss from Collins's failure to continue its New Survey of England after the appearance of W. G. Hoskins's *Devon* in 1954. Nikolaus Pevsner's *Middlesex*, in the Buildings of England, brought the work of the Royal Commission down to 1951 and recorded much that has since disappeared; it has no single successor, since the revised *London 2: South* (1983) dealt with districts in Richmond upon Thames and *London 3: North West* (1991) with Middlesex west of Edgware Road, besides the outer parts of Westminster, leaving the rest to an awaited *London 4*.

Also partly attributable to the local history council was the revival from 1955 of the Middlesex *V.C.H.* Volume three, published in 1963 a few months before the county's demise, resumed a topographical coverage of 'Outer' Middlesex completed in 1982 with volume seven and thereafter continued for the inner parishes, to include Westminster. The whole county, except Westminster, was treated in volume one of 1969. It contained the Domesday text, necessarily including Westminster abbey's holdings, and definitive accounts, summarizing research to date, on archaeology, religion, and aspects of education.

The Middlesex Local History Council's incorporation into L.A.M.A.S. from 1965, like the M.R.O.'s into the G.L.R.O., marks a reabsorption of the history of Middlesex into that of London. If the name is fated to become less common, Middlesex can conveniently be studied as a whole within a clearly defined Greater London, rather than in varying fractions of whatever are taken to be the environs. It is covered, for example, by the *London Journal*, founded in 1975 to broaden out from more localized publications such as *East London Papers* of 1958–73, and included in Edward Jones and Christopher Woodward's *Guide to the Architecture of London* and Ben Weinreb and Christopher Hibbert's *London Encyclopaedia*, both of 1983. Research is served by the Greater London Archives Network (G.L.A.N.), founded in 1982 to bring together archivists and librarians, by the seminars and projects of the Centre for Metropolitan History, founded in 1987 at London University's Institute of Historical Research, and by the London Archive Users Forum (L.A.U.F.), with its newsletter from 1988.

The Friends of the County of Middlesex still hope to keep its name alive.

Feeling for a parish or a suburb has perhaps been stronger than for the county, however, at least since fears were kindled over 160 years ago when George Cruikshank depicted 'the march of bricks and mortar'. Nothing is now more chic than to describe a select residential area, embedded in later suburbia, as a village. Where only a few road lines and a restored church survive from before the 19th century, no history has a wider appeal than that which conjures up the time when they stood for a distinct settlement. Fourteen local history societies announced meetings in the L.A.M.A.S. *Newsletters* of 1992. Some can claim an impressive list of publications, as can many not there advertised including the Camden History Society with its *Camden History Review* from 1973 and the Friends of Hackney Archives with their *Terrier* from 1985. Preservation societies include the successful raiser of subscriptions, in time-honoured fashion, for the first two volumes of David Pam's *History of Enfield* (1990 and 1992). Meanwhile Alan Godfrey's reproduction of large-scale Ordnance Survey maps is widening knowledge of the Victorian scene. With growing local interest, the lack of a learned society for Middlesex itself is no disgrace.

NORFOLK

Hassell Smith and Roger Virgoe

Norfolk was one of the largest English counties and until the 18th century one of the wealthiest and most densely populated, with over 700 rural parishes, more than 1,500 manors, a cathedral city which was one of the largest towns in England, two other substantial boroughs in Great Yarmouth and King's Lynn, and a network of market towns and villages. Although its remoteness from the main routes from London meant that no major battles occurred there and few events of national importance, its inhabitants have played a significant role in most aspects of English history, not least in the development of antiquarian and historical studies. Notoriously litigious and 'full of wiles', Norfolk men, including an exceptionally large number of lawyers, frequently had to conduct research in documents, church memorials, and the like to seek out evidence for their law cases, but by the 15th century antiquarian interest for its own sake began to emerge.

The first historian of Norfolk, William Worcester alias Botoner (1415–?1482), 'the first Englishman to deserve the name of antiquary', was born in Bristol (about which he also wrote), but spent much of his life as a servant of Sir John Fastolf of Caister Castle, Norfolk.[1] Fastolf's household included a number of writers, but Worcester's antiquarian interests were also stimulated by the practical researches concerned with titles to Fastolf's purchased property. His interests were very wide and his collections and notes extensive, but like most of his Norfolk antiquarian successors he seems to have completed very few of the numerous projects for which they were collected. His 'Itinerary', a commonplace-book recording notes made on his travels and other miscellaneous material, particularly relating to Norfolk, was published in the 18th century by John Nasmith and has more recently been edited by John Harvey.[2] Another collection of notes on the families of Norfolk, 'De agri Norfolcensis familiis antiquis', sounds like the predecessor of so many later county histories; though it is said to have survived until the 17th century, only

---

[1] K. B. McFarlane, 'William Worcester: a Preliminary Survey', *Studies presented to Sir Hilary Jenkinson*, ed. J. Conway Davis (1957), 196–221.

[2] *Itineraria Symonis Simeonis et Willelmi de Worcestre*, ed. J. Nasmith (1778); W. Worcester, *Itineraries*, ed. J. H. Harvey (1969).

a few extracts made by Sir Henry Spelman now exist.[3] Although Norwich monks, like those of other counties, had written about the history of their diocese, monasteries, and saints, it is Worcester's collections that stand at the beginning of a long tradition of antiquarian collecting and writing about their county by Norfolk-domiciled men.

Although the great Norfolk-born scholar and manuscript collector Archbishop Matthew Parker (1504–75) showed no particular concern with the history of his home county, in Norfolk, as elsewhere, the Tudor age saw a great increase of interest in antiquities, particularly genealogy and heraldry. Many manuscript pedigrees and collections of extracts bearing on the history of gentry families survive from the period, some certainly produced mainly from antiquarian interest.[4] In the late 16th century both Norfolk and Suffolk received the attention of the anonymous 'Chorographer' (fl. *c.* 1604) who began the 'first surviving attempt at a full-scale topographical survey' of each county with a general description before proceeding to describe some of the features of individual parishes—unfortunately, only a small proportion of those in Norfolk being covered. The period also saw the first two town histories, both of Yarmouth, written by Thomas Damet and Henry Manship.[5]

The interests of Sir Henry Spelman of Narborough (1564–1641) were, like those of his East Anglian contemporaries Sir Robert Cotton and Sir Simonds D'Ewes, far wider and more scholarly than those of the 'Chorographer', but, along with his more general historical work, he retained a considerable interest in his own county. His manuscripts contained many notes on Norfolk places and pedigrees, his 'Icenia sive Norfolciae Descriptio Topographica' was a fairly brief description of Norfolk on the lines of Camden's *Britannia*, and his 'History and Fate of Sacrilege' was based largely on Norfolk evidence. Spelman was influential upon contemporary antiquaries such as Dugdale, but many of his writings did not get into print until edited by Edmund Gibson in 1698.[6] His books and manuscripts were sold off in 1709; some eventually ended

---

[3] McFarlane, 'William Worcester'. The extracts are in Norf. R.O., MS. NRO 7197, ff. 297–9, 304–21.

[4] M. Maclagan, 'Genealogy and Heraldry in 16th and 17th Centuries', in *English Hist. Scholarship in 16th and 17th Centuries*, ed. L. Fox (1956), 31–48. The general scholarly and historical interests of Sir Thomas Knyvett of Ashwellthorpe (d. 1618), for instance, included collecting genealogical and heraldic material for his own family: Norf. R.O., MS. KNY 824–8 etc.; D. J. McKitterick, *Library of Sir Thomas Knyvett* (Cambridge Univ. Library Hist. Bibliography Ser. iii, 1978).

[5] *Chorography of Norf.* ed. C. M. Hood (1938). And see A. Hassell Smith and D. McCulloch, 'Authorship of Chorographies of Norf. and Suff.' *Norf. Arch.* xxxvi (1977), 327–41. For the Yarmouth historians see H. Manship, *Hist. of Great Yarmouth*, ed. C. J. Palmer (1854); P. Rutledge, 'Thomas Damet and Historiography of Great Yarmouth', *Norf. Arch.* xxxiii (1963), 119–30.

[6] *Reliquiae Spelmannianae*, ed. E. Gibson (1698); *English Works of Sir Henry Spelman*, ed. E. Gibson (1723).

in the Bodleian Library but others passed to the Suffolk antiquary Cox
Macro (1683–1767), and in the 19th century to the Norfolk collectors Hudson
Gurney and Dawson Turner. They are now widely dispersed.[7]

The late 17th century and the early 18th saw the great flowering of Norfolk
antiquarian studies. The interests of the two most significant figures, Peter Le
Neve of Great Witchingham (1661–1729) and Thomas Martin of Palgrave near
Diss (1697–1771), like those of many others, crossed the Norfolk-Suffolk
boundary; their vast collections not only recorded much that has since
disappeared but also preserved many manuscripts that might otherwise have
been destroyed.[8] Contemporary with them was Thomas Tanner (1674–1735),
chancellor of Norwich diocese and later bishop of St. Asaph; his interests
transcended Norfolk but much of his manuscript collection now in the
Bodleian Library related to the county, particularly its ecclesiastical history.[9]
John Kirkpatrick (1685–1728), a close friend of both Le Neve and Tanner,
planned a history of Norfolk for which he accumulated copious materials, but
nothing was published in his lifetime: not until 1845 did Dawson Turner edit
his history of the religious orders in Norwich; much else remains in
manuscript.[10] Benjamin Mackerell (d. 1738), librarian of Norwich City
Library for many years, also prepared a history of Norwich, which got much
closer to completion than Kirkpatrick's but has never been published; he did,
however, put into print in the year of his death the first history of King's
Lynn.[11] With Francis Blomefield (1705–52) such men formed what Thomas
Tanner in a letter to Le Neve called a 'little society of Icenian antiquarians';
although they published little, they constantly exchanged manuscripts and
information.[12]

Francis Blomefield's *An Essay Towards a Topographical History of the
County of Norfolk* drew extensively upon the manuscript collections of his
contemporaries and predecessors, as well as upon evidence collected through
a parochial questionnaire.[13] Despite its modest title the work remains one of

---

[7] *Reliquiae Hearnianae* (1869 edn.), iii. 171; Hist. MSS. Com. 27, *12th Report, IX, Gurney*, 116;
Hist. MSS. Com. *Guide to Location of Collections* (1982), 28.

[8] *D.N.B.* s.v. Le Neve; 'Memoirs of Life of Thomas Martin, Gent., by John Fenn, Esq. 1784',
Norf. Arch. xv (1904), 233–66.

[9] *D.N.B.* s.v. Tanner; M. S. Sommerlad, 'Hist. and Antiq. Interests of Thomas Tanner
(1674–1735), Bishop of St Asaph' (Oxford Univ. D.Phil. thesis, 1962).

[10] F. Johnson, 'John Kirkpatrick, Antiquary', *Norf. Arch.* xxiii (1929), 285–304; J. Kirkpatrick,
Hist. of Religious Orders of Norwich, ed. D. Turner (1845).

[11] *D.N.B.* s.v. Mackerell; B. Mackerell, *Hist. and Antiquities of King's Lynn in Norf.* (1738).

[12] Norf. R.O., MS. NRO 425.

[13] F. Blomefield, *Essay towards Topographical Hist. of Norf.* continued by C. Parkin (5 vols.
1739–75; 2nd edn. 11 vols. 1805–10). The origins and formation of the vols. are discussed and
illustrated in the edn. of *Correspondence of Revd. Francis Blomefield*, ed. D. A. Stoker (Norf. Rec.
Soc. lv, 1992).

the great county histories and is still the only major history of Norfolk. At Blomefield's death he had printed and distributed only two volumes out of a projected five. The rest were completed in 1810 with considerably less thoroughness by his contemporary, the Revd. Charles Parkin. The work is best known through the 11-volume edition issued in 1811. Written at a time when England's county 'commonwealths' were ruled by their gentry and its parishes by their squires, Blomefield's *Essay* provided a history of the descent of each manor in the county and of the rise and fall of Norfolk's landed families; the volumes on Norwich still remain the fullest account of the development of the institutions and antiquities, secular and ecclesiastical, of the city.

Peter Le Neve's collections, which provided one of the important sources for Blomefield's work, had been destined for a special library in Norwich, but that plan came to nothing since 'Honest Tom Martin of Palgrave', who was Le Neve's executor, consolidated his hold on the Le Neve East Anglian manuscripts by marrying his widow. Martin did little with them except to continue to collect (notably acquiring Blomefield's own large collections), to make copious notes from his own and borrowed manuscripts, and to do some desultory sorting and cataloguing. On his death the enormous accumulation of the labours of his predecessors and of his own insatiable searches was sold off and over the next century became widely dispersed. The original manuscripts collected by Le Neve, Blomefield, and Martin and the vast compilations of notes and calendars made by them can now be found in scores of public and private libraries, many of those papers, inevitably, having passed at some time through the hands of Sir Thomas Phillipps.[14]

The most famous single group of Martin's manuscripts was the letters and papers of the Paston family taken from Oxnead Hall by Blomefield after the death in 1732 of William Paston, 2nd earl of Yarmouth.[15] They were eventually acquired after Martin's death by John Fenn, 'another smatterer in antiquity but a good sort of man', as Horace Walpole called him.[16] John Fenn (1740–94) of East Dereham, Norfolk, had been a friend of Thomas Martin for some years and long engaged in antiquarian pursuits. In 1787 and 1789 he published meticulous transcripts of the 15th-century letters of the Paston family and their connexions, a further volume being published after his death. His efforts earned him a knighthood from King George III, to whom the early volumes had been dedicated, and they made a great hit in fashionable

---

[14] For Martin's collections and their dispersal see *Norf. Arch.* xv. 233–66; M. F. Serpell, 'Sir John Fenn, his Friends and the Paston Letters', *Antiq. Jnl.* lxiii (1983), 95–121.

[15] *Paston Letters and Papers of 15th Century*, ed. N. Davis (2 vols. 1971–6), i, pp. xxiv–xxxiii.

[16] Serpell, 'Sir John Fenn'; the quotation is from p. 105.

Georgian society; to Walpole they 'make all other letters not worth reading'.[17]
They brought to public and eventually to scholarly attention the earliest
collection of correspondence in English, a source which, since the edition by
J. Gairdner in the 1870s, has made Norfolk the most widely cited county by
nearly all historians of 15th-century England.[18]

Fenn, through his friendship with John Norris, also acquired, sorted, and
bound the numerous transcripts, extracts, and calendars copied (sometimes in
shorthand) from a wide variety of local and central records by John's father
Anthony Norris of Barton Turf, Norfolk (1711–86), who had also intended a
history of the county.[19] Those, like Fenn's own collections, including most of
the Paston material, were sold off in the 19th century by members of the
Frere family, John Fenn's heirs.[20] Again there were many and varied
purchasers but fortunately most of the Paston letters and papers went in time
to the British Museum, allowing the recent edition by Norman Davis to be
far more accurate than Gairdner's could be. Walter Rye bought much of the
Norris material, which is now in Norfolk and Norwich Record Office.[21]

Collectors of manuscripts and annotators of material continued to thrive in
Norfolk until modern times. Perhaps the two most prolific were the
indefatigable writer as well as collector Walter Rye (1843–1929), whose
manuscripts and notes are now mostly in Norwich,[22] and G. A. Carthew
(1807–82), who followed the example of Le Neve and Martin by collecting
numerous manuscripts encountered in private houses during his work as a
solicitor in central Norfolk. He made use of them in two published books;
when his manuscripts were sold off, some of them were purchased by Rye,
but much still remains in private hands.[23]

Carthew's work was very much in the Blomefield tradition, but in many
respects the second edition of Blomefield's *Essay* (1805–10) had marked the
end of an era. New opportunities for historical research had become available

[17] *Original Letters Written During Reign of Henry VI, Edward IV, Edward V, Richard III and
Henry VII by Various Persons of Rank and Consequence* (5 vols. 1787–1823); Serpell, 'Sir John
Fenn'.

[18] *Paston Letters 1422–1509*, ed. J. Gairdner (3 vols. 1872). There were several later—and fuller—
editions.

[19] Serpell, 'Sir John Fenn'.

[20] *Paston Letters and Papers*, ed. Davis, i, pp. xxviii–xxx.

[21] The Norris sale was at Sotheby's in July 1888. The duke of Norfolk also purchased
documents, which are now at Arundel Castle (Suss.). Rye's purchases are now among the Rye
MSS. in Norf. R.O.

[22] G. A. Stephen, *Walter Rye: Memoirs, Bibliography and Catalogue of his Norf. Manuscripts in
Norwich Public Libraries* (1929).

[23] G. A. Carthew, *Hundred of Launditch and Deanery of Brisley in Norf.: Evidences and
Topographical Notes* (3 vols. 1877–9); *Hist., Topographical, Arch., Genealogical and Biographical of
Parishes of West and East Bradenham, with those of Necton and Holme Hale* (1883). Carthew's
MSS. were sold at Sotheby's on 8 Nov. 1883.

with the foundation of the British Museum, and the Public Record Office was to be set up in 1838. New men, sometimes less well rooted in the land, had elbowed their way into county society from among the bankers, manufacturers, and lawyers, and new philosophical ideas were current in the Norwich Literary and Philosophical Society. Ultimately the positivism of Comte prevailed. As a result 19th-century antiquaries viewed the history and antiquities of the county from a different perspective. Principal among them were Dawson Turner (a Yarmouth banker), the Freres of Roydon (variously civil servants and academics), the Gurneys of Earlham, Keswick, and North Runcton (industrialists and bankers), Walter Rye, Edward Beloe, and Basil Cozens-Hardy (solicitors), and H. Bradfer-Lawrence, an estate agent and brewer in King's Lynn. Such men continued the great tradition of manuscript collecting, their interest in private and state papers being heightened by a preoccupation with autographs, but they were also men of wide intellectual interests, combining, particularly in the case of Dawson Turner, interests in natural history, archaeology, art, and history. All of them published extensively, but they preferred to write limited and detailed studies from which they expected that a definitive Norfolk history would be created. The most scholarly was probably Dawson Turner,[24] while Walter Rye became the most prolific. A long-distance runner, which perhaps accounts for his haste, and a controversialist, which perhaps accounts for his inaccuracies, Rye's publications amounted (on a cursory count) to 152 articles and 117 books and pamphlets—surely a record to be envied by historians in university departments whose scholarly achievements are currently measured by quantity rather than quality.

The enduring monuments of 19th- and early 20th-century antiquaries are the Norfolk and Norwich Archaeological Society, the Norwich Castle Museum, and the local studies department of the Norwich Central Library. Each has greatly influenced the development of historical and archaeological studies within the county. From its foundation in 1847 the archaeological society began to publish historical source material in both its annual transactions and in substantial occasional volumes. Its first secretary saw as one of its purposes 'creating a better taste among that class from whence our churchwardens are usually taken', and he clashed frequently with Dawson Turner, but scholarly antiquarianism triumphed and the journal *Norfolk Archaeology* has published over the years an increasing number of important

---

[24] His collection of letters and state papers and drawings of antiquities ran to hundreds of volumes, by no means all of them relating to Norf. Many of those which did are now in the British Library, notably 50 volumes in which he expanded Blomefield's hist. of Norf. by the addition of some 7,000 drawings, engravings, and original documents (B.L. Add. MSS. 20013–23062).

articles on the history and archaeology of the county.[25] Its occasional papers include Walter Rye's *State Papers Relating to Musters, Beacons, Shipmoney etc. from 1626 to the Beginning of the Civil War* (1907) and two volumes of Norfolk pedigrees edited and extensively annotated by G. H. Dashwood and others.[26] By 1928 the society's council had wisely decided that a separate organization was necessary to collect, preserve, and publish manuscripts relating to the history of the county; by 1930 it had founded the Norfolk Record Society which to date has published 56 volumes of county records.

Meanwhile the Norwich Castle Museum (founded in 1894 to house the archaeological and natural history collections of the Norfolk and Norwich Museum) rapidly became the focus of archaeological and art-historical studies thanks to a series of substantial bequests (notably those of J. J. Colman and R. Fitch) and to the enterprise of its departmental keepers. Its leadership in creating a county museums service in 1974 and in integrating the Norfolk Archaeological Unit (founded in 1973) into that service has given further impetus to the study of Norfolk archaeology and topography. The work of the Castle Museum has been complemented by the facilities provided by the local studies department within Norwich Central Library. The gift by Walter Rye of much of his library, together with the bequest of J. J. Colman's collection of local material, has provided Norfolk historians with a reference library of outstanding quality.

Besides those institutions, 19th-century antiquaries, inspired, no doubt, by the great narrative histories of their time, produced some compendious studies, notably of their towns. They were firmly rooted in borough records, some being little more than a narrative compilation of those records. For Norwich the Revd. W. Hudson and J. C. Tingey edited two volumes of *The Records of the City of Norwich* (1904–10). A work of sound scholarship with an extensive introduction, it remains the fundamental source for the history of this city. Yarmouth and King's Lynn were served in similar vein by C. J. Palmer and H. J. Hillen.[27] At parish level, studies by F. G. Davenport and C. M. Hoare on Forncett and Gimingham[28] respectively are outstanding examples of the genre. The county as a whole fared less well. It was left to R. H. Mason, a man who stood outside our group of

[25] B. Cozens-Hardy, 'Early Days of Soc.' *Norf. Arch.* xxix (Centenary Vol. 1946), 1–7.

[26] *Visitation of Norf. 1563*, ed. G. H. Dashwood and others (2 vols. 1878–95).

[27] C. J. Palmer, *Hist. of Great Yarmouth, designed as Continuation of Manship's Hist. of that Town* (1856); *The Perlustration of Great Yarmouth: with Gorleston and Southtown* (3 vols. 1872–5); H. J. Hillen, *Hist. of Borough of King's Lynn* (2 vols. 1907).

[28] F. G. Davenport, *Economic Development of a Norf. Manor 1086–1565* (1906); C. M. Hoare, *Hist. of an East Anglian Soke: Studies in Original Documents* (1910).

antiquaries, to write the only major county history to appear in the 19th century.[29] It was a narrative work drawing heavily upon sources in London repositories and presenting for the first time a centralist's view of Norfolk history, albeit Mason intended it to preface a work which was to deal with the towns and parishes as well. His history was national history writ small and he wrote in reaction against what he regarded as the specialist antiquarian interests of his contemporaries. The latter, he claimed, 'have too often exposed themselves to the interpretation that their works were little more than a series of parish registers'. That was an exaggerated criticism which, needless to say, excluded him from the counsels of the Norfolk and Norwich Archaeological Society.

None the less his criticism presaged a new and socially diverse generation of Norfolk historians who have been influenced both by the fashions which have prevailed among professional historians for much of the 20th century and by a clutch of enterprising promotional societies and institutional support services. Notable among the latter have been the Norfolk Record Office and the Centre of East Anglian Studies. The record office, formally established in 1963, evolved through the initiative of the Norfolk Record Society and the Norwich Public Libraries Committee which, as early as 1931, had appointed an archivist to care for manuscripts which were either collected by the record society or deposited by public-spirited donors. In 1967 the University of East Anglia established its Centre of East Anglian Studies with a brief to encourage and initiate research into the region's history. To date, its impact has been greater in Norfolk than in Suffolk: it has launched six major Norfolk-based research projects as well as publishing 39 books, pamphlets, and historical aids. Notable among the last has been *A Bibliography of Norfolk History*, published in 1975 and updated in 1991.[30] One example of the Centre's role has been a study of the origins and development of Norwich (the Norwich Survey) undertaken jointly with the city and the Castle Museum. It has produced a number of important archaeological reports, but not the hoped-for history of the city.

Among voluntary promotional societies the most dynamic and enduring has been the Norfolk Research Committee. It was founded in 1934 by the initiative of R. Rainbird Clarke to encourage participation in corporate research projects and to attract established scholars to undertake major studies within the county. Among its most successful projects has been an

---

[29] R. H. Mason, *Hist. of Norf.: from Original Recs. and Other Authorities Preserved in Public and Private Collections* (2 vols. 1882–5).

[30] Vol. i compiled and ed. by Elizabeth Darroch and Barry Taylor; vol. ii compiled and ed. by Barry Taylor. There is also an excellent bibliography of the Norf. Broads in M. George, *Land Use, Ecology and Conservation of Broadland* (1992).

investigation into the origins of the Norfolk Broads undertaken by J. N. Jennings and J. M. Lambert.[31] The *Bulletin* of the Research Committee (1949–91) chronicles hard work, excitement, some disappointments, and a great deal of achievement. In a similar vein the Norfolk Archaeological Research Group, with its *NARG News*, was established in 1975 to encourage lay participation in archaeological recording and to provide voluntary support for funded excavations. In 1991 the two societies merged to form the Norfolk Archaeological and Historical Research Group with its journal *The Quarterly*. The activities of the Workers' Educational Association and the University of Cambridge Board of Extra Mural Studies have been important in expanding interest in local history.[32] Other promotional societies include the Norfolk and Norwich Genealogical Society (1968) with its valuable series of record publications (*Norfolk Genealogy*) and its journal (*Norfolk Ancestor*), and the Norfolk Industrial Archaeological Society (1970) with its *Journal*.

Two committees have been created to integrate the activities of local promotional bodies. In 1971 the Scole Committee for Archaeology in East Anglia was established to co-ordinate archaeological research within the region; its series of *East Anglian Archaeological Reports* has provided a vehicle for the publication of 40 major reports on Norfolk archaeology and topography by members of the Norfolk Archaeological Unit and voluntary fieldworkers. In 1988 many local societies within the county jointly established the Federation of Norfolk Historical and Archaeological Organizations. As a co-ordinating body it has started well by bringing together the expertise of 61 scholars to produce and publish, jointly with the Norfolk Museums Service, *An Historical Atlas of Norfolk* (1993).

The quality of Norfolk records, combined with the activities of their promotional bodies, has attracted British and overseas scholars to undertake research into local topics and to encourage their research students to do the same. Some scholars have used Norfolk history to illuminate wide historical themes. Notable in this category are Owen Chadwick's *Victorian Miniature* (1960), Susan Amussen's *An Ordered Society: Gender and Class in Early-Modern England* (1988), and Ralph Houlbrooke's *Church Courts and the People During the English Reformation, 1520–1570* (1979). Others have exploited Norfolk sources to present history from its participants' point of view. Hassell Smith's *County and Court: Government and Politics in Norfolk, 1558–1603* (1974) and Anne Digby's *Pauper Palaces* (1978) exemplify that

---

[31] J. N. Jennings, *Origin of the Broads* (1952); J. M. Lambert and others, *Making of the Broads: a Reconsideration of their Origin in the Light of New Evidence* (1960).

[32] The work of the Board in Norf. has recently passed to the Centre for Continuing Education at the Univ. of East Anglia, Norwich.

approach. Yet others have applied modern research techniques to analyses of local topics, offering their publications as case studies from which sophisticated regional models of English economic, social, urban, and landscape history can be constructed. The series of articles by Bruce Campbell on medieval field systems and farming practices in east Norfolk[33] is a fine example of the genre, as is Eric Fernie's *An Architectural History of Norwich Cathedral* (1993) and John Evans's *Seventeenth Century Norwich: Politics, Religion and Government 1620–1690* (1979).

Besides those professional outpourings, the great tradition of the earlier antiquaries, of Norfolk history written by Norfolk people, has continued with unabated vitality. Outstanding in that category have been the essays and major studies by R. W. Ketton-Cremer, notably his *Norfolk in the Civil War* (1969) and his masterly *Felbrigg, the Story of a House* (1962). Of the same kind, part family, part social history, and both dealing with aspects of the Gurney family are Percy Lubbock's *Earlham* (1922) and Verily Anderson's *The Northrepps Grandchildren* (1968). On Norwich there is John Pound's *Tudor and Stuart Norwich* (1988) and Charles Jewson's *The Jacobin City: a Portrait of Norwich in its Reaction to the French Revolution 1788–1802* (1975); in topographical history David Dymond's *The Norfolk Landscape* (1985) is one of the few recent attempts to write a county-wide study—by an author who is only a Norfolk man by marriage. David Yaxley also has written extensively on aspects of Norfolk's topography, notably in his report (jointly with Peter Wade-Martins) on *Excavations in North Elmham Park* (2 vols. 1967–72). Economic and social history are well represented by Susanna Wade Martins's *A Great Estate at Work: the Holkham Estate and its Inhabitants in the Nineteenth Century* (1978) and by Alun Howkins's *Poor Labouring Men: Rural Radicalism in Norfolk, 1870–1912* (1985).

Despite the efforts of so many individuals and societies, it is disappointing to report that since Francis Blomefield's *Essay* there has been no major study of Norfolk history nor an overview of its main urban centres. No *Victoria County History* volumes have been undertaken since the completion of volume two in 1906, nor have the investigators of the Royal Commission on Historical Monuments given this county a glance, despite its rich ecclesiastical and domestic architecture. Tom Williamson, in *The Origins of Norfolk* (1993), provides new insights into Norfolk's distant past, but for a modern survey of its whole history we are dependent on Susanna Wade

---

[33] B. M. S. Campbell, 'Extent and Layout of Common Fields in Eastern Norf.' *Norf. Arch.* xxxviii (1981), 5–32; 'Regional Uniqueness of English Field Systems? Some Evidence From Eastern Norf.' *Agricultural Hist. Review*, xxix (1981), 16–28; 'Agricultural Progress in Medieval England: some Evidence from Eastern Norf.' *Economic Hist. Review*, 2nd ser. xxxvi (1983), 26–46; 'Arable Productivity in Medieval England: some Evidence from Norf.' *Jnl. of Economic Hist.* xliii (1983), 379–404.

Martins's useful summary in the Darwen County History Series.[34] Similarly, though much research has been published on aspects of Norfolk towns, for instance *Norwich in the Nineteenth Century*, edited by Christopher Barringer (1984), for recent overviews we have only the extended essay by Barbara Green and Rachel Young on Norwich[35] and Paul Richards's all too brief *King's Lynn* (1990). It is to be hoped that the 21st century will see the publication of those comprehensive histories of Norfolk and Norwich to which generations of antiquaries and scholars have aspired and for which they have prepared such sure foundations.

[34] S. Wade Martins, *Hist. of Norf.* (1984).
[35] B. Green and R. M. R. Young, *Norwich: Growth of a City* (1964).

NORTHAMPTONSHIRE

Paul Stamper

It was while working in Northamptonshire in 1591 that the surveyor and cartographer John Norden (*c.* 1548–1625) formed the idea of a 'Speculum Britanniae'.[1] It was to comprise a systematic description, with maps, of every English county, and is the first known series of English county histories. The scheme, however, was over-ambitious, and only two counties (Middlesex and Hertfordshire) were published before Norden died in obscurity. Northamptonshire was one of a further four counties published later. While the title page of the published edition of *Northamptonshire*[2] indicates its compilation in 1610, a surviving manuscript bears the date 1591,[3] suggesting, quite logically given the circumstances, that it was the first county history that Norden drafted.

Norden's is a brief work, but does include sections on Anglo-Saxon history, the aspect of the county, its seats, parks, hundreds, and rivers, and short histories of Northampton and other chief places. Perhaps the best of the sections was that on the derivation of place names such as Thorpe and Deane; that alone, Kendrick argued, ranked Norden as a notable antiquary as well as map-maker.[4]

In 1695 John Morton, a Cambridge graduate, took the curacy of Oxendon, a small country parish near Market Harborough (Leics.).[5] Then aged *c.* 24, he was to remain there, from 1706 as rector,[6] for the rest of his life. By 1695 he had begun to collect fossils and was corresponding with Edward Lhuyd, keeper of the Ashmolean Museum, with whom he later travelled in northern England. In 1703 he was elected F.R.S., and by then or soon after was in regular contact with scholars including John Ray (1627–1705), Dr. John Woodward (1665–1728), and Sir Hans Sloane; to the last of those he professed his intention to produce a *Natural History of Northamptonshire*.

---

[1] Biography of Norden based on *D.N.B.*; M. McKisack, *Medieval Hist. in Tudor Age* (1971), 143–5. This chapter was read by A. E. Brown and G. R. Foard, who are thanked for their comments.

[2] J. Norden, *Speculi Britanniae Pars Altera: or a Delineation of Northants. being a Brief Hist. and Chorographical Description of that County in the Year 1610* (1720).

[3] In the Bibliothèque Nationale, Paris. Photocopy in Northants. Studies Collection.

[4] T. D. Kendrick, *British Antiquity* (1950), 164.

[5] Unless otherwise stated Morton's biography based on *Jnl. Northants. Natural Hist. Soc. and Field Club*, xiv (1908), 259–72, 293–324.

[6] H. I. Longden, *Northants. and Rut. Clergy from 1500* (16 vols. 1938–52), ix. 273.

By 1704 Morton was gathering and ordering materials. His main interest remained Northamptonshire's natural history rather than its antiquities, and his principal models apparently Plot's histories of Oxfordshire and Staffordshire. Nevertheless, Morton had sufficient acumen to recognize the need for his survey to appeal to a wide body of subscribers if it was to succeed, and decided to give a brief account of the county's principal houses. 'Some of the Gentlemen . . . will, perhaps, for that, condescend to look into the book.'[7] By 1705 a further addition was planned, a new survey of Northamptonshire, to be undertaken with Mr. Vincent of Leicestershire.

That expansion in the *History*'s scope is presumably, at least in part, the explanation for its long delayed appearance. Anticipated as imminent in 1704, it was eventually published in 1712.[8] Few natural phenomena escaped Morton's notice: white blackbirds, shoes cut from cherry stones, and a robin which could speak and play the flageolet. History and antiquities, however, formed only a small part of the published work, although a few items, such as a Roman mosaic at Nether Heyford, were reported fairly fully. There was also a pioneering but 'carelessly executed'[9] transcription of the Domesday survey for Northamptonshire.

Morton's work was well received by the scientific establishment, which recognized its contribution to the study of natural history. Antiquaries were apparently less enthusiastic. Thomas Hearne met Morton a month or two after the *History*'s publication, reporting 'I had a pretty deal of discourse with him. He seems to understand little or nothing of Antiquities.' Morton died in 1726 and was buried at Great Oxendon, where an inscribed slab was installed at the instigation of Sir Hans Sloane.

Before his death Morton wrote a memorandum for his son Henry (d. 1737) concerning the preparation of a revised edition of his *History*, to include a much enlarged section on antiquities. Between 1730 and 1733 Henry sought Sloane's assistance in effecting publication of the second edition; in the end, however, the proposal came to nothing.

One factor may have been the knowledge that another, far fuller, history might soon appear. It was the work of John Bridges, who had been born in 1666 at Barton Seagrave, near Kettering, where his father owned an estate.[10] He became a bencher of Lincoln's Inn, and also held various senior administrative posts in the Customs and Excise. In London Bridges was a

---

[7] *Jnl. Northants. Natural Hist. Soc. and Field Club*, xiv (1908), 265.

[8] J. Morton, *Natural Hist. of Northants.*

[9] *V.C.H. Northants.* i, p. xix.

[10] Unless otherwise noted Bridges's biography based on A. E. Brown and G. R. Foard, *Making of a County Hist.: John Bridges and the Hist. and Antiquities of Northants.* (in preparation). I am indebted to Glenn Foard for loan of the TS. of his section of that work.

respected figure in antiquarian circles, and was elected F.R.S. in 1708[11] and F.S.A. in 1718. By then, in common with others of his acquaintance, he had conceived the idea of a county history and begun to collect materials. While Bridges himself did visit archives and undertake extensive parochial visitations, most research was by keepers of archives, such as the Revd. Joseph Sparke, Peterborough cathedral librarian, and David Casley, deputy keeper of the Cottonian library, and especially by paid researchers, notably William Sliford, a professional antiquary, and William Taylor, schoolmaster of Upper Heyford. Other information, requested by Bridges through a printed questionnaire, came from correspondents including John Morton, whose own *History* had appeared in 1712.[12] Thomas Eayre of Kettering was commissioned to produce maps, and Peter Tillemans, at a guinea a day, to make drawings.

No text had been drafted, however, at Bridges's death in 1724. His will required the sale of his exceptional library of books and manuscripts, except those that might be used to produce his *History*. Notable among the latter were 48 notebooks, all now in the Bodleian Library.[13] Ten years were to pass before Bridges's brother William resurrected the project, appointing Samuel Gibbons, a Middle Temple bookseller, as publisher and Dr. Samuel Jebb, physician, author, and historian, of Stratford (Essex), to edit the assembled material. Sliford, Taylor, and Eayre were all re-engaged to complete the compilation of material. Between 1735 and 1737 altogether 8,650 subscription proposals were circulated, offering a two-volume, 500-sheet work at 2*d*. a sheet. The work was to be modelled, the prospectus stated, on Dugdale's *Warwickshire*.

Jebb's work[14] began to appear early in 1739 with a part covering Fawsley hundred. Already, however, there were problems with the enterprise, with disagreements between the contributing parties over areas of responsibility and money. Six parts had appeared by July 1739 covering Fawsley, Chipping Warden, and part of Norton hundreds, but there publication ceased amidst further wrangling. Gibbons's insolvency, probably the root of the problems, came to a head with his bankruptcy in 1742.

The project was revived in 1755 when a committee of 13 gentlemen under the chairmanship of Sir Thomas Cave of Stanford Hall, a keen historian, was appointed at the summer assizes to oversee publication. After an inauspicious start, with the successive appointments, and resignations, as editor of the Revd. Benjamin Buckler (d. 1780) of All Souls College, Oxford, and Dr.

---

[11] Inf. from Mr. Brown.
[12] Above.
[13] Bodl. MSS. Top. Northants. c. 1–39; e. 1–8; f. 1–4. Other materials include B.L. Lansd. MSS. 729, 1042.
[14] *Hist. and Antiquities of County of Northampton.*

Andrew Gifford (d. 1784), the editorship passed late in 1757 to Peter Whalley, rector of Courteenhall and Fellow of St. John's College, Oxford, whose publications included an essay on the manner of writing history.[15]

Whalley reworked Jebb's texts, especially the general introduction and the introductions to each hundred, and brought out the first volume in parts between 1759 and 1763.[16] Five hundred copies were produced, by Daniel Price of the Oxford University Press. The second volume came out in 1768–9 and the third volume only in 1791, a few months after Whalley's death.

The year after completion of Bridges's *History* saw the publication of the county's first printed parish history, the Revd. John Mastin's *History and Antiquities of Naseby*. Mastin's was a remarkable story. He was born in 1747 in Epperstone (Notts.) into a family of modest husbandmen.[17] At 13, after education by dames and writing masters, he entered the service of a succession of clergymen and gentlemen, by 1770 as steward. All the time his self-education continued. In 1772 he eloped to Gretna Green to marry a modestly wealthy minor. The next year a kinsman offered Mastin a curacy if he could qualify himself, which Mastin did in 1777 when he became curate both at Husbands Bosworth (Leics.) and Naseby.

In 1779 Mastin was ordained priest and appointed sequestrator at Naseby, becoming vicar there in 1783. The Mastins moved from Husbands Bosworth to the newly refurbished parsonage at Naseby in 1787. There, four years later, he began to gather notes on the history of the parish; for, as he noted, when a year later and at the instigation of George Ashby, patron of the living, they were published, 'topographical researches are now the spirit of the times, men of the first erudition not thinking them beneath their attention.'[18]

Although the work is conventional (perhaps due to guidance from John Nichols),[19] with sections on soils, fossils, agriculture, and plants, it is very much a product of Mastin's own curiosity and observations. Of Naseby he noted 'The village appears to have extended more to the south, as foundations of buildings continue to be dug up; and the home grounds show vestiges of old fences, which have formerly divided them into parts seemingly calculated for orchards and gardens to houses now entirely dilapidated.'[20] Assisted by his brother, Mastin excavated on the site of a former chapel at Knutcoat, finding a skeleton but being disappointed in his principal endeavour of discovering

---

[15] The first to be offered the editorship was apparently Dr. Andrew Coltee Ducarel (d. 1785). He declined it.

[16] *Hist. and Antiquities of Northants.*

[17] Biography of Mastin based on Northants. R.O., 'Memoirs of Revd. John Mastin' (accession no. 1991/129).

[18] Mastin, *Hist. Naseby*, p. iv.

[19] Ibid.

[20] Ibid. 8.

'some stone with an inscription'.[21] No less interesting are the biographical sketches of Naseby's 'ingeneous mechanics', such as Joshua Ringrose, 'exceedingly clever in compound machinery', and John Tresler, blacksmith, whitesmith, caster of metals, locksmith, and 'manufacturer of steel cross bows for shooting rooks with balls'.[22]

Partly through the influence of Ashby six or seven hundred subscribers were found. The work was sufficiently well received for Mastin to be invited to join the Antiquaries. 'Not wishing to pay for three letters F.S.A. 2 guineas annually', he declined.

Mastin produced a second, illustrated, edition of *Naseby* in 1818, and died in 1829.[23] By then others had begun to produce local histories. One of the most prolific authors of topographical works on the county was John Cole (d. 1848).[24] Born at Weston Favell, he was apprenticed to W. Birdsall, a Northampton bookseller, who in 1815 published the 23-year-old Cole's first work, albeit anonymously, a small popular history of the town.[25] Cole went on to follow an unsuccessful career as bookseller and schoolmaster variously in Lincoln, Hull, and Scarborough before returning to Northampton. In 1835 he moved to Wellingborough, where he opened a small school and offered geological specimens along with apples, bacon, and ham for sale. The townsmen regarded him as eccentric, 'as he and his sons would go out all day and return laden with wild plants etc.'[26] From Wellingborough he moved to east Northamptonshire, seemingly never remaining long in any one place. He produced numerous short local histories.[27] For Northamptonshire they include Ecton (1825), Weston Favell (1827), Wellingborough (1837), and Higham Ferrers with Rushden and Irthlingborough (1838). Manuscript histories exist for a half-dozen other places.[28] Cole also produced (1834) a textbook for use in the county's schools based on *Cooke's Topography of Northampton*, and in 1846 opened his collection of antiquities, minerals, and suchlike to public exhibition at Wellingborough; a 6*d.* entrance fee was charged. He died in poverty at Woodford.

The last single-handed county history was that of George Baker (d. 1851), who was born at Northampton in 1781.[29] By the time he was 13 and a pupil at Mr. Comfield's establishment in Horsemarket, Northampton, he had

[21] Ibid. 13.
[22] Ibid. 53.
[23] Longden, *Northants. and Rut. Clergy*, ix. 171.
[24] *D.N.B.*
[25] [J. Cole], *Hist. of Northampton and Vicinity*.
[26] *D.N.B.*
[27] *B.L. Catalogue of Printed Books*, s.v. Cole.
[28] *Northants. Local Hist. News.* iv (Sept. 1979), 21.
[29] *D.N.B.*; *Gent. Mag.* new ser. xxxvi. 551.

17 George Baker

produced in manuscript a Life of Dr. John Hinchcliffe (d. 1794), bishop of
Peterborough,[30] and a history of Northampton.[31] After leaving school Baker
became a woolstapler,[32] pursuing his antiquarian interests in his spare time,
notably by assisting John Britton (1771–1857) with the Northamptonshire
section of *The Beauties of England and Wales*.[33] That was published in 1810, as
was Baker's own first printed work, *A Catalogue of Books, Poems, Tracts, and
Small Detached Pieces*, produced in an edition of 20 by the Strawberry Hill
Press.

By 1815 Baker was planning a county history. Correspondence suggests
that originally it was conceived as a partnership between himself, Britton,

[30] *Northants. Notes and Queries*, vi (1896), 117.
[31] T. James, *Hist. and Antiquities of Northants.* (1864), 7.
[32] *Northants. Local Hist. News*, iv (Sept. 1979), 20.
[33] Ibid.; J. Britton and E. W. Brayley, *Beauties of England and Wales*, xi (1810); T. E. Jones,
Descriptive Account of Literary Works of John Britton, pts. ii–iii (1849–50), appendix pp. 91–2.

and the leading topographical publisher John Bowyer Nichols (1779–1863).[34] Baker, it was proposed, would be paid 4 guineas a printed sheet for gathering and editing materials: some £315 for a 300-page part. Baker was unclear whether that was supposed to include his travelling expenses; a visit to every parish, he felt, was indispensable. Fortunately, as he pointed out to Britton, 'I travel very economically.'[35] The precise terms arrived at are uncertain, but agreement was apparently reached with Nichols, who was to publish the five parts of Baker's *History* which appeared between 1822 and 1841.

Baker issued a proposal for his work in 1815,[36] presumably the same year that he sent out copies of a printed two-page questionnaire to clergymen and the like.[37] It sought information on numerous points concerned with local agricultural conditions, geology, natural history, manors, antiquities, charities, and worthies. If any one question caught the flavour of Baker's enterprise it was 'Have there been any remarkable Storms? Or are there any curious natural Phenomena, as Echoes, etc.?' Clearly, this was to be a *History* of the most traditional sort. Oddly, no enquiry was made about religious life in the parish; perhaps Baker, a Nonconformist,[38] felt that questions of faith demanded a more delicate and personal approach.[39]

By the time the first part of his *History* appeared in 1822 Baker (elected F.S.A. in 1819)[40] had attracted some 400 subscribers: *c.* 100 for an impression on large paper and 300 for the standard edition.[41] That first part, covering the hundreds of Spelhoe, Nobottle Grove, and Fawsley, was well received, one reviewer considering it 'well digested' and 'truly valuable'. Especially commendable, it was felt, were Baker's dissection and separate presentation of manorial portions (although, perversely, the reviewer commented on how disadvantageously it rendered conspicuous gaps in the descent), his biographical studies of landed proprietors and incumbents, and the 'scientific' descriptions of church fabric based on first-hand investigation including, in the case of the remarkable inscribed font at Little Billing, the removal of encrusted whitewash.[42]

Already, however, there were problems with the enterprise. Some Baker admitted to in his 'Address to the Reader', notably that despite the adoption

[34] *D.N.B.*; *English County Historians*, ed. J. Simmons (1978), 141–2.
[35] Northants. Studies Collection, G. Baker correspondence, including letter to Britton, 1 July 1815.
[36] *Gent. Mag.* new ser. xxxvi. 551.
[37] Copy in Northants. Studies Collection, G. Baker correspondence.
[38] *Gent. Mag.* new ser. xxxvi. 552.
[39] e.g. Northants. R.O., Holt 323, correspondence 27 May 1823, G. Baker to T. Scrafton.
[40] On 2 Dec.: inf. from Soc. of Antiq.
[41] Northants. Studies Collection, G. Baker correspondence, annotated subscription list.
[42] *Gent. Mag.* xc (2), 417–19, 525–9.

of a considerably smaller typeface than was usual for such works, the part was much longer than planned. Even so, a portion of Fawsley hundred had had to be held over for completion in the next part.[43] Already there were doubts about Baker's ability to sustain such a demanding and laborious scheme.[44]

Nevertheless, when the second part of volume one appeared in 1826, comprising the remainder of Fawsley, and Chipping Warden hundreds, all was said to be well. The number of subscribers had increased, and patrons were vying to present engravings for the work's embellishment. Following some trenching at Nether Heyford in 1821 Baker's fieldwork had included further excavations: at Borough Hill near Daventry, where in 1823 'a troop of labourers' was employed to clear a large Roman building and open 17 barrows, at Chipping Warden (1824), and at Thenford.[45] The third and final part of volume one covering King's Sutton hundred and including an index for the whole volume, appeared in 1830. A reviewer begged indulgence for Baker's slow and steady progress: 'topographical manuscript, like wine, is generally the better for keeping'.[46]

Volume two, intended to complete the southern third of the county, began to appear in 1836 with a part covering Norton and Cleley hundreds. Even three years earlier Baker had felt compelled to publish a communication explaining delays in publication, apparently the subject of 'frequent complaint'. 'Fitting up a new residence' had occupied most of 1832, and there had been other, unspecified, diversions of a private nature.[47] Presumably that was an allusion to his active role in the life of the county town, which encompassed the British schools, the Northampton Savings Bank, the General Library, the Artisans' Society, the Mechanics' Institute, and the Victoria Dispensary, as well as from 1836 the office of magistrate of the borough.[48] The slow progress, however, was mainly a product of Baker's continuing 'scrupulous and feverish anxiety to render the [History] as perfect and authentic' as possible. All the same, and for the first time, he was forced to admit that the loss of subscribers by death and 'fluctuations of property' was a worry.[49]

By the latter part of 1837 there was sufficient concern among Baker's supporters about the future of the History—180 subscribers had fallen—for an appeal for additional subscribers to be got up under a committee of the gentry

---

[43] Ibid. 529.
[44] Ibid. 417.
[45] *Gent. Mag.* xcvi (2), 33–4; *Northants. Local Hist. News,* iv (Sept. 1979), 21. For the Borough Hill excavations see also Northants. R.O., NR Pamphlets 1592, p. 76.
[46] *Gent. Mag.* ci (2), 425.
[47] Ibid. ciii (1), 299–300.
[48] Ibid. new ser. xxxvi. 551–2.
[49] Ibid. ciii (1), 299–300. See also Northants. Studies Collection, G. Baker correspondence, copy of prospectus for vol. iv with annotated subscription list.

headed by the marquess of Northampton. It had little success.[50] Four years later the final part of Baker's *History* appeared, on Towcester hundred. Wymersley, intended to come out with it, was omitted.[51] By then 220 subscribers had been lost, and with it Baker's will to see the project through. His health was broken and his fortune exhausted.[52]

Late in 1842 a six-day sale saw the disposal of his collections:[53] books, manuscripts, engravings, coins, antiquities, and the remaining unsold copies of the *History*. The bulk of Baker's manuscripts and notes was purchased by Sir Thomas Phillipps (apparently to the surprise of Lord Spencer, who thought them destined for Althorp)[54] and are today preserved in the Bodleian Library.[55] Baker died in 1851 and was buried in the Independent chapel in King Street, Northampton.[56]

Baker's sole beneficiary was his unmarried sister Anne[57] (d. 1861).[58] Like her brother, she devoted much of her time to matters charitable, improving, and antiquarian, and in 1812, when still in her mid 20s, was among the first to draw attention to the outstanding Romanesque fabric of St. Peter's church, Northampton. To her brother's *History* she contributed much of the botanical and geological material, and supplied a considerable number of the illustrations, some of which she herself engraved.[59] More importantly she was George's constant companion on 'topographical excursions', acting as his amanuensis and artist.[60] Baker's original parish questionnaire had included an enquiry about 'peculiar words', and in due course he suggested to Anne that she produce an independent work bringing together the 'provincialisms' she had recorded. Her *Glossary of Northamptonshire Words and Phrases to which are added, the customs of the county* (2 vols. 1854) eventually appeared three years after her brother's death. Contemporary opinion regarded it as one of the fullest and most satisfactory of the local wordbooks.[61]

Northamptonshire was among the counties where a good start was made to

[50] *Gent. Mag.* new ser. xvi. 614–15; new ser. xxxvi. 551.

[51] Ibid. new ser. xvi. 614.

[52] Ibid. new ser. xxxvi. 551.

[53] Copy of sale catalogue in Northants. R.O., N.R.S. 622.

[54] Northants. R.O., NR Pamphlets 1592, p. 21. Phillipps acted with great charity to the Bakers, to the extent of offering them accommodation at Middle Hill: A. N. L. Munby, *Formation of Phillipps Library from 1841 to 1872* (Phillipps Studies iv, 1956), 20–2.

[55] Bodl. Phillipps catalogue, pp. 69–779. Further Baker correspondence and MSS. are in Northants. Studies Collection.

[56] *Gent. Mag.* new ser. xxxvi. 551–2; *Northampton Herald*, 12 Dec. 1891.

[57] Northants. R.O., X 6169, probate copy of will of G. Baker.

[58] *D.N.B.*; *Gent. Mag.* new ser. xi. 208.

[59] *Gent. Mag.* xc (2), 529; xcvi (2), 33; new ser. xi. 208.

[60] A. E. Baker, *Glossary of Northants. Words and Phrases* (1854), i, p. xii.

[61] *Gent. Mag.* new ser. xi. 208. Some of Miss Baker's correspondence etc. is in Bodl. MS. Phillipps-Robinson c. 529, ff. 36–8.

the *V.C.H.*[62] One volume appeared in 1902 and two, including a special
genealogical one, in 1906. The editors were the Revd. R. M. Serjeantson (d.
1916) and W. Ryland D. Atkins (knighted 1911, d. 1925), the former (and
probably the more important) rector of St. Peter's, Northampton,[63] and the
latter a politician (M.P. 1906–23) and administrator.[64] Some research was still
going on in 1908, but thereafter it came to a halt as the V.C.H. faced financial
reality. Work restarted in 1925 when James Manfield (d. 1925), shoe
manufacturer and local philanthropist,[65] undertook to guarantee costs, thereby
securing the appearance of volume three, edited by William Page, in 1930.
The next, and as yet last volume, was brought out in 1937 by L. F. Salzman.

In 1920, as the Northamptonshire V.C.H. lay dormant, a county record
society was founded.[66] The key figure was Miss Joan Wake (d. 1974), for 43
years not only honorary secretary but also, for most of that time, its general
editor. In 1914, when she was studying under Frank Stenton at Reading
University, he suggested a society along the lines of Lincolnshire's. Together
they began to acquire documents; from the outset it was to be a collecting as
well as a publishing body.[67] Over the years Stenton, his wife, and Miss Wake
published important volumes in the society's main series,[68] as well as
staunchly supporting all its ventures. Those included, from 1948, publication
of *Northamptonshire Past and Present* (of which Miss Wake was editor
1948–62),[69] an important vehicle for articles, notes, and reviews concerning the
county's history. That connexion also produced Stenton's early volume (1933)
on Northamptonshire in the English Place-Name Society's series.[70] Of the
parties' attachment to the county there could be no doubt. One day, while out
on their famous bicycles, the Stentons saw Pytchley signposted, Lady Stenton
casually commenting on the P*i*tchley road. 'You mustn't call it that!' retorted
Sir Frank, 'If Miss Wake heard you call it that she would vomit.'[71]

Between 1920 and 1930 the Northamptonshire Record Society was housed
in Northampton Public Library, in the Borough Museum building. In 1930 a
record room and library were provided at County Hall, which remained open
until the Second World War when the records were dispersed. In 1946–7 the
record office reopened at Lamport Hall through the generosity of Sir Gyles

[62] Northants. Studies Collection has a copy of the draft Northants. prospectus (1900).
[63] *Northampton Independent*, 18 Nov. 1916.
[64] *The Times*, 31 Jan. 1925.
[65] *Northampton Independent*, 11 July 1925.
[66] *Northants. Past and Present*, i (1) (1948), 1.
[67] Ibid. iv (3) (1968/9), 181–2; v (3) (1975), 157–8.
[68] To the soc. Miss Wake contributed all or substantial pts. of vols. i, iii, vii, xxiv, xxvii; Frank
Stenton vol. iv; and Doris Stenton vols. v, xv.
[69] *Northants. Past and Present*, v (3) (1975), 163.
[70] *Place-Names of Northants.* (E.P.N.S. x, 1933).
[71] *Northants. Past and Present*, v (3) (1975), 291.

Isham (created bt. 1941, d. 1976).[72] Sir Gyles, who between the wars had been a professional actor playing Shakespeare on the London stage, and against Garbo in the 1935 Hollywood film *Anna Karenina*, thought the record office a much preferable tenant at Lamport to Italian prisoners of war, its then occupants.[73] There the office remained until a move to Delapré Abbey, Northampton, in 1959,[74] its home until the opening of a purpose-built office at Wootton Hall Park, Northampton, in 1991.[75]

Among the many others who have written in the 20th century on the county's history it would be improper not to mention briefly Henry Isham ('Harry') Longden (d. 1942).[76] Born in 1859, as occupant of a family living, farmer of his own glebe, fox hunter, and above all keen scholar, he was a representative of an age already lost. A prominent early supporter of the V.C.H., contributor to the *D.N.B.*, and editor of the 1681 heralds' visitation of the county,[77] in 1926 he 'created a sensation in the genealogical world' by the identification of Amphillis Washington, the president's ancestor. Most important, however, was his 16-volume biographical study of the clergy of Northamptonshire and Rutland which he began to publish after years of dedicated study in 1938. As Joan Wake observed, the series placed him in the true line of descent from Bridges and Baker.[78]

---

[72] Ibid. i (1) (1948), 7; *The Times*, 30 Jan. 1976, p. 18.
[73] *Northants. Past and Present*, v (3) (1975), 158; vi (3) (1980), 165–73; vii (5) (1987–8), 367.
[74] Ibid. v (3) (1975), 158.
[75] Inf. from the county archivist.
[76] For biography see Longden, *Northants. and Rut. Clergy*, xv, pp. v–xlvii.
[77] *Visitation of Northampton 1681* (Harl. Soc. lxxxvii).
[78] Longden, *Northants. and Rut. Clergy*, xv, p. xlii.

NORTHUMBERLAND

Jane Freeman

Up to Hodgson's time, therefore, there was, strictly speaking, no History of Northumberland worthy of the name; nothing of its 'Origines', no account of its British or Saxon owners or their works, no general detail of descent of property or blood, no parochial description, and the records of the stirring and romantic traditions belonging to its history as a border county, or to its own internal feuds . . . were yet sleeping under a cover of dust in the public or private repositories of the kingdom.

The words were written by James Raine, in celebration of John Hodgson, author of five volumes of an unfinished *History of Northumberland* published between 1820 and 1840. The qualifications 'strictly speaking' and 'worthy of the name' were needed; the comment was preceded by a lengthy discussion of Hodgson's predecessors in the field of Northumberland history.[1] Raine's summary of their works illustrated two major themes in the treatment of the county's history: one was the prominence of Newcastle upon Tyne, to accounts of which brief excursions into the county's past were sometimes added; the other was the fascination exercised by the visible remains of the Roman occupation, and above all by the Roman wall. A third theme is indicated by his reference to Northumberland's 'stirring and romantic traditions', traditions which encompassed both its place on the Anglo-Scottish border and the peculiar reputations for lawlessness held by Tynedale and Redesdale as late as the 18th century. Those traditions were notably explored by Walter Scott, whose *Border Antiquities of England and Scotland* appeared six years before the first of Hodgson's volumes.

Raine's list of local historians begins with William Gray, who in 1649 published a 34-page pamphlet entitled *Chorographia, or a Survey of Newcastle upon Tine*. Gray commended earlier writers, among them 'the Learned Camden, and painful Speed', who had undertaken descriptions of antiquities throughout the country. Contending that it was 'impossible that any one Man, being never so Inquisitive and Laborious, should attain unto the perfect knowledge of all Passages in all Places', he offered an account of his own town. In his few pages he established a pattern followed by later and more

---

[1] J. Raine, *Memoir of John Hodgson* (2 vols. 1857–8), i. 191–7.

prolix historians of Newcastle. Sections devoted to the general history of the town and surrounding area in the pre-Roman, Roman, and Anglo-Saxon periods were followed by a topographical description of the town and a discussion of its trade. In the last five pages he once again turned his attention beyond the town walls, in a section on 'Noble and Ancient Families of the North and their Castles'.

A very similar structure was used by the town's next historian, Henry Bourne, curate of All Saints' church in Newcastle, whose *History of Newcastle upon Tyne*, published in 1736, three years after his death, was a much more substantial work. In a preface couched in very defensive terms, Bourne spoke of his quest for all relevant materials, and complained that rumours had been circulated denigrating his efforts in an attempt to prevent his work achieving public success. The *History*, some 250 pages, was supplied with footnotes and references which give credence to his claims to scholarship. Like Gray, he ventured briefly into the history of the county, giving in footnotes and marginal comments some account of lordships which owed service to the town's castle.[2]

Further histories of Newcastle were apparently planned by a Mr. Akenhead, who published proposals for a two-volume history in 1750, and by James Murray, a Nonconformist minister, who was said to have worked only from printed sources. Both were mentioned by John Brand, whose two volumes of the *History and Antiquities of Newcastle upon Tyne* were published in 1789.[3] Raine described the work as 'a lumbering book . . . into which its author seems to have emptied the gatherings of a long-continued commonplace book, without much selection or condensation.'[4] The criticism had some justice: on many pages more than half of the space was occupied by footnotes, quoting sources in full or elaborating on what was said in the text. The amassing of detail, however, foreshadows Hodgson's volumes; similarly, Brand's use of lengthy appendices in which to print documents relating to the town look forward to Hodgson's interest in the publication of records.

Histories of the county of Northumberland were much slower to appear in print. William Nicolson, bishop of Carlisle 1702–18 and of Derry 1718–27, contributed material on Northumberland to editions of Camden's *Britannia* published in 1695 and 1722 and was said to have compiled an account of the antiquities of Northumberland, which apparently included descriptions of the county's Roman and pre-Conquest history and of its ecclesiastical institutions, and an alphabetical list of towns, villages, and places of note.[5] Its

---

[2] H. Bourne, *Hist. of Newcastle* (1736), 109–21.
[3] J. Brand, *Hist. of Newcastle* (2 vols. 1789), i, pp. vii, ix.
[4] Raine, *Hodgson*, i. 196.
[5] W. Camden, *Britannia* (1722 edn.), i, p. xl; *D.N.B.* s.v. Nicolson.

scope was presumably similar to notes on the county's history collected from 1729 to 1739 by John Horsley, chiefly celebrated as the author of *Britannia Romana*, which included a pioneering study of the Roman wall. Horsley's notes were published in the 19th century.[6] Nicolson's manuscript was reputedly deposited in the library of the dean and chapter of Carlisle; it was sought there but not found by John Wallis, whose *Natural History and Antiquities of Northumberland* was published in 1769.[7] Wallis's two volumes formed the first printed history of the whole county, and also covered Berwick-upon-Tweed and those parts of County Durham which lay north of the Tyne and were known as North Durham. A brief introduction to the first volume outlined the county's early history, described its physical relief, and touched on border raids and the feuding of the surnames of the dales. Much of the rest of the volume was devoted to natural history, Wallis's first love. The second volume was dedicated to 'antiquities', which were described as encountered on three journeys through the county. The work thus had the character of a 'view' rather than a history, but much historical information, including descents and genealogies, was provided. Hodgson himself expressed a restrained admiration for Wallis's volumes: 'considering the scantness of the printed information on the subject when the author published, [it] is certainly not only a copious, but a very correct account'. He particularly welcomed the inclusion of histories of estates and of families.[8]

Writing a few years later than Wallis, William Hutchinson made no pretence of offering more than a view of the county;[9] in the preface to his second volume, replying to challenges to statements published in the first, he claimed allowance for such errors because his work was a view and not a history. Although he began with the customary rehearsal of Roman and Anglo-Saxon history, he presented much of his information as the personal observation of a traveller. In drawing attention to matters of history or antiquity, he frequently cited Wallis, occasionally disagreeing with him,[10] and he also made use of correspondence between a group of notable antiquarians including John Horsley, John Warburton, William Stukeley, Christopher Hunter, and others.[11] Like Wallis, his interest extended to North Durham and to Berwick, and he also touched on Newcastle and on places beyond the Cumberland and Scottish borders.

No other substantial historical work on the county was published before the

---

[6] J. Horsley, *Britannia Romana* (1732); [idem], *Inedited Contributions to Hist. of Northumb.* [1869], i. 1–64.

[7] J. Wallis, *Northumb.* (2 vols. 1769), i, p. x.

[8] J. Hodgson, *Hist. of Northumb.* (5 vols. 1820–40), iii (2), 70.

[9] W. Hutchinson, *View of Northumb.* (2 vols. 1776–8).

[10] e.g. ibid. i. 44.

[11] e.g. ibid. i. 145–61.

first volume of Hodgson's *History*. Other tours and travellers' guides appeared. Hodgson himself contributed the section on Northumberland to John Britton and E. W. Brayley's *Beauties of England and Wales*.[12] His involvement in matters antiquarian seems to have grown in a manner typical of the period from interests in geology and botany. In 1806, when curate of Gateshead, he joined the Newcastle Literary and Philosophical Society. In 1808 he became incumbent of Jarrow and Heworth, and he later held the livings of Kirkwhelpington and Hartburn. By 1810 he had begun to formulate ideas for a history of the Tyne and of the Roman wall, and in 1812 he published, by commission, an 'historical and descriptive guide' to Newcastle.[13] Also in 1812, he was one of seventy gentlemen invited by John Bell, a Newcastle bookseller, to join in forming a local antiquarian society. Although the Newcastle Literary and Philosophical Society had originally expected to include the investigation of antiquities amongst its activities, it offered little to cater to antiquarian tastes, and in 1813 the Society of Antiquaries of Newcastle upon Tyne was formed. The new society took as its chief interest the antiquities of the north of England, especially those of Northumberland, Cumberland, and Durham. Hodgson was immediately elected as one of its two secretaries, and at its second meeting read to his fellow members a discursive paper 'On the study of antiquities'.[14]

Hodgson's prominence among local antiquarians was thus confirmed. The work of the society also provided opportunities to cement his friendship with its first president, Sir John Swinburne of Capheaton, who passed to Hodgson for his use a very large collection of documents relating to the Swinburne family and their estates. With Swinburne's permission, Hodgson made them available to Robert Surtees, who was then working on his *History of Durham*, and with whom he was to correspond and co-operate until the latter's death in 1834.[15]

About the time that the Newcastle Society of Antiquaries was founded, Hodgson began to plan a history of the whole of Northumberland. Between 1814 and the publication of the first volume in 1820, he travelled widely in the county, consulting manuscript collections, viewing and sketching buildings and archaeological remains; in 1819 he paid an extended visit to London, during which he combined negotiations for rebuilding Heworth church with visits to the British Museum and consultation of the public records. By 1818 the scale of the project was beginning to oppress him. He wrote to Swinburne in April that

---

[12] J. Britton and E. W. Brayley, *Beauties of England and Wales*, xii (1) (1813), 1–247.

[13] J. Hodgson, *Picture of Newcastle upon Tyne* (1812); Raine, *Hodgson*, i. 7–8, 51, 63–4, 74, 87; *Archaeologia Aeliana* [hereafter *Arch. Ael.*], 3rd ser. x. 127–8.

[14] Raine, *Hodgson*, i. 120; *Arch. Ael.* [1st ser.] i, pp. ix–xviii; 5th ser. xviii. 197, 215.

[15] Raine, *Hodgson*, i. 125–58; *D.N.B.* s.v. Surtees; above, Co. Dur.

to finish such an undertaking, in a creditable manner, would take me one year's constant residence in Durham, and another in London; and many years of unremitting labour in the county, besides an expense in travelling, etc., etc., which no county history can ever repay.

He considered giving up the *History* in favour of a plan, concerted with Surtees, James Raine, and others, of publishing documents relating to Northumberland and other northern counties in a quarterly journal; in his biography of Hodgson, Raine claimed to have no recollection of such a prototype of the Surtees Society, although the list of documents suitable for publication cited by Hodgson included many which later appeared in that society's volumes. The proposal was set aside, however, and in 1819 a prospectus for Hodgson's *History* was published in the *Gentleman's Magazine*. There were to be six volumes: the first was to be a general history of the county, including sections on agriculture, mining, geology, and natural history; volumes two, three, and four were to comprise 'parochial history'; and there were to be two volumes of historical documents.[16]

The volume published in 1820 was the fifth in the sequence set out in the prospectus; one of two comprising 'Ancient Records and Historical Papers', it included material from the Capheaton manuscripts, the hundred rolls, and other public records, mostly in Latin. Hodgson acknowledged that the contents were 'of a dry and unamusing kind', but justified the decision to begin in that way by the need to avoid introducing material in a foreign language into the parish histories, and by the ease of reference to important sources thus provided for himself and his readers.[17] He was congratulated by Surtees on his bravery in 'laying the foundation stone of Records first', but sales of the volume were, not surprisingly, poor, and Raine, with hindsight, doubted the wisdom of the decision.[18] In 1827 the first volume of parish histories was published; it included accounts of the franchise of Redesdale and of seven parishes. In the preface, Hodgson acknowledged that he had come to realize that the topographical history could not be compressed into the three volumes he had originally proposed.[19] In an effort to save space, much genealogical and biographical matter was presented in annotated pedigrees; they and sections of miscellanea for each of the parishes were printed in smaller type than the main text. The result, especially where the footnotes were long, was a volume in which information was very plentiful but less than clearly presented.

---

[16] Raine, *Hodgson*, i. 125, 190–1, 202–5, 208–69. For Surtees Soc., see above, Co. Dur.; below, this chapter.

[17] Hodgson, *Hist. of Northumb*. iii (1), pp. i–ii.

[18] Raine, *Hodgson*, i. 310.

[19] Hodgson, *Hist. of Northumb*. ii (1), pp. viii–ix.

Another volume of records and papers followed in 1828[20] and a second volume of parish history in 1832.[21] A third volume of parish history, published in 1840 and including a lengthy account of the Roman wall, was written by Hodgson, but he was then frail, and James Raine superintended its progress through the press. Raine also wrote the preface, in which he quoted from notes written by Hodgson, which indicated the latter's disappointment at the poor financial return he had received from previous volumes of the *History*, his uncertainty about the amount of information to include in the parish histories, and his sense that work on the *History* had detracted from performance of his clerical duties.[22] Hodgson produced no further published work for the *History* before his death in 1845.[23]

To complete the *History* as Hodgson had originally conceived it, the volume of general history and parochial histories for much of the county remained to be written. The Newcastle Society of Antiquaries undertook to make good the omissions, firstly by appointing John Hodgson Hinde to compile the introductory volume, which was published in 1858. In the chronological account which occupied most of the volume, Hinde concentrated on the Roman and medieval periods; he included another lengthy discussion of the Roman wall, contributed by Dr. Bruce, and despatched the county's history from the accession of Henry VII in some 70 pages of the total of 400. Although the preface promised owners of the earlier volumes that the society would spare no effort to complete the *History*, no realistic plan was made for its completion until the 1890s. Some gaps were filled piecemeal. James Raine, Hodgson's biographer, had published in 1852 a *History of North Durham*, providing an account of the former Durham parishes north of the Tyne which had by then become part of Northumberland. Hodgson had not treated any of the county's towns; a history of Alnwick, in two volumes and including much record material, was published in 1866–9 and an account of Berwick-upon-Tweed in 1888.[24]

In May 1890 the Newcastle antiquaries were reminded by Dr. Thomas Hodgkin of their promise to bring Hodgson's *History* to completion. On Hodgkin's initiative a committee was formed, subscribers and donors were sought, and an editor, Edward Bateson, was appointed. The intention was to provide histories for all the Northumberland parishes not covered by Hodgson's work; North Durham and Berwick were presumed to lie outside the committee's terms of reference and Alnwick was later omitted, as being

[20] Ibid. iii (2).
[21] Ibid. ii (2).
[22] Ibid. ii (3), pp. iii–vii.
[23] *Arch. Ael.* 3rd ser. x. 128.
[24] G. Tate, *Hist. of Alnwick* (2 vols. 1866–9); J. Scott, *Berwick upon Tweed* (1888).

adequately described in Tate's 1866–9 *History*, from the list of places to be treated.[25] A potential rivalry with the Victoria County History, set in hand a few years after the formation of the Northumberland committee and designed to include all English counties, did not deter the committee from its work. No Northumberland volume was published by the V.C.H., although one on Roman history for the northern counties was projected in 1903–10, and in 1927 most of the material on Northumberland history collected for the V.C.H. was sold to the committee.[26]

Between 1893 and 1940, when its work was completed, the Northumberland County History Committee published 15 volumes and employed six editors; the last three volumes were edited by Madeleine Hope Dodds, the first woman whose name appeared on the title page of a history of the county. Although Hodgson provided the model and inspiration and editors drew on his manuscript collections, there were, naturally, innovations. The geology of each area was described in some detail; for some parishes there were sections on dialect and on agriculture. In 1904–5 archaeological excavations of the site of the monastic house at Tynemouth were undertaken on the committee's behalf: the results were described in volume eight of the *History of Northumberland*.[27] Later volumes recorded other excavations undertaken for the *History*, most notably at Corbridge.[28] Descriptions of such aspects of parish history were often contributed by specialists: all geological sections were written by Edward Garwood, the only contributor to all volumes of the revived *History*. The modernity of the approach did not preclude a strain of romanticism, however. The rescue by Grace and William Darling of survivors from the wreck of the *Forfarshire* in 1838 is celebrated in the account of Bamburghshire: 'the heroism of the Darlings has maintained in the present century the noble traditions of Bamburgh, handed down from an ancient past.'[29]

While Hodgson's work and its completion formed the main strand of historical writing on Northumberland from the 1820s, it was not, of course, the only one. Before his first volume appeared Hodgson reported that an Alnwick bookseller had advertised a rival publication;[30] it is not known to have appeared. The disappointing sales of early volumes of Hodgson's *History* may, however, have been due in part to the publication of an *Historical, Topographical and Descriptive View of Northumberland* by Eneas Mackenzie. The author, the son of a poor Aberdeenshire shoemaker, had pursued a varied

[25] Northumb. County Hist. Committee, *Hist. of Northumb.* (15 vols. 1893–1940), xv, pp. ix–xi.
[26] *V.C.H. General Introduction*, 3, 9, 12.
[27] Northumb. County Hist. Committee, *Hist. of Northumb.* viii, p. vi.
[28] Ibid. x, pp. vi, 474–520.
[29] Ibid. i. 173–4.
[30] Raine, *Hodgson*, i. 294.

career as a Baptist preacher and a shipbroker in Sunderland before becoming a partner in a printing business in Newcastle upon Tyne.[31] His *View* appeared in two volumes in 1825, when Mackenzie described it as an enlarged edition of a work which had first appeared some years earlier. The earlier edition has not been traced, and there is some doubt whether it existed. The *View* provided an outline of the general history of the county and a description of each town and parish, including Berwick and North Durham, but not Newcastle. As the title implied, it included much contemporary description, but its historical coverage was reasonably substantial, and it had a clarity of layout and a geographical comprehensiveness notably at odds with Hodgson's volumes. Mackenzie completed his work with a two-volume *Account of Newcastle upon Tyne* in 1827. Rather differently organized were the *Local Records* compiled by J. Sykes and published in 1833. Sykes presented a chronological list of events and anecdotes from the history of Northumberland, Durham, Newcastle, and Berwick from the Roman settlement until 1832. Much of the two volumes was devoted to the years since 1700 and drawn from newspapers and other periodicals. Sykes apparently saw the *Records* as raw material from which other local historians could work, but they were sufficiently popular in themselves to have two continuations, one by John Latimer, who published a volume in 1857 covering the intervening years, and another by T. Fordyce, who covered the period 1833–75 in volumes published in 1867 and 1876.

In the preface to his *View of Northumberland* Eneas Mackenzie made reference to antiquarians who had denied him access to material; that comment, his free acknowledgement of 'occasional inaccuracies', and the absence of the names of many notable antiquarians from the list of those thanked for their help, bear witness to his place outside the local scholarly and historical establishment.[32] That establishment had as its natural focus the Newcastle Society of Antiquaries. In the first forty years of the society's existence, however, it exhibited few signs of vitality. Mackenzie himself commented on its lack of activity, as did W. S. Gibson, writing on the history of Tynemouth in 1846.[33] The history of the society's publications bears witness to that state of affairs. Provision had been made in its original statutes for the publication of papers and communications, but the first volume of *Archaeologia Aeliana, or Miscellaneous Tracts Relating to Antiquity* did not appear until 1822; John Hodgson was the chief contributor and the volume was prefaced by his paper 'On the study of antiquities'. Only three more volumes had been published by 1855. There followed a surge of activity, with

---

[31] *D.N.B.*; W. Fordyce, *Hist. and Antiquities of County Palatine of Durham* (2 vols. 1855–7), i. 10–11.

[32] E. Mackenzie, *View of Northumb.* (2 vols. 1825), i, pp. iii–iv.

[33] E. Mackenzie, *Account of Newcastle upon Tyne* (2 vols. 1827), ii. 486–7; W. S. Gibson, *Hist. of Tynemouth* (1846), i, pp. iii–iv; *Arch. Ael.* 5th ser. xviii. 199.

six volumes appearing between 1857 and 1865, and the establishment in 1855
of a series of *Proceedings* of the society, which recorded meetings and included
notes on historical and archaeological subjects briefer and less formal than the
papers appearing in *Archaeologia Aeliana*. A period of quiescence after 1865
was followed by another revival in the 1880s, again marked by a vigorous
publication programme; from 1883 *Archaeologia Aeliana* normally appeared
annually.[34] The antiquaries' activity in the mid 19th century coincided with
the foundation in 1862 of the Architectural and Archaeological Society of
Durham and Northumberland, which began publishing its *Transactions* in
1870.[35] The impetus for the new society's formation had come principally
from York and Durham, and although it offered the Newcastle antiquaries
some competition for membership, in later years the two societies were to co-
operate in some of their activities.[36]

John Hodgson's enthusiasm for records publication, particularly his
proposal of 1819 for a journal of historical records, foreshadowed the
establishment in 1834 of the Surtees Society, of which he was a founder
member. That society is discussed in more detail elsewhere in this volume;[37]
its existence did not preclude other ventures in records publication for
Northumberland. One such was a series of *Reprints of Rare Tracts*, published
by M. A. Richardson between 1847 and 1849 in fine but small editions; much
of their content was from the 16th and 17th centuries. Following Hodgson's
example, county histories, up to and including the volumes of the
Northumberland County History Committee, continued to present extensive
extracts from local or national records.[38] The work in Northumberland of the
Durham and Northumberland Parish Register Society, which produced 36
volumes of transcripts of registers between 1898 and 1926, was apparently
closely connected with that of the *History of Northumberland*; transcriptions
of Corbridge and Halton registers, for example, were undertaken during the
preparation of the relevant volume of the *History*.[39] In the early 20th century,
however, the Newcastle Society of Antiquaries still perceived a need for
further initiatives in printing historical records. In 1919 they appointed a
committee to put in hand a series of volumes, relating to Durham,
Northumberland, and Newcastle; the first, published in 1920, was an edition
of the Newcastle council minute book of 1639–56 prepared by Madeleine

[34] *Arch. Ael.* 5th ser. xviii. 205.
[35] From 1984 published as *Durham Arch. Jnl.*
[36] *Trans. Durham and Northumb. Archit. and Arch. Soc.* i, p. iii; *Arch. Ael.* 5th ser. xviii. 205;
Proc. Soc. Antiq. Newcastle-upon-Tyne, 2nd ser. i. 27.
[37] Above, Co. Dur.
[38] e.g. Northumb. County Hist. Committee, *Hist. of Northumb.* i. 49–54.
[39] Ibid. x, p. viii; *Corbridge Register* (Durham and Northumb. Parish Register Soc.
Publications, xxiv).

Hope Dodds. Eleven more volumes, approximately evenly divided in subject matter between Durham and Northumberland (including Newcastle), were produced. In the last, published in 1933, it was recorded that the series could not be continued because there were too few subscribers.[40]

The completion of the work of the Northumberland County History Committee in 1940 marks a natural break in the story of historical writing on the county. As in the rest of England, the later 20th century has seen a burgeoning of interest in local history, fuelled by improved record and library services; early signs of that development included the publication in 1963 of a comprehensive catalogue of printed and manuscript sources for Northumberland's history available in Newcastle upon Tyne[41] and the initiation in 1972 of a series of handbooks prepared for the Northumberland Local History Society.[42] A guide to English local history published in 1992 listed as relevant to the study of Northumberland seven societies, including an umbrella for many more in the form of the Association of Northumberland Local History Societies, and ten journals then in publication.[43] The historians of Northumberland still, to adapt Raine's phrase, sought to awaken those 'records . . . yet sleeping'.

[40] *Renaissance Heraldry of Durham* (Newcastle upon Tyne Rec. Committee Publications, xii), introductory note.
[41] H. A. Taylor, *Northumb. Hist.* (1963).
[42] *Northumb. Handlist of Sources* (Northumb. Local Hist. Soc.), preface.
[43] S. Guy, *English Local Studies Handbook* (1992), 236–7.

NOTTINGHAMSHIRE

Adrian Henstock

The Art of Physick, which I have professed (with competent success) in this County, not being able for any long time to continue the people living in it, I have charitably attempted . . . to practise upon the dead.

D r. Robert Thoroton offered that apology to his readers for compiling Nottinghamshire's first, and greatest, county history. His *Antiquities of Nottinghamshire*, which appeared in 1677, was one of the classic histories of that era, modelled directly on Dugdale's *Warwickshire*.[1] Its author was a country physician who lived in the village of Car Colston on the edge of the Vale of Belvoir, and who had a far-flung practice among the well-to-do of the region. Thoroton's interest seems originally to have been aroused by a fascination with his own family history. Although his family were more yeomen than gentry, Thoroton had proudly traced his ancestry to the Norman baronial family of Lovetot. His expertise in genealogy led him to compile pedigrees for neighbouring gentry families, at least nine of which he researched for Dugdale's heraldic visitation of Nottinghamshire in 1663. It was Dugdale, together with a member of the county gentry, Gervase Pigot, who first encouraged Thoroton to extend his researches and record them in the form of a book. As he reminded Dugdale in an 'epistle dedicatory' to the *Antiquities*, the occasion was 'some very few years after your Visitation of our County, you and I being with our Friend Mr Gervas Pigot, since deceased, at his House at Thrumpton'. Pigot produced a transcript of some ancient records together with antiquarian notes 'that served to give occasion to both your importunities that I should attempt something further in it'.[2] Pigot's notes were written by Thoroton's own father-in-law Gilbert Boun, as the beginnings of a projected 'Description of Nottinghamshire'. Although Thoroton dismissed them rather curtly as being 'only Doomsday Book, and a short note or two on every Town' (i.e. township), Boun deserves more credit than he has been given for providing a basis for Thoroton's work. There survives amongst

---

[1] R. Thoroton, *Antiquities of Notts.* (1677), preface. For a general discussion of Thoroton's life see A. Henstock and K. Train, 'Robert Thoroton, Notts. Antiquary: 1623–1678', *Trans. Thoroton Soc.* lxxxi (1977), 13–32.

[2] Thoroton, *Antiquities*, dedication.

Engraved by W. & I. Walker from the Original Painting in the possession of the Thoroton Esq.

18 Robert Thoroton

Thoroton's historical collections a slim manuscript booklet in another handwriting which comprises a brief description of Rushcliffe hundred and all the lordships in it, giving the Domesday Book entry and details of the descent of the manors. The text is headed 'Chapter the first' and it is dated internally 1641.[3] It is almost certainly in Gilbert Boun's hand and must be the notes, or part of the notes, to which Thoroton referred. It is not possible to say whether Boun completed his work for the whole of Nottinghamshire. As feodary for the county it is likely that he compiled the information initially for practical purposes, but had then arranged it into the draft of a brief history under the name of each manor. Although the work displays none of the depth of research which Thoroton later undertook, it formed a foundation on which he could build.

In researching his book, Thoroton visited many churches, copying inscriptions and sketching coats of arms, but he hardly visited the north of the county farthest from his home. Time was always the enemy, as he made clear in a note next to an unfinished sketch of arms in Holme Pierrepont church, 'which I had not time then to trick out it being night, and I have not been at Holme since'.[4] Most of his research, however, was based on original archives or, in their absence, on transcripts and collections of other antiquaries. Many of those were borrowed from private owners, for example the Rufford abbey cartulary from Lord Halifax, and extracts compiled from the Pipe Rolls by the Yorkshire antiquary Roger Dodsworth. Lord Fairfax lent the latter through the agency of Dr. Vere Harcourt and Gervase Pigot.[5] As a busy doctor and often over-zealous J.P., Thoroton could not visit the major national and regional archives, particularly the public records in London and the diocesan records at York. In his 'epistle dedicatory' he apologized to Dugdale that 'I could never get opportunity to go myself and stay at York, to abstract what might be useful to me from that Registry, as you ever advised me, and others it seems could not well do it for me, for I had several undertakers who all failed in the point'. From York 'one of my agents only brought me the titles of certain records, and another a catalogue of the livings-spiritual in the Arch-deaconry of Nottingham'. After the book's publication Dugdale repeated the point in a letter about Thoroton's work: 'I do esteem the book well worth your buying though had he gone to the fountain of records it might have been better done'.[6]

As with so many antiquarian histories, Thoroton's work is especially helpful as a source of information on his own times. As a young man he had lived through the Civil War, and witnessed at least two of three sieges of

---

[3] Notts. Archives [hereafter N.A.], M 494, ff. 140–53.
[4] N.A., M 493, f. 81.
[5] Henstock and Train, 'Robert Thoroton', 27.
[6] N.A., M 494, ff. 132–9; Hist. MSS. Com. 25, *12th Report, VII, Le Fleming*, pp. 139–40.

Newark; following the third in 1646 he commented that the town 'suffered more by the plague within than the enemy without'.[7] His conservative political views were frequently expressed, especially when railing against the evils of inclosure. An early Tudor inclosure at Thorpe-in-the-Glebe had 'so ruined and depopulated the Town, that in my time, there was not a House left inhabited of this Notable Lordship (except some part of the Hall . . .) but a Shepherd only kept Ale to sell in the church'.[8]

His descriptions of Nottingham, at a time when it was undergoing a post-war boom as a fashionable regional centre, are valuable: 'Many people of good quality from several parts, make choice of habitations here, where they find good accommodation'. He observed with wry amusement the building of fine town houses with elegant façades by the new urban élite, who vied with each other to lead 'the fashionable dance of building new Fronts'.[9]

His *Antiquities* was illustrated with several well executed prospects of Nottingham and Newark, as well as views of notable country houses, churches, and church monuments, mostly drawn by a Nottingham heraldic and monumental mason, Richard Hall, and engraved by Dugdale's engraver, Wenceslaus Hollar.[10]

One feature of the *Antiquities* is the absence of any information on archaeological antiquities. It is the more surprising in that Thoroton's home village, Car Colston, flanked the Roman Fosse Way and there was the site of a small Roman fort and town within a mile of his house. It was left to William Stukeley to draw attention to the significance of the Fosse Way and its forts in the 1720s, but little else about local archaeology was published until the end of the century. Between 1787 and 1790 the Mansfield Woodhouse antiquary Major Hayman Rooke delivered (and later published) three archaeological papers to the Society of Antiquaries.[11]

The very existence of Thoroton's great work in some respects stifled the development of local history in Nottinghamshire, as many writers have simply quoted his facts *ad nauseam*. The first county history to do so was the Revd. Thomas Cox's Nottinghamshire contribution to *Magna Britannia*, which appeared in 1727. The main thrust of the Georgian antiquaries was towards town histories, however, possibly inspired by the best example,

---

[7] Thoroton, *Antiquities*, 198.

[8] Ibid. 39.

[9] Ibid. 499.

[10] For Hall and Hollar see M. W. Barley and K. S. S. Train, introduction to J. Throsby, *Thoroton's Hist. of Notts.* (1790–6, reprinted 1972), and M. W. Barley, 'Richard Hall, Thoroton's Illustrator', *Trans. Thoroton Soc.* xci (1987), 12–13.

[11] H. Rooke, *Account of Remains of Two Roman Villae Discovered near Mansfield Woodhouse* (1787); *Observations on Roman Roads and Camps in Neighbourhood of Mansfield Woodhouse* (1788); *Roman Remains in Sherwood Forest* (1790).

Charles Deering's *Nottinghamia Vetus et Nova*, published in 1751. William Dickinson (alias Rastall)'s histories of *Southwell* (first edition 1767) and *Newark* (1806) were rivalled a few years later by R. P. Shilton's histories of the same two places (1818 and 1820 respectively). They no doubt helped to inspire W. Harrod to publish *Mansfield* (1801), John Blackner *Nottingham* (1815), J. Holland *Worksop* (1826), and John Piercy *Retford* (1828). Most resorted to the formula of dealing with the history of the corporation, charities, parish churches, and old buildings, illustrated with contemporary engravings. Outstanding amongst them was Deering's *Nottingham*, perhaps the second most important work of Nottinghamshire historiography, which broke new ground in its approach. Although Deering, like Thoroton, was a doctor, the two could not have been more dissimilar. Deering was a German and had come to London in 1713 as a diplomat; he later studied medicine in France and for reasons unknown came to Nottingham in 1735. He was an unhappy figure, a failure both in his profession and in local society, but by 1738 had published a catalogue of local flora which was one of the earliest scientific surveys of its type. Encouraged by a member of the town gentry, John Plumptre, he then turned his hand to local history and topography, compiling his major work on Nottingham in under four years, a remarkable achievement for a recently arrived foreigner. Unfortunately he failed to find a publisher, and the work was eventually published, complete with numerous illustrations, after Deering's death in 1749 by local printer George Ayscough.[12] It is chiefly of value for his contemporary descriptions of the town. Deering's scientifically trained, enquiring mind sought out information on such matters as demography, food supply, climate, and local industries; the latter included a detailed drawing and a minute description of the hand-operated stocking-knitting frame. Framework knitting was Nottingham's fastest growing industry.

The centenary in 1777 of the appearance of Thoroton's county history stimulated two proposals to publish a reprint. Those proved abortive, only one resulting in the production of a few copies of the first instalment—mainly Rushcliffe hundred—which were printed by W. Whittingham of King's Lynn in 1781. Nevertheless by 1796 a complete new and updated edition in three volumes had appeared, compiled by the Leicester antiquary and parish clerk John Throsby, already author of three publications on his own county.[13] Throsby made no attempt to revise Thoroton, but under each town or village entry reprinted Thoroton's text verbatim, and then added his own contemporary comments under a separate heading. He expanded the section

[12] A. C. Wood, 'Dr. Charles Deering', *Trans. Thoroton Soc.* xlv (1941), 24–39.
[13] Barley and Train, introduction to Throsby, *Thoroton's Hist. of Notts.*

on Nottingham, adding 'all that is valuable in Deering'. While the approach was sensible, it has been the source of considerable confusion to later historians, who either have not always grasped the distinction or else have not made it clear whether they have been quoting Thoroton's words of the 1670s or Throsby's of the 1790s: many a reference to 'Thoroton' or 'Throsby' is ambiguous.

Throsby apparently began 'following the track of Thoroton' in August 1790 and toured the county, visiting churches and country houses and collecting information from interested local personalities. Like Thoroton's, his work is biased towards the south of the county, no doubt discouraged both by the distance from Leicester and the poor roads in the clay country of the north; the highways around South Leverton he described as 'intolerable for poor curates'. He did not, however, have the entrée into gentry circles that Thoroton had enjoyed and was refused access to certain country houses. He used no original archives, confining himself to printed sources; some parish entries consist of little more than a few factual notes. He had nearly all of Thoroton's engravings redrawn, and added contemporary views of his own, mostly of country seats, in a somewhat crude style.[14]

The early 19th century witnessed the first appearance in Nottinghamshire of that distinctive genre which had appeared in the more 'picturesque' counties earlier in Georgian times: the historically based topography aimed mainly at upper- and middle-class tourists. G. A. Cooke's *Topographical and Statistical Description of Nottinghamshire* appeared in 1810, followed shortly by F. C. Laird's Nottinghamshire section of the *Beauties of England and Wales* in 1813. The Revd. J. Curtis's *Topographical History of Nottinghamshire* (1843–4) quoted extensively from Thoroton, but by that date the first expanded commercial directories had begun to appear, containing an extensive history of the county as well as parish histories. The first Nottinghamshire directory to adopt the wider format was that compiled by William White of Sheffield in 1832, to be followed by updated versions by others in 1844, 1853, and at regular intervals thereafter. A county history with a difference was Thomas Bailey's four-volume *Annals of Nottinghamshire*, published in 1853–5. Bailey set out a narrative history of important events in chronological order. Although a major achievement and a useful work of reference, its value is marred by a complete failure to cite sources and the lack of a running date-heading to his pages. A similar but more useful venture relating only to Nottingham and district was *The Date Book of Remarkable Events* (covering 1750 to 1884), compiled by J. F. Sutton and largely based on newspapers.

Nottinghamshire local historical writing during and since the 19th century has been bedevilled by certain popular themes with a wide appeal, where facts

---

[14] Ibid.

have often been romanticized or even fictionalized. The most notable, the legend of Robin Hood, linked to the history of Sherwood forest, has fascinated amateur antiquaries since the 18th century, and has attracted academic attention in the present century.[15] The tales of Robin Hood's exploits are first referred to in Langland's *Piers Plowman* of 1377, and the search for an historical figure behind the ballads has produced several potential candidates, none supported by conclusive proof, from both Nottinghamshire and Yorkshire. The south Yorkshire antiquary, the Revd. Joseph Hunter, was the first to produce any form of systematic historical enquiry into the story of Robin Hood, and he also turned his attention to another great historical epic, the Pilgrim Fathers.[16] The origins of that separatist group, including several of the leaders such as William Brewster, were to be found in north Nottinghamshire and adjacent parts of Lincolnshire and Yorkshire. That story has also produced a considerable literature.

As with all English counties, the late Victorian and Edwardian era saw a proliferation of local antiquarian works of variable quality. Amongst the potentially most useful were the unfinished *Notes on the Churches of Nottinghamshire* by J. T. Godfrey, an attempt to emulate the Revd. J. C. Cox's similar four-volume work on Derbyshire. Regrettably only two volumes appeared, covering the hundreds of Rushcliffe (1887) and Bingham (1907) in the south of the county. Further town histories included *Worksop* by Edwin Eddison in 1854 and Robert White in 1875, *Mansfield* by W. Horner Groves in 1894, and *Newark* by Cornelius Brown in 1879. The last was later expanded into a monumental two-volume study published in 1904–7, soundly based on the borough archives and other original records. Brown also made the only attempt at a county history in the period, with his contribution to the Popular County History Series, published in 1891. That, however, was more a topographical history of county places. During the Victorian period local libraries, museums, and private collectors began amassing collections of local historical books and manuscripts; they included bodies such as the Bromley House Subscription Library, the Mechanics' Institute, and the public library, all in Nottingham. Several bibliographies of local history were published, some of them listing the contents of those institutions or private libraries, such as those of James Ward (1891 and 1896) and Lord Belper (in 1915 following its gift to the county council).

The growing interest in antiquarian matters, particularly amongst the county gentry and clergy, led to the establishment of learned journals, some of them in conjunction with neighbouring counties. The Lincoln Diocesan Architectural

---

[15] Modern academic works include R. B. Dobson and J. Taylor, *Rymes of Robin Hood: Introduction to the English Outlaw* (1976) and J. Holt, *Robin Hood* (1982).

[16] J. Hunter, *South Yorks.* (1828–31); idem, *Collections Covering Church or Congregation of Protestant Separatists formed at Scrooby in North Notts.* (1854).

Society (later the Lincolnshire and Nottinghamshire Architectural and Archaeological Society) included the county's ecclesiology in its publications, while *Nottinghamshire and Derbyshire Notes and Queries* ran to six volumes between 1893 and 1898. The latter's demise was probably hastened by the founding in 1897 of Nottinghamshire's own antiquarian society, named the Thoroton Society in honour of the county's first historian; its volumes of *Transactions* have since appeared annually.

Those initiatives were paralleled by a movement towards publishing vital archive sources. The first major contribution was the first volume of the *Records of the Borough of Nottingham* (covering 1155 to 1399), edited by William Stevenson in 1882. A further five volumes were published before the First World War, with three more in the 1940s and 1950s, a magnificent achievement covering the whole period from 1155 to 1900. A less ambitious attempt to emulate the series for the county archives was begun by the then clerk of the peace for the county, H. Hampton Copnall, who transcribed the county quarter sessions records from their start in 1604 to the end of the 17th century, and published them in the form of a classified narrative calendar in 1915. That was followed by a companion volume for the 18th-century county records compiled by Copnall's successor, K. Tweedale Meaby, in 1947. In the meantime there were other initiatives. The Thoroton Society launched its separate Record Series in 1903 with an edition of 17th-century bishops' transcripts, the first of 38 volumes published up to 1990. The series has been particularly strong on medieval inquisitions *post mortem* and monastic cartularies and charters, as well as poll books, probate inventories, coroners' inquests, and definitive clergy lists (compiled by K. S. S. Train) for most of the county's churches. It achieved a notable milestone in 1962 by first publishing a 20th-century text (the first county register of motor vehicles for 1903), followed in 1990 by a miners' union minute book of the 1920s and 1930s.

A parallel interest in genealogy gave rise to the published series of pre-1812 marriage register transcripts edited by W. P. W. Phillimore, which eventually covered 219 parishes between 1898 and 1938. A similar but occasional series of complete early register transcripts was also published by G. W. Marshall. Other early independent record publishing ventures included Robert White's *The Dukery Records* of 1904, which transcribed documents relating to the Bassetlaw area, and the edition six years later of the important manuscript Rector's Book of Clayworth, which contains complete population listings of 1674 and 1688; they have provided crucial national evidence for modern historical demographers such as Peter Laslett.[17] Also at that period the

---

[17] *Rector's Book of Clayworth, Notts. 1672–1701*, ed. H. Gill and E. L. Guilford (1901); P. Laslett and J. Harrison, 'Clayworth and Cogenhoe', in *Hist. Essays presented to David Ogg*, ed. H. E. Bell and R. L. Ollard (n.d.).

reports of the Historical Manuscripts Commission drew attention to the wealth of information in private archives, particularly those of the dukes of Portland at Welbeck Abbey (10 vols. 1894–1931) and Lord Middleton at Wollaton Hall (1911).

As in so many counties the appearance of the *Victoria County History* marked the emergence of the first 'modern' county history, even though it carried chapters on hunting, fishing, racing, and other preoccupations of the Victorian gentry. Two volumes, edited by William Page, were published in 1907 and 1910 respectively. They broke new ground by including chapters on social and economic history and industries as well as political history, by basing the research soundly on the public records and other archive sources, and by having major sections written by professional *female* research assistants attached to the V.C.H. staff. The more conventional chapters were entrusted to well known local antiquaries: earthworks to W. Stevenson, and religious houses and forests to the Revd. J. C. Cox, the Derbyshire-focused clergyman with a national reputation for his antiquarian publications. Schools were covered by the educational historian A. F. Leach, and Domesday studies by a rising young scholar of local origin, Frank Stenton. The descendant of an old-established legal family from Southwell, Stenton later became one of the foremost authorities on Anglo-Saxon England. Although his career was spent outside his native county, he retained many local ties, not least his ownership of several strips in the uninclosed common fields of Eakring.[18]

The next village to Eakring is Laxton, where elements of the open-field system survive, uniquely, to this day. Laxton first attracted academic attention in the 1930s, culminating in the classic study *The Open Fields* by Dr. and Mrs. C. S. Orwin (1935). It was a pioneering work, combining the fruits of practical farming experiments with analysis of historical records, notably the outstanding estate map and survey of 1635 in the Bodleian Library, Oxford. Later studies of Laxton by Professors J. D. Chambers (1964) and John Beckett (1989) have extended and updated their work.[19]

Professor Chambers, of Nottingham University, was also responsible for the first modern history of the county in a specific period. His *Nottinghamshire in the Eighteenth Century: A Survey of Life and Labour under the Squirearchy* was published as early as 1932, again employing an innovative approach with an emphasis on the social and economic structure of the county, using new demographic techniques measuring population trends based on parish-register data. He later expanded it *c.* 1957 into a classic

    [18] For Stenton's local links see M. W. Barley, 'Frank Merry Stenton, 1880–1967', *Trans. Thoroton Soc.* lxxi (1967), 11–12.

    [19] J. D. Chambers, *Laxton: the Last English Open Field Village* (1964); J. V. Beckett, *Laxton: England's Last Open Field Village* (1989).

monograph on the newly emerging theme of regional history, with his study of
the economic development and industrialization of the east Midlands, entitled
The Vale of Trent, 1670–1800: A Regional Study of Economic Change.
Chambers's 18th-century study was followed within five years by another but
very different period history, *Nottinghamshire in the Civil War* by Professor
A. C. Wood, also of Nottingham University. That is one of the most exhaustive
studies of the war in any county, examining the social, religious, and political
background of the ruling community as well as providing a detailed
chronological narrative of local events. His task was aided by the existence in
print since 1806 of the lengthy 'Memoirs' of Colonel John Hutchinson, written
by his wife Lucy after the Civil War, which described the career and local
activities of the Parliamentarian governor of Nottingham castle.

Other notable initiatives from the 1930s had a national impact for local
studies. A pamphlet by Arthur Cossons on *The Turnpike Roads of
Nottinghamshire* was the first definitive survey of the county's turnpike
network based on the Acts of Parliament, and was published jointly by the
Historical and Geographical Associations as a national model. At that period
also the left-wing village schoolmaster from Sutton Bonington, W. E. Tate,
began studying the archives held by local parish churches through a series of
W.E.A. classes. He later extended it into a national study which is still a
classic textbook: *The Parish Chest*, published in 1946, contains many
Nottinghamshire examples.

Ten years after his history of the Civil War, Professor Wood published a
new *History of Nottinghamshire*, beginning in Roman times but ending
somewhat abruptly with the Reform Act in 1832, after which, he claimed, 'it is
hardly possible . . . to isolate county history for separate treatment'. The
stated intention of Wood's work was a synthesis of the latest research 'buried'
in local monographs and national histories in order to produce a frankly
popular county history. In that he succeeded, as his book is academically
sound yet eminently readable. It is important as the only analytical history of
the county as a whole, but its approach is traditional, its concern largely with
political, religious, and administrative matters.

Two notable milestones in the further development of county history were
the local volumes of two national surveys. The first was the *Place-Names of
Nottinghamshire*, compiled by J. Gover, A. Mawer, and Frank Stenton (1940)
and the second the county volume of Nikolaus Pevsner's *Buildings of England*
series (1951). Pevsner had already treated the medieval carvings in the chapter
house at Southwell Minster in *The Leaves of Southwell* (1945). The awakening
interest of the 1960s and later in vernacular buildings nationally was partly
inspired by Maurice Barley of Nottingham University, whose *English
Farmhouse and Cottage* appeared in 1961; under his influence numerous
papers appeared in the *Transactions of the Thoroton Society* and other local

publications on the history of smaller buildings throughout the county. As a result of the efforts of both Barley and his friends and colleagues such as Dr. Norman Summers, the number of house histories available in print is the envy of many counties. Recent more general surveys have included David Kaye's *Nottinghamshire* in the Darwen County History Series (1987) and Christopher Weir's *The Nottinghamshire Heritage* (1991).

In concluding this survey of Nottinghamshire historians perhaps one might be forgiven for echoing Thoroton's pleas about his county history: 'I allow no man for a judge who hath not done something of this nature himself'.[20]

---

[20] Thoroton, *Antiquities*, dedication. For a useful select bibliography of the major works of Notts. hist. see M. Dobbin, *Notts. Hist. and Topography: Select Descriptive Bibliography to 1980* (1983).

OXFORDSHIRE

Alan Crossley

Oxfordshire's sole representative on the long shelf of large-scale old county histories was published by an engraver, Joseph Skelton,[1] who supplemented depictions of the county's 'leading specimens of antiquity' with 'succinct notices' of every parish, compiled largely from information supplied by correspondents.[2] The volume, published for subscribers in parts from 1823, contains fine illustrations and may have 'removed the erroneous idea of our county being uninteresting',[3] but the text scarcely fulfilled Skelton's hopes that it would 'lessen the labours of some future historian'.[4]

Skelton's concern and surprise that Oxfordshire, in common with that other 'University county', should lack an adequate history[5] was shared by many writers of the late 18th and early 19th century. Thomas Warton in 1782 declared that, discounting works on the university, he could think of no county that had 'received so little elucidation', despite 'presenting many a topic of useful and amusive speculation'.[6] J. N. Brewer, author of the hastily compiled Oxfordshire volume in the *Beauties of England and Wales* series in 1813, noted its 'want of a regular historian';[7] the patchiness of his derivative compilation reflects the paucity of available secondary works, and perhaps excuses Skelton's failure to acknowledge the existence of the prior publication.

In 1819 the publisher and collector Thomas Phillipps, perhaps also unaware of Brewer's work, referred to 'that long wished-for *desideratum*, a good county history of Oxfordshire'. He hoped to live long enough to remedy the omission,[8] but in the 53 years left to him published only a few monumental

---

[1] *D.N.B.* Some ideas for this chapter were suggested by M. Graham, 'Development of Local Hist. in Oxon.' *Oxon. Local Hist.* ii (8), 290–7.

[2] J. Skelton, *Antiquities of Oxon.* (1823), foreword and preface. The copy in Bodl. (G.A. Fol. A 113) contains printed prospectuses.

[3] Bodl. MS. Eng. Lett. d. 38, ff. 238–9: letter from Skelton to John Dunkin, 1828.

[4] Skelton, *Antiquities of Oxon.* foreword.

[5] Ibid.

[6] T. Warton, *Hist. and Antiquities of Kiddington* (1815, being the 3rd edn. of *Specimen of Hist. of Oxon. [Kiddington]*), original preface (1782), 3, 5.

[7] J. N. Brewer, *Topographical and Hist. Description of Oxon.* (*Beauties of England and Wales*, xii (2), 1813), bibliography.

[8] Birmingham Central Library Archives Department, no. 125537: letter from Phillipps to W. Hamper, 25 Oct. 1819.

inscriptions from those Oxfordshire parishes with the initial letters A–C.[9] The
chasm between ambition and achievement provides a recurrent theme in the
story of Oxfordshire's historiography, but Phillipps's shortfall merits comment if
only for the impressive scope and rapid abandonment of his original plan. In
1818 he was intending to compile a history from answers to 44 questions
covering a range of subjects unsurpassed even in 20th-century county histories.[10]
A year later, however, Phillipps was aiming merely to publish a set of parochial
collections, derived from Bodleian Library and other manuscripts,
supplemented by contributed material on 'eminent persons'.[11]

As an unfulfilled venture Phillipps's was unspectacular compared with that
of Samuel Rush Meyrick (1783–1848), whose 'Oxonia Restaurata', an intended
'chorographical, historical, architectural, monumental, and heraldic survey',
in the end comprised only a few notes in a large, carefully ruled book whose
title page, ironically, bears the maxim *Vox audita perit, Litera scripta manet*.
Meyrick, later a noted historian of arms and armour, and of Cardiganshire,
perceived the county historian's chief difficulties to be 'much labour and
expense' and, in his case, access: concerning ancient records in London
'offices', for example, he had no idea where to go and had 'no Interest at
them'.[12] A century earlier White Kennett (1660–1728), better prepared and
investigating only a single parish, grumbled similarly about labour and
expense, and confessed that courage had failed him at certain 'Courts of
Record' when he found 'the exaction for searching and transcribing to be so
great, and perceiv'd the Notes to be so imperfect'. He recognized that his kind
of work might have been better achieved through public funding and co-
operative effort, an early insight into the future of county historiography.[13]

Probably the most formidable list of the obstacles confronting a county
historian was incorporated by Thomas Symonds (d. 1845), vicar of Eynsham,
in a plan for an Oxfordshire history which, not surprisingly, was never carried
out.[14] The list was not original, having been copied from an early 18th-
century scheme for a history of Durham among the papers of Thomas Carte
(1686–1754);[15] it included gloomy reflections on charges for record searching,
cost of engravings, wide variety of subjects, 'Privacy of Affairs', and the

---

[9] *Oxon. Monumental Inscriptions*, [ed. T. Phillipps] (Evesham, privately printed, 1825): copy in
Bodl. Manning fol. 6.
[10] Bodl. MSS. Phillipps-Robinson b. 197, f. 35; c. 252, pp. 111 sqq.: parochial notes probably
compiled from answers to questionnaire.
[11] Ibid. b. 67, pp. 1–2; b. 104, ff. 185–7. Cf. A. N. L. Munby, *Formation of Phillipps Library to
1840* (Phillipps Studies iii, 1954), 5–6, and plate II; Munby, *Portrait of an Obsession* (1967), 12–13.
[12] Bodl. MS. Top. Oxon. c. 336; *D.N.B.*
[13] W. Kennett, *Parochial Antiquities Attempted in Hist. of Ambrosden, Burcester, and other
Adjacent Parts* (1695), epistle and preface.
[14] Oxon. R.O., DL. I/xii/i, pp. 21–4. For Symonds, *V.C.H. Oxon.* xii. 149.
[15] Bodl. MS. Carte 193, pp. 1–5.

'Incapacity of any Writer in Respect of the universal Learning required'—
none could proceed without the help of 'the Clergy in general . . . a Physician,
a Poet, a Tradesman, an Antiquarian in Records'. The county historian's
task, as thus presented, was intimidating enough, but in addition some writers
were driven by apocalyptic anxieties: Kennett feared that the 'memoirs' of his
parish would soon be 'buried in unsearchable Oblivion';[16] Skelton asserted
that the county's antiquities were 'every year diminishing in number' and
'facts . . . were hastening onward to oblivion'.[17] Henry Hinton (1749–1816)
feared that 'every day will cut off some source of information' as ancient
families died out and historic sites were lost through the 'powerful effect of
modern improvement'.[18]

Unfulfilled ventures owed as much to personal circumstances and
predilections as to any intrinsic difficulties of the task. Richard Rawlinson
(1690–1755), on the brink of publishing a major work on Oxfordshire in 1720,
was seduced by foreign travel and never rekindled his earlier enthusiasm.[19]
Thomas Warton, in 1782 proffering a slim parish history as a 'Specimen of a
History of Oxfordshire', loftily disclaimed any design to write a county
history: he had 'other engagements, and other inclinations'.[20] To modern ears
perhaps the least persuasive excuse was that made for Sir Henry Ellis
(1777–1869), whose Oxfordshire collections, begun with 'industry and skill'
whilst at St. John's College, were curtailed when 'preferment in the British
Museum . . . furnished him with far different avocations'.[21]

The difficulties of writing county history were of course no greater in
Oxfordshire than elsewhere, and indeed some writers argued that the county
offered special advantages. Warton pointed to the 'ample treasures' of the
Bodleian and Ashmolean libraries.[22] In the early 19th century William Upcott
noted that Oxfordshire contained not only 'valuable materials for an
Historiographer' but also competent and resident gentlemen of the university,
to whom, in the vacations, writing a county history should prove 'an agreeable
and instructive amusement'.[23] Cynics might point out that 150 years later,
when the topographical sections of the Oxfordshire *V.C.H.* were in hand,
similar expectations of the Oxford don were sometimes over-optimistic. More

---

[16] Kennett, *Parochial Antiquities* (1695), epistle.

[17] Skelton, *Antiquities of Oxon.* foreword and prospectus in Bodl. copy (G.A. Fol. A 113).

[18] M. Clapinson, 'Topographical Collections of Henry Hinton and James Hunt', *Oxoniensia*,
xxxvii. 216.

[19] B. J. Enright, 'Rawlinson's Proposed Hist. of Oxon.' *Oxoniensia*, xvi. 57–77; *D.N.B.*

[20] Warton, *Kiddington* (1815), original preface (1782), 5.

[21] T. Fuller, *Hist. of Worthies of England*, ed. J. Nichols (2 vols. 1811), ii. 240; *D.N.B.* For his
Oxon. collections, Bodl. MS. Eng. Hist. f. 7.

[22] Warton, *Kiddington* (1815), original preface (1782), 5.

[23] B.L. Add. MS. 15931, f. 1v.

seriously, it has been argued that until modern times the university's presence impeded rather than facilitated Oxfordshire local history, because interest in Oxford overshadowed interest in the county.[24] Certainly the great antiquary Anthony Wood (1632–95) seems to have been deflected from his intention to emulate Dugdale's *Warwickshire* by the bulk and fascination of materials for the history of university and city.[25] Certainly many later compilers of works on Oxfordshire devoted so much space to Oxford that their treatment of the rest of the county has the character of an afterthought: one account published in 1727 devoted over 150 pages to Oxford and only 66 to the other towns and villages;[26] a bibliography published in 1818 comprised 58 pages of works on the city and university, only nine on the rest of the county.[27]

Another explanation for the lack of an Oxfordshire history may have been a weakness of 'county consciousness' among local gentry, attributable in part to the university's dominance in the county town. In most counties the close integration of the 18th-century county community was reinforced by regular gatherings in the county town for quarter sessions, elections, races, and other social events. Oxford was used for such occasions but there are hints that it never quite fulfilled the role of a county town in the manner of, say, Dorchester and Gloucester. The academic community which so dominated Oxford's citizens was hardly likely to make visiting country gentry feel at home; the town houses set up by country gentry in other 18th-century shire towns were noticeably absent in Oxford, and there are few signs of the assertive and self-conscious county community which elsewhere subscribed eagerly to county histories. Although, as William Upcott noted, no county was better provided with notable 'mansions' and with noblemen and gentry of 'ancient family' who ought to subscribe liberally to a county history,[28] in the event they did not do so. Lack of financial backing from the Oxfordshire squirearchy may have been decisive, for without patronage or subscriptions the step from collecting to publishing was as great then as later, for, as Skelton ruefully noted, 'no works answer so ill in a pecuniary point of view as those connected with county or local history'.[29]

In 1811 John Nichols listed the principal published materials for Oxfordshire history (excluding works on Oxford itself) as the *Magna Britannia* (1727), which was mostly a recension of William Camden's *Britannia*, Richard Gough's additions to Camden (1789), Robert Plot's

[24] *Oxon. Domesday* (Alecto Hist. Edns. 1990), introduction, 1.
[25] For his plans for a county hist. see *Wood's Life and Times*, i (Oxford Hist. Soc. xix), 5.
[26] T. Cox, *Magna Britannia et Hibernia* (6 vols. 1720–31), iv. 209–509.
[27] W. Upcott, *Bibliographical Account of English Topography* (3 vols. 1818; facsimile edn. 1 vol. 1978), pp. 1069–1134.
[28] B.L. Add. MS. 15931, f. iv.
[29] Skelton, *Antiquities of Oxon.* foreword.

19 Robert Plot

Natural History of Oxfordshire (1677), and a few parish histories.[30] Such continued reliance on Plot and Camden reflects the poverty of the competition, for by then they had little to offer beyond their early appearance in the field. In Plot's *Natural History* there was only a single chapter on antiquities and his work was soon attracting scholarly derision: Thomas Warton mocked Plot's 'uncommon credulity', his obsession with 'tautological echoes, fanciful petrifications, subterraneous snails, undescribed thunderbolts, cosmetic clay, the altitude of giants, uncommonly prolific cases of Oxfordshire women and cows'.[31] Some of Plot's indiscriminate recording was not, however, without historical importance: his accounts of contemporary industrial processes remain invaluable, while his need precisely to locate an echo in Woodstock park yielded the only useful illustration of the demolished royal palace and its surroundings.[32]

The Oxfordshire section of Camden's *Britannia*, of which editions were published from 1586 until 1806,[33] hardly merited such prolonged exposure at the centre of the county's historiography. Some of Camden's more risible speculations, for example that the Rollright stones were 'haply erected by Rollo the Dane, who afterwards conquered Normandie',[34] were soon refuted, but other nonsense was more persistent; his work became a vehicle for all kinds of additions, ranging from the merely topical to the wilfully misleading. Banbury, credited only with a reputation for cheese in the first edition, soon had the word zeal (in reference to its notorious Puritanism) 'foysted in', according to Camden, 'by some compositor or pressman'.[35] Camden openly disavowed the interpolations made by his first translator, Philemon Holland, in the edition of 1610, urging the authenticity of his 'Latin copie';[36] yet he made no comment on an earlier, stealthy introduction into his Latin edition of 1600 of a preposterous story, mostly from an alleged Asser manuscript, crediting Oxford University with greater antiquity even than its (entirely mythical) foundation by King Alfred.[37] Not surprisingly the 'excellent' Asser manuscript, which provided the story of a 9th-century refoundation by St. Grimbald of a university dating from the 5th century, has never come to light. Whatever Camden's role in this blatant propaganda exercise, the incident

---

[30] Fuller, *Worthies*, ed. Nichols, ii. 240.

[31] Warton, *Kiddington* (1815), original preface (1782), 4.

[32] R. Plot, *Natural Hist. of Oxon.* (1677), plate 1.

[33] For varying counts of edns. cf. Bodl. Catalogue of Printed Books; *Camden's Britannia 1695* (facsimile edn. 1971), introduction, 9; *D.N.B.* s.v. Camden, William.

[34] W. Camden, *Britannia*, trans. P. Holland (1610), 374–5.

[35] W. Camden, *Britannia*, ed. R. Gough (1789), i. 298 n. Earlier it was alleged that Camden himself changed ale to zeal: *Camden's Britannia 1695* (facsimile edn. 1971), 270.

[36] Camden, *Britannia*, ed. Gough (1789), i, pp. vii, 298 n.

[37] The interpolation is discussed in ibid. i. 299–300; J. Parker, *Early Hist. of Oxford* (Oxford Hist. Soc. iii), 39–52.

throws harsh light on scholarly standards of the day and on the integrity of such men as Brian Twyne, keeper of the university archives,[38] who corroborated the manuscript's existence. The choice of Camden's *Britannia* to disseminate the story indicates the book's early prominence; its enduring reputation meant that the Oxford myths and other more innocent pieces of misinformation had a longer life than they deserved.

Most of the myths were finally refuted in Richard Gough's edition of 1789,[39] which has been described as 'really a failure' on the ground that by then Camden's great pioneer work was being replaced by detailed county and regional histories.[40] For Oxfordshire, however, that was not so, and although Gough chose to reproduce much of the irremediable palimpsest of earlier work he also made well annotated additions, based on fieldwork and on the new sources then available, such as the tardily published Leland's *Itinerary* (which contained useful material for a few Oxfordshire places, notably Ewelme and Banbury).[41] Gough was an outstanding collector of books and manuscripts, and his bequest to the Bodleian Library in 1809 provides a measure of how much, or rather how little, Oxfordshire material was then available.[42]

One of Gough's treasured possessions, passed on to his friend Archdeacon Ralph Churton[43] with reversion to the Bodleian Library, was White Kennett's own annotated copy of his history of Ambrosden (1695).[44] Kennett (1660–1728), vicar of Ambrosden and later bishop of Peterborough,[45] might reasonably be described as the founder of parochial historiography. As an undergraduate he had undertaken research for Anthony Wood, and when presented to Ambrosden in 1685 he turned to parochial records to settle uncertainties over a charity; he claimed no other motive than 'love of his Parochial charge, and the benefit of Posterity'. His first 'slow discoveries' inspired such a widening of research that 'Had I propos'd the Antiquities of this whole County, I should perhaps have sooner gathered up sufficient materials for it. But confining my self to such a narrow circuit, I often read much to very little purpose'.[46] Most parish historians would understand that experience. Kennett's range of sources, careful annotations, and judicious

---

[38] S. Gibson, 'Bryan Twyne', *Oxoniensia*, v. 94–114.

[39] Camden, *Britannia*, ed. Gough (1789), i. 299–300.

[40] *Camden's Britannia 1695* (facsimile edn. 1971), introduction, 12.

[41] Camden, *Britannia*, ed. Gough (1789), i. 293–310.

[42] *Summary Catalogue of Western MSS. in Bodl.* iv. 150–296.

[43] *D.N.B.*

[44] Copy of *Parochial Antiquities* (1695) in Bodl. Gough Eccl. Top. 67B: note of loan to Churton in preliminary pages; cf. Kennett, *Parochial Antiquities*, ed. B. Bandinel (1818), i, p. iii. For mistaken identification of Bodl. Don. d. 56 as the author's copy cf. Bodl. Catalogue of Printed Books; *Friends of Bodleian 12th Annual Report* (1936–7), 17.

[45] *D.N.B.*

[46] Kennett, *Parochial Antiquities* (1695), epistle and preface.

approach ('where I wanted authorities, I resolv'd my conjectures should be short and modest') made his pioneer work rightly influential, and justified a new edition as late as 1818.

Another outstanding early Oxfordshire parish history was Thomas Warton's *Kiddington* (1782), again written by the incumbent of the parish, again by no ordinary cleric. Warton (1728–90) was at various times Camden Professor of History at Oxford University, Professor of Poetry there, and Poet Laureate.[47] His *Kiddington* is notable for its scholarly footnotes and for an unusually early awareness of what is now called landscape archaeology. Warton denied that county histories need be dull compilations 'fabricated by the petty diligence of . . . unaspiring Antiquaries'.[48] Although in 1815 Warton's work was 'generally allowed to be one of the most elegant and judicious Accounts of a single Parish that has yet appeared',[49] his suggestion that it should lead on to a scholarly county history was not taken up for over a century.

Nichols's list of notable Oxfordshire books in 1811 also included 'a few detached parishes' in the *Gentleman's Magazine*,[50] and several works on Oxford city and university. In 1739 it was complained that 'our alma mater already has too much waste paper on her hands',[51] and certainly most early work on Oxford was dross concerning its mythical origins. Even its first serious historian, Brian Twyne (?1579–1644), was driven by twin obsessions, to demonstrate that the university was older than Cambridge, and to claim for the university all the privileges held by the city. Consequently his *Antiquitatis Academiae Oxoniensis Apologia* (1608) was of much less value than his vast manuscript collections; they formed the basis, albeit poorly acknowledged, of much of the later work on city and university by Anthony Wood (1632–95). Wood's own great achievements were for long diminished by unhappy editing; during his lifetime only a poor Latin version of his history of the university and part of his biographical studies were published.[52] His work on the city was mangled by Sir John Peshall in an edition of 1773, and the rest did not begin to receive adequate treatment until editions by John Gutch (from 1786) and Philip Bliss (from 1813).[53] Eventually Wood's work on the city and his autobiographical manuscripts were superbly

---

[47] T. Warton, *Specimen of Hist. of Oxon. [Kiddington]* (1782), retitled in 3rd edn. *Hist. and Antiquities of Kiddington* (1815); *D.N.B.*

[48] Warton, *Kiddington* (1815), original preface (1782), 1.

[49] Ibid. preface (1815).

[50] For Oxon. articles, *Gent. Mag. Library, English Topography*, ix, ed. F. A. Milne (1897), 51–236.

[51] Bodl. MS. Willis 45, f. 206.

[52] A. Wood, *Historia et Antiquitates Universitatis Oxoniensis* (1674); idem, *Athenae Oxonienses* (2 vols. 1691).

[53] A. Wood, *Ancient and Present State of City of Oxford* [with additions by J. Peshall] (1773); idem, *Hist. and Antiquities of Colleges and Halls*, ed. J. Gutch (1786); idem, *Hist. and Antiquities of Univ. of Oxford*, ed. J. Gutch (3 vols. 1792–6); idem, *Athenae Oxonienses*, ed. P. Bliss (4 vols. 1813–20).

edited by Andrew Clark (from 1889).[54] Most 18th-century work on Oxford simply repeated Wood, and new ground was not broken until the early 19th century with works by Chalmers, Ackermann, and others.[55]

Oxfordshire's lack of early county histories was compensated to some extent by the survival of important historical collections, most of them in the Bodleian Library. Anthony Wood, in addition to valuable references throughout his diaries, left several volumes of genealogical, heraldic, and topographical notes, including records of visits to most Oxfordshire churches in the 1650s and later.[56] Useful church notes were made by Nathaniel Greenwood and by Matthew Hutton in the 1650s,[57] and the works of John Aubrey (1627–97) contain scattered but important Oxfordshire material.[58] Another great antiquary resident in Oxford, Thomas Hearne (1678–1735), contributed disappointingly little to the county's historiography, but there are valuable references among his diaries and other works.[59] Probably the most useful collections are those of Richard Rawlinson, who in the period 1718–20 was planning to publish a survey of Oxfordshire based on personal visits and a questionnaire.[60] Rawlinson intended to improve on Anthony Wood's notes, and his wide-ranging printed questionnaire, much coveted by later antiquaries such as Richard Gough, covered population, feasts and market days, land ownership, manorial rights, resident gentry, patronage, church building, charities, schools, antiquities, agriculture, local customs (including 'games amongst the vulgar'), and unusual events.[61] Rawlinson's partner in the venture was the London bookseller and publisher Edmund Curll (1675–1747), whose scandalous career seems oddly at variance with his good repute (at least for a while) among antiquaries such as Rawlinson and Browne Willis.[62]

---

[54] *Wood's Hist. of City of Oxford*, ed. A. Clark (Oxford Hist. Soc. xv, xvii, xxxvii); *Life and Times of Anthony Wood*, ed. A. Clark (Oxford Hist. Soc. xix, xxi, xxvi, xxx, xl).

[55] A. Chalmers, *Hist. of Colleges, Halls and Public Buildings attached to Univ. of Oxford* (2 vols. 1810); R. Ackermann, *Hist. of Univ. of Oxford* (3 vols. 1837). For the historiography of Oxford see the present author's article in *Encyclopaedia of Oxford*, ed. C. Hibbert (1988), s.v. Historians.

[56] The chief collections are Bodl. MSS. Wood E. 1; B. 15; C. 10–11, of which most are printed in *Parochial Collections*, i–iii, ed. F. N. Davis (Oxon. Rec. Soc. ii, iv, xi) and *Oxon. Monumental Inscriptions*, [ed. Phillipps]; Bodl. MSS. Wood D. 4, 11, 19 (1); F. 21, 31.

[57] Bodl. MS. Top. Oxon. e. 286; ibid. MS. Rawl. B. 397, ascribed in error in Bodl. *Catalogue of Rawlinson MSS.* to a Michael Hutton. For matching handwriting of Dr. Matthew Hutton (1639–1711) cf. Bodl. MS. Wood F. 42, f. 262.

[58] e.g. Bodl. MS. Top. gen. c. 25; ibid. MS. Aubrey 16.

[59] *Remarks and Collections of Thomas Hearne*, i–xi, ed. C. E. Doble and others (Oxford Hist. Soc. ii, vii, xiii, xxxiv, xlii, xliii, xlviii, l, lxv, lxvii, lxxii); [R. Gough], *British Topography* (2 vols. 1780), ii. 79–180*, *passim*.

[60] B. J. Enright, 'Rawlinson's Proposed Hist. of Oxon.' *Oxoniensia*, xvi. 57–77. Rawlinson's chief Oxon. collections are Bodl. MSS. Rawl. B. 400B, C, E, F, mostly printed in *Parochial Collections*, i–iii.

[61] Bodl. MS. Rawl. D. 1481, ff. 30–1. A copy by Rawlinson of Bodl. MS. Wood E. 1 is in MS. Rawl. B. 400B.

[62] *D.N.B.*; Enright, *Oxoniensia*, xvi. 57–8..

Although there seem to have been few replies to the questionnaire,[63] a county tour undertaken by the partners in 1718 yielded valuable evidence for most Oxfordshire parishes.[64]

Curll's acidic notes[65] also provide amusing reminders that 'fieldwork' then, as now, was an unpredictable experience. At Chalgrove their host, who 'seem'd to have an Inclination to these Kind of Studies' entertained the visitors like 'a true English Gentleman'; by contrast the rector of Charlton, 'por'd over our papers . . . never ask'd us so much as to light', and obliged them to consult his parish registers 'in the Chaise'. At Lewknor the rector's old maid 'very narrowly watch'd the Antiquary', while the rector of Rotherfield Peppard, 'Empty, Proud, Peevish, Pragmatical, Spleenetick, and Mistrustful', took it in 'great dudgeon that we came to catechize him, as he was pleas'd to call it'.[66] Rawlinson's planned publication never appeared, and his recommendation of the project to Oxford University, if indeed ever made, was ignored.[67]

Important collections were compiled by a fairly close-knit group of antiquaries working on Oxfordshire in the early 19th century. The topographer William Upcott (1779–1845), born in Oxford,[68] left fairly negligible Oxfordshire collections,[69] but was a great encourager of others. He was a friend, indeed 'the devoted slave',[70] of John Dunkin (1782–1846), native of Bicester, later a bookseller and printer in Bromley (Kent), who published volumes on Bicester and two Oxfordshire hundreds[71] and compiled voluminous collections for the county as a whole. Although much was taken from now easily available sources in the British Library and public records there is useful original material.[72] Dunkin referred to his 20 or so volumes as 'paltry collections . . . the commencement of a county history'.[73]

Dunkin corresponded with, and contributed to the published works of,

---

[63] For examples see Bodl. MS. Rawl. D. 1481, ff. 30–1, 42, 44; *Parochial Collections*, iii. 370–2.

[64] *Parochial Collections*, i–iii, *passim*. For cautionary remarks on this edn. see Enright, *Oxoniensia*, xvi. 68 n., 70.

[65] Bodl. MS. Rawl. B. 400F, not identified in Bodl. catalogue as Curll's, but in his hand and evidently the duodecimo volume referred to in [Gough], *British Topography*, ii. 80. For Curll's hand see, e.g., Bodl. MS. Rawl. Letters 4, f. 101.

[66] Enright, *Oxoniensia*, xvi. 65–7.

[67] Fuller, *Worthies*, ed. Nichols, ii. 240, states erroneously that Rawlinson's recommendation was in his will.

[68] *D.N.B.*; A. N. L. Munby, *Cult of the Autograph Letter* (1962), 13–32; Upcott, *Bibliographical Account of English Topography*.

[69] B.L. Add. MSS. 15930–1. For Oxon. notes made in collaboration with John Dunkin, Bodl. MS. Dep. d. 74.

[70] Bodl. MS. Eng. Lett. d. 38, *passim*.

[71] J. Dunkin, *Hist. and Antiquities of Bicester* (1816); idem, *Hist. and Antiquities of Hundreds of Bullingdon and Ploughley* (2 vols. 1823).

[72] The chief surviving Dunkin collections are Bodl. MSS. Dep. d. 71–82; ibid. MS. Eng. d. 2102.

[73] Ibid. MS. Eng. Lett. d. 39, f. 175 and v.

both J. N. Brewer and Joseph Skelton.[74] Skelton's notes and correspondence were in turn handed on to Thomas Symonds (d. 1845),[75] whose own Oxfordshire collections eventually filled nine large volumes; sadly he made few original observations, and although resident in Eynsham for nearly half a century commented only in passing on such notable features of his own parish's history as the disappearance of a large medieval village (Tilgarsley).[76] Symonds's collections were later acquired by J. M. Davenport (1809–82), clerk of the peace for the county and author of several useful books on Oxfordshire.[77] Davenport's library of Oxfordshire books and manuscripts, augmented by his son Thomas (d. 1904), also clerk of the peace, has been preserved in the county record office since 1935.[78] Large collections by two Oxford citizens, Henry Hinton (1749–1816), ironmonger, and James Hunt (1795–1857), chemist, were out of circulation from c. 1820, when sold to Sir Thomas Phillipps, until acquired by the Bodleian Library in the 1960s and later. The collections include valuable church notes of the early 19th century.[79] From the same period the drawings of John and his son J. C. Buckler (1770–1851 and 1793–1894), notable for their architectural detail and impressive coverage, are among the greatest assets of a well documented county.[80] Of later Oxfordshire collections the most extensive and useful are those of W. H. Turner (d. 1880), another Oxford chemist,[81] while good collections for smaller areas include those of the Revd. Thomas Delafield (d. 1755) for Haseley, Stokenchurch, and Milton,[82] and of Charles Richardson (d. 1827), chiefly for Combe and Woodstock.[83]

In Victorian Oxfordshire, as elsewhere, books on local history proliferated: educational and social change, cheaper print, improved public transport, all tended to make local history less exclusively the preserve of squire and parson. The trend, however, was towards parish histories and themes such as church architecture rather than towards county history, although J. M. Falkner's *History of Oxfordshire* (1899) provided a popular synthesis.[84]

---

[74] e.g. ibid. d. 38, ff. 46, 52, 188, 200, 202.

[75] Ibid. MSS. Top. Oxon. b. 80; c. 199.

[76] Oxon. R.O., DL I/xii/i–ix. For Symonds, *V.C.H. Oxon.* xii. 149.

[77] Oxon. R.O., introduction to Symonds collection, index; J. M. Davenport, *Oxon. Annals* (1869); [idem], *Lords Lieutenant and High Sheriffs of Oxon.* (1868); [idem], *Oxon. Lords Lieutenant, High Sheriffs, and Members of Parliament*, revised T. M. Davenport (1888). For obituary notice, *Oxford Jnl.* 4 Feb. 1882.

[78] Oxon. R.O., TS. notes on Davenport Library by S. J. Barnes, county archivist, 1976.

[79] M. Clapinson, *Oxoniensia*, xxxvii. 215–20.

[80] H. M. Colvin, *Biographical Dictionary of British Architects* (1978), 155–7.

[81] *Summary Catalogue of Western MSS. in Bodl.* nos. 29019–46; *Oxford Jnl.* 3 July 1880; *Oxford Times*, 27 June 1980.

[82] *Summary Catalogue of Western MSS. in Bodl.* nos. 18139–58, 30538, 34593.

[83] Bodl. MSS. Top. Oxon. d. 171–3.

[84] Some notable individual studies of towns are mentioned in M. Graham, *Oxon. Local Hist.* ii (8), 290–7.

Enthusiasm for Oxfordshire history was focused by several learned societies, of which the earliest was the Oxford Society for Promoting the Study of Gothic Architecture, founded in 1839, renamed the Oxford Archaeological Society in 1848 and the Oxford Archaeological and Historical Society (O.A.H.S.) in 1860. Early obsessions with Gothic architecture and the ecclesiology movement were soon overtaken by wider interests. It promoted an important architectural guide to the Oxford area,[85] and its published *Proceedings* date from the foundation until 1900. After a long lapse the society was revived and in 1936 began the annual publication of *Oxoniensia*, devoted to articles on Oxford and its neighbourhood.[86]

The North Oxfordshire Archaeological Society first met in Banbury in 1853[87] and published *Reports* and *Transactions* from 1856. Its aim was to study and preserve the antiquities of north Oxfordshire and parts of neighbouring counties, avoiding topics of religious and political controversy.[88] In 1887 it became the Oxfordshire Archaeological Society and membership widened. The society was dormant from 1940 until 1949, and was affiliated with the O.A.H.S. in 1954.[89] One of the founder members was William Wing of Steeple Aston (d. 1882), agriculturalist and prolific compiler of parochial 'annals';[90] Wing was strongest on the events of his own day, memorably castigating 'a Goth of a farmer' for blowing up a standing stone.[91] Later the Archaeological Society was dominated by distinguished scholars, including, from 1911, the county's outstanding modern historian, the Revd. H. E. Salter (d. 1951).[92] It was the Oxford Historical Society, however, which provided Salter with 'the main field of his work'.[93] The society was founded in 1884 on principles suggested by J. R. Green (d. 1883),[94] and during the next century it published many of the major sources for Oxford's history, most surviving cartularies of local religious houses, and several distinguished monographs. Salter was involved in as many as 35 volumes in the series. The Oxfordshire Record Society was founded in 1919, largely on the initiative of the Revd. F. N. Davis,

---

[85] *Guide to Archit. Antiquities in Neighbourhood of Oxford*, [ed. J. H. Parker and W. Grey] (4 pts. 1842–6).

[86] W. A. Pantin, 'Oxford Archit. and Hist. Soc. 1839–1939', *Oxoniensia*, iv. 174–94.

[87] A possibly erroneous foundation date of 1852 was printed on later reports: e.g. Oxford Arch. Soc. *Report*, no. 72.

[88] Rules of 1853 and later in ibid. *Reports, passim*.

[89] Ibid. *Transactions* and *Reports*, nos. 1–87 (1853–1949); *Oxoniensia*, xvii/xviii. 257–60 (incorporating *Report*, no. 88).

[90] E. H. Cordeaux and D. H. Merry, *Bibliography of Printed Works Relating to Oxon.* (Oxford Hist. Soc. new ser. xi), index s.v. Wing.

[91] W. Wing, *Annals of Steeple and Westcot Barton* (reprint from *Oxford Chronicle*, 1866), 14.

[92] Oxford Arch. Soc. *Reports*, 1911–37.

[93] W. A. Pantin, 'Herbert Edward Salter, 1863–1951', in *Survey of Oxford*, i (Oxford Hist. Soc. new ser. xiv), pp. xi–xxxiii.

[94] *Objects and Work of Oxford Hist. Soc.* (1900); ibid. (1911).

rector of Crowell and secretary of the Canterbury and York Society, and with strong support from the Oxfordshire Archaeological Society. Since then it has published 57 volumes, making available a wide variety of the major sources for Oxfordshire's history. Salter was chairman of the society 1921–42.[95]

To analyse the large corpus of modern local historical literature is beyond the scope of this article, but it may be noted that the strength of the county's learned societies demonstrates that at last those special advantages mentioned by earlier writers were beginning to influence Oxfordshire's historiography. The presence of the university ensured substantial local support for scholarly ventures, while the Bodleian Library, Ashmolean Museum, and the increasingly accessible university and college archives made Oxfordshire exceptionally rich in materials for local history. The city of Oxford established a local studies library as early as 1890, and the county council upheld that tradition by establishing in 1991 the Centre for Oxfordshire Studies, which brought together the local studies library, a large family history collection, extensive photographic and oral history archives, and a Sites and Monuments Record established as early as 1965.

Thus it was in a favourable climate that the Victoria County History progressed towards that *desideratum* mentioned by Phillipps in 1819, a good county history of Oxfordshire. The local committee formed in 1933 to continue the Oxfordshire *History*, which at that time comprised an isolated volume published in 1907, brought together county landowners and scholars; Oxford colleges contributed generously and the city corporation gave what is thought to have been the first grant made by a local authority to the *History*. A new local committee set up in 1948 after wartime interruption brought representatives of the university and local authorities into partnership with London University, owners of the *History*, and in 1965 Oxfordshire county council took over direct local responsibility for the project.[96] In all 12 volumes have been published covering some two thirds of the county, including two general volumes and two treating the city of Oxford and the university. A similarly ambitious project is the *History of the University of Oxford*, of which five volumes have been published since 1984. These large-scale modern histories are merely the flagships of a vast and busy flotilla. Interest in Oxfordshire history has never been so intense, the sources never so accessible. In 1695 White Kennett, challenging those who might think 'all history to be scraps, and all antiquity to be rust and rubbish', was confident that 'times will come, when persons of better inclination . . . will be glad to find any collection of this nature; and will be ready to supply the defects'.[97] His appeal to posterity was vindicated.

[95] Inf. from S. R. Tomlinson, Hon. Secretary, Oxon. Rec. Soc.
[96] *V.C.H. Oxon.* iii, p. xv; ix, p. xv.
[97] Kennett, *Parochial Antiquities* (1695), epistle.

SHROPSHIRE

G. C. Baugh

Shropshire's greatest native historian—most recently (and meticulously) edited by another native of the county—was Orderic Vitalis, writing *c.* 1114–41. His work is a rich source for the history of Shropshire under the first generation of Norman rulers, but Orderic's themes are wider than local history.[1] No such historical precocity is evident five centuries later, for Shropshire was not the scene of early labours on a county history, though the county town was more creditably treated over the years.[2] In 1636 Dugdale, reviewing the prospects for histories of several midland counties, was in touch with a noted Shropshire antiquary, John Langley of the Amies (in Broseley)—but in hope of obtaining Warwickshire material from him, not with a Shropshire history in mind.[3] And when Richard Gough reviewed matters nearly 150 years later[4] the most substantial publication was T. Phillips's recent *History and Antiquities of Shrewsbury* (1779),[5] to be superseded in the next generation by Hugh Owen's work, to which J. B. Blakeway also contributed.[6]

In identifying the first serious attempt at a Shropshire history it is necessary to consider the work of two kinsmen and namesakes, if only to distinguish them and their different approaches to provincial antiquities.

It would in any case be impossible to overlook the polymath Edward Lhuyd

---

[1] *Ecclesiastical Hist. of Orderic Vitalis*, ed. M. Chibnall (6 vols. 1968–80).

[2] E. Thornes, *Encomium Salopiae* (1616); O. Mathews, 'Scituation, Foundation and Auncient Names of Famous Towne of Sallop' (1616, in T. Hearne, *Hist. of Glastonbury* (1722), 237–71). Town and parish histories, however, are mentioned only incidentally in the following survey, for which Mr. A. M. Carr, Dr. D. C. Cox, Mrs. M. T. Roberts, and Dr. P. A. Stamper kindly provided references. Mr. Carr, Mr. J. B. Lawson, and Dr. J. F. A. Mason are thanked for commenting on a draft of what follows. Antiq. materials (esp. those in B.L.) not specifically referred to here are included in the surveys of topographical sources in *Trans. Salop. Arch. Soc.* [hereafter *T.S.A.S.*], ii. 297–316; 2nd ser. ii. 76–104; D. H. S. Cranage, *Churches of Salop.* x (1912), 1106–7.

[3] *Life, Diary, and Correspondence of Sir William Dugdale*, ed. W. Hamper (1827), 154–6. For Langley cf. ibid. 278–9, 329; *T.S.A.S.* 2nd ser. v. 119–22.

[4] [R. Gough], *British Topography* (2 vols. 1780), ii. 175–86.

[5] On its authorship see below.

[6] *Some Account of Ancient and Present State of Shrewsbury* (1808); Owen's copy in Shrewsbury School library (S.XII.67) is extensively altered in MS., apparently for a 2nd edn.; cf. J. Nightingale, *Topographical and Hist. Description of County of Salop.* (1813), p. v; Bodl. MS. Blakeway 26; below.

(1660–1709), born in Loppington parish the illegitimate son of Edward Lloyd of Llanforda near Oswestry. Lhuyd's mother was a Cardiganshire woman, but he was fostered for nine years at Crew Green (Mont.), just beyond the Shropshire border.[7] Educated at Oswestry grammar school,[8] he may have taught there before going up to Oxford in 1682. In 1696 Lhuyd issued *Parochial Queries*, destined, however, not merely for Shropshire parishes but for all those of Herefordshire and Wales too. Moreover, although they owed much to those devised by the Cumbrian antiquary Thomas Machell—'the first to specify the study of geography, history, and antiquities at the parish level',[9] geography and antiquities formed the subject of only 16 of Lhuyd's *Queries* while 31 were 'towards the Natural History'. In fact Lhuyd was planning (as urged on him at Oxford) a 'British Dictionary, Historical and Geographical', incorporating a natural history of Wales after the fashion of the county and provincial histories of his patron Dr. Robert Plot[10] and others whom Lhuyd encouraged or with whom he kept in touch.[11] Though no mean antiquary and archaeologist,[12] Lhuyd was in fact chiefly important as a scientific observer and systematic classifier of natural-history phenomena: a Baconian scientist especially eminent as a botanist and in the related fields of geology and palaeontology,[13] though Celtic philology[14] formed the subject of one of his most substantial (and pioneering) publications.[15] The Shropshire historian would rejoice to discover Shropshire replies to Lhuyd's *Parochial Queries* but, alas, only that for Oswestry survives.[16] Almost all Lhuyd's papers were burnt:[17] some in 1807 at Thomas Johnes's house at Hafod Uchtryd (Cardig.),[18] some in London being bound for Sir Watkin Williams Wynn.

[7] A. H. Dodd, 'Early days of Edward Lhuyd', *National Library of Wales Jnl.* vi. 305.

[8] *V.C.H. Salop.* ii. 152. For the rest of this para., except where otherwise stated, *Dictionary of Welsh Biography* (1959), 565–7; references to Lhuyd in S. A. E. Mendyk, *'Speculum Britanniae': Regional Study, Antiquarianism, and Science in Britain to 1700* (1989), *passim* but esp. pp. 206–12.

[9] According to F. Emery in *Trans. Honourable Soc. of Cymmrodorion* (1958), 44.

[10] R. Plot, *Oxon.* (1677); idem, *Staffs.* (1686).

[11] e.g. John Aubrey (*Wilts.* ed. J. Britton for Wilts. Topographical Soc. 1847), John Morton (*Northants.* 1698), and Dr. Charles Leigh (*Lancs., Ches., and the Peak in Derb.* 1700).

[12] G. Daniel, 'Edward Lhwyd: Antiquary and Archaeologist', *Welsh Hist. Review*, iii. 345–59, esp. 353 sqq.

[13] E. Lhuyd, *Lithophylacii Britannici Ichnographia* (1699).

[14] V. E. Durkacz, *Decline of Celtic Languages* (1983), 189–90, 214.

[15] E. Lhuyd, *Glossography* (1707): first, but only, vol. of the *Archaeologia Britannica* adumbrated in his projected 'British Dictionary'.

[16] Bodl. MS. Rawl. B. 464, ff. 152v.–158v., printed in *Parochialia*, ed. R. H. Morris, i. 127–32; ii. 9 (1909–10 supplements to *Archaeologia Cambrensis*).

[17] Some are identifiable in *Catalogue of Duplicates and Portion of Library of Sir John Sebright. Also Collection of MSS. collected by Sir Roger Twysden and Mr. E. Lhwyd* (1807), e.g. pp. 45–6, 51–2 (copy in B.L. 269.i.7).

[18] *Dictionary of Welsh Biography*, 442.

Lhuyd's distant kinsman[19] and namesake was working on Shropshire along more conventional county-history lines. The barrister Edward Lloyd (1666–1715), of Drenewydd (in Whittington), spent some of his early years in London studying antiquities and exploring the public records. He had a numerous acquaintance with scholars like Le Neve and 'the Antiquarians Company at the Fountain by Temple Gate'.[20] Retiring to Shropshire he 'digested a part of his extensive collections' into a manuscript 'Antiquities of Shropshire'.[21]

Lloyd's 'Antiquities' circulated in manuscript, and a copy evidently came to Thomas Wilkes, rector of Pitchford 1712–16 and 'a spick and span new antiquary'; he was preparing materials by 1716, but in 1731 he confessed to having 'long ago laid aside my design'. Four or five years later another clergyman, Thomas Loxdale, Staffordshire antiquary and 'not unmindful of the antiquities of Shropshire', was offering help to William Mytton.[22] By then it was clearly Mytton who gave most grounds for hope of a published Shropshire history, though Richard Gough's history of Myddle (written c. 1700, published 1834) and Samuel Garbet's history of Wem (written c. 1750–5, published 1818 ostensibly as the first instalment of a history of part of Bradford hundred) were notable contributions to parochial history.[23]

William Mytton (1693–1746) was a younger son of the family long seated at Halston (in Whittington), neighbours to Edward Lloyd, most of whose papers passed to Mytton. By 1731 Mytton's designs towards a county history were becoming widely known. Between 1732 and 1736 he journeyed around Shropshire with a young assistant, James Bowen, inspecting registers, inscriptions, and title deeds.[24] They visited the Tower records and in 1733 Mytton consulted Dugdale's manuscripts in the Ashmolean. Browne Willis had considered Mytton 'very ingenious' and 'well qualified' in 1734, and by 1741 (when they were corresponding about church dedications)[25] Mytton was circulating proposals for a general history and 'actual survey' of Shropshire. His friend Charles Lyttelton had for years pressed him about progress and

---

[19] Bodl. MS. Top. Salop. c. 1, pp. xvii, xviii; cf. *Alumni Oxonienses, 1500–1714*, ed. J. Foster (4 vols. 1891), iii. 923.

[20] J. Evans, *Hist. of Soc. of Antiq.* (1956), 45–6; Bodl. MS. Blakeway 8, ff. 1–7.

[21] S.P.L. [Local Studies Library, Shrewsbury, formerly Shrewsbury Public Library], MSS. 108, 5705.

[22] Bodl. MS. Blakeway 8, ff. 1–2, 8, 12, 25; T. F. Dukes, *Antiquities of Salop.* (1844), preface; *Staffs. Hist. Collections* [hereafter *S.H.C.*], 4th ser. xi. 77–83.

[23] For Gough, introductions by W. G. Hoskins (1968) and D. Hey (1981 and 1983) to their edns. of *Hist. of Myddle*.

[24] See, except where otherwise stated, Bodl. MS. Blakeway 8, ff. 1–3v., 9–25; S.P.L., MS. 2791, p. 530 (wrongly calling Mytton 'Revd.' and rector of Habberley); MS. 4080, p. 2009; MS. 6688; MS. 6741, p. 123.

[25] Cf. B.L. Add. MS. 30316.

publication, but Mytton, deaf and rheumatic, had become increasingly evasive. An *Inquisitio Parochialis*, with questions on the church, the parish, and the parishioners, had been drawn up[26] but perhaps never circulated: it may be significant that Mytton's 1741 proposals solicited information (to be sent to him directly or through Rogers, a Shrewsbury bookseller) as 'the matter is so confused and dispersed'. He may have intended much reliance on Lloyd's papers which, with his own collections,[27] remain useful sources. The drawings in Mytton's collections probably owe much to the artistry of Bowen (d. 1774), of whom one would willingly know more: 'a very facetious character & the life of the Gullet club', he became a herald painter and undertaker in Shrewsbury and worked on Shrewsbury abbey church and Oswestry church; he had left Mytton in 1737, and Mytton died at Habberley in 1746,[28] having published nothing. Bowen's materials, however, were probably used by his son John as the real author of Phillips's 1779 *History and Antiquities of Shrewsbury*.[29]

Leonard Hotchkiss (headmaster of Shrewsbury School 1735–54) and the Revd. Francis Leighton (1747–1813) also made collections for a Shropshire history but published nothing,[30] and the burden of preparing a topographical county history was next shouldered by two contemporaries of unequal powers and achievement: John Brickdale Blakeway (1765–1826) and William Hardwicke (1772–1843). The younger may be disposed of first. Hardwicke,[31] a Bridgnorth solicitor, became agent to the Whitmores of Apley Park and registrar of their peculiar jurisdiction of St. Mary Magdalen's, Bridgnorth. His profession opened country houses and church vestries and their contents to him; he had ready access, for example, to the Myttons' papers at Halston. From such sources he compiled pedigrees, made collections,[32] and drafted parish histories. He seems early to have decided against publication, and that may help to explain his high reputation as a genealogist[33]—one that does not

[26] At front of Birmingham Univ. Library, MS. 7/ii/1.

[27] Ibid. MSS. 7/ii/1–7; Soc. of Antiq. MS. 477 and Prattinton Collection miscellanea, xxv, pp. 73–85. Mytton's and Lloyd's collections, and Mytton's correspondence with Lyttelton, Browne Willis, and others (extracted in Bodl. MS. Blakeway 8), are in B.L. Add. MSS. 30311–31. The papers now forming Salop. R.O. [hereafter S.R.O.] 4827/1 may include Mytton transcripts from Rymer's *Foedera*.

[28] *V.C.H. Salop.* viii. 240, 243–4.

[29] *Salopian Shreds & Patches*, viii. 208; Bodl. MS. Blakeway 16, note on front endpaper; ibid. MSS. Gough Salop. 1–9, 11–17, 17B, 20.

[30] *V.C.H. Salop.* ii. 155, and sources there cited; *Gent. Mag.* new ser. vi. 302, 398–9; new ser. xxvi. 356.

[31] H. Smith, *Short Memoir of Late Eminent Salop. Genealogist and Antiq. William Hardwicke, Esq.* (1879).

[32] S.P.L., MSS. 4645–7; Bodl. MSS. Top. Salop. b. 1–6; c. 5.

[33] Smith, *Hardwicke*, 28, 38–9.

survive serious attempts to use his pedigrees. His six volumes of parish histories, arranged by hundreds and municipal liberties,[34] were originally loose papers in packets, handy for adding and redrafting as new evidence came to hand. The histories are at all stages of completeness, those with a finished appearance perhaps revealing the coverage he aimed at.[35] Hardwicke seems to have had a greater interest in the landscape and topography of places than any of his predecessors or 19th-century successors, though with a wearying preoccupation with weapon hoards, battlefields (of varying degrees of probability), and Celtic *twms*[36] (whatever they may be) that could endow early British history with colourful scenes of conflict and heroism. His medieval material, though often unreliable, affords clues, but his most complete parish histories preserve much useful and reliable detail from his own time and that of the previous generation.

Hardwicke was a 'valued correspondent' whom J. B. Blakeway often consulted 'upon matters relating to County History',[37] but Blakeway[38] was the greater scholar with a more amply furnished mind. A quick intellect, destined after Oxford (went down 1786) for the bar (called 1789), was diverted by a reverse of fortune to the church. Family connexions made him vicar of St. Mary's, Shrewsbury, in 1794, the year after ordination. Other livings held in plurality soon made him comfortable, and antiquities became his favourite study. Only a small proportion of what he wrote was ever published, and that mostly posthumously.[39] Nevertheless his materials for a topographical history of Shropshire[40] (including the parish questionnaire by then commonplace)[41] reveal an astonishing industry, though they perhaps suggest (thanks to the labours of others in arranging them)[42] more methodical ways than one of his capacious memory was used to employ. His two great works were the two-volume *A History of Shrewsbury* (dated 1825 although the last part was being issued when he died in 1826),[43] written jointly with Archdeacon Owen, and *The Sheriffs of Shropshire* (1831).[44]

'Of all names associated with our local history and antiquities', wrote a well

---

[34] William Salt Library, Stafford [hereafter W.S.L.], 350/1–5/40. Vol. 6 (351/40) in fact contains only Hardwicke's native parish of Worfield.

[35] e.g. W.S.L. 350/2/40, Drayton in Hales; 350/5/40, Church Stretton.

[36] e.g. ibid. 350/5/40, Church Stretton pp. 18–19, 24.

[37] Smith, *Hardwicke*, 31.

[38] *Memoir of late Rev. J. B. Blakeway, F.S.A.* (copy in S.P.L., Watton press cuttings, v. 7).

[39] Notably his topographical hist. of Shrewsbury, ed. W. Phillips for *T.S.A.S.* 3rd ser. v–vii (1905–7).

[40] Bodl. MSS. Blakeway 1–26.

[41] Ibid. 9; cf. the Soc. of Antiq. model questionnaire: copy in Worcester City Library, reference WQ 942.44 (accession 982560).

[42] *Salopian Shreds & Patches*, viii. 208.

[43] *Memoir of Blakeway*, 5, 7.

[44] Ed. W. G. Rowland: Shrewsbury School Library, the Revd. E. Burton's MSS. (3 vols. 1824–33), *passim*.

qualified judge in 1853, 'that of Mr. Blakeway has ever seemed to me entitled to an increasing reverence', and the *History of Shrewsbury* was then justly estimated to be 'of the very highest order of excellence; and that not merely topographically, but as furnishing those very elements towards a general History of England which ought to be ready and available to the national historian'.[45]

The writer of those words kept three local reference works ready to hand during his own study and writing: the *History of Shrewsbury* and *The Sheriffs of Shropshire*, and T. F. Dukes's *Antiquities of Shropshire* (1844).[46] Thus for R. W. Eyton the chain of his most eminent predecessors was complete, for the work published by the Shrewsbury solicitor Thomas Farmer Dukes[47] was none other than Edward Lloyd's manuscript whose attribution to Mytton[48] had so irritated Blakeway;[49] now at last it had appeared with another man's name on the title page, though Lloyd's authorship is acknowledged in the preface.[50] The confusion of authorship by no means detracted from the usefulness (in Eyton's eyes) of a work drawing so largely upon the public records.

Robert William Eyton (1815–81) sprang from two Shropshire families settled early enough on their estates to be (in the Scots phrase) 'of that ilk'. His father was a younger son of Thomas Eyton of Eyton upon the Weald Moors, whose family Eyton himelf believed, albeit on circumstantial (mainly armorial) evidence, to be cadets of the Pantulfs, barons of Wem. His mother was a daughter of E. J. Plowden of Plowden.[51] Eyton was educated at Bridgnorth grammar school (whither his father removed him from Rugby)[52] and Christ Church. His second-class honours in classics (1839) was attributed to undergraduate enthusiasm for English history. Certainly without such early groundwork his twelve years as a Worcestershire curate and Shropshire rector before the first part of his great work appeared might hardly have sufficed for the laying in of that critical and detailed familiarity with the public records[53] which give the *Antiquities of Shropshire* their individual character and high value. It was presumably at Ryton (where he became rector in 1841) that he familiarized himself with the diocesan and country-house muniments,[54] his

[45] R. W. Eyton, *Antiquities of Salop.* i (1854), 13.

[46] Ibid.

[47] E. G. Salisbury, *Border Counties Worthies* (1880), 2nd ser. 95; S.R.O. 665/3/166.

[48] Thomas Pennant, *Tours in Wales* (1810), i. 319–20.

[49] Bodl. MS. Blakeway 8, ff. 3v., 5Av., 8v.; MS. Top. Salop. d. 1, f. 32 and v.

[50] Cf. ibid. MSS. Top. Salop. c. 1–2.

[51] Burke, *Landed Gentry* (1898 edn.), i. 481–2; Eyton, *Antiquities*, viii (1859), 27; xi (1860), 218–21; *V.C.H. Salop.* xi. 139–40, 198.

[52] *V.C.H. Salop.* ii. 143. For what follows, except where otherwise stated, see *D.N.B.*; *T.S.A.S.* x. 1–9; lv. 102–4; *Notes & Queries*, new ser. vii. 444–6; new ser. viii. 322–6.

[53] Eyton, *Antiquities*, i. 2–10; cf. Hubert Smith's copy of the sale catalogue of Eyton's library in S.P.L., accession 1195.

[54] Eyton, *Antiquities*, i. 10–12.

family's respectability (preserved in 1816 by an adroit suppression of the circumstances of his grandfather's death)[55] easing his access.[56]

The first part of the *Antiquities* was sent to subscribers in December 1853. The five volumes planned ran eventually to twelve, the last (1860) consisting largely of indexes. From the first the *Antiquities* found great favour with subscribers (whose interest was sustained by the regular appearance of parts and volumes), the press, and the learned world: Sir William Hardy, later deputy keeper of the public records, placed Eyton far ahead of 'all our County Historians ancient or modern', and the work was singular among county histories chiefly in its single-minded concentration—in a style some found repulsively dry—on the genealogies, properties, and public lives of the feudal landowners between the Conquest and Edward II's reign, the period of which (as William Page justly noted) he 'was peculiarly the master'.[57] Churches were treated perfunctorily, their architecture illustrated mainly in the drawings contributed by the Revd. J. L. Petit,[58] the Revd. John Brooke of Haughton in Shifnal,[59] and others. Nor did landscape and topography interest Eyton; indeed his topographical obtuseness (not too strong a word) occasionally led him into odd errors.[60] Later periods (for whose study his library was well supplied) seem not to have interested him seriously,[61] even if he toyed late in life with the idea of continuing the *Antiquities*. Such limitations, however, enabled Eyton to complete 'the most important single work ever devoted to the history of Shropshire'.[62] His main source of inspiration, unlike that of many other county historians, seems not to have been local patriotism, but (as his comment on Owen and Blakeway's history reveals) a wish to contribute local research to national history. When therefore the *Antiquities* was complete—having paid its expenses[63]—Eyton left Shropshire and turned to early medieval studies of national scope and for other counties.[64]

[55] S.R.O. 665/2/5966, 6017–18; 1066/111, 27 Feb. 1816; *Autobiography of Charles Darwin*, ed. N. Barlow (1958), 40–2; C. Hulbert, *Hist. and Description of Salop.* (1837), ii. 154.

[56] e.g. S.R.O. 2/434; 1224, box 342, Prior Gosnell's register; cf. Loton Hall MSS., Sir Baldwin Leighton's diary 6 May 1865, 8 Sept. 1867.

[57] *V.C.H. Salop.* i, p. xxi. Eyton had originally intended to stop at Henry III's death: *Antiquities*, i. 1.

[58] Author of *Remarks on Church Archit.* (2 vols. 1841), *Archit. Studies in France* (1854), etc.

[59] Burke, *Landed Gentry* (1952 edn.), 271.

[60] e.g. the mislocation of Crudgington (cf. *Antiquities*, x (1860), 308; *T.S.A.S.* lxii. 12 n. 7) or the assertion that Charlton Grange (in Shawbury) 'has no modern representative. The name is lost' (cf. *Antiquities*, viii. 250; O.S. Map 1", index to tithe survey [c. 1851], sheet LXXIII. SW.).

[61] Perhaps because the easily accessible (i.e. printed) recs. gave out at that point: *T.S.A.S.* x. 3–4.

[62] *T.S.A.S.* lv. 104.

[63] Smith, *Hardwicke*, 28.

[64] Eyton's notebooks, transcripts, etc., are in B.L. Add. MSS. 31923–46, 33226; Bodl. MSS. Top. Salop. d. 2–3; S.P.L., MS. 114.

Eyton wrote Shropshire's last single-handed topographical history based on original work. Though Charles Hulbert's 1837 volume on Shrewsbury was only an 'enlarged' edition of Bowen's 1779 work,[65] his companion volume on Shropshire (also 1837)[66] had contained some useful contemporary information, and the Revd. C. H. Hartshorne's *Salopia Antiqua* (1841) had been a genuinely original archaeological synopsis with appendices on place names and Shropshire dialect. When, however, J. C. Anderson published a history in 1864—prompted by little more than the availability of Eyton's plates—it was wholly unoriginal: a mere abridgement of Eyton with a little additional material on Shrewsbury and the archaeology of Wroxeter from Owen and Blakeway and Hartshorne.[67] By then in fact the subjects considered essential for a county history were multiplying, and in 1860—the very year in which Eyton's *Antiquities* was completed—it could be alleged that 'the history of Shropshire, as it is, yet remains to be written'![68]

The future then clearly lay with the organization of local and specialist studies, initially by county societies. That had been true for a generation. When the Shropshire and North Wales Natural History and Antiquarian Society (1835–77)[69] had been founded local antiquarian studies were no longer the lonely pursuit they had been in Hardwicke's day when he was (though a correspondent of Blakeway and Peter Prattinton) 'a solitary antiquary of [his] particular district'.[70] Specialized collections were multiplying. The Revd. Edward Williams (1762–1833), a zealous botanist,[71] transcribed the Shrewsbury and Haughmond abbey cartularies and much other historical material;[72] he united considerable artistic talent[73] to his antiquarian tastes, and artistic and antiquarian interests were combined by others such as David Parkes (1763–1833), schoolmaster, artist, and antiquary.[74] Such combinations occasioned picture books like William Pearson's *Select Views of the Antiquities*

[65] 'Phillips's' (see above), originally printed by Hulbert's father-in-law Thomas Wood, owner of the *Shrewsbury Chronicle*: *T.S.A.S.* xlviii. 195–6.

[66] The *Hist. and Description of Shrewsbury* and of *Salop.*, though differently titled, form one work issued in pts. (some in S.P.L.) 1829–37: cf. S.P.L., MS. 6815; C. A. H[ulbert], *Obituary of Late Mr. Charles Hulbert* (2nd edn. 1860): copy in S.P.L.

[67] Anderson, *Salop.: its Early Hist. and Antiquities*, pp. vii–viii; cf. *V.C.H. Salop.* i, p. xxi; Croydon Natural Hist. and Scientific Soc. Arch. Section, *Newsletter*, lix. 3–6 (copy in S.P.L., BA 54 v.f.).

[68] *Eddowes's Jnl.* 26 Sept. 1860, p. 4.

[69] S.P.L., MS. 6825; *T.S.A.S.* i, pp. ix–xi.

[70] Smith, *Hardwicke*, 9–10; E. A. B. Barnard, *Prattinton Collections of Worcs. Hist.* (1931), 114.

[71] *Salop. Notes & Queries*, vii. 38; *V.C.H. Salop.* i. 53.

[72] S.P.L., MSS. 1, 1A, 2–7; B.L. Add. MSS. 21236–7; Shrewsbury School Library, 'Salop. Registers' (S.X.2).

[73] S.P.L., MS. 372.

[74] H. R. Wilson, *David Parkes 1763–1833* [1978].

of Shropshire [1807] and *A Selection of Antiquities in the County of Salop* (1824),[75] publications that avoided the intractably copious materials for topographical history. John Homes Smith (d. 1868)[76] drew at least 219 churches[77] and, though his talents were not as great as Williams's, the work of both men survives as a valuable record of Shropshire churches in the late 18th and mid 19th centuries. It was George Morris's skill as a draughtsman that caused Blakeway to draw him into antiquarian pursuits, and George (1789–1859) and his brother Joseph Morris (1792–1860) became able and prolific genealogists,[78] Joseph eventually aspiring to write a county history too.[79]

The tendency evident in Pearson's books, to design works of county history around illustrations, persisted into the 20th century,[80] but other collections were being formed with various different motives for which the Shropshire and North Wales Society's library and museum provided a focus. Edward Edwards, innkeeper, bookseller,[81] and writer,[82] formed an 'extensive collection' of topographical records (1,100 volumes and pamphlets) and in 1855 a subscription was opened to buy it[83] for the society's new rooms in Vaughan's Mansion. One of the society's founders,[84] the Revd. W. A. Leighton (1805–89), botanist, antiquary, and Parkes's son-in-law,[85] was a member of the Caradoc and Severn Valley Naturalists' field clubs (founded in 1863 and united in 1893 as the Caradoc and Severn Valley Field Club)[86] and was first editor (1877–86) of the *Transactions* of the Shropshire Archaeological and Natural History Society (founded in 1877).[87] The *Transactions* were an essential new feature of the historical scene, providing an outlet for local and specialist studies—as, for example, H. B. Walters's papers later collected and published as *Church Bells of Shropshire* (1915). The *Transactions* eventually superseded the county

[75] Cf. F. Calvert and W. West, *Picturesque Views in Salop.* (1831).

[76] S.P.L., Capt. R. S. Webb's pedigree (1917) of Smith and Stretton family.

[77] His watercolours are in S.P.L.: *T.S.A.S.* lix. 84, 87.

[78] *V.C.H. Salop.* iii. 312, 325, and sources there cited; R. A. Preston, 'George and Joseph Morris: Genealogists of Salop.' *Salop. Family Hist. Jnl.* x. 102–3; S.P.L., MSS. 282, 2788–95, 4077–86; cf. ibid. MSS. 13–29, 4696. Some of their materials were published posthumously in *T.S.A.S.*

[79] *Eddowes's Jnl.* 26 Sept. 1860, p. 4.

[80] e.g. H. T. Timmins, *Nooks and Corners of Salop.* (1899); Stanley Leighton's projected county hist. (below).

[81] S.P.L., Watton press cuttings, iv. 448–9, 492; xii. 8A.

[82] Author of *Parliamentary Elections of Borough of Shrewsbury from 1282 to 1859* (1859).

[83] S.R.O. 665/3/180.

[84] Ibid. 1041/Ch/48, p. 1 (no. 9); 1041/Ch/52, p. 1 (no. 4: last mention); S.P.L., MSS. 180, 181 (s.a. 1854–5); *T.S.A.S.* lix. 82–3 (wrongly stating that the soc. occupied Vaughan's Mansion from 1835).

[85] *V.C.H. Salop.* i. 53; Wilson, *Parkes*, family tree.

[86] Cf. S.R.O. 4624/1/1–2; 4624/2/1–4; ibid. *Trans.* of both clubs.

[87] *T.S.A.S.* i, pp. v–xi; ix, plate and note preceding p. 1; x, pp. v, xi.

newspapers' antiquarian columns,[88] though not for many years during which they kept local antiquaries in touch with each other.[89] (The historical and antiquarian interests of Shropshire newspaper proprietors, often also booksellers and publishers,[90] and the contributions they and their staff made to county and local history lie beyond the scope of this survey.)

In due course the ranks of local historical scholarship were joined by men of humbler social origins[91] than the gentry and professionals who had preponderated thitherto. Women too began to play their part. Georgina Jackson's and Charlotte Burne's publications on Shropshire dialect and folklore were significant contributions to national work,[92] as were, in a later generation and a rather different sphere, the lifetime's labours of the archaeologist Lily Chitty (1893–1979).[93] Mrs. Stackhouse Acton's *The Castles & Old Mansions of Shropshire* (1868) was more local in its appeal, and others too—Francis Leach,[94] Stanley Leighton,[95] and H. E. Forrest[96]—tackled 'county history' through the country houses and the families who built and lived in them. The Revd. D. H. S. Cranage's 'complete, detailed, and reliable account' of Shropshire churches, issued in parts (eventually with financial help from the Shropshire Archaeological and Natural History Society) between 1894 and 1912, was another specialist work that, *c.* 1956, had been 'neither superseded nor in any essentials found wanting'.[97] In 1897 Stanley Leighton founded the Shropshire Parish Register Society[98] to tackle another specialized aspect of county record publication, at first (until 1906) under the vigorous editorship of W. P. W. Phillimore, a national figure with local roots.[99] The care, listing, and publication

---

[88] 'Bye-Gones relating to Wales and Border Counties', *Oswestry Advertiser*, 1871–1940; 'Salopian Shreds & Patches', *Eddowes's Jnl.* 1874–91; 'Salop. Notes & Queries', *Shrewsbury Chronicle*, 1884–1942.

[89] *Oswestry Advertiser*, centenary supplement 5 Jan. 1949, p. 7.

[90] For Thomas Wood, above, n. 65. For the Eddoweses, owners of *Salopian Jnl.* 1794–41 and later *Eddowes's Jnl.*, and booksellers, B.L. Add. MS. 24569, f. 38; *T.S.A.S.* xlviii. 105–10; S.P.L., MS. 4083, pp. 3634–5. For J. Askew Roberts, *Oswestry Advertiser*, centenary supplement 5 Jan. 1949, esp. pp. 4–5, 7.

[91] e.g. John Randall and William Phillips: below.

[92] G. Ashman, 'Charlotte Sophia Burne', *Talking Folklore*, i. 6–21; J. Wright, *English Dialect Dictionary* (1898–1905).

[93] *T.S.A.S.* lx. 131–3; *Lily F. Chitty Collection: Catalogue of her Arch. Recs. relating to Salop.* [ed. A. M. Carr] (privately printed, 1992), 3–8.

[94] *County Seats of Salop.* (1891).

[95] *Salop. Houses Past & Present* (1901), was intended as the first instalment of a fully illustrated county hist. (ibid. p. vii). The unpublished texts and drawings (microfilm in S.R.O. 1119/1–7) passed to Mr. F. G. Salway of West Felton; there are also drawings at Hodnet Hall.

[96] *Old Houses of Shrewsbury* (4 edns. 1911–35); *Old Houses of Wenlock and Wenlock Edge* (1914); *Some Old Salop. Houses and their Owners* (1924).

[97] N. Pevsner, *Buildings of England: Salop.* (1958), 45–6; D. H. S. Cranage, *Not Only a Dean* (1952), esp. pp. 214–15.

[98] S.R.O. 1314/1, 4; *Salop. Parish Registers: Hereford Diocese*, vi, pp. vii–x.

[99] S.R.O. 1314/10; *Who Was Who, 1897–1915*, 412.

of local records was more generously undertaken as the views of local scholars penetrated official bodies.[1] Shropshire was among the earliest counties to publish its quarter-sessions records and survey parish records.[2]

In such circumstances there was no longer any possibility of an adequate topographical county history based on single-handed original research, and the *Victoria History of the Counties of England* emerged as a national collaborative enterprise.[3] (Though not the first such,[4] it was by far the most ambitious.) Some local specialists or prominent early contributors to local *Transactions* contributed also to volume one (1908) of the Shropshire *V.C.H.*: such were John Randall (1810–1910), artist and autodidact geologist and local historian;[5] William Phillips (1822–1905), botanist and antiquarian;[6] the Revd. C. H. Drinkwater (1831–1923), a 'most diligent' antiquary;[7] Prebendary Thomas Auden (1836–1920);[8] and H. E. Forrest (1858–1942), zoologist and geologist.[9] Randall's intimate knowledge of the east Shropshire coalfield was deeply rooted, deriving—in part at least—from his conversations with Adam Luckock (1727–1831) who knew the Darbys and Coalbrookdale in the mid 18th century.[10] Forrest's geological speculations were crowned by a book on the Atlantean continent.[11]

Work on the Shropshire *V.C.H.* ceased for many years after 1908, and county historical publication was carried on by the societies. The Shropshire Archaeological and Historical Society[12] (with which the Parish Register Society merged in 1922)[13] had published 68 volumes of *Transactions* and some substantial monographs by 1993. The Caradoc and Severn Valley Field Club, whose last *Transactions* appeared in 1973, issued some monographs thereafter. More local and specialist societies, however, were founded, there being some 20 in 1993,[14] and some published.[15] By the time work on the Shropshire *V.C.H.* resumed in 1961

---

[1] *Calendar of Muniments and Recs. of Borough of Shrewsbury* (1896), preface; *T.S.A.S.* 2nd ser. viii, pp. xviii–xxii.

[2] *V.C.H. Salop.* iii. 222–3.

[3] *V.C.H. General Introduction*, 4 sqq.

[4] e.g. Nightingale's *Salop.* (1813) was pt. of J. Britton and E. W. Brayley's *Beauties of England and Wales* (1801–16).

[5] *V.C.H. Salop.* xi. 23, and sources there cited.

[6] Ibid. i. 55.

[7] Vicar of St. George's, Shrewsbury, 1872–1923: *T.S.A.S.* xlii. 221–6.

[8] *T.S.A.S.* xli. 149–54.

[9] Ibid. li. 160 and plate facing p. 138; *Trans. Caradoc and Severn Valley Field Club* [hereafter *T.C.S.V.F.C.*], xi. 237–40.

[10] J. Randall, *Hist. of Madeley* (1880), 286–95; S.R.O. 2280/BRg/3, p. 241 (no. 1921).

[11] *T.C.S.V.F.C.* x. 168; cf. *B.L. Catalogue of Printed Books*, s.v. Forrest.

[12] The soc. dropped 'Natural Hist.' from its title *c.* 1922 and added 'Hist.' in 1987: inf. from the Hon. Secretary.

[13] *T.S.A.S.* 4th ser. ix, pp. xix–xx.

[14] Inf. from S.P.L.

[15] e.g. the Salop. Family Hist. Soc. and the South-West Salop. Hist. and Arch. Soc., whose *Jnls.* first appeared in 1980 and 1989 respectively.

(under the aegis of the county-council Records Committee, which had opened a county record office in 1946)[16] that scheme had expanded: the four Shropshire volumes originally planned were increased to ten topographical and two or three general volumes in 1961 and the topographical volumes were increased to thirteen in 1976.[17] Six volumes had appeared by 1993: three general volumes had been added to volume one and two topographical volumes had appeared; a third topographical volume and a fifth general volume were then well advanced. The *V.C.H.*'s expansion was organized from the centre[18] in response to the increasing range of subjects that had long been considered essential. One of the newest approaches—analysis of the historical landscape—underpinned the work of the writers of volume eight (1968), the second Shropshire *V.C.H.* volume to be published, and was praised by the man who, more than any other, had inspired the growth of landscape studies—Professor W. G. Hoskins.[19]

If, in the 1990s, the *V.C.H.* remained the only hope of completing a topographical history of the county, there was nevertheless a long tradition of individually written single-volume general histories or surveys of Shropshire. Few of them were bad,[20] many were good,[21] and some—professionally written studies in national series—were outstanding.[22] Photography[23] revived the picture-book tradition: local publications naturally tended to cover particular places[24] but books in national series and some local or individual works covered the county[25] or aspects of its history.[26] In the best illustrated works amateurs and professionals were attaining indistinguishable standards by the 1980s. Nor were amateurs (in that word's precise and admirable sense) failing to hold their own in other ways, as the work of H. D. G. Foxall (1911–89) and others, contributors to the *V.C.H.* and the English Place-Name Society's work,[27] demonstrates: the amateur, on whom the writing of local history had depended for centuries, was keeping pace with the professional—so recent, and possibly ephemeral, a figure on the local scene.

[16] *V.C.H. Salop.* iii. 223.

[17] S.R.O. 3763/2/8–9.

[18] C. R. J. Currie, 'Hist. of V.C.H. Ser.' *Some Historians of Lincs.* ed. C. Sturman (Occasional Papers in Lincs. Hist. and Arch. ix, 1992), 90–2.

[19] *Agricultural Hist. Review*, xx. 78–80; S.R.O. 3763/30/6, letter 5 Nov. 1971.

[20] But Augustus J. C. Hare's *Salop.* (1895) is.

[21] J. E. Auden, *Little Guide: Salop.* (1912); *Memorials of Old Salop.* ed. T. Auden (1906).

[22] T. Rowley, *Salop. Landscape* (1972; in *The Making of the English Landscape*, ed. W. G. Hoskins); B. Trinder, *Industrial Revolution in Salop.* (2 edns. 1973, 1981); idem, *Hist. of Salop.* (Darwen County Hist. ser. 1983).

[23] In the early 1890s Cranage decided against re-using the plates from Eyton's *Antiquities* in favour of photographs: *Not Only a Dean*, 214–15.

[24] Many of the 1970s listed in *T.S.A.S.* lx. 123–4; cf. *Salop. Newsletter*, xxxii, p. 2; xxxv, p. 8.

[25] U. Rayska, *Victorian and Edwardian Salop. from Old Photographs* (1977).

[26] I. J. Brown, *Mines of Salop.* (1976); R. Hill and P. Stamper, *Working Countryside 1862–1945* (1993).

[27] *V.C.H. Salop.* iv, p. xv; xi, pp. xiii–xiv; M. Gelling, *Place-Names of Salop.* i (E.P.N.S. lxii/lxiii, 1990), pp. ix–xi. Cf. H. D. G. Foxall, *Salop. Field-Names* (Salop. Arch. Soc. 1980).

SOMERSET

R. W. Dunning

While many other counties were being surveyed by John Norden and his imitators, Thomas Gerard, a gentleman living at Trent on Somerset's southern border, undertook 'a particular description' of Somerset and a 'survey' of Dorset. Of the Somerset manuscript, completed in 1633, only half survives, found with surveys of Norden *c.* 1896[1] and published in 1900.[2] It is arranged topographically, following the county's rivers from the west and revealing the author's awareness of landscape and his interest in family history and heraldry. Gerard's sources were wide-ranging, with an emphasis on public records and the contents of local muniment rooms, but he also used the manuscript collections of Leland, thanks to his friendship with William Burton, and of Sir William Pole.

Gerard's work, although remaining for so long unpublished, was known to a group of antiquarians working in the county in the early years of the 18th century.[3] The interests of the nonjuror Dr. George Harbin (d. 1744)[4] were as much political as antiquarian, but he transcribed two local monastic cartularies[5] and corresponded with and regularly met other members of the group, Thomas Carew (d. 1766) of Crowcombe, Thomas Palmer (d. 1734) of Fairfield, and John Strachey (d. 1743) of Sutton Court.[6] Palmer and Carew, each with antiquarian collections drawn from their own and their neighbours' archives, produced disappointingly modest results: Palmer a draft history of Williton hundred and of some parishes where he had land,[7] Carew some papers which he allowed Strachey to use and which his descendants later offered to John Collinson.[8]

Strachey issued proposals for a work to be entitled 'Somersetshire

[1] *Som. and Dors. Notes and Queries*, v (1897), 97–102.

[2] *Particular Description of Som.* ed. E. H. Bates (Som. Rec. Soc. xv, 1900).

[3] *Som. and Dors. Notes and Queries*, v. 97; Som. R.O., Strachey MS. (DD/SH) 144.

[4] S. W. Rawlins and P. B. G. Binnall, 'Dr. George Harbin', *Proc. Som. Arch. and Natural Hist. Soc.* [hereafter *P.S.A.N.H.S.*], xciii (1947), 68–83.

[5] G. R. C. Davis, *Medieval Cartularies of Great Britain* (1958), 4 (Athelney), 12 (Bruton); *P.S.A.N.H.S.* cxxxvi (1993), 149–60.

[6] Rawlins and Binnall, 'Harbin', 81; Som. R.O., DD/SH 96.

[7] Som. R.O., Acland-Hood MS. (DD/AH) 21.

[8] Strachey's papers are ibid. DD/SH 97–8; Carew's in ibid. DD/TB 19/1–3; 20/1–5; 21/2; 51/1.

Illustrated' in 1736. He had already published geological studies of the Mendip hills and in 1731 *An Alphabetical List of Religious Houses in Somersetshire*.[9] At the time that he issued his proposal for a history he was working on a map of the county, the first on a large scale but one which had serious inaccuracies.[10]

Strachey had contemplated a county history ever since the turn of the century,[11] and his surviving notes reveal a personal knowledge of the public records which culminated in 1739 in an index of their repositories,[12] and a series of extracts from plea rolls, records of the court of wards and liveries, and the patent and decree rolls.[13] The resulting county history was less impressive: 16 sections of drafts in octavo and some folio pages of more finished work.[14]

One other work,[15] probably finished in the 1730s and recently come to light, seems to have been written by a county official. With an occasional foray into false etymology or antiquarianism, it is essentially a survey of the county's hundreds, hundred courts, and rating assessments by someone intimately concerned with the system of local administration and taxation. Future county historians will find it of considerable value.

In August 1742 the *Sherborne Mercury* offered its readers 'A compleat history of Somerset Shire' to be issued in 52 weekly numbers. The contrast between it and the work of Strachey and his friends could not have been more marked, and even its publication was something of a fraud, since it was a reissue,[16] with some omissions not noted in the title page, of part 60 of Thomas Cox's *Magna Britannia*.[17] References to Leland and Camden reveal the general nature of the work, although it includes some contemporary information about the county's charity schools.

Somerset's first individual county history[18] was published in 1791 but it was cast in a traditional and not a revolutionary mould. It bears the sole name of John Collinson on its title page although much of the natural history and topography was the work of Edmund Rack, secretary of the Agricultural and Philosophical societies of Bath. Collinson, then aged only 23, had proposed a history of his native Wiltshire in 1780 after collecting materials in his

---

[9] Ibid. DD/SH 110; E. Green, *Bibliotheca Somersetensis* (1902), iii. 291.
[10] T. Chubb, *Descriptive List of Printed Maps of Som. 1575–1914* (1914), 35.
[11] Som. R.O., DD/SH 97.
[12] Ibid. DD/SH 204.
[13] Ibid. DD/SH 141, 151, 192, 200, 202–3.
[14] Ibid. DD/SH 107–8.
[15] Photocopy in office of editor, V.C.H. Som., County Hall, Taunton.
[16] *Som. County Herald*, 15 June 1940.
[17] T. Cox, *Magna Britannia et Hibernia* (6 vols. 1720–31), iv. 720–912.
[18] J. Collinson, *Hist. and Antiquities of Som.* (3 vols. 1791)

undergraduate days. A year later, when a curate in Cirencester, he was
contemplating instead a history of Somerset, but the idea was abandoned
when he failed to gain access to John Strachey's papers. With Rack's name
behind him, however, the papers became available and new *Proposals* were
issued in 1784. Rack's death and Collinson's own personal circumstances
caused some delays, but the three-volume history was issued within seven
years of its announcement.[19]

Collinson acknowledged the use of the collections of Thomas Palmer and
Thomas Carew, and he probably also used the papers of George Harbin,[20] but
there is no evidence that he had access to Strachey's papers. He certainly
consulted the bishops' registers at Wells, cited manuscripts at Longleat and in
the British Museum, and used the collections of Sir William Pole.

A review and consequent correspondence in the *Gentleman's Magazine*
were not favourable, some writers criticizing the arrangement by hundred and
parish, others the quality of the scholarship.[21] Sir Henry Maxwell Lyte
perhaps came nearest a true assessment a century later when he remarked that
the work was 'meagre and in some sections fundamentally incorrect'.[22]
Nevertheless for a century and more many people clung to Collinson, even
urging a better index rather than any proposed revision.[23] The county
archaeological society published a new index in 1898[24] and in 1939, as a
supplement, those parts of a survey compiled by Richard Locke in the early
1780s to which access had been offered to Edmund Rack.[25] The original
history, the supplement, and the index were reprinted in one volume in 1983.[26]

Collinson remains the only work covering the whole county but in the next
50 years there followed two histories of county sub-divisions and several town
histories. Joshua Toulmin, Taunton's Unitarian minister, published a history
of his own town in 1791 which proved so meagre that it was expanded and
rewritten by James Savage in 1822.[27] Warner's history of Bath appeared in
1801[28] and, by the same hand, a history of Glastonbury which was rather
overshadowed by material on the abbey.[29] James Savage, Toulmin's reviser

---

[19] Biographical and bibliographical inf. from unpaginated introduction to reprint of Collinson's *Hist.* (1983).
[20] Collinson, *Hist.* i, pp. ix–x, 84 n. (second pagination).
[21] *Gent. Mag.* lxiii (1), 148–50, 237; lxiv (1), 497–8; lxiv (2), 621, 701–2, 977–80, 1165–7, 1179.
[22] H. C. Maxwell Lyte, *Hist. of Dunster* (1909), i, p. vi.
[23] Below.
[24] *Index to Collinson's Hist. of Som.* ed. F. W. Weaver and E. H. Bates with J. R. Bramble (1898).
[25] *Supplement to Collinson's Hist. of Som.* ed. F. M. Ward (1939); *Gent. Mag.* lxiv (2), 1179–81.
[26] By Alan Sutton, with an introduction by R. W. Dunning.
[27] J. Toulmin, *Hist. of Town of Taunton* (1791); J. Toulmin, *Hist. of Taunton, new edn. greatly enlarged, and brought down to the present time by James Savage* (1822).
[28] R. Warner, *Hist. of Bath* (1801).
[29] R. Warner, *Hist. of Abbey of Glaston and Town of Glastonbury* (1826).

and librarian to the Taunton Institution, in the course of his professional duties received the volumes of the Record Commission and made good use of them and of the Luttrell manuscripts at Dunster for a history of 15 parishes in west Somerset.[30] Similarly, in 1829 John Rutter, a Shaftesbury publisher, produced a survey of parishes around Weston super Mare based on two excursions and correspondence with local clergy and gentry. Collinson and Sir Richard Colt Hoare's *Modern Wiltshire* proved his inspiration and only the contemporary observation remains of value.[31]

Colt Hoare was also the inspiration for a serious attempt at a new county history which has not received the credit it deserves. The Revd. William Phelps, like Collinson a parochial clergyman and already author of a volume on botany,[32] in 1835 announced and at once began publication of a complete county history, to include both general chapters and parochial histories. In the event the histories covered only 13 hundreds in the centre and south-east of the county. A bibliographical nightmare,[33] the work was issued in eight parts and presumably foundered for financial reasons after 1839. The topographical chapters, including the results of new research and fieldwork, record then recent changes in land ownership and land use, and remain a significant contribution to county history.[34]

Renewed enthusiasm came from the county's archaeological society, formed in 1849 to 'explore the treasures of nature and art . . . and to accumulate a body of facts in aid of the studies of the antiquary and natural historian'.[35] In support of such an aim Dr. William Buckland, geologist and dean of Westminster, proposed for a new county history 'a small monograph—its subterranean antiquities forming one side, and its present natural history the other'. He suggested that the work needed a 'properly qualified person' to organize the returns to the questionnaires sent at first to the clergy and magistrates and later to any interested resident. After a year the survey was proving useless.[36]

In 1859 the current volume of the archaeological society's *Proceedings* was seen as an indication of the progress made towards collecting material for a county history. Two other signs were declared to be the growth of the

---

[30] J. Savage, *Hist. of Hundred of Carhampton* (1829), reprinted with dedication and list of subscribers 1830; an interleaved version of the 1829 edn., in four volumes, with extra material by the author, formerly Phillipps MS. 13675, is in the Local Hist. Library, Taunton Castle.

[31] J. Rutter, *Delineations of North Western Division of Som. and its Antediluvian Bone Caves* (1829).

[32] W. Phelps, *Calendarium Botanicum* (1810).

[33] *Som. and Dors. Notes and Queries*, xxxii (1988), 645–55.

[34] W. Phelps, *Hist. and Antiquities of Som.* (2 vols. 1836–9). Questionnaires and correspondence in Som. R.O., DD/SAS SI 5; DD/DN 293.

[35] *P.S.A.N.H.S.* i (1851), 5.

[36] Ibid. 50; the text of the questionnaires, ibid. 75–85.

society's library and museum, 'one of the best aids towards a good county history', and the activities of a committee charged to revise Collinson.[37] Hopes of several of the society's presidents did not coincide with actual progress noted by the secretary,[38] but individual members contributed in various ways: articles in the *Proceedings*, published monographs including the pioneer work on dialect,[39] the establishment and publications of local antiquarian societies (at Bath in 1867, Wells about 1888, and Wincanton in 1889), the publication of original materials,[40] and the foundation of an antiquarian periodical in 1890[41] and of a county record society in 1887.[42]

The question of a new county history was revived in 1890 by Henry Hobhouse,[43] then president of the county archaeological society, who was supported by Henry (later Sir Henry) Maxwell Lyte, deputy keeper of the public records.[44] The society established a county history committee,[45] but energies were directed rather towards the record society and to the need for a county bibliography of books and prints, a place-name survey, and an inventory of parish records.[46] At least one individual member, himself still wedded to a new edition of Collinson, published his collections of material on 10 parishes near Yeovil, heavily based on legal sources at the Public Record Office.[47] Henry Hobhouse returned to his theme in 1898, pleading for a good county history,[48] and in the following year Sir Edward Fry called members' attention to the work then proceeding on Northumberland.[49] Yet the society as a whole seems to have been unaware of the Victoria County History proposals, and no reference was made to the V.C.H.'s progress, either in Somerset or elsewhere, in its official business. William Page addressed not the archaeological society but county society for support in 1900 when he was intent on forming a Somerset county committee.[50] The lord lieutenant and many of the gentry approached were, after all, the owners of archives to which Page's researchers would have to gain access. In that first foray for county support only Sir John Horner and Hobhouse

---

[37] Ibid. ix (1859), 2–5.
[38] e.g. ibid. x (1860), 2–4.
[39] F. T. Elworthy, *West Som. Word Book* (1866).
[40] e.g. F. Brown, *Abstracts of Som. Wills* (6 vols. 1887–90).
[41] *Som. and Dors. Notes and Queries.*
[42] Som. Rec. Soc.
[43] *P.S.A.N.H.S.* xxxvi (1890), 17–23.
[44] Ibid. 35.
[45] Ibid. xxxvii (1892), 6.
[46] Ibid. xlvi (1900), 9–10, 17; xlviii (1903), 10.
[47] J. Batten, *Hist. and Topographical Collections South Som.* (1894).
[48] *P.S.A.N.H.S.* xliv (1898), 8.
[49] Ibid. xlv (1899), 10–11.
[50] Correspondence in the office of the editor, V.C.H. Som., County Hall, Taunton.

expressed reservations: Sir John preferred a revision of Collinson's *History* to any new initiative and Mr. Hobhouse wanted to know something of Page's plans and who was to be editor. Sir John was not included on the county committee.[51]

Nevertheless, one leading member of the archaeological society, the Revd. E. H. Bates (later Bates-Harbin), became intimately involved in the work of the Victoria History as early as November 1900. He and another scholar with Somerset connexions, Sir Henry Maxwell Lyte, advised, assisted, and read the proofs of the first volume, which appeared in 1906.[52] Bates continued to act as the local contact of the editor, contributing the text of the Somerset Domesday and of the Geld Inquest and revising the work of others in preparation for the second volume, and himself drew up a plan for the completion of the topographical volumes.[53]

For various reasons, largely financial, publication of the second volume of the *Victoria History* was delayed until 1911[54] and the Bates plan for a total of four volumes in ten parts was abandoned in favour of six volumes, of which four were to contain a total of over 470 parishes, each allotted 3½ pages, together with 15 boroughs, of which Bath was to be given 15 pages.[55] Draft histories on that scale were compiled by the Misses E. M. Woodcock and Gladys Bradford,[56] the latter a member of a Somerset family and later the wife of Harold Temperley. Another Somerset antiquarian and architect, Roland Paul, served on the general architectural committee of the Victoria History.[57]

In reply to a correspondent in 1919 William Page admitted that the third volume of the Somerset *V.C.H.* would not be published 'just at present' but expressed the hope that the whole enterprise would before long be started 'with renewed vigour'.[58] No further volumes were forthcoming until the model of local authority patronage established in Wiltshire[59] induced leading members of the county archaeological society, some of them also members of Somerset county council, to begin negotiations with London University in the mid 1960s. Since 1967 a resident local editor, usually with one assistant, has continued the work, on a rather more generous scale than was originally planned. Four volumes appeared between 1974 and 1992, comprising the

[51] *V.C.H.* Som. i (1906), p. xiii.
[52] Ibid. p. xxi.
[53] Correspondence, V.C.H. Som.
[54] *V.C.H. Som.* ii (1911).
[55] Correspondence, V.C.H. Som.
[56] Ibid.
[57] *V.C.H. Som.* i, p. ix.
[58] Correspondence, V.C.H. Som.
[59] *V.C.H. Wilts.* vii, editorial note.

histories of 91 parishes, all within the boundaries of the administrative county established in 1974.[60]

While individual scholars, some of them locally based, worked on their contributions to the *Victoria History* at the turn of the century, others continued a tradition of distinguished monographs or answered the calls made earlier for county-wide aids to research. Among the monographs were those of Charles Chadwyck-Healey on six parishes in west Somerset[61] and Sir Henry Maxwell Lyte on Dunster,[62] and rather less scholarly works on, for instance, Minehead and Kilmersdon.[63] Among the long-needed surveys should be mentioned the county bibliography compiled by Emanuel Green,[64] a bibliography of printed maps,[65] a much less comprehensive though at the time useful survey of parochial records[66] and a continuation of the work on Wellington, the first volume published so long ago as 1889.[67] Two other scholars, both deans of Wells and thus in a long tradition of clerical county historians, made significant contributions. J. Armitage Robinson's studies on the sources for the histories of Wells and Glastonbury[68] led to a wider understanding of the critical analysis of texts and thus to a safer chronology for some key areas of Somerset history. Christopher Woodforde's survey of stained glass[69] was the most distinguished of a group of county-wide studies, covering Saxon charters, Members of Parliament, monumental brasses, and sheriffs, most of which were published as articles or supplements by the archaeological society[70] and which marked the society's return to the concerns for county history that some of its leaders had so forcefully advocated a century before.

[60] *V.C.H. Som.* iii (1974), iv (1978), v (1985), vi (1992).

[61] C. E. H. Chadwyck-Healey, *Hist. of Part of West Som.* (1901).

[62] H. C. Maxwell Lyte, *Hist. of Dunster, and Families of Mohun and Luttrell* (2 vols. 1909).

[63] F. Hancock, *Minehead in Som.: Hist. of Parish, Manor, and Port* (1903); The Lord Hylton, *Notes on Hist. of Parish of Kilmersdon* (1910).

[64] E. Green, *Bibliotheca Somersetensis* (3 vols. 1902).

[65] T. Chubb, *Descriptive List of Printed Maps of Som. 1575–1914* (1914).

[66] T. Scott Holmes, *Report to Convocation of Province of Canterbury on Ecclesiastical Records of Diocese of Bath and Wells* (1914); superseded by *Inventory of Parochial Documents in Diocese of Bath and Wells and County of Som.* ed. J. E. King (1938).

[67] A. L. Humphreys, *Materials for Hist. of Town of Wellington* (1889); idem, *Materials for Hist. of Hundred and Parish of Wellington* (4 vols. 1908–14).

[68] J. A. Robinson, *Som. Historical Essays* (1921).

[69] C. Woodforde, *Stained Glass in Som. 1250–1830* (1946).

[70] G. B. Grundy, 'Saxon Charters of Som.' *P.S.A.N.H.S.* lxxiii–lxxx (1927–34); A. B. Connor, 'Monumental Brasses in Som.' ibid. lxxxvii–xcviii (1931–53); S. W. Bates-Harbin, 'Members of Parliament for County of Som.' ibid. lxxviii–lxxxv (1932–9); S. W. Rawlins, 'Sheriffs of Som.' ibid. cvi–cxi (1962–1966/7).

STAFFORDSHIRE

M. W. Greenslade

Staffordshire's first county historian was Sampson Erdeswick of Sandon, writing at the end of the 16th century.[1] He was born probably in the later 1530s, entered Brasenose College, Oxford, in 1553, and was admitted to the Inner Temple in 1555. He was active in running the Sandon estate even before he succeeded his father in 1596. Both were staunch papists and as such were in constant trouble with the civil and ecclesiastical authorities.

Two years before his death in 1603 Sampson designed his own tomb in the chancel of Sandon church, adorning it with coats of arms and the Erdeswick pedigree from 1086. His family pride and keen interest in heraldry found further expression elsewhere in the chancel. On the north and south walls he had two trees painted, hung with his ancestors' shields. More shields were placed in the east window, and to provide extra space he had two false windows painted on the chancel walls and arms inserted there as well. In addition he had the gallery in Sandon Hall decorated with the names and arms of Staffordshire gentry. He claimed to be the real author of *The True Use of Armorie* (1592), allowing it to be published under the name of his research assistant William Wyrley (1565–1618), Rouge Croix Pursuivant from 1604. Erdeswick was in touch with other antiquaries, notably William Camden, and by 1598 was a member of the first Society of Antiquaries. Camden described him as 'a very eminent person and a great proficient in the study of antiquities'.

His history, entitled 'A View of Staffordshire', was begun *c.* 1593 as part of a larger work intended to cover Cheshire as well. By the time of his death the first draft of the Staffordshire section was finished, but little of the Cheshire part had been written. The View was fairly described by Dugdale as 'a brief but elaborate work' compiled 'from public records and ancient evidences'. It is concerned primarily with genealogy and heraldry, but there is much more to the work than family history. Its form is topographical: Erdeswick arranged

[1] This chapter is based, with some corrections, on M. W. Greenslade, *Staffs. Historians* (Collections for a Hist. of Staffs. 4th ser. xi; Staffs. Rec. Soc. 1982), to which the reader is referred for fuller detail and for sources. Grateful acknowledgement is made to my colleague, Mr. D. A. Johnson, for many helpful comments.

his material place by place along rivers, with a start in the north 'at the head
of the famous river Trent'. It was a scheme which followed Camden's
Britannia. Other topographical features are described, and place names are
discussed. Buildings are mentioned, especially manor houses and castles;
churches are noted mainly for their monuments, although there is a succinct
account of the cathedral and close at Lichfield. Towns are only briefly
noticed: for Stafford the account of the Stafford family and its arms
outweighs the notice of town government, the defences, and the two friaries.
Urban life is mainly a matter of markets, though Stone is also 'a thoroughfare
from London into Ireland, Cheshire and Lancashire' and Uttoxeter 'hath
suffered of late great losses by fire'.

A notable innovative feature was the discussion of sources, documentary,
heraldic, monumental, and oral. That in itself is part of the style of the work,
at once learned, informal, and personal. Erdeswick liked a good story and a
bit of gossip. He disliked the parvenu. He was also a conservationist: it was 'a
great pity' that the bishop was doing nothing to restore the rapidly decaying
paintings in the hall of his palace at Lichfield representing 'the coronation,
marriage, wars, and funeral of Edw. I'—their subject known only from
Erdeswick's brief description. He recorded the removal of the copper from
Sir William Caverswall's monument in Caverswall church with the comment
'such is the iniquity of this age'.

Erdeswick had intended to publish when the Cheshire section was finished,
but he died too soon. Many copies of his work were made over the years, and
in 1717 a poor version was published by Edmund Curll. A scholarly edition
appeared in 1820, the work of Thomas Harwood of Lichfield, with a second
edition in 1844.

A history of Staffordshire was planned by Erdeswick's admirer William
Burton, the historian of Leicestershire, who had a home in both counties; he
died at Fauld, his Staffordshire property, in 1645. By 1636 he had, according
to Dugdale, more than half completed a description of Staffordshire and was
waiting only to see Erdeswick's manuscript before carrying on. Nothing more
is known of the work, and his collections were given by his son to another
Staffordshire antiquary, Walter Chetwynd of Ingestre and also of Grendon in
Warwickshire (1633–93). Erdeswick's collections too passed to Chetwynd,
probably through Chetwynd's aunt who married George Digby, Erdeswick's
stepson and successor at Sandon.

Chetwynd was a man of many parts. A bon viveur noted for his hospitality,
his cook, and his fruit gardens, he was active in Staffordshire affairs as a J.P.,
deputy lieutenant, M.P., sheriff, and even government agent in the early
1680s. A polymath, he was elected a fellow of the Royal Society in 1678. His
rebuilding of Ingestre church in the mid 1670s was almost certainly to the
design of Christopher Wren. He was a friend of Dugdale, his neighbour in

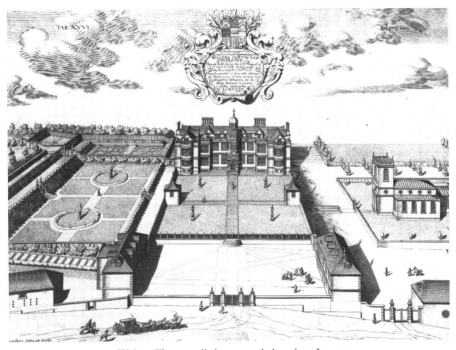

20 Walter Chetwynd's house and church at Ingestre

Warwickshire, and by the early 1660s was working on Staffordshire history. His researches took him into the muniments of the Staffordshire nobility and gentry, the public records, and the libraries of Sir Robert Cotton and Elias Ashmole. He investigated church monuments and windows, transcribed Erdeswick's View, and burrowed into the collections of other local antiquaries. As early as 1664 he wrote an account of Ingestre complete with marginal references. In 1670 he brought the 21-year-old Gregory King from Lichfield to compile a Chetwynd family cartulary in a vellum book, adorned with tricks of seals.

By 1679 Chetwynd was composing 'A Short Survey of Staffordshire'. He continued to work on it in 1680 and added some material in the course of the 1680s. He abandoned it when he had covered only the north-west of the county, but even in its incomplete state it is much longer and more detailed than Erdeswick's View. It is a genealogical account of the manors and churches of the area, generously referenced in the margins from manuscripts and amplified with transcripts of documents in the text. It is very much school of Dugdale, with even more pedigrees than in Dugdale's *Warwickshire*. They are adorned with beautifully drawn coats of arms, evidently the work of

Chetwynd's chaplain Charles King, who also appears to have been the scribe of the fair copy of the Short Survey. The style is drier than Erdeswick's, although Chetwynd's affability comes through with the occasional story.

It is clear from his title and from references in the text that Chetwynd originally intended to cover all the county, and he went on collecting material. In 1690 a new compendium of Chetwynd family deeds was made under the title 'Chetwyndorum Stemma', with tricks of seals and drawings of Ingestre Hall and of the new church and its monuments. In 1692, however, Charles King stated that his master had 'done as much as he designs in the antiquities of this county'. The next year Chetwynd died of smallpox in London. His body was brought to Ingestre and buried in his church.

His work had to wait even longer for publication than Erdeswick's. It was printed in two parts by the William Salt Archaeological Society in 1909 and 1914 with copious notes by the Revd. F. P. Parker. As an edition it leaves something to be desired, even the title being changed to *Collections for a History of Pirehill Hundred*.

Chetwynd also gave much encouragement and help to Robert Plot, the author of *The Natural History of Staffordshire* (1686). The two were kindred spirits, intellectually and convivially. Plot, however, stated that he was first encouraged to turn his attention to Staffordshire by Jane, dowager Lady Gerard, of Gerrard's Bromley, the daughter and heir of Erdeswick's stepson George Digby; she was also Chetwynd's first cousin. Plot was already planning work on Staffordshire in 1675, and he issued a prospectus in 1679, making the first of many visits to the county in July that year.

His book is learnedly and attractively written and has footnotes and an index. Though it is concerned mainly with natural history, two of its ten chapters are devoted to local history; Plot later considered a second edition with considerably more historical material. There are 37 plates, dedicated to the local nobility and gentry who had helped him and including views of their houses. There is also a map embellished with arms keyed to the houses depicted on it. Dated 1682 and published in 1684 in three slightly varying versions, it is on the scale of 2 inches to the mile. It was based on a new survey, in which Gregory King appears to have been involved. It was also the first map of any importance to be engraved by an Englishman, Joseph Browne of Woodchester (Glos.).

Apart from the 1717 edition of Erdeswick, it was over a century before another attempt at a history of Staffordshire appeared in print. In the meantime there were plenty of local antiquaries—gentry, clergymen, professional men—amassing notes and copying and annotating Erdeswick. A full-scale county history eluded them, and most did not aspire to it. One who may have done so was John Huntbach (1639–1705) of Featherstone near Wolverhampton. A nephew of Dugdale's wife, he was also a friend of

Chetwynd. With plans to cover his native Seisdon hundred (south-west Staffordshire) and Cuttlestone hundred to the north, he may have intended to continue where Chetwynd had left off.

The antiquarian who achieved most during the period was Richard Wilkes (1691–1760). Abandoning a Cambridge fellowship and thoughts of a clerical career in his early 30s, he returned to his native Willenhall and built up a county-wide medical practice. His main leisure interest was Staffordshire history, often pursued in conjunction with his professional visits. In the 1730s he compiled an account of British and Romano-British Staffordshire with much topography added. In the 1750s he embarked on a general history of the county to the Norman Conquest followed by a topographical gazetteer. He included economic material as well as genealogy and ecclesiastical history, the whole spiced with his quizzical and down-to-earth approach to life.

His collections passed to a relative, the Revd. Thomas Unett of Stafford, who seems to have planned a history based on them. In 1768 he sold them to Thomas Feilde, vicar of Brewood and master of the grammar school there. That year Feilde had issued a prospectus inviting subscriptions to a proposed history of Staffordshire. Over 40 subscribers came forward, but Feilde abandoned the project in 1770 'through the unhappy situation of my private affairs' and emigrated to Virginia. In 1793 his collections were presented by a relative to a new historian of Staffordshire on condition that the rights of Feilde's subscribers were honoured.

The historian was Stebbing Shaw (1762–1802), a native of Stone whose father became rector of Hartshorne in Derbyshire in 1769. Ordained in 1789, Stebbing returned to Hartshorne in 1791 and succeeded to the rectory on his father's death in 1799. Having already published work on other parts of the country, he embarked on a large-scale history of Staffordshire in 1791. He issued a circular in October, pointing out the repeated expectations which had been raised for a history of the county and the richness of the raw materials, 'almost entirely unpublished'. He also noted that 'in the present enlightened age' family archives were readily available and research was 'facilitated by the wonderful improvement in roads, which renders travelling for personal inspection of places so easy and commodious'. A few months later he produced a prospectus for a history in three volumes with engravings.

For the rest of his life he travelled diligently, searching out sources and making topographical drawings. He also spent much of the year in London where he took a house in Thornhaugh Street near the British Museum. In 1793 he not only acquired Feilde's collections but also bought 13 volumes of the Stafford family's manuscripts and most of the plates engraved for Plot's *Staffordshire*. He also secured access to the Paget family's rich archives at Beaudesert, some of which he was able to borrow. His friend and constant critic Samuel Pipe Wolferstan, the antiquarian squire of Statfold near

Tamworth, recorded how in February 1794 Shaw arrived, having 'filled his pockets with Beaudesert antiques, in great triumph, "such curiosities as Dugdale never saw", etc.' In 1794 Shaw was also in the muniment rooms at Trentham, Swynnerton, Whitmore, and Tixall. In addition he visited industrial sites such as John Wilkinson's ironworks at Bradley near Bilston and Josiah Wedgwood's pottery at Etruria. In 1795 he worked in the Ashmolean Museum in Oxford.

Early in 1796 he started feeding his first volume to his printer, John Nichols of Fleet Street, London. It was published on 8 September 1798. It covered part of Offlow hundred (south-east Staffordshire) and the city of Lichfield. It also included a general history consisting of Wilkes's history up to the Norman Conquest, long extracts from documents illustrating feudal and ecclesiastical history and the Civil War, the text of the Staffordshire portion of Domesday Book reprinted from the 1783 record-type edition, and an account of the county's natural history contributed mainly by other writers including the chemist James Keir. There were numerous engravings, many based on Shaw's own drawings. There was also a map, a half-scale version of William Faden's 1799 edition of William Yates's 1 inch to the mile map of 1775, which Shaw and Pipe Wolferstan had helped to revise. The price of the volume to subscribers was 3 guineas 'common paper' and 4 guineas 'royal paper'; non-subscribers paid an extra 5s. A limited number of 'illuminated' copies, with coloured plates in addition to the other illustrations, were available to subscribers at 10 guineas.

Volume two started to go to press in 1799, but in 1800 Shaw decided to proceed only with part one, covering the rest of Offlow hundred and the whole of Seisdon hundred. It appeared in July 1801. It included Isaac Taylor's 1750 plan of Wolverhampton, and there were again 'illuminated' copies. By the time of Shaw's death in 1802 part of Cuttlestone hundred was in proof.[2]

Doubts had been expressed from the start about Shaw's intellectual and physical adequacy for the work, and in the end his mind gave way. He attributed one of his attacks in 1802 to being 'perplexed' by the History and by 'close attention at the Museum'. Financial worries and adverse criticism deepened his perplexity. Cost and confusion were increased by extensive proof corrections and a large number of pages added at a late stage of printing. The chapter on Bilston in volume two contains the admission that the account of

---

[2] The two volumes of Shaw's *Staffs.* were reprinted in 1976. The reprint includes the coloured drawings in Shaw's 'illuminated' copies as black and white reproductions. Volume one of the reprint has a specially written introduction by M. W. Greenslade and G. C. Baugh. To volume two are added the proofs of Cuttlestone hundred with Shaw's corrections, a brief index printed after the original publication, and a set of plates prepared for the unfinished part of the *Hist.*

the Bradley ironworks supplied by John Wilkinson was 'unfortunately lost for the present'. Lord Bagot's comment in 1833 tersely sums up the general criticism of Shaw's two volumes: 'What he did publish is full of *curious matter*, miserably ill arranged.'

There is truth in such criticism, but it is far from the whole truth. Shaw was the first to attempt a large-scale history of Staffordshire and to publish even part of it. He drew on a much wider range of sources than any previous Staffordshire historian, and he was indefatigable in searching them out. He showed a greater awareness than his predecessors that there is more to local history than genealogy, heraldry, and church monuments. He was also more aware than any of them, except Plot, of the value of illustrations. His harshest critic, James Broughton of Handsacre, admitted that 'Shaw combined with unequalled industry an entire devotion to his task'. It is Staffordshire history's loss that those qualities killed him when his task was only half completed.

Ideas for completing Shaw's work were mooted for many years. Pipe Wolferstan's name was mentioned, but he contented himself with annotating the two published volumes with a view to presenting them to the British Museum. In 1810 he bought Shaw's collections, only to sell them in 1813 to William Hamper, the Birmingham antiquary. In 1821, a year after Pipe Wolferstan's death, his son presented the two annotated volumes to the museum.

Meanwhile the Staffordshire volume in *The Beauties of England and Wales* appeared in 1813; it was written by Joseph Nightingale, a London Unitarian minister who also contributed accounts of Shropshire and Somerset to the series. An even longer work followed in 1817, *A Topographical History of Staffordshire* by the agronomist William Pitt. He was born at Tettenhall in 1749 and published the first of several editions of *General View of the Agriculture of Staffordshire* in 1794. A *History, Gazetteer, and Directory of Staffordshire* was issued in 1834 by William White, a Sheffield printer, with a second edition in 1851. Plot found a successor in Robert Garner (1808–90), a Stoke-upon-Trent doctor who published *The Natural History of the County of Stafford* in 1844. The earlier 19th century also saw several abortive schemes for a county history: James Broughton complained in 1841 that 'scarcely a year elapses but proposals for one are put forth by some empty pretender, without a single requisite for the occupation'.

His strictures were made as part of a correspondence in the *Staffordshire Advertiser*, the county newspaper, discussing the problem of a full-scale county history which, it was claimed, had become too much for a single person to undertake. Concentration on limited areas was one solution proposed, and one that was already being pursued. The earliest Staffordshire example had appeared in 1794, *The History and Antiquities of Shenstone* by

Henry Saunders, assistant curate of Shenstone for 13 years; finished in 1774, it was published after his death by his son. One of the more notable early contributions was *The History and Antiquities of the Church and City of Lichfield* (1806), by Thomas Harwood, headmaster of Lichfield grammar school and perpetual curate of Hammerwich. Many more local works followed, most of them concerned with towns.

In the course of the 19th century local societies began to be formed, likewise focusing on a particular place or area. Burton-upon-Trent claims to have been first in the field: when its Natural History and Archaeological Society was established in 1876 it was stated to be a refoundation of a society established in 1846. Otherwise the honour goes to the North Staffordshire Field Club, founded in 1865 as the North Staffordshire Naturalists' Field Club. From the first it published an annual report which evolved into an annual volume of transactions covering local history and archaeology as well as natural history.

The other solution to the problem of county history propounded in the 1841 correspondence was the creation of a stock of raw material on which historians of particular areas could draw to produce a complete county history on a uniform plan. Such a collection was at that very time being created by William Salt (1808–63), a member of the banking firm of Stevenson, Salt & Co. which had interests in Stafford and London. In 1831 he bought Shaw's collection from Hamper's executors, and he proceeded to add to them, also employing agents to copy Staffordshire items in the manuscripts at the British Museum and in the public records. Already in 1841 Salt's collection, according to Broughton, consisted 'of genealogies, church notes, charters, deeds, visitations, prints, maps, drawings, all printed works relating to the county, Shaw's correspondence, together with his unpublished plates and letter-press'. In 1868 Salt's widow put the collection on sale at Sotheby's but was persuaded to change her mind. She then offered it to the county provided an endowment was raised. In 1872 a house adjoining the family bank in Market Square, Stafford, was acquired as a home for the collection, and in December the William Salt Library Trust was established. In February 1873 a resident librarian was appointed. Staffordshire had what was in effect a county record office 75 years before one was officially established. In 1918 the library moved into a Georgian-fronted house in Eastgate Street, Stafford. When in 1947 the county council established a county record office, it arranged that the post of county archivist should be combined with that of William Salt librarian. The library continues as an independent trust.

The campaign to establish the William Salt Library also produced a scheme for a society to publish Salt's collection. It was put forward in 1870 by Colonel George Wrottesley (1827–1909), described by J. H. Round as the Nestor of genealogists. A younger son of Baron Wrottesley of Wrottesley

21 William Salt

Hall, Tettenhall, he was a member of the committee which established the library. His influence is apparent in its final report in 1872, expressing the hope that the library might 'be the means of giving to Staffordshire a County History unsurpassed in England'. In 1878 Wrottesley was pressing the trustees to organize a set of printed archaeological transactions. Subscribers were secured, and in September 1879 a meeting at the library established the William Salt Archaeological Society with Wrottesley as secretary and *de facto* editor. The society's aim is summarized in the title of its publications, *Collections for a History of Staffordshire*. Wrottesley retired from the army in 1881 with the honorary rank of major-general and devoted the rest of his life to his brainchild as secretary-editor and author. In 1936 the society was renamed the Staffordshire Record Society.

It was fitting that a century of so much activity and publication should also produce a bibliography. In 1883 Rupert Simms (1853–1937), a secondhand bookseller of Newcastle-under-Lyme, began to collect material for his *Bibliotheca Staffordiensis*, published in 1894. Its wide range is indicated by its subtitle: 'a bibliographical account of books and other printed matter relating to—printed or published in—or written by a native, resident, or other person deriving title from—any portion of the County of Stafford'.

The end of the century brought new hope of a large-scale county history with Staffordshire's involvement in the Victoria History of the Counties of England. A local committee was established in 1899, and five volumes were planned, two of general articles, two of parish histories, and one of pedigrees. The first of the general volumes appeared in 1908, but it was then some 40 years before anything further was done.

In 1946 Margaret Midgley, the William Salt librarian and a former assistant to the general editor of the *V.C.H.*, wrote to him asking for facts and figures with a view to resuming work on the Staffordshire volumes. She stated that help was offered by the earl of Shrewsbury and G. P. Mander, the scholarly editor of the Record Society from 1922 to 1946. The general editor's reply mentioned a programme of one general volume and five topographical, a timetable of at least seven years, and the 'formidable' cost of around £9,000. After leaving Staffordshire in 1947 to undertake a survey of ecclesiastical archives for the Pilgrim Trust, Miss Midgley approached Mander about the possibility in due course of a job on a revived Staffordshire V.C.H. Mander set to work, and in 1950 a committee was set up consisting of representatives of the county council, the county boroughs of Burton-upon-Trent, Smethwick, Stoke-upon-Trent, Walsall, West Bromwich, and Wolver-hampton, and London University, along with individual experts. The programme was that put forward by the general editor in 1947, and Miss Midgley was appointed editor, starting work in January 1951.

Staffordshire has shared in the general expansion of local history during the later 20th century. It has had its volume in the many county series. Being the last county to be covered in Sir Nikolaus Pevsner's *Buildings of England*, it has the distinction of possessing the last Building of England, William Butterfield's Old Rectory (1852) at Sheen, where Pevsner completed his series at 10.23 a.m. on Tuesday 6 October 1970.[3] New societies have included the South Staffordshire Archaeological and Historical Society (1957) and the Black Country Society (1967), each of which soon started to publish a journal. In 1984 a new journal, *Staffordshire History*, was launched to publish articles relating to all parts of the county. Keele University has an ever increasing involvement in the local history not only of Staffordshire but of the adjoining parts of Shropshire and Cheshire as well. Many of its ventures are co-ordinated by its Centre for Local History, established in 1978. New repositories of raw material have included a record office at Lichfield opened in 1959 under the joint control of the county, the city, and the diocese, and a county museum at Shugborough opened in 1966. The Staffordshire Victoria History too has shared in the general expansion. In 1972 its committee adopted a plan for 20 volumes, and 10 had been published by 1990. Four of them were general volumes, which go some way towards providing a general history of the county. Until, however, the remaining topographical volumes are completed, Staffordshire will still be awaiting that full-scale history which has eluded it for so long.

In 1993 it seemed that the prospect would recede once more. In spring the Staffordshire V.C.H. committee was faced with a crisis when two of the metropolitan boroughs supporting its work found themselves unable to continue their financial contributions. A solution was found whereby the committee handed over the management of the work to Keele University in partnership with London University, with the staff becoming members of the Keele history department and the county council providing financial support. The new arrangement promises well for the completion of the Staffordshire *History*. Its sponsors could well invoke the words of William Hamper when contemplating a winter journey in 1814 in the cause of Staffordshire history: 'the spirits of Erdeswicke, Burton, and Chetwynd will hover around us and supply an ample protection against the perils of the way.'

---

[3] *The Guardian*, 10 Oct. 1970, p. 8.

SUFFOLK

David Dymond

Of all the counties of England there is possibly none so ill provided with county histories as Suffolk.[1]

Not only does it teem with archaeological sites, listed buildings, and conservation areas, but Suffolk is one of the most historically active counties in England. For example, its county record office is the busiest in the country, and over eighty per cent of its modern parishes have historical recorders. Yet, as Anthony Wagner indicates, it has serious bibliographical disadvantages when compared to its neighbours. It has no major county history published in the 18th or 19th century, to compare with Francis Blomefield's *Norfolk* (1739 and later) and Philip Morant's *Essex* (1768). It has only two introductory volumes from the *Victoria County History*, whereas Cambridgeshire now has an almost complete set of general and topographical volumes. Again, in contrast to Essex and Cambridgeshire, it has received no coverage in inventories of the Royal Commission on Historical Monuments. Nor does it have a modern history in several volumes by different specialists, such as the admirable *History of Lincolnshire*. It does, however, have other categories of history which help to compensate for such deficiencies.

Some writers have always preferred to concentrate on the society in which they themselves were living, in other words to write contemporary history for the benefit of the future, and Suffolk has several examples of that approach.

Robert Reyce wrote his *Breviary of Suffolk* about 1603, and altered and expanded it over the next 30 years; it was eventually published by Lord Francis Hervey in 1902. Although Reyce delved into earlier history his main purpose, inspired by Carew's *Survey of Cornwall* (1602), was to portray Suffolk as it was in his own lifetime. In 'a plaine and familier description of the Country', he gave invaluable comments on Suffolk's landscape, farming, cloth industry, and social distinctions.

Contemporary with Reyce's survey was 'The Chorography of Suffolk', recently reassembled and edited for the Suffolk Records Society by Diarmaid MacCulloch. That survey of individual parishes was written by an unknown

---

[1] A. Wagner, 'Foreword' to J. Corder, *Dictionary of Arms* (Suff. Recs. Soc. vii, 1965).

author, and contains a significant amount of first-hand information mainly on church monuments and inscriptions.

Another widely quoted source is John Kirby's *Suffolk Traveller*, first published in 1735. It was a primitive gazetteer which sometimes made useful comments on, for example, contemporary markets and industries. A second edition of 1764 prepared by Richard Canning was better organized and rather more informative. Another supposed updating by Augustine Page in 1844, subsequently titled *Topographical and Genealogical History of the County of Suffolk*, bore little resemblance to Kirby's book, but gave more detail on manors, churches, and charities. When Norman Scarfe wrote his Shell Guide in 1960 (expanded in 1976), a masterpiece of compact and critical description, he referred to himself as 'The New Suffolk Traveller'.

An outstanding contemporary historian of the 19th century was John Glyde of Ipswich. He had a compassionate yet objective interest in the social and economic problems of his day, and like a true son of the 19th century was fascinated by official statistics. In his *Suffolk in the 19th Century*, published in 1856, he attempted to describe 'the actual condition of Suffolk in 1851' with the aid of 'many important statistical facts' (derived from the census of that year, other official reports, and his own enquiries). He had a burning desire to make statistics speak of the human condition, and dealt with population, family life, crime, poverty, education, farming, and social conditions.

In its unpublished collections Suffolk has fabulous riches, easily comparable in documentary terms to the Mildenhall, Sutton Hoo, and Hoxne treasures, and still largely untapped. Over fifty antiquaries made collections of historical information and materials, and most of them exclusively for Suffolk. Their work was in no sense formal history, and much of it was repetitive and derivative. Nevertheless it could include invaluable contemporary comment, historical evidence which has since been misplaced or destroyed, and many original documents such as charters. It is of course a minefield for the uninitiated, as antiquaries frequently copied the work of their predecessors without acknowledgement, disembowelled books, or chopped up and rearranged the manuscripts of others.[2] Fortunately we have an excellent guide in John Blatchly's *Topographers of Suffolk*, subtitled *Brief Biographies and Specimens of the Hands of Selected Suffolk Antiquaries* (latest edn. 1988).

Only a few examples can be mentioned here. Most collectors specialized in particular subjects or geographical areas; for example Edward Dunthorne, a grocer of Dennington, confined his interests to the hundred of Hoxne, while

---

[2] 'Chorography of Suffolk', written in 1600–5, had been cut up into several hundred fragments, and ended up in at least six different MS. collections: *Chorography of Suff.* ed. D. N. J. MacCulloch (Suff. Recs. Soc. xix, 1976), 1–8.

Thomas Martin of Palgrave (1697–1771) made valuable notes on more than 200 Suffolk churches. Some, however, made collections for the whole county and had dreams of producing some kind of 'history'. Thus Craven Ord (1756–1832) amassed 24 hundredal volumes, regarded as 'Collections for a History of Suffolk'; Henry Jermyn (1767–1820) of Sibton left over 50 volumes of notes, now in the British Museum; W. S. Fitch (1793–1859) compiled 30 bulging scrapbooks on the hundreds of Suffolk and 27 more of illustrations, as 'Materials towards a History of Suffolk'; Edmund Gillingwater (c. 1735–1813) wrote 13 manuscript volumes entitled 'A Topographical History of the County of Suffolk'; and Claude Morley left mountainous typescripts which he called 'Historia Saxonica Suffolciensis' and 'The Medieval History of Suffolk'.

All those examples fade into insignificance when compared to the work of D. E. Davy (1769–1851) of Yoxford and Ufford. His collections were bought by the British Museum in 1852, and include 37 hundredal volumes 'towards a parochial history of Suffolk', 43 volumes of Suffolk pedigrees, 13 volumes of miscellaneous documents and copies, and two volumes called 'A History of the County of Suffolk'. The hundredal volumes are now available on microfilm in the Suffolk Record Office, and so in a sense are a published county history similar in character to the work of Gage and Suckling. They not only contain Davy's own observations based on tireless travelling, but include the transcribed notes of several earlier antiquaries. In 1891–2 R. P. Sanderson of the British Museum wrote 'Of the general collections towards a history of the whole county, none anywhere surpass those of the indefatigable David Elisha Davy.'[3]

Since the early 19th century, three attempts to produce a multi-volumed history of Suffolk have foundered after promising starts. In 1838 John Deck of Bury St. Edmunds published a superlative volume, *The History and Antiquities of Suffolk: Thingoe Hundred* by John Gage of Hengrave Hall. It contains frequent variations of type, family trees, 85 engravings large and small, and numerous footnotes including the sternly patrician *Penes nos*. Gage had an excellent knowledge of sources, particularly the cartularies and registers of Bury abbey, and he frequently included complete transcriptions of, and quotations from, original documents. His book covered only a small hundred, but he hoped to extend the work to the rest of the county. He died, however, in 1842, leaving a large collection of notebooks on Suffolk hundreds which are now in Cambridge University Library. Had his volume of 1838 been the first of a complete series, the development of Suffolk history would surely have been different.

---

[3] I predict that the growing collection of Peter Northeast, with its parish and subject files drawn from a wide range of MS. and printed sources, will ultimately be the most rewarding of all.

In 1846 and 1848 the Revd. Alfred Suckling of Barsham published at his own expense two volumes also entitled *The History and Antiquities of the County of Suffolk*, but this time covering three and a half hundreds in the north-east of the county. He too had intended to cover the whole county but, like Gage, had embarked on the project too late, 'in the days of declining life'.

The two general volumes of the *Victoria County History* appeared for Suffolk in 1907 and 1911, in reverse order. They had been edited by William Page, and included contributions from such eminent writers as George Unwin and J. C. Cox. The sections on religious houses, and on ecclesiastical, industrial, and maritime history, are still of fundamental importance to modern scholars. A county committee had been formed to support the research in 1907: it consisted inevitably of members of the local nobility and gentry, mayors, and leading churchmen, leavened by practising historians such as Edmund Farrer, Claude Morley, and Frederick Warren. Lilian Redstone worked as a 'topographical supervisor' for the *V.C.H.* and actually wrote accounts of 33 parishes in West Suffolk, but none of them ever appeared in print. The impetus of the great work was not maintained beyond the First World War, and the opportunity to revive it with the support of local authorities never arose after 1945.

Suffolk has several one-volumed county histories published in the last hundred years. Canon J. J. Raven of Fressingfield finished his *History of Suffolk* in 1895. He claimed, as befitted a series called Popular County Histories, a commendable 'personal intercourse with all classes'. As in nearly all such books, his coverage began with prehistory, and his purpose was 'the relation of the history of the county to that of the country at large'. In 1930 Lilian Redstone, who later founded the record offices of West and East Suffolk, produced her *Suffolk* in the series known as Borzoi County Histories. It ran to only 96 pages, but was an elegantly written survey of existing knowledge. In similar vein to Raven she justified her study as reducing 'to the sharp outlines of a miniature those great general questions with which the historian is concerned'. The most recent of the genre is *A History of Suffolk* by David Dymond and Peter Northeast (1985) in the Darwen County History Series, which is a heroic attempt, so its authors think, to summarize the huge amount of new research done in the last generation.

In addition to such summary histories, the county has other influential handbooks such as Norman Scarfe's deeply personal *Suffolk Landscape* (1972) and Munro Cautley's irreplaceable *Suffolk Churches and their Treasures* (1937, 1982).

Three widely spaced initiatives in the field of county journals are of fundamental importance. The inaugural meeting of the Bury and West Suffolk Archaeological Institute took place in Bury St. Edmunds in March

1848.[4] The first part of its *Proceedings* was printed in 1849. The organization was widened in 1852 to become the Suffolk Institute of Archaeology and Natural History.[5] Since its foundation, the Institute has published 37 full volumes containing many indispensable articles on most aspects of local archaeology and history. Naturally the balance of subjects within the journal and the backgrounds of contributors have changed over time. For example, volume five (1886) was entirely written by six clergymen!

In 1950 the Suffolk Local History Council was formed, and its journal *The Suffolk Review* first appeared in July 1956.[6] Though always more home-made in character than the *Proceedings*, it has provided a very useful outlet for historians of all kinds. The first volume, for instance, contained articles by George Ewart Evans and George Fussell, both distinguished agricultural historians then resident in the county.

Before the advent of the Suffolk Records Society is discussed, it must be emphasized that transcripts and translations of Suffolk documents had been printed for generations. A fascinating early example was Nathaniel Bacon's *Annalls of Ipswiche*, compiled in 1654 but not published until 1884 (edited by W. H. Richardson). It contained transcripts of court rolls and books, accounts, deeds, and letters, presented chronologically from Norman times to 1649. Bacon's main aim was to dispel ignorance of the laws and customs of the borough. Other good examples are Samuel Tymms's *Wills and Inventories of Bury St. Edmunds* published by the Camden Society in 1850 (frequently quoted in the *O.E.D.*); *Memorials of St. Edmund's Abbey*, edited by Thomas Arnold in three volumes for the Rolls Series, 1890–6; and J. J. Muskett's *Suffolk Manorial Families* (3 vols. 1900–14) which prints many wills, extracts from heraldic visitations, and memorial inscriptions.

Furthermore, some record publications had appeared in serial form. *East Anglian Notes and Queries* (1858–71, edited by Samuel Tymms; second series 1885–1910, edited mainly by C. H. Evelyn-White) largely consisted of transcripts of original documents drawn from Suffolk and surrounding counties. More remarkable still are 22 quarto volumes known as 'Suffolk Green Books', edited by Sydenham Hervey in the period 1894–1915. They contain sources such as parish registers, the subsidy returns of 1327 and 1524, hearth-tax returns of 1674, and the diaries and letters of John Hervey (1665–1751), 1st earl of Bristol.

The Suffolk Records Society was founded in 1958, largely on the initiative

---

[4] Before 1848 there had been a Suffolk Archaeological Association based in Ipswich; it published some *Original Papers* in 1846–8.

[5] In 1954 the Institute dropped the term 'Natural Hist.' from its title, but in 1976 brought back 'Hist.', thus reflecting the changing balance of interests within (and without) its ranks.

[6] Eight duplicated issues preceded vol. i of *Suff. Review* before July 1956.

of Norman Scarfe and Geoffrey Martin, who became its first general editors. The first volume (on Suffolk farming in the 19th century) appeared in the same year, as a memorial to the pioneering work of Lilian and Vincent Redstone. Since then 35 annual publications have appeared, presenting documents ranging over seven centuries.[7] One of the most notable achievements has been the publication in eight volumes of the correspondence and discourses of John Constable. At present, 10 more editions are being prepared, and that will take the society comfortably into the new millenium.

In 1979 the society launched an independent annual series to publish the pre-Reformation charters of Suffolk. That was the initiative of Professor R. Allen Brown, who was general editor until his death in 1989. So far, 12 volumes have appeared dealing with the smaller religious houses, and the series will eventually culminate, in Allen Brown's own words, with 'the ascent of the Everest of Bury'.

In the years 1904–7 W. A. Copinger, assisted by his industrious daughters, produced an extraordinary bibliographical work normally known as *Suffolk Records* (5 vols. besides an index volume). Alphabetically it lists thousands of references to local places, families, and subjects, culled from the calendars, catalogues, and indexes of various collections (including the Public Record Office, British Library, and Bodleian Library)—a treasure trove which immediately makes the historian aware of what exists outside purely local repositories.

In 1970 the Suffolk Local History Council published *Suffolk Local History: A Short Bibliography*, which was prepared by three local archivists then teaching extra-mural classes. Although long out of print, that pamphlet with its critical comments is still a useful introduction to printed works of general significance.

In 1979 a monumental *Suffolk Bibliography* was published as volume 20 of the Suffolk Records Society, prepared by A. V. Steward during 12 years of supposed retirement. It surveys printed works on the county up to the year 1970. Its 8,123 entries, including references to about 2,000 articles in 185 periodicals, are organized by general topics such as economic history and religion, and then by family and locality, on lines similar to the *Norfolk Bibliography* which appeared in 1975 (a rare example of Suffolk following Norfolk). The Suffolk bibliography has obvious value for historians interested in particular places and families, and its more general value has been enhanced by the subsequent production of an index of subjects prepared by Peter Northeast.

In a category of its own is W. A. Copinger's *Manors of Suffolk* (7 vols.

---

[7] Two 'extra' volumes have also appeared: J. Webb, *Great Tooley of Ipswich* (1962) and J. C. Ivy, *Constable and the Critics 1802–37* (1991).

1905–11), which is larger than many multi-volumed histories of other counties. It purported to give a history of every manor in the county, quoting major sources such as Domesday Book and inquisitions *post mortem*. Though notoriously inaccurate, it is still the obvious starting point for anyone wishing to penetrate the manorial world of Suffolk. For the gentry themselves one turns to the distinguished work of Joan Corder: her definitive edition of William Hervy's heraldic visitation of 1561 (Harleian Society new series ii–iii, 1981–4) and her *Dictionary of Suffolk Arms* (1965), for which no other English county has a parallel in print.

Suffolk has many worthy parish and town histories ranging in date from the 18th century to the present, so what follows is only a brief personal selection dwelling mainly on the earliest examples.

An outstanding village history is Sir John Cullum's *History and Antiquities of Hawstead* (1784). Modestly aiming at 'the innocent amusement and happiness' of his readers, Cullum in fact offered a remarkably far-sighted approach to history and contemporary life. For instance, he collected local dialect words, studied local farming, analysed parish registers back to the 16th century (without using the term 'aggregative analysis'), argued that local population had risen in the previous 200 years causing serious overcrowding, and with prescience called for a proper national census.

Three other examples of village histories must suffice. John Gage, previously mentioned for his abortive county history, also wrote *The History and Antiquities of Hengrave* (1822). That sumptuous book is especially noteworthy for quoting the building accounts of Hengrave Hall in the 1520s and 1530s, household accounts from the Elizabethan period, and a detailed inventory of 1603. Sir William Parker's *History of Long Melford* (1873) drew heavily on a wide range of sources (for example, medieval surveys, wills, lists of church goods, and churchwardens' accounts), and was Victorian squirearchical history at its best. F. Barham Zincke in his *Wherstead* (2nd edn. 1893) was certainly self-opinionated and prolix (he had no doubt about 'the torpidity and the benumbing dulness' of medieval life), but he was concerned with 19th-century social problems such as poaching and emigration, and used oral evidence to good effect.

Suffolk has several early histories of towns which repay study. Thomas Gardner wrote his *Historical Account of Dunwich, Blithburgh and Southwold* (1754), which preserved Ralph Agas's famous map, because he was fascinated by nature's destruction of a major port and therefore 'the Instability of sublunary Things'. Edmund Gillingwater wrote factually packed histories of both Lowestoft and Bury St. Edmunds, and argued that local history was useful for preventing future disputes such as the ancient animosity between Yarmouth and Lowestoft. A. G. H. Hollingsworth was one of the more successful town historians of the 19th century; he crammed 32 chapters into his *History of Stowmarket* (1844), based on local archives and diligent reading in the British Museum.

But the most intriguing of the earlier town histories is undoubtedly Robert Loder's *History of Framlingham*. It was published in 1798 but was based on a manuscript history dated 1712 which had been compiled by Robert Hawes, steward of the manor. The book contains a section on the masters and fellows of Pembroke College, Cambridge (from the mid 17th century lords of the manor), which had been begun in the 17th century by Matthew Wren, bishop of Norwich and Ely. Among its transcripts is the important ordinance of 1653 which led to the founding of a workhouse, grammar school, and almshouses.

Traditionally the writing of Suffolk history was dominated by the leisured and professional classes, above all by the clergy. That is why their writings usually concentrated on gentry and clerical families, the descents of manors, heraldry, funerary monuments, and ecclesiastical livings. Nevertheless, after the V.C.H. was created in 1899, academics (particularly academic women) began to open up new areas in a more scholarly way. For example, Beatrice Lees made a translation of the Suffolk Domesday which is still the best available;[8] Gladys Thornton on the basis of a Ph.D. thesis wrote her *History of Clare* (1928), which still provides an excellent introduction to the Suffolk cloth trade; and Mary Lobel, formerly a research student at Girton College, Cambridge, made a masterly analysis of medieval borough government and political tensions in her *Borough of Bury St. Edmunds* (1935).

Since the Second World War the study of local history has boomed, stimulated principally by the proliferation of local societies (now over fifty, large and small), the widespread provision of adult courses led by extra-mural departments and the W.E.A., and the creation of a first-class record office. At the same time books, pamphlets, and journals have poured from the press, some of them admittedly of a poor standard but others enshrining invaluable work on local parishes and towns. For instance, nobody interested in the Breckland can ignore the work of John Munday: over some fifteen years he produced large numbers of duplicated leaflets on a host of subjects connected with Eriswell and surrounding parishes. Similarly Peter May wrote two penetrating studies of the frontier town of Newmarket, from the late 12th century when it emerged as a commercial speculation in a corner of Exning parish, until the 18th century when under royal patronage it had become a major centre of horse-racing and training.[9]

Two county-wide books recently published by the county council may turn out to be influential. The first, compiled by Wendy Goult, is *A Survey of*

---

[8] *V.C.H. Suff.* i. 357–582.

[9] Interestingly Peter May and John Munday were both clergymen of a scholarly type now almost extinct.

Suffolk Parish History (1990). In three volumes it covers every parish in the county, giving basic information under headings like Farming, Church, Occupations, and Recreations, drawn mainly from basic printed sources. The main purpose is to give students a starting-point for their own investigations, and to stress the importance of making local history comparative. The second is *An Historical Atlas of Suffolk*, edited by David Dymond and Edward Martin (1988), in which nearly thirty contributors prepared 62 distribution maps and short explanatory texts on a wide variety of topics ranging from geology and prehistory to the distribution of modern population and 20th-century cinemas.

The academic contribution to county and local history is getting stronger by the year. That is not simply because more national historians are 'looking in', as they always have, to focus on local examples. The main cause lies in the nature of postgraduate research, which may be officially classified as some form of general history (for example, political, economic, or religious) but is frequently focused on local societies and communities, often exploiting major local archives. In fact it is local history in all but name.[10]

Suffolk's classic example is Diarmaid MacCulloch's widely acclaimed *Suffolk and the Tudors* (1986), which is based on an earlier thesis and explores the political and religious life of the county in a turbulent period. Understandably MacCulloch did not aim at 'total' history, for he says little about farming, industry, poverty, and other major themes; his main emphasis is on the government of the county, with particular reference to the leading gentry, and on the struggle between different religious groups. We now need other volumes of its calibre, dealing with the county at other periods and of course stressing links with regional and national history: that would be the best way of achieving a modern version of the multi-volumed county history which Suffolk has always lacked.[11]

---

[10] Suffolk has no university, but is within the obvious influence of the universities of Cambridge, Essex, and East Anglia in the three neighbouring counties.

[11] In writing this chapter I received valuable help from others. Though unwell my wife Mary nobly combed a wide range of books, and four friends gave generous advice: John Blatchly, Peter Northeast, Clive Paine, and Norman Scarfe. I, however, must be held responsible for the opinions expressed and final choices made.

SURREY

Beryl Board

Four major histories of the county of Surrey were prepared and published between 1672 and 1912, and parts of it were treated in histories of London. This chapter is concerned mainly with the four county histories.

In the mid 17th century William Camden's *Britannia* (1586) remained the model for the topographical writer, but it was a new *Britannia*, planned by John Ogilby, that engendered the first history devoted solely to the county. Ogilby, appointed king's cosmographer, intended to publish his *Britannia* in three volumes, the third to be a topographical and historical description.[1] The maps for the first volume were well advanced in the early 1670s when John Aubrey was drawn into the venture, on the recommendation of his friend Christopher Wren, to undertake the topographical descriptions.[2] It is probable that the meetings Ogilby had with Wren, John Hoskyns, Robert Hooke, Gregory King, and Aubrey to consider his printed questionnaire took place at that time.[3] Aubrey had completed a history of Wiltshire, his native county, but, being pursued by creditors, was in dire need of paid employment, and the work as he said 'suited his genius'. Accustomed to 'taking notes of Antiquity and, having a quick draught', drawing 'landskips on horse-back symbolically', he was prepared to 'scurry all over England and Wales for Ogilby'.[4]

In July 1672 he set out from London on his first task, the perambulation of Surrey, bearing an impressive commission from Ogilby. By mid September, after 'the pleasantest pilgrimage that any man has had since the Reformation', Aubrey returned to London with 'a great swab of papers' which would 'make a pretty piece'. He intended to complete his work along the south bank of the Thames in another week or two. When he returned from Richmond he found that Ogilby had changed his mind about the third volume and would not use Aubrey any more, but 'get what scraps he could out of books and by hearsay and not write more than four or five leaves of any county'.[5] Aubrey, who had

---

[1] *D.N.B.*; J. Ogilby, *Britannia* (1675), i, title page.
[2] *Aubrey's Brief Lives*, ed. O. L. Dick (1949), 67.
[3] A. Powell, *John Aubrey and his Friends* (1988 edn.), 152.
[4] *Aubrey's Brief Lives*, ed. Dick, 65, 67.
[5] J. Aubrey, *Natural Hist. and Antiquities of Surr.* (facsimile edn. 1975), i, p. v.

looked forward to further work in Berkshire and Sussex, was disappointed
and out of pocket.

There is no evidence that Ogilby's decision was based on a poor opinion of
Aubrey's work. William Dugdale and Elias Ashmole said that if Ogilby did
not use Aubrey's notes his book would be a 'bauble'; when John Evelyn read
them in the winter of 1675–6 he commended Aubrey's industry, judgement,
and accuracy, although he noted that several places were left out. Ogilby died
in 1676 and his third volume was never published. In 1691 Anthony Wood,
who had borrowed the notes, exhorted Aubrey to transcribe and preserve
them. Aubrey, regretting that he had not done so earlier, visited those places
Evelyn had noted, including Southwark, which he had intended to leave out
because John Stow had published a full account of it. He did not, however,
want the trouble of another transcription. He wrote that his notes were 'set
down tumultuarily, as though tumbled out of a sack, as they came to my hand,
mixing Antiquities and Natural Things as I have done them', an echo of
Evelyn's postscript to the contributions he sent to Aubrey in 1676, 'I have set
things down tumultuarily as they came into my sudden thoughts'.[6]

When Aubrey died in 1697 he had already given the Surrey manuscript
with other books and papers to the Ashmolean Museum, where they were
seen in 1714 by Richard Rawlinson, who was associated with the publisher
Edmund Curll in issuing a series of county and cathedral histories, based on
the work of earlier antiquaries.[7] Rawlinson began to revise Aubrey's work,
using the Ashmolean manuscript and another from a private collection, 'both
in a very confused and immethodical order'. He recruited local help using a
printed questionnaire and in 1717 made a perambulation with his brother
Thomas and Curll. Aubrey's work, revised and brought up to date by
Rawlinson, was published in 1718 as *The Natural History and Antiquities of
Surrey Begun the Year 1673 by John Aubrey and Continued to the Present Time*,
in five octavo volumes. The first volume was arranged in the order of
Aubrey's notes, but thereafter Rawlinson grouped them by their hundreds.
The change of plan caused discrepancies and some duplication.
Rearrangement and correction of Aubrey's notes and insertion of new
material was a complicated editorial task. Rawlinson added material from
local informants, from his own fieldwork, and from published works. He
claimed to have reproduced most of Aubrey's work, but failed to indicate his
own interpolations, so that dating of information is difficult.[8] His misreading
of a cross reference as a parish heading, which led him to site Dorney House

[6] Ibid. i, Aubrey's note to the reader and Evelyn's letter.
[7] B. Enright, 'Richard Rawlinson and Publication of Aubrey's *Natural Hist.*' *Surr. Arch.
Collections*, liv. 124–33.
[8] Ibid.

in Byfleet instead of in Weybridge, may not be an isolated editorial error.[9] He did not include Aubrey's sketches and maps, which may have suited the octavo format better than the illustrations he chose. There is nothing in Rawlinson's edition to justify Richard Gough's supposition that 'the confined and scanty materials Aubrey left make it probable that he made very little progress in Ogilby's plan'.[10]

The value of Aubrey's work lies in his careful observation of the places he visited and in his diligent transcription of epitaphs, many of which were destroyed in the next century. His notes were enlivened by anecdotes, 'curious' matters, and oral traditions. It is likely that he would have accepted many of Rawlinson's amendments; in 1680, in appealing to Richard Blackbourne for advice on a draft of his *Life of Mr. Thomas Hobbes of Malmesburie*, he wrote, 'Pray be my Aristarchus, and correct and marke what you think fitt. First draughts ought to be rude as those of paynters, for he that in his first essay will be curious in refining will certainly be unhappy in invention'.[11] William Bray, who studied Aubrey's and Rawlinson's manuscripts in the Bodleian Library when he was preparing his own county history in the early 19th century, regarded Aubrey as the father of that work.[12] Some antiquities overlooked by Aubrey and Rawlinson were treated by Nathaniel Salmon in his *Antiquities of Surrey* (1736).[13] No rival edition of Aubrey's perambulation has been published and Rawlinson's edition was reissued in facsimile in 1975, with an introduction by J. L. Nevinson.

Richard Gough reviewed the published works and unpublished collections relating to Surrey in his *British Topography* in 1780.[14] He consulted local antiquaries, presumably Owen Manning among them, when he contributed to an edition of Camden's *Britannia* in 1789.[15]

Historians of London, following John Stow, usually included the borough of Southwark in their works.[16] Daniel Lysons, a young curate in Mortlake and Putney, turned his attention to the farther environs of London, beginning in 1790 to study 28 Surrey parishes which lay within *c.* 12 miles of Westminster bridge, for the first volume of his *Environs of London* (1792). He visited every place, noting evidence of epidemics, longevity, and population trends in parish records. His use of baptismal and burial registers in estimating

[9] L. R. Stevens, 'Error in County Histories', *Surr. Arch. Collections*, xlix. 124–5, plate xiv.
[10] [R. Gough], *British Topography* (2 vols. 1780), ii. 262.
[11] *Aubrey's Brief Lives*, ed. Dick, 178–9.
[12] O. Manning and W. Bray, *Hist. and Antiquities of Surr.* (3 vols. 1804–14), ii, p. iv.
[13] Ibid. iii. 686.
[14] [Gough], *British Topography*, ii. 261–84.
[15] *D.N.B.*
[16] Manning and Bray, *Hist. of Surr.* iii. 687–9.

22 Richard Gough

population is noteworthy.[17] His attention to buildings, gardens, and occasional 'curious' and 'superstitious' matters, recalls Aubrey's *Surrey*, to which Lysons referred frequently.[18] Lysons, like Aubrey, copied epitaphs; he included also extracts from borough and parish records.[19] The text was arranged alphabetically by parish, with an appendix containing the account of Bermondsey, and additional information, mainly from escheat bundles.[20] A second edition was published in 1811 and a supplement to the first edition, with important additions and corrections, in the same year.[21]

Lysons seems to have been unaware of the Surrey collections of Owen Manning and William Bray when he wrote his *Environs*, although he acknowledged information received from Bray as treasurer of Henry Smith's

[17] e.g. D. Lysons, *Environs of London*, i (1792), 80–1, 571–2.
[18] Ibid. i. 5–7, 27–8, 309–14, 329, 365.
[19] Ibid. i. 98–100, 113–17, 223–35.
[20] Ibid. i, pp. xi–xii, 541–72.
[21] *D.N.B.*

charity.[22] Manning had been collecting material for a county history since he became vicar of Godalming in 1763. William Bray, lawyer and descendant of a family long settled at Shere in Surrey, started his collection at about the same time. Bray had been appointed to the Board of Green Cloth, a judicial institution of the royal household, and acquired a house in Great Russell Street, from which he conducted his London practice.[23] The association of the two men, which culminated in one of the best county histories of its period, began in 1767 when Manning replied to an enquiry from Bray, written three months earlier, about his plans for a county history. In reply Manning invited Bray to assist him, instead of co-operating with 'Mr. H.', as Bray proposed to do.[24] From that time the two men corresponded, especially on matters of manorial history.[25] Bray's legal practice made him familiar with estate business and his residence in Bloomsbury gave him ready access to London record repositories. In 1772 Bray was admitted to the Society of Antiquaries and contributed frequently to *Archaeologia* on a range of subjects.[26] Until 1772 Manning was occupied in completing Lye's Saxon dictionary[27] and unable to fulfil the hope, expressed in 1767, of proceeding as fast as possible with his history.[28] His study of the Surrey entries in Domesday Book were complete by 1773, however, and he intended to publish a facsimile in his history. In 1779 he wrote of employing a person to list incumbents of the nine peculiars in the county from the archbishops' registers. He was also working on Bray's forebears at Shere, trying to identify Lady Magdalen Bray and to decide whether Mary, wife of Edward Bray, was an Elrington or a Cotton.[29]

The completion of Manning's history was awaited with high expectation, but his eyesight failed and when he died in 1801 little more than his preface was ready for printing. Richard Gough, in his old age, declined to take up the work and it was William Bray who then undertook to edit and publish it for the benefit of Manning's widow and children. The task of digesting Manning's notes and completing the documentary and topographical work occupied much of Bray's time in the following years, and in addition to his professional work he was in 1803 elected treasurer of the Society of Antiquaries.[30] He discussed the Surrey history with Gough and Lysons,

---

[22] Lysons, *Environs*, i. 513.
[23] Manning and Bray, *Hist. of Surr.* (facsimile edn. 1974), i, p. vi; Surr. R.O. 85/1, *passim*; 'Extracts from Diary of William Bray', *Surr. Arch. Collections*, xlvi. 26–58.
[24] Fitzwilliam Museum, Cambridge, Ashcombe collection II. 104. Mr. H. remains unidentified.
[25] Surr. R.O. 85/3/4 (19–21).
[26] *Index to Archaeologia, Vols. I–L* (1889), s.v. Bray.
[27] *D.N.B.*; Surr. R.O. 85/3/4 (19).
[28] Fitzwilliam Museum, Ashcombe collection, II. 104.
[29] Surr. R.O. 85/3/4 (21).
[30] Ibid. 85/3/4; J. Evans, *Hist. of Soc. of Antiq.* (1956), 221, 243.

continued to collect material to fill gaps in Manning's research, and visited
churches throughout the county, always leaving a donation in the church
box.[31] Bray kept a list of sources he used, which survived with his collection
of sale particulars and answers to his enquiries.[32]

In 1804 the first volume of *The History and Antiquities of Surrey* was issued
and contained Manning's long-awaited facsimile of the Surrey entries in
Domesday Book. The parish histories, in hundredal order, comprised
topography, extracts from Domesday Book with a commentary, manorial
descents, pedigrees, the church and living, monumental inscriptions, patrons
and incumbents to 1786, the returns of overseers and charity trustees of 1786,
and population returns from the 1801 census. In the first volume Bray
meticulously marked his own frequent additions and occasional amendments
with 'hooks and asterisks'. He amended the statement in Manning's preface
that 'bounds of parishes are generally . . . commensurate with, and
correspond to, those of one or more manors' with the note 'It has been
observed that this is by no means the case in this county'. In his preface to the
second volume, issued in 1809, Bray called the work 'an historical dictionary'
and, with justification, claimed the qualifications required of its editor:
industry in searching for records and papers, patience in examining them, and
accuracy in extracting them. He defended the inclusion of epitaphs, not only
because Dugdale and Gough approved of them, but because they could
clarify a descent or confirm possession. Publication of the second volume was
delayed until 1809 because 'Mr. Manning's very extensive collection consisted
in notes, put down as they occurred . . . reference to original records was
necessary in many instances; in many a search after others was indispensable'.
Bray lamented the death in February 1809 of Richard Gough, on whose
guidance he had relied.[33] Bray would walk from Bloomsbury, take the coach to
Edmonton, and from there walk to Gough's house at Enfield to discuss the
Surrey project.[34] The third volume, issued in 1814, completed the parish
histories. Appendices listed Acts of Parliament relating to the county, county
rates, gaols, roads, bridges, canals, railways, tradesmen's tokens issued in the
17th century, a continuation of the list of sheriffs to 1814, and the 1811 abstract
of population. Specialists contributed sections on entomology, botany, peat,
fossils, and mineralogy. In one respect only were subscribers disappointed:
the illustrations were dull. In 1819 engravings of 47 Surrey churches by James
Peak, which Bray had dismissed as 'badly executed',[35] were published as *The*

---

[31] Surr. R.O. 85/1/43–6.
[32] Ibid. 85/2/1, 85/2/6, 85/2/8, 85/41/1, 85/3/4 (13).
[33] Manning and Bray, *Hist. of Surr.* ii, p. iv.
[34] Surr. R.O. 85/1/44, 3 Aug. 1802.
[35] Manning and Bray, *Hist of Surr.* iii. 687.

Ecclesiastical Topography of Surrey, and in 1847 Richard Percival completed an illustrated edition of Manning and Bray's *History*, enlarging it with over 6,000 prints and drawings, to 30 volumes.[36] In 1974 a facsimile edition of the original three-volume *History* was issued in collaboration with Surrey County Library, with an introduction by Professor Jack Simmons.

Bray left the Board of Green Cloth in 1810, but he was treasurer of the Society of Antiquaries until 1823.[37] His sight began to fail and from 1828 he could no longer read, but in 1832, at the age of 96, when he was cared for by his daughters and 'seldom left the fireside', he wrote in his own hand to congratulate a former client, Christopher Tower of South Weald (Essex), on the successful outcome of a long legal dispute about Brentwood free school.[38]

Edward Wedlake Brayley (1773–1854),[39] who produced his *Topographical History of Surrey* between 1841 and 1848, had gained his experience of writing topographical works in association with John Britton. Brayley used the works of his predecessors, studying them in detail, as is apparent from the zeal with which he noted their errors, but his *History* was not merely a new edition of Manning and Bray's. To him local history was interesting and important for its connexion with national history and its contribution to the advance of archaeology, geology, agriculture, botany, and other useful sciences. He was interested not only in the past but also in the present.[40] His *History* was first issued in parts and collected in four illustrated volumes in 1850, with a geological section by Gideon Mantell (1790–1852). It was promoted by Robert Best Ede, printer and bookseller of Dorking, who recruited subscribers by offering to insert their armorial bearings in the *History*. Volumes were dedicated successively to Queen Victoria and members of the aristocracy connected with the county. Brayley's lists of 'pleasant villas and cottage residences of a superior class' that had been built in Guildford, Chertsey, and Egham probably helped to elicit subscriptions from the 'gentlemen of respectability and comparative affluence' who lived in them.[41]

The scope and arrangement of Brayley's *History* resembled that of his predecessors, but it had many illustrations, extensive footnotes, and many addenda. The illustrations were mainly of buildings, reflecting the interest of Thomas Allom (1804–72), architect,[42] to whom Brayley entrusted their selection. Many of the engravings were commissioned for the *History* and donated by owners of the buildings they depict. A double-spread map of the

[36] Ibid.; *D.N.B.* s.v. Bray.
[37] Surr. R.O. 85/1/53; Evans, *Hist. of Soc. of Antiq.* 243.
[38] Essex R.O., D/DBg 48/19.
[39] *D.N.B.*; J. Todd, 'Edward Brayley: Surr. Historian', *Surr. Life*, ii (6).
[40] Brayley, *Hist. of Surr.* i, p. 1.
[41] Ibid. i. 400; ii. 220, 273.
[42] *D.N.B.*

river Mole shows elevations of buildings and details of bridges, and the initial letters of chapter headings were decorated with miniature scenes.[43] Initial publication in parts may account for the attachment of addenda at the end of many sections. The main account of the building of Kingston New Town, where there had been built 'about 160 houses, including many detached and coupled villas (stuccoed) in a somewhat capricious style of architecture', ended with the possession by the mortgagees. The later revival of the scheme, to form the neighbourhood of Surbiton, was reported in addenda.[44] Brayley not only inserted addenda but used footnotes also for new information, as well as for transcripts, anecdotes, and opinions. His notes include a list of owners of pews, an account of the cultivation of cedar of Lebanon and of a weeping willow transplanted from the Euphrates, a list of organ stops, an illustrated description of a drainage pipe 'laid down in Wolsey's time', entries from parish registers, an anecdote about a footpad, and a comment that Barbara Villiers was 'the most rapacious of all the king's mistresses'.[45] The notes and addenda reveal the extent of Brayley's assiduous research in many sources and his reluctance to abandon material that could not be inserted in the text, as he strove to bring his drafts up to date at the time of printing. Britton tells how, when pressed by the printer, Brayley 'continued to write 14 to 16 hours with a wet handkerchief round his throbbing head'.[46]

The authors and editors of the histories of Surrey had all drawn on the work of their contemporaries, but none had been based on the principle of co-operative research and writing as was the *Victoria County History*, founded in 1899. In December of that year it seemed that Montague Giuseppi and H. E. Malden would jointly, for a shared fee of £500, compile the topographical history of the parishes and manors of Surrey.[47] Giuseppi seems to have withdrawn from the topographical work, contributing only a section on industry, and Malden became the local editor.

Henry Elliott Malden was the son of Henry Malden, professor of Greek at University College, London, whose family had settled in Putney.[48] At the celebration of the Domesday Book octingentenary in 1886, H. E. Malden contributed a paper on the Surrey entries and he transcribed and annotated the Cely papers in the Camden series for the Royal Historical Society.[49] Under J. H. Round's supervision he contributed the text of Surrey Domesday

[43] Brayley, *Hist. of Surr.* i. 170–1.

[44] Ibid. iii. 52, 167–8.

[45] Ibid. i. 10; ii. 72; iii. 54–6, 440–1, 443.

[46] J. Britton, *Brief Memoir of Edward Wedlake Brayley* (1855).

[47] V.C.H. recs., A 55.

[48] *D.N.B.*

[49] A. T. Milne, *Centenary Guide to Publications of Royal Hist. Soc.* (Royal Hist. Soc. Guides and Handbooks ix, 1968), 51, 138–9.

for the first volume of *V.C.H. Surrey*. He wrote the general descriptions for parish histories and superintended, with William Page, manorial descents prepared by Page's staff of women graduates. He wrote the specialist sections on ecclesiastical, military, social and economic, and political history.[50] The latter was commended by the *Times Literary Supplement* as a model for his colleagues in other counties.[51] Malden was, however, one of those editors said, without further explanation, to have been tried and found wanting.[52] Page, in correspondence with Malden, commented on slackness in not following a manorial descent beyond 1822, the omission of a charity, and the inadequacy of a contributor's draft.[53]

Whatever the failings of the local editor, Page's editorial ability, his training of staff, and recruitment of specialist contributors ensured that *V.C.H. Surrey*, published in four volumes between 1904 and 1912, with an index volume in 1914, was a modern, scholarly history. Surrey, largely isolated by tracts of forest and marsh, was shown to have had an ancient life of its own. Professor F. Haverfield applied reason to the search for the site of Noviomagus, the 'lost' Roman town that had teased earlier historians, suggesting sites of not one, but four 'new towns' in southern England. The county had no bishop of its own, no great town, and no seat of a Norman baron. Guildford was said to be indebted for what importance it possessed to its position in a gap in the chalk uplands, while Southwark in the north was drawn into the suburbs of London. The political arrangements of the 19th century went far to destroy the individuality of the county.[54] It was against that background that the topographical volumes painstakingly treat manorial descents, borough history, and buildings. The architectural emphasis of the text extends to the illustrations. Matters such as natural, military, political, and ecclesiastical history, sport, industries, and schools, scantily treated in or omitted from earlier histories, were concentrated in specialist sections of the general volumes.

None of the major histories that followed Aubrey's perambulation superseded its predecessors entirely. Their contemporary evidence, their variation in style and intent, and even the idiosyncrasies of their authors and editors compel the modern student of local history to study them all. It would be wise to consult the *V.C.H.* in cases where its predecessors disagreed, in the hope of finding a conclusion based on the additional sources that were searched under its methodical system.

[50] *V.C.H. General Introduction*.
[51] *Times Literary Supplement*, 1 Aug. 1902, p. 228.
[52] *V.C.H. General Introduction*, 8.
[53] V.C.H. recs., A 55.
[54] *V.C.H. Surr*. i. 275, 431; iv. 347–9.

The availability of the county histories and the interest they aroused stimulated societies devoted to discussion and research. Many local history societies have been founded within the present county and the London boroughs that absorbed its metropolitan fringe. The oldest survivor is the Surrey Archaeological Society, founded in 1854, which publishes *Surrey Archaeological Collections* and a *Bulletin*. It also maintains a library, a collection of objects and archives, and a programme of landscape survey and excavation. A group of the society, specializing in industrial history, was formed *c.* 1975. Croydon Natural History and Scientific Society, founded in 1877, publishes *Proceedings* (formerly *Transactions*), mainly on archaeology. The Wimbledon Society, formerly the John Evelyn Club, was founded in 1903. It maintains a museum and library and produces occasional publications. The Surrey Parish Register Society, founded in 1903, produced transcripts of registers, and the Surrey Record Society, founded in 1913, produced a series of transcripts of many other archives, sometimes in association with Surrey county council.[55]

No comprehensive bibliography of the county has been published. Standard reference works include sections on Surrey[56] and there are published catalogues of the Minet library of manuscript and printed sources, collected in the late 19th century and preserved in Lambeth Archives Department.[57] Surrey County Library issued an annual *Current Bibliography of Surrey* from 1976 to 1982.[58] *The Story of Surrey in Maps*, the catalogue of an exhibition assembled by the Surrey branch of the Royal Institution of Chartered Surveyors in 1956, provides a useful annotated list. A modern bibliography of the county is needed to provide an essential key to the many books and articles written since the publication of the last county history.

[55] A. W. G. Lowther, 'Brief Hist. of Soc.' *Surr. Arch. Collections*, liii. 1–34; E. L. C. Mullins, *Guide to Hist. and Arch. Publications of Socs.* (1968), pp. 102, 423–7; P. Marcan, *Greater London Local Hist. Directory and Bibliography* (1988); publicity leaflets.
[56] e.g. A. L. Humphreys, *Handbook to County Bibliography* (1917); T. Besterman, *World Bibliography of Bibliographies* (1965–6 edn.); *Bibliography of Hist. Works Issued in U.K.* (1957 and later edns.).
[57] *V.C.H. Surr.* iv. 25; *Catalogues of Collection* (1901, 1910); *Index to Catalogue of Deeds in Library* (1914); inf. from Lambeth Archives Department.
[58] Inf. from Surr. County Library.

SUSSEX

T. P. Hudson

Despite its closeness to London, Sussex was late in attracting serious interest in its history and antiquities.[1] John Leland's mid 16th-century *Itinerary*, for instance, says little beyond a few remarks about Petworth.[2] A rare early visitor with antiquarian interests was Lieut. Hammond, who in 1635 passed through on a tour of the southern and western counties.[3] Later tourists were often deterred by the county's notoriously poor communications; those who did come rarely strayed from a few standard routes which took in Tunbridge Wells, Rye, Lewes, Brighton, Arundel, Petworth, and Chichester.[4]

William Camden's short description of Sussex in *Britannia* (1586), translated into English in 1610, was to be the basis of its published history for more than two centuries, both in amplified editions such as that of Richard Gough (1789) and in the work of others, notably Thomas Cox's *Magna Britannia* of 1730. A 'chorographical description' or gazetteer, intended by John Norden to accompany his map of the county of 1595, remained in manuscript and virtually unknown until the 20th century.[5]

The first to investigate Sussex's history in more detail were two lawyers, representatives of a group often to be involved with the subject because of their access to and familiarity with documents. John Rowe (*c.* 1560–1639), who trained in Lewes, rose to be principal of Clifford's Inn; in connexion with his work as steward to Lord Abergavenny he collected details of manorial rights and customs in Lewes rape both for administrative purposes and out of antiquarian interest.[6] Meanwhile John Smith or Smyth (1567–1641) of Nibley, steward to the Berkeleys of Berkeley castle (Glos.), compiled in 1637 a manuscript history of their manor of Bosham, which he addressed to the 10-year-old George Berkeley with the aim of encouraging pride in his inheritance

[1] Thanks are due to the following for commenting on a draft of this chapter and making valuable suggestions: Colin Brent, John Farrant, Kim Leslie, Tim and Alison McCann, and Christopher Whittick.
[2] *Suss. Arch. Collections*, cxvi. 275.
[3] *Camden Miscellany*, xvi (Camden 3rd ser. lii).
[4] Cf. *Suss. Arch. Collections*, cxvi. 275.
[5] Ibid. 269–74.
[6] Ibid. xxiv. 85–98; *Suss. Rec. Soc.* xxxiv, pp. vii–ix.

and a resolution to maintain it. Though never published, like much of Smith's other historical work, it shows an astonishingly modern use of medieval sources, with numerous references occupying the wide margins of the manuscript.[7]

At the end of the 17th century William Petyt (d. 1707), keeper of records in the Tower of London, collected Sussex references from the medieval rolls in his care, apparently purely for antiquarian use; at his death he left them to the Inner Temple library for the benefit of later antiquaries,[8] the first such gift to a public repository for that purpose. In the 18th century another Sussex attorney, John Elliot (1725–82), made a similar collection, now divided between Eastbourne public library, the library of the Sussex Archaeological Society, and the East Sussex Record Office.[9] Serious study of field antiquities, on the other hand, had to wait until the early 19th century and the activities of Samuel Lysons and the Revd. James Douglas; it was continued more systematically after *c.* 1865 in excavations and fieldwork by the father of modern archaeology, General Pitt-Rivers, and his followers, notably H. S. Toms, curator of Brighton museum, and the Hove doctor E. Cecil Curwen.[10]

The 18th century also saw two abortive attempts to compile for publication a great history on the lines of Dugdale's *Warwickshire*. William Hayley, rector of Brightling (d. 1789), made voluminous extracts relating chiefly to eastern Sussex from books and from manuscripts both public and private, including Domesday Book, the Battle abbey register, and parish registers.[11] A plan of his projected work shows a tripartite division, the first book dealing with 'general' history, natural history, and among other things 'manufactures', the second with church history, and the third with individual places.[12]

Hayley's friend Sir William Burrell, Bt. (1732–96), embraced the same idea.[13] Though belonging to a Sussex family based in the West Grinstead and Cuckfield areas Burrell, a London civil lawyer, never himself lived in the county, retiring to the Deepdene near Dorking (Surr.). Starting with manuscript additions to his copy of Cox, he methodically extracted Sussex references from the national archives, from parish registers, and manor court rolls, and transcribed deeds in private hands; his transcripts, unfortunately,

[7] *D.N.B.*; West Suss. R.O. [hereafter W.S.R.O.], Bosham Manor MSS. (Acc. 939), III/14.

[8] *Suss. Arch. Collections*, xxiii. 320; J. Dallaway, *Hist. of Western Division of Suss.* i (1815), p. iv; J. B. Williamson, *Hist. of the Temple, London* (1925), 649.

[9] *Suss. Arch. Collections*, cxii. 44; cxxiii. 268–70.

[10] *Suss. Arch. Soc. Newsletter*, xli. 353–5.

[11] Dallaway, *Hist. of Western Suss.* i, pp. iv–v; B.L. Add. MSS. 6343–61.

[12] B.L. Add. MS. 6355, ff. 13–15.

[13] Account of Burrell based mainly on *D.N.B.*; *Suss. Views*, ed. W. H. Godfrey and L. F. Salzman (Suss. Rec. Soc. Jubilee vol. 1951), pp. viii–xi; Dallaway, *Hist. of Western Suss.* i, pp. i–iv; *Suss. Arch. Collections*, xxiii. 319.

were not always accurate. Burrell also had 'the helpful, if reprehensible, habit' of initialling documents he had seen.[14]

In pursuit of evidence from buildings and other physical remains, Burrell himself visited nearly every parish in the county, inspecting and making notes on churches, their monuments, and other fittings; he also commissioned three draughtsmen, Samuel Hieronymus Grimm and the two James Lamberts, uncle and nephew, to make detailed drawings of churches, houses, and other buildings and antiquities throughout the county.

Hayley seems to have abandoned his own plans for a history in favour of Burrell's, sending him long letters about places in east Sussex which included transcripts of monumental inscriptions.[15] The onset of paralysis in 1787 prevented the completion of Burrell's work; but at his death he left 42 volumes of his notes and drawings to the library of the British Museum, where they have served ever since as a quarry for researchers. The same library was to be the repository from 1820 for Hayley's notes, and in the early 20th century the most important of those of E. H. W. Dunkin (see below) were given to it, making what is now the Manuscripts Department of the British Library one of the chief sources for Sussex history.

Meanwhile the first histories of individual towns had appeared. The earliest was *The Antiquities of Arundel* (1766), by the local schoolmaster Charles Caraccioli, whose Italian origins are unfortunately obscure.[16] Intended to memorialize the castle, which then seemed to be falling into irreversible decay, it was ineptly compiled from published sources and dealt chiefly with the town's successive lords. In the preface the author engagingly apologized for any errors in his English, only recently acquired. A *History of Chichester* published in 1804 was the work of a clergyman who was also a schoolmaster, Alexander Hay. It too is poor, badly arranged and insufficiently localized,[17] while the *History and Antiquities of Horsham*, written and published with his own crude woodcuts by the 16-year-old Howard Dudley in 1836, is of only slight value. The eastern half of the county fared better, with the Frenchman Paul Dunvan's anonymously published *Ancient and Modern History of Lewes and Brighthelmston* (1795),[18] which used sources well by the standard of the period, and W. G. Moss's detailed *History and Antiquities of Hastings* (1824), the work of a visitor, which included among many

---

[14] *Cowdray Archives*, ed. A. A. Dibben (2 vols. 1960–4), i, p. xxxii n.

[15] B.L. Add. MSS. 6359; 6361, ff. 11–12, 16; T. W. Horsfield, *Hist., Antiquities, and Topography of Suss.* (1835), i. 53–4.

[16] *D.N.B.*

[17] H. Johnstone and F. W. Steer, *Alexander Hay, Historian of Chichester* (1961), 2–3.

[18] The author is identified at M. A. Lower, *Worthies of Suss.* (1865), 333.

illustrations a facsimile of the Domesday entry relating to the town. For other resorts contemporary guidebooks included more or less accurate historical surveys, showing that popular history was already part of the 'leisure experience'.

The idea of a large-scale county history was taken up in the early 19th century by the Revd. James Dallaway (1763–1834),[19] secretary to the 11th duke of Norfolk, who commissioned him in 1811 to write an account of the western half only. Volume one (1815), besides histories of Chichester and Chichester rape, incorporated 166 pages of 'Preliminary History' relating in part to the whole county, and including chapters on prehistoric and Roman remains and on Domesday Book, transcripts of some medieval sources for feudal history, and lists of office holders, together with brief sections covering military and maritime history, communications, forests, 'manufactures', and population. Dallaway's only other contribution was volume two, part one, on Arundel rape, which appeared in 1819.

Both Dallaway's volumes made great use of Burrell's collections, together with other manuscripts in London and Chichester. They are marred, however, by carelessness over details, relying much on local people to supply or check information. The account of Arundel, according to the town's later historian the Revd. Mark Aloysius Tierney, is 'neither full nor accurate in any one of its most essential and important points',[20] while that of Amberley castle contains 'some rather gross blunders' according to Walter Peckham, who also described Dallaway's pedigrees as 'absolutely useless'.[21] Volume two, part one, prints no fewer than 17½ pages of corrections to volume one, besides 6½ pages to its own text; in local history, as Dallaway himself remarked in the preface to his first volume, 'perfect accuracy . . . is not to be commanded'!

The 11th duke of Norfolk left money at his death in 1815 for the work to continue, and the Revd. Edmund Cartwright (d. 1833) was commissioned to complete it. His volume two, part two (1830), on Bramber rape, drew on the records of Magdalen College, Oxford,[22] but was generally no more accurate than Dallaway had been; C. F. Trower in 1875 enumerated 19 separate mistakes in the descent of Findon manor.[23] Cartwright also produced in 1832 a revised edition of volume two, part one, most of the copies of which had

---

[19] Account of Dallaway based mainly on *Suss. Arch. Collections*, ciii. 1–48; Dallaway, *Hist. of Western Suss.* i, pp. i–vii.

[20] W.S.R.O., Burrell MSS., papers of Sir C. M. Burrell, Bt., Misc. Correspondence, 1830–50, no. 10.

[21] *Suss. Arch. Collections*, lxii. 21; ciii. 21.

[22] E. Cartwright, *Parochial Topography of Rape of Bramber in Western Division of Suss.* (1830), pp. v–vi.

[23] *Suss. Arch. Collections*, xxvi. 253–8.

perished in a fire;[24] according to Tierney, it did little more, as regarded Arundel, 'than engraft a fresh stock of errors on those of its predecessor'.[25]

Dallaway and Cartwright's *History* was followed almost immediately by the first history of the whole county, written by the Lewes schoolmaster and Unitarian minister Thomas Walker Horsfield,[26] and priced much more cheaply than its predecessor. Horsfield had brought out a two-volume history of Lewes and its environs between 1824 and 1827; but while volume one of the county history, on eastern Sussex, had much merit, volume two largely followed Dallaway and Cartwright, repeating their mistakes. The introductory chapters of volume one contain good accounts of geology (by the Lewesian Gideon Mantell) and agriculture (by John Ellman, son and namesake of the agricultural improver of Glynde), while five appendices in volume two include a detailed survey of the parliamentary history of both the county and its boroughs (by another Lewes-born lawyer, William Durrant Cooper).[27]

Horsfield's radical outlook is revealed in the article on Warnham by the eulogistic account (also written by W. D. Cooper)[28] of the poet Shelley, then still considered disreputable. Commenting on his sympathy for the 'poor outlaw' Jack Cade, however, the *Gentleman's Magazine* reviewer pointed out that, since they were not contemporaries, Cade had not had the chance to effect 'his act of equal partition on the editor's goods and chattels'.[29] Like Dallaway and Cartwright, Horsfield used Burrell's notes heavily, and like them he sought to spread responsibility, describing himself as 'editor' only: much information had been collected by the publisher, John Baxter of Lewes; much text was written by others; and Horsfield himself claimed not to have seen the proofs. One of the publisher's justifications for the work was that it would induce strangers to visit the county's historic sites: an early example of 'tourism promotion'.

Further town histories appeared during the mid 19th century. Tierney's *History and Antiquities of Arundel* (1834), perhaps the longest for any Sussex town, like Caraccioli's earlier gave disproportionate attention to the owners of the castle. Brighton too was further treated: J. A. Erredge's *Ancient and Modern History of Brighton* (1867) used documentary sources (the author died dramatically at his desk while in conversation with his publisher), while J. G. Bishop's *A Peep into the Past: Brighton in the Olden Time* (1880) was first

[24] E. Cartwright, *Parochial Topography of Rape of Arundel* (1832), p. vii.

[25] W.S.R.O., Burrell MSS., papers of Sir C. M. Burrell, Bt., Misc. Correspondence, 1830–50, no. 10.

[26] Account of Horsfield based mainly on Horsfield, *Hist. of Suss.* i, pp. i–vii; introduction to facsimile edn. (1974) by F. W. Steer.

[27] *Suss. Arch. Collections*, lxxxv. 56.

[28] Horsfield, *Hist. of Suss.* i, p. ii.

[29] *Gent. Mag.* cvi (2), 66.

published as newspaper articles. Both William Holloway's *History and Antiquities of Rye* (1847) and W. D. Cooper's *History of Winchelsea* (1850) remain standard works today. Of other 19th-century town histories F. H. Arnold's of Petworth,[30] though slight, used oral memory concerning events of the previous century, and Dorothea Hurst's of Horsham[31] is carefully compiled. Towns such as Hailsham,[32] East Grinstead,[33] and Shoreham,[34] on the other hand, had to wait until the early 20th century for a comprehensive history. That of Hailsham by Louis Francis Salzmann (later Salzman) is outstanding and shares the systematic thematic approach adopted in the parish articles of the *Victoria County History*, while that of East Grinstead, by W. H. Hills, taps some unusual sources, including records of the Charity Commission and of the London, Brighton, and South Coast Railway. No exhaustive history of Worthing was published until 1980,[35] and in 1993 several Sussex towns, including large or historically important places such as Eastbourne, Littlehampton, and Midhurst, still lacked anything comparable.

The next important stage in Sussex historiography was the foundation of the Sussex Archaeological Society in 1846,[36] among the first of its kind. The promoters included the surveyor and cartographer William Figg (1799–1865), who perhaps derived his interest in the history of the land from his profession; Mark Antony Lower (1813–76), a schoolmaster and the son of a surveyor; and W. H. Blaauw (1793–1870), an eminent historian and antiquarian of private means. One chief aim of the society initially was to publish 'Collections' towards a history of the county,[37] and since 1848 a series of (to date) 130 volumes of *Sussex Archaeological Collections* has appeared, dealing from the first with varied aspects of history and of art and architectural history as well as what would now be called archaeology. Clergymen were at first prominent both as authors of articles and among the membership. Many of the early articles are slight, but the journal has published pioneering work on new subjects, as well as series of studies on particular themes, notably in medieval history.[38] Much such work was encouraged by L. F. Salzman, who served as editor from 1908 to 1958.

A section of 'Notes and Queries' at the back of each volume was separated

[30] F. H. Arnold, *Petworth: Sketch of Hist. and Antiquities* (1864).

[31] D. Hurst, *Horsham: Hist. and Antiquities* (1868); D. Hurst, *Hist. and Antiquities of Horsham* (1889).

[32] L. F. Salzmann, *Hist. of Parish of Hailsham, Abbey of Otham and Priory of Michelham* (1901).

[33] W. H. Hills, *Hist. of East Grinstead* (1906).

[34] H. Cheal, *Story of Shoreham* (1921).

[35] *V.C.H. Suss.* vi (1), 65–129, 270–80.

[36] Account of Suss. Arch. Soc. based mainly on *Suss. Arch. Collections*, lxxxv. 3–76.

[37] Ibid. i. 1–13.

[38] The contents of the first 84 vols. are summarized at ibid. lxxxv. 67–76.

off in 1926 to form a quarterly journal *Sussex Notes and Queries*. After its demise in 1971 its successor the *Sussex Archaeological Society Newsletter* for a time published shorter articles and notes. Five general indexes produced roughly every 25 years have enabled easy access to the information in all three periodicals.

Of equal importance with the publication of articles and notes was the society's work in collecting and preserving documents, a task later to be shared by some urban libraries and museums. Successive 'curators of deeds' calendared the society's large collection, but in the 1980s the documents themselves passed into the care of the West and East Sussex Record Offices which had been founded soon after the Second World War.

M. A. Lower, the third editor of *Collections*, attempted in 1870 to synthesize the new knowledge presented in its first 20 volumes in his *Compendious History of Sussex*, which also included bibliographies of relevant articles in the journal, arranged under places. A work of more lasting value was his *Worthies of Sussex* (1865), the only collective historical biography for the county, offered as one instalment towards a comprehensive county history, which could be complemented by others' work on other subjects. Lower's research included visiting nearly every place in Sussex connected with his 'worthies'— a task made possible, as he acknowledged in the preface, only by the rapid growth of the London, Brighton, and South Coast Railway's network of lines.

Sir William Burrell's role, meanwhile, was taken up by E. H. W. Dunkin (1849–1915), a London-based antiquary of private means who planned both a 'parochial' history of the county and a biographical compendium of Sussex clergy.[39] Taking advantage of the abolition in 1852 of the search fee payable for non-legal enquiries at the newly founded Public Record Office, and of the easier accessibility of some other archives, for instance those of Chichester diocese, Dunkin set about reading and noting everything that could possibly be relevant, not only using available lists and indexes, but also searching at the P.R.O. 'thousands of uncalendared or imperfectly calendared rolls', for instance all plea rolls from Henry III to Henry VIII. His work set a new standard of accuracy of transcription, but making and classifying notes gradually became the end, and the books were never written; the few sections which Dunkin did draft,[40] closely following the wording of the sources used, suggest that they would have been very tedious to read. The best of Dunkin's notes, in 221 volumes, survive today at the British Library,[41] and others are in the library of the Sussex Archaeological Society.

---

[39] Account of Dunkin based on *Suss. Rec. Soc.* xx, pp. xv–xvi; B.L. Add. MSS. 39326 (1), f. 1; 39475B, f. 510; 39476, f. 138; 39545, ff. 1–7.

[40] e.g. B.L. Add. MS. 39338, f. 80.

[41] Ibid. Add. MSS. 39326–546.

In 1900 Dunkin and L. F. Salzman, with the genealogists Lt.-Col. Attree and R. Garraway Rice and others, founded the Sussex Record Society[42] to publish transcripts of original documents—an idea first suggested in 1877. Forty-six volumes appeared in the first 46 years of the society's existence, and by 1992 there were 77. Early ones, often partly or largely financed by individual members, concentrated heavily on genealogy and the descent of manors. They included calendars of all important Feet of Fines relating to the county, all inquisitions *post mortem* after 1485, and marriage licences. Later volumes covered more varied subjects, through church history to social and economic history, with the publication after 1921 of several volumes of court rolls, custumals, and surveys. Two themed volumes collected items from different sources on chantries and on Rye's maritime trade, while four volumes extracting early wills arranged the material by place and subject. Town history was served after 1946 by the publication of important records relating to the borough government of Lewes and Chichester. Several volumes in the series, especially among recent ones, have notable explanatory introductions.

A complete and authoritative history of the county was finally started in the early 20th century, when the first two volumes of the *Victoria County History* for Sussex (1905–7) appeared. They dealt with general subjects, including some never previously covered, such as the social and economic history of the county or its ecclesiastical and secular architecture. In addition, volume one's translation of the Sussex section of Domesday Book remains the easiest version to use. The treatment of such subjects as forestry and sport in volume two, however, reflected the interests of the landed classes at whom the *V.C.H.* was originally aimed.

Four 'topographical' volumes were published in the series under the editorship of L. F. Salzman between 1935 and 1953, including *inter alia* useful accounts of Hastings, Rye, Winchelsea, Lewes, and Chichester, and rather skimpier (but still essential) ones of Brighton, Hove, and Bognor Regis. Three further volumes published since 1980 have exemplified the widening scope of *V.C.H.* topographical articles since 1945, treating new subjects like the history of landscape, seaside resorts, and suburbia. The history of Arundel rape is in progress, leaving only that of Pevensey rape then to be written.

Meanwhile, two short popular histories of Sussex have been produced since the Second World War. Roy Armstrong's of 1961[43] had a traditional approach, though the revised edition of 1974 contains original work on the new subject

---

[42] Account of S.R.S. based on *Suss. Arch. Collections*, lxxxv. 37, 63–5; *Suss. Views*, ed. Godfrey and Salzman, pp. v–vii.
[43] J. R. Armstrong, *Hist. of Suss.* (1961).

of vernacular architecture. John Lowerson's of 1980[44] incorporated the first serious work on the 19th- and 20th-century history of the county as a whole.

The revivification of the *V.C.H.* in Sussex, as elsewhere, was due to local authority patronage, which has also been shown since the Second World War in the foundation and continuation of the two county record offices, principally that of West Sussex, and in the support given to such series of local pamphlets as the magnificent 53 'Chichester papers' on a wide variety of subjects co-ordinated by the Sussex, later West Sussex, county archivist Francis Steer between 1955 and 1977.

Histories of individual places other than towns were rare before 1900, though three ponderous volumes devoted to West Tarring near Worthing by its vicar John Wood Warter in the 1850s and 60s were an eccentric exception.[45] Several rural parishes in West Sussex were given an extended treatment in the first half of the 20th century based on the careful use of original sources: Selsey,[46] Westbourne,[47] Fernhurst,[48] Henfield,[49] Parham,[50] and Pagham.[51] In the traditional way, most of the writers were clergymen or people of private means. The Henfield history was intended to foster a feeling of community in the village, a justification paralleled by Sir Cecil Hurst's extolling of William Albery's history of Horsham published in the same year for its value in inculcating a civic sense.[52] A quarter of a century later the sociologist Peter Ambrose gave a more dispassionate account of the East Sussex village of Ringmer in the later 19th and 20th century,[53] blending sociology and history to show the effect of changes in rural life, with a much wider application than to the immediate locality.

The 20th century has also seen numerous monographs on particular subjects covering either the whole county or individual places. Sir William St. John Hope's magisterial *Cowdray and Easebourne Priory* (1919) and Charles Dawson's similarly lavish production on Hastings castle[54] set a standard for the description of important buildings; Dawson's book includes much on the history of Hastings rape as well. At the same period Sir Charles Thomas-Stanford revived the tradition of patrician county historians with his fine

[44] J. Lowerson, *Short Hist. of Suss.* (1980).

[45] J. W. Warter, *Appendicia et Pertinentiae, or Parochial Fragments relating to Parish of West Tarring* (1853); idem, *The Sea-board and the Down* (2 vols. 1860).

[46] E. Heron-Allen, *Selsey Bill: Historic and Prehistoric* (1911).

[47] J. H. Mee, *Bourne in the Past* (1913), revised and completed by Salzman.

[48] A. M. Tudor, *Fernhurst: Story of a Suss. Village* (1934).

[49] H. de Candole, *Story of Henfield* (1947).

[50] [J. Wentworth-Fitzwilliam], *Parham in Suss.* (1947).

[51] L. Fleming, *Hist. of Pagham in Suss.* (privately printed, 1949–50).

[52] W. Albery, *A Millennium of Facts in Hist. of Horsham and Suss. 947–1947* (1947), p. v.

[53] P. Ambrose, *Quiet Revolution: Social Change in a Suss. Village 1871–1971* (1974).

[54] C. Dawson, *Hist. of Hastings Castle* (1909).

Sussex in the Great Civil War and the Interregnum (1910), which gave full treatment to those episodes, quoting some documents *in extenso* and aiming to reference every important statement. Between the Wars the Horsham saddler and radical William Albery investigated the parliamentary history of his town in massive detail,[55] drawing widely on documents he had himself collected, while the work of Henry Cheal of Shoreham set that place in the context of maritime history.[56] Sussex was treated as part of the wider Wealden area in Ernest Straker's study of the iron industry,[57] as after 1945 in Ivan Margary's work on Roman roads,[58] Hugh Kenyon's on the glass industry,[59] and R. T. Mason's on vernacular buildings.[60] Meanwhile, the two volumes of Allen Mawer and F. M. Stenton's *The Place-Names of Sussex* (1929–30) served later historians of agriculture and settlement; Richard McKinley's *Surnames of Sussex* (1988), also part of a national project, is sure to have a similar role in future.

The advent of salaried professionals, many occupied in higher education teaching, since the Second World War has caused a movement away from the classic themes of old-style county history; some results have been indicated already. Much has been written on the economic, especially agricultural, history of the county, notably by Hugh Kenyon,[61] Peter Brandon,[62] Eleanor Searle,[63] and Nigel Saul;[64] meanwhile, Brandon's *The Sussex Landscape* (1974), part of a national series of county landscape histories, was the first book devoted to that subject. Studies of Sussex to exemplify national themes have included Roger Manning's *Religion and Society in Elizabethan Sussex* (1969), Anthony Fletcher's *A County Community in Peace and War: Sussex 1600–1660* (1975), and Graham Mayhew's *Tudor Rye* (1987), while leisure and resort development have been illuminated by the work of E. W. Gilbert,[65] John Lowerson and John Myerscough,[66] and David Cannadine.[67]

[55] W. Albery, *Parliamentary Hist. of Ancient Borough of Horsham 1295–1885* (1927).

[56] H. Cheal, *Ships and Mariners of Shoreham* (1909).

[57] E. Straker, *Wealden Iron* (1931); cf. H. Cleere and D. Crossley, *Iron Industry of the Weald* (1985).

[58] I. D. Margary, *Roman Ways in the Weald* (1948).

[59] G. H. Kenyon, *Glass Industry of the Weald* (1967).

[60] R. T. Mason, *Framed Buildings of the Weald* (1964).

[61] *Suss. Arch. Collections*, xciii. 78–156; xcvi. 35–107; xcviii. 71–117; xcix. 102–48 (studies of probate inventories of Kirdford and Petworth).

[62] Articles in *Agricultural Hist. Review*, xix. 113–34; *Economic Hist. Review*, xxv. 403–20; *Suss. Arch. Collections*, c. 60–72; cix. 69–93; *Trans. Institute of British Geographers*, xlviii. 135–53; liv. 1–17.

[63] E. Searle, *Lordship and Community: Battle Abbey and its Banlieu, 1066–1538* (1974).

[64] N. Saul, *Scenes from Provincial Life: Knightly Families in Suss. 1280–1400* (1986).

[65] E. W. Gilbert, *Brighton, Old Ocean's Bauble* (1954).

[66] J. Lowerson and J. Myerscough, *Time to Spare in Victorian England* (1977).

[67] D. Cannadine, *Lords and Landlords: Aristocracy and Towns 1774–1967* (1980), 229–388, on Eastbourne.

Working-class history had been foreshadowed before the First World War in three pamphlets on the history of Angmering published by the local builder Edwin A. Harris.[68] Written 'expressly for working men', they vigorously attacked both local landowners and the Church; the first sold nearly 1,000 copies in a few months. The work of Roger Wells[69] and Mick Reed[70] on 19th-century rural history has used much Sussex material, while since 1970 series of pamphlets using oral history techniques have been produced in places as diverse as Brighton and Glynde near Lewes. The Brighton series, published by the co-operative QueenSpark, has *c.* 30 titles, including several working-class autobiographies and most recently a study of post-war gay life in the town.[71]

Some of the numerous historical societies founded since the 1960s have produced journals, publishing important work; the best is perhaps *Sussex Industrial History*. Adult classes in local history, particularly those of the Centre for Continuing Education of Sussex University, have spawned accounts of particular places. Many such histories written by individuals during the same period have in contrast been uncritical and anecdotal, often preferring the reproduction of old photographs or documents to serious analysis.

The bibliography of Sussex history has been a fitful activity. Attempts were made in the later 19th century to record everything published previously;[72] the only modern parallel, albeit on a smaller scale, is the Centre for Continuing Education's three period bibliographies, aimed in the first instance at adult education classes.[73]

---

[68] E. A. Harris, *Angmering: a Study* (1912); *Angmering: a Study* [1914]; *Angmering: a Short Treatise, Shewing its Descent from Congregated Wealth to Congregated Poverty* (1914) (photocopies at W.S.R.O. library; copies of the first and third at Chichester Reference Library); *Kelly's Directory of Suss.* (1913).

[69] e.g. *Victorian Village: Diaries of Revd. John Coker Egerton 1857–1888*, ed. R. Wells (1992).

[70] Articles in *Hist. Workshop*, xviii. 53–76; *Jnl. of Peasant Studies*, xii. 109–23; *Rural Hist.* i. 83–94; *Suss. Arch. Collections*, cxxiii. 225–41.

[71] Brighton Ourstory Project, *Daring Hearts: Lesbian and Gay Lives of the 50s and 60s in Brighton* (1992).

[72] *Suss. Arch. Collections*, xv. 215–30; xvi. 273–90; xvii. 169–84; xviii. 87–110; xxxii. 201–12; xxxiii. 207–12; cf. ibid. lxxxii. 141–52; *General Index to Suss. Arch. Collections Vols. LI–LXXV and to Suss. Notes and Queries Vols. I–IV* (Suss. Arch. Soc. 1936), 487–522.

[73] S. Farrant, *Medieval Suss.: a Bibliography* (1980); C. E. Brent, A. J. Fletcher, and T. J. McCann, *Suss. in 16th and 17th Centuries: a Bibliography* (1974); J. H. Farrant, *Suss. in 18th and 19th Centuries: a Bibliography* (4th edn. 1982).

WARWICKSHIRE

Christopher Day

Rarely has a work dominated a county's historiography to the extent of William Dugdale's *Antiquities of Warwickshire Illustrated*, published in 1656.[1] Dugdale's achievement was hailed by contemporaries,[2] it inspired or overawed his successors,[3] and it commands respect today. Dugdale was not, strictly, Warwickshire's first historian, even discounting John Leland and William Camden, whose national surveys had much to say about the county.[4] John Rous (d. 1491) has a shaky claim to that title. His *History of the Earls of Warwick* said nothing important about the county, but his history of Warwick might have influenced topographical studies had it survived.[5] As it is, his account of Warwickshire villages depopulated in the 15th century has given the county precedence in a subject highly regarded by the 20th.[6]

Early 17th-century Warwickshire proved sympathetic to the precocious young Dugdale,[7] for an 'Antiquities of Warwickshire' was already in the air, its likely author Henry Ferrers (d. 1663) of Baddesley Clinton, member of the

[1] I am indebted to the staff of Birmingham Central Library Archives Department [hereafter B.C.L.A.D.], Shakespeare Birthplace Trust R.O. [hereafter S.B.T.R.O.], and Warws. R.O. for helpfulness well beyond the course of duty. I am also grateful to Dr. D. M. Barratt and Dr. R. Bearman for many helpful comments. They should not, of course, be held responsible for any errors. What follows deals primarily with the historiography of the county, and histories of particular places are noted only in that context.

[2] A. Wood, *Life and Times*, i (Oxford Hist. Soc. xix), 209.

[3] E. Hasted, *Hist. and Topographical Survey of Kent* (1797), i, preface, pp. v–vi; [R. Gough], *British Topography* (2 vols. 1780), ii. 299; *Dugdale's Visitation of Lancs. Part III*, ed. F. R. Raines (Chetham Soc. lxxxviii), 1–40.

[4] J. Leland, *Itinerary*, ed. L. Toulmin Smith (5 vols. 1907–10), ii. 40–52, 165–6; v. 10–12, 150–6; W. Camden, *Britannia* (1586), 316–22.

[5] J. Rous, 'De Antiquitate Verovicensis', noted by Leland, *Itinerary*, ii. 165; T. Kendrick, *British Antiquity* (1950), 19.

[6] J. Rous, *Historia Regum Angliae*, ed. T. Hearne (1716); W. Tate, 'Warws. Inclosure Acts and Awards', *Trans. Birmingham Arch. Soc.* [hereafter *T.B.A.S.*], lxv. 57–60; C. J. Bond, 'Deserted Medieval Villages', *Field and Forest: Hist. Geography of Warws. and Worcs.* ed. T. R. Slater and P. J. Jarvis (1982), 150–2.

[7] *Life, Diary, and Correspondence of Sir William Dugdale*, ed. W. Hamper (1827), 5–9; P. Styles, *Sir Simon Archer, 1581–1662* (Dugdale Soc. Occasional Paper [hereafter D.S.O.P.] vi); revised version in idem, 'Sir Simon Clarke, 1579–1652', *T.B.A.S.* lxvi. 6–34; idem, *Studies in 17th-Century West Midlands Hist.* (1978), 1–41; annotated MS. version in Warws. R.O., CR 1741/4; idem, 'Dugdale's Warws.' (MS. of lecture, in Warws. R.O., CR 1741/49); D. Douglas, *English Scholars, 1660–1730* (1951 edn.), 49.

23 William Dugdale

Society of Antiquaries in the 1580s and highly regarded by Camden and Sampson Erdeswick, the historian of Staffordshire.[8] Though William Hamper, editor of Dugdale's autobiography, saw much Ferrers material that was later destroyed and believed he intended an historical topography in the manner of Lambarde's *Kent*,[9] it now seems doubtful that he was temperamentally capable of progressing beyond a preoccupation with lists and headings.[10] William Burton failed in 1631 to persuade Sir Thomas Shirley of Ettington, whose interests were strictly genealogical, to undertake the task, and by 1634 he was talking vaguely of 'him that will undertake the work'.[11] In 1636 he was pressing Sir Simon Archer (d. 1662) of Umberslade.[12]

Archer, who is credited with first awakening in Warwickshire people 'a consciousness of their past', linked the older generation, represented by Ferrers, with Dugdale.[13] Dugdale found in Archer a patron with the social standing and connexions in Warwickshire and London that he, from a lesser gentry family new to the county, lacked.[14] In 1637 Dugdale began a period of prodigious work in London as Archer's assistant; he emerged from the barely conceivable disorder in which national records then languished the master of them and of his craft. As early as 1638 there were indications in the didactic tone of his correspondence with Archer that he was outgrowing his subordinate position, and he also worried that shortage of funds would compel him to abandon the project to Archer, whose commitment he was beginning to doubt. The project was saved by the intervention of Sir Christopher Hatton, who bore the costs of research, helped Dugdale secure the independence of a position in the College of Arms, and persuaded Archer, a man impressively generous of spirit, to hand over the reins.[15] It was to assist his former protégé that Archer sent out his celebrated prototypal questionnaire requesting information about not just lordships and advowsons but archaeological sites and deserted settlements.[16] If Dugdale bore the brunt of research in national archives, he relied heavily for local material, 'as almost every page in the book will manifest', on Archer and his associates.[17]

---

[8] E. K. Berry, *Henry Ferrers, an Early Warws. Antiquary* (D.S.O.P. xvi); Camden, *Britannia*, 319; ibid. trans. P. Holland (1610), 568; S. Erdeswick, *Survey of Staffs.* (1844 edn.), 441–3, 523.

[9] Hamper, *Life*, 265 n.

[10] Bodl. MS. English Lett. b. 1, f. 239 and v.: printed in Hamper, *Life*, 182–3; Berry, *Henry Ferrers, passim*.

[11] Bodl. MS. English Lett. b. 1, ff. 62, 76, 106.

[12] Hamper, *Life*, 155–6.

[13] Styles, *Sir Simon Archer*, 48.

[14] Hamper, *Life*, 9–10, 155–6, 174.

[15] Ibid. 181–6.

[16] Styles, *Studies*, 22–4; R. Bearman, *Captain James Saunders of Stratford-upon-Avon: a Local Antiquary* (D.S.O.P. xxxiii), 24.

[17] *Warws.* preface. For Archer's collections and their present locations see Styles, *Studies*, 4–5, 18; Bearman, *Captain James Saunders*, 21–5.

Warwickshire became the model for county histories in all but its unconventional lack of a general introduction, which Dugdale replaced with a short introduction to each hundred. *Warwickshire* was arranged by hundreds but, within that framework, conformed to Camden's scheme of following rivers or Roman roads. Each parish was treated separately. Introductory remarks covered topography, etymology, archaeology, and notable events, and there were occasional excursions into general matters such as markets and fairs and local customs, but the bulk of the volume comprised detailed accounts of manors, advowsons, and church monuments. Manorial families only were covered, their descents liberally illustrated with pedigrees and coats of arms. Engravings of houses were included if paid for by their owners, for *Warwickshire* was published at Dugdale's expense. Coverage of towns was largely constitutional and institutional.

Warwickshire was not renowned for its literary style, which can be inelegant to the point of obscurity, nor for its length, though it runs to an impressive 816 folio pages.[18] The mass of information, and details of buildings since altered or demolished, remain invaluable. The book's supremacy derived rather from Dugdale's mastery of sources, his methodology, and his sense of purpose, hurdles at any one of which so many aspiring authors fell.[19] His notebooks display a methodical, selective approach totally at variance with so many random, disordered antiquarian collections.[20]

Dugdale's adoption of the Ciceronian maxim that an historian need not be 'an orator, *satis est non esse mendacem*', was justified by his being the first consistently to cite his sources in the 'margents'. His work was also preceptive, 'my principal aim having been, by setting before you the noble and eminent actions of your worthy ancestors, to incite the present and future ages to a virtuous imitation of them'.[21] *Warwickshire* acquired thereby a magisterial authority: 'there are works which scrupulous accuracy united with stubborn integrity has raised to the rank of legal evidence. Such is Dugdale's *Warwickshire!*'[22] It was cited in support of title and descent: 'this is not the first lawsuit Sir William Dugdale's *Warwickshire* has created', it was remarked in 1678.[23] The connexion remained apparent in 1827 when the *Gentleman's*

---

[18] The pagination, which runs to p. 826, is irregular.

[19] *Warws.* preface; Dugdale, 'Directions for Search of Recs. and Making Use of Them': printed in J. Ives, *Select Papers* (1773), 34–7; M. W. Greenslade, *Staffs. Historians* (Staffs. Rec. Soc. 4th ser. xi), 161–3; Douglas, *English Scholars*, 49; H. A. Cronne, 'Study and Use of Charters by English Scholars', in *English Hist. Scholarship in 16th and 17th Centuries*, ed. L. Fox (1956), 75–91.

[20] Bodl. MSS. Dugdale 2–4, 6–7, 9, 12–15; C. R. Cheney, 'Dugdale Tercentenary', in *English Hist. Scholarship*, ed. Fox, 7–8. For Dugdale's MSS. see F. R. Maddison, D. Styles, and A. Wood, *Sir William Dugdale* (guide to exhibition at Warwick County Museum, 1953).

[21] Bodl. MS. Rawl. C. 146, f. 353; *Warws.* dedicatory preface 'To My Honoured Friends the Gentry of Warws.'

[22] T. D. Whitaker, *Hist. and Antiquities of Deanery of Craven*, preface to 2nd edn. (1812).

[23] Quoted in Styles, *Sir Simon Archer*, 23 n.

Magazine saluted 'that romantic and chivalrous *law-book* (for that is its *real* character)'.[24]

Warwickshire was innovative in other areas, notably, as its title suggests, in the use of maps, views, and engravings of monuments, coins, and archaeological finds. The maps, by Dugdale himself, are not wholly reliable and occasionally contradict the text, but they locate parks, archaeological sites, and deserted settlements.[25] The prospects of towns, by Wenceslaus Hollar, are of obvious topographical importance, particularly that of Warwick, depicted only 38 years before the great fire of 1694.

There are areas where *Warwickshire* has long been found wanting, particularly its failure to notice 'any families, however respectable or ancient, which were not lords of a manor or patrons of a church'.[26] Dugdale, of course, never claimed to write the complete history of a place. Nevertheless, his accounts of towns are particularly unsatisfactory to the modern mind, industrial Birmingham typically receiving a passing nod before we are hurried on to more serious matters: 'being a place very eminent for most commodities made of iron, was in Edward the Confessor's days the freehold of one Ulwin'.[27]

Dugdale did not escape attack for plagiarism and inaccuracy. In 1713 the herald John Anstis berated 'that grand plagiary—I can trace the fellow's guilt through every book he hath printed'.[28] Whatever the doubts over the *Baronage* and the *Monasticon*, there is no evidence that *Warwickshire* is anything but Dugdale's, although its preparation, as he faultlessly acknowledged in his preface, was collaborative.[29] He was condemned for inaccuracy in 1730 by 'snarling' Charles Hornby, an 'ill-natured pedant' from the Pipe Office who clearly got as good as he gave.[30] Against the *Baronage* that charge has stuck, but *Warwickshire* is generally a model of accuracy.

Whereas *Warwickshire*'s appearance served elsewhere to stimulate research, in Dugdale's own county it had the opposite effect, as if nothing more remained to do: 'you have drawn the bridge after you—scarcely leaving any gleanings for the most exact of future undertakers'.[31] Dugdale's lament that 'we are fallen

[24] *Gent. Mag.* xcvii (1), 513.

[25] P. D. A. Harvey and H. Thorpe, *Printed Maps of Warws. 1576–1900* (1959), 11–15, 84.

[26] *Gent. Mag.* lxxxi (1), 39.

[27] *Warws.* 655.

[28] Bodl. MS. Ballard 17, ff. 44v.–45v. in Bodl. *Summary Catalogue of Western MSS.: 1697 Catalogue* (new edn.), p. 1068.

[29] D. Douglas, 'William Dugdale: the Grand Plagiary', *Hist.* new ser. xx. 207–10; idem, *English Scholars*, 47.

[30] C. Hornby, *A Small Specimen of the Many Mistakes in Sir William Dugdale's Baronage* (1730); S. E. Brydges, *Censura Literaria* (10 vols. 1805–9), viii. 113–19; Hamper, *Life*, 495.

[31] William Somner to Dugdale, in Hamper, *Life*, 309.

into an age wherein matters of antiquity are valued but by few'[32] was justified for Warwickshire, where the scholarly enthusiasm so characteristic of the earlier 17th century seems in the later to have declined into indifference.[33]

In 1730 the Revd. William Thomas, rector of Exhall, published a new edition of *Warwickshire* in a handsome, two-volume folio set. The first edition was updated and corrected, and the indexes were improved, but most importantly Thomas used parish and episcopal registers, corporation records, and his own observations to add new material.[34] Richard Gough's slur, 'very careless in his accounts, and took very little pains for his information', has damaged Thomas's reputation unfairly.[35] Perhaps the greatest advance lay in the quality of the maps, by the great surveyor Henry Beighton. Though little appreciated at the time, Beighton's work set new standards, portraying landscape, settlement, and communications with meticulous accuracy, and depicting coal mining for the first time.[36]

There were to be no more revised editions of *Warwickshire*. The 'Coventry' edition, published by John Jones in 1765, was a reprint of the first; its usefulness lay in appearing in 70 weekly parts at 6*d*. each.[37] It was rightly felt by then that Dugdale needed continuation rather than reissue, and that Warwickshire had fallen behind other counties.[38] William Upcott's *English Topography* (1818) lists 26 Warwickshire titles, excluding reprints of Dugdale.[39] All, apart from two agricultural surveys,[40] deal with particular places. Probably the best known, certainly the most entertaining, is William Hutton's *History of Birmingham*, an endearing mix of detail and digression published in 1781. The book's significance stems from its author and readership. Hutton was, unusually, neither a country gentleman nor a clergyman but a paper merchant who turned to writing in middle age. *Birmingham* may not be a scholarly work, but it combines astute observation with a prescient awareness that Birmingham and its Staffordshire and Worcestershire hinterland would increasingly be considered a distinct region.[41] A new readership was already apparent in the 207 subscribers to

---

[32] Hist. MSS. Com. 25, *12th Report, VII, Le Fleming*, p. 80.

[33] A. M. Mimardiere, 'Warws. Gentry, 1660–1730' (Birmingham Univ. M.A. thesis, 1963: copy in Warws. R.O.), 90.

[34] Preface; H. M. Jenkins, *Dr. Thomas's Edn. of Sir William Dugdale's Antiquities of Warws.* (D.S.O.P. iii).

[35] [Gough], *British Topography*, ii. 300; Hamper, *Life*, 485–6.

[36] Harvey and Thorpe, *Printed Maps of Warws.* 19–35, 93–5.

[37] Hamper, *Life*, 486.

[38] *Gent. Mag.* lxxxi (1), 38–9.

[39] W. Upcott, *Bibliographical Account of English Topography* (3 vols. 1818), iii. 1247–82.

[40] J. Wedge, *General View of Agriculture of Warws.* (1794); A. Murray, *General View of Agriculture of Warws.* (1813).

[41] e.g. *Hist. of Birmingham*, 41. For the work's shortcomings see R. Holt, *Early Hist. of Town of Birmingham, 1166–1666* (D.S.O.P. xxx), 1.

Thomas's edition of *Warwickshire*: only 110 comprised the gentry who were Dugdale's dedicatees, and 55 were not Warwickshire residents. Hutton's 297 subscribers included only 40 gentry and 13 clergymen.[42] The public for Warwickshire history would increasingly be the scholar, the interested lay person, and the traveller.[43] The proliferation of guidebooks emphasizes the point. Warwickshire, boasting a glamorous selection of castellations at Warwick, Sir Walter Scott's celebrated ruins at Kenilworth, and Shakespeare's Stratford, was well placed to take advantage of developing taste for tourism and the picturesque. William Moncrieff's *Guide to Leamington Spa* sold 3,000 copies by the time of its third edition in 1824, and Henry Cooke's *Guide to Warwick* ran to 40 editions.[44]

The more the county's archives were scoured to produce a growing mountain of material, the less likely it was that one person could complete the anticipated continuation of *Warwickshire*.[45] There were two serious attempts. William Hamper (d. 1831) was elected to the Society of Antiquaries in 1821 largely on the strength of his reputation as a self-taught runic scholar.[46] In 1827 he published his acclaimed edition of Dugdale's autobiography, and he was known to be collecting towards a new edition of *Warwickshire*. Hamper, partner in a Birmingham brass foundry, claimed that 'commercial concerns and public office' prevented publication.[47] It has since been doubted that he 'ever intended to re-edit *Warwickshire*—though he seemed unwilling for anyone else to undertake the task'.[48] He died young for a Warwickshire antiquary,[49] and it may simply be that Thomas Phillipps's letter to him in 1819 was prophetic: 'many who collect for county histories and wait until they have collected an immense mass of materials too often die before they can publish them'.[50] The destruction of his collections precludes certainty,[51] but his annotated copy of *Warwickshire* suggests that Hamper's Dugdale would have been new but not different,[52] displaying a pious regard, common among Warwickshire antiquaries, that contemplated additions only of the same kind

---

[42] B. J. Ronchetti, 'Antiq. Scholarship in Warws. 1800–60' (Birmingham Univ. M.A. thesis, 1952), 18.

[43] R. B. Wilson, 'Evolution of Local Hist. Writing on Warws.' *T.B.A.S.* lxxi. 65.

[44] Ronchetti, 'Antiq. Scholarship', 19, 30–4, 176 sqq.; P. Morgan, 'Early Booksellers, Printers, and Publishers in Stratford', *T.B.A.S.* lxvii. 59, 63.

[45] Maddison and others, *Sir William Dugdale*, 31–3.

[46] Correspondence in B.C.L.A.D., nos. 117630, 125537–42; Hamper, *Life*; *Gent. Mag.* ci (1), 566–9; S. Timmins, 'William Hamper, F.S.A.' *T.B.A.S.* xxiii. 1–5; H. S. Pearson, 'William Hamper', ibid. xlvi. 49–53; B. Ronchetti, 'William Hamper, 1776–1831', ibid. lxviii. 110–20.

[47] *Gent. Mag.* ci (1), 567–8.

[48] Ronchetti, 'Hamper', 114.

[49] He was 55. Ferrers, Archer, and Dugdale all lived into their 80s.

[50] B.C.L.A.D., no. 125537: letter of 25 Oct. 1819.

[51] Below.

[52] B.L. printed books, C.45.k.2.

and form as the original. The Revd. Thomas Ward (d. 1850) must also be judged on an incomplete record since only part of his material survives.[53] It is less a work of history than an historical source, its notes and drawings rich in valuable, sometimes unique, contemporary detail.[54]

The archetypal 19th-century Warwickshire antiquary was no longer the country squire of convention. If not a clergyman, he was likely to be from the urban, commercial classes, comfortable but not wealthy, educated outside the universities, and a member of his borough corporation, which was necessary to gain access to borough records. The most important groups were centred on Coventry and Stratford. At the former, Thomas Sharp (d. 1841), hatter, William Reader (d. 1852), printer, and George Eld (d. 1862), silk merchant and dyer, were at the heart of a particularly productive circle, Sharp in particular making innovative use of guild records, albeit in limited antiquarian fashion.[55] Although such men worked mainly on their own districts, some also collected and published material for the county. Sharp's last work was the *Epitome of the County of Warwick* (1835), a 200-page handbook. The drawings which he commissioned and collected to illustrate his copy of Dugdale's *Warwickshire* now form the celebrated Aylesford collection, a record of the county before Victorian changes swept across it.[56]

At Stratford, a group led by Robert Wheler (d. 1857), solicitor, had access to council records and to the Archer family papers, whose temporary deposit in the town clerk's office in 1812 created among Warwickshire antiquaries the excitement of an appearance of the grail among King Arthur's knights.[57] Stratford antiquaries were primarily interested in Shakespeare, but they accumulated large quantities of local historical material as a byproduct. Wheler published in 1806 what was long the town's standard history.[58] He also compiled a conventional manuscript volume of Dugdale-like Warwickshire material, drawing heavily on the Archer manuscripts.[59] Wheler's friend James Saunders (d. 1830), a former captain in the Warwickshire militia, compiled the most beautiful of Warwickshire antiquarian collections. His drawings are

[53] B.L. Add. MSS. 29265–6; S.B.T.R.O., DR 272.

[54] B.L. Add. MS. 29265, f. 1; Ronchetti, 'Antiq. Scholarship', 105–7; G. Tyack, 'Thomas Ward and the Warws. Country House', *Archit. Hist.* xxvii. 534–42: I am indebted to Dr. R. Bearman for this reference.

[55] Ronchetti, 'Antiq. Scholarship', 66–70, 109, 119, 126–32; F. L. Colvile, *Worthies of Warws.* (1870), 676–9; M. H. M. Hulton, 'William Reader, Printer and Antiquary', *Warws. Hist.* v. 175–88; *D.N.B.*

[56] B.C.L.A.D., Aylesford Collection; *Gent. Mag.* new ser. xvi. 437; Ronchetti, 'Aylesford Collection', *T.B.A.S.* lxxi. 76–9.

[57] Ronchetti, 'Antiq. Scholarship', 77–81, 109–10, 120–6; eadem, 'Hamper', 116–7; Bearman, *Captain James Saunders*, 7, 21, 27; Colvile, *Warws. Worthies*, 806–7; *D.N.B.*

[58] *Hist. and Antiquities of Stratford-upon-Avon.*

[59] B.L. Add. MS. 28564; S.B.T.R.O., ER1/1–34.

exceptional, his notebooks works of art.[60] Saunders was, as has been noted, a
rare antiquary indeed in showing no interest in his own ancestors,[61] and he
was unusual in Warwickshire at that time in publishing nothing. Yet in many
ways he represented the strengths and weaknesses of that whole period,
particularly the inexhaustible but often uncritical collecting and transcribing
of whatever came to hand, unmindful of the example of their professed
model, William Dugdale. It is not quite enough to say with Hamper's
daughter Lydia that they worked for their 'own private contentation', since so
many were clearly collecting with one eye to posterity.[62] Yet their enthusiasm,
and the artless pleasure which shines from their correspondence, is disarming.
Moreover, their very lack of discrimination has finally benefited Warwickshire
historiography by accidentally preserving in copy much that has since been
lost or destroyed.[63]

William Staunton (d. 1848) of Longbridge Manor was something of a
throwback, being head of an ancient county family. He devotedly put together
the greatest collection of Warwickshire material ever assembled, comprising
2,000 books and manuscripts, 1,500 engravings, and a 'very large' quantity of
ephemera that included eight volumes of Henry Ferrers's manuscripts, some
Archer material, and the greater part of the Sharp and Hamper collections. In
the worst disaster ever to befall Warwickshire historiography, the Staunton
collection, which had been presented to Birmingham in 1875 that it might be
'preserved for ever', was almost totally destroyed when the Birmingham
Reference Library burned down on 11 January 1879.[64]

The centenary of Thomas's edition of *Warwickshire* was marked by the
appearance of two new histories. William Smith claimed his[65] to be in the
Dugdale tradition, insufficient in itself to forestall Hamper's dismissive 'zeal
without knowledge'.[66] Although derivative, and omitting some places
altogether, it is a useful work of reference, particularly well illustrated.
William West's 802-page book[67] is the more significant, despite borrowing all
its historical content, for it contains a pioneering and informative directory,
and descriptive itineraries of roads which West must have known intimately if

[60] Bearman, *Captain James Saunders*, passim; S.B.T.R.O., ER1/61–72, 100–1.
[61] Bearman, *Captain James Saunders*, 1.
[62] Note in Hamper's interleaved copy of the *Life*, p. 1B: B.C.L.A.D., no. 100569.
[63] Bearman, *Captain James Saunders*, 22–5.
[64] Since even the MS. catalogue was lost, the full contents of the collection remain unknown.
See B.C.L.A.D., no. 73128: book of cuttings about the Staunton collection; ibid. MS. 723/1–18:
Staunton correspondence 1815–48; ibid. no. 62569: *Auction Catalogue*, Hamper library (1831);
Ronchetti, 'Antiq. Scholarship', 61, 109, 131–2; A. Andrews, 'Birmingham Reference Library',
Archives i (5), 12; P. B. Chatwin, 'Staunton Collection', *T.B.A.S.* xlviii. 171–6.
[65] *New and Compendious Hist. of County of Warwick* (1830).
[66] Quoted in Ronchetti, 'Antiq. Scholarship', 103.
[67] *Hist., Topography, and Directory of Warws.* (1830).

24 The burning of Birmingham Reference Library

we accept a small fraction of the 10,000 miles he claimed to have walked in obtaining 2,000 subscribers.[68]

Original work on Warwickshire in the 19th century was increasingly the preserve of learned societies and journals. Early Warwickshire societies were scientific, or proto-scientific, and philosophical, with later historical and archaeological offshoots.[69] Thus the Warwickshire Natural History and Archaeological Society was founded in 1836 as a section of the Warwick and Leamington Phrenological Society. It published no journal, though it sponsored the *Churches of Warwickshire* survey (1844–58).[70] The society never established a firm county-wide base and, its membership and finances in

---

[68] Wilson, 'Evolution of Local Hist. Writing', 68.
[69] Ronchetti, 'Antiq. Scholarship', 35–9; S. Piggott, 'Origins of County Arch. Socs.' *T.B.A.S.* lxxxvi. 1–15.
[70] Below.

decline, it failed in the early 20th century. It did, however, establish
Warwickshire's first museum, in Warwick market hall, in 1836. It became the
official county museum in 1951.[71] An archaeological section of the
Birmingham and Midland Institute was formed only in 1870, lending weight
to the argument that such societies were slower to get off the ground in
industrial areas.[72] Its interests were wider than the title implied,
Warwickshire, Worcestershire, and south Staffordshire apparently being
included from the start and its first president anticipating 'many valuable
contributions to our social and industrial history'.[73] The society pioneered the
recording and preservation of historic buildings in the region. Renamed the
Birmingham Archaeological Society in 1898,[74] it became, through its
Transactions, the county's most important historical society, despite its
membership (restricted to men except on excursions) failing to reach 200 until
well into the 20th century. It also published some records following the
demise of John Fetherston's *Warwickshire Antiquarian Magazine*, which had
performed that task during a run of only eight volumes between 1859 and
1877. From the 1920s the *Transactions*' increasingly wide range included work
of national importance. Warwickshire was slow to establish a county record
society, and only with the formation of the Dugdale Society in 1920 did the
county begin to match progress elsewhere.[75] Publication by the county council
of quarter session records under the general title *Warwick County Records*
began in 1935.

Archaeology and ecclesiology commonly overlapped in the 19th century,
and in Warwickshire they came together to considerable effect in the
influential figure of Matthew Bloxam (d. 1888). A disciple of Thomas
Rickman, who transferred his architectural practice to Birmingham in 1820,
Bloxam produced his authoritative *Principles of Gothic Architecture* as a young
man in 1828.[76] His *Churches of Warwickshire* unfortunately never progressed
beyond the deanery of Warwick following the death of his collaborator,
William Staunton. Bloxam's prolific writings on archaeology are now
outdated, though his sardonic descriptions of spurious artefacts and
collections remain a delight.[77]

Advances in typography and illustrative techniques encouraged publication
for the popular market, with mixed results. Some still repay attention.

[71] A. C. Wood, 'Warwick County R.O.' *Archives*, ii (12), 197.
[72] Piggott, 'Origins of County Arch. Socs.' 14.
[73] *T.B.A.S.* i. 5–6.
[74] Ibid. xxiv.
[75] Scrapbooks in S.B.T.R.O., DR 113/1–2.
[76] Ronchetti, 'Antiq. Scholarship', 234–41; P. B. Chatwin, *Incidents in Life of M. H. Bloxam* (D.S.O.P. xiii).
[77] e.g. *The Meteor* (Rugby School Magazine), clxxxviii. 55–7.

Graphic Illustrations of Warwickshire (1829), for example, contains engravings of high quality; Tom Burgess, editor of the *Leamington Courier* and friend of Bloxam, produced in his *History of Warwickshire* (1876) an unusual mixture of original research, analysis, and criticism sugared with fairy tale; and Sam Timmins, president of the Birmingham Archaeological Society, wrote one of the best volumes in the Popular County History series.[78] The traditional author-publisher, crippled by expense and unable to meet popular demand, was largely replaced by local printers and booksellers.[79]

Old-style collections were still made. In terms of quantity none can approach those compiled in the late 19th century and early 20th by the Revd. J. H. Bloom, rector of Whitchurch. Their core comprises an astonishing 115 volumes at Stratford and a further 13 at Birmingham,[80] containing much material that is now readily available elsewhere but is nevertheless usefully brought together. Other notable collections include those of W. B. Bickley, ranging from medieval deeds to a 'Fenian threatening Letter';[81] of J. A. Cossins, whose church notes and drawings, made 1882–90, merit wider attention;[82] of O. Baker (d. 1939);[83] and of E. Woodward Jephcott (d. 1969).[84]

In 1889 the Revd. George Miller, vicar of Radway, produced an underrated history of Warwickshire parishes based on substantial archival research,[85] but a much changed county still lacked a good new large-scale history. The 1,038-page catalogue of Birmingham material published in 1918 indicated the daunting scale of such a project.[86] It could only be tackled collaboratively, as in J. A. Langford's *Warwickshire Past and Present* (1884), which acknowledged two named collaborators and unspecified 'eminent assistants'. Dependence on secondary sources, and an irritating failure to cite them, make the work a disappointment. In a new approach, the Warwickshire Village History Society was established under the umbrella of the Women's Institute in 1926 to compile a history of every village in the county. Seven histories, best described as slight, had been published when the society folded in 1946,[87]

---

[78] S. Timmins, *Hist. Warws.* (1889).

[79] Wilson, 'Evolution of Local Hist. Writing', 68–9; P. Morgan, 'Early Booksellers, Printers, and Publishers in Stratford', *T.B.A.S.* lxvii. 55–70.

[80] S.B.T.R.O., DR 41; B.C.L.A.D., nos. 182240–1, 184961, 185955–6, 190803, 192062–4, 195938, 198614, 204518, 216259.

[81] B.C.L.A.D., no. 331530.

[82] Ibid. nos. 395707–11.

[83] S.B.T.R.O., DR 521.

[84] Warws. R.O., CR 1868.

[85] *Parishes of Worcester Diocese*, i (Warws.). I am indebted to Dr. D. M. Barratt for bringing this work to my attention.

[86] Birmingham Public Libraries, *Catalogue of Birmingham Collection* (1918); *Supplement* (1931); Andrews, 'Birmingham Reference Library', 13–14. The library was rebuilt and restocked with remarkable speed after 1879: ibid. 12.

[87] S.B.T.R.O., DR 351.

overtaken by a project on an altogether more ambitious scale. The first of four
Warwickshire volumes originally planned for the *Victoria County History*
appeared in 1904. A local committee with W. F. S. Dugdale—a nice touch—as
secretary provided support for 17 contributors supervised by the *V.C.H.*'s
London editors, H. A. Doubleday and William Page. After volume two (1908)
there was a hiatus until in 1935 Warwickshire was selected for a pilot project
aimed at raising funds locally. Subventions from the county and borough
councils allowed the appointment in 1937 of Philip Styles as part-time local
editor to supervise the first topographical volume, which appeared in 1945.[88]
Five further topographical volumes followed, edited in London, and in 1969
the series was complete.

The two introductory volumes have familiar strengths and weaknesses:
authoritative and innovative, for example, on archaeology (F. Haverfield) and
Domesday Book (J. H. Round), curiously unbalanced in according modern
political history (on the home ground of Joseph Chamberlain) only slightly
more space than beagling and considerably less than coursing.[89] The first four
topographical volumes, completed, unfortunately, just as *V.C.H.* coverage was
starting to expand, are in general markedly inferior to the last two. Styles's
important account of Stratford[90] contrasts with the perfunctory treatment of
most other towns. Even Stratford lacks the innovative work on demography
and social structure found in Styles's work elsewhere. The account of
Birmingham, occupying the whole of volume seven, was the most ambitious
study of a single place yet undertaken by the V.C.H. Coventry and Warwick
were similarly treated in volume eight. The preponderance of local
contributors had by then given way to V.C.H. staff and leading academic
specialists. Despite complaint that volumes seven and eight comprised 'a
collection of materials for a history yet to be written',[91] reviewers generally
recognized that they marked a significant phase in the *V.C.H.*'s development.[92]

The line of historians in the Dugdale tradition ended with the death in 1964
of P. B. Chatwin, lamented as the last whose erudition covered 'all periods of
prehistory and history and all corners of Warwickshire'.[93] Specialist studies
based on themes or 'problems' are now the norm, especially in social and
economic history, areas which have grown enormously since R. B. Wilson's
Handlist of 1955 listed only 14 Warwickshire titles.[94] The historic county

[88] *V.C.H. General Introduction*, 15.
[89] *V.C.H. Warws.* ii. 383–6, 467.
[90] Ibid. iii. 221–82.
[91] P. Searby, *Urban Hist. Newsletter*, xiv. 7–8.
[92] e.g. W. H. Chaloner, *English Hist. Review*, lxxxi. 419; P. Styles, *Hist.* lii. 410–11.
[93] P. Morgan, 'P. B. Chatwin', in 'Essays in Honour of P. B. Chatwin', *T.B.A.S.* lxxviii.
[94] R. B. Wilson, *Handlist of Books re County of Warwick* (1955).

sometimes features in modern research, as in the landscape studies of M. W. Beresford, H. Thorpe, and their successors,[95] or in the explorations of local medieval society inspired by R. H. Hilton.[96] Recent general histories have aimed at the lay reader.[97] Among non-academics, the quality of work on particular towns, villages, and districts by local societies and university extra-mural classes in particular has never been higher.[98]

A further development has seen the region replace the county as the focus of study. Commentators from Leland on had noted the distinction between the woodland country (the Arden) north of the Avon and the open-field south (the Feldon),[99] later writers on agriculture and industry[1] revealing a more complex diversity which has been further explored in the landscape and settlement studies of the influential school of historical geography at the University of Birmingham.[2] Local government reorganization in 1974 recognized the Birmingham region's exceptional character by creating from neighbouring parts of Warwickshire, Worcestershire, and Staffordshire the county of the West Midlands. That Coventry has always proclaimed its distinctiveness, and indeed was a county of itself from 1451 to 1842,[3] and that Warwickshire has at various times been divided among four dioceses, further underlines the point.[4] Warwickshire has three record offices with extensive county-wide collections. The earliest was established in 1847 at Shakespeare's Birthplace in Stratford.[5] From 1862, when Stratford's borough records were transferred there, it took material on deposit and served as a *de facto* county record office until the formation in 1931 of the county record office at Warwick.[6] The third major repository, the Birmingham Reference (later Central) Library, opened in 1866.[7]

Production of literature on all aspects of Warwickshire history has been so rapid as to deter compilation of up-to-date bibliographies. The *Handlist* of

[95] M. W. Beresford, 'Deserted Villages of Warws.' *T.B.A.S.* lxvi. 49–106; H. Thorpe, 'Lord and Landscape', *T.B.A.S.* lxxx. 38–74; *Field and Forest*, ed. Slater and Jarvis.

[96] R. H. Hilton, *Social Structure of Rural Warws. in Middle Ages* (D.S.O.P. ix); C. Dyer, *Warws. Farming, 1349–c. 1520* (ibid. xxvii).

[97] e.g. Slater, *Hist. Warws.* in the Darwen County Hist. Ser.

[98] *Local Hist. Research in Progress* (1977), published by Univ. of Birmingham Extra-mural Department, gives a general outline.

[99] Leland, *Itinerary*, ii. 47; Camden, *Britannia*, 316–17.

[1] e.g. Wedge, *Agriculture of Warws.*; Murray, *Agriculture of Warws.*; *Resources, Products, and Industrial Hist. of Birmingham and Midland Hardware District*, ed. S. Timmins (1866).

[2] *Birmingham and its Regional Setting* (1950); T. R. Slater, 'Harry Thorpe', *Field and Forest*, 17.

[3] *V.C.H. Warws.* vii. 3–4.

[4] A. C. Wood, 'Warwick County R.O.' 195, 201.

[5] L. Fox, 'Shakespeare Birthplace Library', *Archives*, v (25), 90–9.

[6] Inf. from Dr. R. Bearman; *Collection and Preservation of Local Hist. Recs. at Shire Hall, Warwick* (Warws. County Council Records Committee, 1935).

[7] Andrews, 'Birmingham Reference Library', 11–12.

1955 was compiled just as the pace was quickening.[8] The most comprehensive bibliography remains the unpublished catalogue at the Birmingham Central Library. An excellent survey of work in progress in 1977[9] has not been updated, but *Warwickshire History*, the journal of the Warwickshire Local History Society, has since 1980 included an annual bibliography. The great unpublished collections of the past are unlikely to be emulated. Although much of what they contain is now redundant, they provide an irreplaceable insight into one of the longest and most distinguished historiographical traditions in England.

[8] Wilson, *Handlist*.
[9] *Local Hist. Research in Progress.*

WILTSHIRE

Ken Rogers and Douglas Crowley

T he first proposal to write a history of Wiltshire was made at a meeting of the gentlemen of the county held at Devizes in March 1660. The main purpose of the meeting was to choose two candidates for the county at the coming parliamentary election, but some of those present expressed the wish that Wiltshire, 'wherein are many observable antiquities', should be surveyed in the manner of Dugdale's *Antiquities of Warwickshire*, which had been published in 1656.[1]

Our knowledge of the proposal comes from John Aubrey, who was born in 1626 at Easton Piercy in Kington St. Michael parish. 'I was much inclined by my genius from childhood, to the love of antiquities', he wrote, 'and my fate dropped me in a country most suitable for such enquiries'. He had already been fascinated by the great monument at Avebury and later compiled the first account of it in his manuscript 'Monumenta Britannica', first published in full only in 1980.[2] It may be supposed that Aubrey himself put forward the proposal made in 1660, which captured the interest of several others present at the meeting, and some sort of scheme was drawn up. William Yorke of Basset Down was to take the middle division of the county and Aubrey the northern; three others undertook to assist. Judge Robert Nicholas, who had extensive notes from ancient deeds, was also to be involved.

If Aubrey initiated the scheme, he also wrote its epitaph: 'this good design vanished *in fumo tabaci* and was never thought of since'. It did, however, bear some fruit: Aubrey himself collected material in two manuscript volumes which he called 'An Essay towards the Description of the North Division of Wiltshire'.[3] Far from being that, the material consists of notes, of varying value, arranged by parish, which attained the status of a partial county history only when expanded and printed in the 19th century. Aubrey's lack of method and application, perhaps partly due to his frequent absence from the county in later years, makes his information exasperatingly scrappy. Its brevity, however, is not entirely Aubrey's fault: in 1703 the keeper of the Ashmolean

---

[1] *Wilts. Topographical Collections of John Aubrey*, ed. J. E. Jackson (1862), 3.
[2] J. Aubrey, *Monumenta Britannica*, ed. J. Fowles (2 vols. 1980–2), 17.
[3] *Wilts. Topographical Collections*, ed. Jackson, 1, 3.

Museum lent one of the manuscript volumes, which was never returned and
has been lost sight of since *c.* 1834.[4] The thinness of Aubrey's surviving work
is all the more exasperating because he had real insight as a topographer, as
shown by his account of his own birthplace:

> Easton Pierse was anciently a parish of itself. It was a little manor: where is yet to
> be seen . . . tofts. In the time of Henry VII a world of little manors over England
> were destroyed . . . The chapel was pulled down about forty years since. The toft
> where it stood is still called the chapel-hay . . . They did bury here.

The preface to his Wiltshire collections, about life in Wiltshire in earlier
times, much of it related to him by his grandfather and other old people, is
also a vivid piece of writing.[5] Aubrey also compiled a natural history of
Wiltshire which, too, was not printed until the 19th century.[6] It is a matter of
constant regret that such a sensitive, enquiring, and attractive man produced
no finished work on his native county, but he has at least been the subject of a
superb modern biography, Anthony Powell's *John Aubrey and his Friends*
(1948).

In the 18th century there are known to have been four schemes to write the
history of Wiltshire but all came to nothing. In 1714 Thomas Tanner, son of a
vicar of Market Lavington and author of *Notitia Monastica* (1695), produced a
printed *Scheme of the Intended History of Wiltshire*.[7] Nothing is known of any
action taken on it, and Tanner's own notes, although they found a resting
place in the Bodleian Library,[8] are of little value.

In 1780 the Revd. John Collinson, a native of Bromham, published his
*Proposals for Printing by Subscription the History, Antiquities and Geographical
Description of the County of Wilts*. He indicated that he had been working on
the history of the county for three years and claimed that he had acquired
'many curious and valuable manuscripts containing a series of interesting
particulars' relating to it. He also implied that the work was virtually ready
for the press. Subscriptions of 2 guineas were called for, half to be paid in
advance, and the history was to be published in two quarto volumes.[9] Why
that apparently promising venture came to nothing is obscure. Its failure may
not be ascribed to indolence or incompetence on Collinson's part, for he
published a three-volume history of Somerset in 1791.

---

[4] Ibid. p. v; A. Hollaender, 'Jackson's Copy of Aubrey's Wilts. Collections', *Wilts. Arch.
Magazine*, xlix. 545, 549–50.
[5] *Wilts. Topographical Collections*, ed. Jackson, 7–17, 235–6.
[6] J. Aubrey, *Natural Hist. of Wilts*. ed. J. Britton (1847).
[7] J. Britton, *Essay on Topography* (an appendix to J. E. Jackson, *Hist. of Grittleton* (1843)), p.
viii.
[8] *D.N.B.*
[9] Wilts. R.O. 9.

MARLBOROUGH, JULY 14, 1780.

PROPOSALS

FOR PRINTING BY SUBSCRIPTION,

THE

History, Antiquities, and Geographical Description,

OF THE

COUNTY of WILTS.

CONTAINING

I. A copious Detail of its civil, military, and ecclesiastical Transactions, deduced from the Æra of the Roman Invasion to the Year 1780, with a circumstantial Account of every Remnant of ancient Art now extant in the County.

II. A general Survey of the County, divided into Twenty-nine Hundreds, in which are considered its Situation, Air, Soil, natural Productions, Manufacture, &c. Its City, Boroughs, Market Towns, Villages, Hamlets, Seats of the Nobility, Baronets and Gentry, Pedigrees of Families, public Foundations, Charters, Churches, with their Values, Patrons Names, and Monuments.

Adorned with an accurate Map, elegant Views of Churches, Ruins of Castles, Monasteries, and romantic Landscapes.

By the Rev. J. COLLINSON,

Author of the Beauties of British Antiquity.

TO THE PUBLIC.

AMong a Variety of Publications descriptive of particular Counties, *WILTSHIRE* has hitherto escaped unnoticed, which, (considering Circumstances in its Favour) is rather a Matter of Surprize. It is now Three Years since the Author of the present Work first formed a Design of rescuing this important Part of the Kingdom from Oblivion: The Success he met with in the Course of his first Enquiries exceeded his Expectations, and encouraged him to persist in the Pursuit; for besides the Information collected from Books of established Authority, he procured many curious and valuable Manuscripts, containing a Series of interesting Particulars relative to this County. These Advantages, and the unsolicited Assistance of several Gentlemen well known in the Literary World, have enabled the Author to offer to the Public a complete HISTORY and DESCRIPTION of *WILTSHIRE*. The Method of this Work differs little from that of other similar Productions. The Ancient History of the County is placed first; its Antiquities follow, and after that the general Survey. No Article, even of the smallest Importance to a *Wiltshire* Reader, is omitted; nor has any thing crept in which may be judged foreign to the Purpose. The descriptive Part is the Result of the Author's own recent Observation. Thus much only it was judged necessary to premise in Favour of this Undertaking, the Utility of which will be obvious to every one; and it is presumed the Work itself will be altogether acceptable to the Public.

That nothing may be wanting either of Ornament or Entertainment, a Number of Plates engraved by the most eminent Artists, from Drawings taken on the Spot, will be interspersed throughout the Volumes.

CONDITIONS.

I. That the Work shall be neatly printed in Two large Volumes in *Quarto*, on a superfine Paper, and new Type cast for the Purpose.

II. The Price to Subscribers will be Two Guineas, one-half to be paid at the Time of subscribing, and the Remainder on the Delivery of the Book in Boards.

III. As soon as a Number are subscribed for, sufficient to bear the Expence of Printing, the Subscription will be closed, of which Notice will be given, and the Book will be immediately put to the Press.

IV. To each Subscriber will be given a Receipt for the Money, specifying at the same time that the Money will be returned if any thing should prevent the Publication of the Work.

SUBSCRIPTIONS are taken in, and Receipts delivered, by Mr. LONGMAN, Bookseller, *Pater-noster*

In 1788 another plan for a general history of the county was proposed, by
Henry Penruddocke Wyndham in the preface to his edition of the Wiltshire
Domesday.[10] Wyndham's appreciation of the difficulties of compiling a
county history may seem exaggerated in the light of Collinson's *Somerset*, but
rings depressingly true today:

> Few people can be expected to engage in an operation, the trouble and expense of
> which would be certain, and the termination of which could scarcely be hoped for
> during the existence of a single life. And where shall we find a man whose
> abilities and circumstances would enable him singly to persevere in so
> complicated an operation? If a man of proper abilities should venture upon the
> work, and depend upon a proper subscription to support its expenses, it is much
> to be apprehended that few people would risk subscriptions on the precarious
> uncertainty of ever seeing the history; particularly as it would not only depend
> upon the honesty and industry of the undertaker, but would also be liable to a
> total miscarriage by the intervention of death or illness that might happen to him.

To disperse such clouds Wyndham proposed to raise money by offering
subscribers one or more copies of the work and a share in any ultimate profits.
When £1,500 or £2,000 had been raised a committee was to engage 'able
historians, antiquarians, draughtsmen, heralds, botanists, engravers, etc., etc.'
and incredibly, Wyndham considered that the project might easily be completed
in three or four years. Nothing came of the scheme, which Wyndham perhaps
doomed by his mixture of deep pessimism and reckless optimism.

The last of the 18th-century proposals was made by James Davidson,
curate of Froxfield, in 1799. Davidson claimed to have already made
considerable progress in collecting materials and invited answers to a series of
27 questions.[11] It is a sorry reflection on the gentry of Wiltshire that at the end
of the century, apart from the national compilations, there had appeared no
book dealing with the history of the county as a whole or any considerable
part of it. There were descriptions of Salisbury and its cathedral and of
Wilton House, and books of little value on Salisbury and Devizes; otherwise
published work on local history was almost entirely lacking.

The deficiency was partly remedied in 1801 by the appearance of the first
two of three volumes of John Britton's *Beauties of Wiltshire*. Britton was, like
Aubrey, a native of Kington St. Michael. His father, a baker, maltster,
shopkeeper, and small farmer, for some years provided a good living, but later
the businesses failed and the family fell into poverty. In his *Autobiography*
Britton gave a lively account of life in Kington St. Michael, and drew a bitter
contrast with the idyllic picture presented by Mary Russell Mitford in *Our*

---

[10] H. P. Wyndham, *Wilts. Extracted from Domesday Book* (1788), pp. xxi–xxv.
[11] Britton, *Essay on Topography*, p. ix; Wilts. R.O. 1635/5.

26 John Britton

Village. In 1787, when he was 16, he was apprenticed to a London wine merchant. He hated the drudgery of his work and learned very little, but he managed to read widely and made the acquaintance of literary and artistic people. In later employments, in the wine trade, as a lawyer's clerk, as a writer for the theatre, and as a reciter and singer on the stage (on the same bill as a 'learned dog'), he also found time for historical writing.[12]

Britton was industrious and pertinacious, and the volumes brought out in 1801 contained over 600 pages on Wiltshire topography. Their defects are obvious, and later were acknowledged by Britton himself when he called them 'my juvenile and very imperfect work'.[13] Much space is devoted to the county seats, with lengthy descriptions of their contents; much less than the whole of Wiltshire is dealt with; descriptions of places are brief and conventional; Stonehenge is attributed to 5th-century Romanized Britons. Only occasionally, as when he wrote from personal knowledge of the Chippenham clothiers, does Britton have independent value.

The *Beauties of Wiltshire* set the course of Britton's life after 1801. In the preface he referred to his intended co-operation with E. W. Brayley to publish a series, the *Beauties of England and Wales*. Brayley was another ex-apprentice who had forced his way into the literary world and had already co-operated with Britton to produce a broadside ballad, *The Guinea Pig*, which sold 70,000 copies, though most of them were pirated. The partnership produced not only the *Beauties* series, but others dealing with cathedral and architectural antiquities.

By the time the Wiltshire volume of the *Beauties of England and Wales* appeared in 1814, as part two of volume 15, Britton, the sole author, still found himself lamenting that no essential progress had been made towards a county history. That volume, however, of over 700 pages, was a great advance on his earlier attempt, and can itself claim to be the first history of the county. It also takes a prominent place in the ranks of literary curiosities, for few books can have been launched on the world with such a condemnation of an author by his publisher. In reply to a veiled reference in Britton's preface to 'circumstances connected with its publication which it is unnecessary to notice', the publishers inserted a final leaf bearing a tirade against Britton and Brayley:

had that gentleman [Britton] been as expeditious in the execution of the task allotted to him, as they [the publishers] have been liberal in rewarding him, the public would have had no cause for complaint, but such has been the turpitude of Mr. Britton and his co-adjutor, that every obstacle they could invent has been

---

[12] J. Britton, *Autobiography* (1850); cf. M. R. Mitford, *Our Village* (1986).
[13] Britton, *Essay on Topography*, p. viii.

practised to impede its progress, and even now . . . they have thought proper . . .
to throw out aspersions against the late worthy and respected, though
unfortunate, publisher, which shows a malevolence of heart, only known, it is
hoped, to persons like themselves. It would occupy too much of our own time
now to reply to the scandalous insinuations of these ANTIQUARIAN
QUACKS.

Britton mentioned in 1814 that the third volume of his *Beauties of Wiltshire*
was being prepared and would soon be published: it did not come out until
1825.[14]

The help of William Cunnington of Heytesbury concerning monuments on
Salisbury Plain was acknowledged by Britton in 1801. Cunnington, a
woolstapler, had been advised to ride on the downs to benefit his health and
had become interested in prehistoric remains. By 1800 he was working with
the Revd. William Coxe, who employed Crocker & Sons of Frome (Som.) to
survey earthworks and Roman roads. Sir Richard Colt Hoare, Bt. (1758–1838),
joined in the work. He was a member of the London banking family; his
father Richard Hoare had married a cousin, the daughter and heir of Henry
Hoare who laid out the gardens at Stourhead; and he was very wealthy. After
the death of his wife in 1785, leaving a baby son, he spent several years on the
Continent, where he developed an interest in, and a knowledge of, paintings
and antiquities. Later he spent much time touring in Wales, and only in 1801,
in co-operation with Cunnington, did he begin to study the antiquities of
Wiltshire. In 1803, when Coxe said that he was 'barrow-mad', Hoare took
over from Coxe a plan to write a history of ancient Wiltshire. Cunnington
contributed much of the fieldwork and excavation, Hoare the finance and a
rapidly growing interest and knowledge. The first of three parts of volume
one of *The Ancient History of Wiltshire* appeared in 1810, shortly before
Cunnington's death, and the volume was completed in 1812. The final part of
the second volume appeared in 1821.[15]

Before his preoccupation with prehistoric Wiltshire, Hoare had formed a
library which included 'almost every book relating to the history and
topography of his own country, concerning the subject generally and each
individual county'. His purpose was to enable a work on the history of
Wiltshire to be written without recourse to other libraries, and it seems that
he intended to be the author. Britton's second volume of 1801 was dedicated
to him, and he wrote to congratulate Britton, but it is possible that Britton's
work gave Hoare little pleasure. Soon after 1801 he was refusing to send
information, and by 1804 a breach had opened between them. Not until 1818,

---

[14] J. H. Pafford, 'John Britton: Bibliographical Note', *Wilts. Arch. Magazine*, liv. 441.
[15] K. A. Woodbridge, *Landscape and Antiquity* (1970), 187–234.

however, did Hoare formally propose a county history. He then issued a pamphlet, *Hints on the Topography of Wiltshire*, in which he suggested a co-operative approach to compile one, dividing the work by hundreds. In 1819 several hundreds were being worked on, and in 1822 *Mere*, his own hundred, in which Stourhead lay, was published as the first part of *The History of Modern Wiltshire*. A recent writer has said that it set 'a typographical standard for what was to be the most handsome county history yet to be produced'.[16] It may be pleasant to a bibliophile to see about two thirds of each page, when uncut, to consist of margin, but generations of users have ruefully agreed with Britton's words: 'I very much object to its unwieldy, unpleasant, and expensive size'.[17]

The histories of 15 hundreds, all in south Wiltshire, were completed. Hoare compiled six himself and his name appears on the title page of each of six others, presumably because he wrote or edited parts. Of 11 other authors named, one, the Revd. John Offer, was a salaried employee rescued by Hoare from 'the drudgery of a school' at Imber and sent to London, Oxford, and elsewhere to consult documents. It was a great blow to the series when Offer died in 1822. Another author, W. H. Black, was a practised palaeographer and a sub-commissioner of the public records. Others, such as James Arundell, Lord Arundell, of Wardour Castle, were landowners, and the histories of the two hundreds, Warminster and Westbury, which contained some of the industrial areas of west Wiltshire, were written by clothiers.[18]

It is difficult to evaluate *Modern Wiltshire* as a whole. Ostensibly it is systematic: there is an article on each parish in each hundred, and for each parish the Domesday Book entry, a plan of the church, monumental inscriptions, and material from the available Record Commission publications are normally to be found. There was, however, no consistency in what additional material was included: some parishes were treated very briefly, others at much greater length with copious extracts from documents, some of them not very old. The article on Westbury, for example, includes abstracts of many 18th-century title deeds. Much apparently depended on what interested the compiler. Hoare himself gave no detail of the building of his own house at Stourhead, of the laying out of the grounds, or of how his ancestors added to the estate of the Stourton family. On the other hand, he printed a paper on forestry which he gave to the Bath Agricultural Society in 1814, and a letter of 1814 on botany thought to have been the last dictated by the Empress Josephine.[19] As editor he apparently exerted an influence which, according to some later tastes, may have diminished the work. The original draft of Richard Harris's account of

---

[16] Ibid. 251–8.
[17] Ibid. 229.
[18] Ibid. 251–8.
[19] R. C. Hoare, *Modern Wilts.* (1822–44), Mere, 86–8; Heytesbury, 214–15.

Westbury still exists,[20] and on two valuable pages, which did not appear in print, gives information, some of it unique, on the woollen industry in the town. One volume stands above the others in the series, and perhaps above any other for a place in England of similar size. Robert Benson and Henry Hatcher's *Salisbury*, which appeared in 1843, runs to nearly 900 pages; its main part is a chronological narrative in which the histories of England, Salisbury cathedral, and the city are mingled, and there is a lengthy appendix of charters and documents.[21] On the publication of George Matcham's *Frustfield* in 1844 *Modern Wiltshire* was completed for the southern half of the county.

As early as 1821 it was understood that the northern half would be undertaken by Sir Thomas Phillipps, Bt., and Phillipps contributed to John Offer's salary.[22] He may have been taking preliminary steps in preparation for the volumes when he printed in 1821 some of Aubrey's material ('without note, arrangement, or heraldic illustration'); in 1822 in two volumes but only six copies of each, the monumental inscriptions from the majority of Wiltshire churches; and in 1825 a list of the institutions of Wiltshire parish clergy. He continued to print Wiltshire manuscripts and pedigrees in numbers so small that no complete bibliography has ever been compiled, and in 1838 printed the remainder of Aubrey's material.[23] In 1837 he was still collecting materials for a history of north Wiltshire but he could not afford to spend £2,000 a year on the project as Hoare had done and was doubtful if anyone would buy his work if it was printed.[24] Even in 1843 Phillipps declared that he had not relinquished the intention of publishing on north Wiltshire,[25] but no history of a north Wiltshire hundred appeared.

In 1839 John Britton took a lead in forming the Wiltshire Topographical Society, and declared his aims in doing so in an *Essay on Topography*, which he claimed was 'the first attempt in forming a sort of *Grammar and Dictionary of the Science of Topography*'. As he had in 1801, he commended the scheme to write a history of Wiltshire proposed by Wyndham in 1788, and he expressed the view that the history of a county would best be recorded by the compilation of detailed and complete histories of individual parishes. His essay was written as a guide to method and sources for the members of the society who had undertaken to write parish histories. In it he published his misgivings about the value of Hoare's work, describing it as 'Historical Collections', although he claimed to do so 'cautiously and . . . correctly: for it

---

[20] Wilts. R.O. 540/320.

[21] Hatcher was the principal author; for his dispute with Benson: Britton, *Autobiography*, ii. 21–2.

[22] Woodbridge, *Landscape and Antiquity*, 255, 257.

[23] *Wilts. Topographical Collections*, ed. Jackson, p. viii, n.; T. Phillipps, *Monumental Inscriptions of Wilts.* (1822); T. Phillipps, *Institutiones Clericorum in Comitatu Wiltoniae* (1825).

[24] *Wilts. Arch. Magazine*, liv. 246–7.

[25] J. Stratford, *Catalogue of Jackson Collection in Royal Library* (1981), 36.

is admitted and lamented by the best topographical critics that the amiable, generous, and zealous patron of Wiltshire topography has not succeeded in producing full and complete histories of the . . . parishes'. Britton's judgement of *Modern Wiltshire* may be understandable but the Wiltshire Topographical Society could not supplant it. The *History of Grittleton*, by the Revd. J. E. Jackson, published in 1843 with Britton's essay as a 66-page appendix, was the only parish history produced by the society. Its introductory matter includes a list of *c.* 140 members and details of 13 forthcoming articles, of which three were 'preparing for speedy publication'. All that came out, however, were Britton's *Memoir of John Aubrey* (1845) and his edition of Aubrey's *Natural History of Wiltshire* (1847). In 1850 the society's activities were suspended; Britton recorded in the minutes his 'regret and mortification' at the failure, which he blamed on the 'little assistance and co-operation from other gentlemen of the county'.[26]

In 1852, when he was 80, Britton wrote to William Cunnington of Devizes, the grandson of Hoare's collaborator, offering to dispose of his Wiltshire books and manuscripts to a public society in the county. A public meeting was held and £150 was raised to pay for the collection, which was placed in Devizes town hall. The purchase led directly to the founding of the Wiltshire Archaeological and Natural History Society (W.A.S.) in 1853; Britton addressed the inaugural meeting and lived to see the society well established and the first two editions of its magazine (*W.A.M.*) published. Thenceforward, especially after 1874 when a permanent home for its library was found, part of the present museum in Devizes, the society and *W.A.M.* have been of crucial importance for the study of local history in the county.[27]

In its early days none contributed more to *W.A.M.* than Canon Jackson, the author of *Grittleton*. Born in Yorkshire in 1805, Jackson went to live with his brother James, curate of Farleigh Hungerford (Som.). In 1834 he succeeded him as curate and lived there for most of the time until 1845. Interest in the former owners, the Hungerfords, developed into what Jackson called a mania; it remained with him for life, but he also became an omnivorous collector of information and printed and manuscript material on all aspects of Wiltshire history. Removal to Leigh Delamere in 1845 took Jackson to the same corner of Wiltshire which gave birth to both Aubrey and Britton, and their mantles may be said to have fallen on him. The muniment rooms in many of the great Wiltshire houses were open to him, especially that at Longleat, and Wiltshire historians and archivists are familiar with his bold and legible handwriting on deeds and papers. His best known work is his edition of Aubrey's

---

[26] Britton, *Essay on Topography*, pp. v–vi; Britton, *Autobiography*, ii. 22–6; C. W. Pugh, *Wilts. Arch. and Natural Hist. Soc. Centenary Hist.* (1953), 5–6.

[27] Pugh, *Centenary Hist. passim.*

Topographical Collections, published by W.A.S. in 1862, in which his own contributions outweigh the original many times. Few issues of *W.A.M.* until Jackson's death in 1891 were without an article from him, in many cases lengthy and learned.[28] Although such a prolific writer, Jackson was unable to make full use of all the evidence he collected, and for reasons that are now obscure he failed to ensure that it was preserved in Wiltshire. By a decision which has hampered all Wiltshire-based historians after him he left 14 large volumes of topographically arranged notes and papers to the Society of Antiquaries, and the rest of his library was sold. By good fortune the Hungerford collections, for many years in private hands, were purchased by W.A.S. in 1958.[29]

The society's library remained a focal point for Wiltshire studies, and *W.A.M.* has been the vehicle for the publication of much valuable material; the Revd. E. H. Goddard, secretary, editor, and librarian for 40 years, compiled a *Wiltshire Bibliography* published by Wiltshire county council in 1929. From its earliest days the society had given a home in its library to original records, and by 1945 a considerable quantity was held. Some publication of original texts appeared in *W.A.M.*, especially a useful series of reports between 1898 and 1941 on records in the society's own keeping; co-operation with the British Record Society resulted in the publication of three volumes of *Inquisitiones post mortem* (1901–14);[30] and the society itself published a two-volume edition of the *Tropenell Cartulary* (1908).[31] Extracts from and lists of original documents also appeared in *Wiltshire Notes and Queries*, a quarterly antiquarian and genealogical magazine published 1893–1916 from the office of the *Wiltshire Gazette* at Devizes: the magazine carried genealogical notes and articles on local history but eschewed archaeology. Independently of both *W.A.M.* and *W.N. & Q.* a Wiltshire Record Society was set up, and produced three volumes between 1896 and 1902.[32]

Regular publishing of historical documents for Wiltshire was first achieved, after the Second World War, by the Records Branch of the Wiltshire Archaeological and Natural History Society, which re-formed itself as the Wiltshire Record Society in 1967: since 1947 an edited text has been published

---

[28] Stratford, *Jackson Collection*, contains a memoir of Jackson and a list of his publications.

[29] Hollaender, 'Aubrey's Collections', *Wilts. Arch. Magazine*, xlix. 547–8; R. E. Sandell, 'Jackson Papers', *Wilts. Arch. Magazine*, lvii. 263–4.

[30] *Abstracts of Wilts. Inquisitiones post mortem, 1242–1326*, ed. E. A. Fry (Index Library, xxxvii); *Abstracts of Wilts. Inquisitiones post mortem, 1327–77*, ed. E. Stokes (Index Library, xlviii); *Abstracts of Wilts. Inquisitiones post mortem, 1625–49*, ed. G. S. and E. A. Fry (Index Library, xxiii).

[31] *Tropenell Cartulary*, ed. J. S. Davies.

[32] Pugh, *Centenary Hist.* 34–5.

nearly every year and the series displays outstanding professionalism. R. B. Pugh (1910–82) was a leader in forming the branch in 1937. Though not a native of Wiltshire, Pugh's family had lived at Devizes, his uncle C. W. Pugh was the librarian of W.A.S., and he adopted Wiltshire as a special interest. If the leadership of the Wiltshire Record Society, which was begun while he was an assistant keeper of the public records, and for which he himself edited four texts, was a great contribution to the study of Wiltshire, Pugh's part in setting up V.C.H. Wiltshire was a greater one. He was one of the architects of the partnership between the University of London and local authorities in Wiltshire, of which the publication of 15 volumes of *V.C.H. Wiltshire* (1953–91) is the fruit so far, and, as general editor of the *V.C.H.* from 1949 to 1977, made Wiltshire a pattern for other counties.[33]

[33] *Wilts. Coroners' Bills, 1752–96*, ed. R. F. Hunnisett (Wilts. Rec. Soc. xxxvi), pp. xiii–xvii.

WORCESTERSHIRE

D. C. Cox

Worcestershire's first topographer was Thomas Habington of Hindlip, a Catholic gentleman born in 1560.[1] He had been lucky to survive implication in the Babington and Gunpowder plots and had suffered both imprisonment and economic persecution. As an old man,[2] already the author of some works of national history, he embarked on a 'Description' of Worcestershire designed to refute a remark that the county 'contained few gentlemen of antiquity' and inspired by William Burton's *Description of Leicestershire* of 1622.[3] There had been an heraldic visitation of Worcestershire in 1569 but many gentlemen saw the heralds as social inferiors and had withheld co-operation.[4] Pedigrees were therefore often imperfectly recorded, and Habington's policy was to avoid them 'as dangerous rocks either to offend the gentlemen if I say too little or hazard my credit if I say too much'.[5] Forced to construct a new framework from original sources, he began by collecting notes from the Exchequer records, and then proceeded to make his own heraldic visitation by transcribing the arms and monuments in every church, a task begun by October 1634[6] and still unfinished in 1637.[7]

As he travelled he also made notes of oral evidence.[8] At Middle Littleton, 'enquiring of an inhabitant here, who though very plain in appearance yet was witty and not unlearned, how many in succession were lords of Middle Littleton since the abbey's ruin, he answered the owners changed so often as they confounded his memory'.[9] Habington thus learnt to be wary of 'vulgar reports or private conceits' and distanced himself from oral information whenever forced to cite it, 'for I will not pawn my credit upon reports'.[10] That

---

[1] On Habington's life, family, and MSS. see *D.N.B.*; *Survey of Worcs. by Thomas Habington*, ed. J. Amphlett (Worcs. Hist. Soc.) [hereafter *Surv.*], i. 1–26 (all references are to that edn.); J. Humphreys, *Studies in Worcs. Hist.* (1938), 67–86. The author is indebted to Mr. C. D. Gilbert of Kidderminster for information derived from his unpublished research on Habington.

[2] *Surv.* i. 62 n.

[3] Ibid. i. 30, 34, 196.

[4] Ibid. i. 192.

[5] Ibid. i. 428.

[6] *Trans. Worcs. Arch. Soc.* [hereafter *T.W.A.S.*], new ser. xviii. 29.

[7] *Surv.* ii. 173.

[8] e.g. ibid. i. 174–5, 183, 382; ii. 17, 63, 120, 125, 175, 226.

[9] Ibid. i. 323.

[10] Ibid. i. 205, 268.

may be why he rarely mentioned archaeological finds; it was certainly not from indifference, for he recorded in detail the discovery of an ancient burial at Crowle that he had seen for himself as a young man.[11] On his perambulations Habington noted many antiquities—a moated house, a ruined chapel, or a great park—and appraised the landscape's economic condition.[12] Broadwas was 'shut up with incommodious ways, but this is abundantly recompensed with a bountiful dower of fruitful ground lying on Teme's bank, whose pastures for riches compare with the best'.[13] At Dudley, 'whither we ascend over hills resembling with their black colour the Moors who are scorched with the sun', the miners 'have all of them the reputation of bold spirited men'.[14] At Droitwich he reported minutely the topography and techniques of salt making.[15] Indeed the spectacle of man's works in Creation sometimes lifted his rich prose to a lyrical, even metaphysical, plane. At Cowleigh, on the slope of the Malverns, he found 'a mansion where the springs descending from above with a soft murmur delight the senses, a seat for the Muses, but better for devotion; for lifted on high if you look one way you see nothing but the hills and the heavens, if the other, below you behold a vast prospect of this perishing world'.[16]

There came a time when Habington 'despaired ever to be able to compass the whole work of the county' and was ready to leave it 'to some such learned men as Mr. Burton'. He was encouraged to go on, however, when the capitular (formerly conventual), and later the episcopal, records at Worcester were opened to him.[17] Of the five capitular registers on which he relied[18] four remain.[19] The fifth, the 'ledger of demises or leases' (or 'ledger of dimissions'), which included deeds of the mid 15th century,[20] was later lost.[21] A sixth 'ledger' (Hemming's Cartulary), which Habington believed lost,[22] was cited, for its charters, from notes by Thomas Talbot[23] and, for its narrative, from an unidentified manuscript.[24] In the episcopal archives Habington relied almost entirely on the Red and White books, the former being 'the most

[11] Ibid. i. 135–6.
[12] Ibid. i. 142, 450; ii. 275.
[13] Ibid. i. 108.
[14] Ibid. i. 195.
[15] Ibid. ii. 295–8.
[16] Ibid. i. 329.
[17] Ibid. i. 29, 34.
[18] Ibid. i. 334.
[19] G. R. C. Davis, *Medieval Cartularies of Great Britain* (1958), nos. 1070–1, 1075–6.
[20] *Surv.* i. 280, 552; ii. 62, 371–2.
[21] Not recorded in Hist. MSS. Com. 37, *14th Report, VIII, Worcester Dean and Chapter*, pp. 176–80.
[22] It was owned privately in the late 16th century: Davis, *Medieval Cartularies*, no. 1068.
[23] *Surv.* i. 285, 334, 355–6, corresponding to P. H. Sawyer, *Anglo-Saxon Charters: Annotated List and Bibliography* (Royal Hist. Soc. Guides and Handbooks viii), nos. 179, 55, 113.
[24] e.g. *Surv.* i. 248, 360, 490.

authentical ledger of this bishopric' and 'my special director in this work'.[25] Well provided with ecclesiastical material, Habington lacked adequate records of lay estates[26] until Sir Simon Archer, followed by others,[27] furnished him with 'abundance of royal records'[28] and William Dugdale supplied extracts from the Beauchamp cartulary,[29] Domesday Book, etc.[30] Habington made little use of private title deeds ('evidences'), which he considered less reliable than public records and which, in any case, most owners 'neglected' to make available.[31]

It seems that Habington's early want of lay records influenced the order of the complete 'Description', for which we have his written plan.[32] It was to be in two books, the first beginning with a history of the church of Worcester to the Dissolution, followed by a survey of the cathedral church and then, in deference to the king,[33] by Worcester city and the royal boroughs of Droitwich, Bromsgrove, and Bewdley. The rest of book one, however, was assigned to the 'patrimony of Christ':[34] a history of each estate of the bishop and of the cathedral priory, followed by a history of each of the other religious houses and of its estates. It was the ecclesiastical part of book one that Habington, 'wanting records of the secular state of this shire', drafted first.[35] Book two was thus left to cover the bulk of the pre-Dissolution lay estates. Those of the Beauchamps, earls of Warwick and barons of Elmley, were to form its opening section;[36] the other estates were to follow under their respective hundreds. In both books the manorial descents were continued beyond the Dissolution. But no text of the entire 'Description' is known. Instead we have drafts, each with some writing in Habington's hand and some in those of his scribes. No draft follows his outline plan and, while there is much duplication within and between the drafts, a few places do not appear at all. In July 1641, however, Habington considered the work complete. The following April Sir Simon Archer was encouraging him to have it printed, but soon war broke out and Hindlip was plundered.[37] Fortunately some, perhaps all, of the drafts were saved and

[25] Ibid. i. 56, 255.
[26] Ibid. ii. 106.
[27] Ibid. i. 117 n., 183, 314; ii. 124.
[28] Ibid. i. 34.
[29] Life, Diary, and Correspondence of Sir William Dugdale, ed. W. Hamper (1827), p. 198.
[30] P. Styles, Studies in 17th-Century West Midlands Hist. (1978), 20.
[31] Surv. i. 35; ii. 50 n., 129. For exceptions see i. 81, 190, 300, 399, 445; ii. 105, 115, 160, 286, 292.
[32] Ibid. i. 27–32; cf. i. 388–9; ii. 1, 106.
[33] Ibid. i. 27 n.; ii. 530.
[34] Ibid. i. 388.
[35] Ibid. i. 106.
[36] Ibid. i. 30; ii. 250–2.
[37] Styles, Studies, 20.

Habington continued to add notes in them until 1647, within a few weeks of his death.[38]

The manuscripts then passed to his son William, the poet. In 1653 Sir Simon Archer wished Dugdale to persuade William Habington to have the 'Description' printed,[39] but William died the following year. The manuscripts passed to his son Thomas,[40] during whose long life there were several moves towards publication; but the matter became increasingly difficult, for standards of research continued to rise, with Dugdale's *Warwickshire* (1656) the new model, and taste in written prose became more austere. Nathanael Tomkins (d. 1681), a prebendary of Worcester from 1629,[41] knew Habington the antiquary, and at Staunton church had helped him to read an ancient inscription.[42] He wrote 'Observations of Mr. Abington's Antiquities of Worcestershire', and on Tomkins's work Dr. William Hopkins (d. 1700), a Worcester prebendary from 1676,[43] added his own 'Observations'.[44] Those texts are now probably lost.[45] In the 1690s Anthony Wood recorded that Habington's manuscripts were still in his grandson's hands and 'might be useful for the public, if in others'.[46] Thomas Habington did try to have Wood revise and edit the papers, but without success. He then seems to have made a fruitless approach to James Wright, the historian of Rutland.[47] In 1695 Dr. Hopkins contributed the translation of and 'Additions' to the Worcestershire part of Gibson's Camden,[48] and in a footnote[49] referred to Thomas Habington's ownership of his grandfather's 'Description', 'the publication whereof hath been impatiently expected of him above these 20 years'. William Nicolson proposed to Hopkins that he edit the 'Description' for publication, but Hopkins declined, having by then concluded that it contained 'great defects and errors'.[50] In 1717 Richard Rawlinson did publish extracts, 'Mr. Abingdon's Survey of the Cathedral Church of Worcester' and 'An Account of Great Malvern Priory in Worcestershire', but only in the setting of a larger compilation.[51]

---

[38] *Surv.* i. 289, 429; ii. 207, 227.
[39] *Life of Dugdale*, ed. Hamper, p. 273.
[40] In possession *c.* 1675: W. Camden, *Britannia*, ed. E. Gibson (1695), cols. 521–2, note.
[41] *D.N.B.*
[42] *Surv.* i. 378.
[43] *D.N.B.*
[44] Hist. MSS. Com. 1, *1st Report, Winnington*, p. 53.
[45] The MS. presumably perished in the Stanford Court fire: *Surv.* i. 21 n.
[46] *Athenae Oxonienses*, ed. P. Bliss (4 vols. 1813–20), iii (1817), col. 225.
[47] Inf. from Mr. Gilbert.
[48] Camden, *Britannia*, ed. Gibson, preface.
[49] Ibid. cols. 521–2.
[50] *Collections for Hist. of Worcs.* ed. T. Nash, i (1781), introduction, p. ii.
[51] *Antiquities of Cathedral Church of Worcester* (1717). For Rawlinson's editorship of this see his *D.N.B.* entry.

Thomas Habington the younger died childless in 1721 and in the same year the Revd. William Thomas settled in Worcester.[52] It may have been then that he bought the elder Habington's manuscripts;[53] in his *Antiquitates Prioratus Majoris Malverne* (1725) Thomas cited the survey of the priory church by Habington, 'antiquarius noster Wigorniensis'. In 1730 he published a new edition of Dugdale's *Warwickshire*,[54] an excellent preparation for the 'History of Worcestershire' with which he was thought to be 'obliging the world'.[55] Habington, however, had not provided so ample a base as Dugdale, and in 1735 Thomas told Charles Lyttelton 'I am in no haste of printing, and when I shall begin I don't know, but in the mean time shall be writing fair and perfectly the copy of the Antiquities of Worcestershire now lying by me'.[56] He 'hardly allowed himself time for sleep, meals, or amusement'[57] and by 1738 his additions to Habington included many transcripts from the episcopal and capitular registers,[58] lists of patrons and incumbents for every parish,[59] and all the new church inscriptions and heraldry.[60] In that year, however, he died, and the Habington-Thomas manuscripts were then sold to Lyttelton.[61] He added fuller histories of parishes that had Lyttelton connexions[62] and died bishop of Carlisle in 1768, leaving such of the manuscripts as were in his possession, together with his own Worcestershire manuscripts, to the Society of Antiquaries.[63] Some of the Habington manuscripts had already been dispersed, including a folio draft of the 'Description' that Thomas and Lyttelton had handled;[64] after 1768 it remained with the bishop's brother at Hagley.[65]

Among the first to show an interest in the Lyttelton bequest was the Revd. Dr. Treadway Nash (1725–1811), an Oxford don who had come into a large

[52] *D.N.B.*
[53] Wood, *Athenae*, ed. Bliss, iii, col. 225.
[54] H. M. Jenkins, *Dr. Thomas's Edn. of Sir William Dugdale's Antiquities of Warws.* (Dugdale Soc. Occasional Paper iii, 1931).
[55] London, Soc. of Antiq. MS. 143, ii, f. 2 (Penyston Hastings to Thomas, 11 Dec. 1732).
[56] Ibid. MS. 149, f. 16 (Thomas to Lyttelton, 24 Dec. 1735).
[57] J. Chambers, *Biographical Illustrations of Worcs.* (1820), 338.
[58] e.g. Soc. of Antiq. MS. 149.
[59] A few survive in ibid. MS. 143. Thomas's MS. 'Patroni et Incumbentes Ecclesiarum in Agro Wigorn.' (Soc. of Antiq. minutes, xi, p. 5) has not been traced.
[60] Chambers, *Biographical Illustrations of Worcs.* 338.
[61] Ibid. 436. On him see *D.N.B.*
[62] Soc. of Antiq. MS. 139, ff. 1–28, 30–46, 48–55, 114–56; MS. 143, i, ff. 37–63v., 328–34; ii, ff. 197–238; MS. 152.
[63] Ibid. MSS. 139–40, 143–52.
[64] *Surv.* i. 470 n.; ii. 3 n.
[65] In 1978 his successor, Viscount Cobham, offered it for sale (Sotheby Parke Bernet & Co. *Catalogue of Lyttelton Papers*, 12 Dec. 1978, pp. 68–9, lot 61) but withdrew it before the auction: *Friends of Worcester R.O. Newsletter*, ii. [3].

Worcestershire estate.[66] Having moved to the county, he missed the scholarly
life and, without any topographical research to his name, formed the ambition
of revising the manuscripts for the press. He began in 1774 by having a clerk
copy out Habington's 'Description', together with the additions of Thomas
and Lyttelton, in blank 'books', one for each parish. Only then did he see that
the text needed more revision than he had bargained for. Though based in the
provinces, heavily committed to county business and the management of his
estate, and reluctant to spend money, Nash was nevertheless determined to
publish. He therefore decided not to correct the parish books systematically
but merely to amplify them from a short list of readily available sources and
to appeal for additional facts by questionnaire, advertisement, and personal
letter. Eventually he was forced to undertake fieldwork too, and visited many
churches for new inscriptions. His most valuable contribution, however, was a
generous flow of information, anecdote, and opinion (fearlessly expressed)
about 18th-century Worcestershire. Sadly, he soon tired of the job. The
Society of Antiquaries urged him to do more research, but he was unwilling
and instead contracted John Nichols to print the work. Nash offered Richard
Gough, director of the Antiquaries, the chance to correct and improve the
proofs, and Gough, unable to persuade him that corrections should be made
in the copy first, reluctantly agreed. The two folio volumes of Nash's
Collections for the History of Worcestershire appeared in 1781 and 1782, and a
Supplement of corrections and additions in 1799. Nash was careful not to claim
that the *Collections* were a 'history' (a continuous narrative aspiring to literary
excellence) or that he was any more than their 'editor'.

Dissatisfied with what Nash had done,[67] Peter Prattinton (b. 1771) of
Bewdley began to form his own collection 'for illustrating Mr. Habington's
survey of the county of Worcester'. He was a rich bachelor and untroubled by
any haste to publish, so spent his life transcribing and collecting. He died in
1840, leaving the collection to the Society of Antiquaries, where it consists of
81 volumes and five boxes.[68] Its scope and quality have allowed few
Worcestershire historians to pass it by. Prattinton, however, was the last
practising antiquary to use Habington's 'Description' for a starting point, and
in 1856 John Noake endorsed Nash's weary conclusion that such a

[66] On Nash and his work see D. C. Cox, '*This Foolish Business': Dr. Nash and Worcs. Collections*
(Worcs. Hist. Soc. Occasional Publication vii, 1993) and sources there cited.

[67] Bodl. MS. Douce d. 21, f. 242 (Prattinton to Francis Douce, 23 Dec. 1809). Miss Isobel
Morcom (Mrs. D. B. Robinson) is thanked for this reference.

[68] On Prattinton, his collections, and the means of reference to them see E. A. B. Barnard,
Prattinton Collections of Worcs. Hist. (1931); *T.W.A.S.* new ser. viii. 67–73; xiv. 61–8; xvi. 56–7;
xviii. 58; xxx. 83. A microfilm of the parish notes and illustrations and of the 'Miscellanea' is in
Hereford and Worcester R.O. (St. Helen's), ref. 989.9:91 BA 10509. Extracts relating to churches
have been published: *T.W.A.S.* new ser. vii. 83–93; ix. 100–6; x. 80–7; xi. 119–30; xii. 56–60.

compilation could never be a 'history'; the county needed 'a picture of the life and manners of our ancestors, and not a mere record of names and dates and crude undigested facts'.[69] Noake (1816–94), a talented journalist,[70] wrote widely-read miscellanies based on primary sources,[71] and in 1877 hoped that the time was 'not far distant' for a collaborative county history, more 'popular' than any previously attempted.[72] Earl Beauchamp, too, as president (1875–88) of the Worcester Diocesan Architectural and Archaeological Society, wanted a new county history[73] and in 1892, at the urging of J. W. Willis Bund, the society appointed a committee to frame a scheme for a county record society, whose publications would be the foundation for such a work. Thus was formed in 1893 the Worcestershire Historical Society. The plan of the new history was left undecided; Willis Bund knew only that the work of Habington and his successors was 'a parochial record, not a county history'.[74]

Willis Bund (d. 1928)[75] and John Amphlett (d. 1918)[76] edited 16 volumes between them. The vision of a new and better kind of county history, however, did not become any less nebulous as record publications accumulated, and there was scope meanwhile for an improved 'parochial record'. When the *Victoria History of the Counties of England* was begun in 1899, Willis Bund was therefore willing to become local editor. The Worcestershire volumes[77] did include 'general' articles, but he freely acknowledged that some of those would be found premature.[78] Nevertheless it was among the achievements of the Worcestershire *V.C.H.* (and among Nash's failures) to define accurately the current state of knowledge. Hardly any of the Worcestershire *V.C.H.* was written by local authors, and in fact its publication marked the first acquisition by professionals of the high ground in Worcestershire history and archaeology. By the 1920s it was rare for residents to have a sufficiency of both learning and leisure. The Worcestershire Parish Register Society, founded *c.* 1913, had managed to produce only five volumes, the last in 1916,[79] and after Willis Bund's death the Historical Society

[69] *Notes and Queries for Worcs.* p. vii.

[70] *D.N.B.*

[71] *Notes and Queries for Worcs.* (1856); *Worcs. Relics* (1877); *Worcs. Nuggets* (1894).

[72] *Worcs. Relics*, preface.

[73] *T.W.A.S.* new ser. xxx. 12.

[74] *Associated Archit. Socs.' Reports and Papers*, xxi. 119–29.

[75] On whom see *T.W.A.S.* new ser. iv. 111–17. His Worcs. collection is in Worcester City Library.

[76] On whom see Worcs. Naturalists' Club *Trans.* viii (1), 46–56. His diaries, 1864–1918 (described in *T.W.A.S.* new ser. xviii. 57–8), are at Worcester College, Oxford.

[77] *V.C.H. Worcs.* (5 vols. 1901–26). The Worcs. *Hist.* was almost complete by 1915 but publication of the fourth and index vols. was delayed by the war: ibid. iv, p. xix.

[78] Ibid. i, p. xix.

[79] The Worcs. Arch. Soc. launched a 'second series' of registers but only those of Upton Snodsbury (1950) and St. Michael's in Bedwardine (1954) appeared. Some Worcs. registers have since been published by the Birmingham and Midland Soc. for Genealogy and Heraldry.

published only four volumes (in seven parts) before 1960. Its membership had dwindled to a mere handful by the end of the Second World War, but J. F. Parker, honorary secretary and treasurer 1949–59, retrieved the society's finances almost single-handed and thus made possible its revival in 1959.[80] By then the universities, adult education, and the archive profession had expanded, to produce more potential editors and more demand for texts, and new publication grants had become available. The first general editor of the society's new series was Mr. (now Professor) P. H. Sawyer, then of Birmingham University, and his successors have all been professional scholars. In its first hundred years the society has published 55 volumes and (from 1977) some *Occasional Publications*. A new county history, however, is no longer the aim.

Even in Nash's time it was apparent that lone antiquaries were better able to publish on single places and subjects than on a whole county. Places were favoured first: Worcester by Valentine Green (1764 and 1796),[81] Evesham by William Tindal (1794)[82] and George May (1834 and 1845),[83] and Bewdley (1883)[84] and Kidderminster (1890)[85] by J. R. Burton. Thematic books appeared from the early 19th century, on biography,[86] field archaeology,[87] ecclesiology,[88] heraldry,[89] church plate,[90] parliamentary representation,[91] bibliography,[92] place names,[93] agriculture,[94] architecture,[95] and so on. Meanwhile the fruits of even

[80] *Court Rolls of Manor of Bromsgrove and King's Norton*, ed. A. F. C. Baber (Worcs. Hist. Soc. new ser. [iii], 1963), p. v.

[81] *Survey of City of Worcester* (1764); *Hist. and Antiquities of City and Suburbs of Worcester* (2 vols. 1796).

[82] *Hist. and Antiquities of Abbey and Borough of Evesham*.

[83] *Hist. of Evesham* (1834); *Descriptive Hist. of Town of Evesham* (1845).

[84] *Hist. of Bewdley; with Concise Accounts of some Neighbouring Parishes*.

[85] *Hist. of Kidderminster, with Short Accounts of some Neighbouring Parishes*.

[86] Chambers, *Biographical Illustrations of Worcs.*; E. O. Browne and J. R. Burton, *Short Biographies of Worthies of Worcs.* (1916).

[87] J. Allies, *On the Ancient British, Roman, and Saxon Antiquities of Worcs.* (1840); a revised edn., *British, Roman, and Saxon Antiquities and Folk-Lore of Worcs.* (1856), was one of the earliest works to use tithe surveys for field-name evidence.

[88] J. Noake, *The Rambler in Worcs., or Stray Notes on Churches and Congregations* (3 vols. 1846–54).

[89] H. S. Grazebrook, *Heraldry of Worcs.* (2 vols. 1873).

[90] W. Lea, *Church Plate in Archdeaconry of Worcester* (1884); W. A. and W. R. H. Peplow, *Church Plate of Archdeaconry of Worcester* (1967).

[91] W. R. Williams, *Parliamentary Hist. of County of Worcester* (privately printed, 1897).

[92] C. L. Nichols, *Bibliography of Worcs.* (1899); J. R. Burton, F. S. Pearson, and J. Humphreys, *Bibliography of Worcs.* (3 pts. Worcs. Hist. Soc. 1898–1907). Of the latter, pt. 1 covers Acts of Parliament, pt. 2 works relating to the county as a whole, and pt. 3 botanical works.

[93] W. H. Duignan, *Worcs. Place-Names* (1905); A. Mawer and F. M. Stenton, *Place-Names of Worcs.* (E.P.N.S. iv, 1927).

[94] R. C. Gaut, *Hist. of Worcs. Agriculture and Rural Evolution* (1939).

[95] F. T. S. Houghton, *Little Guide: Worcs.* (1922, 3rd edn. 1952); J. Lees-Milne, *Worcs.: Shell Guide* (1964); N. Pevsner, *Buildings of England: Worcs.* (1968).

narrower independent research could be garnered in the transactions of county societies. Upon the completion in 1854 of Noake's *Rambler*, which exposed the state of church architecture and liturgy in the county, E. A. H. Lechmere founded the Worcester Diocesan Architectural Society in order to promote Camdenian ecclesiology. Only Anglicans could belong.[96] Its transactions were published from 1854 in the *Reports and Papers* of the Associated Architectural Societies,[97] but from 1870 many Worcestershire articles appeared in the *Transactions and Proceedings* of the Birmingham Archaeological Society,[98] and slighter ones from 1897 in the *Transactions* of the Worcestershire Naturalists' Club. The diocesan society gradually broadened its interests, especially as the pace of church building and restoration slackened, and it was accordingly renamed the Worcester Diocesan Architectural and Archaeological Society in 1875 and the Worcestershire Archaeological Society in 1910, when non-Anglicans were first admitted.

Membership more than doubled between 1914 and 1924[99] and made possible the publication of a separate 'new series' of *Transactions* from 1924. They were edited until 1949 by E. A. B. Barnard (d. 1953), who had begun his antiquarian career in Evesham in the 1890s.[1] An urbane and astonishingly productive antiquary, he was, like his readers, politely but persistently inquisitive about individual people and places in the 'Four Shires', especially in the 16th–18th centuries. He had a talent for finding documents (though not for correctly transcribing or listing them) and a gift for presenting his discoveries enjoyably; like Noake, he wrote much for local newspapers. A full bibliography of his books and articles from the 1890s to the 1950s would be immense, and his many pieces in the *Transactions*, together with series by other contributors on church bells, monumental brasses, and stained glass, sustained the journal through the difficult 1930s and 1940s. During the Second World War, however, the volumes became shorter, and after the war were kept short by printing costs. From 1949 there was also some discontinuity of editorship, and annual publication ceased in 1964. That failure coincided with the new opportunities offered to archaeologists by the redevelopment of town centres, nowhere more sweeping than at Worcester, and their only other local outlet was then the relatively ephemeral *West Midlands Archaeological News Sheet*. In 1967 Mr. P. A. Barker,[2] a professional

---

[96] For its hist. see *T.W.A.S.* new ser. xxx. 2–15.
[97] A subject index to the titles of the Worcs. articles is ibid. 48–53.
[98] List (to 1936), ibid. xvii. 50–60.
[99] Ibid. ii, p. xiii.
[1] On him see *Vale of Evesham Hist. Soc. Research Papers*, i. 47–53 (with select bibliography). His diaries are in Hereford and Worcester R.O. (St. Helen's), ref. 705:673 BA 5821/1–3.
[2] On whom see *From Roman Town to Norman Castle: Papers in Honour of Philip Barker*, ed. A. Burl (1988), 1–10, 68–76, 82–4.

archaeologist who had taken the lead in 'rescue' excavation at Worcester, became honorary editor of the Archaeological Society and launched a biennial 'third series' of *Transactions*. Under his editorship a higher proportion of space was filled by excavation reports than in any equivalent period, but excavation methods had so advanced as virtually to exclude the amateur, both as practitioner and as intelligent reader, and later editors have therefore been careful to print a good measure of non-archaeological material.

The limitations placed upon practical archaeologists by the *Transactions'* reduced frequency, and by its editors' need to include articles for other members, were partly compensated when Worcester City Museum launched the *Worcestershire Archaeology Newsletter* (later the *Worcestershire Archaeology and Local History Newsletter*) in 1967, and other special interests have been served at county level by *The Worcestershire Recusant*, published by the Worcestershire Catholic History Society from 1963 and incorporated in 1991 in *Midland Catholic History*, and by the reports (in the *Newsletter*) of the Hereford and Worcester Architectural Record Group formed in 1975. During the local-history revival of the 1960s the most ambitious journal to emerge below county level was probably the *Vale of Evesham Historical Society Research Papers*, launched in 1967 but wound up for economic reasons in 1979. By the 1990s Worcestershire's past had long ceased to be imagined as an intelligible unity; the hard experience of Nash and his successors established that no such unity ever existed. It is therefore natural and right that Thomas Habington's deep interest in landed estates has since been matched in intensity by many other specialisms. Each of them takes a narrow view of local history, but together they proclaim the subject's endless possibilities.

YORKSHIRE

G. C. F. Forster

Yorkshire has yet to be written: for, to a well-informed historian, Yorkshire is a whole kingdom.[1]

Those words of Professor Jack Simmons neatly provide the key to the historiography of England's largest historic county. Early references to Yorkshire's history can, however, be found in the writings of Bede, his continuators, and Alcuin, and in the important chronicles composed in Yorkshire religious houses from the 12th century onwards there is material about church affairs and the doings of churchmen in the diocese, historical writing which has also served as source material for later historians.[2] The flowering of English topographical writing from the later 15th century produced no work exclusively on Yorkshire, but there is much of value both in the record of John Leland's journeys and in William Camden's *Britannia*.[3] A more direct advance was made by the Yorkshire-born Christopher Saxton, whose map of Yorkshire (1577) provided a pioneering, basic survey in use for about a century and laid the foundation of Yorkshire cartography which was continued by John Warburton's new survey (1720) and improved upon by Thomas Jefferys's map of 1772, which itself held the field until Christopher Greenwood's map of 1817–18 and the Ordnance Survey.[4] If those influential map-makers made their own contribution to the county's history, so too did the early travellers and diarists—from Celia Fiennes to Arthur Young—who visited Yorkshire during the 17th and 18th centuries; they were not writing history, but they contributed to it by recording their observations of the landscape, buildings, farming, industries, and markets.[5]

[1] J. Simmons, 'Writing of English County Hist.' *English County Historians*, ed. J. Simmons (1978), 2.

[2] A. Gransden, *Hist. Writing in England, c. 550–c. 1307* (1974), 67–91, 269–95, 519–21; J. Taylor, *Medieval Hist. Writing in Yorks.* (St. Anthony's Hall Publication xix, 1961), 4–5, 7, 12–14.

[3] J. Leland, *Itinerary*, ed. L. Toulmin Smith (5 vols. 1907–10), esp. i and vi; W. Camden, *Britannia* (1586, English translation 1610), *passim*.

[4] A. Raistrick, *Yorks. Maps and Map-Makers* (1969), 14–15, 24, 28, 41, 46, 51; *Descriptive List of Printed Maps of Yorks. and Ridings, 1577–1900* (Yorks. Arch. Soc. Record Ser. lxxxvi), pp. vi–xiii.

[5] E. Moir, *Discovery of Britain: English Tourists, 1540–1840* (1964), 159–78, a convenient list of travel writings.

Historical recording of a different kind flourished in 17th-century Yorkshire, where several antiquaries collected and copied documents, noted monuments, inscriptions, and heraldry, and constructed pedigrees. Most prominent among them was Roger Dodsworth, 'one of the greatest of English antiquaries', who transcribed great numbers of charters and manorial rolls, copied the surviving manuscripts of Yorkshire monasteries and made innumerable notes on local churches. A highly industrious and careful scholar, Dodsworth had in mind three projects, a Monasticon, a Baronage, and a history of Yorkshire, but he published nothing under his own name, though his invaluable collections (which went ultimately to the Bodleian Library) underlay the work of others, notably Sir William Dugdale, Thomas Tanner, and John Burton.[6] Among other Yorkshire antiquaries who carried on Dodsworth's great work were John Hopkinson (1610–80), a lawyer and herald's deputy who assisted Dugdale; Dr. Nathaniel Johnston (1627–1705), an assiduous collector of material for a 50-volume history of the county, a plan which not surprisingly proved abortive; James Torre (1649–99), who catalogued Dodsworth's manuscripts and built up several volumes of manuscript evidences for the diocese of York and its cathedral, material later used for a similar survey by Archbishop John Sharp; and Abraham de la Pryme (1672–1704). Even if the achievements of those men lay in collection rather than publication, they made their contribution to the history of Yorkshire by exchanging information with others of similar interests, and by transcribing or collecting documents and thus preserving evidence which might otherwise have been lost.[7]

Although Heneage Dering, dean of Ripon, composed *Reliquiae Eboracenses* (1743), an elegant poem in Latin hexameters, he stopped short with the Romans, and the county's antiquarian tradition languished after 1730, apart from the life's work of Dr. John Burton. He was a well known philanthropist, physician, and man-midwife in York; allegedly a Jacobite, he was satirized as Dr. Slop in Sterne's *Tristram Shandy*. He became a notable antiquary: in preparing his work on Yorkshire monasticism he used a great variety of

---

[6] N. Denholm-Young and H. H. E. Craster, 'Roger Dodsworth (1585–1654) and his Circle', *Yorks. Arch. Jnl.* xxxii. 5–32; B. A. English and C. B. L. Barr, 'Recs. formerly in St. Mary's Tower, York, pt. i', ibid. xlii. 198–235; J. Simmons, 'English County Historians', *Trans. Hunter Arch. Soc.* viii. 281; F. Madan, H. H. E. Craster, N. Denholm-Young, *Summary Catalogue of Western MSS. in Bodl.* 865–72.

[7] G. C. F. Forster, 'First Medievalist in Leeds: Ralph Thoresby, F.R.S., 1658–1725', *Church and Chronicle in Middle Ages*, ed. I. Wood and G. A. Loud (1991), 260; E. W. Crossley, 'MSS. of Nathaniel Johnston, M.D., of Pontefract', *Yorks. Arch. Jnl.* xxxii. 429–41; York Minster Library, Dean and Chapter muniments, L 1 (6–10); Borthwick Institute of Hist. Research, York, Bp. Dio. 1–3; *D.N.B.* The compilations of Torre and Sharp were used by George Lawton in his invaluable work of reference for benefices, patronage, and charities in the historic diocese of York, *Collectio Rerum Ecclesiasticarum de Diocesi Eboracensi* (1840). For Pryme, below, Yorkshire East Riding.

printed sources, manuscripts lent by private owners (including the archives of Fountains Abbey), records in the Tower of London, and the collections of Dodsworth and his circle. The first volume of Burton's *Monasticon Eboracense* (1758–9) comprised a history of the early Church in the diocese, accounts of the religious orders in the county, their churches, endowments, patrons, and abbots, and information on parish churches. It was well received but the proposed second volume was not published, and Burton's collections were sold to William Constable of Burton Constable (Yorks. E.R.). Burton had other projects in mind: a plan to establish in York a repository for records and representative antiquities from the whole county; a proposal for a society to collect information on Yorkshire by means of a detailed questionnaire enquiring about natural resources, population, institutions, manufactures, and buildings; an ambition to write a general county history. Nothing was accomplished, and Burton's work marks the end of an epoch.[8]

The years from 1760 to 1830 were a vintage period for the study of county history in many parts of the country, but not in Yorkshire, where historical and literary pursuits were focused on individual places or on the production of more general works with a severely practical purpose, such as gazetteers and directories. Among them were E. Hargrove's *Yorkshire Gazetteer* (1806, 1812) and T. Langdale's *Topographical Dictionary of Yorkshire* (1809), both of them conveniently arranged, with historical material as well as contemporary facts. More important was the *History, Directory and Gazetteer of the County of York* (2 vols. 1822, reprinted 1969) by Edward Baines the elder, a printer who became owner-editor of the *Leeds Mercury*. Baines was a careful writer who provided for each place a general historical description drawn from the available published literature. Some of the more popular topographical works on the county published at that time were influenced by the Romantics, with their interest in scenery and picturesque detail: one was John Bigland's contribution to the *Beauties of England and Wales* series, *A Topographical and Historical Description of the County of York* (1812), a large, illustrated work to be used only with great caution; another was Thomas Allen's *New and Complete History of the County of York* (3 vols. 1829–31), containing perfunctory and derivative information on all parishes but described by a later critic as a 'Catch-penny Work . . . to call it a complete history . . . is a deception; the plates are on a par with the book'.[9]

Illustrations were by then regarded as more important than ever before, both as a record and as a stimulus to the reader's historical imagination. One famous example was George Walker's *The Costume of Yorkshire* (1814), 40

---

[8] J. Burton, *Monasticon Eboracense* (1758–9); R. Davies, 'Memoir of John Burton', *Yorks. Arch. Jnl.* ii. 416 sqq.; *V.C.H. City of York*, 242, 248–9.
[9] W. Boyne, *Yorks. Library* (1869), 14.

coloured plates with descriptions, in English and French, of men and women in a variety of occupations, from a spinner to a jockey, a whalebone scraper to a cutler. Another, more circumscribed, was *Monastic Ruins of Yorkshire* (2 vols. 1843) from drawings by William Richardson—fine plates but mean text. Most important of all, however, would have been the illustrations arranged for the projected 'General History of the County of York' in seven folio volumes, announced by the author, the Revd. Thomas Dunham Whitaker, in the *Leeds Intelligencer* in 1816. Whitaker had already published, or sent to the press, large volumes on extensive areas of the West Riding; he proposed to deal with other parts of the county on a more limited, though still elaborate, scale, using a vast range of sources, personal fieldwork, and material supplied by others, to provide a history of manners as well as of places and buildings. The books were to include landscape drawings by J. M. W. Turner and architectural subjects drawn by J. C. Buckler. It was an over-ambitious and too costly enterprise which seems to have unnerved the publishers (Longman) and frightened potential subscribers before it foundered because of Whitaker's failing health, and death in 1821, with only the volume on Richmondshire completed to show what the author was attempting.[10]

Historical work on the county had so far been undertaken by individuals, sometimes collaborating, often labouring alone, rather than by organizations. By Whitaker's time, however, change was in the air, first marked in the county by the foundation in 1820 of the Yorkshire Philosophical Society: collecting, rather than research and writing, was its main activity but it brought together men with scholarly interests in a wide range of subjects.[11] During the second quarter of the 19th century major advances were made nationally and locally in provision for historical study, developments in tune with the intellectual climate of the time, not least the interest in things medieval and the concern to rescue and preserve the remains of the past—buildings, artefacts, documents, and traditions—threatened by the rapid changes of the period.[12] The needs of serious historical scholars and the general interests of the educated encouraged the establishment of societies to investigate the past and publish its records. In the North the first was the Surtees Society, founded in April 1834 by friends of Robert Surtees to publish documents 'illustrative of the intellectual, the moral, the religious, and the social condition' of those parts of England and Scotland which had formed the kingdom of Northumbria. The society flourished from the start and quickly became a leader in the field, publishing an extensive range of Yorkshire material

[10] *Leeds Intelligencer*, 25 Mar. 1816; D. Hill, *In Turner's Footsteps* (1984), 23–6; below, Yorkshire East Riding; Yorkshire North Riding.

[11] J. Biggins, *Historians of York* (St. Anthony's Hall Publication x, 1956), 11.

[12] C. Dellheim, *The Face of the Past* (1982), 1–31, 54.

including wills, diaries, chantry certificates, and archbishops' registers, as well as the records of major religious houses and the great minster churches of York, Ripon, and Beverley. The achievements of the Surtees Society's early decades owed much to James Raine and his son, also James, whose editorial industry was prodigious even if sometimes marred by errors and unacknowledged omissions.[13]

From the 1840s there was a rapid, country-wide proliferation of county archaeological societies, but it was not until 1863 that there was founded in Huddersfield the society which, taking the whole historic county for its province, would eventually be named the Yorkshire Archaeological Society. Its purposes were to explore the county's past, to collect, investigate, and preserve its antiquities and records, and to work towards a history of the county. Guided by earnest amateur scholars, many of them clergymen, the Yorkshire Archaeological Society had made rapid progress by 1870, drawing members from all over Yorkshire, establishing a library, and launching a journal. From the early years until the 1930s the predominant contents of the *Yorkshire Archaeological Journal* reflected the society's main concerns: Roman remains and other archaeological finds; historic buildings, especially churches and their monuments, plate, bells, and glass; coins and tokens; heraldry and pedigrees; manuscripts. The publication of documents by the society became a major activity after 1884 with the establishment of the Record Series, which issued 45 volumes within 25 years: Feet of Fines, deeds, subsidy rolls, inquisitions, royalist composition papers, court rolls, cartularies, assize rolls, and wills. In 1899 the society made a further important contribution to the study of records by forming another society for the publication of the county's parish records.[14] Moreover, all those activities were supplemented by individual ventures such as J. J. Cartwright's valuable collection of Yorkshire material from the State Papers, and by Joseph Foster's large volumes of Yorkshire pedigrees.[15]

By the time William Boyne had published his pioneering and still invaluable bibliography, *The Yorkshire Library* (1869), there was already a formidable amount of material about the county's history in print, and the list

---

[13] A. Hamilton Thompson, *The Surtees Soc. 1834–1934* (Surtees Soc. cl), 1–2, 14, 23, 26, 29–30; P. Levine, *The Amateur and the Professional: Antiquarians, Historians and Archaeologists in Victorian England* (1986), 41, 44–5; *D.N.B.*

[14] S. Piggott, 'Origins of English County Arch. Socs.' idem, *Ruins in a Landscape* (1976), 171–95, esp. 190; Levine, *Amateur and Professional*, 46, 48, 51; Dellheim, *Face of Past*, 43, 51, 53, 55–7; J. W. Walker, *Hist. of Yorks. Arch. Soc.* (n.d.), 3 sqq., 9, 13; C. T. Clay, *Catalogue of Publications of Rec. Ser. 1885–1946* (Yorks. Arch. Soc. Rec. Ser. cxiii), pp. vii–xi, xiii sqq.; G. C. F. Forster, 'Yorks. Arch. Jnl., vols. 1–50', *Yorks. Arch. Jnl.* l. 1–6.

[15] J. J. Cartwright, *Chapters in Hist. of Yorks.* (1872); J. Foster, *Pedigrees of County Families of Yorks.* (2 vols. 1874).

continued to grow, inevitably with unevenness of quality. Some works showed little acquaintance with the original sources now increasingly available in print: Henry Schroeder's *Annals of Yorkshire* (2 vols. 1851–2) could be described as a 'contemptible work', 'a jumble', 'the work of the scissors and paste-brush', and John Mayhall's *Annals* (1860) was scarcely better.[16] In the 1880s and 1890s there was a spate of popular antiquarian periodicals, dealing with different aspects of the county's past; they were short-lived, as they deserved to be.[17] Even the 10 volumes entitled *Old Yorkshire* (1888–91), edited variously by W. Smith and W. Wheater and purporting to provide notes and extracts from original sources, similarly lacked reliability. Other historical works on the county scale were more careful and can still be useful. *Yorkshire Past and Present* (2 vols. 1871–7; 4 vols. 1870–5) by Thomas Baines (son of Edward Baines the elder) drew upon the publications of the Record Commission, the Public Record Office, the Surtees Society, the collections printed by Rushworth and Rymer, printed chronicles, and Blue Books; it presented a coherent survey of events in Yorkshire from the earliest times, a classic account of the woollen industry by the author's brother Edward Baines the younger, and historical descriptions of the main towns; it also included valuable contemporary data. Another effective work was J. S. Fletcher's *Picturesque History of Yorkshire* (3 vols. 1899–1901), which was particularly useful for its topographical descriptions, current information, and personal observations. In contrast, the most bizarre undertaking was that of the eccentric genealogist and copyist, the self-styled Marshal-General G. H. de S. N. Plantagenet-Harrison, who planned a six-volume general history of Yorkshire; having been refused a reader's ticket to the reading room of the British Museum for applying under the title of duke of Lancaster, he set himself the task of searching and recording for every place all relevant material in the public records; not surprisingly he only published one (highly indigestible) volume on Gilling West (Yorks. N.R.).[18]

Those endeavours marked the end of attempts by 'a single man to encompass the whole range of material available for the history of one English county', even with the limited, chronological narratives of events favoured by 19th-century writers.[19] The necessary degree of collaboration amongst a number of contributors was achieved by the Victoria County History, which produced between 1907 and 1913 three general volumes on the history of

[16] Boyne, *Yorks. Library*, 29–30.
[17] Conveniently listed in *Catalogue of Printed Books and Pamphlets in Library of Yorks. Arch. Soc.* (1935), ii. 264–5.
[18] G. H. de S. N. Plantagenet-Harrison, *Hist. Yorks.* (1885), i, pp. vii–viii; A. L. Morton, 'The Hero as Genealogist', *Yorks. Arch. Jnl.* xl. 351–70.
[19] Simmons, *County Historians*, 16.

Yorkshire. It faced the problem of writing the history of the county as a whole by presenting coherent accounts of political, ecclesiastical, and economic history and by treating some other subjects (Domesday Book, industries, sport, for example) on a county-wide basis.

A great improvement on earlier publications, *V.C.H. Yorkshire* was matched by other advances in the study of the county's history. The Yorkshire Archaeological Society Record Series continued its important editions of texts, many of them prepared by very distinguished editors: J. W. Clay, J. T. Fowler, William Brown, A. Hamilton Thompson (a professor at Leeds and a man 'of rare distinction'), and, above all, Sir Charles Clay (son of J. W.), whose *Early Yorkshire Charters* and numerous other editions made him 'one of the most distinguished editors of medieval charters this country has produced'.[20] More local manuscripts became available too: the Y.A.S. has been collecting documents from the whole of Yorkshire since 1867, thus serving as a general county record office; during the present century the county's university libraries have developed record repositories; and in the 1950s the establishment of the Borthwick Institute of Historical Research at St. Anthony's Hall, York, has made the vast records of the diocese of York accessible to scholars.[21]

The availability of a wider range of original sources has been reflected in the contents of the *Yorkshire Archaeological Journal* which, since the 1930s, has published more varied papers on the county's political, military, ecclesiastical, agrarian, and architectural history.[22] Moreover, the foundation of a new journal, *Northern History*, at the University of Leeds in 1966 has facilitated the publication of articles setting Yorkshire's history in a wider regional context. Since the 1920s scholars have produced a growing body of specialized monographs on different aspects of the whole county's history—on the Reformation, the cloth industry, Puritanism and recusancy, the gentry, architecture, and transport, to mention only a few. Yet there is no new, large-scale, up-to-date history of the entire county for, in the words of the late Professor G. R. Potter, 'Yorkshire is too big . . . in reality, three counties, the three Ridings being thoroughly separable, while remaining part of a whole'.[23]

[20] See obituaries, *Yorks. Arch. Jnl.* xxv. 124–6; xxviii. 107–33; xxxviii. 266–8; l. 189–90; lii. 1–18.
[21] J. S. Purvis, *Archives of York Diocesan Registry* (St. Anthony's Hall Publication ii, 1952), 7–8.
[22] Forster, *Yorks. Arch. Jnl.* l. 1–6.
[23] G. R. Potter, 'Introduction', in J. Hunter, *South Yorks.* (reprinted 1974), i, p. v.

YORKSHIRE: THE EAST RIDING

G. H. R. Kent

The history and topography of the East Riding of Yorkshire and Hull began to be written in the 16th century but the area was for long discussed in general works, dealing either with the United Kingdom as a whole or with Yorkshire, and it was only in the 18th century that works of genuine *local* history started to appear and not until the 19th that major histories were published.

The chronicle of Thomas Burton, abbot of Meaux, written in the later 14th century, included topographical information, notably on the drainage and the erosion of the coast, and genealogical detail, but those subjects were incidental to his main concern, the history of the abbey and its estates.[1] The novel idea that the locality was of interest in itself lay behind the work of John Leland, 'the father of English topography'. The excursions he made *c.* 1535 into the East Riding from York were limited in scope: he journeyed to Beverley, Hull, and into Holderness, before returning to York through Howden. Much of his description was of the towns, particularly of their ecclesiastical buildings, some of which he would have had to visit as a Crown commissioner. He did, however, comment more generally, noting in Beverley the canal 'cut from the town to . . . Hull river, whereby pretty vessels come thither' and in both of the earl of Northumberland's houses at Leconfield and Wressle a 'studying chamber . . . called Paradise'.[2] Leland's work had a formative influence on topographical writing by being incorporated into the publications of his successors, notably William Camden's *Britannia*, first published in 1586.[3] Despite the additions introduced by its various editors, the account of the East Riding in *Britannia* remained brief on the eve of the 19th century, in contrast to that of its western neighbour. Camden's work in turn spawned similar volumes, like Defoe's *Tour Through the Whole Island of Great Britain* (1724–7), which merely reproduced much of Edmund Gibson's edition of *Britannia*.[4] Better was Thomas Cox's *Magna Britannia et Hibernia*

---

[1] *Chronica Monasterii de Melsa* (Rolls Ser. xliii, 3 vols. 1866–8), ed. E. A. Bond.
[2] The standard modern edn. of the 'Itinerary' is that ed. by L. Toulmin Smith (5 vols. 1907–10).
[3] W. Camden, *Britain*, trans. P. Holland (1610).
[4] Also R. Blome, *Britannia* (1673).

(1720–31), which added information from other sources, and noticed in Beverley the houses then being built there by the local gentry.

Leland's example as traveller and commentator was followed by several visitors to the area in the 17th century and later.[5] Their accounts once again concentrate on the towns of Beverley and Hull, though Celia Fiennes also described enthusiastically her kinsman's house at Burton Agnes in 1697.[6] The most useful of the early travellers' tales is probably that of John Ray, who visited in 1661. His wide-ranging description of Hull deals with its principal church, defences, government, school, trade, and waterworks,[7] besides discussing (correctly) the town's origin. Concentration upon 'the sights' resulted in a limiting repetition in the descriptions: most commentators for instance noticed as a curiosity a kayak from Greenland, where Hull had recently established itself in whale fishing.[8] Those memoirs were nevertheless significant contributions to knowledge of the area, and, though long unprinted, some were evidently circulated and incorporated into the general works, Ray's account appearing in Cox's *Magna Britannia*.[9]

Of greater immediate importance than the visitors' accounts were perhaps the maps and plans which from the earlier 16th century guided the visitors and excited interest.[10] The first county map, showing the several deer parks of the East Riding, was produced in 1577 by Christopher Saxton.[11] It was copied and reproduced in early 17th-century editions of Camden, and served as the basis for later maps, like John Speed's map of the North and East Ridings of 1610, published with Speed's other county maps in the very successful *Theatre of the Empire of Great Britain*, which first appeared in 1611. The early maps did not show roads but that lack was remedied later in the 17th century, John Ogilby surveying and describing the principal routes in his *Britannia* (1675) and that information being depicted on Philip Lea's 1687 edition of Saxton.[12]

Another advance, the copying, classification, and dissemination of information from major caches of records, was at first directed towards monastic and diocesan sources covering all Yorkshire rather than just the East

---

[5] Accounts of the area from and including Leland's to those of 19th-century fact-finders are collected in *Descriptions of East Yorks.: Leland to Defoe*, ed. D. Woodward (East Yorks. Local Hist. Ser. xxxix) and *Descriptions of East Yorks.: De La Pryme to Head*, ed. J. Crowther (East Yorks. Local Hist. Ser. xlv).

[6] C. Fiennes, *Journeys*, ed. C. Morris (1947), 86–91. See also 'Thos. Baskerville's Journeys in England, Temp. Car. II', Hist. MSS. Com. 29, *13th Report, II, Portland*, ii, pp. 313–14.

[7] *V.C.H. Yorks. E.R.* i. 371–2.

[8] *Select Remains of the Learned John Ray*, ed. W. Derham (1760), 139–47; Fiennes, *Journeys*, 88–9; *Life of Marmaduke Rawdon of York* (Camden Soc. [old ser.] lxxxv), 147–9; *V.C.H. Yorks. E.R.* i. 136.

[9] T. Cox, *Magna Britannia et Hibernia* (6 vols. 1720–31).

[10] H. Whitaker, *Descriptive List of Printed Maps of Yorks.* (Yorks. Arch. Soc. Rec. Ser. lxxxvi).

[11] Published in 1579 in C. Saxton, *Atlas of England and Wales*.

[12] P. Lea, *Traveller's Guide, being the Best Map of England and Wales* (1687).

Riding.[13] Local topographical writing began in Hull, which had been described pictorially by Speed in 1610 and *c.* 1640 by Wenceslaus Hollar.[14] During his incumbency of the curacy of Holy Trinity church, Hull, from 1698 until 1701, Abraham de la Pryme, member of a Huguenot family settled at Hatfield (Yorks. W.R.),[15] catalogued the corporation records and by order of the mayor and aldermen produced an outline history of the town. In 1703 de la Pryme said that the history remained unfinished and 'neither must I dare to publish it, till some be dead that are now living'. After his death in 1704 some of the manuscripts relating to Hull were bought by the corporation; many of his other topographical collections, including material on Hull[16] and collections on Hedon and the East Riding,[17] and the West Riding,[18] were acquired by John Warburton, the cartographer[19] and herald,[20] before being bought by the marquess of Lansdowne and eventually deposited in the British Museum library. De la Pryme's work on Hull was published later in the 18th century in three histories of the town, the earliest being that of Thomas Gent, a York printer.[21] John Tickell acknowledged his debt to de la Pryme, citing as sources, besides the corporation and Trinity House records, three manuscript volumes lent by Lord Lansdowne. The plan adopted for all three histories—and for later histories of Hull and Beverley—was of a chronological survey of events, followed by an account of particular aspects of the town's life and institutions. Tickell's history included a town plan of 1791 by Anthony Bower. All three printed many excerpts from records, amply fulfilling Gent's object of crowding in 'as much anecdote and narrative . . . as possible'; 'even the index', he promised, 'is full of amusement'.[22] Altogether superior to the rambling 18th-century compilations was Charles Frost's discussion of the medieval town, supported by documents which corrected earlier erroneous discussion of the town's origin.[23] Tickell and Frost were both used by J. J. Sheahan for a later account, chiefly valuable for its wealth of information on Victorian Hull.[24]

Frost's sources included the manuscripts in the library at nearby Burton

[13] Above, Yorks.

[14] *V.C.H. Yorks. E.R.* i, plate facing p. 132.

[15] *Diary of Abraham de la Pryme* (Surtees Soc. liv), pp. xii, xv, xviii–xx, 204 n.; *V.C.H. Yorks. E.R.* i. 124, 165, 214, 290.

[16] B.L. Lansd. MSS. 890–1.

[17] Ibid. Lansd. MS. 894.

[18] Ibid. Lansd. MSS. 897–8.

[19] Whitaker, *Descriptive List of Printed Maps of Yorks.* 51.

[20] *D.N.B.*

[21] T. Gent, *Annales Regioduni Hullini* (1735); G. Hadley, *New and Complete Hist. of Town and County of Town of Kingston-upon-Hull* (1788); J. Tickell, *Hist. of Town and County of Kingston upon Hull* (1798).

[22] Gent, *Annales Regioduni Hullini* (1869 edn.).

[23] C. Frost, *Notices relative to Early Hist. of Town and Port of Hull* (1827).

[24] J. J. Sheahan, *Hist. of Town and Port of Kingston-upon-Hull* (1864).

Constable, where an important collection had been assembled by Cuthbert Constable (d. 1747) and his son William (d. 1791).[25] John Burton, heir to James Torre's work on the St. Mary's manuscripts and to nearly 2,000 of the charters, sold his collections to William Constable, and copies of government records relating to the lordship of Holderness were also gathered there, in part to assist in the Constables' litigation over reclaimed land in the Humber and other matters.[26] Among the antiquarians given access to the library was the Revd. William Dade, rector of Barmston in Holderness, who at his death in 1790 left an unfinished manuscript history of Holderness, which was promptly added to the library and used by Tickell and by Thomas Thompson for his preliminary sketches on Holderness.[27] Greater use of Dade's manuscript was made by George Poulson, whose two-volume *History and Antiquities of the Seigniory of Holderness* based upon it appeared in 1840–1.[28] The work is largely a parish-by-parish account of the area, arranged under the constituent bailiwicks of the wapentake of Holderness, following on brief introductory chapters on politics, religion, and, an important physical feature of the area, the drainage. A later writer's judgement on Poulson's work as 'slip-shod and unsatisfactory'[29] seems unduly harsh for a work of such detail and scale. Though much of the information presented has since been published in record volumes, without the frequent mistakes of transcription, translation, and dating of Poulson's volumes, some valuable evidences are not to be found elsewhere and have probably been lost in the original.

No other surveys on the scale of Poulson's *Holderness* were attempted before the 20th century. It is true that several general works appeared in which Hull and the riding's parishes were discussed, but the treatment was cursory and they are now valued for their contemporary detail rather than their history.[30] From the early 19th century, however, accounts of particular places proliferated.[31] The early writers were often clergymen or professionals living on estates close to the larger towns, and the publications ranged from

[25] J. Burton, *Monasticon Eboracense* (1758), p. vi; J. Foster, *Pedigrees of County Families of Yorks.* (2 vols. 1874), ii, s.v. Constable of Constable Burton [*recte* Burton Constable].

[26] Hull Univ. Library, DCC (papers relating to Attorney General v. Constable 1879 and subsequent actions); Humberside A.O., DDCC.

[27] T. Thompson, *Ocellum Promontorium* (1821–4). In 1828 Thompson visited France for antiquarian study, died in Paris, and was buried in the Père-Lachaise cemetery: addition to Hull Central Library copy.

[28] B. A. English and C. B. L. Barr, 'Recs. formerly in St. Mary's Tower, York, pt. 1', *Yorks. Arch. Jnl.* xlii. 224, 226–8; Poulson, *Hist. and Antiquities of Seigniory of Holderness*, i, preface.

[29] J. R. Boyle, *Early Hist. of Town and Port of Hedon* (1895).

[30] T. Allen, *New and Complete Hist. of County of York* (1828–31); J. J. Sheahan and T. Whellan, *Hist. and Topography of City of York, Ainsty Wapentake, and East Riding of Yorks.* (1855–6); T. Bulmer & Co. *Hist., Topography, and Dir. of East Yorks.* (1892).

[31] Many of those works are discussed in A. G. Dickens and K. A. MacMahon, *Guide to Regional Studies on East Riding of Yorks. and City of Hull* (1956).

small volumes much concerned with the local church—and in at least one case, Thomas Clarke's history of Howden, written to fund its restoration[32]— to comprehensive histories supported by extensive excerpts from local and other records. The earliest work of local history outside Hull—and atypically one concerned with a large rural parish—came from the industrious John Burton, who appended a mostly tenurial and ecclesiastical history of Hemingbrough, where his wife had an estate, to his *Monasticon Eboracense* (1758). Burton's history was intended as an exemplar of accounts to be produced under his scheme for a history of the county; the account had little influence before the 19th century and was itself superseded by the detailed and scholarly history of Thomas Burton, which appeared posthumously in 1888 in an edition enlarged by the Revd. James Raine, son and namesake of the antiquary.[33] Other noteworthy local histories were those devoted to Beverley and Hedon. Materials for a history of Beverley were collected *c.* 1700 by de la Pryme[34] and two aldermen of Beverley, Matthew Ashmole and Marmaduke Nelson,[35] and early the next century by the Beverley publisher Matthew Turner. Turner's project was eventually entrusted to the Revd. George Oliver, whose *History and Antiquities of the Town and Minster of Beverley* appeared in May 1829.[36] Oliver's work was no doubt hastened by the preparation of a rival, George Poulson's *Beverlac*, which George Scaum of Beverley published late that year or early in 1830.[37] Both histories followed the pattern established for town histories of narrative followed by thematic description, and Oliver's history also included selective information on the area around Beverley. Poulson was assisted by the historian of Hull, Charles Frost, and his history is reckoned the better of the two. The decayed port of Hedon also had its history told in two works which appeared virtually together. J. R. Boyle, the later translator of Hull's records,[38] supported his history with excerpts from the national records and from those of Hedon corporation, then recently clawed back from the heirs of a less-than-scrupulous local antiquary, Gillyat Sumner.[39] G. R. Park carried the history of the borough beyond the medieval limit of Boyle's account but his work was less scholarly.[40]

---

[32] T. Clarke, *Hist. of Church, Parish, and Manor of Howden* (1850).

[33] The two Burtons were evidently not related: T. Burton, *Hist. and Antiquities of Hemingbrough* (1888), 283–4 and *passim*; *D.N.B.* s.vv. Burton; Raine.

[34] B.L. Lansd. MS. 896.

[35] *V.C.H. Yorks. E.R.* vi. 202.

[36] *Hull Advertiser*, 15 May 1829. The work was remaindered in 1836: ibid. 9 Sep. 1836.

[37] Poulson's history is dated 1829. *Hull Advertiser*, 13 Nov. 1829; 12 Feb. 1830; *English Catalogue of Books, 1801–36*, p. 465.

[38] J. R. Boyle, *Charters and Letters Patent Granted to Kingston upon Hull* (1905).

[39] J. R. Boyle, *Early Hist. of Town and Port of Hedon* (1895), pp. vi–ix and *passim*.

[40] G. R. Park, *Hist. of Ancient Borough of Hedon* (1895).

The accumulation of printed local histories was aided and informed by parallel developments: the writing and publication of reports on various aspects of the riding's life, those on agriculture being particularly important for a predominantly rural area,[41] and the growing accessibility of central and local sources. The efforts of national bodies like the Record Commissioners and the Historical Manuscripts Commission were complemented by those of regional societies. In 1835 the Surtees Society produced its first volume in what was to be a distinguished series devoted to the ecclesiastical and other records of north-east England. Among the earlier volumes was de la Pryme's diary, detailing his indefatigible investigation of the area around Hull and his correspondence with antiquaries like Thoresby.[42] The Yorkshire Archaeological Society, originally a West Riding body, has provided a wealth of evidence for all parts of the county, as well as several volumes specifically concerned with the East Riding, in its record series, established in 1885 as 'a contribution of materials toward the History and Antiquities of Yorkshire'.[43] Another great achievement of the society has been the continuation of William Farrer's monumental *Early Yorkshire Charters*.[44] In the present century a mass of important material held by local record offices, including the ecclesiastical collections in the Borthwick Institute and the Minster Library at York, has been described in mostly unprinted calendars and lists, and a further aid in searching printed material and the major manuscript collections has been provided by the creation at Hull University of a widely available computerized index, the East Yorkshire Bibliography. Besides their record work, local societies also published contributions to the history of the area in their journals. Articles ranging from the scholarly to the distinctly 'folksy' appeared in the *Transactions* of the East Riding Antiquarian Society from 1893 until the society foundered under the dual blows of the Second World War and the death in 1941 of the editor, Thomas Sheppard, a prolific author of local studies and the director of Hull's museums. An offshoot of the Antiquarian Society, the East Yorkshire Georgian Society, published useful architectural studies from 1937 until 1963, and some of the best writing on the area continues to appear in the booklets of the East Yorkshire Local History Society, begun in the 1950s.

John Burton's proposals in 1758 for a county history, involving the employment of persons 'to observe and collect what is remarkable and

---

[41] A. Young, *Six Months' Tour through North of England* (1770); W. Marshall, *Rural Economy of Yorks.* (1788); I. Leatham, *General View of Agriculture of East Riding of Yorks.* (1794); H. Strickland, *General View of Agriculture of East Riding of Yorks.* (1812). Excerpts printed in *Descriptions of East Yorks.* ed. Crowther.

[42] *Diary of Abraham de la Pryme* (Surtees Soc. liv).

[43] Preface to Yorks. Arch. Soc. Rec. Ser. i.

[44] Vols. i–iii (privately printed, 1914–16); iv–xii, index to i–iii (Yorks. Arch. Soc. 1935–65).

curious',[45] only began to be realized in the 20th century. The Victoria History
of the Counties of England, founded in 1899,[46] produced a general history of
Yorkshire in the early years of the present century,[47] but it was only about
1960, with funding from local government, that work was begun on the task of
writing a parish-by-parish survey of the East Riding and Hull. The first
volume of the East Riding set, published in 1969 and devoted to Hull,[48] was
greeted as 'one of the most brilliantly detailed full-length urban portraits yet
done in this country'.[49] Since then a further five volumes have appeared,
providing histories of Beverley, Bridlington, Hemingbrough, Hedon, and
many rural parishes in all parts of the former riding. Work is proceeding on 27
parishes in Holderness, which will be published as the seventh volume in the
series.

[45] *Monasticon Eboracense*, 426.
[46] *V.C.H. General Introduction*, 1.
[47] *V.C.H. Yorks.* i (1907); ii (1912); iii (1913); index (1925).
[48] *V.C.H. Yorks. E.R.* i (ed. K. J. Allison).
[49] H. J. Dyos in *British Book News*, Aug. 1973.

YORKSHIRE: THE NORTH RIDING AND THE CITY OF YORK

W. J. Sheils

THE NORTH RIDING

The extensive acres of the North Riding have attracted most of the well known antiquarian and literary tourists since John Leland in the 1540s but, in the absence of any large town, it has been the dramatic coastline, the vast landscapes of the moors and dales, and the monastic sites which have brought forth most comment. Indeed that tradition can be traced back to the 1170s with Walter Daniel's description of the young Ailred's arrival at Rievaulx, written shortly after the saint's death:

> the spot was by a powerful stream called the Rie in a broad valley stretching on either side. The name of their little settlement and of the place where it lies derived from the name of the stream and the valley, Rievaulx. High hills surround the valley encircling it like a crown. These are clothed by trees of various sorts and maintain in pleasant retreats the privacy of the vale, providing for the monks a kind of second paradise of wooded delight. From the loftiest rocks the waters wind and tumble down to the valley below, and as they make their hasty way through the lesser passages and narrower beds and spread themselves in wider rills, they give out a gentle murmur of soft sound and join together in the sweet notes of a delicious melody.[1]

Similar responses were to be evoked once more at the end of the 18th century when the county was a rich source of inspiration for romantics in search of the picturesque. Perhaps the most celebrated account from those travellers is that of Dorothy Wordsworth, who traversed the county from east to west with her brother William and his new bride, Mary Hutchinson, in October 1802. Coming down Sutton Bank she wrote

> We had not wanted fair prospects before us, as we drove along the flat plain of the high hill, far far off us, in the western sky, we saw shapes of Castles, Ruins among

---

[1] *Life of Ailred of Rievaulx by Walter Daniel*, ed. F. M. Powicke (1950), 12–13.

groves, a great spreading wood, rocks and single trees, a minster with its tower unusually distinct, minarets in another quarter, and a round grecian temple also . . . As we descended the hill there was no distinct view, but of a great space . . .

and her brother was moved to write a sonnet on the darkening scene.[2] Those two excerpts stand in the tradition of English landscape literature, but there were other visitors with more specific interests, such as the agriculturalist Arthur Young, who described the country around Rievaulx in very different terms in 1771:

> Now it is highly worthy of remark that the husbandry of these farmers is universally bad:—their fields lie in a slovenly condition; and of no little encouragement to them is the lowness of their rents, that many large tracts of land that yielded good crops of corn, within 30 years, are now over-run with whins, brakes, and other trumpery. The farmers are a poor wretched sort of people.
> If it be demanded, how such ill courses are to be stopped: I answer, Raise their rents. First with moderation; and if that does not bring forth industry, double them.[3]

Since the North Riding forms part of the county of Yorkshire and lies within the ancient diocese of York, the sources for its history reflect those for the whole county, and especially noteworthy are the printed records of the numerous monastic houses and the series of volumes of *Early Yorkshire Charters*.[4] Within the riding there were a number of smaller administrative or topographical areas: the ancient jurisdiction of Northallertonshire belonged to the bishopric of Durham, whose records are to be found at the Prior's Kitchen, Durham; the archdeaconry of Richmond, transferred to the newly created diocese of Chester in 1539, had always enjoyed a large degree of autonomy which was also reflected in the secular name, Richmondshire, given to the northern part of the archdeaconry from the 1130s;[5] and the northern boundary of the county, known as Cleveland, also attracted its own particular loyalty, though that was never expressed administratively until 1974.[6] It was those units, rather than the riding itself, which drew the attention of the earlier local historians.

Yet the North Riding Record Society was founded in 1881, largely through the efforts of the Revd. J. C. Atkinson, a noted antiquarian and folklorist

---

[2] *Journals of Dorothy Wordsworth*, ed. M. Moorman (2nd edn. 1971), 156; the sonnet 'Dark and More Dark the Shades of Evening Fall' is at p. 221.

[3] A. Young, *Six Months' Tour through North of England* (4 vols. 1967 edn.), ii. 80–3.

[4] Vols. iv and v of *Early Yorks. Charters* cover the honor of Richmond.

[5] A. Hamilton Thompson, 'Registers of Archdeaconry of Richmond, 1361–1442', *Yorks. Arch. Jnl.* xxv (1931), 129–68; *Early Yorks. Charters*, v. 13.

[6] The county of Cleveland was formed from the North Riding and Co. Dur. in 1974.

whose autobiographical account of his ministry at Danby in Cleveland, *Forty Years in a Moorland Parish*, is a classic account of local traditions and customs.[7] The society published only 13 volumes, nine devoted to quarter sessions records and edited by Atkinson, and four on the forest and honor of Pickering, culled from the duchy of Lancaster records, before it ceased in 1897.[8] The task of writing the county history was then taken up by the V.C.H., which, having published three volumes devoted to Yorkshire between 1907 and 1913, published two topographical volumes covering the North Riding in 1914 and 1924.[9] A county record office was established at Northallerton in 1949 to care for the records of the quarter sessions and also the registry of deeds, established in the county in 1735, and it has remained the chief archive repository of the area, incorporating the wider dimensions of North Yorkshire on the reorganization of local government in 1974. Annual reports, including short articles on local topics and lists of important deposits, have been published since 1966, and in 1974 the office began its own record publication series, having produced 50 volumes of a somewhat variable quality to date.[10]

Detailed accounts of those ecclesiastical parishes in the diocese of York can be gleaned from the manuscripts of James Torre, currently deposited at the York Minster Library. Torre's work was used by Archbishop John Sharp at the end of the 17th century and both were incorporated into the parochial directory published by George Lawton in 1840.[11] The Richmond parishes were excluded from detailed consideration in those works but a similar compilation was made *c.* 1718 by Francis Gastrell, bishop of Chester, and has recently been published.[12]

The most celebrated of the earlier county historians is probably Thomas Dunham Whitaker, whose *History of Richmondshire* was published posthumously in 1823 and has been described as the 'least satisfactory, though the most pretentious' of his works. It was embellished with 32 engravings by J. M. W. Turner and the portrait of the area conveyed by the work probably owed more to them than to the text which they were designed to accompany,[13] the view of Wycliffe near Rokeby, the reputed birthplace of John Wyclif,

---

[7] Published in 1891.

[8] Details in E. L. C. Mullins, *Texts and Calendars*, [i] (Royal Hist. Soc. Guides and Handbooks vii, 1958), 491–3.

[9] *V.C.H. General Introduction*, 33.

[10] North Riding R.O. *Annual Report* (1966); a full list of publications can be obtained from North Yorks. R.O., Northallerton.

[11] G. Lawton, *Collectio Rerum Ecclesiasticarum de Diocesi Eboracensi* (1840).

[12] *Archdeaconry of Richmond in 18th Century*, ed. L. A. S. Butler (Yorks. Arch. Soc. Rec. Ser. cxlvi, 1990).

[13] *D.N.B.* s.v. Whitaker. The full title is *Hist. of Richmondshire in North Riding of County of York*.

being full of religious symbolism.[14] The *History of Cleveland* produced by
John Graves in 1808 was less celebrated but provided readers with valuable
information from recently published works such as John Tuke's agricultural
survey and the 1801 census, from which Graves included the relevant sections
of Rickman's abstracts in order to make some contribution to the
contemporary debate on population.[15] Graves's *History* was followed by that
of J. W. Ord, published in 1846, which made extensive use of the manuscipts
of Sir Thomas Phillipps, especially in its lengthy account of Guisborough
priory.[16] By the date of Ord's history the area had become the fastest growing
industrial region in Britain, a fact not reflected in the author's concerns, and
Middlesbrough had to wait until 1881 when a *Jubilee History* was published. A
modern history of the industrial city, by W. Lillie, appeared in 1968, from
which time both the urban and rural past of the region have been the subject
of the annual *Bulletin of the Cleveland and Teesside Local History Society*.[17]

The towns of the county had attracted historians from the 17th century,
when the interest in bathing encouraged a York bookseller to publish a 214-
page encomium to Scarborough entitled *Scarbrough-Spaw, or a Description of
the Nature and Vertues of the Spaw at Scarbrough, Yorkshire*.[18] The
antiquarian Roger Gale published a brief history of Northallerton, the county
town, in 1739,[19] but it was not until the later 18th century that more serious
historical works appeared. James Langdale's *History of Northallerton* was
published in 1788 but was both poorer in quality and later than the detailed
History of Whitby by Lionel Clarkson, which devoted most of its 362 pages to
a history of the abbey but also included a useful account of the years between
1540 and 1776. Clarkson was a mathematical teacher in the town and reflected
the importance of seafaring to the community in his work, a theme taken up
and treated more extensively by the Revd. G. Young in his two-volume
history, published in 1817 with 300 pages of appendices and the following
observation in the preface:

> Correct views of a country are not to be gained from the hasty remarks of the
> tourist, who skims over its surface in a few days; but from the patient researches
> and mature observation of local writers.[20]

---

[14] E. Shanes, *Turner's Picturesque Views in England and Wales, 1825–38* (1979), 21–2.

[15] J. Graves, *Hist. of Cleveland in North Riding of County of York* (1808).

[16] J. W. Ord, *Hist. and Antiquities of Cleveland, comprising Wapentake of East and West Langbargh, North Riding* (1846).

[17] H. G. Reid, *Middlesbrough and its Jubilee, a Hist. of Iron and Steel Industries* (1881); W. Lillie, *Hist. of Middlesbrough, an Illustration of Evolution of English Industry* (1968).

[18] *Noble City of York*, ed. A. Stacpoole (1972), 929.

[19] *D.N.B.* The volume contained 13 pages.

[20] L. Clarkson, *Hist. of Whitby and Abbey* (1779); G. Young, *Hist. of Whitby and Streonshalh Abbey with Statistical Survey of Vicinity to Distance of 24 Miles* (2 vols. 1817).

Almost contemporary with Young was the impecunious publisher and failed businessman John Cole who, having left Northamptonshire, published during the 1820s a series of short and well printed historical and topographical sketches of Scarborough which, together with the more substantial history first published by Thomas Hinderwell in 1798, formed the basis of much later writing about the town as its reputation as a resort grew.[21] Histories of Richmond and Thirsk also appeared in that decade, Clarkson's on Richmond being the more significant addition to knowledge.[22]

Although some of those histories attempted to place their towns in the context of the region the rural areas of the riding were poorly chronicled in comparison to other counties by the mid 19th century. The works of Gill (1852) and Grainge (1859) attempted to remedy that for the fertile vale of York,[23] but the recovery of the rural past of the region has been the concern of relatively recent historians, some of whom follow in the tradition of J. C. Atkinson. The farming and country crafts of the upland regions have been documented by Marie Hartley and Joan Ingilby in their *Life and Tradition* volumes on the Dales and the North York Moors, which incorporate photographic and oral evidence, and whose collection of artefacts is housed in the Upper Dales Museum at Hawes.[24] The industrial history of the Dales has been recorded in a series of books on lead mining by Arthur Raistrick,[25] and vernacular building of the region has been the subject of two recent studies, recalling Arthur Young's earlier comment on the housing of Cleveland: 'upon descending into Cleveland, one circumstance must strike every traveller; the admirable manner in which all farmhouses are built'.[26] The presence of local historical societies, such as that at Helmsley which, since 1965, has produced *The Ryedale Historian*, and the fact that the county contains two extensive area of National Park, mean that the current generation is conscious of the past, and much research is promoted by local institutions of higher education.[27] Within that framework, however, tourism

---

[21] *D.N.B.*; T. Hinderwell, *Hist. and Antiquities of Scarborough* (1798).

[22] C. Clarkson, *Hist. of Richmond in County of York* (1821); C. Jefferson, *Hist. of Thirsk and Other Remains of Antiquity in Neighbourhood* (1821).

[23] T. Gill, *Vallis Eboracensis comprising Hist. and Antiquities of Easingwold and Neighbourhood* (1852); W. Grainge, *Vale of Mowbray: Historical and Topographical Account of Thirsk and Neighbourhood* (1859).

[24] Published in 1968 and 1972 respectively.

[25] A. Raistrick and B. Jennings, *Hist. of Leadmining in Pennines* (1965); A. Raistrick, *Lead Industry in Wensleydale and Swaledale* (1975).

[26] B. J. D. Harrison and B. Hutton, *Vernacular Houses in North Yorks. and Cleveland* (1984); Royal Com. on Hist. Monuments (England), *Houses of North York Moors* (1987); Young, *Six Months' Tour*, ii. 94.

[27] Both York and Teesside universities offer courses leading to qualifications in regional and local hist.

and the heritage industry make for uneasy companions, fostering the scholarly work of English Heritage and the National Trust at one level whilst at the same time characterizing a large tract of the county as James Herriot country, in which the nostalgic adventures of a local vet are given a topographical gloss embellished by romantic photography.[28] The new leisured classes pose much the same dilemma to the contemporary local historian as their forebears did in the early 19th century to their predecessors.

THE CITY OF YORK

The antiquity of the city of York, and the richness of the surviving traces of its past, have attracted the historian ever since the beginnings of modern historical writing in the 17th century. The first historian of the city was not, however, the first to be published. Sir Thomas Widdrington, M.P. for the city in 1660, offered to dedicate his *Analecta Eboracensia* to the members of the corporation, but their blunt refusal of the offer ('a good purse is better than a long story') meant that Widdrington refused to allow his discursive but thoroughly researched history to be published, and it remained in manuscript until 1897.[29] The first published history followed soon after, when Christopher Hildyard's modest *A List and Catalogue of all the Mayors and Bayliffs, Lord Mayors and Sheriffs* appeared in 1664. It commanded the market until the history brought out by the eccentric Irishman Thomas Gent in 1731. The volume was poorly produced and based largely on the sepulchral monuments in the city churches, but Gent justified his efforts in bringing the dead to life as a way of gaining that sustenance denied to him by the living![30] The book was well received but was soon eclipsed by the most distinguished of the early York histories, Francis Drake's *Eboracum or the History and Antiquities of the City of York*, published in 1736. Drake made extensive use of the civic and minster records and his text has remained an essential source for all later historians of the city, despite the author's tendency to display his Tory sympathies and a proclivity to attribute anything of antiquity to the Romans.[31] Various abbreviations of Drake were published later in the century, and his work formed the basis of the next substantial history of the city, by William Hargrove in 1818. Hargrove was editor of the *York Herald*, in whose columns he and his sons continued to write articles on the city's history throughout the 19th century.

[28] *James Herriot's Yorks.* (1979).
[29] York's historiography has been discussed at greater length in J. M. Biggins, *Historians of York* (St. Anthony's Hall Publication x, 1956); Widdrington's hist. was edited by C. Caine.
[30] Biggins, *Historians*, 5–6; *Noble City*, ed. Stacpoole, 931.
[31] Drake's hist. was reprinted in 1978, with an introduction by K. J. Allison.

That century was noted more for the editorial output of scholars working on the York records than for new histories. The minster fire of 1829 stressed the importance of systematically recording the ornaments, glass, and architectural features of the church, a task taken on by John Browne, whose massive history in two volumes, one consisting of plates, appeared in 1847. Many of Browne's conclusions were challenged by Robert Willis, whose history was published in 1848,[32] and more seriously by James Raine, in his edition of the *Fabric Rolls* (1859), whose work caused Browne to issue a revised edition of his history in 1863. Raine and his father, also James, were responsible for an enormous output of edited material in the later 19th century, though the quantity was not always matched by the quality of the work produced. Nevertheless they and others like them, such as Francis Collins, editor of the freemen's rolls, Robert Skaife, the compiler of lists of civic officers and transcriber of several parish registers, and Maud Sellers, editor of Merchant Adventurers' and other financial records, laid the foundations for the work undertaken by professional historians later.[33] Those editions were concerned with the past of the city, and a guide to the ancient records of the corporation was published in 1908, followed shortly by a bibliography of printed sources held in the city library, which also housed the archives.[34] They were greatly extended by the range of responsibilities undertaken by local authorities in the 19th century and further contemporary material is contained in the columns of the newspapers published in the city from 1719.[35] At the end of the century the pioneering social investigation of poverty in York by B. S. Rowntree, followed by another in 1936, created important materials for the social historian.[36]

One 19th-century historian who broke new ground was Robert Davies, town clerk from 1828, whose *History of the York Press* remains a valuable source book and whose *Antiquarian Walks Through the City of York* was to set a style for future writers.[37] Early in the present century a number of substantial histories of variable quality appeared, with that of Angelo Raine, city archivist and editor of the valuable series of House Books, being

---

[32] J. Browne, *Hist. of Metropolitan Church of St. Peter, York* (2 vols. 1847); R. Willis, *Archit. Hist. of York Cathedral* (1848).

[33] The edns. were mostly for the Surtees Soc. and the Yorks. Arch. Soc. and are listed in Mullins, *Texts and Calendars*; Skaife's list of civic dignitaries is available in MS. in York Reference Library.

[34] W. Giles, *Catalogue of Charters, House Books, Freemans Rolls and other Old Documents belonging to Corporation of York* (1908); *List of Books in Local Collection relating to City and County of York* (1912).

[35] *Noble City*, ed. Stacpoole, 934, 944–51.

[36] *Poverty, a Study of Town Life* (1901); *Poverty and Progress* (1939).

[37] Published in 1866 and, posthumously, in 1880 respectively.

outstanding.[38] The appearance of the *City of York* volume of the *V.C.H.* in 1961, however, marked a definitive point in the city's historiography. Written by professional historians and organized by period it marks both an end and a beginning.[39] The first of the Royal Commission on Historical Monuments's volumes on the city, concerned with the Roman remains, was published in the following year, and has been followed by a volume on the city defences and three topographical inventories.[40] A number of scholarly monographs, notably on the 16th and 19th centuries, have appeared in recent years,[41] and a collaborative volume was published in 1981 to commemorate the 150th anniversary of the British Association for the Advancement of Science, which held its first meeting in the city in 1831.[42] Many of the contributors to that volume were staff at the University of York, founded in 1961, and they were also prominent in the *History of York Minster* published in 1977.[43] Restoration work on the minster in the 1970s stimulated further work on the fabric, which has resulted in a volume devoted to the Norman church built by Archbishop Thomas and the first volume on York for the *Corpus Vitrearum Medii Aevi*.[44] The rich archival sources for the city have been exploited in many doctoral dissertations and learned articles in recent years, but the long tradition of locally inspired writing on the city survives and is encouraged by an essay prize awarded annually, and by *The York Historian*, established by the Yorkshire Architectural and York Archaeological Society in 1976.[45]

All those developments have built on the work of the early scholars, but perhaps the most innovative of the recent approaches to the city's past has been that of the York Archaeological Trust, founded by Dr. P. V. Addyman in 1972. The trust employs a mixture of private sponsorship, public funding, and scholarly grants to undertake its extensive excavations, the results of which are to appear in a 17-volume *Archaeology of York*, several fascicules of which have already been published.[46] The trust also publishes other studies for a

---

[38] The House Books have been published by the Yorks. Arch. Soc. Rec. Ser.; A. Raine, *Mediaeval York: a Topographical Hist.* (1955).

[39] *V.C.H. City of York*, ed. P. M. Tillott.

[40] *City of York*, i, *Eburacum* (1962); ii, *The Defences* (1972); iii, *South and West of the Ouse* (1972); iv, *North and East of the City* (1976); v, *Central Area* (1981).

[41] e.g. D. M. Palliser, *Tudor York* (1979); A. Armstrong, *Stability and Change in an English Country Town: a Social Study of York 1801–1851* (1974); F. E. Finnegan, *Poverty and Prostitution: a Study of Victorian Prostitutes in York* (1979); idem, *Poverty and Prejudice: Irish Immigrants in York 1840–1875* (1982).

[42] *York, 1831–1981: 150 Years of Scientific Endeavour and Social Change*, ed. C. Feinstein (1981).

[43] *Hist. of York Minster*, ed. G. E. Aylmer and R. Cant (1977).

[44] D. Phillips, *Excavations at York Minster*, ii (1985); T. W. French and D. O'Connor, *York Minster: West Windows of the Nave* (1989).

[45] The Oliver Sheldon Prize, established 1978; winning entries are published in the *York Historian*.

[46] Published by C.B.A

more general audience and is itself a commercial fundraiser with retail outlets, a coffee shop, and the nationally known re-creation of Viking York, time cars included, at the Jorvik Centre. Those activities help to finance its scholarly work, and the mixture of public and private resourcing, together with the academic and popular output, make the trust a reflection of the place of scholarship in a rapidly changing society deeply conscious of, but uncertain how to treat, its past. It remains to be seen whether the successful model adopted at York can be transferred to other localities.

YORKSHIRE: THE WEST RIDING

G. C. F. Forster

Aspects of the history of the West Riding are mentioned in the early histories and chronicles, as well as in the recorded observations of diarists and travellers, and very important West Riding material is to be found in the collections of Roger Dodsworth and others in Yorkshire antiquarian circles.[1] Nevertheless, much of our knowledge of the riding's history rests upon the foundations laid by three men: Ralph Thoresby, Thomas Dunham Whitaker, and Joseph Hunter. Faced with the daunting size of both the whole county and the West Riding itself those men 'were sensible in carving for themselves great subdivisions . . . and treating them thoroughly'.[2]

The first of the three, Ralph Thoresby, was a Leeds cloth merchant who gave up business to pursue historical interests, becoming an ardent collector of manuscripts, books, pedigrees, inscriptions, and coins, and building a wide circle of acquaintance with other antiquaries in Yorkshire and beyond. During the closing decades of the 17th century, the common interests of many scholars country-wide were engaged with a new, collaborative edition of Camden's *Britannia* for which the editor, Edmund Gibson, invited Thoresby to contribute to the section on the West Riding. His contribution was a substantial one, comprising corrections and additions to repair omissions and bring the main text up to date.

Thoresby had already embarked on his main work, the history of Leeds and its neighbourhood, and was examining documents, genealogies, and monumental inscriptions, and borrowing material from the collections of other Yorkshire antiquaries. He decided to produce first a topographical survey, which was eventually published as *Ducatus Leodiensis* (1715), a competent work in the form of a perambulation, affording a description of the town, the parish church, and other buildings, with shorter accounts of the places in the vicinity. Thoresby then turned to the historical part of the undertaking, beginning with the ecclesiastical history which was published as *Vicaria Leodiensis* (1724), a limited but useful book which attracted less attention than the *Ducatus*. His political history was left unfinished at his

---

[1] Above, Yorks.
[2] J. Simmons, 'Writing of English County Hist.' *English County Historians*, ed. J. Simmons (1978), 2.

death, but a fragment of his survey of 'these Northern parts' almost to the end of the 6th century was published posthumously in *Biographia Britannica*. Thoresby's writings were restricted in scope and frequently unselective and uncritical, but they retain their usefulness, they preserve evidence which might otherwise have been lost, and they have won for him a modest but deserved place in the historiography of the West Riding.[3]

By the time of Thoresby's death the pace of local antiquarian activity was slowing and few writers followed his example, though mention may be made of two other works from the period: the West Riding section of Thomas Cox's *Magna Britannia*, a topographical description arranged by wapentake and place;[4] and *The Ancient and Modern History of the Loyal Town of Ripon* (1733), a not wholly reliable medley by that interesting figure, Thomas Gent, author, artist, printer, publisher, and eccentric.

Towards the end of the 18th century the study of topography and local history in the West Riding was revived by the Revd. Thomas Dunham Whitaker, whose labours produced volumes of lasting value, if often too detailed and diffuse.[5] Beginning with his *History of the Original Parish of Whalley and Honor of Clitheroe* (1801), Whitaker worked on a much bigger scale than his predecessors. His *History and Antiquities of the Deanery of Craven* (1805) was well reviewed and proved to be much in demand.[6] In preparing it Whitaker drew not only upon published records and general histories but also upon the muniments of the principal landowners in the area; the work comprises a general historical description, including comments on the landscape and the damage wrought by the new manufactories, and a parish-by-parish account. Whitaker then turned his attention to the Leeds district, producing a corrected, annotated edition of Thoresby's *Ducatus Leodiensis* (1816) and also publishing his own *Loidis and Elmete* (1816), which discussed 'the Districts described in those words by Bede', a region supposedly embracing lower Airedale and Wharfedale, as well as Calderdale. In that book he claims to have reduced the volume of detail, and he tries to expound a clearer historical outline, particularly in the section about Leeds. With the completion of topographical works covering such a wide area of the West Riding it was perhaps natural that Whitaker should have wished to expand his studies to include the remainder of the county, a scheme which encountered difficulties before being cut short by his death. Nevertheless, the work which he did accomplish remains a significant

[3] For full references to Thoresby's work see G. C. F. Forster, 'First Medievalist in Leeds', *Church and Chronicle in Middle Ages*, ed. I. Wood and G. A. Loud (1991), 251–70.

[4] T. Cox, *Magna Britannia et Hibernia* (6 vols. 1720–31), vi. 331 sqq.

[5] R. V. Taylor, *Biographia Leodiensis* (1865), 286–92; G. R. Potter, 'Introduction', in J. Hunter, *South Yorks.* (reprinted 1974), i, p. v; D. Hill, *In Turner's Footsteps* (1984), 23–6; *D.N.B.*

[6] 2nd edn. (1812); 3rd edn. by A. W. Morant (1878).

achievement, and the scale of it entitles him to a place in 'the company of county historians'.[7]

The same can be said of the Revd. Joseph Hunter, author of two massive local histories.[8] Born in Sheffield, Hunter began collecting notes on churches, inscriptions, genealogy, and heraldry while still a schoolboy. After more than 20 years as a Presbyterian minister in Bath he became an assistant keeper of the public records in 1838; from then onwards he worked on the Pipe Rolls and other Exchequer records, becoming 'one of the great archivists'. Before that he had long maintained a wide-ranging correspondence with other antiquaries and had acquired a varied historical knowledge. 'Impelled to write by a passion for the study of antiquity', Hunter edited Thoresby's *Diary* (1830) and published two large works on the history of those parts of the West Riding he knew best: *Hallamshire* (1819) and *South Yorkshire* (2 vols. 1828–31). For both books he drew on the fruits of his youthful collecting, used the transcripts and notes of Dodsworth and his circle, worked on manuscripts in the British Museum, the Tower, and the College of Arms, examined the records held by the main local landowning families, and made personal observations in each place mentioned.

Hallamshire comprises some general chapters on trade, ecclesiastical affairs and Dissent, the grammar school, and local charities, with a township-by-township survey of Sheffield itself and the neighbouring parishes of the ancient division of Hallamshire. The topographical sections contain invaluable information but the material on the cutlery trades and the local economy has long since been superseded. *South Yorkshire* has some claim to be Hunter's most notable historical work: it again presents general material and an account arranged topographically; it includes very careful descriptions of changing property ownership, accurate pedigrees, effective illustrations, and two detailed maps. It is a great repository of carefully expounded information, and although it did not do justice to the significance of the region's coal deposits, canals, and drainage schemes, it still has 'meaning, interest, and value'. By his formidable scholarship, his skill with records, his neatly arranged historical works, and his economical style, therefore, Hunter earned for himself a deservedly large reputation in the learned world.

Hunter himself supplied many notes for a second, enlarged edition of his *Hallamshire* (1869), to which the editor, the Revd. Dr. A. Gatty, added

---

[7] Simmons, *County Historians*, 2.

[8] P. Levine, *The Amateur and the Professional: Antiquarians, Historians and Archaeologists in Victorian England* (1986), 19–20, 71; D. Evans, 'Joseph Hunter, Assistant Keeper of the Recs. 1838–1861', *Trans. Hunter Arch. Soc.* viii. 263–71; G. R. Potter, 'Joseph Hunter Centenary', ibid. 288–96; D. Crook, 'Joseph Hunter and Public Recs.' ibid. xii. 1–6, 8–9; G. R. Potter, 'Introduction', in Hunter, *South Yorks.* (reprinted 1974), i, pp. vii–xi.

contemporary information, especially about industry, and that basic work on the Sheffield region was later complemented by R. E. Leader's compendious *History of the Company of Cutlers in Hallamshire* (2 vols. 1905–6). Historical works (with varying degrees of interest and reliability) were published on other rising industrial towns of the West Riding during the 19th century.[9] Among the most useful were J. James's *History and Topography of Bradford* (1841, with a *Continuation*, 1860), to which more recent students of the town's history are still indebted, and J. Wardell's *Municipal History of the Borough of Leeds* (1846), valued for its translations of charters and excerpts from municipal records. The various town histories shared the same characteristics: detailed factual treatment; extracts from records, often without references; unacknowledged use of secondary sources; minimal discussion and comment; and usefulness for contemporary data.

The local patriotism and interest represented by the town histories is faithfully reflected in the proliferation of historical societies between the 1870s and 1914: the Bradford Historical and Antiquarian Society led the way in 1878, to be followed by the Thoresby Society in Leeds in 1889; the Halifax Antiquarian Society held its inaugural meeting in 1901; and in Sheffield the Hunter Archaeological Society was founded in 1912. All those societies set themselves to organize lecture programmes, collect locally relevant books and records, and issue publications. Their journals have continued to appear, offering to members and the wider public a wealth of articles and printed documents: 'a veritable library of Leeds' is one description of the Thoresby Society's publications.[10] At the same time research on individual places has been greatly assisted by the collections of local records brought together in the public libraries of the main towns; the importance of those, and the university and Yorkshire Archaeological Society's repositories, was increasingly appreciated in the absence of a county record office in the West Riding until after the changes in local government of 1974.

Historical work on the numerous towns in the West Riding both generated, and responded to, scholarly and public interest, but by the end of the 19th century there were renewed advances in work on wider regions, a development which has endured. Four well known examples may be cited: the works of Harry Speight, who wrote discursively but carefully on Wharfedale, Nidderdale, and Craven, producing topographically organized surveys based

---

[9] Conveniently listed in W. Boyne, *Yorks. Library* (1869), 71–151, and in *Yorks. Arch. Soc. Library Catalogue*, i and ii, *passim*.

[10] Levine, *Amateur and Professional*, 179–83; C. Dellheim, *The Face of the Past* (1982), 73–130; J. Reynolds and W. F. Baines, *One Hundred Years of Local Hist.: Bradford Hist. and Antiq. Soc. 1878–1978* (1978), *passim*; *Trans. Hunter Arch. Soc.* i. 10–11, 125, 133; W. B. Trigg, *Hist. of Halifax Antiq. Soc. 1900–1950* (1950), 4–15; G. C. F. Forster, *Centenary Hist. of Thoresby Soc.* (Thoresby Soc. Publications, forthcoming).

partly on primary sources;[11] the serious, if semi-popular, descriptions of topography and folk life in the Dales written by Ella Pontefract, Marie Hartley, and Joan Ingilby;[12] the numerous detailed studies by Arthur Raistrick, partly summed up in his *Old Yorkshire Dales* (1967) and his landscape history, *West Riding of Yorkshire* (1970); the collaborative volumes on the Dales prepared from primary sources and fieldwork by various adult classes and edited by Bernard Jennings, and offering in each case a topical and thematic treatment.[13] On a much larger scale, *West Yorkshire: an Archaeological Survey to A.D. 1500*, edited by M. L. Faull and S. A. Moorhouse (3 vols. 1981), comprises a synthesis of archaeological data, an account of the administrative and tenurial framework with manorial descents, and a survey of the rural landscape. Those contributions to the history of the West Riding have been matched by more publications devoted to individual towns, including specialized monographs and two large, collaborative volumes, *A History of Modern Leeds* (1980), edited by Derek Fraser, and *Huddersfield: a Most Handsome Town* (1993), edited by E. A. Hilary Haigh. What the West Riding still lacks is a *V.C.H.* series building upon what has already been achieved.

[11] *Upper Wharfedale* (1900); *Lower Wharfedale* (1902); *Nidderdale* (1906); *Craven and North-West Yorks. Highlands* (1892) and other works listed in *Yorks. Arch. Soc. Library Catalogue*, ii. 152–3.
[12] E. Pontefract and M. Hartley, *Wharfedale* (1936); M. Hartley and J. Ingilby, *Yorks. Dales* (1956); M. Hartley and J. Ingilby, *Life and Tradition in West Yorks.* (1976).
[13] *Hist. of Nidderdale* (1967); *Hist. of Harrogate and Knaresborough* (1970); *Pennine Valley: Hist. of Upper Calderdale* (1992).

INDEX

The index covers persons, places, and institutions. Places are identified by the ancient counties in which they lay. Periodicals and journals are in general indexed only when their provenance is not obvious or their contents span several counties. An italic page number denotes an illustration.

Burton Constable (Yorks. E.R.), 435, 442–3
Burton-upon-Trent Natural History and
  Archaeological Society, 362
Bury (Lancs.), 220 n
Bury and West Suffolk Archaeological Institute, see
  Suffolk Institute of Archaeology and History
Bury St. Edmunds (Suff.), 370, 372–3
Butterworth, Edwin, 222
Buxton (Derb.), 109

Calderdale (Yorks. W.R.), 457
Caley, John, 46, 248 n
Cam, Helen, 68
Cambridge, 63, 66; R.C.H.M. inventory, 28;
  Stourbridge fair, 63
Cambridge Antiquarian Society, 66–8, 203, 205
Cambridge Camden Society, see Ecclesiological
  Society
Cambridge University, 66, 330; Archaeological
  Museum, 67; Board of Extra Mural Studies, 288;
  Pembroke College, 373
Cambridgeshire, 27, 62–70, 197, 205, 207; learned
  societies, 66–8; R.C.H.M. inventory, 28, 30;
  V.C.H., 68–70
Cambridgeshire and Huntingdonshire
  Archaeological Society, 67–8, 205–6
Cambridgeshire Local History Council, 68
Camden, William, 12, 13, 14–15, 18, 32, 42, 72, 85,
  132, 142, 271, 302–3, 326, 328–9, 355–6, 385, 396,
  398–9, 433, 440
Camden (London borough), 279
Camp, John, 58
Campbell, Bruce, 289; Douglas Sutherland,
  marquess of Lorne, later duke of Argyll, 22
Camulodunum, 142; and see Colchester
Cannadine, David, 394
Canning, Richard, 367
Cansick, Frederick, 277
Canterbury (Kent), 210–11, 213; archbishop, see
  Parker, Matthew
Canvey Island (Essex), 143
Capel-Coningsby, George, Viscount Malden, 181
Car Colston, see Colston
Caraccioli, Charles, 387, 389
Caradoc and Severn Valley Field Club, 344, 346
Caradoc Field Club, 344
Cardiganshire, 324
Carew, Richard, 86–7, 366; Thomas, 348, 350
Carlisle (Cumb.), 100; bishops, see Lyttelton,
  Charles; Nicolson, William; Robinson, Henry;
  Tullie House museum, 101
Carpenter-Turner, Barbara, 173
Carruthers, Robert, 202
Carte, Samuel, 234; Thomas, 324
Carter, Edmund, 63–4; John, 262
Carthew, George A., 284
Cartmel (Lancs.), 218–19
cartography, see under county names
Cartwright, Edmund, 388–9; James Joel, 437

Cash, Margaret, 175
Casley, David, 293
Cautley, Munro, 369
Cave, Sir Thomas, 293
Caverswall, Sir William, 356
Caverswall (Staffs.), 356
Cecil, William, Baron Burghley, 10, 12, 14,
  142
Centre for Metropolitan History, see London
  University
Chadwick, Owen, 288
Chadwyck-Healey, Charles E. H., 354
Chalgrove (Oxon.), 332
Chalklin, Christopher William, 214
Chalmers, Alexander, 331
Chaloner, Thomas, 73; William Henry, 83
Chambers, Jonathan David, 320–1
Chancellor, Frederic, 148, 150
Chandos, duke of, see Brydges
Channel Islands, 168; and see Guernsey; Jersey;
  Sark
Chantrey, Sir Francis Legatt, 111
Chapman, John, 151
Chapple, Thomas, 119
Charlton (Oxon.), 332
Charnwood forest (Leics.), 242
Chatsworth (Derb.), 110
Chatterton, Thomas, 163
Chatwin, Philip B., 408
Chauncy, Sir Henry, 186–7
Cheal, Henry, 394
Cheffins, Joshua, 250
Chelsea (Mdx.), 272, 274
Cheltenham (Glos.), 160
Chertsey (Surr.), 381
Chesham (Bucks.), 57
Cheshire, 71–84, 217, 223–4, 355–6, 365; learned
  societies, 81–3, 223–7; V.C.H., 82, 84
Cheshire Rural Community Council, 83
Cheshire Sheaf, 82, 225
Chess Valley Archaeological and Historical Society,
  57 n
Chester, 71–4, 80, 224; bishop, see Gastrell
Chester and North Wales, Architectural,
  Archaeological, and Historic Society of, 82
Chetham Society, 81–2, 222–7
Chetham's Library, see Manchester
Chetwynd, Walter, 17, 356–9
Chetwynd-Talbot, John George Charles Henry
  Alton Alexander Chetwynd, earl of Shrewsbury,
  364
Chibnall, Albert C., 59; Marjorie, 336
Chichester (Suss.), 385, 387–8, 392
Chicksands (Beds.), 35
Chilton (Bucks.), 54
Chippenham (Wilts.), 416
Chipping Warden, see Warden
Chipping Wycombe, see Wycombe
Chiswick (Mdx.), 274